French Baroque Music

Premiere Journeé.

Dies primus.

Alceste, Tragedie en musique, ornée d'entrées de Ballet, representeé à Versailles dans la cour de marbre du Chasteau eclaire depuis le haut jusqu'en bas d'vne infinité de lumieres.

Alcestis Tragœdia, perpetuo cantu et variis saltationibus decorata, in marmoreo Palatij Versaliarum caucedio, vndequaque facibus accensis illuminati, acta.

Frontispiece: Performance of Lully's *Alceste* on 4 July 1674 in the Cour de Marbre at Versailles (Bibliothèque Nationale, Cabinet des Estampes).

French Baroque Music

from Beaujoyeulx to Rameau

REVISED AND EXPANDED EDITION

James R. Anthony

AMADEUS PRESS
Reinhard G. Pauly, General Editor
Portland, Oregon

Printed in Hong Kong

AMADEUS PRESS
The Haseltine Building
133 S.W. Second Avenue, Suite 450
Portland, Oregon 97204, U.S.A.

Library of Congress Cataloging-in-Publication Data
Anthony, James R.
    French Baroque Music from Beaujoyeulx to Rameau / James R.
Anthony. —Rev. and expanded ed.
    p. cm.
Includes bibliographical references and index.
ISBN 1-57467-021-2
    1. Music—France—16th century—History and criticism.
    2. Music—France—17th century—History and criticism.
    3. Music—France—18th century—History and criticism.
    I. Title.
ML270.2.A6 1997
780'.944'09032—dc20   96-38352
                                                             CIP
                                                             MN

Contents

Plates follow page 240.

Plates

Tables

$\mathscr{P}reface$

$\mathscr{T}$he Amadeus Press edition of *French Baroque Music* brings this book up to date and makes it available in English once again. A veritable explosion of interest in French Baroque music has taken place since B. T. Batsford in London and W. W. Norton in New York published the first and second (revised) editions in 1974 and 1978. The first French edition (*La musique en France à l'époque baroque*) published by Flammarion in Paris in 1981 included some new material and some new entries in the bibliography, and many corrections to the references. In 1992 Flammarion published a "*nouvelle édition*" that contains a short new essay (a "postface") after the main text, a greatly enhanced bibliography, and an index. None but the last French edition remains in print.

The complete revision undertaken in this third English edition attempts to incorporate all new significant research of the last two decades in a systematic way. This is particularly reflected in the bibliography. The majority of its 798 new titles date from the decade 1981–1991, that is, since the publication of the French edition. In spite of its 1304 entries, the bibliography makes no claim for completeness. When one realizes that by 1975 a single scholar, Norbert Dufourcq, had written more than 100 articles dealing with French music of the seventeenth and eighteenth centuries, it becomes clear that even an extended bibliography of this general survey must be highly selective. Inevitably, one chooses those titles that have best served one's research, those articles or books that synthesize, that shed light upon the thorny problems of archival studies, deal with social and economic considerations, extend biographical knowledge, advance stylistic insights, and, yes, merely entertain. A selective number of doctoral theses are included. I have opted, however, to exclude a thesis if its author has carried over the essence from his study into a book or an extended article and left behind the chaff of academia.

The interested reader will find scattered throughout the bibliography what Laurence Dreyfus referred to as the "raucous polemics about over-dotting, vibrato, and the performance of trills" (and, one might add, the performance of the appoggiatura). Although the first volley in the battle of the double dot was fired by Frederick Neumann, writing in French (1965b), all subsequent articles have appeared in English.

On a more elevated note, the rich, archival studies of early twentieth-century scholars such as Michel Brenet, Lionel de La Laurencie, and Romain Rolland have been continued by Marcelle Benoit and, most recently, by Jérôme de La Gorce and Catherine Massip, among others.

The chronological boundaries of the book are, of course, respected in the bibliography. They remain generally fixed from about 1581 (*Ballet comique de la reine*) to about 1733 (death of François Couperin and first performance of Rameau's *Hippolyte et Aricie*). Whereas it is not possible to posit a specific date to mark stylistic change, any general survey of a stylistic period must have a beginning point and cannot be totally open-ended. The *Ballet comique* is the first court ballet to adumbrate French Baroque opera. It is not uncommon to find the time span of a book to be framed by its most important people ("from Monteverdi to Bach," for example). François Couperin, if not the most representative composer of the *grand siècle*, was arguably the greatest composer of the declining years of the *Roi Soleil* and of the Regency. The choice of the first performance date of Rameau's opera as a terminal point begs explanation. Although elements of *Hippolyte* refer back to Lullian models and more particularly to *préramiste** experiments, changes in *Hippolyte* were perceived as a break with tradition, a sea change in the music of the French Baroque. For the *Almanach des spectacles* of 1765, *Hippolyte* marked the date of a "revolution" in French music. One year earlier in the *Éloge de M. Rameau*, Michel-Paul Guy de Chabanon had written, "This revolution was sudden; the opera *Hippolyte* began it; *Les Indes galantes* continued it" (1764). The ensuing battles between the *Lullistes* and the *Ramistes* and the mid-century *Querelle des bouffons* belong to a later period that culminated in the classical language of Gluck. For this reason, Rameau sources are generally restricted in this bibliography to his keyboard music, motets, and cantatas—nearly all composed before *Hippolyte et Aricie*.

"La musique baroque française, existe-t-elle?" This pointed question, found in a review of *La musique en France à l'époque baroque* in a Swiss journal (*Construire*, 8 December 1982), was posed in many French language reviews of this book. It highlights the fact that there is no consensus regarding the coupling of the terms *French* and

Baroque. To the end of his life, Norbert Dufourcq (d. 1990) remained the most forceful (and eloquent) opponent of the concept of "French Baroque music." In a review of *Jean-Baptiste Lully and the Music of the French Baroque*, in the pages of the important journal that he founded, he wrote:

> *Concerning this subject, we will not reopen this quarrel, vain as it is useless, over acceptance of the word* baroque. *Let the foreigner give our music the appellation he has chosen, while the French school generally means by* classique *the entire period that extends from 1661 to Berlioz" (1988–1990* Recherches sur la musique française classique *26:236, note 5).*

It is ironic that at Versailles itself, the *sanctum sanctorum* of the *Roi Soleil*, a Centre de Musique Baroque de Versailles (CMBV) was established in 1987. An important component of the Centre is the "Atelier d'études sur la musique française des XVIIe & XVIIIe siècles" directed by Jean Duron, which has impressive tools for database and library research. The CMBV has enlarged the parameters of French "Baroque" music from 1581–1733 to 1589–1789, which increases overlap with Dufourcq's French "Classical" music (1661 to Berlioz).

To be sure, the use of the term *Baroque* is an over-simplification. Few will deny that French music of the seventeenth and early eighteenth centuries reflects the classical (with a small "c") bias of the *grand siècle* in the plastic and visual arts, architecture, drama, literature, and the history of ideas. Yet there is an extended meaning of *Baroque* (with a capital B) that embraces purely musical practices, such as the *basse continue* or the *stile concertato*, and relates the French Baroque musical experience to that of Germany, Italy, and England. The contrast between the *petit choeur* in trio texture and the five-part *tous* found in the introductory *symphonie* of Lully's Te Deum owes as much to the *stile concertato* of the Italian Baroque as Armide's recitative, "Enfin, il est en ma puissance," owes to the classical declamation of Racine. There appears to be more tolerance today in France, if not for total acceptance of the term *Baroque* (hardly desirable in any case), at least for the coexistence of *Baroque* and *Classical*. The simplest and most accurate way of defining this period is to follow Marcelle Benoit, who changed the name of the dictionary published by Fayard under her direction from *Dictionnaire de la musique classique en France, 1589–1789* to *Dictionnaire de la musique en France aux XVIIe et XVIIIe siècles.*

Tangible evidence of increased interest in French Baroque music extends far beyond a statistical study of the lengthened bibliography. Herbert Schneider's *Lully Werke Verzeichnis* (LWV) was published in

1981, the year *French Baroque Music* was translated into French. H. Wiley Hitchcock's *Catalogue raisonné* of the complete works of Marc-Antoine Charpentier appeared the following year. In preparation or already completed are the *Catalogues raisonnés* of the complete works of Michel-Richard Delalande (Lionel Sawkins), Sébastien de Brossard (Jean Duron), Michel Lambert (Catherine Massip), Henry Du Mont (Jean Lionnet), Daniel Daniélis (Catherine Cessac), Guillaume Bouzignac (Marie Joelle Ebtinger), and Nicolas Bernier (Nathalie Berton). A *Catalogue thématique des sources du grand motet français* was published under the direction of Jean Mongrédien in 1984. A *Catalogue raisonné* by Carl Schmidt of the *livrets* of Lully's *tragédies lyriques* was published in 1995. Unfortunately, in the face of mounting economic difficulties and in spite of the unstinting efforts of Marcelle Benoit, *Recherches sur la musique française classique* is in grave danger of ceasing publication. *XVIIᵉ siècle* devotes an occasional issue to some aspect of the music of this period. More recently, through its database and annual *Bulletin*, the *Atelier d'études sur la musique française des XVIIᵉ & XVIIIᵉ siècles* serves as an important clearing house for all information on current research.

The past decade has witnessed a steady proliferation of performance and facsimile editions of French Baroque music. Happily, it is no longer possible to state, for example, that the motets and Masses by Marc-Antoine Charpentier "slumber today undisturbed in the archives of the Bibliothèque Nationale and the Bibliothèque Municipale of Versailles" (*French Baroque Music*, 1974, 185). A sampling of recent performance editions of Charpentier's music could include the opera *Médée*; the opera *David et Jonathas*; *Neuf leçons de ténèbres*; Charpentier's music for Molière's comedies; and motets, Masses, and oratorios published by CMBV, Éditions des Abbesses, and Musica Gallica.

Complementing musical editions of Charpentier's work is a body of important articles and theses, two studies of life and works (a long monograph by Catherine Cessac, and a highly concentrated biography by H. Wiley Hitchcock), a semiannual *Bulletin de la Société Marc-Antoine Charpentier* (ed. Cessac), the first volumes of the projected thirty-volume *Mélanges autographes* (Minkoff), and an impressive discography.

A selected list of music editions would also note that within the last twelve years, a few *grands motets* by Henry Desmarest have been edited by Jean Duron, and *grands motets* by Michel-Richard Delalande have been edited by Lionel Sawkins and by Philippe Oboussier. The *Dialogus de anima* by Henry Du Mont (ed. Jean Lionnet) is the first volume of the complete works of Du Mont to be published by the CMBV. The two volumes of Du Mont's *Mélanges à II, III, IV, et*

V parties (ed. J. Quitin) have been published by the Société Liégeoise de Musicologie, and the *Corpus des luthistes français* (CNRS) continues its monumental task of publishing the complete French lute repertory.

With very few exceptions, on the other hand, high-caliber performance editions of the music of Jean-Baptiste Lully and Jean-Philippe Rameau, the two giants of the seventeenth and eighteenth centuries, respectively, have malingered in limbo. In spite of the *Jean-Baptiste Lully. Actes du colloque* (1990), *Jean-Baptiste Lully and the Music of the French Baroque* (1989), and *Jean-Philippe Rameau. Actes du colloque* (1986), when it comes to the music, itself, we have hardly progressed beyond the incomplete Lully *Oeuvres complètes* edited by Prunières in the 1930s and the flawed Rameau *Oeuvres complètes* edited by Saint-Saëns in the early years of this century. There is hope in the fact that committees recently formed in France have undertaken the responsibility of preparing new editions of the complete works of Lully (committee headed by Jérôme de La Gorce and Herbert Schneider) and Rameau (committee headed by Silvie Boissou).

In the late 1960s, Gregg Press published facsimile editions of certain French Baroque operas that now, sadly, are out of print (for example, Charpentier's *Médée*, Campra's *L'Europe galante*, and Destouches's *Amadis de Grèce*). The 1970s saw ambitious projects such as facsimiles of the *Manuscrit Bauyn* (Minkoff), the *Pièces de clavecin* by François Couperin, and the *Pièces de clavecin* by Rameau (Broude Trust).

Chief among the facsimile editions of the 1980s and 1990s are *The Eighteenth-Century French Cantata* (Garland) in seventeen volumes with commentary by David Tunley, *French Opera in the Seventeenth and Eighteenth Centuries* edited by Barry S. Brook in seventy-five volumes (eleven of which have already been published by Pendragon Press), and the *Mélanges autographs* by Charpentier in thirty volumes, mentioned above (Minkoff). Of great importance for any study of primary sources are the more than 700 facsimile editions of treatises and music scores (see, for example, the twenty-nine volumes of *clavecinistes français du XVIIIe siècle*) published by Minkoff.

Knowledge for its own sake is valuable and its accumulation can be justified, but ideally the research involved in books and articles and in musical editions should lead to performance. French Baroque music demands much from the professional and amateur performer. Without becoming distracted by the "raucous polemics" of performance authenticity regarding the use of period versus modern instruments, the performer must have some understanding of rhythmic alterations, of the appropriate and refined application of ornaments that is one step removed from improvisation, of correct declamation, and, above all, an appreciation of the central importance of dance gesture to all of this music. Accurate reading of the notes on the page is not enough. "If one plays Lully as written," writes Marc Minkowski, "without ornaments, without declamatory energy, it can very quickly lead to deadly boredom" ("Lully au Théâtre des Champs-Élysées," *Diapason harmonie, décembre* 1991).

On the other hand, a performance rooted in clear understanding of the basic principles of French Baroque music can fire the imagination and bring the music of the *grand siècle* to life for late twentieth-century audiences. A fine example of this is the performance of Lully's *Atys* by "Les Arts florissants" under the direction of William Christie. This *tragédie en musique*, a favorite of Louis XIV, has been performed more than seventy times since 1986 for enthusiastic audiences in Florence, Paris, Montpellier, Versailles, and Brooklyn. This presents an interesting, though not unprecedented, example of research lagging behind practice, for there is no modern, printed full score of *Atys*. There exists only a piano-voice reduction dating from the 1880s (*Chefs-d'oeuvres classiques de l'opéra français*) and a 1987 facsimile of a 1709 short score (Société de Musicologie du Languedoc). Therefore, the full score that was used had to be assembled from the scores and separate parts found in the Bibliothèque Nationale and the Bibliothèque de l'Opéra.

In addition to William Christie, Jean-Claude Malgloire ("La Grande Écurie et la Chambre du Roy"), Mark Minkowski ("Musiciens du Louvre"), Gustav Leonhardt ("La Petite Bande"), Philippe Herreweghe ("Ensemble Vocal et instrumental de la Chapelle Royale"), and, more recently, Jeffrey Skidmore ("Ex Cathedra") and Christophe Rousset ("Les Talens lyriques"), among others, have made of French Baroque music a vital listening experience. In so doing, they have translated the research listed in my bibliography into sound for stage, chamber, and chapel.

I wish to express my deepest gratitude to the following individuals who made the preparation of this final edition of *French Baroque Music* possible. First and foremost, I acknowledge the careful and painstaking work of my wife Louise in the computer preparation of the manuscript and for her rigorous attention to problems of style and content. Without her, I would not have had the courage to continue. I wish to thank the library staff at the Département de la Musique at the Bibliothèque Nationale for their most generous, conscientious work with Jean-Michel Nectoux in verifying and correcting many references for the French edition of 1981, and for their continued patience and many kindnesses. I owe a great debt to Lionel Sawkins, Jean Duron, Catherine Massip, Marcelle Benoit, Jean Mongrédien, and Catherine Cessac for their encouragement and many insights. I must thank Kathy Krauss of Tucson for her invaluable assistance in the early stages of this revision. I take pleasure in thanking Reinhard

Pauly, General Editor, Karen Kirtley, former Editorial Director, and Suzanne Copenhagen, Line Editor—all of Amadeus Press—for their expert guidance and strong support.

In conclusion, I wish to thank the Bibliothèque Nationale, the Bibliothèque de l'Opéra, the Special Collections at the University of California at Los Angeles for permission to reproduce illustrations, and the Musée du Louvre for permission to reproduce the painting *Le Concert* by Nicolas Tournier on the cover.

Unless otherwise indicated, all translations are mine. I have included the original French for extracts from poetry. Throughout the book, I have employed the original French spelling, and in my translations I have kept the often bizarre capitalizations of the old French to preserve some of its flavor and any emphases that might have been intended.

Préramiste is the term generally used for the period after the death of Lully and before the advent of Rameau as an opera composer, that is, from 1687 to 1733.

≈ *Chapter 1* ≈

Institutions and Organizations
of the Grand Siècle

*A*ny study of the music of the seventeenth and early eighteenth centuries in France must also be a study of the institutions from which much of the music issued. Surely no other nation has known the all-pervasive, hierarchial organization that characterized the France of Louis XIV.

On 9 March 1661, Cardinal Mazarin died; and Louis XIV, at age twenty-three, took unto himself the destiny of France. He chose to become his own first minister, thus eliminating the threat of another power-hungry Cardinal Richelieu or Mazarin. "Above all," he wrote in his *Mémoires,* "I was resolved not to have a prime minister . . . there being nothing more shameful than to see, on the one hand, all the power and, on the other, the mere title of king" (Louis XIV, ed. of 1978, 44).

To help him govern and direct policy, he appointed talented and ambitious men from the middle class (among whom were Jean-Baptiste Colbert, Michel Le Tellier, and the Marquis de Louvois), thus inaugurating, in the Duc de Saint-Simon's words, the reign of the vile bourgeoisie. By eliminating the nobility from his councils, he neutralized their power and, in effect, reduced the *princes du sang* to decorative impotency.

In exercising his passion for order at all levels of society, Colbert, between 1661 and his death in 1683, completed the creation of royal academies that were to systematize the artistic and intellectual life of the regime. In 1661 only the Académie Française (established by Cardinal Richelieu in 1635) and the Académie Royale de Peinture et de Sculpture (1648) existed. Within the next decade, Colbert approved the founding of five more academies: Académie Royale de

Danse (1661), Académie des Inscriptions et Belles Lettres (1663), Académie des Sciences (1666), Académies d'Opéra (1669, which later became the Académie Royale de Musique [1672]), and the Académie Royale d'Architecture (1671).

It is hardly surprising that many facets of musical life of the *grand siècle* would also fall under a hierarchal administration which reflected the centralized bias of the regime. The phrase, composed or printed "by express order of His Majesty" graced many scores ranging from *pièces d'occasion*, such as the *Airs de trompettes, timbales et hautbois fait par Mr. de Luly* for the *carrousel* of Monseigneur (the *grand Dauphin*) in 1686, to the *grands motets* composed for the Royal Chapel by Henry Du Mont, Pierre Robert, and Jean-Baptiste Lully.

The king, except for some ability on the lute and guitar, made little mark as a performing musician. He was, however, musically literate and possessed a fair amount of critical acumen.

He was considerably more than an aristocratic abstraction dispensing royal privileges and patents from the splendor of a Versailles council chamber. More than any other monarch of his time, he became personally involved in the music for his court, especially in the years following the final move to Versailles in 1682. He chose the music instructors for his family and relatives with care: Michel-Richard Delalande to teach Mlle de Nantes and Mlle de Blois, his daughters by Mme de Montespan; and Marc-Antoine Charpentier to teach composition to his nephew, Philippe II de Bourbon (Duc de Chartres until 1701, then Duc d'Orléans to 1723, Regent of France 1715–1723). François Couperin, in the preface to his first book of *Pièces de clavecin* (1713), relates that "for the last twenty years I have had the honor to be in the King's employ and, during most of this time, to be teaching Monseigneur the Dauphin, the Duc de Bourgogne, and six princes and princesses of the Royal Family." Louis XIV suggested to Philippe Quinault and Lully the subject matter of certain *tragédies en musiques* (*Roland, Amadis, Armide*); and according to Évrard Titon du Tillet (1677–1762),[1] gave Louis-Nicolas Clérambault the texts (authors unknown) for several cantatas that were later performed in the apartments of Mme de Maintenon.

The king's attitude is well expressed by the archival comment apropos of a vacancy among the musicians of his Chamber: "When places become available, His Majesty, in line with his plan to appoint individuals experienced in their profession to his Chamber, does not tolerate anyone who lacks these qualities and all the experience necessary to acquit himself of the task perfectly" (Écorcheville 1906c, 1:26).

In order to find individuals "experienced in their profession," he established a series of competitions: the first, to choose four *sous-maîtres* for his Royal Chapel in 1663 (Du Mont, Gabriel Expilly,

Robert, Thomas Gobert), was followed fifteen years later by another competition for the positions of four organists for the Royal Chapel (Guillaume-Gabriel Nivers, Nicolas-Antoine Lebègue, Jacques Thomelin, Jean-Baptiste Buterne); the most impressive of all was the great *concours* of 1683, again for the Royal Chapel *sous-maîtres*, in which more than thirty-five applicants from all over the realm competed (see Chapter 13). In choosing Jean-Baptiste Lully as *Surintendant et Compositeur de la Musique de la Chambre du Roi* in 1661 and in authorizing Lully's "letters of naturalization" in December of the same year, Louis XIV was assured of an efficient and ruthless agent whose absolutism, in fact, paralleled his own.

The King's Music[2]

Music at the court of Louis XIV was organized, from an administrative point of view, into three large divisions: Music of the Chamber (*Musique de la Chambre*), Music of the Great Stable (*Musique de la Grande Écurie*), and Music of the Royal Chapel (*Musique de la Chapelle Royale*). In addition, the *Vingt-quatre Violons du Roi* (also referred to as the *Grande Bande*) and the *Petits Violons du Roi* (referred to as the *Petite Bande* and later in the century as the *Violons du Cabinet*), although technically under the administration of the Chamber, were virtually autonomous because of their great prestige. The number of the king's musicians varied at any given time, but, by the end of the reign of Louis XIV, it ranged between 150 and 200 individuals. These were collectively referred to as *Musiciens du Roi*, or *Officiers de la Maison du Roi*, or, simply, as *Violon de la Chambre du Roi* or *Hautbois du Roi*. To be an *officier* of the king, one had to fullfill three conditions: to be of good moral character; to profess and practice the Roman Catholic religion; and to possess sufficient funds to buy the post, assuming the other conditions were met. Once installed, the *officier* soon took active part in choosing his replacement. Succession upon retirement or death was usually accomplished by a *survivance* in which the *officier* gave the right to inherit his post to a designated relative, or the right to purchase his post to a friend or, possibly, a student. At Versailles, this was one of the ways to build dynasties of musicians such as the Hotteterre, Philidor, Rebel, or Boesset families. Jean-Baptiste Boesset, for example, was named *survancier* at age twenty-one by his father, Antoine, in 1635. He then passed the right to the position on to his own son (aged two) in 1667.

Those court musicians who could not qualify for *officier* were divided into three categories: *musiciens ordinaires*; *musiciens extra-ordinaires* (musicians not regularly employed at court but used for certain occasions—town musicians or foreigners, for example); and *musiciens suivant la cour*, made up of minor artists or, occasionally, students completing their years of apprenticeship.

Music of the Chamber

The source of the music both of the Chamber and the Stable may be traced back to François I. This most pleasure-loving of the Valois kings, who was receptive both to spectacular *fêtes* and to the more intimate and contemplative arts, created two categories for his court music. For the music of his Chamber, he chose soloists: singers (for madrigals and chansons), lutenists, and virtuosi cornett players from Italy. Organists, harpsichordists, and viol players joined them later. For his Stable, he chose ensemble instruments appropriate for outdoor performances; they included oboes, sackbuts, and violins for the parades and lavish ceremonies that lent colorful accents to his gentle Loire valley.

At some point before 1571 during the reign of Charles IX, the two families of bowed strings (viols and violins) moved from the Stable to the Chamber. In 1592 under Henri IV, the position of *Surintendant de la Musique de la Chambre* was created. During the seventeenth and eighteenth centuries, two men were appointed to hold this position simultaneously. Each served for one of the two terms of the year. In addition to administrative functions, they were responsible for the choice of music and for the overall organization of all nonreligious musical performances at court. Aiding the *Surintendant* was the *Maître de Musique de la Chambre*, who was also responsible for the musical education as well as the nourishment and even some of the clothing of the *pages* (boys) assigned to the Chamber. There were three *pages* in the Chamber and eight assigned to the Royal Chapel (see Sawkins 1987, 316–317). The third administrative division was that of *Compositeur de la Chambre*, whose special task was often reflected in such titles as *Compositeur de la musique instrumentale de la Chambre* or *Compositeur des entrées des ballets*. Occasionally, one individual controlled all three divisions. Lully and Delalande, for example, each reigned in isolated splendor during certain periods of their tenure.

By 1590, discouraged by poor pay and the interminable wars of religion, many Italian violinists who had been brought to the court of Catherine de Médici by the Maréchal de Brissac and who had acquitted themselves so nobly in the first court ballet, the *Ballet comique de la Reine* (1581), returned home. French performers now formed the nucleus of players who eventually staffed the most important ensemble groups: the *Douze Hautbois* and the *Vingt-quatre Violons*. By 1609 there were twenty-two *Violons ordinaires de la Chambre du Roi*; by 1626 this group, which then numbered twenty-four, was given official recognition by Louis XIII as the *Vingt-quatre Violons du Roi*. Some of the best of these violinists came from the Parisian popular orchestras of the Guild (Confrérie) of Saint-Julien. They traded the rough and ready life of the streets for a more genteel existence as a *Violon de la Chambre du Roi*.

Hidden away in the archival records of the *Minutier Central* are many success stories of *Violons de la Chambre* such as one Jean de La Motte who entered the king's Chamber as a *Violon* in 1606 and by 1622 was also dancing teacher of the *pages* assigned to the Great Stable, and who ended up owning five houses in the Paris suburbs.[3]

The *Vingt-quatre Violons*, often reinforced by the *Douze Grands Hautbois* of the Great Stable, constitute the first, formally established orchestra to be built around a group of stringed instruments. The distribution of parts within the typical *a*5 (five-part) texture of French seventeenth-century instrumental music was as follows: six first violins (*dessus*), six basses (the *basse de violon*, not the violoncello), and four each of the three inner parts all tuned as the modern viola, but each with its own clef; the inner parts (or the *parties de remplissage*) were known as *haute-contre*, *taille*, and *quinte*.

According to Bernard Bardet, the *Petits Violons* ensemble served Louis XIV personally and was created for this purpose about 1648 while he was still a boy.[4] In March 1653, Lully was appointed *Compositeur de la musique instrumentale*. At some point after this date, the king assigned the *Petits Violons* to Lully, who had found fault with the performance of the *Grande Bande* ostensibly on the grounds of their sloppiness and undisciplined use of ornaments. In actuality, Lully probably wanted a group of his own to test his ideas of orchestral performance techniques, which twenty years later were to make his opera orchestra the envy of all Europe.

The *Petits Violons* appeared for the first time under Lully's direction in the court ballet *La Galanterie du temps* (1656), and, for six years, the new group was used almost to the exclusion of the *Vingt-quatre Violons*. After 1661 Lully apparently reconciled his differences with the *Grande Bande*, and the ensembles were even combined from time to time for special court performances. The *Petits Violons* were suppressed about 1715, but the *Vingt-quatre Violons* continued in existence until 1761.

The division of labor between the two groups is difficult to determine. However, in an extract from the *État de la France*[5] for the year 1686, Prunières discovered the following:

> *The* Grande Bande *of the* Vingt-quatre Violons, *always so labeled although they are at present twenty-five . . . plays for the dinner of the King, for Ballets and for Comedies. The* Petits

> Violons *which number twenty-four . . . follow the King on his journeys to the country, usually play for his supper, for Balls and the Recreation of His Majesty. They also play for Ballets (1920, 130).*

The musicians of the king's Chamber were the most renowned of the age. Among the singers were the wife of Delalande, Anne Rebel, his two daughters (Anne and Jeanne), François Couperin's cousin, Marguerite-Louise, Anne de La Barre, and Michel Lambert's sister-in-law, Hilaire Dupuy. Sébastien Le Camus and Pierre Chabançeau de La Barre excelled on the lute and theorbo; Robert de Visée, on the guitar and theorbo and as a singer. Among the flutists were Philibert Rebillé, René Descoteaux, and Michel de La Barre. Chief among the viol players were Marin Marais and Antoine Forqueray. The court harpsichordists were Jacques-Champion de Chambonnières, Jean-Henry D'Anglebert, and François Couperin. The king also took special pleasure in the keyboard performances of Elisabeth Jacquet, Marie-Françoise Certain, and another daughter of François Couperin, Marguerite-Antoinette.

Music of the Great Stable

For the man in the street in the twentieth century, the word *stable* evokes a dark and malodorous place. For the seventeenth-century man who gazed at the magnificent, semicircular stables at Versailles built by Hardouin-Mansart in 1682, the Great Stable meant much more than housing for the king's horses. Among the many *officiers du roi* attached to the Great Stable were the musicians traditionally associated with military and outdoor pageantry. These musicians were some of Louis XIV's best wind, brass, and timpani players, who orchestrated the pomp and ceremony of court life: the royal births, marriages, and funerals; the heralding of the king's arrival in towns and villages throughout the realm; and the welcoming of such foreign dignitaries as the envoys from Siam in 1686 and the Persian ambassadors in 1715. They crossed administrative boundaries to join the musicians of the Chamber in performances of ballets and *divertissements*, or to join the musicians of the Royal Chapel in performances of *grands motets*. They were available for parades, *carrousels* (equestrian ballets organized at court, generally on allegorical subjects) and other outdoor *fêtes*. They accompanied the king to parliament; their fanfares were heard both on the battlefield and at the hunt. The people reveled in the sight of the colorful, mounted trumpeters whose remote descendants in the *Garde Républicaine* quicken the pulse of parade watchers today as they play their trumpets at a gallop down the Champs-Élysées on Bastille Day.

From the 1540s, the instrumentalists of the Stable were already grouped into three categories including twelve, five, and seven musicians, respectively: (1) *saqueboutes et joueurs d'instruments* (sackbuts and instrumentalists), (2) *fiffres et tabourins* (fifes and drums), and (3) *trompettes* (see Écorcheville 1900–1901).

Although *joueurs d'instruments* originally referred in the main to wind instruments (oboes and cornetts), violinists were also included in the music of the Stable, which reminds us that at that time the violin was considered appropriate for music *en plein air*. As we have already seen, however, most bowed strings were transferred from the Stable to the Chamber by 1571.[6]

By 1571 the Stable had at its disposal twelve trumpets, eight fifes and drums, fifteen sackbuts, oboes, and cornetts, one musette, and, according to Henry Prunières, one "undetermined player." The divisions remained essentially the same under Louis XIV. In the *État des officiers de la Maison du Roi* for 1689 (see Benoit 1971a, 121), the following administrative units of the Stable are itemized: *trompettes* (twelve players); *joueurs de violon, hautbois, saqueboutes et cornets* (twelve players); *hautbois et musettes de Poictou* (six players); *joueurs de fifres et tambour* (eight players); and *cromornes et trompettes marines* (six players). Tradition apparently decreed that the administrative title of each category remain fixed long after certain instruments had fallen out of favor. Sackbuts, for example, were no longer employed during the period of Louis XIV, cornetts were used primarily to double the sopranos of the Royal Chapel, and crumhorns (*cromornes*) were used sparingly in some court ballets. On the other hand, the trumpet marine (*trompette marine*), the large, one-stringed, bowed instrument favored by Monsieur Jourdain, had its following to the middle years of the eighteenth century.

The four best trumpet players, the *trompettes ordinaires*, were always expected to be available and to precede the royal coach on horseback in uniform. The eight remaining were used for performances of Te Deums, funerals, coronations, arrivals of visiting dignitaries, and the like.

The category "sackbuts and instrumentalists" included some of the best performers who were prepared to play on a variety of wind instruments. In the second half of the seventeenth century, the category became known as the *Douze Grands Hautbois*. These were actually ten (not twelve) instruments of the oboe family and two bassoons. They had only three official functions a year to meet: the rising (*lever*) of the king on the first day of January and May, and on 24 August for Saint Louis's day. The remainder of the time they combined with other groups, such as the *Vingt-quatre Violons*, for performances of court ballets, *divertissements*, operas, and so forth.

The music of the Stable entered a long decline after 1690. Jules Écorcheville estimates that there were scarcely six or eight musicians out of forty-three who served effectively by the time of the Regency. Yet, even at the end of his long life, Louis XIV took some comfort from their music, and "on Saint Louis's day, 1715, a few days before his death, the drums and oboes [of the Great Stable] were in place under his window" (Écorcheville 1900–1901, 641).

In truth, the significance of the Great Stable to a history of French Baroque music does not lie with its spectacular "orchestration" of the ceremonies, the *carrousels,* and *fêtes* performed for the pleasure of the king and the royal family; its historical function, in retrospect, was to provide an invaluable proving ground for the great family dynasties of wind players. Generations of Hotteterres and Philidors were blessed with economic security and ample opportunity for extensive performance on their chosen instruments. This in turn not only led to the betterment of performance techniques, but also, and most importantly, it stimulated needed reforms in the construction of the instruments themselves to the point that, soon after the turn of the century, French oboes and flutes were the most admired in Europe.

Music of the Royal Chapel

At the time François I ascended the throne (1515), he inherited from his predecessor, Louis XII, a Royal Chapel that was "impressive in both size and quality" (see Brobeck 1995, 188) It changed little during the late sixteenth and early seventeenth centuries. In principle, it was a stronghold of musical conservatism and thereby merely reflected the state of religious music in France until Louis XIV initiated some reforms after 1679.

As late as 1645, when Guillaume du Peyrat published his formidable *Histoire ecclésiastique de la cour ou les antiquitez et recherches de la chapelle et oratoire du Roy de France depuis Clovis Ier jusques à nostre temps, divisée en trois livres* (Ecclesiastical history of the court, or Early histories and studies of the chapel and oratory of the King of France from Clovis the First to our time, divided into three books), the Royal Chapel consisted of "two *sous-maîtres,* six boy sopranos, a first cornettist [*cornet ordinaire*], another cornettist, two falsettists [*dessus mués*], eight basses, eight tenors, eight *hautes-contres,*[7] eight chaplains, four chapel clerks and two grammar instructors for the children" (482).

The important post of *sous-maître,* which also could carry the title *Compositeur de la Chapelle,* had authority comparable to the *Surintendant de la Musique de la Chambre.* The *sous-maître* trained the choir and chose and composed music for the king's Mass and other important ceremonies. His immediate superior's position, *Maître de la Chapelle,* was usually an honorary appointment to the Royal Chapel and given to a highly placed ecclesiastic, such as the Archbishop of Paris or of Rheims, rather than to a musician.

In 1678 the Treaty of Nijmegen, which made Louis XIV the most powerful of Europe's monarchs for the next decade, gave him some respite from following his armies. At this time, he turned his attention to the transformation of Versailles, which had begun as early as 1661, and to his Royal Chapel.

The first chapel at Versailles was the chapel opposite the kitchens, dating from 1663 to 1670 and little larger than a salon; the second, a large one-storied salon located in the queen's wing, existed from 1670 to 1673. A third chapel was built in the king's wing on the site of the Salle du Sacré and was used from 1673 to 1682. The fourth chapel was inaugurated in 1682 when the king and his court made their permanent residence at Versailles. It was designed on two levels and was located in the king's wing on the site of the present Salon d'Hercule.[8] The magnificent final chapel, begun by Hardouin-Mansart and completed by Robert de Cotte, dates from the end of the aging monarch's rule (1710).

The *grand motet*, the *ne plus ultra* of French Baroque religious music, owes its very existence to the king's concept of music appropriate for the chapel of Europe's most powerful monarch. The 1708 *État de la France* lists, under "Musique de la Chapelle," eleven sopranos, eighteen *hautes-contres*, twenty-three tenors, twenty-four baritones, and fourteen basses (Morby 1971, 226). This suggests that the balance of the soprano section was made up of the young male *pages* assigned to the Chapel but not carried on the official roles in the seventeenth century. Cornetts were employed when necessary to lend support to the soprano section. Male sopranos, then, included falsettists, castrati (called *dessus italiens*), and boys.

The role of female singers at the Royal Chapel in the period of Louis XIV has not been well researched. According to Norbert Dufourcq, women "seem to have been introduced to the Royal Chapel at the time of Lully."[9] However, none were registered as *officiers* in the seventeenth century, so their names do not appear in the archives. Evidence of their presence lies in certain of the *grands motets* of Delalande gathered and copied in Philidor's *atelier* in 1689 and 1690. In *Exaudi Deus deprecationem*, for example, the copyist identified a "Mlle Delalande" as the singer of a twelve-measure soprano solo in the opening chorus. Jacques Bonnet certainly acknowledged the presence of female singers when he wrote, in 1715, that "the King's Music is ordinarily composed of 100 or 120 male and female musicians under the jurisdiction of the *Maître de la Musique de la Chapelle*" (423–424).

Instrumentalists, labeled *symphonists* or *concertants*, infiltrated the Royal Chapel in the late 1660s, due, perhaps, to the influence of early *grands motets* by Lully such as the *Miserere* of 1664, which was particularly favored by the king. The instrumentalists were never carried on the official lists of the *États des officiers de la Maison du Roi* pertaining to the Royal Chapel; no one would have dared create official Chapel positions for these musicians—especially for violinists destined to play for ballets and *divertissements*. Nonetheless, the 1708 *État de la France* enumerates the following instrumentalists for the "Musique de la Chapelle": six violins and violas, three bass violins, one *"grosse basse de violon,"* one theorbo, two flutes, two oboes, one bass crumhorn, two serpents, and one bassoon.[10]

In 1678, the king established a competition to choose four organists for his Chapel where there had previously been but one. The winners were Guillaume-Gabriel Nivers, Nicolas-Antoine Lebègue, Jacques Thomelin, and Jean-Baptiste Buterne. Succeeding his teacher, Thomelin, in 1693, François Couperin held this post until 1730. The salary of six hundred *livres* for each quarter was second only to that of the *sous-maîtres*, yet the only organs at Versailles appear to have been modest, positive instruments until the completion in 1709 of the *grand orgue* built by Étienne Enoc and Robert Clicquot.

From the sixteenth century to the Revolution, the kings of France were to demand, for their own Chapel, the best singers from Paris churches, such as Notre-Dame and the Sainte-Chapelle. Often the choir directors of the churches in Paris were themselves members of the Royal Chapel, which brought about an irregularity of service in their own parishes.[11] At the Sainte-Chapelle responsibility for the direction of the choir and the composition of the music lay with the *Maître de Musique des Enfants*, a position held by Marc-Antoine Charpentier for the last six years of his life.

The broad lines of demarcation placed between institutions constituting the king's music were artificial. They served administrative ends only. Members of each institution passed freely from one group to another, and several smaller, more nebulous groups were also marked for performance. Thus, the oboes that played at balls and *divertissements* might be drawn from the two companies of musketeers quartered at Versailles, each of whom boasted four oboists and six drummers. Trumpets could be supplied by the Stable as well as by the *Trompettes des Menus Plaisirs*, who were players drawn from the king's corps of bodyguards.

Performances by combined groups were common, especially for such ceremonies as coronations, royal births and deaths, marriages, and so on. Once a year on Saint Louis's eve, free public concerts were held in the Tuileries gardens. At this time the *Vingt-quatre Violons*, the trumpets and drums of the Great Stable, and the orchestra of the Académie Royale de Musique all joined together. In a sense it was the king's gift to the city of Paris, and for the poor of the teeming metropolis, it was a rare opportunity to catch a glimpse of delights taken for granted by the rich. The thrust of the crowds was such that on one occasion, we read in the *Mercure* of August 1719,[12] "After the fireworks, the crowd pushing to the gates of the Tuileries was so great that it cost the lives of six or eight women who were suffocated or crushed to death" (168).

Before taking leave of the king's music, we should acknowledge the role of Philidor, *l'âiné* (the elder), whose *atelier* preserved in manuscript so much of the music heard at Versailles during the reign of Louis XIV. André Danican Philidor, *l'âiné* (ca. 1652–1730), was the *Garde de la Bibliothèque de la Musique du Roi*. He served in the same capacity for the Count of Toulouse, Louis XIV's son by Mme de Montespan. We do not know when Philidor officially was appointed the king's music librarian. The archives do not show payment to him or to his *atelier* before 1684. Who were the copyists who worked side by side with Philidor? We know four by name: violinist François Fossard; Philidor's son-in-law, Jean-Louis Schwartzenberg, called Le Noble; one of the three known Ferriers who were wind players at the court; and the eldest of Philidor's twenty-one children, his son Anne Danican Philidor. We know that, at times, the *atelier* employed at least nine copyists in addition to Philidor and Fossard. Marcelle Benoit noted the following record of payment under the "comptes de la maison du roi" for the year 1697: "126 *livres* to Fossard and Philidor for nine copyists who worked for three days and two nights to copy the music of the pastorale *ISSÉ* by le sieur Destouches."[13]

The Town's Music

J'entends déjà par tout les charrettes courir,
Les massons travailler, les boutiques s'ouvrir;
Tandis que dans les airs mille cloches émues,
D'un funèbre concert font retentir les nues,
Et se mêlant au bruit de la grêle & des vents,
Pour honorer les morts, font mourir les vivans *(Nicolas Boileau-Despréaux*, Satire VI: Les Embarras de Paris*)*.

I already hear the carts rolling everywhere,
The masons working, the shops opening;
While in the air a thousand bells, touched by the emotion
Of a funeral concert, make the clouds resound,
And mingling with the noise of hail and winds
To honor the dead, make the living die.

The music of Paris in the *grand siècle* was more than the sound of Lully's orchestra at the Académie Royale de Musique, more than a

Charpentier Te Deum at the Sainte-Chapelle or a Couperin organ Mass at Saint-Gervais. It was the music of *mille cloches* (a thousand church bells), the music of the street punctuated by the cries of the hawkers. "There is not a city in the world," wrote Louis-Sébastien Mercier in his *Tableau de Paris* (1781), "where street sellers possess shriller or more piercing voices . . . . Sounds from their gullets drown out the noise and din of city squares" (cited by Lacroix 1875, 335).

Paris in the seventeenth century was still very much a medieval city: noisy, crowded, and malodorous. The stench of refuse from Les Halles was no respecter of royalty housed in the dark and uncomfortable apartments of the nearby Louvre. In 1706, according to the king's chief engineer, Sébastien Le Prestre de Vauban, the greater metropolitan area had 856,938 souls, and to Charles de Secondat, Baron de Montesquieu's Persian it must have seemed that all of them were concentrated in the center of town:

> *The houses are so high here, that one would judge them to be occupied only by astrologers. You well know that a city built in the air, which has six or seven houses one on top of the other, is extremely crowded, and that, when everybody goes down into the streets, there is great confusion (Montesquieu. 1721. "Lettre XXIV." In Lettres persanes).*

Yet the music of the streets was also heard in the sounds of the king's masons and carpenters at work lifting the face of the old city and creating, for an eternity to admire, the monuments of the age of Louis XIV. There was geometry in André Le Nôtre's garden of the Tuileries and in the closed forms of the royal squares (Place des Victoires and Place Louis-le-Grand). The classicism of Claude Perrault's colonnade of the Louvre was softened by Italian decoration. In the church of the Val-de-Grâce, the College of Mazarin, and the chapel of the Invalides, Italian Baroque exuberance was restrained by the same French classical spirit.

Much of the musical life of the city centered on an area bounded on the north by Les Halles, on the east by Saint-Gervais at the entrance to the Marais, on the west by the Tuileries, and on the south, across the Seine, by Saint-Severin and the Latin Quarter. Here were the most important churches: Saint-Merri, Saint-Gervais, Saint-Germain-l'Auxerrois, the Oratoire, Saint-Jean-en-Grève, Saint-Jacques-de-la-Boucherie, Notre Dame, the Sainte-Chapelle, and Saint-Severin. Within the same area were the Académie Royale de Musique and the home of the Concert Spirituel and the Concerts Italiens. Here too were the shops of the makers of stringed instruments (*luthiers*) and the builders of harpsichords and organs; and here in Montesquieu's "city built in the air," bordering on the Rue Saint-Martin near the hospital of Saint-Julien-des-Ménétriers, lived most of the musicians of the Confrérie of Saint-Julien.

Confrérie de Saint-Julien-des-Ménétriers

From 1321, when thirty-seven minstrels registered with the Provost of Paris to establish a musicians' guild, there was powerful, paternalistic protection for Parisian *"maîtres à danser et joueurs d'instruments tant haut que bas"* (dancing masters and the players of instruments both loud and soft).

During the sixteenth and seventeenth centuries, the purpose of the group was to protect its members against exploitation and to assure equal profit sharing. The articles governing the corporation, many of which are found in the documents of the *Minutier Central*, assured a remarkable degree of protection for the members of what was, in actuality, one of the first musicians' unions. If engaged for an *aubade* (or *réveil*—a dawn serenade), for example, members were supposed to share their profits with those who did not participate. All were required to give an accurate report of their earnings under pain of expulsion, and the members even enjoyed a type of medical insurance whereby those who were sick would be paid "as if they had worked" unless the illness were reported to be "shameful" (*honteuse*).[14]

The leader of the Confrérie was known as the *Roi des Ménétriers* and, later in the seventeenth century, as the *Roi des Violons.* The high point of the syndicate, both quantitatively and qualitatively, was reached in the late years of the sixteenth century and the early years of the seventeenth before the exodus of many of the best players from the Confrérie to the king's Chamber. The pages of the *Minutier Central* are filled with documentation of the syndicate's activities. It is curious that a series of legal papers, couched in the abstruse, archaic language of minor functionaries, can make flesh and blood of the Parisian *joueurs d'instruments.* The din and clamor of street life, the hand-to-mouth existence of these often illiterate musicians, are all recorded here. One can imagine the torrent of abuse and invective—the result of the frustrations of daily living—that must have motivated an item of 17 July 1602 whereby, if any member of the association "swears and blasphemes the name of God in anger or otherwise, or picks a quarrel with anyone else, in such a case the said individual must pay to the injured the sum of two crowns" (see Jurgens 1969).

For the town musician who was called upon to perform for weddings, engagement parties, banquets, masquerades, dawn and evening street serenades, and formal concerts, the notarized contracts were designed for protection from his fellows as much as from any outside exploitation. Thus, the eleven *joueurs d'instruments* who in 1618 formed an association to play together for thirteen years levied a fine of sixteen *sols* should any member miss the scheduled Friday afternoon rehearsals. The contracts carefully spelled out these instruments and their designated performers; in one instance we read that this was done to make sure that no one would change his part "without the consent of all his companions."

After the midyears of the seventeenth century, with many of its best players now affluent members of the *Vingt-quatre Violons du Roi*, the *Petits Violons*, the Stable, or, after 1673, the Opera orchestra, the Confrérie declined in importance. It had become fat, lazy, and complacent; worse, it had been corrupted by power. Secure behind its impressive array of royal patents and notarized articles, it lashed out in a series of power plays to force an even greater number of musicians into its orbit of control.

After the death of Louis Constantin in 1657, the *Roi des Violons* was the powerful Guillaume Dumanoir (1615–1697), who also signed himself "*Joueur de violon du Cabinet de Sa Majesté, l'un des Vingt-quatre Violons de sa Grande Bande, et pourvu aussi de l'office de Roy des joueurs d'instrumens et des maîtres à danser de France*" (Player in the *Violons du Cabinet* of His Majesty, one of the Twenty-four Violinists of his *Grande Bande*, and also has filled the post of King of instrumental players and masters of dance in France) (Dumanoir 1664; ed. of 1870, vii). In 1660 Guillaume I, as he was called with heavy sarcasm by Besche *l'aîné*,[15] was at the height of his power with some two hundred performers and composers under his command. He basked in the praise of Louis XIV (*"Notre très cher et bien-aimé Guillaume Dumanoir"*), yet one year later his fortune changed. The king effectively isolated him by appointing Lully to a position of unprecedented power, and thirteen of the *Maîtres de Danse* of the Confrérie actively revolted. In an *opera-buffa* atmosphere of charge and countercharge (satirized by Molière in the *maître de musique* and the *maître de danse* scenes from *Le Bourgeois gentilhomme*), the dancers petitioned for a royal patent to establish an Académie Royale de Danse. Their success in March 1661 gave them a position of strength from which to woo others of their colleagues away from the strictures of the Confrérie. The statutes state that in the city and suburbs, other master teachers of dance can aspire to join the founders and be received into the Academy should they be judged "worthy and capable." If a son of a dancer, they pay the sum of fifty *livres*; otherwise, they must pay three hundred *livres*.

The insistence of "Guillaume I" that the new academicians be subject to the rules of the Confrérie and his efforts to prevent their *Lettres Patentes* from being registered in Parliament resulted in a long series of polemics on both sides. Typical is a *Discours académique*

(Paris, 1663) prepared by the Académie Royale de Danse to prove that dance, in its nobility, has "no need of Instruments of Music and that it is totally independent of the Violin" (cited by Loubet de Sceaury 1949, 80). In a Pyrrhic victory of sorts, Dumanoir had the last word in his polemic of 1664, *Le Mariage de la musique avec la dance*: "In a word, who does not know that the Dance is not, properly speaking, an Art, but only an exercise" (ed. of 1870, 71).

In 1668 "Guillaume I" relinquished his throne to his son, "Guillaume II," who had learned little from his father's mistakes. The establishment of the Académie Royale de Musique in 1672 introduced a new, competitive element that worked to the disadvantage of the Confrérie. In a decree of 14 August 1673, Lully, who clearly took care of his own, gave his orchestral musicians permission to "play for balls, weddings, serenades, and other public *fêtes* and to take the salary paid them without any harassment from the *Maîtres* [i.e., the Confrérie]" (Loubet de Sceaury 1949, 99). This was the worst blow yet to the syndicate, for it found itself reduced to exercising its authority over café musicians from the bottom of the barrel.

In a final bid for power, the Confrérie blurred the lines of distinction found on all patents between the *maîtres à danser et joueurs d'instruments*, on the one hand, for example, and the *compositeurs de musique, organistes et professeurs de clavessin*, on the other, in order to bring the latter group under the jurisdiction of the Confrérie. However, the "composers of music, organists, and professors of harpsichord" had no intention of submitting to the abusive restrictions of the syndicate. In a document, quoted by Écorcheville, entitled *Raisons qui prouvent manifestement que les compositeurs et joueurs d'instruments d'harmonie ne peuvent être de la communauté des Ménestriers* (Reasons which manifestly prove that composers and players of keyboard instruments cannot be members of the *Ménétriers*), they stated:

> *The* maîtres *have taught violin to all the lackeys of Paris. They have played with riffraff* [racaille] *in order to get out of sharing profits with other* maîtres. *They have allowed most of their* maîtres *to play in cabarets against Article VI of their Statutes. They have accepted as* maîtres *all sorts of vagabonds and even coachmen to whom they have issued false credentials, although they have never filled a term of apprenticeship in the home of a* maître *(1906c, 28).*

Even religious organizations recognized the potential threat to their organists and composers. In a letter of 1692 addressed to the Lieutenant General of Police, a certain Sister Marguerite de Jésus of the Couvent de la Croix in the Faubourg Saint-Antoine wrote: "It takes only three or four years to master dance and violin playing. It takes fifteen and twenty years to form organists and to learn how to play the harpsichord" (Benoit and Dufourcq 1957, 42).

The king's organists, Lebègue, Nivers, Buterne, and François Couperin, petitioned the king for *Lettres Patentes* which would permanently remove the threat of coercion and economic privation initiated by the Confrérie. The king supported his organists and, in a royal patent of 25 June 1707, dealt a crushing blow to the Confrérie of Saint-Julien. The *Lettres Patentes* read, in part:

> *Wishing to treat favorably the organists of our chapel and others, who make their living teaching composition, and performers of the above mentioned* instruments d'harmonie, *and to maintain them in the free exercise of their profession, We have, by these presents, signed by Our hand . . . forbidden the so-called* maîtres à danser, joueurs d'instruments tant haut que bas et hautbois, *to trouble the petitioners in the exercise of their profession (Dumanoir 1664; ed. of 1870, 117).*

Ringing words, these, to emanate from an absolute monarch, and in the opinion of Besche, "the Organists of the King and those of the Capital were the first to undertake the defence of freedom in the Musical Art" (1774, 8). The Confrérie, now a butt of musical jokes, was immortalized a few years later (1717) in the satiric program suite of François Couperin, "Les Fastes de la grande et ancienne Mxnxstrxndxsx" (*Ménestrandise*).

In summary, however, it should be emphasized that the Confrérie had served an important role in the history of French instrumental music. In their best days members not only kept their ranks filled by means of a careful system of apprenticeship, but they also trained fine performers who made up the bulk of the king's instrumentalists. By showing instrumental distributions between 1583 and 1625, François Lesure has demonstrated that the *Vingt-quatre Violons* transferred to the court the scoring practices of the Confrérie orchestra with their predilection for many treble and bass instruments (1954, 52).

The Confrérie de Saint-Julien-des-Ménétriers "had suffered diverse fortunes" since its founding in the fourteenth century as Écorcheville points out, "but its church, its hospital, a concert hall, and, above all, a solid syndical organization still rendered service to those whose métier was music" (1906c, 21).[16]

Académie Royale de Musique[17]

In the *Lettres Patentes* of 28 June 1669, Louis XIV accorded "Our well-loved and faithful Pierre Perrin" the sole privilege of establishing "Académies d'Opéra" in the realm for performances "en Musique en langue françoise" modeled on academies that had been established in Italy "for several years" (cited by Loubet de Sceaury 1949, 92).

Little matter that there were no such royal academies for the performance of opera in Italy or in Germany and England as Perrin had claimed. He had touched a point of national pride in Colbert and maneuvered the creation of yet another institution. Perrin now had a guaranteed, twelve-year dictatorship over opera production in France.

The sordid tale of his misadventures (see Chapter 6) reached a climax with the unfortunate man's imprisonment for debt. Impatiently awaiting just such a chance was Jean-Baptiste Lully, who had committed one of the few errors of judgment in his career by refusing to believe that the French wanted a national opera. Now, acting with dispatch, Lully purchased the entire privilege from Perrin, promising him a pension for life and paying him a sum sufficient to repay his creditors and to be released from debtor's prison. The king was informed of this move, presumably by Mme de Montespan, and before 16 March 1672 he formally transferred the privilege to his *Surintendant de Musique:* "In order to assure greater success, We believed it appropriate to give control (of the opera) to an individual whose experience and capacity We know well . . . " (cited by Loubet de Sceaury 1949, 93). To avoid duplication and perhaps to assure a fresh beginning, the king changed the name of the organization from the Académies d'Opéra to the Académie Royale de Musique, and further, he extended the privilege from a dozen years to the lifetime of Lully and his heirs. In actuality after Lully's death, the privilege passed in and out of the hands of Jean-Nicolas Francine, Lully's son-in-law, until his retirement in 1728, when the opera came under the direction of André Cardinal Destouches, who was followed in quick succession by Gruer in 1730, Lecomte in 1731, Armand-Eugène de Thuret in 1733, and François Berger from 1744 to 1747.

More clever and more ruthless than Perrin, Lully succeeded in obtaining additional, repressive patents that assured him absolute power over French stage music and effectively immobilized potential rivals (see Chapter 5).

In Jacques-Bernard Durey de Noinville's *Histoire du théâtre de l'Académie Royale de Musique en France*, we may read the many articles issued by the king at Versailles and Marly in 1713 and 1714 to assure more effective administrative control over the Paris Opera. These regulations obviously grew from the smooth-running and efficient organization that Lully had made of the Académie Royale de Musique. Among other items we learn that free schools of music and dance were established (Article II); a lucrative pension system for singers and dancers was created (Article XIII); and medical coverage was provided, assuring a pension to those "crippled in the service of the Opera" (Article XLI).

For almost one hundred years (1674–1763) the home of French opera was the Grande Salle of the Palais Royal that had been occupied by Molière's troupe at the time of that great playwright's death in 1673. Inaugurated in 1641, the hall was one of two built for Cardinal Richelieu in the Palais Royal (known also as the Palais Cardinal). Lully modified it with the 3000 *livres* given to him by Louis XIV. It was renovated in 1732 and again in 1749, then destroyed by fire in 1763. Barely satisfactory for the type of spectacle envisioned by Lully and later by Rameau, it was much longer than wide with a parterre, a gallery (amphitheater), three rows of loges (the last row labeled *Paradis*), and a double balcony. The theater was cramped. Henri Lagrave (1972, 86) estimated that the hall would accommodate between 1300 and 1400 spectators, although there were only 1270 seats. Its stage was small. From the English translation of Luigi Riccoboni's *Réflexions historiques et critiques sur les différens théâtres de l'Europe* (1738), we read:

> *The Decorations of the Stage of the Opera are very handsome, but not to be compared with those of Italy, the Smallness of the Stage not admitting of their being either so large or so magnificent as those of the vast Theaters of Venice, Milan, etc. (1741, 152).*

In his satiric pamphlet of 1753, the Baron F. W. von Grimm had his *"petit prophète de Boehmisch-Broda"* describe the Paris Opera as a marionette theater. Charles De Brosses, after visiting Naples in 1739, commented that the stage alone of San Carlo was larger than the entire Paris Opera (see Paul-Marie Masson 1930, 117).

The price remained fairly uniform and was "double that of any other Entertainment, in proportion to the Preference of Places" according to Riccoboni (1741, 153). Writing in his preface to Volume 6 of Rameau's complete works (*Oeuvres complètes de J.-P, Rameau* 1900, xxv), Charles Malherbe informs us that at the beginning of the eighteenth century, admission to the balcony or on the stage was eleven *livres*, ten *sols*; seven *livres*, four *sols* for the first loges and gallery; three *livres*, twelve *sols* for the second loges; one *livre*, sixteen *sols* for the third loges (the *Paradis*) and the parterre. The printed *livret* (libretto) was sold for thirty *sols* at the door of the theater before each performance.

Joachim Christoph Nemeitz, an affluent German traveler, included much information in his *Séjour de Paris* (1727) regarding the Paris musical scene of the 1720s as seen through the eyes of a class-conscious young *galant*. In his "faithful Instruction for Travelers of Means," he ranked seating arrangements in the Paris theaters as follows:

> At the Comedies [Comédie Française and Comédie Italienne] a man of quality takes his place on the Stage and in one of the first Loges, or in the Parterre, if there are not too many people. But rarely in the second Loge which is for the bourgeois, and never in the Amphitheater where all sorts of riffraff are assembled. But the Amphitheater of the Opera is honorable and has the rank of the first Loge. The second Loge is still passable. But no one would willingly seat himself in the alleged Paradis, excepting the Balcony which is on the side. The Balcony, below, to the side of the stage, is for gentlemen of distinction and costs ten livres per person. But the Parterre is sometimes visited by people even of the first quality, since one has the advantage there of being able to enter or to leave freely without disturbing anyone. When one is in the Parterre of the Comédie or the Opera, one takes care to whistle at some Actor or to clap his hands in order to mock him. This gives rise sometimes to disagreements (1727, 105).

In general, *tragédies lyriques* (called *tragédies en musique* at that time) and *opéras-ballets* were performed at five o'clock in the afternoon on Sundays, Tuesdays, Thursdays, and Fridays during the winter; the summer schedule omitted Thursday performances. Out of deference to the wishes of the church, the Opera closed twenty-three days during the Easter season and eleven days annually for solemn religious feasts.

In 1712 Louis XIV ordered the construction of the Magasin, an annex to the Académie Royale de Musique, which provided rehearsal space, schools of singing and dance, administrative offices, a library, and a ballroom. In 1715 the Académie Royale de Musique received permission to sponsor public balls in the theater from 11 November until Advent and from Epiphany to Shrove Tuesday. The royal patent specifically stated that "His Majesty very expressly forbade entrance to anyone who is not masked." According to Durey de Noinville, the balls began at eleven o'clock at night and ended at six or seven o'clock the next morning. Thirty musicians assembled half an hour before the dancing commenced to give a concert "of large-scale pieces of instrumental music *[symphonie]* by the best masters" (1757, 1:164).

The Concert Spirituel[18]

"The taste for music," we read in the *Mercure de France*, "has never been so universal. In Paris and in the smallest provincial towns, Concerts and Academies of Music have been maintained at considerable cost, and new ones are established each day" (April 1727, 747). The first permanent concert organization to give series of subscription concerts on a commercial basis came into being in Paris two years earlier. It was the Concert Spirituel founded in 1725 by Anne Danican Philidor (1681–1728), the eldest son of André Danican Philidor, *l'aîné*. In order to circumvent the notorious privilege created for Lully that prevented anyone without written permission from singing any piece in its entirety whether in French or other languages, Philidor agreed to pay the sum of ten thousand *livres* per year for three years to Francine, administrative head of the Académie Royale de Musique and Lully's son-in-law. Philidor further agreed to prevent the performance of operatic fragments or pieces with French texts.

The concerts took place on religious holidays when the Académie Royale de Musique was closed. Durey de Noinville (1757, 170) stated that this amounted to about twenty-four concerts a year and included the following feast days: Feast of the Purification of the Virgin (2 February), Feast of the Annunciation (25 March), from Passion Sunday (two Sundays before Easter) to Quasimodo (one Sunday after Easter) inclusive, Ascension Day, Pentecost, Corpus Christi, Feast of the Assumption of the Virgin (15 August), Nativity of the Virgin (8 September), All Saints Day (1 November), Conception of the Virgin (8 December), Christmas Eve, and Christmas Day.

The inaugural concert was held on 18 March (Passion Sunday) 1725 in the Salle des Suisses of the Tuileries Palace. This hall was a gift from Louis XV and remained the home of the Concert Spirituel until 1784. The first program included a suite of airs for strings by Delalande; the *grands motets Confitebor tibi* and *Cantate Domino*, also by Delalande; and the "Christmas" Concerto (Opus 6, No. 8) by Arcangelo Corelli.

The performers at the Concert Spirituel were usually first-rate; the vocal soloists came from the Opera, and the chorus was made up of some of the best singers of the Royal Chapel and the principal churches of Paris. Motets by Lully, Nicolas Bernier, Louis Marchand, Destouches, Jean-François Lalouette, Jean Gilles, François Petouille, Henry Desmarest, Michel Pignolet de Montéclair, Louis-Antoine Dornel, François Colin de Blamont, André Campra, and many others were performed; but throughout the history of the Concert Spirituel, the motets of Delalande remained the examples of this genre most in demand.

Like the early history of the Opéra Comique, the story of the Concert Spirituel is that of an organization acclaimed by audiences and performers alike, yet beset by financial woes and impossible restrictions brought about, in part, by jealous rivals. Philidor resigned in 1728 a few months before his death, and the enterprise was taken over by Michel Delannoy, Pierre Simart, and the composer Jean-Joseph Mouret. During this administration, the complexion of the concerts changed somewhat: Italian performers and compositions were much in vogue; instrumental music began to achieve a significance that would contribute substantially to the development of the sonata and the concerto in France. Among the violinists were Jean-Baptiste Anet, a student of Corelli's, and Jean-Pierre Guignon, the *Roi des Violons* who specialized in the sonatas and concertos of Antonio Vivaldi and who was rivaled at the concerts by the great French composer-performer, Jean-Marie Leclair.

Financially, this administration fared no better than that of Philidor, and on 25 December 1734, the Académie Royale de Musique moved in to take control of the Concert Spirituel. The musical direction was wisely given to violinist-composer Jean-Féry Rebel and to François Francolar. Although each concert included at least one *grand motet*, the main significance of the Concert Spirituel lay more and more in the domain of instrumental music. Each program contained at least one sonata or concerto for violin played by Guignon or Leclair, and Italian and German symphonies began to appear on the programs in the late 1740s.

Under the direction of Joseph-Nicolas-Pancrace Royer, Gabriel Capperan, and, after the death of Royer in 1755, Joseph Cassanéa de Mondonville, the instrumental and vocal forces of the Concert Spirituel (according to Durey de Noinville 1757, 173–176) were as follows: vocal soloists included four sopranos, one *haute-contre*, and three baritones; and the chorus was made up of twelve sopranos, fourteen *hautes-contres*, seven tenors, and five lower voices (basses and baritones). The particular distribution of parts demonstrates the domination of the *haute-contre* over the tenor in French vocal writing of the Baroque period. The *Symphonie* consisted of sixteen violins, two violas, six basses, two double basses, five flutes and oboes, and three bassoons. This reflects the strong emphasis on treble and bass instruments that characterized French scoring practices during the same period.

The Concert Spirituel existed for sixty-six years. It provided an important forum for new music: vocal and instrumental, religious and secular. It thereby contributed in no small way to the formation of new musical attitudes on the part of French composers, performers, and consumers of music in the eighteenth century.

Coexisting with the Concert Spirituel in its early days were two additional concert series: the so-called Concerts Français and the Concerts Italiens. Philidor established the Concerts Français just six months before his resignation from the directorship of the Concert Spirituel. Its concerts were held in the Tuileries on Saturdays and Sundays during the winter season. This series had a big advantage in having obtained the services of two of the best singers at the Opera: Mlle Catherine-Nicole Le Maure and Mlle Marie Antier. The programs included *divertissements* and cantatas, for the most part in French. Over one hundred concerts were given from 1727 to November 1730, when, except for scattered concerts, the series terminated.[19]

The Concerts Français competed directly with the Concerts Italiens (founded in 1724 by Pierre Crozat and the Marquise de Prie), which also gave subscription concerts in the Tuileries—theirs on Thursdays and Saturdays. We learn from Titon du Tillet that at the Concerts Italiens:

> *They only performed Italian music; they were almost entirely Italian musicians, with some Frenchmen who had been in Italy . . . Several* Amateurs de la Musique Italienne *. . ., such as M. Crozat, M. Gaudiori, Guardian of the Royal Treasury, and others, established this Concert [series], whose expenses they underwrote (1732, 677).*

Thus was inaugurated the age of the wealthy middle-class entrepreneur that reached its height in Rameau's sponsor, the financier Alexandre-Jean-Joseph Le Riche de La Pouplinière (1693–1762). Financier Antoine Crozat (1655–1738), whom Saint-Simon deemed "the richest man in Paris," gave concerts at his home on the Rue de Richelieu from 1715 to 1724 (Daval 1961, 114). Then, for thirty-one years (1731–1762), private concerts under the financial direction of La Pouplinière presented to the Parisian musical world some of the most important performers and compositions of the period.

⁓ Part One ⁓

Stage Music

Chapter 2

Ballet de Cour I: *From Beaujoyeulx to Lully*

On the evening of 15 October 1581 from ten at night to half past three in the morning, the *Balet comique de la Royne* (as the title was originally written) was performed at the Petit Bourbon palace in Paris. This first court ballet[1] was part of the second day's festivities celebrating the marriage of the Duc de Joyeuse and the queen's sister, Marguerite de Vaudémont. There is no evidence that the spectators, numbering in an exaggerated estimate by Beaujoyeulx as being between "nine or ten thousand," heard an "*invention moderne*" (Beaujoyeulx 1582, "Au lecteur") in this long performance, nor is there any reason to suppose that the queen mother, Catherine de Médici, or that Henry III's queen, Louise de Lorraine, realized that their favorite project, carried out by Beaujoyeulx at the staggering cost of close to 200,000 pounds, was the most important attempt to date in France to unify poetry, dance, music, and decor within one continuous action.

To all appearances, the *Ballet comique de la reine* (as it was later referred to) was one more ambitious *fête* in the tradition of sixteenth-century entertainments at the court of the Valois kings. The mythological personages, the nymphs and satyrs, the political allusions, the eulogies of the monarch, and the elaborate machinery had their counterparts in earlier *fêtes* at Fontainebleau and Bayonne, which, in their turn, had been modeled on Italian masquerades and pastorales.

Two immediate forerunners of the *Ballet comique de la reine* were the *divertissement Le Paradis d'amour* and the *Ballet des Polonais*. *Le Paradis d'amour* (text by Pierre de Ronsard) was presented on 20 August 1572 as part of the celebration of the marriage of Henri de Navarre and Marguerite de Valois. On the night of 19 August 1573, sixteen royal ladies representing the sixteen provinces of France danced the *Ballet des Polonais*, which Catherine de Médici had commissioned from Beaujoyeulx to honor the Polish ambassadors.

In its allegorical character, its vocal solos, its machinery, and its dancing, *Le Paradis d'amour* evokes much of the same atmosphere as the later *Ballet comique de la reine*. More importantly, this episodic ballet does have a central plot in which allegory had the Huguenot bridegroom and his followers sent to Hell by the Catholic defenders of Paradise: Charles IX and his brothers. A fateful acting-out of the smoldering hostilities exploded only four days after the performance in the Massacre of Saint Bartholomew's Eve (see Yates 1947, 254–259).

In spite of the unity of action exhibited by *Le Paradis d'amour*, it is the later, more elaborate *Ballet comique de la reine* that in the opinion of later aestheticians and historians deserves a significant place in the development of French dramatic music. Typical is the comment of Pierre-Louis d'Aquin de Château-Lyon, who described the *Ballet comique* as the first work in France to give "some idea of the musical theater" (1753, 1:156). For some, the *Ballet comique* was not only the first example of a dramatic representation in music and dance, it was also the first work of this genre to demonstrate the ubiquitous, albeit ill-defined, "good taste" or "*le bon goût*" of the seventeenth- and eighteenth-centuries (see, for example, Germain Boffrand 1715, 1:27).

It is impossible to determine how many writers of later generations were actually familiar with the text and music of the *Ballet comique* and how many were echoing, often verbatim, the opinions of others. The 1582 edition printed in Paris by Adrian Le Roy, Robert Ballard, and Mamert Patisson was well known in later times.[2] Claude-François Ménestrier summarized the action and included textual fragments from it in his *Des représentations en musique anciennes et modernes* (1681). Charles Burney owned a copy, and Jean-Benjamin de La Borde in his *Essai sur la musique ancienne et moderne* (1780) mentioned its availability in the king's library. Did the brothers Claude and François Parfaict, those meticulous compilers of all manner of information on the French theater, write from direct observation when they invited all to "read again the singing *vers* of the ballet of 1582 . . . you will observe there the birth of '*le bon goût*,'" or were they merely quoting Jean-Laurent Lecerf de la Viéville's work, where the identical sentence is found?[3]

In writing the 1582 preface, Beaujoyeulx was aware that he had indeed created an *invention moderne*, for he stated that "never has a ballet been printed in which the word *comique* was employed" (1582, "Au lecteur"). He saw the necessity of justifying his coupling of *ballet* and *comique*. It follows in this context that *comique* describes a work containing dramatic unity. In like manner did Saint-Hubert in his *La Manière de composer et faire réussir les ballets* (1641) define ballet as "*comédie muette*," an apt description appropriated forty years later by Ménestrier in his *Des ballets anciens et modernes*.

The *Ballet comique de la reine* had a clear relationship to the concept of humanism as formulated by the *Pléiade* and by Jean-Antoine de Baïf's Académie de Poésie et de Musique (which had become the Académie du Palais under Henri III). This is not surprising. The Duc de Joyeuse had been a financial supporter of Baïf's Académie; and Lambert Beaulieu, the chief composer of the *Ballet comique*, was closely associated with the co-founder of the Académie, Thibaud de Courville. The commendatory poem found at the beginning of the printed edition supports the humanistic mystique of the ballet in the lines:

> Et la façon tant estimée
> De nos poètes anciens,
> Les Vers avecques la musique,
> Le Balet confus mesuré,
> Démonstrant du ciel azuré
> L'Accord par un effect mystique.
>
> *And the manner so esteemed*
> *Of our former poets—*
> *The verses with music,*
> *The disordered ballet measured,*
> *Demonstrating accord*
> *From azure heavens by a mystical effect.*

The syllabic choruses do resemble the *vers mesuré à l'antique* (see Example 2-1); and the carefully planned, geometric figures of the concluding *grand ballet* graphically represent the Pythagorean-Platonic bias of the Académie. In defining ballet in his preface as a "geometric mingling of several dancers," Beaujoyeulx viewed his project as being within the humanistic milieu of the Académie (1582; rpt. 1971, "Au lecteur").

The *Ballet comique* owes its existence to many hands. The exact role of the Huguenot poet Agrippa d'Aubigny is still in doubt. He claimed to have been the real author of the ballet (see Yates 1947, 257). Most scholars, however, credit Beaujoyeulx with its master plan and the overall organization of the dances.

Baltasar de Beaujoyeulx (born Baltazarini da Belgiojoso, died ca. 1587) arrived in France about 1555. According to Pierre Bourdeille, Seigneur de Brantôme, it was the Maréchal de Brissac who sent

Beaujoyeulx from Piedmont with his *"bande de viollons très exquise"* to be employed by Catherine de Médici as a *valet de chambre*. Brantôme, who, it should be remembered, was a close personal friend of the musician, also informs us that Beaujoyeulx was the *"meilleur viollon de la chrestienté"* (cited by Prunières 1914, 78). Beaujoyeulx had arranged the dances in the *Ballet des Polonais*. Now he was assisted in the creation of the *Ballet comique* by Lambert Beaulieu and Jacques Salmon, who were responsible for the music. La Chesnaye wrote the text, and Jacques Patin, *"peintre du Roy,"* designed the stage sets and costumes.

The 1582 edition reveals French lyric drama in embryo. There is a single line of dramatic action: to destroy the power of the enchantress, Circé, through the intervention of Mercury, Pallas, Pan, and Jupiter in order to re-establish harmony, reason, and order. This theme is coupled with adulatory references to the king—political propagandists and flatterers have been finding their own values in art for a long time.

The extant music includes eight choruses (one *a*4, five *a*5, and two *a*6), two vocal solos, two duos with choral refrains, and two sets of instrumental dances. Accompaniments for the vocal solos and duos were not printed. The 1582 edition, which gives many details regarding the action and setting, is very vague concerning specific instrumentation. Flageolets, *orgues doulces* (soft organs), harps, lutes, lyres, oboes, cornetts, sackbuts, recorders, *violons* (generic term for all strings of the violin family), and *"aultres doux instrumens"* (other soft instruments) are mentioned throughout the score; and we are told that during the descent of Jupiter, forty musicians (vocalists and instrumentalists) performed in the *voûte dorée* (a cloud machine which was illuminated inside). The dances, scored in five-part texture, were performed by ten *violons* and constitute the earliest printed music of the violin family.

The intrinsic musical value of the *Ballet comique* is not commensurate with its historical position. The choral music is square and rigidly homophonic, with only an occasional cross relation to lend some harmonic interest (Example 2-1).

Example 2-1. Extract from Chorus, "Allez, filles d'Achellois," *Ballet comique de la Reine* (after ed. of 1582).

The dances, however—especially the famous "Son de la clochette"—have formal charm despite the almost geometric regularity of their phrase groupings. The long dialogue between Glauque and Tethys is one of the earliest examples of declamatory singing in stage music, but the long melismas on inconsequential and unaccented words indicate a general lack of concern with either the rules of prosody or a dramatic rendering of the text.

The components of a typical seventeenth-century court ballet are the following: *récits, vers, entrées*, and usually a concluding *grand ballet*. The word *récit* should not be confused with *récitatif*. As a generic term, it was used to characterize "that which is sung by only one voice" (Furetière 1690, 3:unpaged). Therefore, a *récitatif* is a particular type of *récit*. In the Baroque period, the term applied as well to passages for solo instruments such as a *récit de viol*. In the court ballet, *récits* were at first declaimed, but beginning with the *Ballet de la reine* of 1609 and the *Ballet de Monseigneur le Duc de Vendôme* of 1610, vocal solos substituted for declamation. Such *récits* generally occurred at the beginning of each section of the ballet and separated the ballet into acts. They were most often performed by characters who did not dance. Similar to the *air de cour* in structure and melodic shape, they commented on the dramatic action. It is important to emphasize that the vocal music of court ballets also included choruses and polyphonic airs as well as solo *récits*. These airs were provided by the most important composers of court airs, including Pierre Guédron, Antoine Boesset, and Étienne Moulinié. Boesset, for example, contributed over seventy polyphonic airs and solo *récits* to twenty-five court ballets (see Durosoir 1991, 240–249).

Vers pour les personnages were rhymed verses distributed among the spectators. They were included in the *livre du ballet* (later known as the *livret*) and occasionally contained indiscreet references to the royal dancers. The publication of detailed descriptions of the *mise-en-scène* and identification of the dancers in *livrets* became customary after 1610. Michel de Pure complained that the *vers* were the "weakest and least important part of the ballet . . . an ornamental pastiche" (1668, 296).

Entrées, which separated the acts into scenes, began with the entry of elaborately costumed and masked dancers who were identified not only by their pantomime, their dances, and characteristic music, but also by the *vers* and *récits*. The *danses de caractère*, which made up many of the *entrées*, were dances believed to be characteristic of certain countries or regions. Jean-Baptiste Dubos defined the term as referring to a dance whose "melody and rhythm imitate a specific style and which is, therefore, assumed to be appropriate for certain peoples"

(1719; ed. of 1770, 3:184). Ménestrier commented in his *Remarques pour la conduite des ballets* that "melody has different characteristics in different countries; it is heavy in Germany, serious and forceful in Spain, lively in Italy, and regular in France" (1658; rpt. as appendix 1967, 224).

The *grand ballet*, a forerunner of the operatic finale, concluded the ballet and was danced by the *grands seigneurs* and, at least once each year, by the king himself. It was distinguished from the other *entrées* by an "*atmosphère de luxe*," often in marked contrast to the limited abilities of its dancers (La Laurencie 1920, 76). Michel de Pure, a witness of the collaboration between Lully and Benserade in the composition of court ballets, described the frustration of Lully, who was continually embarrassed by the "stupidity of most of the *grands Seigneurs*" (1668, 248), many of whom appeared quite incapable of mastering the more rapid steps. The dancers, who generally remained masked throughout, were members of the court plus a few professionals in the service of the king. In "ballets of the king," men took the roles of female characters; in "ballets of the queen," women of the court were permitted to dance.

From the late sixteenth century to the death of Lully in 1687, court ballets were performed in Paris at the Grande Salle of the Louvre, the Grand Salon of the Tuileries Palace, the Palais Royal, the Hôtel de Ville, and, until its destruction in 1660, at the Salle du Petit Bourbon (between the Louvre and the church of St.-Germain-l'Auxerrois). Outside Paris, performances took place at the royal chateaux at Compiègne, Fontainebleau, Chantilly, Vincennes, St.-Germain-en-Laye, and Chambord.

All court ballets resulted from the collaboration of a royal patron, poets for the *vers* and *récits*, at least two composers responsible for the vocal and instrumental music, and a machinist to plan and execute the elaborate stage machinery. The patron determined the subject matter (*sujet*) and the distribution of labor.

The role of Louis XIII in the choice and treatment of the *sujet* must not be underestimated. In the *Ballet de la Merlaison* performed at Chantilly on 15 March 1635, the choreography, airs, and even the costumes were "all the invention of His Majesty" (Lacroix 1868, 5:113). The king also chose the subject for the *Ballet de la délivrance de Renaud*, performed on 29 January 1617, for which he created his own role as a demon of fire. This popular theme of deliverance, adapted from Tasso's *Gerusalemme liberata*, is also the subject of the *Ballet de l'aventure de Tancrède en la forêt enchantée*, which was performed in the Grande Salle of the Louvre on 12 February 1619. It took little imagination to interpret the combat of Tancrède and his cavaliers against the monsters of the enchanted forest as an allegorical representation of Louis XIII and his favorite *grand seigneur*, Charles d'Albert de Luynes, delivering France from her enemies.

The Jesuits also were quick to realize the propaganda potential of ballet, and at Rheims in 1628 they mounted a production of *La Conquête du char de la gloire* in which giants of the black tower (Huguenots of La Rochelle) hold captive the knights, who are eventually liberated by the shepherd, Caspis (Richelieu), after Théandre (Louis XIII) has killed the dragon of the tower (see Chastel in Christout 1967, 3).

Jacques de Gouy suggested, in the preface to his *Airs à quatre parties sur la paraphrase des psaumes de Godeau* (Paris 1650, fol. iii), that Louis XIII would have much preferred spending all his time in the preparation and performance of ballets if only the "cares of governing so many people in such difficult times had allowed him leisure commensurate with his zeal." The appendix to the present book translates a description of the preparation of the *Ballet du grand bal de la Douairière de Billebahaut* danced by Louis XIII at the Hôtel de Ville in Paris on 25 February 1626. The order to prepare the Hôtel de Ville for this performance had been given by the king to his *Conseiller d'État* at the Louvre on 4 February, and all subordinates in the complex chain of command went feverishly to work to build the elaborate machines, construct platforms, and prepare the banquet halls and rooms of the Hôtel de Ville. From this description, found in the *Histoire de la ville de Paris* (1725) by Dom Michel Félibien and Guy-Alexis Lobineau, it is clear that neither labor nor expense was stinted in the preparation of a court ballet.

Too often, poets of second rank composed the verses for the *vers*, *récits*, and *airs*, although Jean Bertaut, François de Malherbe, Sigongnes, Pierre de L'Estoile, Charles Sorel, Jean Bordier, Racan, Théophile de Viau, and Vincent Voiture are known to have supplied texts for the music of Pierre Guédron, Gabriel Bataille, Vincent, the Boessets (Antoine and Jean-Baptiste), Moulinié, François Richard, François de Chancy, Louis de Mollier, Michel Lambert, and Jean de Cambefort.

The machinists, usually brought in from Italy, held a position second to none in the creation of court ballets. Enthusiastic descriptions of complex, quick scene changes are plentiful in seventeenth-century sources. "In rapid succession one saw the Plain of Casale, the snow-covered Alps, the stormy sea, the yawning pit of Hell, and the opening of the sky with Jupiter descending," wrote Michel de Marolles in describing the long *Ballet de la prospérité des armes de la France* (five acts, thirty-six *entrées*), which was performed 7 February 1641 (1656 1:126). From time to time voices were raised against an opulence that too often indicated "more of purse than intelligence" (Michel de Pure

1668, 303). It is refreshing in the midst of such excesses to read both Marolles and Saint-Hubert, who singled out the *Ballet des doubles femmes* (1626) as an example of a successful ballet which cost little to produce and which contained none of those "large machines and long perspectives which, rather than adding grace to the setting, often acted as detriments to the performers" (Marolles 1645; 1656 1:71).

Saint-Hubert's *La Manière de composer et faire réussir les ballets* is one of the earliest and most informative sources for a study of the seventeenth-century court ballet. According to Saint-Hubert, ballet, riding, and fencing were the three proper forms of exercise for the nobility. He recognized two principal types of ballets: the serious and the grotesque; and he acknowledged the possibility of their coexisting within the same ballet. He classified ballets by their length: a *"ballet royal"* ordinarily included thirty *entrées*, a *"beau"* ballet had at least twenty *entrées*, and a *"petit"* had ten to twelve. He enumerated six necessary components for the creation of a worthy ballet: subject, airs, dances, costumes, machinery, and organization. Calling attention to the danger of rushing through preparation for a ballet and perhaps admonishing those among the nobility who were too lazy to "exercise," Saint-Hubert added:

> It is very necessary to take time to study the steps and the entrées. That which is improvised never succeeds well; fifteen days for a grand ballet and eight days for a petit ballet would not be too much time to spend in preparation (1641, 17).

About 1620, Michel Henry, a violinist of the Royal Chamber, copied an important collection of ballet music. Unfortunately, the music in Henry's hand is not extant, but his list enumerates 117 ballets of which 96 were performed between 1597 and 1618, thus giving some gauge of the popularity of the genre (see Lesure 1956). Charles Chevalier, Pierre Beauchamps, and Pierre-Francisque Caroubel are three of eleven men whom Henry identifed as composers of the dance music for thirty-three of these ballets. The structural significance of the single, unifying dramatic plot of the *Ballet comique de la reine* had little impact on those responsible for most of the ballets on Henry's list. These works, which borrowed liberally from the *mascarades à l'italienne* and the court *fêtes*, included many *entrées* of colorful and grotesque characters with no relation to any central plot. Such titles as *Mascarade des foux* (1596), *Ballet des barbiers* (1598), *Ballet des sorciers*(1601), *Ballet des garçons de taverne* (1603), *Ballet des paysans et des grenouilles* (1607), *Ballet des filles de joye* (1608), and *Ballet des ivrognes* (1609) illustrate the preoccupation at the turn of the century with burlesque elements (crazy people, barbers, sorcerers, tavern waiters, peasants, prostitutes, and drunks).

Not until 1609, with the *Ballet de la reine* (*vers* by Malherbe), and 1610, with the *Ballet d'Alcine ou de Monsieur de Vendôme*, was there a return to the unified dramatic action established twenty-nine years before by Beaujoyeulx. This type of ballet, labeled *ballet mélodramatique* by Prunières, remained in vogue for about a decade. At its best in such works as the *Ballet de Minerve* (1615), *Ballet de la délivrance de Renaud* (1617), *Ballet de l'aventure de Tancrède . . .* (1619), and *Ballet de Psyché* (1619), the *ballet mélodramatique* was a convincing dramatic spectacle, although the *récits* composed by Pierre Guédron (1565–1621) for *Renaud* and *Tancrède* rarely approach dramatic declamation.[4] Oddly enough, Guédron's genuine dramatic gifts may be better observed in such late *récits* as "Quel excès de douleur" and "Toi de qui la rigueur" (in Book 9 of *Airs de cour mis en tablature de luth par Anthoine Boesset* [1620]), which are totally independent of any known court ballet.

Although there is little information regarding the use of specific instruments in the *Ballet de la délivrance de Renaud* and the *Ballet de l'aventure de Tancrède . . .* , the *livret* to *Renaud* (printed by Ballard in 1617) describes the "concert" at the beginning of the ballet as having been performed by "sixty-four voices, twenty-eight viols, and fourteen lutes conducted by *le sieur* Mauduit" (Lacroix 1868, 2:102). By the time of *Tancrède* the large number of treble instruments (four cornetts, four oboes, and six flutes) that characterized French operatic scoring until the time of Rameau was already in place. With its unified plot, use of chorus, and spectacular theatrical finales, the *ballet mélodramatique* bordered on opera.

In 1621, after the death of Louis XIII's favorite patron of the ballet, the Duc de Luynes, the *ballet mélodramatique* was superseded by the *ballet à entrées*, which, as the name implies, was a purely choreographic spectacle: a succession of tableaux and pantomimes and a steady procession of elaborately costumed figures. The unity of plot established by Beaujoyeulx and nurtured by the *ballet mélodramatique* was discarded. The apparent abruptness of this change has perplexed many modern historians, who have speculated widely on the causes.

Their attention is perhaps unwarranted, for almost from its inception, decorative elements had threatened any tendencies towards dramatic unity in the *ballet de cour*. The structural differences described by Prunières and others apparently escaped the notice of such keen observers as Saint-Hubert or Marolles, who could not have anticipated the significance twentieth-century historians would attach to the *ballet mélodramatique* as an important precursor of French opera.

Yet in fact, under the patronage of a musically sophisticated monarch, the *ballet mélodramatique* pointed towards opera up to the time of the death of Luynes and Guédron. All the necessary constituents were included, not least of which was a composer who, if judged by his late *récits*, exhibited real dramatic flair. Why, indeed, was French opera not created some fifty years before Lully's *Cadmus et Hermione?*

The mixture of serious and grotesque elements would not have disturbed audiences of that time, who were accustomed to this "baroque" juxtaposition in the plays of Jean de Schelandre and Alexandre Hardy. In his preface to the *tragi-comédie Tyr et Sidon* (1628) by Schelandre, François Ogier condoned the mixture of "grave things with those less serious" and added that theater existed only for "pleasure and diversion."

Almost sixty years later, Ménestrier defined his generation's concept of theater in *Des ballets anciens et modernes selon des règles du théâtre*. By then distinct differences were established, at least in principle, between tragedy, comedy, and ballet: "Tragedy and Comedy were created for instructional purposes . . . and the Ballet for *pleasure and diversion*" (emphasis added) (1682, 291).

Ménestrier's airtight classifications were perhaps the product more of his Jesuit training than of empirical observation. However, the years that separated Ogier from Ménestrier had witnessed the establishment of French classical drama, with its impressive super-structure of rules and regulations and its seat of authority centered in the Académie Française founded by Richelieu in 1635. In this rarefied atmosphere of Cartesian rationalism and imagined or real academy control, the *ballet de cour* could be accepted only as "exercise" or royal "diversion." It was understandable that it would relinquish any dramatic pretensions. It had lost, if indeed it had ever possessed, the single-mindedness of purpose rooted in the Renaissance humanism of the Florentine Camerata.

Ménestrier shows the distance between the dramaturgical rules of French classical theater and the ballets of the mid-seventeenth-century:

> *The subjects of ballets are drawn ordinarily from the Fable, from History, from the properties of natural or moral existence, or from caprice . . . . The Fable . . . need not resemble reality . . . . It demands no other unity but that of a plan that assures that different* entrées *have some rapport with a Subject . . . . Unity of time and place, which the Tragedy observes with so much care, is almost never found . . . . The principal condition of the Fable of a Ballet is that it be ingenious and agreeable (1658; rpt. as appendix 1967, 222).*

For the royal participants and spectators, it was sufficient that the ballet entertain on a lavish scale. Through it they could act out the role of ideal courtier and thereby, it was hoped, be noticed by their king. The court ballet was, in fact, a political arm of the monarchy, a means of domesticating the nobility and praising the centralized power and control of the regime (see Bridgeman 1957, 14). For king and courtier alike, it is doubtful that the fine distinctions of Père Ménestrier and other aestheticians even existed.

A more compelling reason that prevented the evolution of the *ballet mélodramatique* into opera after the death of Guédron was the lack of a composer of dramatic instincts. There was no Claudio Monteverdi in France to build on the models of *Tancrède* or *Renaud*. In spite of the melodic gifts of Antoine Boesset and Cambefort, no one prior to Lully really tried to exploit the dramatic potential of the ballet. Marin Mersenne clearly understood this deficiency. In "Livre sixièsme de l'art de bien chanter" in his *Harmonie universelle*, he acknowledged the critical role of Peri in introducing theatrical declamation into music and added: "Our musicians are, it would seem, too timid to introduce this manner of declamation in France" (1636; rpt. 1965, 2:357).

The *ballet à entrées*, under the aegis of the fat and gout-ridden Duc de Nemours, was a choreographic spectacle composed of several parts. Each part had its own subject matter and characters; each part, however, related in some manner to a collective idea expressed in the title. In the *Ballet du grand bal de la Douairière de Billabahaut* (1626), for example, the four corners of the world each send delegates to the Ball of the Douairière. Each part of the world has its own ballet preceded by *récits* and including several *entrées*. The *Ballet des quatres Monarchies Chrestiennes* (1635) is a spectacular ethnographic ballet, with Italy, Spain, Germany, and France constituting its four sections.

In spite of the fragmentary state of much of the music and the questionable taste of many of the *entrées*, the *ballet à entrées* is worthy of special study. Its influence far exceeded its intrinsic musico-poetic value. Structurally, it is the most important antecedent of the later *opéra-ballet*. André Campra's *L'Europe galante* (1697), although substituting *galanterie* for the *bouffonerie* of the *Ballet du grand bal*, is, nonetheless, in a direct line of descent from this type of ethnographic ballet. Even in its decline, the *ballet à entrées* helped sustain the interest of French audiences in a merger of music, dance, and spectacle. Its short binary airs (their poetic structure based generally on a quatrain or a six-line stanza), the homophonic choruses, and the variety of dance types contributed to the formation of the *tragédie lyrique*. The history of the French overture may be traced in the scores of pre-Lully *ballets à entrées*. After 1640, most ballets included overtures. In the *Ballet de Mademoiselle* (1640), the *Ballet des rues de Paris* (1643), and the *Ballet des fêtes de Bacchus* (1651), there are already overtures that suggest the type later standardized by Lully in 1658 in his *Ballet d'Alcidiane* (see Prunières 1910a–1911).

The extant music of the pre-Lully court ballets is scattered among many sources. Vocal airs and *récits* are found in the collections of *airs de cour*. In an exhaustive survey of these collections, André Verchaly (1957) has succeeded in identifying 177 airs and *récits* from 56 ballets, all composed before 1643. He insists that there is no vocal music left from court ballets between the *Ballet comique de la reine* of 1581 and Guédron's first book (in actuality the second book) of *Airs de cour à quatre et cinq parties* of 1608.

The sources for instrumental music are equally diffused. Some appear where least expected, for example, in such collections as Robert Ballard's first and second books of lute pieces (1611 and 1614). The Philidor manuscript collection at the Bibliothèque Nationale (especially *Rés.* F496 and *Rés.* F497) is an important source. The king's librarian-copyist made this collection of dances, overtures, and *entrées* from more than one hundred ballets, "*dancéz sous les règnes de Henry IV et Louis XIII.*" With few exceptions, Philidor copied only the treble and bass lines, which were probably all that were available to him. Other important sources for instrumental music are the *Terpsichore Musarum* of Michael Praetorius and Pierre-Francisque Caroubel, the Kassel manuscript (a collection of music written between 1650 and 1670 and edited by Écorcheville as *Vingt suites d'orchestre du xviie siècle français* in 1906), the Uppsala Library manuscript of dances performed at the court of Queen Christina of Sweden between 1644 and 1654, and the *Pièces pour le violon à quatre parties* printed by Ballard in 1665. Chapter 19 contains a more detailed discussion of these sources.

On 26 February 1651 the *Ballet de Cassandre* inaugurated the court ballet of the period of Louis XIV. The twelve-year-old monarch danced for the first time in this ballet, and Isaac de Benserade (1613–1691) made his debut as a poet of superior literary talents (see Silin 1940 regarding Benserade). Charles Perrault, in his *Les Hommes illustres qui ont paru en France pendant ce siècle*, defined the basic change in concept that Benserade brought to his *vers*. Before him, the *vers* were concerned primarily with the characters portrayed onstage rather than with those who were performing the roles. "M. de Benserade," wrote Perrault, "conceived of the *vers* in such a manner that they applied equally to one as to the other" (1696–1700, 1:80). Occasionally with a touch of sarcasm, with a suspicion of malice or a raised eyebrow, Benserade illuminated in elegant verse the political and amorous intrigues of those who danced with the king.

After years of stagnation, the *ballet de cour* was given new life by the *Ballet de la nuit*, performed at the Petit Bourbon on 23 February 1653. Benserade provided texts for the *vers*; the vocal music was composed by Jean de Cambefort (1605–1661), Jean-Baptiste Boesset

(1614–1685), and Michel Lambert (1610–1696); and the instrumental music, according to Philidor, was composed by professional dancers Louis de Mollier (ca. 1615–1688) and Verpré (dates unknown) and violinist Michel Mazuel (1603–1676) (see Silin 1940, 218). Giacomo Torelli (1608–1678) was responsible for the elaborate machines. The ballet was divided into four parts and forty-five *entrées*.

The music by Cambefort is of interest. The "Récit de la nuit" constituting the prologue (Example 2-2) resembles the declamatory style of Guédron more than the *récits* of Jean-Baptiste Boesset or Lambert. Already present is the insistent, anapestic, rhythmic formula so characteristic of the recitatives in Lully's ballets and operas.

Languis – san – te clar – té, Cachez vous dessous l'on – de

Example 2-2. Cambefort: Extract from "Récit de la nuit," *Ballet de la Nuit* (after Philidor manuscript copy).

In the second part of the ballet, which represents the *divertissements* that "reign between nine in the evening to midnight," the dancers included the king, Mollier, Lambert, and Lully. The fourth part ("From three in the morning until the rising of the Sun") introduced Louis XIV, *le Roi Soleil* (the Sun King) in the symbolism of the "rising sun" for the first time, as may be observed in Plate 1.[5] The ballet ended dramatically:

> *Dawn, pulled on a superb chariot, brings in the most beautiful Sun one has ever seen, which first disperses the clouds and then promises the grandest and most beautiful day in the world; Spirits come to render him homage; and all that forms the grand Ballet. The subject is vast and, in all of its expanse, sufficiently worthy to exercise the steps of our young Monarch, without detracting from the scheme* (Ballet de la nuit 1653, *from Ballard manuscript in the Bibliothèque Mazarine*).

So it was that a 20-year-old Florentine, Giambattista Lulli (1632–1687), found himself onstage dancing next to the King of France. Less than one month later, on 16 March, Lully was appointed *Compositeur de la Musique instrumentale du roi*, a position left vacant by the death of Lazarini. The year 1653 had double significance for the creator of French opera: it was the beginning of a productive collaboration with the poet Benserade, which lasted until 1681; and, more important for Lully, it marked the beginning of his "grandest and most beautiful day in the world" in friendship with Europe's most powerful monarch, *le Roi Soleil*.

Chapter 3

Ballet de Cour II: The Period of Lully

Twenty years' apprenticeship as a composer of *ballets de cour* and *comédies-ballets* prepared Lully for his role as creator of the *tragédie en musique*. *Cadmus et Hermione* is inconceivable without the background of the *Ballet d'Alcidiane* or *Psyché*.

Jean-Baptiste Lully[1] was first brought to the attention of the court as dancer and violinist. He had arrived in Paris in 1646, a boy of fourteen sent from his native Florence by the Chevalier de Guise to serve as a *garçon de chambre* to Guise's cousin Anne Marie Louise d'Orléans, Duchesse de Monpensier (*la Grande Mademoiselle*), who wished to perfect her Italian. Lully requested his release from her staff in 1652 at the time she was exiled from Paris for her participation in the Fronde. She granted this without protest, because, as she wrote in her *Mémoires*, "he is a great dancer."

With his appointment in 1653 as a court composer of instrumental music, Lully's position appeared secure, and he devoted his full attention to the composition of court ballets. From 1654 to 1671, he provided music for twenty-six court ballets whose titles and performance details can be found in Herbert Schneider's article on Lully in the *Dictionnaire de la musique française aux XVIIe et XVIIIe siècles* (1992, 416). The court ballet served Lully as a testing ground where he learned to differentiate between the respective styles of his native and adopted lands and where he could observe the reaction of the young king and Cardinal Mazarin to his efforts.

Lully's genuine gift for comedy, which was later snuffed out at the insistence of the Académie des Inscriptions et Belles Lettres, became apparent as early as 1655 in a "Récit grotesque italien" from the *Ballet des bienvenus* performed at Compiègne in May to celebrate the marriage of Cardinal Mazarin's niece to the Duke of Modena. No French air by Lully can be authenticated before 1657 ("Que les jaloux" from the *Ballet de l'amour malade*).

In 1656 Cardinal Mazarin commissioned Lully to compose a ballet to be presented before the king and queen at the Louvre during carnival season. Lully's music for the *mascarade, Galanterie du temps*, has not survived. It included Italian airs and dances and, according to Jean Loret, was performed by a "symphony of more than twenty-five instruments."[2] It marks the first appearance under Lully's direction of the *Petits Violons* which soon surpassed its parent organization, the *Vingt-quatre Violons du Roi*. Perrault described one of the reforms initiated by Lully and executed by his *Petits Violons*:

> *Before him, only the soprano line was considered important in string pieces; the bass and inner parts were a simple accompaniment or a heavy counterpoint often composed on the spot by the performers themselves . . . but Lully made all the parts sing together as agreeably as the soprano (1696–1700, 1:85).*

The first ballet for which Lully supplied all the music is the *Ballet de l'amour malade* first seen at the Louvre on 17 January 1657. Loret informed us that this ballet was performed by "more than sixty instruments with the rare and beautiful voices of three men and three women" (1658; 1857–1878, 2:290). Lully danced the role of Scaramouche in the fifth *entrée*.

The *Ballet d'Alcidiane*, performed at court on 14 February 1658, is the first of Lully's ballets to lead directly to the development of French opera. Lully composed all of the instrumental music and most of the vocal music. The overture, with its dotted rhythms, its wide melodic profile, and its fugal second section, bears the classical stamp of all subsequent French overtures. In his letter of 16 February, Loret described it as being played by more than eighty instruments including thirty-six violins, flutes, viols, harpsichords, guitars, lutes, and theorbos.[3] The trumpet-like flourishes and slow harmonic rhythm of the combat music prefigure the type of military *divertissement* found in *Thésée* or *Bellérophon*. The "Chaconne des Maures," which concludes the ballet, assumes the same grand proportions and structural significance of the chaconnes found in the *tragédies lyriques*.

Most of the independent instrumental music of *Alcidiane* and all of its dances, excepting the *petite chaconne*, employ the five-part texture which Lully later used in the *tragédie lyrique*. There is no reason to look for influences from Venetian opera; as observed earlier, five-part texture was used in French dance music at least as early as the *Ballet comique de la Reine*.

The French *récits* in the second and third parts of *Alcidiane* were probably composed by Jean-Baptiste Boesset, but the *récit*, "Que votre empire," from the first part of the ballet has been attributed to Lully (see Prunières's introduction to *Les Ballets*, vol. 2 of *Oeuvres complètes de J.-B. Lully*). It illustrates how well the Florentine had already mastered the style of the French *air de cour* and how he had surpassed his French colleagues in dramatic expressiveness. The bass line, with its consecutive downward leaps of two major sevenths, is bolder than the more static basses of his contemporaries (see Example 3-1 below).

Example 3-1. Lully: Extract from "Que votre empire," *Ballet d'Alcidiane* (after Philidor manuscript copy).

The years 1661 and 1662 marked a turning point in Lully's career. In May 1661, he was appointed to the important position of *Surintendant de la Musique de la Chambre du Roi*; in December that same year he received his letters of naturalization. On 16 July 1662 he was appointed *Maître de la Musique de la Famille Royale*, and eight days later at the church of Saint-Eustache he ensured his naturalization by marrying Madeleine Lambert, daughter of the court composer Michel Lambert. The marriage contract gives us an insight into the character of Lully, who was not beyond eliminating his modest origins with a stroke of a pen. Thus came about the metamorphosis of a miller's son into "Jean-Baptiste Lully, Esquire, son of Laurent de Lulli, Florentine gentleman." That Jean-Baptiste was well entrenched at court is evidenced by the fact that Louis XIV, his queen and queen mother (Marie Thérèse and Anne d'Autriche), Colbert, and such well-known performers as the dancer Louis Hesselin and the singers Pierre de Nyert and Hilaire Dupuis, all signed the contract.

Lully's musical naturalization kept pace with these events. The French *air de cour*, especially as composed by his father-in-law, remained the chief model for the vocal music in his ballets in the 1660s. Already present, however, were his first attempts to synthesize Italian laments (modeled in a general way on those of Luigi Rossi) with French *airs de cour* or *récits* of a more elegiac nature.

Armida's lament, "Ah, Rinaldo, e dove sei?" from the *Ballet des Amours déguisés* (1664), is the prototype for the *plaintes* found in the *Ballet de la naissance de Vénus* (1665) and in the *Ballet de Flore* (1669). Through the "Plainte de Vénus" in the *Ballet de Flore*, Lully moved closer to the spirit of the French *air sérieux*, which had become a more personal and expressive genre under the influence of the singer Pierre de Nyert (ca. 1597–1682). With its lack of long, vocal melismas, its restrained chromaticism, dramatic use of rests and such affective intervals as the descending diminished seventh, this lament closely resembles "Languir se plaindre," an *air sérieux* composed by Jean Sicard (dates unknown) and published the preceding year (see Example 3-2).

Example 3-2. (a) Lully: Extract from "Plainte de Vénus," *Ballet de Flore* (after Philidor manuscript copy). (b) Sicard: "Languir," *Airs à boire et sérieux*, Book 3 (Paris, 1668).

Lully quickly assimilated the long heritage of French dances into his dance music and introduced new dances that were coming into fashion. Abbé Dubos credited Lully with the addition of more fast dances (*airs de vitesse*) in the court ballet:

> *As the dancers . . . were obliged to move with greater speed and more action than had been common up to that point, and as there were those who maintained that this was a corruption of good taste*

in the dance . . . Lully himself was obliged to compose the steps that he wished the dancers to execute (1719; 7th ed. 1770, 3:167).

In the ballets composed up to 1673 (the year of *Cadmus*), Lully used the following dances in order of priority: bourrées (twenty-six), minuets (twenty-one), sarabandes (nineteen), gavottes (sixteen), canaries (six), chaconnes (five), courantes (four), galliards (three), and loure (one) (Ellis 1969, 30–31).

Purely musical features of the ballet gradually usurped the position of dance. In the words of Pierre-Jean-Baptiste Nougaret:

Only ballets in which a little vocal music had been introduced used to be appropriate for performance at his [Louis XIV's] court; but the eventual result was that vocal music took supremacy over dance; this latter found itself to be no more than an accessory (1769, 2:230).

Ballets such as the *Ballet des Muses* (1666) and the *Ballet de Flore* (1669) best illustrate these changes. The preeminence of vocal airs, ensembles, and choruses, rather than any organizational principle in the *Ballet des Muses*, must have caused Sébastien de Brossard's comment: "From all appearances it is this Ballet that gave rise to the idea of composing operas in French."[4]

The choral finale to the prologue of the *Ballet des Muses* expresses the same sentiments found in any number of subsequent operatic prologues: "*Rien n'est si doux que de vivre à la cour de Louis le plus parfait des Roys*" (Nothing is sweeter than to live at the court of Louis, the most perfect of kings). The music for this fatuous text is square and pompous and already tradition-bound (see Example 3-3). It was to remain the official gesture of adoration throughout the *grand siècle*.[5]

From the standpoint of its fluid structure, the *Ballet des Muses* is a fine illustration of the improvisatory nature of several court ballets. It went through six stages of development, from the first performance on 2 December 1666 to the final performance on 19 February 1667, necessitating six different *livrets*. New material was constantly added on a trial and error basis to render the ballet "still more agreeable" (Anthony 1987b, 337). By 14 February the boundaries of the original court ballet had been stretched to include two of Molière's *comédies-ballets*: *La Pastorale comique* and *Le Sicilien*.

The *Ballet des Muses* also shows Lully well on the way to the creation of French recitative that approximated the declamatory practices of the French stage. According to Lecerf, Lully modeled his recitative on the intonation of Jean Racine's mistress, Marie Desmares, Dame de La Champmeslé, at the Hôtel de Bourgogne. Yet even before her earliest triumphs, Lully—in the recitative "Arreste, malheureux" from the *Ballet des Muses*, for example—had introduced the predominately anapestic rhythmic organization and the division of the Alexandrine into hemistiches that were to characterize the recitatives of French opera (see Example 3-4).

Example 3-3. Lully: Extract from chorus, "Rien n'est si doux," *Ballet des Muses* (after Philidor manuscript copy).

Example 3-4. Lully: "Recitative" from *Ballet des Muses* (after Philidor manuscript copy).

In addition to containing the earliest examples of Lully's recitatives, the court ballets also introduced a type of binary air that would assume pride of place in Lully's *tragédies en musique*. This is the so-called extended binary air (ABB'). The text is most commonly a quatrain whose last two lines are repeated. The first two lines of the quatrain constitute the A section musically. The next two lines of text likewise form the B section of the music. The textual repetition of B, however, always generates a musical variant, B', whose note values and melodic shape may be similar to but are never an exact repetition of the music in the B section (see Chapter 7). This type of binary organization is rare in the airs of Lully's French contemporaries. On the other hand, mid-seventeenth-century Italian composers such as Luigi Rossi, Mario Savioni, Carlo Caproli, and Giacomo Carissimi favored the extended binary air in their operas and cantatas. Lully could easily have come across such airs in manuscript copies which began circulating in Paris in the middle of the century. The earliest example of an extended binary air by Lully is "Bel art qui retardez" from the *Ballet des arts* (1663). After this date, there is a gradual increase in the number of such airs in Robert Ballard's collections of *Livre d'airs de différents autheurs*, with many examples drawn from Lully's court ballets (see Anthony 1987a, 126–129).

Lully had already composed eight *tragédies en musique* before returning again to the court ballet. *Le Triomphe de l'Amour* (1681) and *Le Temple de la Paix* (1685) bear only a structural resemblance to earlier court ballets. Hard pressed to find a proper category for *Le Triomphe de l'Amour*, the Parfaict brothers wrote: "Properly speaking, it is neither an opera nor a ballet but a collection of *entrées* mixed with *récits*" (ca. 1741, 1:47).

Le Triomphe de l'Amour was first performed before the court at Saint-Germain-en-Laye on 21 January 1681 after a record thirty-nine days of rehearsal (including Christmas Day). It was performed by sixty-four dancers, forty-eight vocalists, and seventy-five or seventy-six instrumentalists (see Coeyman 1990a, 525). The entire production was moved to the Académie Royale de Musique in May of 1681, thus making this the first court ballet to be seen on the stage of the Paris Opera. The most important aspect of the Paris performance was the appearance of professional female dancers on stage. Included among these were Mlles de La Fontaine, Pasant, Carré, and Leclercq. Mlle de La Fontaine, who remained at the Opera until 1692, was the outstanding performer of her age. With her began the incredible star system which dominated the French stage throughout the eighteenth century and gave rise to dancers such as Mlles Françoise Prévost, Guyot, Marie-Thérèse Perdou de Subligny, Marie Sallé, and Marie-Anne Cupis de Camargo (see Levinson 1925).

Musically, *Le Triomphe de l'Amour* resembles the *tragédie en musique* more than the court ballet. It is characterized by a more imaginative approach to instrumentation than is generally the case—even in Lully's later works. The "Prélude pour l'Amour" is scored for both transverse flutes and recorders (*taille*, *quinte*, *petite basse*, and *grande basse*),[6] and there are directions in the Ballard printed edition of 1681 giving precise performance instructions. For example, in the *ritournelle* and the air of Venus in the first *entrée*, the string players are told to play "softly, almost without touching the strings," and in the "Prélude pour la Nuit," Lully instructed all players to use mutes and to "play softly, particularly during the vocal solos."

Récits in *Le Triomphe de l'Amour* lost their independent existence, for they were carefully integrated into its dramatic action. There are sixteen *récits* for the twenty *entrées*, a ratio far larger than in any earlier ballet. The chorus is prominent. It is a large double chorus whose two sections remain on opposite sides of the stage throughout the performance. The dance is a mere accessory.

Lully's last court ballet, *Le Temple de la Paix*, was first performed before the court at Fontainebleau on 20 October 1685. It reached the stage of the Académie Royale de Musique one month later. "The Peace," wrote Lully in its preface, "Which Your Majesty has so generously given to his vanquished Enemies, is the subject of this Ballet . . . . Could I find a more fitting subject for which to compose some *chants extraordinaires*?" Little matter that the peace was of short duration. Three years later, Louis XIV embarked on the disastrous War of the League of Augsburg that saw Austria, Holland, Spain, and England in powerful alliance against France. *Le Temple de la Paix*, then, is a late example of politically inspired ballets such as the *Ballet des quatres monarchies chrestiennes* (1635) and the *Ballet de la prospérité des armes de France* (1641). In emphasizing his "*chants extraordinaires*," Lully gave recognition to the non-choreographic elements that dominate this ballet to an even greater degree than in *Le Triomphe de l'Amour*.

Louis XIV appeared on the stage for the last time in 1670, dancing in *Les Amants magnifiques*. Although not so passionately committed to the ballet as his father had been, the king had taken much pleasure in participating in *ballets de cour*. Whether or not his general education had been neglected as Saint-Simon insisted, he had taken special pains to be well instructed in the dance. The financial account for the year 1660 shows that the king's dancing master, Pierre Beauchamps, received two thousand *livres* whereas only three hundred *livres* were allotted to his writing teacher (Despois 1874, 329). By the 1680s, the *ballet de cour* had lost most of its identification with the court; the elaborate procedures of composition and performance detailed by Saint-Hubert and Marolles were already part of the legacy of the past.

By the early years of the eighteenth century, the *ballet de cour* was looked upon as archaic and in questionable taste. Louis de Cahusac, writing in the 1750s, stated unequivocally that it was a "genre which no longer exists" (1754, preface). It was exhumed at court from time to time for a special occasion. Delalande had used it for both the *Ballet de la jeunesse*, which was first performed at Versailles on 28 January 1686 as the court's principal entertainment for Carnival season, and for *Le Palais de Flore*, which was first performed at the Grand Trianon on 5 January 1689 to welcome home the Grand Dauphin from the War of the League of Augsburg. These two ballets have much in common with Lully's two court ballets of the 1680s. The *Ballet de la jeunesse* is a synthesis between opera and ballet. The long poem, about 250 lines, is divided into three episodes, devoted, respectively, to Mercury, Pallas, and Philis and Tircis. The music is rich in *symphonies*, recitatives, airs, choruses, and dances. At the center of the work is the "Chaconne de la jeunesse" whose sixty-one variations are built on the eight-measure bass line. From Lully, Delalande had learned how to organize an entire scene around the chaconne pattern. The theme and twenty-eight of the variations are instrumental; the balance of the variations are for vocal solo, ensemble, and chorus.[7]

In the second decade of the eighteenth century the court ballet, by then a relic of a bygone day, was revived again, possibly as a way of linking the ten-year-old king with his Bourbon past. Louis XV's brief appearance as a dancer was limited to three ballets, all performed at the Tuileries Palace: *L'Inconnu*, *Les Folies de Cardenio*, and *Les Éléments*. Delalande wrote the music for *L'Inconnu* which took place for the first time on 8 February 1720. Dances, rather than vocal music, dominate this work as if to give a final salute to the glorious tradition of the court ballet. Delalande also wrote the music to *Les Folies de Cardenio*, which was performed between 10 December 1720 and 27 January 1721. This was a much more elaborate production, which required the immense spaces of the Salle des Machines of the Tuileries. *Les Éléments*, first performed on 21 December 1721, is the only court ballet of this period that subsequently reached the stage of the Académie Royale de Musique (1725). André Cardinal Destouches composed the greater part of the music of this last court ballet although Delalande contributed the overture and some numbers in the prologue and in the first *entrée*. In its operatic version, *Les Éléments* was an important forerunner of the *ballet héroïque* (see Chapter 10).

At the Jesuit College Louis-le-Grand, the ballet was maintained to 1764, the date of the expulsion of the Jesuits from France. It was part of the annual ceremony marking the end of the year's work. Nemeitz described it as follows:

The Students of the Jesuits perform a Latin Tragedy at the College Louis-le-Grand once a year at the beginning of August. As the Fathers wish to excel in all their actions, they omit nothing to augment the magnificence of their Spectacle. Not content merely to adorn the stage with the most beautiful Decorations and to clothe the Actors in the richest garments, they even bring in the best people of the Opera whether for dancing or for playing in the Orchestra. They mount a Ballet between each act, which is usually directed by Mons. Blondi. The Stage is erected outdoors in the Court of the College. . . . All the area of this spacious court is full of benches for the Spectators, of which there is such a great number that not only are all places occupied, but all the windows of the College that overlook the court are filled with people from top to bottom. At the conclusion of the play, some books are distributed to the Students as a prize for their industry (1727, 107–109).

All manner of musical performances and ballets served as *inter-mèdes* that were inserted between the acts of Latin tragedies.[8] Some ballets were closely aligned with the action of their tragedies and may be considered early examples of the *danse en action.* Thus, the tragedy *Aurelius,* performed at the College 2 August 1668, included a ballet "based on the action of the Latin tragedy" (Lowe 1966, 178). Among the composers who wrote *intermèdes* for the Jesuits were Pierre Beauchamps, Campra, Charpentier, Clérambault, Pascal Collasse, Delalande, Desmarest, Claude Desmatins, Lalouette, Claude Oudot, and Royer. Music for ten ballets composed in the 1680s and performed at the College was copied in 1690 by Philidor in a collection entitled *Les Ballets des Jesuits, composés par Messieurs Beauchant [sic], Desmatins et Collasse.*

Genuine *tragédies en musique* were composed for the College beginning in 1684. These works, which include *Demetrius* (1685) by Claude Oudot (music lost), *Celse martyre* (1687) by Charpentier (music lost), and Charpentier's *David et Jonathas* (1688), developed from the ballets, the *pastorales en musique,* and other *intermèdes;* and their evolution paralleled in miniature the development of French opera from the *ballet de cour.*

For more than a century, the *ballet de cour* served king and courtier as a luxurious diversion and a legitimate excuse for royal exercise. It served its purpose well; its overtures and prologues, its spectacular finales, its vocal airs, ensembles, and choruses, its dances and independent instrumental *symphonies,* and its sense of ceremonial gesture all live on in the *tragédie lyrique.*

≈ *Chapter 4* ≈

Italian Opera in France

$\mathscr{I}$talian influence on French art during the sixteenth century was in constant ebb and flow. From their first invasion of Italy, the Valois kings brought back Italian decorators for their chateaux: the gardener Pacello was at Amboise; Il Boccador contributed much to the decoration of Chambord, Blois, and the Hôtel de Ville in Paris; and the great Leonardo da Vinci died in the manor house at Amboise in 1519.

Chateaux of the Loire valley are a happy synthesis between French forms and Italian decoration. The shape of the old medieval fortress can still be discerned underneath the flamboyant decoration of Chambord, while the austere keep at Chenonceaux tempers the elegance there.

Although a love-hate relationship with Italy persisted throughout the *grand siècle*, there remained constant an assertive French classical spirit. The chronological distance between Joachim Du Bellay's *Défense et illustration de la langue française* (1549) and Boileau's *L'Art poétique* (1672) is great, but the order and discipline of French classicism unite them. "Avoid these excesses," wrote Boileau, "leave to Italy all this false brilliance and foolish glitter."

French classical genius tempered and modified Italian baroque exuberance. Louis-Jean Lemercier's Sorbonne chapel and Jules-Hardouin Mansart's Val-de-Grâce church owe as much to this spirit as they do to the so-called Jesuit style; the rejection of Gian Lorenzo Bernini's plans for the rebuilding of the Louvre partially reflected the classical bias of both Louis XIV and Colbert.

Partisans of Italian music during the first half of the seventeenth century were much more numerous than we have heretofore believed. The inventories of music libraries of middle-class Parisians cited by Madeleine Jurgens in the *Documents du Minutier Central* (1969, 1:865–894) reveal that long before the days of the Italophile Nicolas Mathieu, curé of Saint-André-des-Arts, there were impressive private collections of Italian madrigals and motets. In fact, in the collections described by Mme Jurgens, the ultramontane examples far outnumber the French *airs de cour*.

Marin Mersenne and André Maugars were among the first in France to try to classify the stylistic differences between French and Italian music. Yet, it was still an age of innocence, of peaceful co-existence; the polemics of François Raguenet and Lecerf de la Viéville were far in the future. Probably not too many composers took offence at or even heeded the advice of Maugars, found at the end of his *Response faite à un curieux sur le sentiment de la musique d'Italie*, to travel and listen to "foreign music" in order to "emancipate themselves from their pedantic rules" (1639; rpt. 1993, 28).

The role played by seventeenth-century Italian opera in the development of the French lyric theater at mid-century must be seen against this background of a gradually increasing awareness of rival styles. Cardinal Mazarin (*né* Giulio Rainmondo Mazzarini, 1602–1661) tried in vain for sixteen years to establish a permanent Italian opera troupe in Paris. Not even unlimited funds, the support of the queen mother, or the glamour of the most prominent names among Italian composers and performers convinced French audiences that this foreign importation could be nationalized.

Cardinal Mazarin's wish to promote Italian opera in France was due partly to nostalgia and partly to practical politics. He had formerly been in the service of Cardinal Antonio Barberini in Rome and had witnessed the production of Stefano Landi's *Sant' Alessio* that inaugurated the Barberini palace in 1632. In 1643, after the death of Louis XIII, Mazarin was made a member of the Regency during the minority of Louis XIV. He envisioned opera in France as a political arm of the government, with Italian musicians, poets, and machinists potentially involved in state intrigues, and the court so diverted by the spectacle that his own political machinations might pass unnoticed.

The first Italian work performed at the Palais Royal (on 28 February 1645) was identified in the *Gazette de France* (4 March 1645) as an Italian comedy and ballet danced by the gentlemen of the court. Prunières conjectured that the work was *Nicandro e Fileno* (1913, 62–64), but Paul-Marie Masson identified *Nicandro e Fileno* as an Italian pastorale composed by Paolo Lorenzani on a poem by the Duc de Nevers and first performed at Fontainebleau in September of 1681 (1930, 27). Neal Zaslaw (1989) has marshalled evidence that suggests that the identity of the 1645 "Italian comedy and ballet" may have been the "drama in musica," *Il giudizio della Ragione tra la Belta e l'Affetto*, whose text and music were written by Francesco Buti and Marco Marazzoli, respectively.[1] Two ballet *entr'actes* separate the three acts that follow the prologue. *Il giudizi* was first performed in

Rome during Carnival of 1643. Its allegorical subject matter and hidden political agenda have much in common with other seventeenth-century stage works.

Marazzoli had arrived in Paris in December 1643, followed in April 1644 by the *virtuosa* Leonora Baroni (reputedly a former mistress of Mazarin). In November of that same year, the composer, impresario, alto castrato, and secret agent Atto Melani, his brother Jacopo, and the singer Anna Francesca Costa all joined Mazarin's Italian troupe. By the end of 1646 through the active assistance of the queen mother herself, the French court became a refuge for Cardinal Barberini and his secretary, the poet Francesco Buti, who were escaping the political vicissitudes of the papacy. More importantly, in June 1645 the *grand sorcier* among the Italian machinists, Giacomo (or Jacopo) Torelli (1608–1678), reached the French capital.[2]

On 14 December 1645 at the Petit Bourbon palace, there was a performance of *La finta pazza* with music by Francesco Sacrati and text by Giulio Strozzi. This was a revised version of a work first heard in Venice in 1641. Torelli adapted the original to suit the taste of seven-year-old Louis XIV by adding ballets choreographed by G. B. Balbi for monkeys, eunuchs, negroes, and ostriches. The *livret* and music excited little comment, and the audience appeared less interested in the poetry and music than in the stage sets, machines, and rapid scene changes.

Mazarin's next venture, a performance on 13 February 1646 of Francesco Cavalli's *Egisto* (text by Giovanni Faustini), failed precisely because it was mounted with no complicated *mise-en-scène*. This was false economy from the cardinal's point of view, and he was quick to realize that the French audience, except for those few committed to Italian music for its own intrinsic merits, would demand musical productions on a lavish scale. Already unpopular with some powerful members of the royalty, he could ill afford comments similar to those of Mme de Motteville who wrote with reference to *Egisto* that "we were only twenty or thirty and we almost died of boredom and the cold" (1723, 2:168). Jacques Vanuxem suggests that because of a conflict in scheduling that cost *Egisto* most of its audience, Mme de Motteville's oft-quoted remarks may have been a reaction to the situation rather than a value judgment (1967, 32), for she immediately added that "*Divertissements* of this nature require a large audience, and solitude has no rapport with the stage."

Luigi Rossi's *Orfeo* (text by Buti) provided the image of Italian opera so badly needed by Mazarin. It was performed eight times at the Palais Royal between 2 March and 8 May 1647. The role of Orpheus was sung by the castrato Atto Melani; that of Euridice, by soprano

Anna Francesca Costa. Charles-Louis-Étienne Truinet and Antoine Ernest Roquet quote a contemporary observer who wrote:

> *One does not know which to admire the most, the beauty of its invention, the grace of the solo voices, or the magnificence of the costumes; because by the variety of scenes, the diverse stage decorations, and the novelty of the machines, it surpasses all admiration (1886, xxix).*

Abbé Buti, well aware of French interest in the dance, attempted a liaison between the subject matter of *Orfeo* and that of its ballet *entrées*. "From the moment of its appearance in France," wrote Prunières, "opera was wed to ballet."[3] The ballet music is missing from the manuscript score but was presumably written by French court ballet composers.

The poem is a curious mixture of burlesque ballets of owls, tortoises, and snails, of clowns and satyrs embellishing the simple tale. The music, however, is Luigi Rossi at his best. The prologue is totally independent of the legend of Orpheus and foreshadows the panegyric prologues of *Alceste* and *Thésée*. A chariot, suspended above the French armies, holds "*La Victoire*," who sings verses in praise of the queen mother, "Great Anne whose beautiful hands hold the scepter and hurl thunderbolts." In the words of Ménestrier, this prologue is a "*pièce détachée* unrelated to the story of Orpheus . . . . We have retained this liberty in France, & almost all Prologues to pieces of Music that have been performed are in praise of the King" (1681, 196).

In spite of the general approbation that greeted *Orfeo*, there were scarcely disguised rumblings of discontent from two powerful factions: parliament and the church. The parliament, employing Mazarin's tactics, attempted to divert attention from its own grave fiscal problems by emphasizing and distorting the admittedly exorbitant costs of the production of *Orfeo*. Thus, Guy Joli, an historian and adviser to parliament, carried out this strategy in his *Mémoires* covering 1648–1665 (published 1718), in which he estimated the cost of the production to have been as high as 500,000 *écus*, a figure regarded by Truinet and Roquet as "absurd and untruthful" (1886, xxxvii). Public opinion, as reflected in many of the satirical anti-Mazarin songs, the "*mazarinades*," deduced a clear cause-and-effect relationship between the economic miseries of the state and the cost of an Italian opera staged by an Italian machinist and sponsored by an Italian so-called cardinal.

The second faction was the conservative clergy and their supporters at the Sorbonne who were offended by all stage productions. In her *Mémoires*, Mme de Motteville mentioned an unidentified curé of

Saint-Germain-des-Près who, with the support of seven doctors of the Sorbonne, warned Anne d'Autriche in 1647 that she was in danger of committing a "mortal sin" should she continue to support this type of *divertissement*.

The Fronde (1648–1652) temporarily upset Mazarin's plans to establish a base in France for Italian opera. Italians who remained in France were threatened or, as in the case of Torelli, actually imprisoned. However, with the defeat of the *frondeurs* and the triumphant return of Mazarin to Paris in February 1653, plans for a new Italian opera were made.

That inveterate observer, Loret, noted in *La Muze historique* (letter of 31 January 1654):

> J'apris hier, en mangeant ma soupe,
> Qu'une belle et gaillarde troupe
> De très rare comédiens,
> Et mesmies grands muziciens,
> Arriva lundy de Mantoue,
> Naples, Turin, Rome et Padoue.

> *I learned yesterday, while eating my soup,*
> *That a handsome and lively troupe*
> *Of very rare actors,*
> *And even great musicians,*
> *Arrived Monday from Mantua,*
> *Naples, Turin, Rome, and Padua.*

The "*belle et gaillarde troupe*" was placed under the direction of the composer Carlo Caproli ("Carlo del violino"), and on 14 April 1654 at the Petit Bourbon, his opera *Le Nozze di Peleo e di Teti* (libretto by Buti) was performed. On the title page of the libretto we read, "*comédie italienne en musique entremeslée d'un ballet sur le mesme sujet*" (Italian comedy in music interspersed with a ballet [based] on the same subject). This important concession to French taste resulted in a strange and not entirely convincing attempt to graft French *ballet de cour* onto Italian opera. The Duc de Saint-Aignan and Benserade created ten ballet *entrées* suggested by several scenes from the opera. The music of the opera is lost; that of the ballet is in the Philidor Collection without any attribution. Young Louis XIV danced in six *entrées*; for one, he was garbed in an elaborate and completely fanciful Indian costume and was joined by Jean-Baptiste Lully, who had been in his service for one year.

Mazarin was now at the peak of his political power. The Treaty of Paris and the Peace of the Pyrenées were both signed in 1659. Yet he was unable to establish a permanent Italian company in Paris. After each opera, the Italian troupe disbanded, and the musicians went back to Italy. It was often difficult and expensive to plan and execute return trips. The letters that passed between Mazarin and Buti, who was recruiting in Italy during this period, show the extent of the cardinal's stubborn commitment to his *idée fixe*. Money was no object. In a letter of 8 August 1659 he wrote:

> *I ask you only to examine most carefully anyone whom you choose to sing or play the violin and other instruments; because it is necessary that each be outstanding in his métier . . . . I would rather have such performers and spend more money than have those of ordinary talent at a cheaper price (ed. of 1872–1906, 9:225).*

To celebrate both the marriage of Louis XIV with Marie Thérèse and the Peace of the Pyrenées, Mazarin commissioned the famous Francesco Cavalli (1602–1676) to compose the opera *Ercole amante* on a *livret* by Buti. After much bickering, Cavalli arrived in Paris in June 1660, but neither his opera nor the new Théâtre des Machines at the Tuileries Palace was ready.

Substitution of an earlier Cavalli opera, *Serse* (*Xerses*) with a text by Niccolo Minato, was hastily arranged for performance on 22 November 1660 at the Louvre. The composer made many alterations, spreading the action over five instead of three acts. Mazarin gave Lully the task of supplying ballet music for six *entrées*. Pressed for time, Lully used materials he had already composed, making no effort to coordinate their subject matter with the opera. He did, however, compose a new, magnificent French overture which is a more elaborate work than his first essay in this genre two years earlier (*Alcidiane*). The *fugato* (*gai*) in triple meter precedes a concluding section in which the meter (C), tempo (*modéré*), and general character resemble the opening part of the overture.

The reaction to *Serse* was predictable. The public applauded the dances and the *mise-en-scène* but virtually ignored Cavalli's music. The curious casting, which assigned a castrato to the role of Princess Amastris, lover of King Xerses (also a castrato), and then paraded "her" in male disguise, may have offended the French audience which was already ill-disposed towards castrati.

Mazarin did not live to see the performance of *Ercole amante*, which finally took place on 7 February 1662 almost one year after his death. It served as an inauguration piece for the Salle des Machines built for Mazarin by the septuagenarian architect Gaspare Vigarani and his two sons, Carlo and Lodovico.[4]

The performance of *Ercole amante* lasted for six hours; each act terminated with a spectacular ballet. The final ballet, called the "Ballet de sept planètes," included more than twenty *entrées*. The audience paid little heed to Cavalli's music but revelled instead in the flamboyance of Italian Baroque stage design with its long perspectives and its changes of scene. Shown in rapid succession were a rocky coastline, a royal palace, a grotto, an elaborate garden, a fortress, sepulchers midst cypress trees, Hell, the temple of Juno, and Mount Olympus with the assembly of gods. Loret devoted 210 lines to *Ercole amante* in his *La Muze historique* (see above) but dismissed the poem and music in a few words. Undoubtedly the poor acoustics of the new theater and the audience's general lack of interest in the dramatic intrigue contributed to the failure of this opera, which had required three years' preparation and which may have cost as much as 88,700 *livres* to produce. Prunières conjectured that the majority of the audience was not receptive to a work performed in a language that very few understood (1913, 304), although, as Ménestrier stated, Buti's *livret* "was translated into French verse for the satisfaction of those who did not understand Italian" (1681, 205). Musically, *Ercole amante* was at the mercy of its own monstrous stage machinery, and it is difficult to imagine even the best voices competing with those gigantic machines that descended from the sky groaning under the weight of 150 people.

With the exception of Lorenzani's *Nicandro e Fileno* of 1681, there was a 37-year hiatus that saw no Italian opera in Paris between Cavalli's *Ercole amante* of 1662 and the one-act, Italian opera *Orfeo nell' inferni* that forms part of the final *divertissement* of André Campra's lyric comedy *Le Carnaval de Venise* of 1699. Despite Mazarin's failure to establish a permanent, Italian opera troupe in Paris, the influence of Italian opera on the development of the French lyric drama was far from marginal. At the very least, it made clear that a dramatic composition could be sung from beginning to end, and it stimulated the French to seek solutions to the problem more in keeping with their own traditions.

It is difficult to pinpoint the influence of seventeenth-century Italian opera on Lully. There is little evidence that he was familiar with the masterpieces of the Venetian or Roman schools other than those Italian operas in France with which he was personally involved. The patina of Italianisms that remained in his compositions after 1673—*fugati* in the French overtures, imitative *ritournelles*, extended binary airs, independent comic scenes—was either modified by the predominantly French style or, in the case of the comic scenes, expunged from all operas subsequent to *Thésée*. He was surely familiar with Rossi's *Orfeo* even though he was only fifteen at the time of its Paris performance. The *sommeil* trio of *Les Amants magnifiques* (1670),

"Dormez, dormez beaux yeux" (third *intermède*), and the subsequent *sommeils* of the *tragédie lyrique* derive from the trio, "Dormite, begli occhi," of *Orfeo* (Act II, scene ix).[5]

It is less difficult to point out the influence of Italian opera on Lully's librettist, Philippe Quinault (1635–1688). The scenes of sacrifice and combat, the funeral ceremonies, the evocations of monsters and furies, and the baroque mixture of comic and pathetic characters come as much from Italian opera as from the *ballet de cour* (see Gros 1926, 591). In planning the format of the *livret* for the *tragédie lyrique*, Quinault and Lully both must have remembered the applause that greeted the staging of *Ercole amante*.

Perhaps the experience of *Serse* and *Ercole amante* had the effect of strengthening Lully's basically conservative approach to dramatic music. Mazarin's futile attempts should have convinced Lully that French audiences would accept dramatic works with continuous music only if sung in French, but Brossard relates that even after the impressive success of Perrin and Cambert and the establishment of the Académie d'Opéra, "Lully railed against Perrin's Académie and affirmed many times that the French language was not proper for these large works" (1724; 1725–1730, 220).

~ Chapter 5 ~

The Comédie-Ballet and Related Genres

Comédie-Ballet

In August 1661, Nicolas Fouquet, *Surintendant des Finances*, gave an Italian *fête* at his palace at Vaux-le-Vicomte to honor "the greatest king in the world."[1] Molière wrote *Les Fâcheux* in fifteen days for part of the celebration. Pierre Beauchamps composed the music for this *comédie-ballet*—the first of twelve such works by Jean-Baptiste Poquelin, called Molière (1622--1673), who in this case had had to work with a limited number of dancers. Molière explained in his preface that to make the most economical use of the dancers he had decided to relate the *entrées* to the subject of the play and thereby "make ballet and comedy one." He added that this "*mélange* is something new for the stage . . . and can serve as a plan for other works conceived in more leisure."

Molière was inaccurate. As we have seen, Abbé Buti had introduced ballet *entrées* in *Orfeo* in 1647, and *Le nozze di Peleo e di Teti* was described as an "Italian comedy in music interspersed with a ballet [based] on the same subject."

The active collaboration of Molière and Lully in the composition of *comédies-ballets* began in 1664 with *Le Mariage forcé* and terminated in 1670 with *Le Bourgeois gentilhomme*.[2] Modern productions of the Molière-Lully *comédies-ballets* cut Lully's music severely—even at the Comédie Française, yet in their day, "les deux grands Baptistes" were considered equal partners. By adroit exploitation of Louis XIV's interest in the dance, Lully gained a distinct advantage, which is reflected in a contemporary's description of *Le Bourgeois gentilhomme* as a "ballet composed of six *entrées* accompanied by a comedy" (*Gazette de France*, 18 October 1670).

Molière thought of music and dance as complementing the main action of a comedy, and this idea contributed to the evolution of the later *opéra comique*. Through *intermèdes*, he introduced subplots that emphasized, mirrored, or contrasted with the principal plot. He and Lully first put this dramatic principle to use in the introductory *intermède* of *La Princesse d'Élide*, a *comédie-ballet*. They achieved better fusion between music and spoken verse in *Le Sicilien*, where music and dance penetrate the action with natural ease and are not restricted to *intermèdes*—the latter being essentially interludes following the acts of the comedy.

The use of music and dance within the comedy proper, as well as within *intermèdes*, is perhaps best seen in *Le Bourgeois gentilhomme*, first performed at Chambord on 14 October 1670. Table 5-1 below shows the distribution of music and dance throughout this five-act *comédie-ballet*. The full manuscript score in the Philidor Collection contains the annotations presented in the Table. The airs and ensembles of Acts I, II, and IV are closely aligned with the dramatic action of the comedy. Each of the first three *intermèdes* moves forward the action developed in the preceding scene. By the time we reach the fourth *intermède*, the "Turkish Ceremony," music and dance have totally usurped the role of spoken comedy. At the conclusion of Act V, scene vi, we understand that the entire comedy to this point has been a gigantic prologue to the main event, which is a court ballet, entitled the *Ballet des nations*, having nothing to do with the preceding play. This long ballet (six *entrées)* symbolizes Lully's burgeoning power over Molière, whose characters are reduced to mere onstage spectators, forced at the end to sing banalities: "Quels spectacles charmants." See Table 5-1.

Lully brought to *comédie-ballet* the skills already tested in his *ballets de cour*. In the *entrées* of many of his *ballets à entrées*, he held to the tradition of burlesque and exoticism. Compare, for example, the ballet of the Grand Turc Mahomet in the ballet of the *Grand bal de la Douairière de Billebahaut* with the Turkish ceremony from *Le Bourgeois gentilhomme*. The format of the *comédie-ballet* gave him further opportunity to develop his comic gifts in French and Italian *buffo* scenes. That the Italian *buffo* style was a more natural expression for him at first is evident from the contrast between the comic sections of *L'Amour malade* (to take a *ballet de cour)* and the bass solos of the magician in *Le Mariage forcé*, where his initial attempts to create a French *style bouffe* are stiff and clumsy. French comic scenes he composed five years later for *Monsieur de Pourceaugnac* show no such awkward self-consciousness. The amusing polygamy duet sung by two lawyers in the second act illustrates this well-developed French comic style.

A more subtle comic style is found in the quasi-prologue or preamble to *Le Bourgeois gentilhomme*. A student of the *Maître de Musique* is busy composing an air, requested by Monsieur Jourdain, which becomes "Je languis" sung in scene ii of Act I. Is this the original prototype for those scenes in Hollywood movies of the 1930s and 1940s in which composers are seen at the piano, manuscript paper and pens in disarray, frantically setting down the words and music of an immortal tune? Usually an invisible orchestra suddenly replaces the piano. In this scene, was there a harpsichord onstage? The score mentions only a table (see Table 5-1). Did a bass viol and harpsichord suddenly materialize? In a manner reminiscent of George Gershwin's "Blah, blah, blah," the student composer sings "ou, ou, ou" and repeats this in longer note values to give himself time to write down the words which have just popped into his head (see Auld 1990, 25–28). Humor was surely heightened in the original performance of the role by Monsieur Gaye, a virtuoso baritone. The scene is written in soprano clef, suggesting that Gaye sang the part in a high, squeaky falsetto.

Table 5-1. Music and dance distribution in *Le Bourgeois gentilhomme*.

Overture
("by a large group of instruments")

Prologue
("Seated at a table, a student of the *Maître de Musique* composes an air requested by the Bourgeois.")

Act I
Scene ii
  1. Air: "Je languis" ("*La musicienne*")
  2. Air (by Sablières and Perrin): "Je croyais Jeanneton" (Monsieur Jourdain)
  3. "*Dialogue en musique*"
    a) Ritournelle and air: "Un Coeur" ("*La musicienne*")
    b) Ritournelle and air: "Il n'est rien" ("*Premier musicien*")
    c) Ritournelle and air: "Il serait doux" ("*Second musicien*")
    d) Ritournelle and trio: "Aimable ardeur" (all three)

"Premier Intermède" (follows Act I, scene ii)
Dance: ("Four dancers perform all the different movements and steps requested by the *Maître à Danser*.")

Act II
Scene i
  Dance: Minuet from *Les Amants magnigiques*
Scene v
  Dance: ("A master tailor brings a new costume and has his six assistants, '*garcons tailleurs*,' dress Monsieur Jourdain in time with the music.")

"Second Intermède" (follows Act II, scene v)
Dance: ("The assistant tailors celebrate by dancing.")

Act III

"Troisième Intermède" (follows Act III, scene vi)
Dance: Passepied and two rigaudons ("Six cooks, who prepare the festive meal, dance together.")
Note: Music not extant.

Act IV
Scene i ("The musiciens take their glasses and sing two *chansons à boire* accompanied by the orchestra.")
1. Duo: "Un petit doigt"
2. Duo: "Buvons, buvons chers amis" and trio: "Sus, sus du vin partout"

"Quatrième Intermède" (follows Act IV, scene v)
("The Turkish ceremony to ennoble the Bourgeois takes place with dance and music.")
1. March [1st air]
2. Chorus: "Alla"
3. Air: "Se ti sabir" (Mufti)
4. Dialogue (Mufti and chorus)
5. Air: "Mahametta per Giordina" (Mufti)
6. Dialogue (Mufti and chorus)
7. Dance: "2e air"
8. Choral response: "Ou, ou"
9. Dialogue (Mufti and chorus)
10. Dance: "3^e air"
11. Air: "Ti star nobile" (Mufti)
12. Chorus: "Ti star nobile"
13. Dance: "4e air"
14. Air: "Da ra" (Mufti and chorus)
15. Air: "Non tener honta" (Mufti and chorus)

Act V
("The comedy ends with a small [sic] ballet which has already been prepared.")

Ballet des Nations (follows Act V, scene vi)
Entrée 1 ("A man distributes *livrets* for the ballet; he is at first overwhelmed by the number of people from different regions, who cry out in music for the *livrets*, and by the three pests [*importuns*] who are constantly under foot" [8 numbers].)
Entrée 2 ("Three pests dance")
Entrée 3 ("Three Spaniards" [8 numbers])
Entrée 4 ("Italians" [6 numbers])
Entrée 5 ("French" [4 numbers])
Entrée 6 ("All is concluded by the three nations and by all of those in the audience, who give their approbation in song and dance singing: 'Quels spectacles charmants'.")

The *comédie-ballet* is a virtual compendium of musical forms and practices later used by Lully in his *tragédies lyriques*. Monsieur Jourdain's *Maître de Musique* makes no secret of polite society's preference in solo voices for the soprano, *haute-contre*, and bass (*Le Bourgeois gentilhomme*, Act II, scene i). No tenor is mentioned, thus providing further evidence of the lowly status of this voice during the seventeenth century in France.

Recitative-like passages scattered throughout the *comédies-ballets* display the predominantly anapestic rhythms of fully developed French recitative (see Example 5-1 below). In fact, according to Étienne Gros, Quinault modeled his poetry for the *tragédie lyrique* on Molière's verses for the *comédie-ballet* (1926, 711).

Et ce   sexe in constant trop indig —ne du   jour

Example 5-1. Lully: Extract from *Le Bourgeois gentilhomme* (after Philidor manuscript copy).

The airs of the *comédie-ballet*, like those of the *ballet de cour*, generally follow the tradition of the court airs of Lambert, Boesset, and others. The relatively restricted range, the discreet affective intervals, frequent cadence points, anapestic rhythms, and syllabic rendering of the text, all show us a Lully rapidly absorbing the style of his adopted land and removing traces of his Italian origins. Some of his more lively drinking songs became very well known. We learn from Lecerf that one of these, "Buvons, chers amis, buvons" (*Le Bourgeois gentilhomme*), was one of the airs that Lully "loved the most throughout his life" (1725; rpt. 1966, 3:114). Nevertheless, the Italianate extended binary air, first used by Lully in his *Ballet des arts* of 1663, is no stranger to the *comédies-ballets*. A classic example of this binary air configuration is "Je languis" from *Le Bourgeois gentilhomme* (Act I, scene ii).

Lully also used the dance song in his *comédie-ballets*. Dance songs are airs that are almost literal transcriptions of the dances they follow or precede (see Masson 1930, 222). They underscore the close relationship between vocal air and dance. The dance song was absorbed into the *divertissements* of the *tragédie lyrique* and *opéra-ballet*, where it was often part of a larger complex in which dance, vocal solo, and ensemble were unified thematically (see, for example, the minuets in the prologue to *Cadmus et Hermione*.

The *comédie-ballet* also contains examples of airs written for bass voice and two obbligato instruments, which were aptly described by Manfred Bukofzer (1947, 158) as "doubled continuo" airs; that is, airs in which the bass voice serves simultaneously as vocal melody and bass support. In effect, the upper two obbligato strings (or flutes or oboes) carry the melody. This curious but enduring type of bass air may be traced back to the French *airs de cour* (see Gérold 1921, 162) and was not restricted to France; it is found both in Venetian opera (see Pluto's air, "Pur troppo inequali" from Cesti's *Il pomo d'oro*) and in bass solos of Heinrich Schütz (see "Herr nun lässest du deinen Diener" for two violins, bass, and continuo).

Dialogue airs, which often generate duos and trios, were used more frequently in the *comédie-ballet* than in the court ballet. If anything, the duos and trios of the *comédie-ballet* are less rigidly homophonic than those of the *tragédie lyrique* and are closer to those found in Venetian opera.

The independent instrumental *symphonies* and dances of the *ballet de cour* have their counterpart in the *comédie-ballet*. In addition to titled dances, there are several *airs de danse* with no fixed choreographic intent. These dances, in particular, often show remarkable freedom in their phase groupings and in the use of counter-rhythms in the inner voices (see, for example, the "2e Air" from the Turkish Ceremony of *Le Bourgeois gentilhomme*).

As was true with the *ballet de cour*, the *comédie-ballet* was a haven for all manner of instruments before the relative standardization of the French opera orchestra. At times it was a large, rather heterogeneous orchestra with exotic and colorful instruments. The *livret* of *La Princesse d'Élide* mentions "several hunting horns and trumpets" in concert with the strings, and at one point describes a "large tree machine in which there are sixteen *Faunes*, eight of whom play flutes, the others, violin . . . . Thirty violins answer them from the orchestra with six other harpsichord and theorbo soloists." The rustic sounds of the *hautbois de Poitou* are called for in *Ballet des Nations*. This instrument, first described by Mersenne in 1636, was actually the detached and capped chanter of a bagpipe (see Haynes 1988, 333–334).

In *comédies-ballets* such as *George Dandin* and *Les Amants magnifiques*, musical features tend to dominate and their link with the dramatic action is compromised. In *Les Amants magnifiques*, we are on the very threshold of the *tragédie en musique*. The text by Molière could function as an operatic *livret*; the prologue is sung throughout. Here again the "kingly" prologue of the *tragédie lyrique* is foreshadowed by the use of more unified musical material; the instrumental introduction to the chorus "Ouvrons tous nos yeux" engenders the final dance, the "Menuet des trompettes." The finale is a decorative and sumptuous operatic celebration of the Pythian games. Written in the brilliant key of D major and scored in part for trumpets and drums, it is climaxed by the entrance of Apollo, whose part was danced by the king, thus combining *comédie-ballet* and *ballet de cour*.

Decorative elements in the guise of elaborate stage machinery and costumes remind us that the *comédies-ballets* were originally part of court *divertissements*. In his *Recueil de descriptions de peintures et d'autres ouvrages faits pour le roi* Félibien described the effects of Vigarani's machines in *George Dandin*—the rapid scene changes for which the Italian machinists were so well known:

> *Here, the decoration of the stage is changed in an instant, and one can not imagine how it is that all the real fountains disappear and by what artifice one sees on the stage only large rocks intermixed with trees where several shepherds sing and play all sorts of instruments (1689, 222).*

The open antagonism between Molière and Lully, which ended their collaboration on *comédies-ballets*, may be dated from the bid by Lully to obtain the royal privilege for the establishment of the Académie Royale de Musique. It was not in character for Lully to remain on the sidelines after observing the successes of Robert Cambert and Pierre Perrin with the *Pastorale d'Issy* (1659) and above all with *Pomone* (1671). After buying the royal privilege from Perrin, Lully then managed to obtain a series of patents and ordinances from the king that Molière took as a very real threat to his comedians. The patent dated before 16 March 1672, which gave Lully the authority to establish an "Académie Royale de Musique," at the same time forbade any performance of any work that was sung throughout unless Lully gave written permission—under penalty of a ten thousand *livres* fine and confiscation of the theater, machines, decorations, costumes, etc. An ordinance of 30 April 1673 reduced to eight (two voices, six instrumentalists) the number of musicians who could appear in productions independent of the Académie Royale de Musique and limited these to musicians (and dancers) not in the employ of the Académie. Particularly ominous for Molière was the patent of 20 September 1672 in which Lully received permission to have printed "all and each of the airs composed by him, as well as the verses, texts, subjects, plans, and works for which the above mentioned airs have been composed—with no exceptions" (see Truinet and Roquet 1886; rpt. 1972, 281).

Molière countered by collaborating with Marc-Antoine Charpentier (1634–1704), who composed new music for a performance of *Le Mariage forcé* on 8 July 1672.[3] Molière's final work, the *comédie-ballet Le Malade imaginaire*, included *intermèdes* also composed by Charpentier. In order to meet the restrictions of Lully's patents, Charpentier was forced to recast the music three times. Charpentier's struggle is summed up in the titles borne by the three manuscript versions found scattered through the Charpentier *Meslanges autographes*

in the Bibliothèque Nationale: (1) *Le Malade imaginaire avant les deffences*; (2) *Le Malade imaginaire avec les deffences*; and (3) *Le Malade
imaginaire rajusté autrement pour la 3ᵉ fois.*

The final triumph of Lully's scheming came about fortuitously
with the sudden death of Molière following the fourth performance of
Le Malade imaginaire on 17 February 1673. Lully had been renting a
theater, Jeu de Paume de Bel Air (Rue de Vaugirard, today between
the Odéon theater and the Luxemburg gardens), in which his pas-
torale-pastiche, *Les Fêtes de l'Amour et de Bacchus*, and his first *tragédie
en musique*, *Cadmus et Hermione*, had already been performed. Once
Molière was out of the way, Lully was able to get the king's permission to take over, at no cost, the hall of the Palais Royal which had
served Molière and his troupe so well (ordinance of 28 April 1673).
The king also gave Lully three thousand *livres* to convert this theater,
so Lully found himself with an opera house in one of the wings of the
Palais Royal on the rue Saint-Honoré. A poignant postscript to these
events appears in an annotation in Charles Varlet, Sieur de La
Grange's *Registre* for 1673: "Those actors and actresses [of Molière's
troupe] who remained behind found themselves not only without a
troupe but without a theater as well, which obliged them to seek out
another establishment" (1659–1685; rpt. 1947, 1:[147]).[4]

The *comédie-ballet* was sacrificed to Lully's ambition. It left its
mark on the French lyric theater, however. Richard Oliver has illustrated how its general plan shaped *Cadmus et Hermione* (1947,
361–362). It bequeathed its basic format to the *opéra comique*, and in
the hands of Lully and Molière, it was perhaps the only combination
of poetry and music that pleased both partisans of song and champions
of spoken words. Saint-Évremond advised playwrights to return to
"our excellent Comedies, where one may introduce some dances, some
Music which detracts nothing from the representation . . . ; it is thus
that you would discover what satisfies both the senses and the mind"
(1684b; in *Oeuvres meslées*, 1714, 11:92–93). For Saint-Évremond, certainly, this mixed genre of spoken comedy, music, and dance afforded
no ambiguity.

Such was not the case for the term *comédie-ballet*, itself, which falls
so easily on the ear for us. In fact, *Le Bourgeois gentilhomme* is the only
example of this genre that bears the title "*comédie-ballet*" in the original
printed edition. Even Molière's final essay in this form, *Le Malade
imaginaire*, is labeled "*comédie mélée de musique et de danse.*" We have
seen how the *Gazette de France*, reporting from Chambord, first
described *Le Bourgeois gentilhomme* as a "ballet composed of six *entrées*
accompanied by comedy," yet the same journal on 23 October 1670
labeled the work a "comedy accompanied by a ballet." One is reminded of Charles Robinet's *Lettre en vers à Madame* of 15 February 1670 in

which, in the space of five lines, he defines the *comédie-ballet Les Amants magnifiques* as *"un ballet en comédie . . . ou bien, une comédie en ballet."*

Tragédie-Ballet

Qu'il est vrai que ce grand spectacle,
Qui faisoit la crier: Miracle!
Ce beau spectacle tout royal
Est encore ici sans égal *(Robinet, "Lettres en vers à Monsieur," August, 1671).*

It is true that this grand spectacle,
which causes the cry: Miracle!
This beautiful spectacle, all royal,
Is still here without equal.

With these words, Robinet was describing *Psyché*, a large-scale collaborative effort with Lully as composer and Molière, Quinault, and Pierre Corneille responsible for the text. The *livret* of 1671 labeled *Psyché* a *"tragédie ballet."* It was cast in a prologue and five *intermèdes*, and of all the works discussed in this chapter, it most closely resembles the *tragédie en musique*. By enlarging the role of the gods and making other minor alterations, and by adding recitatives, Lully and Thomas Corneille were able to convert the 1671 *tragédie ballet* into the 1678 *tragédie en musique* in only three weeks' time.

Psyché owes its existence to the desire of Louis XIV to see Vigarani's machines for *Ercole amante* once more—especially those that represented Hell. In 1671 he asked Molière, Racine, and Quinault for a subject that would necessarily include the machinery for Hell. Racine proposed an *Orphée*; Quinault, a *Proserpine*; and Molière, the *Psyché* (see Vanuxem 1967, 40). For the descent of Venus in the prologue, Vigarani created cloud machinery, which made a tremendous impression on Robinet and others. The 1671 livret describes it as follows: "A large machine descends from the sky in between two smaller machines. All three are enveloped at first in clouds which, in descending, undulate, open, and extend themselves until they occupy the entire stage."

The idea of music and dance as dramatic agents came straight from the *comédie-ballet*. The *"concerts lugubres"* and dances marked by "violent despair" of the *"pompe funèbre"* in *Psyché* (Act I, scene vi) prefigure the *"pompe funèbre"* of *Alceste* (Act III, scene v). Although by 1671 the use of Italian was already archaic, the beautiful lament "Deh, piangete al pianto" from the first *intermède* is, in my view, a synthesis between Italian expressiveness and French restraint, in which French elements tend to dominate. In spite of an Italian repetition of text, the range is narrow, the vocal melismas discreet, and the use of dissonance restrained (see Example 5-2). Furthermore, following it is a *double* (probably by Lambert) and a recitative that accommodates French changes of meter and even an Alexandrine couplet. It is worth recalling that, for Lecerf, this lament showed Lully banishing Italian vocal excesses to leave only a "beautiful melody based on French tones" (1725; rpt. 1966, 2:93).

Example 5-2. Lully: Extract from "Deh, piangete," *Psyché* (after Manuscript in Bibliothèque Nationale [MS Vm⁶ 5]).

The spectacular operatic finale that celebrates the marriage of Love and Psyche was never surpassed by Lully, not even in his operas. In this final *intermède*, Apollo, Bacchus, Momus, Mars, and their followers are united. Trumpets and drums combine with voices to articulate the closing lines of this unique *tragédie ballet*:

Chantons les plaisirs charmants
Des heureux amants.
Répondez-nous, trompettes.
Timbales et tambours;
Accordez-vous toujours
Avec le doux son des musettes,
Accordez-vous toujours
Avec le doux chant des amours.

Let us sing of the charming pleasures
Of happy lovers.
Reply to us, trumpets,
Kettledrums and side drums;
Tune yourselves always
To the soft sound of the musettes,
Tune yourselves always
To love's sweet song.

Tragédie à Machines

"The Théâtre du Marais could be considered the cradle of the Académie Royale de Musique," wrote Victor Fournel (1875, 3:24). If we recognize that machines had played a significant role in many French stage productions dating back to the Italianate pastorales of the late sixteenth century, Fournel's opinion has merit, for it is true that the taste of the French audience for intricate stage machinery was consistently and skillfully manipulated for twenty years by impresarios eager to fill the coffers of the Marais theater, which in time became known as the "Théâtre des Machines." It is equally true that, under the influence of Italian opera and court ballet, music and dance invaded the domain of the "machine tragedy" and, in conjunction with the *mise-en-scène*, forced it ever closer to opera.

Like the *tragi-comédie*, the *tragédie à machines* was one of the mixed genres that rendered the French stage "very rich and at the same time very confused" between the 1640s and 1660s (Adam 1949, 2:334). Always popular with the audiences, if not with the academicians, it only gradually gave way before the law of unities and the establishment of French classical drama.

In 1640 Chapoton's tragedy, *La Descente d'Orphée aux Enfers*, was performed at the Palais Royal. Noting the success of this machine tragedy with interest, the comedians of the Marais performed a new version entitled, *La Grande journée des machines ou le mariage d'Orphée et d'Euridice*, in 1648. According to the *livret*, the machinist Denis Buffequin had contrived the "most beautiful and most extraordinary machines that the artifice of our century and past centuries could invent." Much new music was added to the three songs of Orpheus in the original production.

Pierre Corneille's machine tragedy, *Andromède*, has more literary merit. It was initially commissioned by Anne d'Autriche and Cardinal Mazarin and performed at the Petit Bourbon during carnival season in 1650. A reading of the author's preface negates the supposition that by virtue of this work, Corneille, in the words of the *Grand Larousse* encyclopedia, was an "initiator of modern opera" (1960, 1:394). On the contrary, he aligned himself firmly on the side of such later critics of opera as Saint-Évremond by stating that sung words are poorly understood and that therefore he had taken care to have nothing sung that was necessary for comprehension. The music (lost) by Charles Coypeau (called Dassoucy) was employed only to "satisfy the ears of the spectators while the eyes are engaged watching the descent or ascent of a machine." Torelli's machines, however, were far from being "detached ornaments" like the music. They were considered essential to the action. Only in choral commentaries found in such scenes as the combat between Persée and the monster ("Le Monstre est mort, crions victoire," Act III, scene iii) do we come closer to the spirit of opera.[5]

Much nearer to opera is Claude Boyer's *Les Amours de Jupiter et de Sémélé*, performed at the Marais in 1666, in which the spoken drama itself is subordinated to the music (by Louis de Mollier), dance, and machine. The prologue describes the rivalry between Melpomène (tragic Muse), Thalie (comic Muse), and Euterpe (pastoral Muse). In the best operatic manner, each Muse is assigned her characteristic music. Melpomène enters to the "loud sounds of bugles and trumpets"; Thalie plays a "Basque drum, with which mixes a concert of strings"; and Euterpe descends from Mount Parnassus while the musettes and oboes play an air "composed expressly for the pastorale." A more highly developed characterization of a similar situation occurs much later in the prologue to Mouret's *opéra-ballet*, *Les Fêtes de Thalie* of 1714 (see Chapter 10).

If we allow for some hyperbole, Boyer sums up the contribution of the *tragédie à machines* to the French lyric stage in his *Dessein de la tragédie des amours de Jupiter et Sémélé* (1666, 16): "Here is a small idea of our Play, which we might call an Aggregation of all that is astonishing in Music and, finally, of all that is the most powerful and *galant* in Poetry."

Containing at least as much music as the pastorales of Perrin and Cambert, and resembling the subject matter, if not the treatment, of Quinault's *tragédies lyriques*, the *tragédies à machines* may be considered an "imperfect and rough reflection of opera" (Gros 1928, 174).

Chapter 6

The Pastorale

As was true for the court ballet, the sources of the French pastorale lay outside of France. The Italian dramatic pastorale, with its love of classical mythology, and the Spanish pastorale, with its conventionalized shepherds and shepherdesses and its chivalrous trappings, come together in the French pastorale. The first French dramatic pastorales appeared in the late sixteenth century and were based in the main on Italian models. French translations of Torquato Tasso's *L'Aminta* (1581) and Giambattista Guarini's *Il Pastor fido* (1585) appeared as early as 1584 and 1595, respectively.

In subject matter and in decor, French dramatic pastorales contributed certain elements to the lyric stage that were to remain constant up to the eve of the Revolution. Of central importance was the world of the *merveilleux* (a collective term for miraculous, supernatural, and magical events) where the magician, so significant in the *livrets* of Quinault, played a leading role. Magic fountains, apparitions, magic potions, and rapid metamorphoses were everywhere in evidence. The deities mixed in the affairs of mortals, as would the gods of Quinault. Reading Jules Marsan's description of the dramatic pastorale *Arimène* by Nicolas de Montreux, one envisions its choruses and dances, its monsters and magic, and its cloud machines transporting Jupiter and Perseus—a *mise-en-scène* of 1597 that was to have its counterpart 100 years later at the Académie Royale de Musique (1905, 214–215).

L'Astrée, the 5000-page *roman pastoral* by Honoré d'Urfé, exerted considerable influence on the literature and manners of the period. Its first three volumes were in print by 1613. Among the dramatic pastorales based upon it was Honorat de Racan's *Les Bergeries* (1625), which bordered on preciousness and further exploited the cult of shepherd and shepherdess that had been a fixed staple of the French lyric stage and was to remain so through to the end of the eighteenth century.

Elements of the pastorale appeared in the *ballet de cour* as early as the *Ballet comique de la Reine.* Both the *ballet mélodramatique* and the *ballet à entrées* used its subject matter. By 1619 the *ballet mélodramatique* was in *"plein pastorale"* in the sylvan decor of the *Ballet de l'aventure de Tancrède en la forêt enchantée* (La Laurencie 1912, 141). With the appearance of French classical drama, the pastorale was practically eliminated as a dramatic genre—a fate similar to that of the *ballet mélodramatique.* It found refuge in the *ballet de cour* and in the tentative beginnings of French opera.

The pastorale was well adapted for its role in the creation of French opera. It contributed its symmetrically balanced dialogues, which were already a kind of "music without music" (La Laurencie, 1912, 142). Its tender, occasionally melancholy subject matter was ideally suited to the lyric stage; and its use of sorcerers, satyrs, buffoons, shepherds, and shepherdesses in close proximity to the gods introduced the opportunity for contrast, which is essential for effective musical theater.

In 1650 at the height of the Fronde, Charles Dassoucy wrote the pastorale *Les Amours d'Apollon et de Daphné.* This *comédie en musique,* which was probably never performed, included about a dozen *chansons* interspersed among 550 lines of poetry. All of Dassoucy's music for *Andromède* (which he composed that same year for Corneille) and for *Les Amours d'Apollon et de Daphné* is lost except for some extracts found in the collection of his *Airs à quatre parties* published by Robert Ballard in 1653 (see Lila Maurice-Amour, 1955, 46 and 61). Although we know that Dassoucy played theorbo for the performances of Cavalli's *Egisto* and Rossi's *Orfeo,* we can only guess at the extent of Italian influence on this first French *comédie en musique.*

Le Triomphe de l'Amour sur des bergers et bergères, by Charles de Bey and Michel de La Guerre, is the first pastorale that was entirely sung. It was performed at the Louvre on 22 January 1655, probably in a concert version, and was staged two years later with two characters (Tirsis and Philis) added to the original five (Cupid, two shepherds, and two shepherdesses). De Bey's dedicatory letter to the king refers to the pastorale as a *"Comédie françoise en Musique"* and comments on the "novelty of this Piece whose format is my invention, and which is, in effect, the first work of its kind ever to have appeared in this Realm." The *Argument* from the *Avertissement* of the 1655 version is quoted by Henri Quittard and is a classic example of a pastorale plot:

Climène scorns Lysis who loves her; Philandre scorns Climène who loves him; Cloris loves Lysis; Lysis scorns her; Philandre loves Cloris; Cloris scorns Philandre . . . Lysis, Philandre, Climène and Cloris agree . . . to keep their freedom and to renounce love. Cupid

appears with his bow and arrows; . . . all remain together in the
Empire of Love (1908, 379–380).

Louis Auld claims that the lack of connective dialogue results in a
totally non-theatrical format for *Le Triomphe de l'Amour sur des bergers*
et bergères even though it was sung throughout (1986, 1:88). Since no
records of the stage version survived, there is no way of knowing
whether or not changes rendered it more dramatic.

Although little is known about the tragedy *Acébar, Roi du Mogol*,
performed in Carpentras in 1646 with music by Abbé Mailly, we cannot dismiss this work out-of-hand as a contender for being the first
French opera. At the very least, some attention should be given to
Ménestrier's cryptic comments concerning Abbé Mailly: "an excellent
composer" in Carpentras who "sought out this type of Dramatic
Music that has only existed for the last few years" and who composed
some "scenes in *musique récitative* for a tragedy, *Achébar, Roi du Mogol*,
and who accompanied these *récits* with a *Symphonie* of diverse instruments" (1681, 177–178).

The talented organist, Robert Cambert (ca. 1627–1677) may have
been familiar with de Bey's and Michel de La Guerre's *Le Triomphe de*
l'Amour sur des bergers et bergères, for in a letter quoted by Truinet and
Roquet he wrote:

> *Having always had the thought of introducing comedies in music as*
> *are found in Italy, I began to compose an elegy in 1658 for three*
> *contrasting voices in dialogue . . . and this elegy was called the*
> Muette ingratte. *M. Perrin having heard this piece which was*
> *very successful . . . wished to compose a small pastorale (1886, 33).*

The first important result of the collaboration between Cambert
and Pierre Perrin (1620–1675) was the so-called *Pastorale d'Issy*.
Ignoring the earlier efforts of Dassoucy and Michel de La Guerre,
Perrin presumptuously titled his work in the Ballard printed edition of
1659, "*Première comédie française en musique représentée en France.*
Pastorale. Mise en musique par Monsieur Camber [sic], organiste de l'église
collégiale de Saint-Honoré à Paris." Only the *livret* of this pastorale is
extant. The verses of Perrin are banal; the form, however, is less rigid
than that of the "*Comédie françoise en musique*" of de Bey. Quite by
design and apparently to achieve the greatest possible contrast with
Italian opera, the poet "banished all serious thought" ("*raisonnements*
grave") and even all plot from his pastorale in five acts and fourteen
scenes. According to Ménestrier, the work contained songs which
were "linked together following no law but that of expressing beautiful verse and music. . . . All succeeded admirably, because the

Symphonie was beautiful, the performers, handsome, and everyone was in good voice" (1681, 209). This blanket approbation casts some doubt on the Jesuit's critical acumen. Titon du Tillet's comment on the *Pastorale d'Issy* is perhaps closer to the truth: "A number of distinguished persons were very satisfied with the work, although the text left much to be desired" (1732; Supplement 1743, 49).

Certainly, in Saint-Évremond's words, it had the *"agrément de la nouveauté"* (charm of novelty), for it was performed eight or ten times in 1659 at the village of Issy in the country home of Monsieur de La Haye, and a performance was arranged in May the same year at Vincennes before the king, the queen, and Cardinal Mazarin. In spite of his absorption in Italian opera, Mazarin suggested afterwards to Cambert that he and Perrin compose another pastorale on a larger scale. The result was *Ariane ou Le Mariage de Bacchus* (music lost), which was only performed in a revised version with new music by Cambert (?) and Louis Grabu in London on 30 March 1674 (see Bashford 1991). If we may trust Saint-Évremond's judgment based on the Paris rehearsals in 1659, we have been deprived of "Cambert's masterpiece," whose laments were the "equal of Lully's best music" (1684a; 4th ed. 1726, 3:340–341).

On 28 June 1669, Perrin received his twelve-year privilege to establish an Académie d'Opéra, which was inaugurated 3 March 1671 with a performance of the pastorale *Pomone*. Perhaps under the direct influence of the Lully-Molière *comédie-ballet*, Perrin and Cambert created in *Pomone* a much more ambitious and theatrical work than the *Pastorale d'Issy*. It was well received and was performed 146 times, although Cambert with understandable pique wrote afterwards that he would have preferred less success, because "there would not have been so many envious people, and I would not have found myself without employment by virtue of having succeeded too well" (Truinet and Roquet 1886, 157). Saint-Évremond has a character in his comedy *Les Opéra* (Act II, scene iv) describe *Pomone* as follows:

> *Pomone is the first French Opera to appear on Stage. The Poetry in it is very bad, the Music beautiful. Monsieur de Sourdéac built the Machines; this is enough to give you some idea of their beauty; one observed the Machines with surprise, the Dances with pleasure; one listened to the Songs with delight, to the Words with disgust (1684a; 4th ed. 1726, 3:339–340).*

Only the overture, the prologue (subtitled "à la louange du Roi" and labeled Act I), and five pages of Act II remain. Cambert's scoring is more progressive than Lully's; that is, he avoided the heavy $a5$ string writing characteristic of the Florentine and preferred an $a4$ or trio texture. The expressive beginning of Act II (Example 6-1), its bass line rising a diminished fourth to create a poignant dissonant harmony with the melody on the word *soupire*, shows a composer sensitive to the affective nature of Baroque recitative.

Example 6-1. Cambert: *Pomone*, beginning of Act II (after Ballard manuscript ed. in Bibliothèque Nationale).

Following *Pomone*, a second *pastorale-opéra*, *Les Amours de Diane et d'Endymion*, was performed at Versailles on 3 November 1671 (music lost). Its composer, Jean Granouilhet de Sablières, and its librettist, Henry Guichard, were to become Lully's main rivals in the establishment of a permanent French opera. The three-act opera was performed at Saint-Germain-en-Laye on 18 February 1672 with two added *intermèdes* exploiting scene changes and dance (see La Gorce 1984).

All the confusing details of Perrin's relationships with the business manager of his Académie d'Opéra, the talented but unscrupulous Marquis de Sourdéac, and with the Marquis's flunky, the former sergeant, Sieur de Champeron, have been told many times and need not be repeated here.[1] Because of the intrigues of Sourdéac and Champeron, Perrin found himself in debtor's prison, and in June 1672 the theater was closed. Robinet summed up this sorry state of affairs in his "Lettres en vers à Monsieur" of 20 June:

Le Grand Opéra plus n'opère,
Dont maint ici se desespère.
La Discorde aux poils couleuvrins,
Qui se nourrit de noirs chagrins
Et des Plaisirs est l'ennemie,
En a troublé l'Académie,
Les Intendants et les Auteurs, . . .

Tous sont tombez en guerre atroce,
En guerre incivile et féroce.

The Grand Opera operates no more,
For which many here are in despair.
Discord with her snaking hair,
Who feeds on black grief
And of Pleasures is the enemy,
Has troubled the Academy.
The managers and the composers, . . .
All have fallen into war atrocious,
Into war uncivil and ferocious.

Although Perrin continued to languish in jail, a partial resolution of economic difficulties saw the doors of the Académie open again in the winter of 1672 for a performance of a *pastorale héroïque, Les Peines et les Plaisirs de l'Amour*, which Cambert composed to a *livret* by Gabriel Gilbert. The performances must have ended by 1 April, on which date the Académie was again closed by royal decree because Sourdéac and Champeron had failed to pay any wages. As we have seen, Lully chose this moment to secure the royal privilege for himself despite Perrin's having sold two thirds of his privilege to Sablières and Guichard. Molière, and Sablières and Guichard in company with Sourdeac and Champeron, all attempted to block Lully's privilege. With the power of the throne behind him, Lully had little to fear. In buying the privilege from Perrin, he made it possible for the poet to regain his freedom but impossible for Cambert to find any further employment in France as a dramatic composer. Cambert followed his former student, Louis Grabu, to London, where he established a short-lived "Royall Academy of Musick" and where he died in 1677.[2]

Mediocre poet notwithstanding, Pierre Perrin's role in the creation of French opera must not be minimized. His clear understanding of the basic difference between stage drama and opera, as expressed in his letter (30 April 1659) to Girolamo Delle Rovera, Archbishop of Turin, would have found favor with Lorenzo Da Ponte more than a century later:

Such a form of theater [lyric theater] has all the advantages of
spoken theater, and the further advantage over it of expressing
the passions in a more touching manner by the rise and fall of the
voice; of having several things repeated in a pleasing way and
impressing them more forcibly upon the imagination and memory;
of allowing several persons to say the same thing at the same time,
and to express by concerted voices, the unanimity of their spirits,

feelings and thoughts; sometimes even by saying the same things in different notes, to express diverse sentiments at the same time; and other beauties little known until now but admirably effective (Auld 1986, 1:104).

Although Lully must be considered the founder of French serious opera, it was Perrin who provided us with the first *livret* for a tragic opera. *La Mort d'Adonis*, written before 1666, appears as a *tragédie en musique* in Perrin's *Recueil de paroles de musique* (in Auld 1986, 3:123–145). Unfortunately, the music for this *tragédie*, composed by Jean-Baptiste Boesset, has not survived. With some exaggeration, Perrin characterized Boesset's music as the "most learned, the most varied and the most moving that has been heard, I do not say in France but in all Europe, for several centuries" (Auld 1986, 2:33). The *livret* illustrates how close we are to Lully's *tragédies en musique*. It contains references to battle music (Act II, scene v); hunting music (Act IV, scene i); a *Symphonie lugubre* (Act II, scene iv); a *pompe funèbre* (Act V, scene i); a *sommeil* (Act III, scene i): a final *divertissement*; and, just after the *sommeil*, a startling adumbration of Armide's great monologue "Enfin, il est en ma puissance" in which Falsirène, with "dagger in hand," is unable to strike the sleeping Adonis (Act III, scene ii).

The *pastorale héroïque Les Peines et les Plaisirs de l'Amour*, by Cambert and Gilbert, shows a marked advance over *Pomone*. Superior to Perrin as a poet, Gilbert realized certain dramatic advantages in having the gods involve themselves in the affairs of men; Apollo's love for a mortal shepherdess is rendered in a genuinely pathetic tone. Here unfortunately, as is the case with *Pomone*, Cambert's dramatic talents must be evaluated on the basis of the remaining fragments: the overture, prologue, and fourteen pages of Act I. The overture, unlike that to *Pomone*, is not *à la française*. It is more like a multi-sectioned Italian *canzona*. Judging from the extant bits, Cambert appears to have been less concerned with textual elements than Lully but well on the way to creating a French recitative that would have been more genuinely musical. The expressive melismas found in Example 6-2 almost never occur in the syllabic recitatives of Lully.

Example 6-2. Cambert: Extract from Astérie's recitative in *Les Peines et les Plaisirs de l'Amour* (after Ballard manuscript ed. in Bibliothèque Nationale).

Armed with his new royal patent of March 1672, "our dear and well-loved Jean-Baptiste Lully" lost no time in activating the new Académie Royale de Musique. The inaugural choice was a pastorale in three acts, *Les Fêtes de l'Amour et de Bacchus*, performed on 15 November 1672. Evidently thrown together in great haste, this pastiche of several earlier works shows no advance over the pastorales of Cambert. In fact, it is less developed from the dramatic point of view due to its lack of a consistent plot. According to the *Avant-Propos*, it was Quinault's task to "connect these diverse fragments"; Vigarani was responsible for the décor and Des Brosses, for the ballets.

For Étienne Gros, *Les Fêtes de l'Amour et de Bacchus* "marks the end of the pastorale in music rather than the advent of the *tragédie lyrique*." He added that Lully did not favor the *"genre bucolique"* and that while pastoral elements were dispersed in the prologues and *divertissements* of the *tragédies lyriques*, the "pastorale in music disappeared from the stage of the Académie Royale de Musique" (1926, 517).

Surely this is too harsh a judgment. Lully's final completed work, *Acis et Galatée* (1686), is a *pastorale héroïque*, a genre which also had particular appeal for composers of the Regency.[3] The third *intermède* of *Les Amants magnifiques* is a masterpiece, entirely in the *genre buccolique*, for which Molière reduced the confusing numbers of lovers and rejected suitors to a single pair: one shepherd and one shepherdess. The *divertissement* in Act IV of the *tragédie en musique Roland* is dramatically integrated into the plot and is effective precisely because it *is* a pastorale (see Chapter 7).

The pastorale in the generation between Lully and Rameau continued to play an important role in French opera. It was not by accident that Campra chose a pastorale to represent "La France" in his *opéra-ballet, L'Europe galante*. From the beginning of the pastorale, poets used its maxims to comment on the social mores of their time. Musical pastorales found in the *opéras-ballets* of the Regency also use the unreal world of shepherd and shepherdess to illuminate the all-too-real world of the last days of Louis XIV and the Regency. An accusing finger is pointed at the innumerable intrigues and deceits that plagued the court at Versailles. In a simple air from the first *entrée* ("La Pastorale") in Campra's *opéra-ballet, Les Muses*, Silvie sings:

Parmy les grandeurs de la Cour,
À taire ses secrets, chacun sçait se contraindre;
Mais, dans ce tranquile séjour,
Nous n'aprenons point l'art de feindre.

Among the grandeurs of the court,
Everyone knows to constrain himself, to conceal his secrets;

> *But in this tranquil abode,*
> *We learn nothing of the art of feigning.*

The most famous dancers of the post-Lully operatic world were often given solo roles as shepherds and shepherdesses. In 1729 Le Sieur Dumoulin and Mlle Camargo, two of the most popular dancers of the period, were featured as shepherd and shepherdess in Jean-Baptiste Quinault's *Les Amours des Déesses*; eighteen years later the same pair starred as shepherd and shepherdess in Mouret's *Les Amours des Dieux*.

In 1706 in a brief summary of the literary pastorale, Joseph Mervesin described how the French poets

> *imitated the Italian and Spanish poets, learning from them how to compose villanelles; these are songs in which Shepherds and Shepherdesses speak with tenderness. They soon became very much à la mode, and since that time have been used in France to express maxims of love, morality and all that is motivated by gentleness and tenderness (137).*

This summary serves also for the musical pastorale. From the *Ballet comique de la Reine* to the beginnings of French opera, from the *tragédie lyrique* to the *opéra-ballet*, from the magic scenes in Jean-Philippe Rameau's *Dardanus* (1739) to the shepherd Lysis wearing his carmagnole and red turban in André-Ernest-Modeste Grétry's *La Rosière républicaine* (1794), the pastorale is the Ariadne's thread of the French lyric theater.

Chapter 7

Tragédie en Musique I: *Dramatic Organization and Vocal Music*

Avec toute sa pompe & son riche appareil,
La Musique en nos jours ne fait rien de pareil,
Ce bel Art tout divin par ces douces merveilles,
Ne se contente pas de charmer les oreilles,
N'y d'aller jusqu'au coeur par ces expressions,
Émouvoir à son gré toutes les passions:
Il va, passant plus loin par sa beauté suprême,
Au plus haut de l'esprit charmer la raison mesme (Perrault 1687, 19).

With all its pomp and rich display,
The music of our time has no equal,
This beautiful Art, divine in its sweet marvels,
Not content with charming the ears,
Nor with piercing to the heart, by its expressiveness,
To move all passions at its will:
But passing further because of its supreme beauty, it goes
To the height of mind to charm reason itself.

The *Gazette de France* of 29 April 1673 described the first performance of *Cadmus et Hermione*, Lully's first *tragédie en musique*, as follows:

On the 27th, His Majesty, accompanied by Monsieur, Mademoiselle and Mademoiselle d'Orléans, went to the Faubourg Saint-Germain to hear the divertissement *of the Opera of the Académie Royale de Musique established by Sieur Batiste Lully, so celebrated in this Art; and the group left extraordinarily satisfied with this superb spectacle in which the Tragedy of Cadmus and Hermione, a very beautiful work by Sieur Quinault, was performed with astonishing machines and decorations whose invention and operation we owe to Sieur Vigarani, gentleman of Modena.*[1]

Thus, ninety-two years after the performance of the *Ballet comique de la reine*, French stage music had swept full circle. *Cadmus et Hermione* synthesized elements borrowed from the court ballet, pastorale, comedy ballet, tragedy ballet, the machine tragedy, and Italian opera into a large-scale work; and, at least in principle, subordinated all to an overall dramatic unity. In so doing, it eclipsed the earlier attempts of Perrin and Cambert to establish a national opera. "The *grand Opéra* of *Cadmus*, which everyone wished to see," wrote Jean-Nicolas Du Tralage in 1687, "made it easy to forget the operas *Pomone* and *Les Plaisirs de l'Amour*" (cited by Mélèse 1934a, 157).

Cadmus et Hermione opens with a French overture (already familiar by 1673) followed in the routine fashion of that day by an allegorical-political prologue. Loosely based on Ovid (eighth Fable of the *Metamorphoses*), the prologue alludes to the successful conclusion of the Dutch wars. Shepherds and shepherdesses mix with nymphs and pastoral deities such as Palès, Mélisse, and the god Pan. "Le Soleil" destroys a monstrous serpent, and the chorus sings "Répandons le bruit de sa gloire, Jusques au bout de l'Univers." The *livret* informs us that the "allegorical meaning of this subject is so clear that it is pointless to explain it."

A pair of lovers, one or more rivals (often including at least one god or goddess), and the critical mingling of gods and goddesses in the affairs of their mortal protégés formed a ground plan that with minor variants served Quinault for all subsequent *livrets*. Illustrating how carefully Lully incorporated a national style designed to please both court and academy are the inclusion of a *divertissement* of songs and dances in nearly every act, the presence of short binary and rondeau airs, the domination by recitative, the conspicuous chorus, and the full use of spectacular machinery made by Vigarani and (after 1680, by Jean Berain) to accommodate the *merveilleux*.

Livret

From 1673 to 1687, the year of his death, Lully composed an annual opera[2] for which Philippe Quinault (1635–1688) furnished eleven *livrets*. Each *livret* resulted from a threefold collaboration between composer, poet, and the Académie des Inscriptions et Belles Lettres. In spite of the generous four thousand *livres* that Quinault received for each *livret*, evidence suggests that the division of labor was far from equitable. Lecerf's comments illuminate what must have been a complex relationship between an intelligent, imperious composer and his more malleable librettist against the background of the impersonal dicta of the Académie des Inscriptions et Belles Lettres:

> *Quinault wrote out a plan for the action of the Piece. He gave a copy of this plot to Lully, and Lully, seeing the subject of each Act, prepared some* divertissements *from his imagination . . . . Quinault composed his Scenes; as soon as he had finished writing several, he presented them to the Académie Françoise [Académie des Inscriptions et Belles Lettres], with which you are familiar; after having gathered and put to use the advice of the Academy, he brought the scenes to Lully . . . [who] examined this previously reviewed and corrected poetry word by word, which he corrected further or from which he cut out half when he judged it appropriate . . . . He sent* Phaëton *back twenty times, for example, to have entire scenes changed that had been approved by the Académie Françoise. Quinault [with Academy approval] had fashioned an excessively harsh* Phaëton, *who truly spoke abusively to Théone . . . . Lully . . . wanted Quinault to make* Phaëton *ambitious but not brutal; [for Bellérophon] for five or six hundred Verses . . . . M. de Lîle [T. Corneille] was forced to write two thousand (Lecerf 1725; rpt. 1966, 3:195, 197–198).*

Although he rarely attended performances in Paris, the king became an enthusiastic partisan of opera. Mme de Maintenon, who thought the *galant* maxims of Quinault a direct threat to Christian morality, conceded that Louis XIV was interested only in the beauty of the music and that, because of his pleasure in an air, he would go so far as to "sing his own praises as though they had been written for another" (cited by Écorcheville 1906c, 27). He was said to have preferred *Atys* to all others, but he personally chose the subject matter for *Roland, Armide,* and *Amadis.* The dedication found in the first edition of *Phaëton* (1683) suggests that the king's interest even embraced the *mise-en-scène.* Lully thanked his benefactor for having paid attention to all his worries even "down to the costumes, one of the principal parts of this type of Spectacle."

Most commonly, Quinault's *livrets* were judged first and foremost as poetry quite apart from any musical merit. The works were often referred to as Quinault's *tragédies en musique* or Quinault's *Opéra.*[3] In principle, there was no question but that poetry should be the dominant force no matter how modified to fit its lyric setting. "Although the Musician may have more talent than the Poet; although by the force of his genius he may assure the success of an Opera, his art," wrote de Rochemont, "is regarded in France as always secondary to that of poetry" (1754, 25). The concept of operatic music's becoming popular *qua* music was similarly dismissed by Abbé Mably:

> *Many are still persuaded that the success of an Opera depends only upon the Music . . . . An excellent Poem is absolutely essential for the long range success of an Opera. The Music, all by itself, can only give it a passing vogue as a novelty (1741, 6).*

In actuality, as Saint-Évremond complained, "One thinks one hundred times more of Baptiste (Lully) than of Thésée or Cadmus" (1684b; in *Oeuvres meslées*, 1714, 11:87); and although Quinault's verse was praised by many for its adaptability to music, Boileau, no friend to opera, wrote in his *Réflexions critiques* that it was the very weakness of the verses that "rendered them suitable for the musician" (1694, 3:151).

In the tight compartmentalization of dramatic genres characteristic of the *grand siècle*, there was no niche ready-made to accommodate lyric tragedy. Gradually an aesthetic was developed that conceived of opera as having its own laws independent from tragedy and comedy. Ménestrier wrote that because opera was "designed to please and divert rather than to instruct, one seeks there the *merveilleux* more than verisimilitude. It is for this reason that the machines and the extraordinary decorations are appropriate" (1681, 170).

It must be emphasized, however, that this aesthetic was not accepted by all. Perrault wrote:

> *Operas or* Pièces de Machines, *not having been invented at the time of Horace, can hardly be subjected to laws made at that time . . . . Nothing is less bearable in a Comedy than to resolve the Intrigue by a miracle or by the arrival of a god in a machine; and nothing is more beautiful in the Operas than these sorts of miracles and appearances of Divinities when there is some basis for introducing them (1674, 69–70).*

For others, the idea of tragedy as a form of instruction was too strongly ingrained for them to accept any compromises. Samuel Chappuzeau admitted the "agreeable mixture" of Vigarani's machines, dances, and music, and then complained that these "beautiful spectacles are only for the eyes and ears but do not touch the depths of the soul . . . . One can say that he has seen and heard but that he has not been instructed" (1674, 1:53). The *merveilleux* was rejected by such professional opera haters as Saint-Évremond, Boileau, and Jean de La Bruyère. For the latter, machines were "only amusements for children, appropriate for the [Théâtre des] Marionettes" (1688; ed. of 1865, 1:134). Saint-Évremond, somewhat in the position of a secular latter-day Saint Augustine, admitted to having enjoyed the *merveilleux* and having been moved by the music of the opera, but he was forced to conclude that as long as the mind went unchallenged, it was to no avail to flatter the ears or charm the eyes. "It [opera] is nonsense. Nonsense," he added, "filled with music, dance, with machines, and decorations: a magnificent nonsense, but nonsense nonetheless (1684b; in *Oeuvres meslées*, 1714, 11:83).

The pre-eminent position of the *merveilleux* was not seriously challenged, however, until the mid-eighteenth century when it became a natural focal point for the attacks from partisans of the Italian *opera buffa* who wished to banish "the demons and shades, and fairies and genies, and all monsters" from the stage.[4]

Until then, there was general agreement that the unities of time and place, those imperious handmaidens of classical drama, could be overlooked in opera if for no other reason than to justify the introduction of the *merveilleux*. In his *Dissertation critique sur l'Iliade d'Homère*, Jean Terrasson wrote: "The Miraculous or the Supernatural, which reign in all Operas, authorizes . . . changes of Scene, since machines can transport the actors in an instant from one end of the world to the other" (1715, 1:208).

At the same time, Quinault was expected to observe unity of action. Few objected to the successive scene changes in *Isis* from the "pleasant meadows" of Greece to the "most frozen places of Scythia." The scene changes in *Thésée*, from a "frightful desert" to "an enchanted island," offended no one, whereas the affair between two minor characters, Arcas and Cléon, which paralleled the main plot involving Thésée and Aeglé, was "a little puerile" according to Toussaint Rémond de Saint-Mard (1741, 28).

Sacrificed to the demands of unity of action was the development of comic scenes along the lines of those found in *Cadmus*, *Alceste*, and *Thésée*. This mixture of genres, a direct derivative of Roman and Venetian opera, was an anathema to most academicians. The scene between Charon and the unfortunate shades who must pay tribute to cross the river Styx (*Alceste*, Act IV, scene i) is as fine a piece of comic writing and sharp social satire as exists anywhere in French stage music. A remarkably fluid scene, it is constructed around three short, highly contrasted airs separated by *ritournelles*, dialogue recitatives, and brief ensemble responses. The scene pivots around the second air in which Charon, singing only "Donne, passe, donne, passe," resembles the ticket taker at a cinema box office.

Such a scene forces the conclusion that, by silencing Lully's comic muse, official French taste delayed the development of any indigenous *opéra bouffe*. In fact as late as 1714, many were scandalized when Mouret chose the stage of the Paris opera house as the setting for the prologue to his *opéra-ballet Les Fêtes de Thalie* and had the comic muse, Thalie, usurp the position of the tragic muse, Melpomène (see Chapter 10).

Quinault's subject matter derived either from mythology (*Cadmus et Hermione, Alceste, Thésée, Atys, Isis, Psyché, Bellérophon, Proserpine, Persée, Phaëton*) or from familiar legends of chivalry (*Amadis, Roland, Armide*). The dramatic format of the *tragédie lyrique* remained fairly constant, consisting of the entanglement of an amorous couple and one or more rivals (who often included at least one god or goddess) and a complex system of confidants and followers. (Quinault's earlier *tragédies en musique* have a secondary, parallel plot involving person-ages of lesser rank.) Gods and goddesses, magicians and enchantresses compete among themselves and interfere in mortal affairs. When these miraculous interventions bring about a denouement, there is a resemblance to the later "rescue opera." Minerva arrives in Act V of *Thésée* just in time to break the spell of Médée, and the enchantress Urgande in *Amadis* appears in the nick of time to save Amadis and Oriane from the clutches of Arcabonne.

In time-honored fashion, most prologues are divorced from the subject matter of the tragedies. The prologue to *Thésée* leaps into the seventeenth century, setting Venus, Mars, Bacchus, and Ceres at the palace of Versailles—gardens and facade visible onstage. The pro-logue to *Isis* glorifies the naval victories of Jean Bart and Abraham Duquesne, while that of *Persée* alludes to the king's victories in the Dutch wars. Perhaps towards the end of their collaboration, Lully and Quinault had thoughts of modifying the purely panegyric, decorative prologues to link them closer to the dramas. In the prologue to *Amadis*, mention of the death of Amadis precipitates the fatuous com-ment that the destiny of the world now depends on a hero "still more glorious." The two main characters of the prologue, Urgande and Alquif, appear in the tragedy itself.

The scenes of sacrifice, of combat, sleep scenes, funeral cere-monies, and the evocation of monsters, serpents, and furies all stem from a variety of sources, including dramatic pastorales, court ballets, and Italian opera. Quinault was not adverse to "borrowing" Abbé Buti's dancing statues (*Ercole amante*) for the second act of his *Cadmus*. However, in giving the whole a greater dramatic unity and in conceiv-ing of the *divertissement* as a possible dramatic agent, Quinault nation-alized these heterogeneous and baroque elements.

Little is genuinely heroic or tragic in a Quinault *livret*. Only *Atys* would qualify as a tragedy in the classical sense of the word. The famous monologue from Act II of *Armide* ("Enfin il est en ma puissance") was the subject of much contemporary comment, precisely because it is a unique example of heightened dramatic intensity achieved by the perfect union of text and music. Only in some of the later operas did Quinault emphasize the more tragic and heroic elements inherent in his subjects. The conflict between glory and duty on the one hand and love on the other is the dramatic core of *Roland* and of *Armide*. The political implications for the nobility of this Corneillian theme were of sufficient importance to receive full didactic treatment in each prologue:

Du célèbre Roland renouvellons l'histoire.
La France luy donna le jour.
Montrons les erreurs où l'Amour
Peut engager un coeur qui néglige la Gloire (Roland).

Of famous Roland let us revive the story.
France gave him birth.
Let us show the errors whereby Love
Can engage a heart that neglects Glory.

Nous y verrons Renaud malgré la volupté
Suivre un conseil fidèle & sage,
Nous le verrons sortir du Palais enchanté,
Où par l'amour d'Armide il estoit arresté,
Et voler où la gloire appelle son courage (Armide).

There we see Renaud, despite sensual pleasure,
Follow a counsel loyal and wise,
We see him leave the enchanted Palace,
Where he has stopped for love for Armide,
And fly where glory calls his courage.

The amorous intrigues of gods and men are generally more *galant* than heroic in tone, a condition which precipitated many of the later attacks on Quinault's operas by the clergy and the conservative Sorbonne. Ironically, Quinault himself apparently succumbed to this repressive moral climate. After *Armide*, he retired from the stage and wrote a long poem on the extinction of heresy in the realm which begins:

Je n'ai que trop chanté les Jeux & les Amours,
Sur un ton plus sublime, il faut me faire entendre:

Je vous dis adieu, Muse tendre,
Je vous dis adieu, pour toujours (see Gros 1926, 168).

I have sung only too long of games and loves.
On a tone more sublime I must make myself heard;
I bid you adieu, tender Muse,
I bid you adieu forever.

Lully certainly had the utmost confidence in Quinault as a librettist. It will be recalled that because Mme de Montespan had viewed the goddess Juno in *Isis* as an unflattering caricature of herself, Lully was forced to dismiss Quinault and seek another librettist for his next two operas, *Psyché* and *Bellérophon* (see Gros 1926, 119–130). Lecerf informs us that Thomas Corneille was reduced to despair by Lully, who forced him to write two thousand lines of text for *Bellérophon* before finally settling on five or six hundred lines. "Lully," wrote Lecerf, "recognized the superiority of Quinault with regard to Poetry" (1725; rpt. 1966, 3:202).

Musico-dramatic Organization

The interludes of song and dance found in most acts of the *tragédies lyriques* were not called *divertissements* before Campra. Lully and Quinault gave the *divertissements* of the *tragédies lyrique* two mutually exclusive functions: first, as a decorative but nonessential and dramatically neutral ornament; and second, as a decorative but integral part of the dramatic action itself. Both functions shared the panoply of spectacle: dance, chorus, songs, costumes, and machines. In a sense, the second function of the *divertissement* is an amalgamation of the *ballet mélodramatique* and the *ballet à entrées* under the protective canopy of the *tragédie lyrique*. As spectacle and dramatic agent, it is a feature of the musico-dramatic organization of the *tragédie lyrique* too often overlooked or minimized by contemporary scholars. During the *grand siècle* and much of the eighteenth century, this Lullian fusion of the arts, a virtual pre-Wagnerian *Gesamtkunstwerk*, was often cited as a model to be emulated.

Lully had learned much from his long association with Molière, and his own court ballets show close liaison between dance and plot. There was, however, no purely operatic model for composer and librettist to follow. The alignment of dance with plot in the Italian operas performed during the time of Mazarin was sporadic, and it is unlikely that Lully had any knowledge of the dramatic "wholeness" of the operas of Monteverdi. "There were no written rules," wrote librettist Pierre-Charles Roy in his *Lettre sur l'Opéra*. He continued:

If only Quinault had left us his reflections on the art he invented and perfected; if he had followed the example of the great Corneille, . . . but we lack this resource. What remains to be done? It is necessary to draw out from Quinault, himself, his secret by analysis of his dramatic art; it is necessary to break down all his operas, to examine the inner workings, to reconstruct the play; it is necessary to compare the help and obstacles a particular subject has given him; . . . to appreciate the adroitness of his expositions, always fashioned within the plot, always condensed (because sung Tragedy does not have the conveniences of declaimed Tragedy); to be conscious of the liaisons between the divertissements *and the plot, and to be conscious of his singular skill in deriving an interesting situation from a decorative element (1749, 2:15–16).*

Perhaps the most notable example of a *divertissement*'s functioning as spectacle and dramatic agent is the village wedding that encompasses scenes iii through v in Act IV of *Roland*. This even won the approbation of Grimm. Jean-François Marmontel considered it a masterpiece "unique in this genre" ("Pantomime" in *Éléments de littérature*, 1787). The *divertissement* is anticipated in scene ii, where Roland wanders alone in a secluded glade looking for his beloved Angélique. He hears the distant sounds of "*musique champestre*," played by a *trio des hautbois* (two oboes plus a bassoon), which is actually the trio of the minuet to be heard in its entirety in the next scene. Scene iii is the "Nopces de village" (village wedding), a pastoral *divertissement*, which includes a march, chorus, minuet, dance songs, and *entrées* of shepherds and shepherdesses. The bridal pair, a shepherd and shepherdess, in all innocence sing a duo in scene iv commenting on the departure of another happy bridal couple, whom they identify as Angélique and Médor. Hidden, Roland overhears this confirmation of Angélique's betrayal and learns the identity of his rival.

The contrast between the mounting anger of the distraught hero and the bucolic levity of the *fête* heightens in scene v, where Roland interrupts the chorus "Bénissons l'amour d'Angélique, Bénissons l'amour de Médor" (Bless the love of Angélique, bless the love of Médor) with his cries, "Taisez-vous, malheureux" (Be quiet, wretches). The pastoral mood is shattered, and the end of the *divertissement* "Ah fuyons, fuyons tous" (Ah, flee, flee, everyone) merges with Roland's vengeance air "Je suis trahi" (I am betrayed) of scene vi. The act ends on a note of despair in the accompanied recitative "Ah! Je suis descendu dans la nuit du tombeau" (Ah! I have descended into the night of the tomb). Lully's scheme of tonalities throws this conflict of mood into high relief. The act opens in C major and closes in B-flat major. Scene four, the scene of revelation, is critical dramatically and also serves as a harmonic pivot, shifting the tonality from C major to B-flat through the dominant minor key of G.

In most instances, however, *divertissements* are used to sustain a prevailing mood rather than to contrast two opposing moods. This is true of the drummed and trumpeted bellicose *divertissements* of *Thésée*, *Bellérophon*, *Cadmus*, and *Amadis*, which Jean de La Fontaine so vividly described in his *Épître à M. Niert sur l'opéra* of 1677:

> Ses concerts d'instrumens ont le bruit du tonnerre
> Et ses concerts de voix ressemblent aux éclats
> Qu'en un jour du combat font les cris des soldats.
>
> *His instrumental concerts have the noise of thunder,*
> *And his vocal concerts resemble the outbursts*
> *That soldiers' shouts make on a day of combat.*

It is also true of the *divertissement* in Act III (scenes iv through viii) of *Thésée* in which the inhabitants of Hell are catapulted into the action to dramatize the power of Médée against her rival, Aeglé, and of the "Sommeil" from *Atys* and the impressive funeral corteges of *Psyché* and *Amadis*. In the "Pompe funèbre" of *Alceste* (Act III, scenes v and vi), prelude and dramatic symphony substitute for titled dances, and the chorus of grief-stricken women and distressed men helps to sustain the somber mood.

Following a dramatic composer's natural inclination, Lully often used a *divertissement* to conclude his operas in a blaze of spectacle and sound. This practice was not universally admired. Even Lecerf, an ardent supporter, characterized as unfortunate the operas such as *Amadis*, *Persée*, *Atys*, or *Acis et Galatée* that end with "a *divertissement*, a chaconne, or passacaille." For an example of a good ending, he singled out the final act of *Armide*: "There is nothing so perfect. It is an Opera in itself. The *divertissement* occurs at mid-point and leaves the attention of the listener free for the events that follow" (1725; rpt. 1966, 3:13–14). By virtue of its contrast, its economy, and the directness of its action, this act deserves the approbation accorded it during the eighteenth century.

The recall of previously used musical material is a musico-dramatic device employed by Lully that has been little studied. Although used sparingly and generally in a nonsystematic manner, this primitive leitmotif technique undoubtedly served as a model for further development at the hands of such pre-Rameau (*préramiste*) composers as Campra and Mouret. A short vocal phrase of distinctive melodic shape, a "motto" *ritournelle,* or a choral fragment may be subject to later recall. In *Thésée,* the refrain "Revenez, revenez, Amours revenez" from Venus's air in the prologue is first stated in the *ritournelle* and is interpolated into the recitative that follows the air. In the same opera, a fragment of the chorus "Il faut périr, Il faut vaincre ou mourir," first used in Act I, scene i, penetrates Aeglé's recitative in scene ii and is used at the conclusion of both scenes iii and v. In Act I of *Atys,* the opening *ritournelle* generates much of the ensemble music of scenes i to iii. In *Persée,* the entire first scene of Act V is organized around Mérope's opening phrase "O Mort! Venez finir mon destin déplorable." In Act I of *Alceste,* the choral fragment "Vivez, vivez, heureux époux" in scene i is interlaced with recitatives and recurs in scene vi of the same act.

Act III of *Alceste* illustrates the most systematic use of musical recall in the operas of Lully. Each scene builds to the "Pompe funèbre" of scenes v and vi. Each scene is effectively organized around a few short ensemble or choral fragments which recur between *ritour-nelles,* recitatives, and short airs. The fragment "Alceste est morte" from scene iv was often parodied and is certainly the source for Rameau's similar "Hippolyte n'est plus" from Act IV, scene iv of *Hippolyte et Aricie* (see Example 7-1a, b, below).

Example 7-1. (a) *Alceste,* Act III, scene iv (after 1708 ed.). (b) *Hippolyte,* Act IV, scene iv (after 1742 Ballard manuscript ed.).

Related to musical recall is Lully's exploitation of an ostinato bass line pattern as an organizing agent. There are seventeen such cha-conne-airs in Lully's *tragédies en musique.* In most cases, the decision to employ a strophic bass as a form determinant appears to have been arbitrary. However, the text may have governed this decision in a pair of dialogue chaconne-airs: one in *Persée* and another in *Roland.* In *Persée* (Act II, scene v), the same chaconne bass ties together the dialogue airs of Andromède and Mérope, who are rivals for Persée's love. Mérope's text "Unissons nos regrets, le même amour nous lie" (Let us unite our sorrows, the same love links us) suggests such a composi-tional liaison. Similarly, in *Roland* (Act III, scene iv), Roland and Angélique both sing in a pair of chaconne-airs: the first in G major and the second in G minor. In each air, Angélique sings "Que votre destinée est unie à la mienne" (That your destiny is united to mine).

In his late operas, Lully employed a chaconne or passacaille bass pattern to create inner musical unity for an entire scene. In the much admired *divertissement* of scene ii in the final act of *Armide*, a passacaille provides the organizational force for the entire scene, generating three vocal airs, a dance, and three choruses. It is dramatically silenced at the end by Renaud's recitative "Allez, éloignez-vous de moi" (Go, withdraw from me). Finally, in his last complete opera, *Acis et Galathée*, Lully used a chaconne (Act II) and passacaille (Act III) to generate solos, ensembles, and choruses.

Solo Voice Distribution

All soloists at the Académie Royale de Musique were known as *acteurs* and *actrices pour les rolles* (actors and actresses for the roles). Solo parts were identified as the *parties récitants* to distinguish them from the *parties du choeur*. Lecerf summarized the association of vocal range with dramatic role as follows:

> *A third of the leading roles in the Operas of Lully are those of ordinary tenors* ("simple tailles") .... *Our women are always women; our basses ordinarily sing the roles of Kings, scorned lovers, Magicians, serious, older Heroes, etc.; and our tenors and* hautes-contres, *whose voices are as high and as flexible as nature allows and wants them to be, are the young,* galant *Heroes, who ought to be loved, the Gods amorous and gay, etc.* (1725; rpt. 1966, 2:112 and 121).

Evidence from the scores themselves and from contemporary references to performers, however, make it difficult to sustain Lecerf's observations regarding the percentages of roles assigned to "*simple tailles.*" The majority of the leading roles for high male voice in the operas of Lully are written in the alto clef, the normal clef for the *haute-contre*, although, to be sure, Brossard identified this clef (as well as the tenor clef) as appropriate for the "*Hautes ou Premières Tailles.*" Singers such as Bernard Clédière and Du Mesny, who sang leading roles in *Alceste*, *Thésée*, *Bellérophon*, *Proserpine*, *Persée*, and *Acis et Galathée*, were normally identified as *hautes-contres*. It is certain that, no matter what Lully's intention may have been, eighteenth-century revivals of his operas used only the *haute-contre* voice in the leading roles for high male voices.

The royal ordinance issued at Versailles on 11 January 1713, which gives the annual salary in *livres* for the first, second, and third lead singers at the Opera, is a measure of a long-standing tradition of the French lyric stage. The favored high male voice was the *haute-contre*, as seen in Table 7-1 below adapted from Durey de Noinville, *Histoire du théâtre de l'Académie Royale de Musique*; judging from the salary scale and the distribution of leading roles, however, the bass was equally favored. The table clearly exposes the subordinate role of Lecerf's *"simple tailles"* in French Baroque opera; there is no subdivision into a first and second singer, and both tenors received less money than the lowest paid soprano!

Table 7-1. Annual salary in *livres* for the first, second, and third *acteurs* and *actrices pour les rolles*.

Acteurs pour les Rolles	*Actrices pour les Rolles*
Basses-tailles (basses)	*Dessus* (sopranos)
1 *à* 1500	1 *à* 1500
1 *à* 1200	1 *à* 1200
1 *à* 1000	1 *à* 1000
	1 *à* 900
Hautes-contres	1 *à* 800
1 *à* 1500	1 *à* 700
1 *à* 1200	
1 *à* 1000	
Tailles (tenors)	
1 *à* 600	
1 *à* 600	

The contralto voice is absent from the *actrices pour les rolles* in this table. The role of Clorinde in André Campra's *Tancrède* (1702) is exceptional and was created by the composer to capitalize on the timbre of voice and histrionic ability of Mlle Maupin. The range of her voice in *Tancrède* (from d' to e") is actually that of a mezzo-soprano *(bas-dessus)* rather than a true contralto.

In terms of preferred vocal timbre and range, there was obviously a great difference between French and Italian taste in the period from Lully to Gluck. Jean-Jacques Rousseau wrote in his *Dictionnaire de musique*:

> *In France, where they prefer the bass and the* haute-contre *and where they make no use of the mezzo-soprano, male voices take on different characteristics, and female voices keep only one; but in Italy, where they make as much use of a good mezzo-soprano as they do of a higher voice, . . . there is only one featured male voice (1768, 545).*

Although one may concur with Masson that the French concept "remains more dramatic than the Italian" (1930, 261), the tradition that rejected the contralto brought about a convention in France that challenged verisimilitude as much as did the use of the castrato in Italy. In almost every instance in the generation following Lully, the roles of nurses and confidantes, ideally suited to the contralto voice, were given to the *haute-contre* (see, for example, the role of Nérine in "L'Amour saltimbanque" from Campra's *Les Fêtes vénitiennes*).

Recitative

The central position of recitative in French opera from its inception in Lully throughout the eighteenth century is amply attested to by contemporary sources. Le Brun wrote for many when he expressed horror at the thought of those "capricious ignorant ones' who would destroy recitative. "Without recitative," he questioned, "how is it possible to expose and develop a dramatic situation?" (1712, 16–17).

Recitatives from Lully to Gluck most clearly differentiate French from Italian opera. The careful distinction found in Italy between *recitativo secco* and the aria did not exist in France, where lines of demarcation blur. There, the recitative was nourished by the restrained melodic patterns of the air, and the air never completely abandoned the declamatory bias of the recitative. "Our recitative sings too much; our airs, not enough," wrote Charles-Henri de Blainville (1754, 52).

As we have seen, Lully was well on his way to creating a convincing French declamatory style in music before he began his visits to the Hôtel de Bourgogne to hear La Champmeslé declaim the Alexandrines of Racine. Certainly because of this exposure, the composer was motivated to render in music the declamatory practices in vogue at the theater. There is some reason to believe that the twelve-syllable Alexandrine couplets of Racine's verse may have resembled a musical line in La Champmeslé's performance. If Abbé Dubos's description is accurate, Racine himself instructed his mistress to "lower the pitch of her voice when saying '*Nous nous aimions*' [from *Mithridate*] so that she could easily reach a tone one octave above that when pronouncing '*Seigneur, vous changez de visage*'" (1719; 7th ed. 1770, 3:143).[5]

Unlike Racine, Quinault chose a fluctuating number of syllables per line (from two to twelve) for his opera librettos. He rarely employed more than three Alexandrines successively. Buford Norman illustrates how in Act I, scene iii of *Alceste*, Quinault used a varying number of syllables per line to aid in the characterization of Straton and Céphise during their lovers' quarrel. When it becomes clear that Céphise will not marry him, there is a change from Alexandrines to shorter and shorter lines (1989, 189). Still, there are times when Lully (and Rameau) adhered too rigidly to the anapestic rhythms and the two symmetrical hexameters of the French Alexandrine, and the result is monotonous. Example 7-2, below, from *Alceste* shows the most routine application of this declamatory principle.

Tu me vois ar-rê-té   sur le point de partir,   Par les

tris – tes clameurs qu'on entend re-ten – tir.

Example 7-2. Lully: Extract from recitative, *Alceste* (after 1708 ed.).

One way to break up this symmetry was to introduce a changing number of feet per line. This in turn necessitated the use of fluctuating meters to align the strongest syllables (the rhyme syllable and the caesura) with the strongest beats of the measure. Fluctuating meters assured rhythmic variety and remained the most characteristic aspect of French recitative from Lully to Gluck. "The changes in meter cause no difficulty for the French," wrote Telemann, who added, "Their recitative flows continuously, bubbling forth like champagne" (cited by Rosow 1983, 468). "The recitative has neither a uniform rhythm nor melody," wrote Marmontel in Denis Diderot's *Encyclopédie*. "It is ruled exclusively by the caesura and the text phrases" (1751–1780, 2:587). Curiously, in spite of its shifting meters, this type of simple recitative was called "unmeasured" ("*non-mesuré*") by the French, the better to distinguish it from Italian recitative, which was "measured" throughout by the use of a single meter sign.

There remains some confusion over the exact metrical relationships between the constantly shifting meters of French recitative. Among the many seventeenth- and eighteenth-century sources that deal with this problem (often in a confusing and contradictory manner), Michel de Saint-Lambert (*Les Principes du clavecin*, 1702) and Étienne Loulié (supplement to *Éléments ou principes de musique*, ca. 1696) document the principle that "the time-value of a beat in one meter should be equal to that of a beat in the other, even though the note values are not equal" (Loulié cited by Launay 1965, 185); that is, the quarter-note in C, the quarter-note in 3, and the half-note in ₵ all have the same duration.[6]

There is some evidence that, as long as the "built-in" conditions of correct prosody were respected, there was little attempt made to force rhythmically precise rendering of the recitative in performance. Jean-Léonard le Gallois de Grimarest commented that during the most dramatic moments of a recitative "one must not beat time,

because the Actor must be the master of his song and allow it to conform to his expression" (1707, 219).

During Lully's lifetime his recitative was probably performed
crisply—"quickly without appearing bizarre" (Lecerf). Unlike eighteenth-century performances, little ornamentation was added. Lecerf
quoted Lully as stating "no embellishments; my recitative is made
only for speaking" (1725; rpt. 1966, 3:188).

The *récitatif simple* or *ordinaire* is the most common type of recitative found in the operas of Lully. It was generally used along with
short dialogue airs to expedite the action, and it is accompanied only
by the continuo. "In the *récitatif ordinaire*," wrote François-Jean de
Chastellux, "the Musician must not be concerned about charming the
ear." He noted three characteristics of this type of recitative that
remained constant from Lully until Gluck:

> *(1) It must not employ a constant rhythm or meter; (2) it must not
> make use of an accompaniment that in a natural and rapid
> dialogue would prevent the comprehension of the text; and (3) it
> must not tire the actor by exploiting his most brilliant vocal sounds
> (1765, 22).*

Beginning with *Atys*, Lully's recitative becomes more expressive,
more fluid, and better able to mirror the text without sacrificing the
laws of prosody. Example 7-3a–d, below, presents several recitative
fragments from the later operas of Lully. Yet, despite the greater flexibility, increase in range, and more deliberate attempts to dramatize
the text (see an example of the rare use by Lully of text painting in the
Proserpine extract), some of his later *récitatifs ordinaires* lack spontaneity
and genuine dramatic sense. The filled-in descending melodic diminished seventh becomes a cliché formula generally serviceable for the
most impassioned outbursts, and what composer with a natural gift for
dramatic expression would have sanctioned the neutralizing effect of
two descending diminished seventh chords from the same pitch level
within as many measures?

At its best, Lully's *récitatif ordinaire* both stimulates action and
defines character. In the great monologue from *Armide* (Act II, scene v,
reprinted in *The Norton Anthology of Western Music*, 3rd edition, 1996,
401–407), Armide's inner conflict is rendered by music and not seen
merely in terms of standard seventeenth-century declamatory practice.
Here, rests result not only from text caesurae but also, and more
importantly, from Armide's hesitation and her confusion, which they
dramatize. Here, too, wider melodic profile and greater awareness of
harmony produce a telling dramatic effect.

Example 7-3. (a) *Atys* (after 1689 ed.). (b) *Bellérophon* (after 1679 ed.). (c) *Proserpine* (after 1680 ed.). (d) *Armide* (after 1686 ed.).

The eighteenth century rightfully considered this scene a model for the best in French recitative. Rameau printed the entire monologue in his *Nouveau système de musique théorique* (1726, 80–90), used it again in his *Observations sur notre instinct pour la musique* (1754, 69–122) to combat Jean-Jacques Rousseau's criticism of French recitative, and finally, in *Code de musique pratique* (1760, 168–170), Rameau included a detailed harmonic analysis of its opening measures (for a discussion of Rameau's analysis, see Dill 1994).

Armide's monologue was also considered a testing ground for the performer. If we may accept Titon du Tillet's description, few could equal the performance of Mlle Marie Rochois, who created the role in 1686.

> When she began to move and sing, one saw only her onstage. This struck me above all in the Opera Armide, in which she played the grandest, most powerful Role in our Opera . . . . What rapture to see her in the fifth scene of the second Act of the same Opera, dagger in hand, ready to pierce the breast of Renaud sleeping upon a bed of verdure! Fury animated her features, love took hold of her heart; the one and the other agitated her in turn, pity and tenderness succeeded at the end, and love was left the victor. What beautiful poses and true! What different movements and expressions in her eyes and on her face during this monologue of twenty-nine lines . . . . One can say that it is the greatest piece in all our Opera

and the most difficult to perform well *(1732; supplement 1743, 791–792).*

Lully's musical inventiveness may be seen to best advantage in his accompanied recitative *(récitatif obligé)*, which first appeared in *Bellérophon.* Textual declamation, while not neglected, is subordinated to heightened musical expression. The accompanied recitative borrows from the air its greater melodic amplitude and often its tighter musical organization. The orchestra is an ever-present background, which after establishing the mood in a *ritournelle* or prelude, freely penetrates the recitative itself.

The second scene of Act IV of *Roland* and the third scene of Act II of *Armide* are composed entirely of long accompanied recitatives in which the orchestra has prime importance in determining the mood. The difference between accompanied air and accompanied recitative becomes more and more difficult to define. As if to confound classification, there are extended passages of accompanied recitative that lack the typical meter fluctuation of simple French recitative. Often reserved for the most expressive or dramatic moments, this type of recitative is a musical hybrid for which there is no adequate term in French. At the time of Rameau, it was called *récitatif mesuré* or simply *mesuré.* Perhaps the Italian term *arioso* is the most appropriate. Brossard had already defined *récitatif mesuré* as "in the same *mouvement* [no change of meter] as though singing an air."

In *Amadis* the orchestra is the main protagonist in the accompanied recitatives sung by the magician Arcalaus (Act II, scene iii) and the enchantress Arcabonne (Act III, end of scene ii). In both instances, strong rhythms and upbeat *tirades* borrowed from the French overture characterize the supernatural powers of the magicians. Such scenes are the point of departure for the magician Ismenor's accompanied recitative at the beginning of Act II of Rameau's *Dardanus.* Scene vii of the third act of *Acis et Galathée* is an accompanied recitative over 160 measures long sung by Galathée. The orchestra plays continually; there are five internal "preludes" that initiate shifts of mood that then transfer to the voice with great subtlety. Similarly, Act V, scene ii of *Persée* is a long accompanied recitative unified by means of a motto prelude and Mérope's recurring phrase *"O Mort venez finir mon destin déplorable."*

Air

The lack of clear distinction between recitative and air in French Baroque opera is nowhere better illustrated than in the following description by Carlo Goldoni of his first visit to the Académie Royale de Musique:

*I waited for the arias . . . . The dancers appeared; I thought the act
was over, not an aria. I spoke of this to my neighbor who scoffed at
me and assured me that there had been six arias in the different
scenes which I had just heard. How could this be, say I, I am not
deaf; instruments always accompanied the voice . . . , but I took it
all for recitative (1787, 3:38).*

Similar was the reaction of Johann Joachim Quantz, who in summing up impressions of his visit to France during 1726–1727, wrote:
"Their recitatives sing too much, and their arias, too little, so much so
that one is in real difficulty to guess whether a recitative or an arioso is
being heard in an opera (cited by Reilly 1963, 173).

The French operatic air from Lully to Rameau was born of the *air
de cour* and nurtured in the court and comedy ballets. Lully learned
from Lambert, who may have learned from François Richard,
François de Chancy, and others, how to organize a small "scene"
around a series of short dialogue airs. As early as 1637 in Richard's
Airs de cour avec la tablature de luth, there is such a miniature "scene"
("Cloris attends un peu"), which even culminates in an "operatic" duo.

Ménestrier, writing only eight years after *Cadmus et Hermione*,
unequivocally stated that the dialogues of Lambert, Boesset, Le
Camus, and others served as models for what he called *"Musique d'action & de Théâtre"* (1681, 178). In order to illustrate how such *"petites
chansons"* prefigure operatic dialogue airs, he quoted the text of a dialogue between Silvie and Tyrsis by Lambert (178–179).

From Lully to Christoph Willibald Gluck, the French operatic air
may be classified by function into four main types: dialogue air, monologue air, maxim air, and dance song (see Masson 1930, 202–237). A
further classification may be made on the basis of formal structure.
Most airs are in the tradition of short binary, ternary, and rondeau
structures. Binary airs far outnumber the other categories. On the
basis of my calculations, Lully's *tragédies en musique* contain 432 binary
airs, 83 rondeau airs, and 55 ternary airs in addition to 17 chaconne
airs and a small number of through-composed airs that defy structural
analysis (Anthony 1990, 74). These numbers refer only to autonomous
airs and do not take into account either the several airs that serve as
contrasting couplets in choruses or the air fragments that are interspersed with recitatives. What is surprising is the two-to-one domination of the extended binary air (ABB') over its nearest rival, the simple
binary air (AB). As we have seen in Chapter 3, the extended binary air
based on Italian models may have been introduced into France by
Lully himself. Part BB' of the extended binary air from *Atys* (in
Example 7-4 below) includes a textual but not a musical repetition of
the last two lines of poetry. In no other air structure is the alliance

between dance and air so clearly articulated. Their extended binary structures share the characteristically longer second part, which in the dance form generally achieves its subdivision by means of an internal cadence in a related key.

Example 7-4. Extended binary air, "Vous braviez à tort," *Atys*, Act II, scene iii (after 1689 ed.).

Lully skillfully used the dialogue air to move the action forward. He constructed entire scenes around chains of dialogue airs interspersed with recitatives. Thus, he organized Act I, scene i, of *Amadis* around seven dialogue airs that sum up the various types of binary, ternary, and rondeau airs found in French Baroque opera.

The dialogue air is too short to permit genuine characterization ("Un Prix qui me doit charmer" from *Persée*, for example has only ten measures). The strength of affective intervals placed at the beginning of a phrase tends to dissipate rapidly in what is too often a routine cadence formula (see Example 7-5 below). This is certainly due to the characteristic use of short-breathed vocal lines with syllabic treatment of text and the concomitant avoidance of melismas that might have given more amplitude to the vocal line. The continuo reflects this practice by rapid modulations through short, stereotyped cadential progressions to closely related keys.

Example 7-5. Lully: Beginning of Idas's air, "Amants qui vous plaignez," *Atys* (after 1689 ed.).

The static, monologue air was reserved for moments of deep feeling when the actor is "alone and speaks only with himself" (Rousseau). In function, if not in style, it approaches most closely the Italian aria, although in French opera it usually fills an entire scene, while in Italian opera, the scene builds towards the aria. The monologue air is based on a single affection and in Lully's later operas is often accompanied by the orchestra, which gave him a legitimate opportunity to exploit purely musical devices such as long "motto" preludes and instrumental interludes.

The celebrated monologue air "Bois épais" (*Amadis*, Act II, scene iv)[7] is a simple binary air with each part repeated and the whole preceded by a fifteen-measure anticipatory prelude for five-part strings. Its source may be traced back to the many elegiac court airs. It is one of the few melodies by Lully that have the melodic refinement and naturalness of the best airs by Moulinié, Antoine Boesset, or Michel Lambert.

How much did Lambert influence his son-in-law's vocal style? The speculation has been considerable. Certainly the relationship was a close one, and Lully appeared to have had genuine respect for the older man's musical attainments. As is so often the case, it is conceivable that the influence worked both ways. Lully's monologue "Atys est trop heureux" (*Atys*, Act I, scene 4), which is interspersed with recitatives and constructed over a chaconne bass, may well have been the source for Lambert's "Ma bergère est tendre et fidelle" from his 1689 collection of court airs.

Renaud's monologue air "Plus j'observe ces lieux" from *Armide* (Act II, scene iii) illustrates Lully's skill in organizing a large-scale air that borders on being through-composed. Constantly repeated eighth-note pairs in the orchestra represent the gently flowing stream. Their unifying effect is reinforced by a short, repeated note motive that transfers from orchestra to voice at an ever higher pitch level. At no place, however, is there an exact repetition of any portion of the air. Its long prelude is based on the same eighth-note accompaniment figure found in the air and must be played with mutes. Prelude and air form one of Lully's most enchanting nature scenes.

Most maxim airs make general observations and practical comments on the art of amorous dalliance. Normally sung by secondary
characters, they relate more to lovers' intrigues at court than to the
mythological personages on stage; they may be regarded, therefore, as
a commentary upon the *galant* mores of the *grand siècle*. In this, they
are like the old *vers* of the court ballet. It is not surprising that Mme
de Montespan recognized herself in the character of jealous Juno in
Isis. Such *galant* sentiments as "Mais la pluspart des Amants sont sujets
à faire bien des faux sermens" (But most Lovers are subject to swear-
ing false allegiance) (*Thésée*, Act I, scene v) or "Mais rien n'est si char-
mant qu'une inconstance mutuelle" (But nothing is so charming as a
mutual inconstancy) (*Thésée*, Act II, scene ii) incurred the enmity of
the clergy and the conservative professors of the Sorbonne. In the late
seventeenth century, as Jacques Bénigne Bossuet described in his
Satire X of 1692, they attacked "tous ces lieux communs de Morale
lubrique, Que Lully réchauffa des sons de sa musique" (all those common places of lascivious Morality, That Lully reheated with the
sounds of his music). In his 1694 *Maximes et réflexions sur la comédie*,
Bossuet railed against "corruption reduced to maxims . . . in the
operas of Quinault with all their false tenderness and misleading invi-
tations to enjoy one's youth." Mme de Maintenon contemplated the
bad effects of continual exposure to the "detestable maxims" found in
operatic airs (see Garros 1943, 10). It did not seem to matter that also
sprinkled throughout Quinault's poetry were morally acceptable maxims such as "*Un Hymen qui peut plaire, Ne coûte guère . . . . Rien n'est
plus aisé que de faire Un Époux d'un amant aimé*" (*Alceste*, Act II, scene i).
(A marriage that can please, Costs but little . . . . Nothing is easier
than to espouse a beloved lover). Nor did it matter that "Perseus
teaches us to respect the Gods; Phaeton teaches us to moderate our
ambition; Alceste is an example of the duties of conjugal love"
(Antoine-Louis Le Brun 1712, 23).

The dance songs in Lully's *tragédies en musique* form part of each
divertissement. It is a truism that they are the clearest example of the
close alliance between dance and song. Their roots lie in the *brunettes*,
the *airs tendres*, and in the many airs based on dance rhythms found in
the collections of seventeenth-century *airs de cour*.

Lully had learned how to use his dances as models for dance songs
in the *comédie-ballet*. In the *tragédie lyrique* as in the *comédie-ballet*, the
simplest treatment is an addition of text to a direct repetition of the
instrumental dance. There are, however, several examples of dance
songs in which Lully freely varied the vocal version of the dance
model by (1) contracting or elongating the phrase structure or by
(2) retaining the phrase grouping and rhythmic structure of the
model while changing either the melodic organization, the harmonic

organization, or both of these (see, for example, the "Second Air" and the song of the two old men based on it in *Thésée*, Act II, scene vii). On occasion the normal procedure reverses, and the dance song itself serves as model. The prologue of *Cadmus et Hermione*, for example, closes with a minuet that is an instrumental version of a preceding dance song and chorus.

Vocal Ensembles

The duo, the long-favored small vocal ensemble in French opera, did not come under direct criticism until a later generation when Grimm and Rousseau spearheaded an attack against its "unnaturalness." According to Rousseau, "Nothing is less natural than to see two people speaking at the same time" (1768, 179–180). This allegation is comparable to the attacks on the use of song instead of speech by Saint-Évremond, Boileau, Fénelon, and La Bruyère. The latter also labored the obvious by insisting that it is not "natural" to die singing. These critics were judging opera—by its very nature unnatural—according to the standards reserved for spoken drama.

The duo reached French opera by the same route as the air. Dialogues that include duos are found in many court air collections, and the duo was employed in pastorales and in court and comedy ballets.

Duos in the operas of Lully range from brief fragments, simple strophic dance songs, and maxim airs to a duo-air-recitative complex that may dominate an entire scene. Most are strictly homophonic; the points of imitation are found often at the beginning of phrases—a type of sham polyphony that by the second measure has already stabilized into a note-against-note style. This lack of polyphony is consistent with a word-born style and predictably dominates all ensemble writing in Lully's operas. What Masson, in his *Opéra de Rameau*, called the "divergent duo" expresses the opposing sentiments of two individuals. It is rare in French opera before Rameau. *Proserpine* (Act IV, scene iv) includes a duo, "Voyez couler mes larmes," which highlights the conflict between Pluto and Proserpine and is close to a "divergent duo" (see Example 7-6 below). What Rousseau labeled a "duo en dialogue" here leads naturally into the formal duo itself in which there is a genuine attempt at musical characterization.

A trio, "Dormons, dormons tous," is the heart of the "sommeil" in *Atys* (Act III, scene iv). Scored for *haute-contre*, tenor, and bass, it is modeled on the trio "Dormez, dormez, beaux yeux" from the *comédie-ballet Les Amants magnifiques* of 1670. The quartet "Venez vous livrer au supplice" from *Atys* (Act V, scene ii) is in fact a type of divergent duo in which one pair crying for vengeance (Celaenus and Cybel) alternates with another, the lovers (Atys and Sangaride).

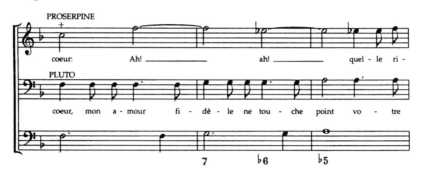

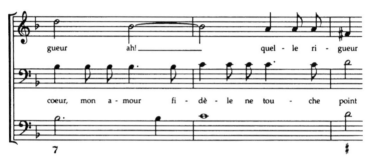

Example 7-6. Lully: extract from duo, "Voyez couler mes larmes," *Proserpine* (Act IV, scene iv) (after Ballard 1680 ed.).

Chorus

Along with dance, the chorus had been an important component of French stage music since the *Ballet comique de la reine*. It served a decorative function in the panegyric prologues of court ballets and in the spectacular finales of many comedy and tragedy ballets. The chorus in the *tragédie lyrique*, in addition to being the crowning embellishment of the *divertissement*, could also be involved in the dramatic action—mainly as a passive commentator. There is little evidence that it participated in the action in seventeenth-century French opera. Rather, it appears to have been lined up on the left and right sides of the stage, identified in *livrets* as the "Côte de la Reine" and the "Côte du Roi," respectively (see Rosow 1987, 329–331).[8] Dancers received the burden of representing the action called for by the choral text. The *livrets* are often quite specific regarding this division of labor. In Act III, scene iii of *Isis*, for example, we read that "one group of Nymphs dances at the same time that another sings." On the other hand, a 1703 *livret* of the same opera introduces some ambiguity in the famous "shivering chorus" scene that opens Act IV. Directly above the "Chorus of people from freezing climes" is written "The people appear to be transformed by the cold, and some of them hide in small caravans (*"petites maisons roulantes"*).

Whether or not the chorus itself participated, it is allowed a forceful musical statement of the action. Witness the vivid description of an attacking monster and the attempts to escape him in the chorus "Tout est perdue" from *Bellérophon* (Act IV, scene ii). Meter changes in themselves generate tempo changes, thereby creating exciting musical contrast. This is intensified by orchestral interjections that overlap but do not coincide with the chorus, thus resulting in a rare use of independent, non-doubling orchestral accompaniment (see Example 7-7).

Example 7-7. Lully: extract from chorus, "Tout est perdue," *Bellérophon* (after 1679 ed.).

In Act IV, scene iv of *Atys*, the chorus witnesses the murder of Sangaride by Atys, and its haunting refrain "Atys, Atys luy même Fait périr ce qu'il aime" (Atys, Atys himself has killed the one he loves) comments on the deed in the manner of an ancient Greek chorus. Act III of *Isis* is made up almost entirely of choruses, some of which employ antiphonal and echo devices. Chorus and orchestra with trumpets and drums combine in the "Choeur des combatans" from *Thésée* (Act I, scene i), in which the primitive use of speech rhythms and repeated notes creates an impressive, bellicose sound-painting.

Choral fragments made from cries of exhortation or supplication are everywhere in evidence. Along with bits of ensemble, recitatives, short airs, and air fragments, they virtually deny the use of any closed musical forms and make difficult the definition of structural divisions. As fragments, they are elements in a scene complex in which they are subordinated to the dramatic flow. They illustrate the dramatist in Lully dominating the musician. The through-composed as opposed to the set piece concept in organizing an operatic scene shows Lully making a virtue of his limitations. That he accomplished what he did in the creation of French opera was due more to superior musical intelligence than to natural, spontaneous musical genius. The long, nonfunctional choruses of the *divertissements* and the sung "chaconnes" (see, for example the finale of *Amadis*), like the sustained choruses of the *grands motets*, are too often repetitive and monotonous.

The French operatic chorus from Lully to Rameau was divided into a *grand* and a *petit choeur*—an organization based on the Italianate *coro ripieno* and *coro concertato* division of much seventeenth-century religious choral writing. The *petit choeur* had less than four parts. Trio texture was favored, and the combination of two sopranos and *haute-contre* became the norm. Indeed, the Diderot *Encyclopédie* definition firmly states that the *petit choeur* "is composed of three parts only: namely, two sopranos and *haute-contre*, which serves them as a bass" (1753, 3:362). Brossard informs us that the *petit choeur* was composed of the "best singers." Unfortunately, he is silent regarding their number. We have no way of knowing whether it was simply a smaller group than the *grand choeur* or whether it was composed only of solo voices, as was usually the case in the *grands motets*.

The composition of the *grand choeur* scarcely varied in seventeenth- and early eighteenth-century French choral writing. The male voices included *haute-contre*, tenor, and bass; the female, only the soprano. (Judging from early eighteenth-century *livrets*, the soprano section also included a small number of male sopranos or falsettists.) This disposition of voices had already occurred in the early *Miserere* by Lully (1664, without female sopranos) and in most of the large choruses of the court ballets. When the texture thickened to five voices in the *grands motets*, the added part was normally the baritone.

The domination by male voices is a musical fact of life which must be faced in modern editions and performances of French choral music of the period. It indicates the lack of interest in the contralto voice in France. Modern substitution of a female alto for the *haute-contre* is no solution, for the "softer" blend achieved by an alto is, in fact, a distinct distortion of the penetrating, shrill quality, the "*voix aiguë*," of the *haute-contre*. A possible compromise suggested by some modern editors is the use of at least one tenor singing in falsetto among the contraltos.[9]

Predictably, the texture of most Lully choruses is homophonic. Rigid note-against-note, syllabic choral writing, when doubled by the orchestra, gives a massive sound complex appropriate for the many allegorical apotheoses to "the greatest of Heroes." There are brief excursions into the neighborhood of polyphony, which never achieve the inner tension and independent part writing necessary in true polyphony. These few measures, when they do occur, are the result of a certain word (such as *volez, fuyons, brillez, coulez,* etc.) rendered musically by an extended melisma that invites imitative treatment.

The routine, often dull, part-writing in some choral and instrumental extracts from Lully's operas may be explained by his use of students to fill in the inner voices, although Lecerf insisted that "Lully himself composed all the parts of his principal choruses and important Duos, Trios, and Quartets." He qualified this by adding that outside of these large pieces, Lully "only composed the treble and the bass and left the inner parts for his *Secrétaires*. However, when the chorus was fugal, Lully always marked the entrances" (1725; rpt. 1966, 3:118–119).

Because seventeenth-century operatic *livrets* did not print full cast lists, it is difficult to fix the exact number of musicians who sang in the Opera chorus during Lully's period. One can say with certitude that the number proliferated during the eighteenth century and ranged from a chorus of fifteen in the earliest days of Perrin's Académie d'Opéra to fifty in 1778. The fluctuating numbers in the first decade of the eighteenth century (thirty in 1701, twenty-two in 1704, thirty-two in 1706) reflect the economic woes of the Opera administration under the direction of Lully's son-in-law, Jean-Nicolas Francine (see La Gorce 1979, 177). Royal ordinances, royal privileges, and printed *livrets* are the sources for most of the available information. According to the Royal Ordinance of 1713, the chorus of the Académie Royale de Musique that year included twenty-two men and twelve women (Durey de Noinville 1757, 1:120). This did not represent maximum strength, however, because Article 21 adds that "All the actors and actresses, with the exception of those who hold the eight *premiers roles*, must sing in the chorus."

Opinion was unanimous with regard to the importance of the chorus in French Baroque opera. It was the one point of agreement in France between partisans of French and partisans of Italian opera. Even Rousseau (writing to Grimm in 1750, three years before the much better known "Lettre sur la musique française") admonished the Italians because of their lack of a genuine chorus: "The few choruses that are in their operas and sung only by the principal performers are not worthy of the name" (cited by Jansen 1884, 463). Lecerf made the same observation almost fifty years earlier when he wrote sarcastically: "Those marvelous opera companies in Venice, Naples, and Rome consist of seven or eight voices" (1725; rpt. 1966, 2:75).

Chapter 8

Tragédie en Musique II:
Instrumental Music and the Dance

The first time that you go to the Paris Opera, when the large orchestra begins to play, pay attention to the overall effect: full, gentle, and dazzling all at the same time; you will conclude . . . that to all appearances, no orchestra in Europe is the equal of the Paris Opera orchestra (Lecerf de La Viéville 1725; rpt. 1966, 3:107).

In his *Dictionnaire de musique*, Brossard defined *symphonie* as "any composition written for instruments." Thus, in French Baroque opera, all instrumental music, whether used independently or in conjunction with the voice, comes under the generic heading of *symphonie*.

All operatic instrumental music, except for the overture, was expected to have some link with the dramatic or choreographic action, for the concept of independent instrumental music was an anathema to most French aestheticians and critics far into the eighteenth century. Fear that Lully's *symphonies* might be considered abstract instrumental music must have precipitated Lecerf's comment that the *symphonie* is the "least essential part of the Music, because it can not express the meaning and sentiment of the tragedy" (1725; rpt. 1966, 2:143).

Lully's dramatic *symphonies* are more advanced than those in Venetian or Roman opera. These instrumental works accompany stage action or help to establish mood. They stand at the beginning of a development that reached a high point in the operas of Rameau. They conform to the all-embracing theory of imitation that dominated the aesthetics of the eighteenth century—an aesthetic that viewed the operatic *symphonie* as an example of the expressive power of music when used to imitate nature or, by extension, states of mind.

Perhaps the most complete statement of this doctrine is found in the *Réflexions critiques sur la poésie et sur la peinture* by Dubos. His definition of *symphonie* emphasizes its descriptive potential.

> *Music uses only instruments to imitate these sounds [of nature], . . . and we commonly call these imitations* symphonies *. . . . The true measure of the imitation of a* symphonie *consists in its resemblance to the sound which it pretends to imitate (1719; ed. of 1770, 1:470–471).*

A psychological dimension was added to the doctrine by Dubos when he suggested that these *symphonies* "are able to agitate us, calm us, move us; in short, they act upon us in the same manner as the verses of Racine and Corneille." Dubos, always the *arbiter elegantiae*, left little doubt as to where his sympathies lay, without seeming to attack abstract music.

> *These same pieces which move us so perceptibly when they are allied with dramatic action, perhaps would only please us moderately were we to hear them played as Sonatas, . . . and consequently we might judge them without knowledge of their greater merit; that is, their relationship to the action, where, so to speak, they play a role (1719; ed. of 1770, 1:483–484).*

Lully's Opera Orchestra

Lully's opera orchestra seems to have been born full grown in *Cadmus et Hermione* and scarcely ever varied thereafter. Institutionalized and rigidly structured from its inception, it parallels other institutions conceived during the reign of Louis XIV. It is conservative, predictable, hierarchal, with little room for trial and error or experimentation. It exploits strong, rather primitive primary colors. Rarely did Lully try to realize the individuality of families of instruments: oboes, flutes, violins, bassoons, even trumpets all share like material. Strings, winds, brass, timpani contrast their basic timbres, but one cannot hear in Lully's *symphonies* the great variation in orchestral textures so deftly used years later by Rameau.

The court and comedy ballets gave Lully an ideal proving ground where he learned how to deal with a variety of instruments. His opera orchestra may be seen as a simplification and refinement of his earlier efforts. He eliminated several of the more exotic instruments, for which the court ballet had been the traditional repository, improved the performance level of his musicians, and, in some cases, encouraged improvement to the instruments themselves. His keen interest in the woodwinds and the availability of some of the best players in the *Grand Écurie* stimulated the development of more flexible and pleasing instruments, although the previously held view that Lully had used the modern oboe as early as 1657 (in *L'Amour malade*) must now be modified in light of recent research. Bruce Haynes has convincingly shown that Lully "may never have known the true oboe [as opposed to the shawm], since its definitive form took shape only at the end of his life" (1988, 336; see also Harris-Warrick 1990b, 97–106).

Grand choeur and *Petit choeur*

Unfortunately, specific information on the exact composition of the Paris Opera orchestra under Lully is lacking. We are, therefore, forced to turn to various privileges and royal ordinances dating from the early eighteenth century and to modify the information they offer with that found in *livrets* and in the writings of contemporary observers. The earliest known source that gives specific information about the Opera orchestra is an archival document of 1704 (see La Gorce 1979, 160–191). Like the chorus, the orchestra was divided into a *grand* and *petit choeur*. The *grand choeur* consisted of ten violins (*dessus de violon*), eight violas (three *hautes-contres de violon*, three *tailles de violon*, two *quintes de violon*), eight bass violins (*basses de violon*), eight winds (oboes, flutes [usually recorders], and bassoons), and one set of kettle drums. The *grand choeur* was used for all *symphonies* designated *tous* (or simply *violons*) as well as for all accompaniments to choruses. Implied in the common appellation *tous* (or *violons*) is the doubling of the outer voices by oboes and/or flutes and bassoons, the string choir being reserved for pieces marked *violons seuls*.

In 1704 the *petit choeur* was made up from the best instrumentalists, who formed their own orchestra around their own harpsichord. It consisted of two violins (*dessus de violon*), two bass violins (*basses de violon*), two bass viols (*basses de viole*) and *contrebasse* (?) (see La Gorce 1979, 178; see also Wood 1981b–1982, 27), one harpsichord, two theorbos, and one conductor *(batteur de mesure)*. The *Privilège . . . pour l'Académie Royale de Musique pour l'année 1712–1713* reveals that two transverse flutes (*flûtes allemandes*) were added to the *petit choeur* at that time (Eppelsheim 1961, 150).

In terms of both numbers and specific kinds of instruments used, the above documents raise more questions than they answer, especially when one attempts to apply them indiscriminately to Lully's Opera orchestra of the 1670s and 1680s. Parts for trumpets abound in Lully's scores, for example, yet the instruments are not included as a part of the *grand choeur*; they were probably played by two of the wind players. Similarly, there is no mention of special instruments such as musettes and cromornes—the *"Instruments champestres"* called for in the *livrets* of *Thésée* and *Atys*. Supernumeraries must have been hired to play when these instruments were needed. It is quite possible that at times the Paris Opera orchestra approached the fifty or sixty members described by Lecerf. In fact, for some listeners, the Opera orchestra overpowered the voices. François de Callières wrote, "One hears only weak voices almost completely covered by the accompaniment of the *clavecin* or of *Theorbes* and other instruments of the orchestra; because of this, part of an air is lost and almost all the words" (1688, 264).

Strings

The *a*5 string orchestra formed the basis of the *grand choeur*. In creating his Opera orchestra, Lully rejected the four-part scoring (violin, two viola parts, and bass violin) used by Cambert in *Pomone* and *Les Peines et les Plaisirs de l'Amour*. Lully opted instead for the five-part scoring already found in his court ballets and comedy ballets. The three "filler parts" (*parties de remplissage*) of the *grand choeur* were the *haute-contre, taille,* and *quinte de violon*. These were three types of violas, all tuned a fifth below the violin. The *haute-contre* employed the C-clef on the first line; the *taille*, the C-clef on the second line; and the *quinte*, the C-clef on the third line. It is worth noting that the first violin part (*dessus*) used what is referred to as the French violin clef, that is, G on the first line. We learn from Georg Muffat that violins did not play the *haute-contre* part, although it was normally well within their range. Drawing on his firsthand experience as a performer in Lully's ballet orchestra from 1663 to 1669, Muffat wrote that the *haute-contre* part, "*Violetta* in Italian, sounds better played on a medium-sized viola, slightly smaller in build than the *taille*, than it does when played on a violin" (1698, preface).

In the eighteenth century, the *parties de remplissage* were gradually reduced to a single viola line by eliminating the *quinte* and fusing the *haute-contre* with the *taille*. The resulting *a*4 texture (violins I, II; viola; cello) was common elsewhere in Europe. The first printed example of such a scoring appears to be *Les Plaisirs de la campagne* of 1719, an *opéra-ballet* by Bertin de la Doué (see La Gorce 1990b, 30), although a manuscript full score of Lacoste's *Créuse* (1712) shows the overture written in four parts (see Wood 1981b–1982, 29). Rameau still distinguished between the *haute-contre* and *taille de violon* in 1763 in his last opera, *Les Boréades* (Sadler 1981–1982, 50).

Evidence supports Eppelsheim's conclusions that the string orchestra of the *grand choeur* was made up of members of the violin family and that the bass viol, with its greater flexibility and range, was restricted to the *petit choeur*.

The question of definition of the *basse de violon* reveals the loose terminology characteristic of the seventeenth and eighteenth centuries. Muffat referred to the *"petite basse à la Française"* and equated it with the Italian *"violoncino"* in the preface to his *Florilegium secundum* (1698); Brossard equated the *basse de violon* with *violone* (the Italian term for double bass) in his dictionary article "Violone," but as though pained by his own ambiguity, he immediately added "or better, [the *violone*] is a Double Bass and sounds one octave lower than the ordinary *Basses de Violons*" (1703). Johann Mattheson also confused the *basse de violon* with the Italian *violone* but did not correct himself in *Das neu-eröffnete Orchestre* (1713); and Michel Corrette described the violoncello in his *Méthode théorique et practique pour apprendre en peu de tems le violoncelle* (1741) as a *"grosse basse de violon."*

There were two types of *basses de violon* used in Lully's orchestra. The first was an instrument slightly larger than a violoncello with four strings (B-flat, F c, g) tuned a whole tone lower than the violoncello. The second, a smaller instrument, had five strings: four tuned like the violoncello and one higher string (C, G, d, a, d') (see Lemaître 1986b,116–123; see also Cyr 1982, 158). If we may believe Corrette, the violoncello superseded the *basse de violon* some twenty or thirty years before the 1741 date of his treatise on the violoncello, that is, sometime between 1710 and 1720; and by 1736 Rameau thought of the violoncello as the normal bass instrument of the *symphonie* even though in some scores it was still referred to as the *basse de violon* (see Masson 1930, 516).

Corrette stated that "Messers Montéclair and Saggioni were the first to play the *contrebasse* at the Paris Opera . . . . At the time of Lulli this instrument was unknown" (1781, preface). Titon du Tillet gives 1700 as the date on which Montéclair entered the Paris Opera orchestra as the first member to play the *contrebasse*. The use of this instrument was called for by Theobaldi di Gatti in *Scylla* (1701) and Campra in *Tancrède* (1702) before its heretofore supposed first appearance in the famous tempest from Marais's *Alcyone* of 1706 (see Barthélemy 1969, 62 and Milliot 1964, 226).

Lully's writing for string orchestra is extremely conservative when compared to that by his contemporaries in Italy and Germany. In seventeenth-century France, violinists held their instruments in the so-called chest (or breast) position. Consequently, the violin part remained in the first position (any other being very difficult to play), and the rare use of a c''' was achieved by extending the little finger on the *chanterelle*. This understood, we can better appreciate Mersenne's comment in "Livre quatriesme des instruments" in his *Harmonie universelle*: "We play almost exclusively on the *chanterelle* and second string of the violin" (1636; rpt. 1965, 3:183). Wide leaps, multiple stops, string crossings, and typically violinistic figurations that appear in Italian music as early as Biagio Marini were foreign to the French style. The dramatic *symphonies* by Lully and his contemporaries seem generally restricted to conjunct motion, with little or no crossing of voices. More violent action is expressed through the kinetic sense suggested by dotted rhythms and *tirades*, which make French music of this period quite different from the mechanical rhythmic pulsations of Italian music in this same period.

Lully must have completely subordinated problems of technique to the problems of rhythmic accuracy and finesse in performance. How else can one explain the choice of "Entrée des songes funestes" (*Atys*, Act III, scene iv) as an audition test for potential members in the opera orchestra? Technically, the piece poses few problems (see Example 8-1 below), but rhythmic accuracy and an intimate knowledge of performance practices (especially as regards rhythmic alterations) are definitely required.

Example 8-1. Lully. Extract from audition test piece, "Entrée des songes funestes," *Atys*, Act III, scene iv (after 1689 ed.).

Winds

When we consider the winds either independently or in conjunction with the string choir, the problems of recreating Lully's exact instrumentation are manifold. It is reasonable to assume, for example, that when the score calls for *flûtes* it refers only to recorders. The prestigious position in the *petit choeur* of the two transverse flutes mentioned in the Royal Privilege of 1712–1713 reflects the increased popularity of the improved transverse flute in the early eighteenth century and bears out Jacques Hotteterre's description of the instrument in the preface to his *Principes de la flûte traversière* (1707) as one of the "most agreeable and most *à la mode*."

During Lully's time the two instruments coexisted—at least in the famous "Prélude pour l'Amour" from *Le Triomphe de l'Amour* (1681), in which transverse flutes (*flûtes d'Allemagne*) are supported by tenor recorders (*quinte de flûtes*), bass recorders (*petite basse de flûtes*), and great bass recorders (*grande basse de flûtes*). According to Jane Bowers, the first specific mention of transverse flutes after Lully's *Le Triomphe de l'Amour* is found in Charpentier's *Médée* of 1693 where, in Act II, scene ii, he calls for two transverse flutes along with *a5* strings (1979, 44).

The writing for recorders is indistinguishable in range and melodic shape from that of the violin. At first glance the use of two *flûtes* in dialogue and in concert with the string choir, as found in the prelude to the "Sommeil" from *Atys* (Act III, scene iv), appears to be a classic example of the *stile concertato*. Yet if one consults the *livret* of 1676, one learns that six *flûtes* were employed in this prelude in what was obviously a three-plus-three combination. The reason for this may have been a practical one, to wit, to boost the weak sound of a single recorder against a string orchestra. In any case, the result would be a sound complex different from that indicated by the score, and is but one example of how the *livret* for a specific revival of a Lully opera may throw light on actual performance practices that are scarcely evident from a reading of the score.

The oboes and bassoons were the work horses of the opera orchestra. Not only did they function independently in dance episodes and *concertato*-like alternations with the strings, but they also apparently doubled the outer voices of the string choir. The ubiquitous *trio des hautbois* (two oboes and bassoon) was ideal for pastoral scenes and for achieving marked color contrast when used in alternation with the string orchestra. As mentioned above, the oboe used by Lully was an instrument in transition between the shawm and the modern oboe, which only came into existence at the end of his life (see Haynes 1988). It undoubtedly still resembled the instrument described by Mersenne as having the "strongest and most *violent* tone of all instruments with the exception of the trumpet" (1636; rpt. 1965, 3:303). When used in substantial numbers, the oboes must have dominated the string timbre. "We have the hautboys," wrote Raguenet in 1702, "which by their sounds, equally mellow and piercing, have infinite advantage over the violins in all the brisk, lively airs" (cited by Strunk 1950, 475).

Neither the 1704 document nor the Royal Ordinance of 1712–1713 is clear regarding the distribution of parts for the eight *"hautbois, flûtes ou bassons."* Presumably there were eight performers who could double on the three wind instruments and perhaps on the trumpet as well when required to do so. In the preface to the Michaelis edition of Destouches's *Les Éléments*, Vincent D'Indy commented that in 1725 the woodwinds of the *grand choeur* comprised five oboes, five bassoons, and two transverse flutes; in 1756 they included four oboes, five bassoons, and two transverse flutes (see Masson 1930, 513). If the members of the *petit choeur* doubled the *grand choeur* in tutti sections, an "extreme disproportion of sonorities" (D'Indy) would have resulted. Melody instruments (fourteen violins, two flutes, four or five oboes, and bass instruments (ten *basses de violon*, one bass viol, two theorbos, five bassoons) would have completely dominated the three *parties de remplissage* consisting of only seven violas and the harpsichord.

Example 8-2 below shows one of the very few places where Lully used more than two oboes in a solo group. This extract from *Atys* also illustrates how clear Lully could sometimes be in indicating exact instrumentation. It is therefore disconcerting to consult the *livret* of 1676 and learn that the *a*4 episode was performed by five oboes and three cromornes, a testimony that lends credence to Joseph Marx's observation that "To determine the instrumentation of Lully's scores is a very complicated and often impossible task" (1951, 14).

Example 8-2. Lully. Extract from the "Entrée des Zéphirs," *Atys* (after 1689 ed.).

The trio texture of two flutes or recorders "accompanied" by violin (or viola), so favored by *préramiste* composers and by Rameau himself, is rare in Lully. One example lies in the instrumental interludes that alternate with the *a*3 chorus (two sopranos, one *haute-contre*) "La Beauté la plus sévère" in Act IV, scene v of *Atys*. The particularly high sonority of this instrumental combination helps define French *douceur* and was no doubt modeled on the texture of the choral *petit choeur* (two sopranos and one *haute-contre*).

Continuo Instruments

The continuo instruments of the *petit choeur* (two theorbos, harpsichord, two *basses de violon*, and two *basses de viole*) were used to accompany the *récitatif ordinaire* and for solo airs and ensembles. The continuo instruments of the *grand choeur* (eight *basses de violon*, bassoons, and [after 1700] *contrebasses*) joined those of the *petit choeur* for the *a5 symphonies*, dances, accompanied airs, and choruses.

In 1932 in the preface to the second volume of "Opéras" in the *Oeuvres complètes de J.-B. Lully*, Prunières noted that "Unless they were explicitly indicated, the harpsichord and wind instruments did not take part in the execution of the *airs de ballet* [dances] . . . as may be seen by examining the separate part books for *Isis* published by Ballard in 1677." In this set of part books, the *basse continue* part (from which the harpsichordist read) and the *basse de violon* part are separate. The *basse continue* title page reads: "*Basse continue*, which includes the entire piece except the *Airs de Danse* which are found in the *Basse de Violon* part*" (cited by Sadler 1980, 155). Research by Graham Sadler has carried Prunières's observations a step further. In the full scores of Lully that were published by Ballard during his lifetime,[1] figures occur above the bass line (implying harpsichord participation) where the words *Basse Continue* appear. Unfigured parts that lack the *basse continue* rubric are limited to dances, *a5 symphonies*, orchestral accompaniments to choruses, and, generally, the overture, thereby suggesting that the harpsichord, which could hardly have been heard anyway, was silent (see Sadler 1980).

Symphonies

The *symphonies* of French Baroque opera may be divided into three categories: (1) overtures, (2) dramatic *symphonies*, and (3) dances.

Overtures

The overture in most French stage music from Lully to Rameau is the typical *ouverture à la française*, whose sharply pointed rhythms (*rythmes saccadés*) and dramatic upbeat *tirades* soon transcended national boundaries. It reached the *tragédie lyrique* via court and comedy ballet with its three principal components intact: it retained its pompous introduction in duple or quadruple meter with dotted rhythms; it kept its lightly fugal and faster contrasting section that was loosely modeled on the Venetian *canzona*; and it generally employed a third section to recapture the mood, if not the music, of the first section. It was the "kingly" introduction *par excellence* and was usually repeated after the prologue as if to suggest that the requisite encomium to Louis XIV had ended and the drama itself might now unfold. There is at least one case of a composer's providing a second overture after the prologue instead of relying upon the usual repeat of the opening overture. Henry Desmarest has left us two overtures in his *Didon* of 1693: the first in G minor and the second in D major, which is closer to the key of the first act.

Frozen by tradition, this type of overture remained in French opera long after its *raison d'être* had ceased to be. It was elevated to a rarified atmosphere by Lecerf. ("Lully's overtures contain beauties that will be new and admirable in all centuries" (1725; rpt. 1966, 2:62). In spite of the built-in bias of a later age against an earlier generation, there is much truth in Jean Le Rond D'Alembert's observation in his *De la liberté de la musique* concerning the French overture: "The [overtures] of Lully, completely insipid and all fashioned from the same mold, have been the unchanging model for over sixty years for those who have followed; during all this time, there has been only one overture at the Opera" (1758; 1821–1822 in *Oeuvres* 1:544–545).

The overture's formal rigidity and aristocratic bearing were anachronistic in the more relaxed days of the Regency, and it remained for Rameau to bring more dramatic as well as musical significance to the genre (Girdlestone 1957, 307). When Rameau suppressed the prologue to *Zoroastre* in 1749, the way was opened to justify a strong dramatic liaison between overture and drama to follow. In the *livret* we learn that the overture "serves as a prologue." The overture to *Zoroastre* relates dramatically (though not musically) to the drama. It is a true program overture that sums up the drama, the details of which are spelled out by the composer himself and printed in the score (see Girdlestone 1957, 299).

The influence of the French overture beyond the boundaries of France far exceeded its intrinsic musical worth in the operas of Lully and his successors. Johann Sigismund Kusser (Cousser), who spent most of the decade 1672–1682 in Paris, was the first in Germany to add the French overture to the German orchestral suite. His *Composition de musique, suivant la méthode françoise contenant six ouvertures de théâtre accompagnées de plusieurs airs* was printed in Stuttgart in 1682. The preface acknowledges the composer's debt to Lully, "whose works at present give pleasure to all the courts of Europe." Not surprisingly, other Germans followed Kusser's lead. Georg Muffat used the French overture to begin five of his six orchestral suites in *Florilegium primum* (1695) and seven of his eight suites in *Florilegium secundum* (1698). All eight of J. C. F. Fischer's orchestral suites in his *Journal du printemps* (1695) begin with a French overture. All the above pieces share the scoring practices and *a5* texture of Lully. Agostino Steffani, who may have witnessed the first performance of *Bellérophon* in Paris in 1679, used the French overture for most of the operas he composed for Munich and Hanover. Overtures and dances from six of his Hanover operas were arranged by him as *sonate da camera* and published later by Étienne Roger in Amsterdam (1710). Before the turn of the century, Georg Böhm had already transferred the orchestral overture to the keyboard, thus anticipating the three keyboard overtures by J. S. Bach (BWV 820, 822, 831). Handel favored the French overture from the time of his first opera for Hamburg, *Almira* (1705). For Bach, it had no limitations of medium or genre; it introduced four orchestral suites and a keyboard partita (No. 4 in D major); it served as a prelude (No. 5, WTC, II), a fugue (No. 5, WTC, I), an important structural division in a set of variations (Variation 16 from the *Goldberg Variations*); and it even combined with a German chorale tune, this time in praise of a heavenly king (Cantata No. 61, *Nun komm der Heiden Heiland*).

England heard the French overture perhaps as early as the 1660s in the repertory of Charles II's band of twenty-four violins that were modeled on Louis XIV's *Vingt-Quatre Violons*. The overture to John Blow's *Venus and Adonis* dates from the lifetime of Lully and is a highly developed French overture, harmonically richer than its models and going so far as to exhibit a thematic liaison with the final chorus of the opera.

In Italy the influence of the French overture was felt in the Concerti Grossi of Corelli's Opus 6 (see, for example, No. 3 in C minor). Rousseau, writing in 1768, stated that the French overture had been introduced into Italy sixty years before. He claimed to have been familiar with "several old Italian operas that were preceded by a Lully overture" (357). After 1700, however, the more homophonic *sinfonia* gradually superseded the conservative French overture in Italy, although Handel used the French overture for two operas produced during his two-year Italian sojourn. *Rodrigo* (1707) includes an overture followed by a dance suite; *Agrippina* (1709) is introduced by an elaborate *sinfonia* that combines the French overture and elements borrowed from the Baroque concerto in the manner of Bach's orchestral overtures.

The *grave* opening section of the French overture could still be heard in the late eighteenth century in yet another role, that of introducing the first movement of the symphonies of Haydn and, less frequently, of Mozart. On into the time of Beethoven, it was recalled in the introduction to his early "Pathétique" sonata and again in the introduction to his last sonata, Opus 111. By then, it was a dimly remembered echo from the remote past: its double dotted rhythms and its *tirades* now both precisely notated, and its formality now lost in overwhelming personal expression.

Dramatic *Symphonies*

The preludes and *ritournelles* found in French Baroque opera serve two functions: they may be used in a purely musical way to introduce a scene, an act, an air, or an ensemble; or they may be linked dramatically to the action onstage.

Both functions show up clearly in *Amadis*, for example. The preludes to the popular airs, "Amour que veux-tu de moi?" and "Bois
épais," simply state the entire air in an instrumental version having no
discernible dramatic function; but the two preludes in Act III, scene ii,
are true dramatic *symphonies* that accompany specific, onstage action
that is unmistakably defined in both score and *livret*. During the first
prelude, Arcabonne is "carried into the air by demons and descends
onto the ruined palace," and during the second, "The jailers open the
cells, and the captives leave."

The two terms *prélude* and *ritournelle* were scarcely distinguishable
during the seventeenth century. In the broadest possible manner,
Brossard defined *Preludio* as a "*symphonie* that served to introduce or to
prepare what follows." He included both overture and *ritournelle*
under this generic heading.

In terms of musical function, however, the word *ritournelle* has
three possible meanings. It may refer to the instrumental episodes that
recur between sections of extended airs or vocal ensembles; it may be
used "*en manière de prélude*" (Rousseau) where it is usually scored for
strings in trio texture; and it may conclude an air or ensemble.

Independent dramatic *symphonies* that "imitate" stage action are
found in the operas of Lully under such titles as "Bruit de trompettes,"
"Bruit de combat," "Les Vents," "Entrée des Aquilons," "Pompes
funèbres," and "Sommeil." It remained for the *préramiste* period and,
above all, for Rameau to develop imitations of natural phenomena
such as thunder storms (especially at sea), tempests, and earthquakes.

Dances[2]

*All Europe knows what a Capacity and Genius the French have for
dancing, and how universally it is admired and followed. (Riccoboni
1738, 110).*

Lully brought to the dances of his *tragédies lyriques* the fruitful
results of a long apprenticeship both as a dancer and a composer of
court and comedy ballets. He had always considered the dance an
expressive medium and a legitimate dramatic tool. Quinault's *livrets*
forced a modification of the nondramatic, purely decorative *entrées* of
the *ballet à entrées*. No "Sauvages Américains" or "Ballet des
Autruches" interrupt the intrigue; and few loosely organized, random-
ly chosen character dances or *danses du bal* occur in the *tragédies
lyriques*. Often the "jeux champêtres," the "fêtes marines," or the
"noces de village" function dramatically—if only because of their
heightened contrast with the plot material.

This liaison between dance and drama provoked the most comment by contemporaries close enough to have witnessed or heard about its implementation. Even the Italophile François Raguenet conceded French superiority in the domain of the dance. He gave scenes from *Isis* and *Atys* as examples in which dance and action are closely linked.

Although it would appear that Pierre Beauchamps, who was responsible for the "composition of the ballets" at the Paris Opera from 1673 to 1687, received much of the credit for choreographing Lully's operas, the division of labor between him and the other choreographer-dancers, Des Brosses, Hilaire Dolivet, and Lully himself, may never be known. According to Lecerf, it was Lully who "reformed the *entrées* and conceived the expressive steps (*pas d'expression*) that related to the subject" (1725; rpt. 1966, 3:209). This is confirmed by Abbé Dubos, who wrote that Lully gave a lot of attention to pantomime and drew upon the talents of Louis Hilaire Dolivet, a "*maître de danse particulier*," for this purpose, while using Des Brosses and Beauchamps to compose the "*ballets ordinaires*."

Untitled dances, less bound by choreographic conventions, afforded the best opportunity to link dance with plot. Surely many preludes and *ritournelles* were also converted into genuine dramatic *symphonies* by means of dance pantomimes, although the scores and even the *livrets* are singularly uncommunicative in this regard. We have word only from 1719 from the keen mind of Abbé Dubos, who gives us just enough information to tantalize and make us regret all the more the lack of some choreographic source that would throw light on the innovative *danse en action* conceived by Dolivet and Lully.

> I have heard tell of some ballets almost without dance, but composed, rather, of gesture and of demonstrations; in a word, a pantomime [jeu muet], that Lully had created for the funeral ceremonies in Psyché and Alceste, in the second act of Thésée where the Poet had introduced the dancing old men, in the ballet of the fourth act of Atys [Songes funestes], and in the first scene of the fourth act of Isis [Choeur des peuples des climats glacez] (1719; 7th ed. 1770, 3:265–266).

Dubos added that the "shivering chorus" and presumably the preceding dance from *Isis* were composed "uniquely of the gestures and demonstrations of people seized with cold. Not a single dance step from our ordinary dance was employed."

By the time Dubos had "heard tell" of Lully's use of dramatic pantomime, this innovation had already been lost in the proliferation of character dances and titled dances during the *préramiste* period. It is therefore understandable that later eighteenth-century aestheticians of the dance often indiscriminately lumped together the dances of the court ballet, the *tragédie lyrique*, and the *opéra-ballet* of the *préramiste* period and labeled them all examples of *"danse simple."* Louis de Cahusac fancied himself to have been the first to have created the *danse en action* in Rameau's *Fêtes de l'Hymen et de l'Amour* (1747). Jean-Georges Noverre, in his *Lettres sur la danse* (1760, 140), considered the dances of Lully to be "devoid of any expression and sentiment. The languid music of Lully rules the dancers' movements and conveys a feeling of sadness calculated more to bore the public than to interest it." This sentiment is echoed by Charles Compan, who, writing one hundred years after Lully's death, characterized his music and dances as "cold, monotonous, without character" (1787, xi).

Table 8-1, adapted in part from Meredith Ellis (1969, 30–31), sums up Lully's use of titled dances in his ballets and *tragédies en musique*.

Table 8-1. Titled dances in Lully's ballets and *Tragédies lyriques*.

Titled dances	Ballet categories	*Tragédies lyriques*
Bourrée	28	8
Gavotte	19	17
Sarabande	24	4
Minuet	36	47
Passepied	2	2
Gigue	5	10
Canarie	10	5
Loure	3	2
Galliard	3	0
Chaconne	9	8
Passacaille	0	4
Rigaudon	0	2

If it is recalled that the ballet categories generally precede the operas in chronology, Table 8-1 illustrates the changing taste in court and stage dances over more than thirty years. It shows the remarkable growth in popularity of the minuet and gigue and conversely the rapid decline of the galliard. Lully wrote his first titled minuet in 1661 for the *Ballet de l'impatience*. In 1665 he included four minuets in the *Ballet de la naissance de Vénus*, and by 1681 he had doubled this number in the ballet *Le Triomphe de l'Amour*. In 1668 Michel de Pure still thought of the minuet, along with the bourrée, as a "new invention" (1668, 279). Ten years later it had become the most popular operatic dance: *Cadmus*, *Alceste*, *Atys*, *Isis*, *Bellérophon*, and *Roland* each have four minuets, and *Phaëton* has six.

What we know about the tempo of Lully's stage dances derives in part from the experiments of a number of theorists with pendulum devices and chronometers. Such are the treatises of Michel L'Affilard (1694), Étienne Loulié (1696), and Jacques-Alexandre de La Chapelle (1736–1752), and the description by Louis-Léon Pajot of a "machine for beating the measure and giving the tempo for all sorts of airs" (cited in Cohen 1981, 69), which had been presented to the Académie Royale des Sciences in 1732. Although helpful, seventeenth- and eighteenth-century sources too often conflict with one another, as do modern scholars who attempt to supply fixed metronome markings.[3] Not only did tempos change depending on time and place, but also an idealized dance for lute or keyboard with its plethora of ornaments could differ markedly from a stage dance with fixed choreography, from a less involved ballroom dance, or from a sung dance. Adopting a classification based on meter and relative tempo, moving from slow to fast, seems best, therefore, in discussing each of the dances found in Lully's operas and listed in the outline above.

Dances in Duple or Quadruple Meter

Loure

Rather slow dance, the loure is normally in 6/4 meter and usually begins with an anacrusis. Some sources refer to it as a "slow gigue," although it may include a shift of pulse from 6/4 to 3/2 as in the "Loure pour les pêcheurs" from *Alceste*.

Gavotte

In both the gavotte and the bourrée, the beat is normally the half-note. The first section begins with two quarter-notes or one half-note before the first complete measure. According to Brossard, it is sometimes *gai* and sometimes *grave*. This lack of consistent tempo is also mentioned by Rousseau, who described the dance as "ordinarily graceful, often gay, and sometimes rather slow and tender."

Bourrée

A dance of popular origins used less frequently than the gavotte on the operatic stage, the bourée was often replaced by the rigaudon in the post-Lully period. Charles Masson noted this association with the rigaudon as early as 1697 when he wrote his *Nouveau traité des règles de la composition de la musique*. He also commented that the bourrée should carry the word *vite* to indicate a faster tempo than the gavotte or galliard. Each of the thirty-four bourrées by Lully begins with an upbeat equal to one quarter-note.

Rigaudon

First danced at the Paris Opera in Lully's *Acis et Galatée*, the rigaudon is a fast dance in duple meter, which, according to Compan, was "very popular in Provence" (1787, 322). It closely resembles the bourrée, although its phrase structure is simpler, and it almost always begins with two half-notes following the quarter-note upbeat.

Gigue

A dance "full of dotted notes and syncopations" (Brossard), the gigue was described by D'Alembert in Diderot's *Encyclopédie* as a "type of accelerated loure." A distinction between the *"gigue française"* and the *"gigue italienne"* was made by Rameau in his *Traité de l'harmonie*; the latter may be in 9/8 or 12/8 whereas the French gigue is most often found in 6/8. Some gigues display a sham polyphony with staggered points of imitation that often result in longer and more asymmetrical phrase lengths than are normally found in French stage dances. The gigue remained popular throughout the Regency, then gradually passed from favor. In 1768 Rousseau observed simply that it had "entirely passed out of fashion; it is not found at all in Italy and scarcely in France."

Canarie

The canarie may be found in both triple meter (3 or 3/8) and compound meter (6/8 or 6/4). According to Charles Masson, the "Canaries and the gigues that have a 6/8 meter sign are conducted in 2 equal beats; it is well to note that the Canarie is a bit faster than the gigue" (1697; 2nd ed. 1699, 8).

Dances in Triple Meter

For discussion of dances in triple meter, we turn to the classification by Masson found in his *Nouveau traité des règles de la composition de la musique*. Throughout the short treatise, Masson draws upon extracts from Lully's operas for illustrative purposes. He writes:

> *In triple meter, there are five sorts of tempo; that is, very slow (fort grave), slow (grave), moderate (léger), quick (vite), and very quick (très vite) . . . . The Sarabande, Passacaille, and Courante must be slow. The Chaconne, moderate; the Minuet, quick; and the Passepied, very quick (1697; 2nd ed. 1699, 7).*

Sarabande

According to Brossard, the sarabande is only a minuet whose tempo is slow and whose mood is serious. Rémond de Saint-Mard adds in his *Réflexions sur l'Opéra* that it is "always melancholy and exudes a delicate yet serious tenderness" (1741, 59). Typically, the sarabande is structured in four-measure phrases, often with a heavily accented second beat and with a hemiola occasionally found in the measures preceding a cadence. A faster type of sarabande, sometimes labeled *"sarabande légère"* was related to the chaconne (see, for example, the *"Sarabande légère"* marked "Mouvement de Chaconne" in Montéclair's *Principes de musique divisez en quatre parties*, 1736).

Passacaille

Brossard confirms Masson's ordering of the passacaille by writing that the "only difference between this dance and the chaconne is that the tempo is usually slower and the melody more expressive and tender" (1703). Both dances are organized in phrases of four or eight measures and are composed of continuous variations over a repeated bass line pattern. Typically, both use the diatonic and chromatic versions of the descending tetrachord pattern, often in close juxtaposition; both contain contrasting episodes in trio combination in which the bass line may be altered or missing altogether (see, for example, the chaconne from *Thésée*, Act IV, scene viii); and both exploit hemiola patterns at cadence points. Montéclair claimed that the passacaille "always begins on the first beat of the measure" and that the chaconne "always begins on the second beat of the measure" (1736, 39–40). When applied to Lully, this observation holds true in the four passacailles (all late works) and in all but one of the eight operatic chaconnes composed after *Psyché* (1698). Like the French overture, the chaconnes and passacailles by Lully remained a fixed entity in French opera until Gluck, and they too were rapidly assimilated beyond the borders of France.

Chaconne

See Passacaille, above.

Minuet

Masson's "quick" tempo designation for the minuet is supported by most early eighteenth-century sources. For Brossard, the minuet was a "very gay dance that originated in Poitou. We should imitate the Italians and use a 3/8 or 6/8 meter sign, which always means very gay and very fast; but we employ instead the simple 3." Lacombe wrote in 1752 that the minuet was in a "moderate triple meter." By 1768, Rousseau found the tempo to be "more moderate than quick, and it is the least gay of dances used at balls." He added, however, that "it is something else again on the stage," which may imply that the faster stage dance may have persisted throughout the eighteenth century. In any case, understanding these comments would prevent modern interpreters of early eighteenth-century music from using the slower *Don Giovanni* minuet as the prototype for all such dances.[4] The late seventeenth-century stage minuet already has the uniform four-measure phrase structure commonly found in the following century. On the other hand, some of the minuets from Lully's early operas are organized in asymmetrical, irregular phrase lengths and often in three-measure phrase groupings more typical of the so-called *menuet de Poitou* (see, for example,the minuet from *Atys*, Act III, scene iv).[5]

Passepied

For Brossard the passepied was merely a "minuet with a very fast tempo." It is normally in 3/8 meter, and the dance patterns themselves are similar to those used in its slightly slower sister dance. Phrases of the passepied are typically extended in Part B by a characteristic hemiola pattern. Lully used the title "Passepied" in *Atys*, *Persée*, and *Le Temple de la Paix*; there is an untitled dance from *Phaëton* that exhibits all the characteristics of this dance. The passepied reached its greatest popularity during the *préramiste* period and after the middle of the century was already in decline. Rousseau flatly stated that "it is no longer in use."

March

In addition to the above-named titled dances, it is necessary to add the Lully march. The march is closely related to the dance and was often used as an *entrée* to move dancers and singers onstage. It is found in both triple and duple meter. Often scored with trumpets (doubling the violins) and drums, it is a primitive, but nonetheless effective musical expression of the pomp and ceremony of the *grand siècle*.

Lully and his followers favored binary structure for the dance, with a repeat of either or both of the two parts. They composed their remaining dances in rondeau form or some other type of formal organization.

The *a*5 string orchestra with occasional contrasting episodes in trio texture served Lully as the basic scoring principle in his dances. Trio episodes are usually scored for recorders and violin (or viola), or for oboes and bassoon, or for three solo strings from the *petit choeur*. The scoring of the minuet from the prologue to *Armide* is an interesting deviation from the norm, in which the opening measures of the dance are played by a trio of recorders and viola followed by the *a*5 string ensemble.

The only stage music source with all its choreography intact is the one-act *mascarade Le Mariage de la Grosse Cathos* (Fat Kate's wedding) by André Danican Philidor, which was performed in 1688. Jean Favier indicated his choreography for all the dances and for two choruses (see Harris-Warrick and Marsh 1994).

Certain manuals dating from the turn of the century give specific choreography for French court dances and, by extension, stage dances. They contain graphic representations of the steps appropriate for each dance and include collections of dances in score as well. The most important and most comprehensive notational system was invented by Pierre Beauchamps and appropriated without acknowledgement by Raoul-Auger Feuillet for his *Chorégraphie ou l'art de décrire la dance par caractères, figures et signes démonstratifs* (first edition, 1700; later editions, 1701, 1709, and 1713). In Brossard's words, "Everyone knows that the late M. de Beaucampt [sic] is the true and first inventor of the notation" (1724; 1725–1730, 24). The system notated all dance steps in diagram and illustrated the position of the feet and the direction of their movement (see Little 1975b). Feuillet explained the word *figures* in the title of his manual as follows: "The 'figure' is the path (*chemin*) one follows in dancing . . . . The path is a line along which one dances" (1700, 2). Plate 2, taken from the 1713 edition of the treatise, affords the modern reader some idea of the complexity of Beauchamps's system, which was widely disseminated via Feuillet and was the basis of most choreographic notation of the early eighteenth century.

Throughout the seventeenth and eighteenth centuries, French music was increasingly dominated by the dance. It spread from court ballet and opera stage to the lute and harpsichord and even to the organ. The rhythm of the minuet, the sarabande, the bourrée, or passepied invaded Chamber and Chapel alike.

Georg Muffat, who went so far as to give detailed rules for bowing his "Airs de balet à la françoise,"[6] concluded that knowledge of the art of the dance is a great aid: "Most of the best violinists in France understand [the dance] very well, and it is not surprising that they are able to find and maintain the *mouvement* of the measure (1698, preface).[7]

Chapter 9

Tragédie en Musique III: *From Lully to Rameau*

At the time of his death on 22 March 1687, Lully's position as a key candidate for the French Parnassus seemed secure. An ordinance of 17 August 1684 had forbidden establishment of opera companies in France without his permission. One month before, on 8 July, he had granted Pierre Gautier of Marseilles permission to establish an Academy of Music there for the performance of operas by Lully and others. Gautier had also received permission to perform in various other unidentified provincial cities. In 1686 Marseilles witnessed performances by Gautier's Academy of *Phaëton* and *Armide*, with *Atys* and *Bellérophon* following in 1687. During the summer of 1687 Gautier brought his troupe to Avignon to perform *Phaëton* and *Armide*. In 1688, Lully's heirs permitted the establishment of an Académie Royale de Musique in Lyons. In the 1690s privileges to form opera companies were granted to Montpellier, Grenoble, Dijon, Chalon, Avignon, Toulouse, and Bordeaux. Seventeenth-century documented performances of Lully's stage works occurred in Rennes,[1] Rouen, Lunéville, Nancy, Metz, Dijon, Lille, and Strasbourg (see Schmidt 1989).

Beyond the borders of France, Lully was perceived as the composer most representative of French music. In England, Roger North praised his *entrées* and observed that "All the compositions of the towne were strained to imitate Babtist's [sic] vein" (1728; 1959, 350). During the heyday of Charles II's aping French institutions and manners, he sent Pelham Humfrey to France as well as to Italy, presumably to absorb their national styles. Humfrey may well have heard some of Lully's court ballets and the 1664 *Miserere*. He returned to England in any case, according to Samuel Pepys, "an absolute Monsieur." In February 1686, a French company performed *Cadmus et Hermione* in London, where the music was considered "indeed very fine"

(Lawrence 1936). Among the listeners may have been young Henry Purcell, who many years later "borrowed" the "Entrée de l'Envie" from the prologue for his own instrumental music in *The Tempest*.

By Purcell's time, however, the influence of French music was on the wane in England. English music was "yet but in its Nonage," he wrote. " Tis now learning *Italian*, which is its best Master, and studying a little of the *French* air, to give it somewhat more of Gayety and Fashion" (preface to *Dioclesian*, 1690). It should be stated that in addition to "Gayety and Fashion" Purcell found in Lully's *Isis* the model for his famous "Frost Scene" in *King Arthur*, Act IV.)

The geographic spread of Lully's operas in the last two decades of the seventeenth century is remarkable considering the relative lack of mobility of opera at that time, but Versailles swept Europe. Many German princely courts of the seventeenth century mimicked its architecture, décor, and gardens and showed a strong predilection for French language and culture. The court at Celle, for example, became a bastion of French taste and manners. After Georg Wilhelm, Duke of Braunschweig-Lüneburg, married Eléanore Desmier d'Olbreuse of Poitou in 1675, there was refuge there for French Huguenots who especially needed it after 1685 when Louis XIV revoked the Edict of Nantes. The court boasted a theater and orchestra which during its best days numbered sixteen players, seven of whom were oboists in the tradition of the Paris Opera orchestra.

The extent to which French style had penetrated German music by the early years of the eighteenth century may be seen from Telemann's comment that "French airs have replaced the former vogue for the Italian cantata here. I have known German, English, Russians, Poles, and even Jews who know whole passages from Lully's *Bellérophon* and *Atys* by heart" (quoted by Mellers 1950, 280, translation mine). Carl Schmidt, basing his research mainly on printed *livrets*, gives 1683 as the date of the first performance of an opera by Lully in Germany (*Isis* in Regensburg). The excellent theater at Wolfenbüttel saw performances of *Psyché* (1686) and *Thésée* (1687). In 1686, ten Lully operas were given in Ansbach. Hamburg and Stuttgart both enjoyed performances of *Acis et Galatée*: Hamburg in 1689 and in 1695; and Stuttgart in 1698.

Multiple performances of Lully's operas were common in The Hague and in Amsterdam beginning with the season of 1686–1687. Between 1682 and 1721 all of Lully's *tragédies-en-musique* were performed there.

In Italy, French dance music and *symphonies* were absorbed into chamber sonatas; Italian composers characteristically expressed little interest in French vocal music. Titon du Tillet tells us that the Italian composer Theobaldo di Gatti decided to go to France, because he had been so charmed by some of the instrumental music from the first operas of Lully to reach Florence, and he "wished to meet the composer" (1732, 621). Titon also quotes a French cardinal who claimed that Corelli himself responded to the cardinal's praise for his sonatas with the remark that "it is because I have studied Lully" (1732, 396). Only two performances of Lully's operas in Italy can be documented: *Psyché* in Modena (1683) and *Armide* in Rome (1690).

Back in France, Italian music only appeared to have been driven underground during the time of Lully's iron-clad control of the lyric theater. Lully was unable or unwilling to prevent the performance of an Italian pastorale at Fontainebleau in 1681 before the king. It was *Nicandro e Fileno* by the popular Roman composer Paolo Lorenzani (1640–1713), who had been in France since 1678 and who had been appointed *Surintendant de la Musique de la Reine* in 1679. From 1685 to 1687 as *Maître de Chapelle* of Sainte-Anne-la-Royale (the church of the Théatine order), Lorenzani organized his *Saluts en musique* "in the manner of Roman oratorios" (see Picard 1981, 252).

Nearby in Saint-Germain-en-Laye, the Italian composer Innocenzo Fede (born 1661) served as Master of Music to the Stuart kings, James II and James III, during their twenty-two-year exile in France. Italian arias, sonatas, and cantatas made up a large part of the repertory of the English court in France (see Corp 1995). In the very heart of Paris, Italian music was performed and disseminated by a small but active group surrounding the dilettante priest of Saint-André-des-Arts, Nicolas Matthieu. Jean de Serré de Rieux described this milieu: "M. Matthieu, curé of Saint-André-des-Arts, established a weekly concert at his home during several years of the last century where only Latin music, composed in Italy after 1650 by the greatest masters, was performed" (1734, 112). Helpfully, de Rieux included the names of the following masters: Luigi Rossi, Cavalli, Maurizio Cazzati, Giacomo Carissimi, Giovanni Legrenzi, Giovanni Paolo Colonna, Alessandro Melani, Alessandro Stradella, and Giovanni Battista Bassani—a cross section of the most important composers of the early and middle Italian Baroque. He added, "It was through the curé of Saint-André-des-Arts that these great works were first known in Paris."

The library of Abbé Mathieu contained some two hundred compositions, over two-thirds of which were by Italian composers (see Le Moël 1963). Unfortunately, the majority of the Italian holdings were catalogued simply as "*paquets de motets à 1, 2 ou 3 voix, de différens autheurs d'Italie*" or "*plusieurs pièces de simphonies de diverse autheurs d'Italie.*" Passing in and out of this heady Italianate atmosphere, which was just across the city from Lully's Académie Royale de Musique, were the composer-monks Claude Nicaise and René Ouvrard (both of whom had made Italian tours), Claude Oudot (who was the musical director of the Académie Française), and the composers Marc-Antoine Charpentier (back from his Italian sojourn by the early 1670s) and Michel-Richard Delalande (to whom Abbé Matthieu bequeathed several Italian motets and cantatas).

After Lully's death, most important French composers moved toward a rapprochement with the invading Italian style. Three Italian airs made a timid appearance in Collasse's *tragédie en musique*, *Astrée* (1691). Charpentier's *Médée* (1694) includes an air written in Italian for a female character identified only as "an Italian." In 1695 Philidor and Fossard, the king's copyists, brought out a volume of *airs italiens* published by Pierre Ballard. In the same year, Christophe Ballard published a collection of *Airs italiens de Monsieur Lorenzani*. André Campra's *L'Europe galante* of 1697 is the first stage work to contain Italian arias overtly similar to those by contemporary Italians such as Scarlatti or Stradella. Ballard brought out the third edition of this *opéra-ballet* in 1699. After his table of *Airs à chanter* he noted:

> *Several Italian airs have been added during the long period of time that this work has been performed. They will be found in the* Recueil des meilleurs airs italiens, *so there is no point in including them in the above table.*

He had already published his first *Recueil des meilleurs airs italiens* that very year. (Four more *recueils* followed it in 1701, 1703, 1705, and 1708.) Campra composed a short, self-contained Italian opera in 1699, *Orfeo nell'inferni*, as part of his lyric comedy, *Le Carnaval de Venise*. One year into the eighteenth century, Corelli's Opus 5 had its first Paris printing, and Brossard not only organized his *Dictionnaire de musique* around Italian terms but also included a *"Traité de la manière de bien prononcer les Mots Italiens,"* which opens: "Never has there been more taste and passion for Italian music than exists now in France." In 1706 the first book of *Cantates françaises* by Jean-Baptiste Morin began the fashion for French adaptations of the Italian cantata. By 1713 the *Mercure galant* admitted that hardly a Musician arrived in Paris without Italian sonatas or cantatas in his pocket, and the following year the November issue of the same journal blamed the "cantatas and sonatas that have flooded all Paris" for the marked change of taste from the "rich simplicity that is the true character of our language and our genius" (201).

With Louis XIV rarely attending court productions of plays or operas, with Versailles taking on more and more the "demeanor of a convent" under the powerful aegis of Mme de Maintenon (Gros 1926, 142), with such powerful members of the royalty as Philippe d'Orléans, the future Regent, declaring (in Raguenet's words) a "definite taste for Italian music" (1705, 51), and with the barriers down to let in cantatas, sonatas, and concertos from across the Alps, partisans of French music prepared to mount a counterattack.

So it was that Lully, a living legend during his lifetime, was rapidly canonized after his death as the patron saint of French music. Just as Giovanni Pierluigi da Palestrina had been seen by a later generation through the eyes of Giuseppi Baini as the savior of Catholic church music (a bias that we are still struggling to overcome), so Lully through the writings of Lecerf de la Viéville emerges as the very epitome of French style.

In reading Lecerf, one must constantly try to discriminate between anecdote, perceptive analysis, and mythology, for certainly the life of the Florentine miller's son, who became the most powerful and wealthy musical dictator of the *grand siècle*, contains all the raw materials from which legends are spun. Lecerf assuredly had absorbed a Lully mystique that placed the composer at the very center of a concentric system, to remain immutable amidst controversy. The system tolerated coexistence but could never concede the presence of a serious rival for its center. Lecerf found himself committed to criticize deviants from the system, those who heard the transalpine call and became "ardent imitators of the Italian manner of composition" (1725; rpt. 1966, 3:318); yet he was obliged to admit that Charpentier, Collasse, Campra, Destouches, and other composers had been "reduced" to seeking "bizarre effects" by the very fact that they wished to avoid being accused of imitating or plagiarizing Lully so soon after his demise. The thought that composers may have wished to "imitate" the Italian manner because of intrinsic musical merits was apparently an anathema to the stubborn Norman.

We should not, however, assume that no criticism was leveled against Lully in France during his lifetime or soon after his death. There were, of course, the professional opera haters, Boileau and Bossuet, backed by the conservative clergy; and those like Louvois, who feared that Lully's rapport with Louis XIV might result in political pressures detrimental to their own interests; also La Fontaine, who, although admitting that coaches lined the Faubourg Saint-Honoré on the days that Lully's operas were performed (1677), was not above mounting a savage personal attack against Lully in *Le Florentin* (1674): "He is lewd and disagreeable, and he devours all . . . . His wife, children, and all others large and small recite morning and night in their prayers 'Lord in your bountiful goodness, Deliver us from the Florentine.'"

Others, who were less concerned with Lully's rancor, weaknesses of character, or homosexual liaisons than with his musical legacy, also sought deliverance. François de Callières attacked the sacrosanct Lully recitative outspokenly one year after the composer's death: "If you were to hear those long, dull recitatives that take up the greatest part of the spectacle in these Operas, you would be surprised at the complaisance and patience of this good Nation" (1688, 266).

Lully received adulation and treatment as though he were larger than life. This was due as much to his usefulness as a symbol of the highest attainments of French music as to the merits of his music itself. In spite of rumblings of discontent, coaches continued to fill the Faubourg Saint-Honoré carrying their aristocratic burdens to performances of *Alceste*, *Thésée*, or *Armide*, and Lully's name became a battle cry for the rapidly forming resistance to Italian influence. Titon du Tillet described Lully as the "father of our beautiful French music, which he carried to its perfection, completely abandoning any taste for Italian music" (1732, 47).

In their oversimplified view of the matter, French aestheticians described French music over and over again with key words or phrases whose antonyms, tainted with partisan bias, were reserved for describing Italian music. The list of adjectives and nouns found below was gathered at random from sources ranging from Mersenne's *Harmonie universelle* (1636) to Louis de Bollioud de Mermet's *De la corruption du goust dans la musique françoise* (1746). The words recur in source after source for more than 100 years. Since it is easier and greater sport to hurl invective than to engage in self-appraisal, the Italian list is longer than the French. From the French point of view, it goes without saying, the sum of the parts under the French column equal *le bon goût* and, under the Italian column, equal *la corruption du goût*.

French Music	*Italian Music*	
beauté	baroque	fureur
calme	bizarre	gaieté
charme	brillant	licence
délicate	bruit	peu naturel
douceur	chargé	rage
élégant	colère	recherché
grâce	défiguré	savant
intelligent	dépit	singulier
naturel	détourné	variété
netteté	diversité	vif
noble	excès	violence
régularité	extravagance	vivacité
(la belle) simplicité		
tendresse		
touchant		

The term *savant* as a term of deprecation perhaps needs an explanation. In his oft-quoted letter to Houdar de La Motte, Rameau defined a *savant musicien* as one who "neglects nothing in the different combinations of notes but is thought to be so completely absorbed by these combinations that he sacrifices everything: good sense, mind, and feeling" (cited in Rameau's *Oeuvres complètes* 6:33). Ironically, the same charge was hurled by the *Lullistes* against the *Ramistes* in the continuation of the interminable polemic between the ancients and the moderns and between French and Italian styles that was brought to a boil by the performances of Rameau's *tragédies lyriques* and *opéras-ballets*. In 1736 one *Lulliste*, Cartaud de la Villatte, even complained that Rameau's harmonies "take on a geometrical tone which frightens the heart" (cited by Girdlestone 1957, 481).

In general it was the aestheticians, the arbiters of *le bon goût*, and not the more discriminating among the *préramiste* composers and performers, who were opposed to the concept of a discreet *goûts réunis*. Whereas André Campra wrote that he had tried to "mix the vivacity of Italian music with the gentleness of the French" (preface to Volume 1 of *Cantates françaises*, 1708), and Couperin recalled with awkward bluntness that Italian and French tastes had "shared the Republic of Music in France for a long time" and declared that he always "esteemed those things that merited it without regard to composer or nation" (preface to *Les Goûts réunis*, 1724); whereas Jacques Aubert admitted to adding some lively and gay touches to the "graceful" and "beautiful simplicity" of French melody (preface to *Suites de concerts de symphonie en trio*, 1730), the critics from Lecerf to Louis de Bollioud de Mermet found this mixture displeasing. "But how well aware one has become," wrote Bollioud de Mermet,

> *that taste is gradually degenerating—almost imperceptibly! . . . They admire that which is bizarre, that which is singular, that which surprises, that which astonishes . . . . The most natural and complete Harmony moves [them] less . . . than an overworked Composition, bristling with obstacles, which in the last analysis makes more noise than an impression (1746, 14–15).*

We must view the changes in performances of Lully's operas after his death and throughout the eighteenth century against this background. That these changes were considerable, especially after 1750, is a matter of record. Their purpose?—to make the genre more palatable to the Parisians' changing taste. There was much contemporary concern at the broadening of tempo and the introduction of what many considered excessive ornamentation into the airs and recitatives. Abbé Dubos remarked that this slowing down of tempo rendered Lully's recitatives "soulless" and increased the length of his operas (1719; 7th ed. 1770 3:343).

Many extant Ballard scores of Lully's operas served as actual performance scores for various eighteenth-century revivals. These scores, many housed today in the Bibliothèque de l'Opéra, are mute testimony to the lack of respect accorded the printed page of a composition— even by the revered master, Lully. Ballard printed the full score of *Alceste* in 1708. For a revival, handwritten changes to one copy (A. 5a, Bibliothèque de l'Opéra) add a new overture, cut Scene 3 of Act I, eliminate pages of recitatives, and replace the choral exclamation "Triomphez, triomphez" that concludes *Alceste* with a sarabande, musette, march, *ariette*, and chaconne.

The 1679 Ballard full score of *Bellérophon* at the Bibliothèque de l'Opéra (A. 11a) is a "copy used for performances," in this case for the revival of 1773. Lois Rosow has identified Pierre-Montan Berton as the one responsible for the numerous changes in this score. Berton, one of two composers appointed to the directorship of the Opera in 1767, edited ten Lully operas between 1759 and 1773 (1987a, 304–305). Example 9-1 illustrates the many additions of ornaments as well as Berton's rewriting and rescoring of *Bellérophon* for the 1773 revival.

Other non-structural changes in the performances of Lully's works were a natural by-product of the sudden release of Académie performers from years of disciplined behavior demanded by Lully. Lecerf, longing for the halcyon days when the director would break a violin over the back of an errant musician, wrote that "Under Lully's control the female singers did not have colds for six months out of the year, and the male performers were not drunk four days out of the week" (1725; rpt. 1966, 3:212). The fact that stringent rules governing the deportment of members of the Académie Royale were drawn up as part of the Royal Ordinance of 1713 verifies Lecerf's observations.

Disenchantment with Lully's *tragédie lyrique* became more and more evident as the eighteenth century progressed. The Parfaicts, referring to the December 1705 revival of *Bellérophon*, wrote: "This opera which had such a brilliant success when new was received rather poorly at this revival" (ca. 1741, 1:114). The revival of *Roland* in 1709 "was not a happy one, in spite of a small Italian air performed by Mlle Dun" (ca.1741, 1:118). In commenting on the season of 1709, the Parfaicts concluded that "It is necessary to confess that this year was not a good one for the revivals of old operas" (ca. 1741, 118). To be fair, it should be recalled that 1709 was a particularly unsettled year. In Kafka-like fashion, Lully's gods and heroes performed their *galants* roles in counterpoint against the rioting, hungry street mobs of Paris. The Duchesse d'Orléans, we read in the *Journal* of the Bibliothèque de l'Opéra[2] "returned to Versailles [from the opera] during the revolt caused by the scarcity of bread—forty persons killed" (entry of 24 August 1709).

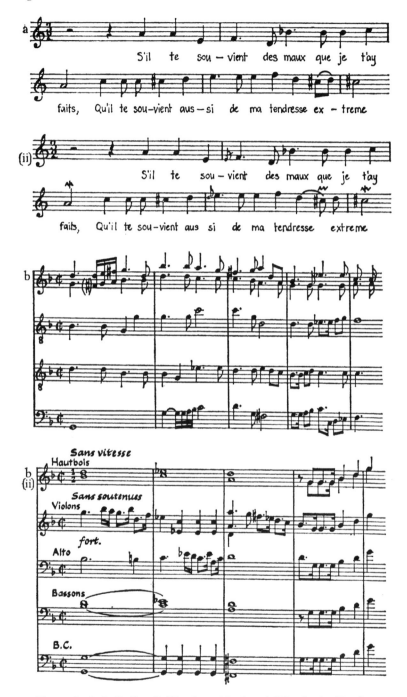

Example 9-1. Lully. *Bellérophon:* (a) after 1679 ed., (a, ii) after Bibliothèque de l'Ópéra, A.11a, (b) after 1679 ed., (b, ii) after Bibliothèque de L'Opéra, A11a).

In the pages of the *Mercure* for November 1714 we read:

It is incontestable that no one has succeeded better than Lully in writing this genre of music [tragédie lyrique], *It is no less true that Quinault surpassed all who worked after him in this genre of poetry. Yet, how many of these great masters' works remain that sustain their initial brilliance; we could easily count them, and I know no others save* Armide, Roland, Alceste, *and* Phaëton. *It isn't that* Bellérophon, Thésée *and* Atys *are inferior to the above,* . . . *but* Bellérophon *has appeared too tragic, we have found* Thésée *listless, and to the shame of our century, we have seen ladies leave during the fifth act of* Atys *(198–200).*

To read these words is to conclude that the days when the soul of Mme de La Fayette was "alarmed" by the "prodigious beauty" of a Lully opera had passed.[3] Predictably, the *Mercure* writer attributed this state of affairs to the change of taste brought about by the surging influence of Italian music.

We must beware of such comments, for in spite of the increasing popularity of an attractive new genre, the *opéra-ballet*, Lully's *tragédies lyriques* continued to hold the stage with remarkable tenacity throughout the eighteenth century. In terms of the longevity of certain Lully operas, our writer was a poor prophet, because *Thésée*, "listless" or not, was performed until 1779, for a period of 104 years; *Armide* was performed for seventy-eight years until 1764, just thirteen years before Gluck's opera on the same Quinault *livret*; and *Amadis*, an opera not even mentioned by the *Mercure* author, remained in the repertory of the Paris Opera for eighty-seven years.

Perhaps it is just this remarkable staying power of Lully's *tragédie lyrique* that lured the *préramiste* composers into trying their luck with the same genre. How else can one explain why André Campra and Jean-Joseph Mouret, for example, continued to compose *tragédies lyriques* even after the popular successes of their *opéras-ballets*? It is clear that the pleasure-loving Regency audience was not in itself powerful enough to overthrow the aesthetic dogmas of a glorious past age. The prestige of the *tragédie lyrique* carried over into a period basically antithetical to it. Sought-after librettists such as Antoine Danchet and La Motte understood the controversial nature of comedy at the Académie Royale de Musique. They knew that they would be judged, like Quinault, by their tragedies. Certain administrative procedures reflect this. Articles XVI and XVIII from the 1713 Ordinances state that the author and composer of a five-act tragedy would receive 100 *livres* for each of the first ten performances, whereas the author and composer of "ballets" (opéras-ballets) would only receive sixty livres.[4] Danchet quite possibly convinced Campra that it was worth more to them in prestige and remuneration to repeat the successes of *Hésione* and *Tancrède* rather than those of *L'Europe galante* or *Les Fêtes vénitiennes*.

A similar situation existed in painting after the death of the court painter Charles Le Brun in 1690. Despite the great popularity of the portrait (the *Salon* of 1699 included 100 portraits and 150 historical paintings), painters of large, historical canvasses remained the "aristocracy of the brush." Jean-Marc Nattier, therefore, devised the mythological portrait in an attempt to gain more prestige for the art of portraiture (see Louis Réau 1925, 1:64).

In the forty-six years that separate Lully's last opera, *Acis et Galatée* (1687), from Rameau's first, *Hippolyte et Aricie* (1733), the *tragédie lyrique* proved a chimera for most *préramiste* composers and librettists. Fifty-eight of their *tragédies-en-musique* were performed at the Académie Royale de Musique. This was fourteen more than all other types of their stage works combined, but only fourteen of the fifty-eight enjoyed three or more revivals, and none could match the longevity of Lully's eight most popular operas.

In the preface to his *Recueil de cantates* (1728), Bachelier reports that he questioned a Parisian with regard to the failure of two *tragédies en musique* written by violoncellist Batistin Stuck. If the response was typical, it shows a hedonistic Regency audience more interested in a pretty air and coquettish singer than in the high-flown poetry and one-dimensional characters of the *tragédie lyrique*:

> *In so far as the* Parterre *cannot sing along with the short, independent airs that are sung in the Operas, these works will always fail. Why on earth does Mr Batistin take it into his head to ornament these little independent airs, which serve to revive the languishing beauty of a scene that sometimes puts us to sleep? . . . If these gentlemen design to please, let them give us pieces such as "Qui sert la fierté dans ces belles," "Nos plaisirs seront peu durable," . . . & innumerable others of this sort, by means of which the slightest little Soubrette, who steps out of character, renders herself worthy of esteem at the Opera by cajoling them [the audience] with a little, disengaged air and, by joining little sidelong glances thereto, creates a Hubbub in the* Parterre, *who judge the beauty of a Piece only by the simperings of she who executes it & who give it the seal of their approval by repeating the same Air in Chorus.*

Among Lully's students, only Pascal Collasse (1649–1709) succeeded in mounting a *tragédie en musique* that was an unqualified success (*Thétis et Pélée*, 1689), and poor Collasse must have grown desperate to repeat this initial triumph. His *Énée et Lavinie* of 1690 had no revivals; nor did his *Astrée* (1692), or *Jason ou la toison d'or* (1696), or *Canente* (1700), or *Polyxène et Pyrrhus* (1706). He ended by abandoning music for alchemy and dying "poor and half insane" in 1709 (Lajarte 1878, 1:72).

After a promising debut with *Didon* (1693), Lully's most talented pupil, Henry Desmarest (1661–1741), knew failures followed by only one moderate success, *Vénus et Adonis* (1697). Desmarest never completed *Iphigénie en Tauride*, his most important work for the lyric stage. Campra finished it with his librettist, Danchet.[5] First performed at the Paris Opera in 1704, it enjoyed many revivals up to 1780, one year after the first performance of Gluck's opera of the same name.

Through scheming that removed all possible rivals, Lully had indeed created an empire, but an empire which did not provide for heirs. The most important composers of the day had, perforce, chosen other routes to success. Delalande, as the most successful court and Chapel composer, wisely restricted his stage music to ballets and *divertissements* (*pièces d'occasion* performed in the gardens of Versailles) until at the end of his career he collaborated with Destouches in the composition of the *opéra-ballet Les Eléments* (1721). François Couperin was essentially a miniaturist and instrumental composer.

Marc-Antoine Charpentier's situation was more complicated. He was Lully's strongest potential rival and no stranger to stage music. After the death of Molière, he continued to compose for the Comédie Française.

One year after Lully's death, on 25 February 1688, a *tragédie en musique* by Charpentier was performed in the theater of the Jesuit College, Louis-le-Grand, where Charpentier had been a *Maître de Musique* since 1684. This sacred opera, *David et Jonathas*, was written forty-four years before Montéclair's more popular *Jephté* and incurred the displeasure of Lecerf who was already ill-disposed towards Charpentier for being an "ardent imitator of the Italian manner." In proselytizing for the idea of a "Christian Opera," Lecerf concluded that Charpentier's *David et Jonathas* "only half merited the name Opera . . . for it was too dry, too denuded of the sentiments of morality and piety" (1725; rpt. 1966, 4:4–5).

It is true that it suffers from a mediocre libretto, but the copy of the score that we have from Philidor's *atelier*, flawed though it may be,[6] proves that *David et Jonathas* is a product of Charpentier's most mature period. Its many choruses are more polyphonic than those by Lully, and there is rich part writing and harmonic audacity as opposed to Lully's note-against-note style and simple diatonicism. The instrumental texture is predominately *a*4 (in contrast to the Lullian *a*5 texture found in Charpentier's later *Médée*), although, as Jean Duron has pointed out, Charpentier's *a*4 texture remains in the main *à la française*, that is, the two inner voices are played by violas and not by the combination more common in *a*4 texture elsewhere in Europe of second violins and violas (1986b, 27–28). Example 9-2 is taken from the impresive air of David, "Ciel, quel triste combat," in Act I, scene iii. This long air is really an air complex that is freely organized in three sections preceded by a prelude. Example 9-2a shows the opening of the prelude; Example 9-2b is an extract from the concluding measures of Part C. The dissonant part writing and parallel fifths in measure two of Example 9-2b are common in the music of Charpentier.

Charpentier did not attempt a breakthrough at the Académie Royale de Musique until 1693 with *Médée*. Damned by Lecerf as the "*méchant opéra de Médée*" (1725; rpt. 1966, 4:121), it was enthusiastically hailed by Brossard as the opera "of all operas" (1724; 1725–1730, 227–228). Lully's chief apologist need not have fretted, for *Médée* is completely in the Lullian mold; witness its homophonic choruses, its accompanied monologue airs, and its chains of short binary airs that organize entire scenes (Act III, scene v, for example). Even the juggling of its *a*5 string texture to darken the color for Créon's monologue air "Noires divinitez" (Act IV, scene ix) is foreshadowed in Epaphie's monologue "Dieu qui vous declarez mon père" in Lully's *Phaëton* (Act IV, scene ii). At the same time, the harmonic language of *Médée* is more varied; the inner voices, more carefully crafted and more vital; and the depth of characterization, richer. This is especially evident in the great monologue of Act III, scene iii, "Quel prix de mon amour."

Although labeled *pastorale*, Charpentier's *Actéon* is in truth a miniature *tragédie en musique* in six scenes lightly scored for two violins and continuo. The climax of the little drama occurs in scene iv beginning at the tragic outburst of Actéon ("Mon coeur autre fois intrepide"), as he sees himself being changed into a stag, and continuing through the subsequent long instrumental lament in C minor.

Charpentier composed a three-act chamber opera, *La Descente d'Orphée aux Enfers* for Mlle de Guise. Only two acts are extant. The score calls for nine singers, including Charpentier himself, as well as two viols, two violins, and continuo. Charpentier also composed two one-act operas: *Les Plaisirs de Versailles* (1680s) and *Les Arts florissants* (1685–1686). Sung throughout, they have been called "operatic divertissements" by Hitchcock.[7]

Example 9-2. Charpentier: "Ciel, quel triste combat," *David et Jonathas* (after Philidor copy). (a) Prelude. (b) Conclusion.

A careful study of the *tragédies lyriques* composed after Lully and before Rameau convinces me that, in addition to the Charpentier operas mentioned above, there is much that is worthwhile in such works as Collasse's *Thétis et Pélée*, Campra's *Tancrède* and *Idoménée*, Desmarest's *Didon* and (with Campra) *Iphigénie en Tauride*, Destouches's *Omphale* and *Amadis de Grèce*, Marais's *Alcyone* and *Sémélé*, and Montéclair's *Jephté*. To be sure, there are pages and pages of imitation Lully, of hack music written to tired formulae. Yet the tendency to group all *préramiste* composers together as "pale imitators of Lully" (Chouquet 1873, 127) or to consider all the *tragédies en musique* by Collasse, Desmarest, Campra, and Destouches indiscriminately in one brief paragraph and to find them "slavishly imitative" of Lully (Haas 1929, 229) seems excessive.

Simply stated, the weakness of most *tragédies lyriques* of the *préramiste* period is their near total subordination of drama to decoration—a change in emphasis that roughly parallels the change in Venetian opera after the death of Monteverdi. The domination of composer over librettist did much to break down the clean dramatic lines of *livrets* even though their subject matter scarcely differs from that of their Quinault antecedents.

On the positive side, this departure from the restrictions of the dramatist released some purely musical forces that contributed to the operatic vocabulary of Jean-Philippe Rameau. Taken as a whole, *préramiste* stage music presents a more daring harmonic language than was evident in Lully. The static basses and slow harmonic rhythm characteristic of Lully gave way gradually before more extensive use of chromaticism and more rapid modulations. Diminished and half-diminished sevenths and secondary dominants such as are found in the accompanied recitative from Montéclair's *Jephté* (Act I, scene vi) became common (see Example 9-3).

Example 9-3. Montéclair: Extract from accompanied recitative, *Jephté* (after 1733 ed.).

Example 9-4. Destouches: Extract from *ritournelle, Amadis de Grèce* (after 1712 ed.).

Examples similar to Example 9-4, from the *ritournelle* in Destouches's *Amadis de Grèce* (Act IV, scene i), are unthinkable in the music of Lully and are clearly a byproduct of the Italian trio sonata. This *ritournelle*, with its suspension chains and its circle of fifths, would have been considered "bizarre" and "peu naturel" by those committed to the "simple," "naturel" style of Lully. Also considered too "recherché" and "savant" would have been the more pronounced use of distant keys such as the shift to B-flat minor in the final scene of Campra's *Idoménée*.

Expanded use of the orchestra is apparent in many *tragédies lyriques* of the *préramiste* period. The great musical frescoes of nature in turmoil, the tempests and earthquakes of Rameau stem from the first use of such program music in Collasse's *Thétis et Pélée*. There is no precedent for Collasse's tempest, which spans the final three scenes of Act II and pierces the chorus and the recitatives of Neptune and Jupiter. Before *Thétis et Pélée* there is only "Les Vents," the descriptive *symphonie*, twenty-eight measures long, near the close of the first act of Lully's *Alceste*. The *Thétis et Pélée* model was followed by Campra in Act IV of *Hésione* (1700), by Desmarest in *Iphigenie en Tauride* (1704), and by Marin Marais in *Alcyone* (1706). The prototype for all later operatic tempests seems to have been the "Tempête" from Act IV, scene iv of *Alcyone* (see Example 9-5). Brossard observed that it inspired a "prodigious number of others: not only in Opera, but also in Cantatas and even in Church Music" (1724; 1725–1730, 243). Marais's orchestral storm, an extended descriptive *symphonie* of almost one hundred measures interrupted from time to time by choral exclamation, was described by Titon du Tillet:

> *One cannot help speaking of the tempest in this opera* [Alcyone], *so vaunted by all the Connoisseurs and which has such an astounding effect. Marais planned to have the bass performed not only by bassoons and ordinary basses de violons, but also by loosely strung drums that rolled continually, forming a muffled, lugubrious sound, which, joined with the high pitched, piercing notes coming from the high part of the top string of the violins and from the oboes, together made one feel all the fury and all the horror of a rough sea.* (1732, 626).

As may be seen from the photocopy in Example 9-5 taken from a Ballard manuscript edition of *Alcyone* in the Bibliothèque de l'Opéra, *contrebasses* and bassoons are found on the line below Titon du Tillet's *basses de violons*.

Préramiste scores show the orchestra functioning as a mood determinant even more than it did in compositions by Lully. At times it dominates a scene. In Act I, scene iv of Campra's *Tancrède*, the orchestral description of an earthquake's sound is totally independent of the chorus. A motive heard in the orchestra dominates the big storm choruses in Campra's *Idoménée*, and the prelude to Act III shows a similar orchestral motive characterizing the "storm" raging in the heart of Idoménée. In Act II, scene i of the same opera, the orchestra participates actively in the shipwreck scene and cuts through the recitative of Neptune, "Vents orageux, Cessez." This scene includes an offstage chorus of "shipwrecked people who are heard but not seen"—a device used earlier by Charpentier in *Médée* and many years later by Rameau in *Zoroastre* (1749).

Example 9-5. Marais: beginning of "Tempeste," *Alcyone* (Bibliothèque de l'Opéra, MS A.69a).

Greater awareness of the coloristic possibilities of the orchestra is also evident in some *tragédies lyriques* of the *préramiste* period (see Borrel 1955, Barthélemy 1955, and Lemaître 1977). The range of the violins increased. There was a modest attempt to exploit the idiomatic features of solo instruments and greater use of obbligato instruments—an influence from the Italian concertos beginning to be heard in France with greater frequency during the early years of the eighteenth century. Witness, for example, the thoroughly idiomatic violoncello obbligato in Venus's air "Coulez ruisseau" from Campra's *Idoménée* (prologue, scene iii) or the independent bassoon line in

Ocean's air "Tremble Thoas" from Desmarest's *Iphigenie en Tauride* (Act III, scene vi). Observe also the frequent use of the transverse flute as an obbligato instrument. "Descendez cher amant," for example, from Marais's *Sémélé* (Act V, scene i) may owe something to similar airs with flute obbligatos found in the early French cantata repertory. At the same time, the recorder was not entirely put aside. As late a source as Montéclair's *Jephté* (1732) makes use of the recorder (*flute à bec*) both in combination with strings and with transverse flute.

Composers became increasingly sensitive to color combinations. The preferred high voice trio texture of two sopranos and a *haute-contre* found in the *petit choeur* of Lully's operas transferred to the orchestra during the *préramiste* period. It is most often found in two flute lines "accompanied" by violins, or it is found in combinations of flutes and violins. The trio texture of flutes and violins in "Cessez mes yeux," from Act III of Campra's *Tancrède* (1702), clearly adumbrates Aricie's air "Hippolyte amoureux" which Rameau composed thirty-one years later for *Hippolyte et Aricie* (Act I). In *Tancrède*, Campra also experimented with the darker colors found in voices of lower range. He scored the main female role for mezzo-soprano and, in spite of the popularity of the *haute-contre* voice, scored all the male roles for bass or baritone. This inevitably resulted in ensembles such as the duo for two basses "Suivons la fureur" (Act I, scene ii). Campra had already combined three basses in the remarkable trio "Joignons nos voix" in *Le Carnaval de Venise* of 1699 (prologue, scene iii).

Given Marin Marais's exploitation of color in his music for solo viols, it should come as no surprise that he was also a master at achieving color contrasts in the orchestral music of his operas. Arguably the most interesting example may be the chaconne from Act II, scene iii of *Sémélé* (see Milliot and La Gorce 1991, 248–249). This long dance (340 measures) is loosely organized into eight sections defined by orchestration and by changes in meter and tempo. Trio sections of flute and violins alternate with full orchestra[8] and with bass duos of cello and bassoon. Unusual shifts of meter (3 to ¢) that generate tempo changes are found throughout, and at one point, measures in 6/8 are superimposed over the prevailing ¢ meter. This results in a highly original cross rhythm (see Example 9-6).

Example 9-6. Marais: chaconne from *Sémélé* (Act II, scene iii) (after engraved ed. of 1709).

In vocal writing, the *préramiste* recitative closely follows the model established by Lully, with some small differences worth noting. There is freer use of the anapestic formula; more rests and sudden changes of tempo underscore the action or state of mind; expressive use of orchestral *ritournelles* helps establish continuity or contrast of mood; the melodic range is greater; and there is dramatic use of affective intervals and dissonant harmonies. Example 9-7a–c shows extracts from Destouches's *Omphale* and *Amadis de Grèce* and Campra's *Tancrède*. The ascending minor sixth, the ascending diminished seventh, and the diminished octave are melodic intervals rarely found in Lully.

Example 9-7. (a) Destouches: *Omphale* (after 1701 ed.). (b) Destouches: *Amadis de Grèce* (after 1712 ed.). (c) Campra: *Tancrède* (after 1702 ed.).

Destouches in particular reveals a highly developed expressive and dramatic sense in his recitatives. The dramatic pauses and orchestral interpolations of Zoroastre's recitatives from Act III of *Sémiramis* prefigure Rameau's own *Zoroastre*, composed thirty years later. Perhaps taking Lully's late accompanied recitatives as models, Destouches fashioned a flexible, "singing" type of musical declamation which approached the Italian arioso. Even while attacking Destouches's *Omphale* (*Lettre sur Omphale*, 1752), F. M. von Grimm admitted that the composer's recitatives were "still esteemed" (see Masson 1945).

Ironically, some of the best examples of *préramiste* recitative are not found in a five-act *tragédie en musique* but rather in the one-act "La Tragédie" from Campra's *opéra-ballet Les Muses* (1703). Superficially, this tragic tale, taken from Ovid's *Metamorphoses*, resembles a Lully-Quinault opera in miniature. Danchet simplified the action and reduced the number of characters to those essential to plot development. Example 9-8a,b contrasts Althée's recitative "Vous noires Déitez" from scene ii of "La Tragédie" with Phèdre's "Dieux cruels" from Act IV, scene v of *Hippolyte* by Rameau. If anything, Campra's example makes more conspicuous use of affective intervals. The main female characters calling upon the "black" and "Cruel gods" in both extracts and the striking use of a diminished seventh chord superimposed over a pedal tone establishes a close relationship in subject as well as in musical treatment.

Example 9-8. (a) Campra: Althée's recitative, *Les Muses* (after 1703 ed.). (b) Rameau: Phèdre's recitative, *Hippolyte et Aricie* (after the De Gland engraved ed. of 1733).

Although most *préramiste* airs follow the Lully tradition of short binary and rondeau structures, there is a marked tendency toward a more expressive vocal line, greater melodic range, and longer phrases. Such is the accompanied monologue air "Sombres forêts" from *Tancrède* (Act IV, scene i), which approaches Handel in its long-breathed melody and depth of expression. Such melodies "sing" more, and textual repetitions for musical reasons are more common. In this connection, the Italian *aria da capo* made its appearance in the *divertissements* of French operas—especially after its use in Campra's *L'Europe galante* (1697). Beginning abruptly in 1707, the French *ariette* took over the role of the Italian aria da capo in operatic *divertissements* (see, for example, Campra's brilliant "Trompettes éclartez," which he added to Collasse's *Thétis et Pélée* in 1708). In no other vocal form of the period is the Italian influence more clearly marked than in the *ariette*. In fact, the *ariette* is the French aria da capo. In French hands, the Italian model was stripped of dramatic significance and was relegated to the dramatically impotent *divertissement* as a mere decorative element. In that capacity, it gave the composer his best opportunity to write virtuoso vocal music.

The *ariette* made its appearance in French opera about the same time that the cantata in the Italian style came into vogue. The aria da capo, then, reached French opera not through direct contact with Neapolitan opera but by the circuitous route of the cantatas. By 1710 we find three cantatas quite naturally so labeled in the score of Campra's *opéra-ballet Les Fêtes vénitiennes*.

The word *ariette*, a French diminutive, is totally inadequate to describe this large formal structure—an anomaly well recognized by most eighteenth-century writers. Cahusac, describing the Italian aria da capo, wrote: "We title them, improperly, *ariette*. The true translation is air" (1754, 3:60). Nougaret, however, was careful to make a clear distinction between *ariette* and air in France.

> The French word, Ariette, comes from the Italian Aria. One means by this term a certain number of lines of verse that are sung and whose melody is extremely ornate. The piece of music which in France we call simply air is a unified and gentle melody. The French musician spends his all in the Ariette to show off his talents and the voice of a singer; instead of composing an air, he only applies himself to express a sentiment (1769, 2:297).

For Rousseau, ambiguous terminology was just one more weapon in his arsenal.

> One may judge the idea our musicians have of the nature of an opera by the singularity of their nomenclature. Those grand pieces of Italian music which ravish the soul, those masterpieces of genius which draw tears . . . the French call ariettes (from "Lettre sur la musique française," translated by Strunk 1950, 649).

Common to most eighteenth-century definitions of the *ariette* are the following ideas: it was composed to show off the voice (*faire briller la voix*); and it was normally found to be organized *en rondeau* (ABA or da capo).

The *tragédie lyrique* of Lully and Quinault underwent critical changes in the hands of the *préramistes*: dances proliferated and the *divertissement* became even more important and increasingly decorative. Campra was accused by one of his contemporaries of "completely drowning the subject [of *Achille et Déidame* (1735)] in *divertissements*. No one wished to honor it [the opera] by calling it a Tragedy" (quoted by Barthélemy 1957a, 147). That Rameau shared the *préramiste* composers' predilection for dance and even increased its use in his own *tragédies lyriques* is indicated in Table 9-1, which shows the number of dances in Lully's *Amadis* (1684), Campra's *Tancrède* (1702), and Rameau's *Dardanus* (revival of 1744).

Table 9-1. Use of dance in *tragédies lyriques*.

	Amadis	*Tancrède*	*Dardanus*
Prologue	3	6	7
Act I	3	2	4
Act II	2	4	2
Act III	2	4	7
Act IV	2	2	4
Act V	1	5	6
Totals	13	23	30

In the closing years of the *préramiste* period, the Paris Opera became a veritable graveyard for the *tragédie en musique*. This trend was checked in 1732, one year before *Hippolyte*, with an opera whose prologue is set on the stage of the Académie Royale de Musique itself: Michel Pignolet de Montéclair's *Jephté*, a "Tragedy taken from Holy Scripture," which in spite of, or perhaps because of, the condemnation of the opera by the Archbishop of Paris, was a great success. From the standpoint of musical and dramatic treatment of the subject, the opera has much to recommend it. "Tout tremble devant le Seigneur" (Act I), a large chorus in which both Jephté and Phinée participate, was highly regarded by Rameau. The same act also includes an unaccompanied chorus, rare for the period, "O Gloire! O force d'Israël." Both Acts I and III contain long double choruses. Variety like this is unusual in choral writing for opera and makes us regret all the more the loss of several of Montéclair's motets and his *Messe de Requiem*. In the final act of *Jephté*, there is an interesting example of musical recall: the opening music that accompanies Jephté's mother as she approaches the sacrificial altar recurs in scene vi as Iphise walks towards the same altar.

Then came *Hippolyte*. "My Lord, there is enough music in this opera to make ten of them; this man will eclipse us all," so prophesied the ageing André Campra to the Prince de Conti (cited by Girdlestone 1957, 193) after the first performance of Jean-Philippe Rameau's *Hippolyte et Aricie* on 1 October 1733. This then is the date that precipitously concludes the *préramiste* period, and this is the date that fixes the outer chronological and stylistic boundaries of our study.

The break with the past sensed by Campra was not lost on other contemporary observers. We read in the *Mercure de France* of October 1733: "They found the music of this opera a little difficult to execute . . . . In his [Rameau's] first work for the lyric stage, he has created an harmonious and virile Music of a new character" (cited in the *Oeuvres complètes de J.-P. Rameau*, 6:lvi). In point of fact, the singers and members of the orchestra were incapable of performing the magnificent second "Trio des Parques" (Act II) whose exciting enharmonic modulation shifts the music in semitones from G minor to D minor (see Girdlestone 1957, 154–155). Rameau was aware that he had pushed far beyond the harmonic limitations of his predecessors. In *Génération harmonique* (1737, 155), he discussed this trio and his disappointment at having been forced to change it for the stage performance. One part prophetic visionary, one part practical musician with the limitations of his performers in mind, he concluded sadly that, because of indifference towards those who invent and because of lack of sufficient research, the "infinite variety to which Music is susceptible, is as yet unknown."

Giving a backward glance over Rameau's career as dramatic composer one year after his death, the *Almanach des spectacles* of 1765, viewed *Hippolyte* as marking the date of the

> revolution which took place in music in France and [the date] of its new advancement. We were astonished at first by music so much more complex and fertile in images than we were accustomed to hearing at the theater. Nonetheless, we tasted this new genre, and we ended by applauding it" (cited in the Oeuvres complètes de J. P. Rameau, 6:lix).

There is little question, then, that Rameau's contemporaries saw *Hippolyte et Aricie* as bringing about a "sea change" in French music of the period.

It is well to acknowledge that Rameau created much of the originality of *Hippolyte* out of the *préramiste* composers' vastly expanded and enriched musical vocabulary. "The great Rameau," wrote Renée Viollier, "is only the logical and magnificent issue of the labor and researches of his immediate predecessors" (1950, Introduction). He parallels Bach in that he culminates a style, in his case, that of the *grand siècle*; but more than Bach, he portends and in places even creates the sound of the future. In the *tragédies lyriques* and *opéras-ballets* of Rameau, the old and the new coexist—sometimes gracefully, sometimes, as the bitter attacks of the Lullistes reveal, to the detriment of their Lullian models.

The *récitatif simple*, although given more melodic and harmonic significance, remains essentially unchanged in Rameau's music as do certain scoring practices such as the *trio des hautbois* and the doubled continuo air. New to French music were his use of independent second violin and viola parts (see *Hippolyte et Aricie*, prelude to Act I, scene i) and his use of sustained winds in pairs to support the strings (see prelude to Act II, scene v and the "Tonnerre" from Act I). In accompanied recitatives such as Phèdre's "Quelle plainte en ces lieux m'appelle" that closes Act IV, we may observe Rameau's progressive features to best advantage. In this scene, we are on the threshold of high classical opera. Rameau's Phèdre and Gluck's Iphigénie and Clytemnestra speak the same language, and it is no longer the language of Lully's Armide.

Rameau's orchestra participates more directly with the vocal music to form entire scene complexes. The orchestra of the second "Trio des Parques" is the true unifying agent. Motifs first heard in the opening *ritournelle* augment the words *sudden horror* by forming a relentless, almost symphonic, counterpoint to the vocal trio. *Préramiste* tempests pale beside the chorus "Quel bruit! Quels vents!" in Act IV, scene iii, where shrill wind passages punctuate angry strings. The orchestra sounds curiously "Viennese" and looks ahead to the sea monster scene in Mozart's *Idomeneo*. (On Rameau's orchestra, see Sadler 1981–1982.)

The supremacy of musician over poet in music like this was the core of frequently bitter arguments between the *Lullistes* and *Ramistes* that divided the Paris musical scene after 1733. In Masson's words, whether Rameau was attacked for his too complicated harmonies, his difficult melodies, his lack of interest in the *livret*, or for his Italianisms, "all this could be reduced to one basic reproach: too much music" (1911, 213).

In the last analysis, the reputation of Rameau in the galaxy of great composers must be based on his stage works.[9] He is the greatest composer of the French eighteenth century. Among all the first-line composers of that century of giants, he, until recently, is the one least performed today. Within the past decade, live performances and/or subsequent recordings of *Hippolyte et Aricie, Castor et Pollux, Zoroastre, Les Indes galantes, Naïs, Pygmalion,* and *Les Paladins* call into question Donald Grout's observation that Rameau's operas "cannot be revived as a living art without reviving the age of Louis XV" (1965, 173). The question persists: Is Rameau's operatic style actually more "dead" than that of Handel, any more frozen in time than that of Gluck? Anyone who has listened to Anthony Lewis's performance of *Hippolyte* (recorded by L'Oiseau-Lyre) must, I believe, conclude that questions concerning a "dead operatic style" are curiously irrelevant when confronted with the "living art" that is Rameau's music.

∼ *Chapter 10* ∼

The Opéra-Ballet

Ce sont de jolis Watteau, des miniatures piquantes, qui exigent toute la précision du dessin, les grâces du pinceau et tout le brillant du coloris (Cahusac 1754, 3:108; transl. below).

*T*he *grand siècle* of Louis XIV had reached its apogee by 1689. The years 1690 to the end of the king's reign in 1715 were marked by endless wars, economic and social crises, and a mood of grim austerity at the court, brought about in part by the appalling personal losses sustained by its aging monarch. François de Salignac de La Mothe Fénelon stated baldly: "All of France is no more than a large poorhouse, desolated and without provisions" (*Lettre à Louis XIV*, 1694). The court *divertissements* and Chapel Te Deums designed to commemorate a happy event, a victory, or a royal birth had an increasingly hollow ring. There were few happy events to commemorate; no Te Deums were sung for the humiliating French defeats at Blenheim (1704), Ramillies (1706), and Oudenarde (1708); and with the loss of three Dauphins in eleven short months, the pall of death hung over Versailles.[1]

The very concept of the divine right of kings was under attack. Contemporary chansons reflected the general mood of discontent and disenchantment with the *grand monarque* and his family:

Le grand-père est un fanfaron,
Le fils un imbécile,
Le petit-fils un grand poltron,
Ohé! la belle famille!

The grandfather is a braggart,
The son, an imbecile,
The grandson, a coward,
O! the belle famille!

More and more, Louis XIV withdrew from active social life at Versailles. Perhaps in so doing he followed the wishes of the pious Mme de Maintenon and her confessors more than his own natural inclinations. It is clear that Mme de Maintenon welcomed the king's interest in religious music. She arranged musicales almost every evening for him in the intimacy of her own apartments. Entries in the *Journal* of the Marquis de Dangeau, begun in 1684 and cut off by his death in 1720, give a vivid picture of the daily life at court. It is clear from the quotations below[2] that the king never entirely relinquished his love of music and the theater but that the days of public display were a thing of the past. No more the pomp and ceremony attendant upon royal presence or privileged guests at court performances of *tragédies lyriques*.

2 October 1694: *After dinner in his chamber the King heard some paraphrases by Racine based on some verses from Saint Paul. Moreau composed the music.*

14 October 1703: *Fontainebleau. During the evening, the new opera of Destouches, the subject of which is the marriage of Carnival and Madness* [Le Carnaval et la Folie], *was performed. As the King rather likes the music of Destouches, it had been hoped that His Majesty would attend. But he has almost entirely renounced such performances.*

9 October 1704: *The King never attends public concerts or the Theater.*

5 November 1712: *In the evenings there is always music at Mme de Maintenon's on the days when the King is not working with his ministers.*

21 December 1712: *This evening there was much music at Mme de Maintenon's. The King had some of his musicians perform scenes from* Le Bourgeois gentilhomme. *They were even in the costumes of actors, and the King found that they played the parts very well.*

As the king withdrew from his role as arbiter of fashion, Versailles itself became less important to the nobility and even to members of the royal family. Gradually, Paris took precedence over Versailles; town house or country chateau now substituted for the centralized court. Among the king's family, the Princesse de Conti, Comte de Toulouse, and the Duc d'Antin (all avid music lovers) bought town houses; and the famous *grandes nuits* at Sceaux at the chateau of the Duchesse du Maine reached their peak in 1714–1715.

The style of the *grand siècle* succumbed to modifications more in keeping with the tastes of a pleasure-loving public. The physical discomforts and aloof grandeur of Versailles were happily exchanged for more ease and intimacy. *Petits appartements* and *salons*, often designed in oval and circular shapes, decorated with mirrors and with furniture arranged for intimate conversation, contrasted markedly with the cold, formal *grandes galeries* of the palace about which even Mme de Maintenon complained: "There is only grandeur, magnificence and symmetry. One must suffer all the drafts from doors that must be face to face. We must die in symmetry" (cited by Réau 1946, 46).

In the art of painting, the mode of the theater in amorous dalliance or in *fête galante* rivalled the heroic poses and big battle pieces of the king's official painter, Charles Lebrun. The new style is best seen in the feminine arabesques and *chinoiseries* of Claude Audran, in p..inted scenes from the *comédie italienne* by Claude Gillot and above all in the *fêtes galantes* of Antoine Watteau. Indeed, if the painting of Watteau may be considered the quintessence of the so-called Regency style and the antithesis of the style of Louis XIV, it should be pointed out that the major part of his work was completed before the death of Louis XIV. "In reality," wrote Louis Réau, "the art that we call Louis the Fourteenth was dying well before the actual setting of the Sun King" (1946, 17). Réau dates the beginning of this change from the end of the "dictatorship of the king's first painter, Lebrun" (died 1690).

Similarly in music, the style of Louis XIV underwent several modifications following the end of the "dictatorship" of the king's first composer, Jean-Baptiste Lully. In the preceding chapter we have discussed the ramifications of these changes as they affected Lullian *tragédies en musique*. In the *opéra-ballet*, however, we come face-to-face with Regency style during Louis XIV's reign. It is the André Campra of *L'Europe galante* and *Les Fêtes vénitiennes* rather than of *Tancrède* or *Aréthuse*, it is the Jean-Joseph Mouret of *Les Fêtes de Thalie* rather than of *Ariane* that most clearly display a Regency style before the chronological beginning of the Regency itself.

A study of the writings of the aestheticians and encyclopedists, a perusal of the influential *Mercure de France*, and a careful reading of *livret* prefaces attest that, in the opinion of the eighteenth century, André Campra and Houdar de La Motte had created a new genre in 1697 with their *opéra-ballet L'Europe galante*. In his "Ballet" article for Diderot, Cahusac described it as "completely new" (*Encyclopédie* 1751–1780, 2:45).

Confusing, vague, and contradictory attempts to define the *opéra-ballet* in many nineteenth- and twentieth-century sources make turning to the eighteenth century for clarification necessary. La Motte admitted that the title of Destouches's *Le Carnaval et la Folie* (1703) announces only "a *bagatelle*, and perhaps all Opera is really nothing else" (preface)—an unthinkable comment if applied to a Quinault *tragédie en musique*. Cahusac contrasted the new genre with the *tragédie en musique* as follows:

> *The opera conceived by Quinault is composed of one central, dramatic action over the course of five acts. It is a vast concept, such as that of Raphael and Michelangelo. The spectacle created by La Motte is composed of several different acts, each representing a single action and including* divertissements *of song and dance. These are pretty Watteaus, piquant miniatures that demand precision of design, grace of brushstroke, and brilliance of color* [French original cited at beginning of this chapter].

A contemporary of André Campra, the librettist and poet Pierre-Charles Roy, best summed up the wide gulf that separates the overall dramatic unity of Lullian *tragédie lyrique* from the *opéra-ballet*: "[The latter] sort of Drama, which assembles three or four [dramas] in the same framework, which presents subjects treated individually, each one in an act with a *divertissement*, . . . pleases by its variety and sympathizes with French impatience" (1749, 2:18). Roy had concluded that Regency audiences were tired of having to follow a continuous five-act plot and preferred lighter diversion. "Separate plots are less fatiguing for the attention than a piece in several acts and make the introduction of *divertissements* easier" (preface to *Les Éléments* of 1725 by Destouches). The definition by Marmontel in Diderot's *Encyclopédie* is typical: "*Opéra-ballet* [is] a spectacle composed of acts independent from one another as regards plot, but united under a collective idea such as the Senses, the Elements" (1751–1780, 2:231). "*Opéras-ballets,*" wrote Nougaret, "are composed of several Acts that have no connection whatsoever with each other" (1769, 2:231). Jean-Jacques Rousseau defined the genre as a "bizarre type of opera . . . the Acts each form a different subject related to one another only in a general way" (1768, 38).

Most eighteenth-century definitions emphasized two structural features of the *opéra-ballet*: (1) each act or *entrée* has its own independent plot which relates very loosely to an overall idea expressed in the title of the *opéra-ballet* (the terms *acte* and *entrée* were interchangeable when referring to the *opéra-ballet*); and (2) each act includes at least one *divertissement* of songs and dances. Therefore, the roots of the genre may be traced to the seventeenth-century *ballet à entrées*, in which each section developed its own plot.

The heart of the confusion in later definitions lies in the way the name *opéra-ballet* was actually used. It seems to have been rarely used in the early eighteenth century and was not used consistently even after 1750. Because of the increased emphasis on *divertissements* in *opéra-ballet* and because of the basic relationship between the new genre and the *ballet à entrées*, many eighteenth-century writers quite naturally used the generic term *ballet* to include the new form. The term *opéra-ballet* came into more general use in the nineteenth century, and the distinctions which characterize the genre, so carefully delineated by eighteenth-century writers, were quickly forgotten. Thus, in the eighteenth century a general, ambiguous title was accorded a precise definition; in the nineteenth century, a title inherently precise was used by most writers in a general and ambiguous way. The basic structural distinction—that of an independent dramatic action for each entrée—was seldom recognized.

The twentieth century inherited the careless application of the term that had plagued the preceding century. Perhaps the most important and successful attempt to classify the term *opéra-ballet*, as well as such related genres as the *ballet héroïque*, *acte de ballet*, and *fragments*, is found in Paul-Marie Masson's brilliant study of the *ballet héroïque*. Quite properly, Masson insisted that the term *opéra-ballet* be reserved for works that lack continuous dramatic action and have "as many different plots as there are acts" (1928, 133).[3]

Eighteen *opéras-ballets* conforming to the eighteenth-century definition were performed at the Académie Royale de Musique from 1697 (*L'Europe galante*) through 1735 (*Les Indes galantes*). Table 10-1 lists them in chronological order, giving title, first performance at the Paris Opera, composer, and librettist. Although the *préramiste* period ends with Rameau's *Hippolyte et Aricie* in 1733, *Les Indes galantes* of 1735 is his first *opéra-ballet*.

A subclassification of these *opéras-ballets* is possible on the basis of subject matter. *Opéras-ballets* written from 1697 through 1719 constitute the first period of *opéra-ballet*. *Opéras-ballets* of the second period from 1723 through 1735 were called *ballets héroïques*.

Except for *Le Triomphe des Arts*, the first nine *opéras-ballets* that form the first period substituted at least some believable contemporary characters for the mythological deities, allegorical figures, and heroes of the *tragédie lyrique* and, with the further exception of *L'Europe galante*, they also introduced genuine comic plot to the French lyric theater as opposed to an occasional comic scene. The fops (*petits-maîtres*), the amorous ladies, and their watchful confidantes engaged in superficial banter, thus giving to the Regency a medium through which it could observe, in ideal reflection, its own hedonistic pursuits.

Table 10-1. Title, chronology, composer, and librettist of *opéras-ballets* performed at the Paris Opera from 1697 through 1735.

Title	First performance	Composer	Librettist
1. *L'Europe galante*	24 Oct. 1697	Campra	La Motte
2. *Le Triomphe des Arts*	16 May 1700	La Barre	La Motte
3. *Les Muses*	28 Oct. 1703	Campra	Danchet
4. *Les Fêtes vénitiennes*	17 Jun. 1710	Campra	Danchet
5. *Les Amours déguisés*	22 Aug. 1713	Bourgeois	Fuzelier
6. *Les Fêtes de Thalie*	19 Aug. 1714	Mouret	La Font
7. *Les Fêtes de l'été*	12 Jun. 1716	Montéclair	Pellegrin
8. *Les Ages*	9 Oct. 1718	Campra	Fuzelier
9. *Les Plaisirs de la campagne*	10 Aug. 1719	Bertin de La Doué	Pellegrin
10. *Les Fêtes grecques et romaines*	13 Jul. 1723	Colin de Blamont	Fuzelier
11. *Les Éléments* (1st perf. 22 Dec. 1721 Tuileries)	29 May 1725	Destouches	Roy
12. *Les Stratagèmes de l'Amour*	28 Mar. 1726	Destouches	Roy
13. *Les Amours des Dieux*	14 Sep. 1727	Mouret	Fuzelier
14. *Les Amours des Déesses*	9 Aug. 1729	Quinault, J.-B.	Fuzelier
15. *Le Triomphe des sens*	5 Jun. 1732	Mouret	Roy
16. *L'Empire de l'Amour*	14 Apr. 1733	de Brassac	Moncrif
17. *Les Grâces*	5 May 1735	Moure	Roy
18. *Les Indes galantes*	23 Aug. 1735	Rameau	Fuzelier

L'Europe galante, first performed in October 1697, may rightly be considered the first *opéra-ballet* due to its subject matter. The immediate structural model for it was undoubtedly Pascal Collasse's *Ballet des Saisons* (*livret* by Abbé Jean Pic), which had been performed at the Paris Opera two years earlier in October and was to hold the stage until 1722.[4] The *Ballet des Saisons* contains a separate plot for each act. Indeed, the Parfaict brothers noted this innovation by pointing out that "This is the first Ballet composed of *Entrées*, each of which has an entire subject separated [from the others]" (ca. 1741, 1:85). Unlike *L'Europe galante*, it restricts its material to the mythological-allegorical personages so characteristic of the *grand siècle*, and its prologue includes a forty-page chorus addressed to "Louis le plus parfait des Roys." Collasse had actually lifted this panegyric from an earlier chorus composed by Lully for the prologue to the *Ballet des Muses* (see Chapter 3). The real innovation of André Campra (1660–1744) and his librettists was to retain the formal structure of the *Ballet des Saisons* and the earlier *ballets à entrées* but to dethrone their deities and shopworn cast. Only the prologues and an occasional *entrée* remained for the odd assortment of characters borrowed by French librettists from allegory and from their *galant* version of classical mythology. The action of *L'Europe galante* does not take place in ancient times, nor is it rooted in myths. On the contrary, Campra and La Motte rendered precise, contemporary stereotypes of courtship as practiced in four European nations. La Motte's summary for the opera appears after the prologue in Ballard's full score of 1724:

> *We have chosen those Nations that are most contrasting and that offer the greatest potential for stage treatment:* France, Spain, Italy & Turkey. *We have followed what is normally considered to be characteristic behavior of their Inhabitants.*
> The Frenchman *is portrayed as fickle, indiscreet & amorous.*
> The Spaniard, *as faithful and romantic.*
> The Italian, *as jealous, shrewd & violent.*
> *Finally, we have expressed, within the limitations of the stage, the haughtiness and supreme authority of the* Sultan *and the passionate nature of the* Sultanas.

In eschewing mythological or allegorical subject matter in the body of the work, La Motte and Campra also had reasonable grounds for avoiding the elaborate machinery and the concomitant paraphernalia of the *merveilleux*, thus introducing a degree of verisimilitude into the French lyric theater.

These innovations were not lost on contemporary audiences. A letter from the Princess Palatine written on 10 November 1697 noted:

> *It is in truth only a Ballet, but it is charming. It is called* L'Europe galante. *They show how the French, Spanish, Italians and Turks pursue love; the character of these nationalities is so properly expressed that one is amused (cited by Barthélemy 1957a, 49).*

The comments of Dr Martin Lister in his entertaining and informative *A Journey to Paris in the Year 1698* not only reveal the esteem with which Campra's first *opéra-ballet* was held, it also substantiates audience participation:

> *I was at the Opera, called* l'Europe galante, *several times, and it is lookt upon as one of the very best. It is extremely fine, and the Musick and Singing admirable: The Stage large and magnificent, and well filled with Actors: The Scenes well suited to the thing, and as quick in the removal of them, as can be thought: The dancing*

exquisite, as being performed by the best Masters of that Profession in Town: The clothing rich, proper, and with great variety.

It is to be wondered, that these Operas are so frequented. There are great numbers of the Nobility that come daily to them, and some that can Sing them all. And it was one thing that was troublesome to us Strangers, to disturb the Box by these voluntary Songs of some parts of the Opera or other (1699, 170–171).

Cahusac, a partisan of La Motte, questioned the absence of the *merveilleux*: "Has La Motte perhaps made a mistake in creating the *ballet*? Quinault felt that the *merveilleux* was the very basis of opera. Why could not it also be the basis of the *ballet*?" (Diderot's *Encyclopédie* 1751–1780, 2:45). The tradition of the *merveilleux* proved, in fact, too powerful to allow *opéra-ballet* permanent exemption. Modification of the subject matter of first-period *opéra-ballet* resulted in the creation of the *ballet héroïque* in 1723. Cahusac nevertheless did recognize the innovative nature of *L'Europe galante*. He stated categorically: "In creating a completely new genre, La Motte gained the advantage of being copied in turn . . . . *L'Europe galante* is the first of our Lyric Works that bears no resemblance to the Operas of Quinault" (1754, 3:108–110). The key words "completely new" and "no resemblance to the operas of Quinault" must have referred to more than just the formal structure of the *opéras-ballets*. Are they not a musical parallel to Cahusac's own happy image of "pretty Watteaus"? Watteau did not usually people his work with mythological or heroic figures or give them supernatural forces, nor did Campra, Mouret, or Montéclair do so in their *opéras-ballets*.

Beginning with *Les Muses* (1703), first-period *opéra-ballet* and its sister, lyric comedy (see Chapter 11), gave French opera its first introduction to fully developed comic opera. It is not a question here of unrelated, comic episodes similar to those that Lully had already employed in his early *tragédies lyriques*. To be sure, there are comic implications in *L'Europe galante*, such as Silvandre's efforts in "La France" to extricate himself from Céphise's accusations of fickleness, but a continuous comic plot is not found within any act of that first *opéra-ballet*.

"La Comédie," the fourth entrée from Campra and Danchet's *opéra-ballet Les Muses* (1703), is the first French operatic comedy to have had an unqualified success. A one-act comic opera of considerable charm, "La Comédie" is an improbable pastiche made up of elements from Molière's *L'Amour médecin* (1665) and an episode described in Plutarch's *Lives* between Antiochus and his beautiful stepmother, Stratonice.

In the minds of most eighteenth-century observers, however, the first work to exploit comedy on the lyric stage was Campra's *Les Fêtes vénitiennes* (1710). Cahusac wrote:

> *In following the plan given by La Motte* (L'Europe galante), *Danchet invented comic entrées; we owe this genre to him . . . .* Les Fêtes vénitiennes *opened a new course for poets and musicians who had the courage to believe that the theater of the* merveilleux *could also be the theater of comedy (Diderot's* Encyclopédie *1751–1780, 2:45).*

Working on a trial-and-error basis from June to December of 1710, Campra composed a prologue and eight *entrées* in an artful combination of fantasy and comedy that made this *opéra-ballet* a most kaleidoscopic translation of "French impatience." *Les Fêtes vénitiennes* was a great success throughout the eighteenth century in France, causing Voltaire to complain that whereas Corneille's tragedy *Cinna* was performed one or two times, *Les Fêtes vénitiennes* played for three months (*Dissertation sur la tragédie ancienne et moderne*, 1749).

Critics of the *opéra-ballet*, including those aestheticians who held that the *tragédie lyrique* was the only legitimate genre for the lyric stage, were spoiling for a fight. The opportunity came on 19 August 1714 with the first performance of Jean-Joseph Mouret and Joseph de La Font's *Les Fêtes de Thalie*. The humiliating defeat of Melpomène (muse of tragedy) at the hands of Thalie (muse of comedy) in the prologue of this *opéra-ballet*, which the librettist had boldly set on the stage of the Paris Opera itself, resulted in a *succès de scandale*. Apollo, as arbiter of the quarrel between his tragic and comic muses, asks Melpomène why she could not coexist with Thalie "as formerly." (Is this an oblique reference to Lully's comic scenes in *Cadmus* and *Alceste*?) Apollo continues with a topical reference to contemporary Italian opera: "This *mélange* still charms Italy today." Pressure was such that the authors were obliged to change the original title of *Les Fêtes ou le triomphe de Thalie* to *Les Fêtes de Thalie* and to add a new *entrée*, "La Critique des Fêtes de Thalie," for the twenty-fifth performance on 9 October 1714 in order to justify their audacity.

Rémond de Saint-Mard understood the full significance of the subject matter of the *opéra-ballet* for a public grown weary of the heroic gestures and pretensions of the *grand siècle*:

> *Because, Monsieur, one has reached the point where one almost wants Ballets* [opéras-ballets] *only . . . . Neither does one need this strong, pathetic action demanded by the tragic. In the Ballet, all*

laughs . . . . Each act must contain a fast moving, light, and, if you wish, a rather galant *plot . . . . Two or three scenes, and short scenes take care of the business . . . . The rest of the action is in* Ariettes, Fêtes, Spectacles *and in all ways made agreeable . . . . These small* divertissements *are much better executed than our* Operas [tragédies en musique] *. . . . Take* L'Europe galante, *take* Les Éléments, *take* Les Fêtes vénitiennes: *you will find some* idées galantes *there, some graceful melodies, and what I particularly like, some agreeable words without their ceasing, for all that, to be natural and simple . . . . You also will find there the painting of our mores; they are in truth rather disagreeable* (vilaines); *but they are ours, and that is sufficient to interest us. Finally, Monsieur, the Ballet is an extremely agreeable spectacle for us. Nothing is better made for our lightness of spirit, nothing agrees better with our character (1741, 94–96).*

Playful maxims and *galanteries* abound in *Les Fêtes vénitiennes, Les Fêtes de Thalie* and *Les Fêtes de l'été.* These works take a pragmatic approach to the art of love. The acute observations of the librettists, La Font and Danchet, contain a touch of cynicism and an almost total lack of sentimentality. Although they borrowed turns of phrase from the vocabulary of *préciosité,* there is no need here for Mlle de Scudéry's metaphorical *carte de tendre.* Rather, they seem to have attempted to mirror the world of the country *seigneur* and the *petits-maîtres,* the elegant ladies and their amorous confidantes, and to render with some accuracy the social and cultural mores, no matter how "*vilaines,*" of the final years of the reign of Louis XIV and the Regency of Philippe d'Orléans.

The flesh-and-blood characters of *opéra-ballet* are found in recognizable contemporary settings. "L'Opéra" from *Les Fêtes vénitiennes,* for example, takes place in the theater of the Grimani Palace in Venice; "Les Ages rivaux" of *Les Ages* is set in Hamburg; and Marseilles is the location of the first *entrée* of Mouret's *Les Fêtes de Thalie.* In the preface to the latter, librettist La Font wrote: "I believe this to be the first Opera in which the women are dressed *à la française.*" In "La Provençale," a new *entrée* added to *Les Fêtes de Thalie* in 1722, Mouret used local costumes, local musical instruments, and popular meridional tunes sung in Provencal dialect.

Campra's *Les Fêtes vénitiennes* also included some topical musical references to certain popular operas performed at the Académie Royale de Musique in the first decade of the eighteenth century. In "L'Opéra," the Neapolitan soldier Damire is an opera buff who describes with vivid intensity the performance of his adored Léontine as Armide in the famous scene from Act II of Lully's *tragédie lyrique*. In the amusing, informative second scene of "Le Bal," Campra parodied well-known extracts from famous operas of the time. Unlike Mozart in the finale to *Don Giovanni*, Campra did not identify his borrowed material but simply stated in his *Avertissement* to the 1714 edition that he had used "some melodies and *Symphonies* of our most skillful composers."[5]

Significantly, as we move into the years of the Regency, we find more and more emphasis placed on the allegorical role assigned to "La Folie" (Madness) in the prologues and *divertissements* of many *opéras-ballets*. La Motte defined "La Folie" as a goddess who "although she did nothing reasonable, at the same time did nothing for which one could not find examples in human behavior" (preface, *Le Carnaval et la Folie* by Destouches). In the prologue to *Les Fêtes vénitiennes* she joins forces with "le Carnaval," and together they triumph over "severe reason." Eight years later "La Folie" is deified and placed above "Love" in the hierarchy of pleasures in *Les Ages* (1718), the only *opéra-ballet* Campra wrote after the beginning of the Regency.[6] Its reckless proliferation of dances and airs are musical excesses commensurate with the extravagant tastes of the Regency. The *fête galante* of *Les Ages* bears approximately the same relationship to *Les Fêtes vénitiennes* as does the grimace of a Lancret to the smile of a Watteau.

First-period *opéra-ballet* gave composer and librettist alike the opportunity to experiment with new and varied forms. The introduction of comic plot and characters drawn in part from French and other European societies stimulated this experimentation. The opportunity apparently ended with the death of the Regent in 1723. Louis XV became officially King of France at age thirteen. On 13 July 1723 the first performance of Colin de Blamont's *ballet héroïque*, *Les Fêtes grecques et romaines*, took place at the Académie Royale de Musique. The end of the first-period *opéra-ballet* and the end of the Regency followed closely one upon the other.

One may only speculate on the reasons for the sudden demise of the first-period opéra-ballet. Was it because of the continued opposition of many aestheticians to comedy on the French lyric stage; was it the return of a king, albeit a boy king, to the French throne; or was it the elusive tragic muse that diverted librettist and composer alike? The revealing discussion by Cahusac of La Motte's defection from the opéra-ballet to tragedy suggests the latter consideration:

> *It is indeed strange that he [La Motte] has not given us a greater number of works in such a charming genre. Only* L'Europe galante *among his works holds the stage today. He undoubtedly believed that that which is called* grand opéra [tragédie en

musique] *was alone worthy of his consideration. His originality was better served, however, in a genre all his own. He excels only in the genre he created. (Diderot's* Encyclopédie *1751–1780, 2:45).*

In any case the *ballet héroïque*, with all the trappings of monarchical opera, evicted the fickle Léandres from the banks of the Seine. They and the Don Pedros, the Léonores, the lively *petits-mâitres*, and the watchful confidantes of the first-period *opéra-ballet* were forced to seek refuge in parodies, *vaudevilles*, and the budding *opéra comique*. The structure of the *ballet héroïque* is the same as that of the *opéra-ballet*; therefore, it may legitimately be considered a specific type of *opéra-ballet* that made up the second and final period of the genre.[7]

In the preface to Colin de Blamont's *Les Fêtes grecques et romaines*, Louis Fuzelier discussed the new aspects of his *livret*:

> Les Fêtes grecques et romaines *is a completely new type of Ballet* [opéra-ballet] . . . . *France has up to now only used the Fable as subject matter appropriate for music [sic]. In a more daring manner, Italy his taken events from History for her operas. The Scarlattis and Bononcinis have had their Heroes sing that which Corneille and Racine would have declaimed* . . . .

> *We have brought together in this Ballet the best-known Festivals of Antiquity [*"Les Jeux olympiques," "Les Bacchanales," "Les Saturnales"*] which appeared to be most adaptable to the stage and to music* . . . .

> *In this Ballet we have neglected the* merveilleux, *the enchantments, and the descents of Divinities. We have deviated from a well-worn and not always well-followed path; we shall learn only too soon whether or not we have lost our way* (also found in Recueil général des opéra *1734, 13:265–270).*

Fuzelier made a full-fledged return to mythological subject matter in his second *ballet héroïque*, *Les Amours des dieux* (1727, music by Mouret). Somewhat apologetically and as though to convince himself, Fuzelier wrote in the preface that, in spite of the use of mythological characters, "the work . . . is absolutely in the heroic genre."

The list of *ballets héroïques* performed at the Académie Royale de Musique from 1723 through 1735 testifies to the end of the first period of *opéra-ballet* (see Table 10-1). All but one of these nine *opéras-ballets* are definitely in the format of the *ballet héroïque*. The librettist Roy succeeded in introducing comic plots into Destouches's *Les Stratagèmes de l'Amour* of 1726. Roy found it necessary, however, to justify this himself in the preface: "The public has decided that if Comedy is allowed on the stage, it may only be a noble Comedy which bears the character of Antiquity."

At its best, the first-period *opéra-ballet* exceeds the second in dramatic originality and freshness of musical idiom. Of the nine in the first period, the four by André Campra, Mouret's *Les Fêtes de Thalie*, and Montéclair's *Les Fêtes de l'été* contain much that is worth reviving,[8] whereas only Destouches's *Les Éléments* among the *ballets héroïques* of the second period has sufficient musical merit to warrant revival. By virtue of the date of its first performance (31 December 1721 at the Tuileries), *Les Éléments* could fit neatly into first-period *opéra-ballet*, but its subject matter prefigures the *ballet héroïque*. Its music gives further evidence of Destouches's sensitivity to harmonic color in the occasional use of unprepared dissonances and parallel seventh and ninth chords. However, efforts to make him a harbinger of musical impressionism show lack of familiarity with other *préramiste* composers whose scores contain similar harmonic effects. Lionel de La Laurencie, for example, singled out the chord in bar three of Leucosie's air "La Mer était tranquille" (*Entrée* II, scene i) as "altogether extraordinary for the period." Yet, this chord is none other than the mediant $\frac{9}{7}_{\#5}$ chord found also in the music of Charpentier, Delalande, and others (see Chapter 13).[9]

The main problem that confronts the modern scholar in dealing with the *opéra-ballet* is the lack of printed editions in full score (*partition générale*). With the exception of the full score of *L'Europe galante* printed by Ballard in 1724 as an *édition de luxe* (see Anthony 1970), all others exist only in the notorious short score (*partition réduite*) favored by the Ballard printing monopoly for *opéras-ballets* of the *préramiste* period. The general practice in preparing a short score seems to have been to eliminate the inner voices. However, this principle was far from universally applied. Vocal and instrumental extracts in trio, for example, were printed in full. Thus, a "*trio des hautbois*" contains three printed parts, but the dance in which it serves as "trio" was printed with only melody and bass!

Even so, one may explore the musical *terra incognita* that is the first-period *opéra-ballet* armed with short scores, collections of separate instrumental and vocal parts (*parties séparées*), and some manuscript full scores (often prepared long after the first performance by someone other than the composer).

Originality of subject matter may well have stimulated originality in the musico-dramatic devices employed by Campra, Mouret, and Montéclair in the first-period *opéra-ballet*. Three forms of musical repetition for dramatic ends may be found in their *opéras-ballets*: repetition of (1) a general melodic shape and rhythmic organization; (2) a phrase of music and text from a particularly important air or ensemble; and (3) an instrumental fragment or an entire instrumental selection.

The most striking example of the first type of musical repetition is found in the last scene of *L'Europe galante* (*Entrée* IV, scene vi). It is an abridged version of the "Prélude pour la Discorde," which interrupts the *divertissement* of the prologue (scene ii). This is the one extract from the dramatic music of Campra chosen by La Laurencie to show a "germ of the leitmotif" (Lavignac and La Laurencie's *Encyclopédie de la musique et Dictionnaire du Conservatoire* 1913–1931, Part 1, 3:1365). The D major key of the prelude becomes D minor; the harmonic underpinning is simplified; the dotted rhythms and string tirades remain. There is also a striking parallel between the musical and textual elements that make up Discord's words in both scenes. By converting the authoritative ascending fourth in the prologue (Example 10-1a) to the more pathetic ascending minor sixth in the last *entrée* (Example 10-1b) and by changing Discord's defiant "C'est en vain" to a resigned "C'en est fait," Campra maintained the textual and general melodic shape but totally altered their meaning. However, judging from copies of the 1724 full score of *L'Europe galante* that served as editions for actual performances, this innovation was lost on the audiences and impresarios of the later eighteenth century. The copies in the Bibliothèque de l'Opéra (A. 45[1]) and the Bibliothèque de Versailles (MSD. 78) have excised the entire final scene of the opera!

Example 10-1. Campra: Thematic recurrences in *L'Europe galante* (after the 1724 ed.). (a) Prologue. (b) Final scene.

The second device, the recurrence of musical and textual fragments, has gone virtually unnoticed, yet it occurs in *Les Muses, Les Fêtes vénitiennes, Les Fêtes de Thalie,* and *Les Fêtes de l'été.* Here, Campra, Mouret, and Montéclair have given greater dramatic focus to a device already introduced by Lully in certain of his *tragédies en musiques* (see, for example, Venus's air "Revenez, revenez, Amours revenez" from the prologue to *Thésée*). Typical is a phrase in scene ii from "L'Amour saltimbanque" (*Les Fêtes vénitiennes*) that is first heard in the prelude (Example 10-2a). It recurs in the main theme of Nérine's air, "Songez, songez" (Example 10-2b). Nérine, the confidante of a young Venetian woman, Léonore, tries to poison her mistress's mind against all lovers. The phrase from the prelude returns twice more—always with the same accompaniment that was heard in Nérine's air. It comes back in the recitative following her air (Example 10-2c), and it interrupts the recitative of Léonore to close the scene (Example 10-2d).

Example 10-2. Campra: Thematic recurrences in "L'Amour saltimbanque," *Les Fêtes vénitiennes* (after ed. of 1711). (a) Prelude. (b) Air. (c, d) Recitative.

One of the best examples of the reappearance of an instrumental fragment or an entire instrumental extract for dramatic purposes is found in scenes iii and iv of "Les Devins de la Place St Marc" (*Les Fêtes vénitiennes*). The *ritournelle* that begins scene iii is presented only in fragments, each fragment interrupted by recitatives. The entire composition, with its fragments connected, becomes the "Marche" that is the entrance music for scene iv. Campra used this same procedure later on in the attractive horoscope scene, which must have influenced Mouret who used the same tool and closely related melodic material for Thalie's entrance music in the prologue to *Les Fêtes de Thalie*.

The increased power of musician over poet shows up in the monologues and Italianate *ariettes* of the *opéra-ballet*. Undoubtedly, the general, nondramatic subject matter and the lack of continuous plot encouraged the creation of these purely decorative yet often musically sophisticated airs.

Italian influence may be seen not only in the increased use of vocal melismas, repeated texts, and concerto-like driving rhythms, but even in the use of the cantata itself as an organizational medium. Thus, the *divertissement* of "Les Devins de la Place Saint Marc" (*Les Fêtes vénitiennes*) was carefully built around what Campra labeled a *cantate*.[10] Campra's cantata is a nice synthesis of Italian aria da capo and French recitative and dance. He organized the components in a large diptych: Recitative / *Ariette* / Dance | | Recitative / *Ariette* / Dance. In each half, the *ariette* forms the basis for the dance that follows. Campra framed the entire cantata with two other dances: the first relates the *divertissement* to the action of the previous scene, the second links the *divertissement* to the scene that comes next. This helps unify the entire *entrée* musically and dramatically.

The *divertissement* of songs and dances is of central importance in the structure of the *opéra-ballet*. Every *entrée* was designed to build toward its *divertissement*. That each *entrée* has its own set of characters helps bring about a measure of contrast between *divertissements*.

The *divertissement* of the *préramiste* period's *opéra-ballet* and *tragédie lyrique* is a repository of the most popular dance types of the early eighteenth century. Sometimes with ennui, often with brilliance, it offers to later generations a summary of the dances that formed an integral part of the operatic milieu following Lully. The forlana, contredanse, and musette, although certainly known in the seventeenth century, were not in general use on the operatic stage until this period, when they joined the dances by Lully discussed in Chapter 8. In *L'Europe galante* (1697), Campra was the first to make use of the forlana, a dance from northern Italy that may be thought of as a fast loure. The contredanse made its debut the same year in the lyric comedy *Aricie* by La Coste, three years before Feuillet included it in his *Recueil de dances, composées par M. Feuillet* (Paris, 1700). This lively dance of English origin is often in compound duple meter and, like the bourrée, it begins on the second beat of the measure. We learn from Rousseau's *Dictionnaire* that the contredanse was a ballroom dance for "four, six, or eight people" (1768, 122). Perhaps the involvement of so many dancers made it a natural choice for a finale. It often concluded a final *divertissement* (see, for example, the contredanse from *Les Fêtes vénitiennes* by Campra).

The musette, a French bagpipe, had been a popular folk instrument throughout the seventeenth century. The first tutor dates from 1672 (Borjon de Scellery, *Traité de la musette*). In the late seventeenth century the name of the instrument became the name of the dance that simulated the sound of the bagpipe's drone. This dance appears to have been first used onstage in Lully's *Alceste* of 1678, where it is called for in the *livret* (prologue, scene iv). It appears in the score to Campra's *opéra-ballet Les Muses* (1703 *entrée* "La Pastorale").

In stage music of this period, the number of dances that bear choreographic or descriptive titles or are simply called *airs* staggers the imagination. There are 123 dances in the four *opéras-ballets* by Campra! One can only wonder how this plethora of dances was used. Were they all grouped indiscriminately in the *divertissements* as decorative entertainment or was some attempt made to relate them to the dramatic action?

Simply stated, dance functioned in two ways in the *opéra-ballet* as it did in the *tragédie lyrique*: as a decorative *agrément* with no discernible relationship to the action; and as a valid dramatic agent either to expedite the action or to lend some emphasis to a salient feature of the scene. Faced with an audience primarily interested in light diversion, the *préramiste* composer stressed dance as *agrément*. As Cahusac pointed out with some irritation, "La Motte only knew the simple Dance . . . . There are only *divertissements* in which one dances just to dance" (1754, 3:153).

Sometimes, however, the dance as *agrément* and the dance as dramatic agent converge in a manner not usually associated with the *opéra-ballet*. The dramatic action of the third *entrée* of *L'Europe galante* ("L'Italie") focuses on the *divertissement* during which the identity of the secret suitor of Olimpia is revealed to his jealous rival, Octavio.

The dance underscores a prevailing mood in several first-period *opéras-ballets*. In scene i of the prologue to Mouret's *Les Fêtes de Thalie*, the "Air des Suivants de Melpomène" emphasizes the severe dignity of the tragic muse. Example 10-3a below shows the typical dotted rhythms and upbeat tirades borrowed from the *tragédie lyrique*. Example 10-3b shows an extract from the dance associated with Thalie. This dance, which appears in its entirety in scene v, is introduced in fragments in scene ii and offers the greatest possible contrast to the stern measures of Melpomène's dance.

Example 10-3. Mouret: Extracts from Prologue to *Les Fêtes de Thalie* (after 1714 ed.). (a) Melpomène. (b) Thalie.

Campra's dances bear out Wilfrid Mellers's observation that he was "perhaps the most enchanting of dance composers" (1950, 78). Witness the gestic directness of his minuets with their strong rhythms and triadic melodies that almost suggest Haydn. Witness the unbuttoned humor of his rigaudons with their unabashed parallel fifths reflecting, perhaps, the rustic dances of his meridional homeland. Witness the kinetic energy of his contredanses and forlanas with an extra measure thrown in here and there to break up symmetrical phrase grouping.

The *opéra-ballet* after *L'Europe galante* became a kind of *pièce d'occasion* directed toward the specific taste of a specific audience. It is to the credit of Campra, Mouret, Montéclair, and Destouches that although totally committed to this aesthetic, they were able to transcend the limited, superficial pleasures of the Duc d'Orléans and his entourage. These are minor masters, poets in miniature who, at their best, like Watteau, created a world half real, half fantasy in the first period of *opéra-ballet.*

Chapter 11

From Divertissement to Opéra Comique

Divertissement

*N*o single definition of a *divertissement* is possible within the context of the seventeenth and early eighteenth centuries. As we have noted, one use of the term refers to the portion of a *tragédie en musique* or *opéra-ballet* that is composed primarily of songs and dances. For a period that could scarcely claim consistency of terminology as a virtue, it is amusing to find some authors insisting with semantic righteousness that *divertissement* be reserved for the *opéra-ballet* whereas *fête* be employed for the *tragédie en musique* (see Compan 1787, 154). *Divertissements* were also found in productions of the Fair Theaters, parodies, *opéras comiques*, and between the acts of pastorales. They were often closely aligned with the action in spoken drama, whether within or between the acts, where they were sometimes labeled *intermèdes*. Delalande, Campra, Charpentier, Collasse, Desmarest, Clérambault, Oudot, Royer, and de Blainville composed *divertissements* for insertion between the acts of Latin tragedies performed at the Jesuit college Louis-le-Grand.

Once we have left the stage, we must abandon any effort to classify *divertissements* by type. A simple pastorale could be labeled a *divertissement*, and an entire week's or even month's entertainment of which the pastorale was but one modest part could be labeled collectively a *divertissement*; a chamber cantata might be subtitled "*Divertissement*," and all six volumes of the music composed by Mouret for the Nouveau Théâtre Italien are grouped generically under the term *Divertissements*.

During the height of the *grand siècle*, Louis XIV ordered so-called *grands divertissements* in 1664, 1668, and 1674 (see Isherwood 1973, 265–280). These *divertissements* commemorated welcome events such as victories and royal births, or merely satisfied a yen on the part of king to parade his affluence. They were a natural outgrowth of the elaborate type of court ballet traditionally presented during the carnival season.

The pages of André Félibien's *Relation de la Feste de Versailles* (1668) and his *Les Divertissemens de Versailles* (1674, 4 with engravings by Chauveau) bring to life as do no other sources the extravagant pomp thought appropriate for the court of the *Roi Soleil*. The preparation of a court *divertissement* was as tightly organized and hierarchal as the production of a court ballet. For the *Divertissement* of 18 July 1668, we read that the Duc de Créqui, as First Gentleman of the Chamber, was charged with everything concerning the comedy; Maréchal de Bellefond, as First Minister of the Hôtel du Roi, took charge of the food; even the great Colbert was responsible, as Superintendent of Buildings, for decorations, outdoor platforms, and preparation for the fireworks; Vigarani was instructed to build a theater for the comedy; and Le Vau, the king's First Architect, was to erect another large edifice for the Court Ball.

That men of this caliber, trained in the arts of fortification, architecture, or government, should at the same time be pressed almost whimsically into service to supervise and build the trappings and symbols of a king's pleasure, should come as no surprise. The progenitors of the Versailles *divertissements* are found in the elaborate *fêtes* of Renaissance Italy and may be traced back to the courts of the Dukes of Burgundy.

According to Félibien, Louis XIV had chosen well:

> *One of the things one ought to admire in the* Fêtes *and* Divertissements *with which the King entertains his Court is the promptitude that accompanies their magnificence: because his orders are executed with so much diligence in the care taken in their application, particularly on the part of those in direct command, everyone believes it could all happen only by a miracle. How surprised we are to see a Theater erected in a moment without our having even been aware of it, glades decorated and embellished with fountains and statues, refreshments ready for the eating and a thousand other things that seem possible only with a long period of time and the bother of an infinite number of workers (1674,4).*

Félibien described the outdoor tables groaning with food—conspicuous consumption at its worst:

> *One of the tables represented a mountain, where within the various caves one might find diverse sorts of cold meats; another was a façade*

of a Palace built with marzipans and other sweet doughs . . . . In the center of these tables was a fountain, the water reaching more than thirty feet in height, the sound of which was very agreeable . . . . After their Majesties had spent some time in this charming place and after the Ladies had refreshed themselves, the King abandoned the Tables to pillage by the people who followed; the destruction of such beautiful arrangements served also as an agreeable divertissement *for the entire Court in the eagerness and confusion of those who demolished the pastry palace and the mountains of preserves (1668, ed. of 1679, 7–11).*

Versailles, 1668, or Las Vegas, 1968? The *divertissement* given by the king for all his court after the triumphant return from the Franche-Comté campaign (1674) lasted from 4 July to 31 August! Included in the *divertissement* were Lully's *Alceste* (4 July), Molière's *L'Églogue de Versailles* (11 July) and *Le Malade imaginaire* (19 July), Lully's *Les Festes de l'Amour et de Bacchus* (28 July), and the inevitable fireworks over the Grand Canal. Félibien was silent concerning the entertainment of the last day (31 August) except to mention that the insatiable king wanted to be shown "beauties to be seen that had never yet been viewed" (1674, 27).

Félibien's account of the performances of *Les Festes de l'Amour et de Bacchus* demonstrates once again that Lully's conception of the ballet as a *danse en action* came long before Mouret and La Motte's creations for the Duchesse du Maine (see below) and long before Cahusac introduced it into the operas of Rameau:

One can say that in this work, Lully has found the secret to satisfy and to charm everyone . . . . If one observes the dances, there is not a step that does not give the sign of the plot that the dancers must dance, and not a step whose gestures be not as good as words to make themselves understood (1668, ed. of 1679, 22).

Félibien's poetic description of a nocturnal *fête* on the Grand Canal strangely evokes the language and imagery of a *Fête galante* by Paul Verlaine:

The King followed by all his Court embarked on the great expanse of water where, in the deep of night, one heard the violins that followed the Vessel of His Majesty. The sound of these instruments seemed to give life to all the statues whose dim lighting also lent a certain grace to the symphonie, *which it would in no way have had in total darkness . . . . These great expanses of water, lit only here and there by so many luminous statues, resembled long galleries and large* salons *enriched & adorned with Architecture & statues of an artifice & beauty unknown until now (1674, 109–110).*

The elaborate court *divertissements* described above suffered an eclipse as the reign of Louis XIV entered its long decline. The shift from month-long *divertissements* of the 1660s and 1670s to a series of playful, court masquerades anticipated the shift from the *tragédie en musique* to the *opéra-ballet* in the period between Lully and Rameau. The *Mercure galant* of March 1688 relates the genesis and fall of the court *divertissement* in a few short pages (25–28) and in so doing gives us a capsule history of the stage music of the *grand siècle*:

> *The custom formerly at the Court was to have a* grand divertissement *that lasted throughout carnival season. This was usually a grand* Ballet en machines, *mixed with vocal solos all relating to some subject such as the* Ballet des Arts, *the* Ballet de la Nuit . . . . *Then, the famous Molière introduced Comedies mixed with dances and vocal solos. These divertissements still please more than ever did the Ballets. Operas succeeded these kinds of Comedies; I am not speaking of those spectacles, they are presently à la mode . . . . However, for some years, the Court has not presented these* divertissements *during carnival season; this is not to save expense, but because it found that the same diversion for a month was too uniform a pleasure. Thus, in place of these Operas, [the court] had diverse, little Masquerades, which scarcely cost less but whose diversity . . . made them more touching and more agreeable. This is what they have done for the last three or four years.*

As entertaining shifted its center of gravity from the court at Versailles to Parisian townhouses or country chateaux, financial support shifted from the king to noblemen and even wealthy middle-class gentlemen, who became patrons of *divertissements*.

Pastoral, mythological, and allegorical themes dominated most *divertissements*. The stag hunt was also favorite subject matter. *La Chasse du Cerf*, a *divertissement* in seven scenes performed before the king at Fontainebleau on 25 August 1708 with music by Jean-Baptiste Morin, was published by Ballard in 1709. The *Avis*, as is so often the case, tells us much about the practical considerations of achieving maximum results from minimal means:

> *No matter how fast and light, the execution is very easy; I have reduced everything to a simple Trio with a violin part to be doubled*

as much as one can. This is a group easy to assemble in any country; the Singing Roles are composed in such a manner that Dessus, Haute-contre, *or* Haute-taille, *which are the most common voices, can sing them. I have marked the places where the hunting horn or trumpet may play; but since these instruments are rarely in concert groups, oboes or violins do just as well. I have used the hunting calls and trumpet fanfares most often heard during a stag hunt and have interwoven them among the Choruses.*

The magnificent chateau at Sceaux built by Claude Perrault and acquired by Louis-August de Bourbon, the Duc du Maine, was the scene in the closing years of Louis XIV's reign of a series of *divertissements* known as the *Grandes Nuits de Sceaux.* Anne-Louise-Bénédicte de Bourbon, the Duchesse du Maine, who had taken up residence at the chateau in 1700, surrounded herself with a *pléiade* of well-known musicians and poets. Writing in 1712 two years before the *Grandes Nuits*, Abbé Charles-Claude Genest described her *divertissements* that had begun as early as 1702 as "pure amusement, unrehearsed . . . a type of impromptu entertainment appropriate only for the occasion" (preface to *Les Divertissemens de Sceaux*). We are told that these playful charades were devised by and for the Duchesse to help endure insomnia. At the same time, some productions were rather ambitious, such as the three short operas composed by Jean-Baptiste Matho (music lost) and performed by several of the best of the king's musicians and dancers. Genest left us a description in *Les Divertissements de Sceaux* (230) of the outdoor theater, which had seating arrangements for three hundred spectators under a tent.

The famous *Grandes Nuits* were on a much more lavish scale. The most important of these took place during sixteen evenings between 31 July 1714 and 15 May 1715. The music for the *Grandes Nuits* was provided by well-known composers: Mouret, Bernier, Colin de Blamont, and Philippe Courbois. It is difficult to ascertain the program for each of the sixteen *Grandes Nuits*. Lyric comedies, plays, dramatic *divertissements, ballets en action*, even cantatas were performed in an enchanting garden setting designed by Le Nôtre. For the thirteenth night, Mouret and Néricault-Destouches's lyric comedy *Les Amours de Ragonde* was performed: and on the fourteenth night with the help of two of the best dancers of the Paris Opera (Le Sieur Balon and Mlle Prévost), Mouret and La Motte presented a pantomime, a true *ballet en action* based on the murder of Camille by Horace in the fourth act of Corneille's *Horace*.

Nicolas Bernier's fifth book of French cantatas was dedicated to the Duchesse du Maine. Significantly, its title page reads: *Les Nuits de Sceaux // Concerts de chambre // ou Cantates françoises // à plusieurs voix // En manière de divertissements // meslez d'airs de violon et autres symphonies //.*

The cantatas of the collection are linked to stage music. They include independent instrumental music such as overtures, dances, and a *sommeil*; they have vocal airs, ensembles, recitatives, and one (*L'Aurore*) ends with a large chorus. It is conceivable that as part of the *Grandes Nuits*, these cantatas may actually have been staged "in the manner of *divertissements.*"

Lyric Comedy

The six lyric comedies of the *préramiste* period were generally classified along with *opéra-ballet* under the single rubric, *Ballet*. The Parfaict brothers were the first to employ the term *comédie lyrique* to describe a work like *Les Amours de Ragonde* by Mouret. Lyric comedies treat their subjects in a comic or, more often, romantic vein. Like *opéra-ballet*, they make use of contemporary characters; but unlike *opéra-ballet*, they all have one continuous plot.

Campra's lyric comedy *Le Carnaval de Venise* (1699) may be seen as a study for his later *opéra-ballet*, *Les Fêtes vénitiennes* (1710). One need not be taken in by the title page of the Ballard 1699 edition that asserts that the music of *Le Carnaval de Venise* is by "M. Campra le Cadet." André Campra at the time was *Maître de Musique* at Notre-Dame cathedral. Given the repressive climate at court, it is easy to see why he tried to mask his success as a stage composer and pass off his secular works as compositions by his younger brother Joseph, a violinist in the Opera orchestra.[1]

Both *Le Carnaval de Venise* and *Les Fêtes vénitiennes* have "La Place Saint-Marc" as a setting, and in both operas Campra used the device of a play within a play. In *Le Carnaval de Venise*, the play within a play is a one-act Italian opera, *Orfeo nell'inferni* at the end of Act III. *Le Carnaval de Venise* also contains a strikingly original *divertissement* (Act III, scene iv) that celebrates the victory of the "Castellans" over their rival street gang, the "Nicoletti."

The most important lyric comedy is undeniably Rameau's *Platée* (1745), which was characterized by Grimm in his *Lettre sur Omphale* (1752) as the "sublime work in a genre which M. Rameau created in France [sic]." Six other lyric comedies besides *Le Carnaval de Venise* were performed before *Platée*: *Aricie* of 1697 (Louis de La Coste and Abbé Pic), *Les Fêtes galantes* of 1698 (Desmarest and Duché), *Le Carnaval et la Folie* of 1703 (Destouches and La Motte), *La Vénitienne* of 1705 (La Barre and La Motte), *Les Amours de Ragonde* of 1714 (Mouret and Néricault-Destouches), and *Don Quichotte chez la duchesse* of 1743 (Joseph Bodin de Boismortier and Charles-Simon Favart).[2]

Of these works, the most significant musically is Mouret's *Les Amours de Ragonde* created for the *Nuits de Sceaux* in 1714 and not performed at the Paris Opera until 1742 in a presumably revised version (only the *livret* of the 1714 edition is extant). Although a genuine lyric comedy, and so labeled by the Parfaicts, it was called a *"comédie-ballet"* in the score, a *"comédie en musique"* in the Ballard *livret* of 1742, and a *"divertissement comique"* by François Auguste Paradis de Moncrif in his *Approbation* (at the end of the same *livret*)—all of which shows the loose terminology of the time.

Musically, *Les Amours de Ragonde* is a charming, though slight score. In eliminating the nonessential prologue, it antedates Rameau's *Zoroastre* by thirty-five years. In its use of a concluding *vaudeville* and popular tunes, it owes much to the music of the contemporary Fair Theaters. One such melody in which each of three characters sings a different story is reproduced in Example 11-1.

Example 11-1. Mouret: Extract from *vaudeville* Les Amours de Ragonde (after ed. "chez la veuve Mouret," n.d.).

Opéra Comique[3]

Both the *tragédie lyrique* and the *opéra comique* in France are indebted to imports from across the Alps. Italian operas mounted in Paris during the time of Mazarin demonstrated that the French would accept a spectacle with continuous music, albeit with many modifications. At the same time, songs and dances never lost their appeal as incidental music in spoken comedies. The popularity of the Molière-Lully *comédie-ballet* has already been discussed. Even more in demand were the Italian comedians who, with Scaramouche at their head, appeared at the Palais Royal in 1660 and soon became a permanent troupe sharing the hall with Molière. From the pay scale it is quite obvious that the king favored the Italians; Scaramouche's troupe received sixteen thousand *livres* annually in contrast to the six thousand allotted Molière and the twelve thousand for the home of French tragedy, the Hôtel de Bourgogne.

The repertory of the Ancien Théâtre Italien from 1682 to 1687 is preserved in the six-volume *Recueil général de toutes les comédies et scènes françoises jouées par les comédiens italiens du roy* published in 1700 by Evaristo Gherardi. The author's informative preface reveals that the Italian comedians as in the old *commedia dell'arte* "learn nothing by heart, and that to play a Comedy, it suffices to have read the plot out-line *["sujet"]* a moment before going on stage."

French scenes, apparently written by several hands, were woven with the Italian and gradually replaced the latter. In the later volumes of the collection, music is much more important, even though, due to Lully's monopoly, the performers were restricted for several years to six instrumentalists, two singers, and two dancers. Out of the fifty-five plays found in Gherardi's *Recueil*, forty-three use music extensively.

The music of the Italian Comedy was of three types: *vaudevilles*, parodies of operas, and original compositions. A *vaudeville* was any song whose melody had long since passed into public domain. It was identified by a title called a *timbre*, which was usually based on the first line of the refrain or first couplet by which the original tune was gen-erally known. The entire melody of the song, tagged by this *timbre*, was known as a *fredon*. The tunes were folk-like, with repeated, simple rhythmic patterns and a narrow melodic range; they were popularly called "Pont Neuf tunes" after the famous bridge over the Seine, which, because of its great width, was a favorite meeting-place for local minstrels. Any tune that caught the public's fancy was a likely candidate for the growing stockpile of *fredons*. Many of the simpler tunes from Lully's operas, such as "Dans ces lieux tout rit sans cesse" from *Phaëton*, lived on far into the eighteenth century as *fredons*.

The Italian Comedy by no means originated the *vaudeville*. The first use of the term goes far back into the early years of the sixteenth century. It was known by such terms as *voix de ville*, *vau de ville* and *vau de vire*, and it became one of the principal antecedents of the court air. There is no compelling evidence for the statement found in many eighteenth-century sources that a certain Olivier Basselin, a fuller from Vaudevire in Normandy, invented the *vaudeville*.

The definition by Mersenne in the "Livre second du chants" in his *Harmonie universelle* is typical: "The *chanson* that we call *vaudeville* is the simplest of all Airs that adapts to any kind of Poetry and that is sung note-against-note" (1636; rpt. 1965, 2:164). Along with the *ari-ette* and *villanelle*, *vaudeville* exemplified the "natural style" for Brossard "that everyone can sing, almost without art" (1703). It was summed up by Boileau in his *L'Art poétique* of 1674 as follows:

D'un trait de ce poème, en bon mots si fertile,
Le Français, né malin, forma le Vaudeville,
Agréable, indiscret qui, conduit par le chant,
Passe de bouche en bouche, et s'accroit en marchant.

From a line of this poem, in good words so fertile,
The Frenchman, born wicked, formed the Vaudeville,

Agreeable, indiscreet, carried by song.
From mouth to mouth, grows as it passes along.

In the Ancien Théâtre Italien, *chansons*, noels, *brunettes*, dances, and, above all, opera airs were used as *timbres*. *Fredons* stemming from these sources became *vaudevilles*. The opera airs were parodied as well. Naturally, the operas of Lully and Quinault were a primary source far into the eighteenth century. Certain scenes, already popular in their original versions, were great favorites. Although clichéd themes (such as the conflict between love and glory) and the general pomposity of *tragédies en musique* made them ideal targets for satire, the parodies themselves underscored the popularity of the originals. Not only were the texts and music parodied, but the best-known performers of the Opera were mimicked as well.

After having enjoyed many years of success in the healthy art of parody, the Ancien Théâtre Italien overstepped the bounds of decorum on 8 January 1696 when it produced a satire called *La Fausse prude*, a thinly disguised attack on Mme de Maintenon, who was already over-sensitive. The king closed the Italian Comedy sixteen months later on 13 May 1697 and expelled the players from the realm. They were gone for nearly twenty years to return only under the more tolerant and relaxed atmosphere of the Regency as the Nouveau Théâtre Italien.

The vacuum created by their departure was rapidly filled by the Fair Theaters (Théâtres de la Foire), which took over the repertory of the Italian Comedy and continued the Italians' tradition of satire and parody against seemingly insurmountable odds, for now they were in direct competition with the French Comedy. The two important fairs, La Foire Saint-Germain and La Foire Saint-Laurent, had been the scene of popular farces and acrobatic displays since the Middle Ages. The Foire Saint-Germain began early in February and continued until Palm Sunday; the Foire Saint-Laurent played from July until the end of September. Paul Scarron's description of La Foire Saint-Germain in 1643 (88) gives us the confusion of jostling mobs, the air punctuated by shrill voices of hawkers and sounds of music. He documented the wide use of musical instruments in the days before Lully's restrictive ordinances:

Le bruit des pénétrants sifflets,
Des flustes & des flageolets,
Des cornets, haultbois & musettes,
Des vendeurs & des achepteurs,
Se mesle à celui des sauteurs

Et des tabourins à sonnettes,
Des joueurs de Marionnettes
Que le peuple tient pour enchanteurs.

The noise of penetrating whistles,
Of flutes and of flageolets,
Of cornetts, oboes & musettes
Of vendors and of buyers,
Mingle themselves with that of tumblers,
And of tambourines,
Of Marionetteers
Whom the people take for magicians.

The impresarios of the first Fair Theaters were themselves often acrobats or tight-rope walkers. In fact, the important theater of the Foire Saint-Germain was under the direction of two tumblers, Claude and Pierre Alard in 1678.

Among the important playwrights for the Fair Theaters were Alain Le Sage, d'Orneval, and Fuzelier, who from 1724 to 1737 collaborated in publishing a collection of ten volumes of plays including musical extracts (*Théâtre de la Foire ou l'opéra comique*). Let Le Sage's preface sum up the genealogy of the *opéra comique* and review the frustrations in the Fair Theatres' struggle to stay alive:

The Fair Theater began with the farces that the tight-rope dancers would mix with their feats. Following this, we presented fragments from the old Italian Plays. The French comedians, however, forced us to stop these performances . . . & obtained Interdictions that prohibited the Fair Actors from giving any comedy by Monologue or by Dialogue. The Fair Performers, not being able to speak, resorted to writing, that is, each Actor had his text written in large letters on placards that he showed to the Spectators. These inscriptions first appeared in prose [in 1710]. Later, they were set to tunes that the Orchestra played and the audience accustomed itself to sing. But, since the Placards [Écriteaux"] encumbered the Stage, the Actors were audacious enough to lower them from waist height . . . . The Fair Actors, seeing that the audience took pleasure in this Spectacle in song imagined with reason that, if the Fair Actors themselves sang the vaudevilles, *it would be even more pleasing. They entered into an agreement with the Opera which, by virtue of its patents, accorded them permission to sing [December 1714]. We immediately began to compose plays purely in* vaudeville; *and the*

Spectacle then took the name of Opéra Comique *[term first used on the publicity posters of 1715]. Little by little, we mingled prose with the verses . . . . So that imperceptibly, the Plays became mixed. They were so when the* Opéra Comique *finally succumbed under the blows of its enemies.*

The first work to bear the title *ópera comique* was Le Sage's *Télémaque* (1715), a parody of Destouches's opera. We learn from the pages of the *Mercure* (July 1715) that the new *opéra comique*, a mixed genre of sung *vaudeville* and prose dialogue, had a popular success that could only bring about retaliatory action from its powerful, jealous rivals: "On this same day [25 July 1715, opening of La Foire Saint-Laurent], the Comédie and the Opera were deserted."

A troupe of Italian players under the direction of Luigi Riccoboni was summoned to Paris by the Regent in 1716. They were known as the Nouveau Théâtre Italien and took up residence in the Hôtel de Bourgogne in the Marais. When in 1719, the Comédie Française suppressed all performances at the Fair Theatres with the exception of tight-rope dancers and marionetteers, the Nouveau Théâtre Italien took advantage of this new repression and filled the gap at La Foire Saint-Laurent with regular performances from 1721 to 1723.

In spite of these vicissitudes, the Opéra Comique managed to survive and even to expand. Its director from 1743 to 1744 and from 1752 to 1757 was Jean Monnet, who had a theater built at the Foire Saint-Laurent. He hired a first class literary talent, Charles-Simon Favart, who brought the genre to its highest point of development from literary and musical points of view.

The subject matter of the *opéra comique* and the new Italian comedy was based on the crude realities of daily life, upon opera parodies, and, especially after 1717, upon the conflicts between the two comedy theaters and the tribulations of the Fair Theatres. In *La Désolation des deux Comédies* (1718) by Riccoboni and Dominique, the character, "Opéra," communicates only by singing; "Opéra Comique," by means of *vaudevilles*; and "Comédie Française," in verses declaimed in Alexandrine couplets. *Funérailles de la Foire* (1718) parodies the well-known "Alceste est morte" from the funeral ceremony in *Alceste* (Act III, scene iv, see Chapter 7) by substituting the words *La Foire* for the word *Alceste* (see Example 11-2). The play was so successful that it was performed at the Palais Royal before the Regent, who, according to the Parfaict brothers, commented that the *opéra comique* resembled a swan "who never sings so melodiously as when he is about to die" (1743, 1:215).

La Foire est mor— te

La Foire est mor — te

Example 11-2. *Alceste* parody from *Funérailles de la Foire* (after Le Sage, Vol. 3).

It would be foolish to claim for the *opéra comique*, before the days of Egidio Romualdo Duni, François-André Danican Philidor, and Pierre-Alexandre Monsigny, musical importance comparable to that of the earlier *comédie-ballet* or the *opéra-ballet* of the *préramiste* period. The plays in the ten volumes of Le Sage's *Le Théâtre de la Foire ou l'opéra comique* lean heavily on the system of *vaudevilles* taken over from the Ancien Théâtre Italien, although descriptive *symphonies*, dances, overtures, and *vaudeville* finales became common in the later plays of the collection. There are more than fifteen hundred tunes reproduced in *Le Théâtre de la Foire ou l'opéra comique*. Eleven hundred of them served as *vaudevilles*.

Le Sage and above all Favart were very skillful in choosing among the vast stockpile of *vaudeville* tunes. A specific *fredon* was often used in the same situation from one play to the next and functioned somewhat as a primitive leitmotif. Speaking of Favart's gift for *fredon* selection, Auguste Font noted:

> *These* vaudevilles *translate with minute exactitude successive degrees of the same sentiment and the most rapid, minute shifts within one action. Thus, the sleep of a shepherdess and the pursuit of a kiss could scarcely be rendered with such delicate truth by newly composed music (1894, 240).*

Some airs from contemporary *tragédies lyriques* or *opéras-ballets* were rapidly absorbed into the *opéra comique* as *fredons*, each with its own *timbre*. The rondeau air from the end of the second *entrée* of Mouret's *Les Fêtes de Thalie*, for example, was a popular *fredon* for more than forty years. Example 11-3a–e below shows its first use (in 1714 in Mouret's *opéra-ballet*) and selected later appearances up through Gluck's *opéra comique Le Diable à quatre* of 1756.

Example 11-3. (a) *Les Fêtes de Thalie* (1714). (b) *Arlequin traitant* (1716). (c) *L'École des Amans* (1716). (d) *La Querelle des théâtres* (1718). (e) *Le Diable à quatre* (1756).

The Opéra Comique used originally composed tunes more and more. These were labeled *ariettes* to distinguish them from the pre-existent *fredons*. Although Favart encouraged the composition of new music, The Parfaict brothers spoke for many when they wrote:

> No matter how agreeable Music composed expressly [for a play] may be, it is impossible to consider it the equivalent of Vaudevilles whose words are known by all . . . and . . . consecrated by usage, . . . explain to the Spectator what the Actor is trying to convey by gesture—even as to his innermost thoughts (1756, 6:71).

Among, the composers of *ariettes* and dances for the Opéra Comique were Jean-Claude Gillier (1667–1737), Jacques Aubert (1689–1753), and the great Rameau himself. Collaborating with librettist Alexis Piron, Rameau apparently composed four works for the Fair Theater (most of this music has disappeared): *L'Endriague* (1723), *L'Enrôlement d'Arlequin* (1726), *La P[ucelle] ou la Rose* (1726), and *La Robe de dissension ou le faux prodigue* (1726).[4]

Although forced by Lully to restrict their musical forces to "two singers and six instrumentalists," the successors of Molière gave music a role in the plays they produced at the Comédie Française. Among the composers who provided vocal and instrumental airs were

Charpentier, the brothers Pierre and Jean-Claude Gillier, Mouret, and Jean-Baptiste Maurice Quinault (see Schneider 1994, 176).

From 1717 until his death, Jean-Joseph Mouret (1682–1738) was the most important composer attached to the Nouveau Théâtre Italien. His active collaboration with the Italians began in 1718 with the French comedy *Le Naufrage au port à l'anglais,* which was also the first French language comedy to be performed on the stage of the Nouveau Théâtre Italien. The success of this production convinced the director Luigi Riccoboni that only works performed in French with occasional Italian scenes would succeed. Six volumes of *Divertissements du Nouveau Théâtre Italien* collect all the "simphonies, accompagnemens, airs de violons et de flûtes, hautbois, de musettes, airs italiens" composed by Mouret for that theater. The 142 *divertissements* found in this work attest to the industry of the "*musicien des grâces.*"

It is fitting to close this chapter with Example 11-4, an extract from *Le Procès des Théâtres* (1718), text by Riccoboni and Dominique, in which Mouret cleverly characterizes the quarrelsome protagonists in the battle for supremacy in the theatrical world in a manner reminiscent of the prologue to *Les Fêtes de Thalie.* Here, the musical fragments assigned to each theater are but six or eight measures long and elide almost imperceptibly with one another.

Example 11-4. Mouret: Fragments from *Le Procès des Théâtres.*

Part Two

Religious Music

☞ *Chapter 12* ☜

From Du Caurroy to Du Mont

*A*ny study of sacred polyphony in France from the death of
Eustache Du Caurroy (1609) to the death of Cardinal Mazarin (1661)
and the beginning of the personal rule of Louis XIV[1] is plagued by an
appaling lack of primary sources. The modern scholar is placed in the
frustrating position of being able to document, through seventeenth-
century accounts, the existence of an impressive amount of religious
music from this period and yet, because of a staggering mortality rate,
being unable to have direct contact with the music itself. Implicated in
this sad state of affairs is the Ballard family's printing monopoly.
Pierre and his son Robert Ballard were more interested in printing
musical settings of psalms, in the fashionable paraphrases by Antoine
Godeau and Philippe Desportes, and the many religious parodies of
airs de cour than they were in printing Masses or motets.

Where are the three Masses by Du Caurroy described by
Mersenne? What has happened to the Cambrai Masses and motets for
double choir composed between 1612 and 1647 by Valérien Gonet, J.
Solon, or Antoine Penne? Only the music for one choir is extant.
Where are the Masses *"avec symphonies"* that Jehan Titelouze performed in the Cathedral of Rouen in 1632 and the motets of Cambert
mentioned by Robinet and Loret? And the late motets by Moulinié?
Where are the motets by Jean Mignon that La Borde informs us were
"judged excellent"? Because not one note of music by Eustache Picot
survives, we are at a loss to know whether or not he carried on some of
the innovations of Nicolas Formé, whom he succeeded in 1638 at the
Sainte-Chapelle. Where and what are the *"Antiennes récitatives"* for
two voices and continuo by Thomas Gobert that he mentioned in his
1646 correspondence with Constantin Huygens? Do the dialogues
between solo and chorus in the motets of Guillaume Bouzignac reflect
the assimilative power of one man exposed to Roman and Catalan

church music, or was Bouzignac the leader of a provincial school whose existence was ignored by the Ballards in Paris?

Based on a study of the extant music, it is clear that the conflict between the religious *stile antico* and *stile moderno*, which took place in Italy soon after the turn of the century, was slow to materialize in France. French composers writing for the church in the first fifty years of the seventeenth century were conservative as a group.

Much of the extant music by Eustache Du Caurroy (1549–1609), praised by Mersenne for its "impressive harmony and rich counterpoint" (1636; rpt. 1965, 3:61), is in the tradition of the international Franco-Netherlands school. Many of the twenty-three motets (from *a*4 to *a*7) found in Book I of Du Caurroy's *Preces ecclesiasticae* (1609) call for equal-voiced double choruses that dialogue and then unite from time to time. Du Caurroy tended to develop each choir in the high Renaissance tradition, treating text phrases in imitative counterpoint. In the *Victimae paschali* (Book II of *Preces ecclesiasticae* found in the *Anthologie du motet latin polyphonique en France [1609–1661]* edited by Denise Launay 1963, 22–27) there are two choirs: one made up of soprano, *haute-contre*, tenor, and bass; the other of soprano, *haute-contre*, and tenor. They come together at the conclusion in seven independent parts of real Netherlandish polyphony that may have stimulated Mersenne's comment: "All the composers of France take him [Du Caurroy] for their master" (1636; rpt. 1965, 3:61). Du Caurroy's *a*5 *Missa pro defunctis*[2] was printed by Ballard in 1636 (privilege date) and performed at the funeral of Henry IV, who was assassinated in 1610. Its performance became a traditional part of the obsequies of kings and princes. Brossard tells us that this custom remained in effect at Saint-Denis in the eighteenth century (1724; 1725–1730, 12).

It is quite likely that double choruses were still somewhat of a novelty in France at the time of Du Caurroy. Specific sources of information on the *concertato* use of a *grand choeur* and a *petit choeur* come from a later time—nearly mid-century. Thomas Gobert differentiated the two groups in a letter to Constantin Huygens dated 17 October 1646: "The *grand choeur*, which is *a*5, is always sung by many voices. The *petit choeur* is composed only of solo voices" (cited in Jonckbloet and Land 1882, ccxvii). The archaic, equal-voiced form of double chorus and the *concertato* treatment of double chorus co-existed as late as 1670. René Ouvrard, *Maître des Enfants* at the Sainte-Chapelle from about 1663 to 1679, wrote:

> *When one composes for two, three or more choirs, these choirs may be equally voiced, that is, they may have the same quantity and quality of voice parts; however, one may choose to have one chorus composed of the ordinary soprano,* haute-contre, tenor *and* bass

which is reinforced by a multiplicity of voices and is called the grand *or* gros choeur; *the other [chorus]* . . . *may have fewer voices or may have no doubling at all, and this we title* . . . *the* petit choeur *or the* voix de récit (La Musique rétablie depuis ses origines, *no date, cited in Launay 1957, 179).*

French composers were also conservative in the use of instruments accompanying the chorus, although eye-witness accounts of performances often seem to contradict official documents and printed editions. Unlike Italian scores of the period, French scores did not have separately printed instrumental parts. As late as 1645, the instrumentalists employed in the Royal Chapel consisted of two cornett players. The serpent gradually replaced the cornett, and solo instruments made a timid appearance at the Sainte-Chapelle in the 1680s. Not until the very end of the century, however, was André Campra allowed to introduce violins at Notre-Dame Cathedral—some twenty years after he had successfully used them at Saint-Étienne in Toulouse. As late as 1689 influential members of the clergy were opposed to the use of a *symphonie* for ceremonies at the Cathedral of Senlis; and far into the eighteenth century the twenty-four Masses of Henri Hardouin (1727–1808), *Maître de Musique* at Rheims from 1748 to 1791, were performed a cappella. On the other hand, soon after 1626, the Cathedral of Rouen purchased three bass viols, a serpent, bassoon, cornett, sackbut, and violins to accompany the *Lamentations* (see Launay 1963, 191). By 1655, Chartres had a serpent, bassoon, and double-bass.

Why some churches and some religious orders were musically progressive while others remained bastions of conservatism is difficult to say. Did the pockets of Italian influence in Provence enrich the musical resources of some of the Toulouse churches? Certainly in Paris, where the Theatine priests were called the "Pères du chant" and where music was under the direction of Paolo Lorenzani for a time, the Theatines' chapel welcomed musical elements borrowed from secular sources, as did the monastic chapels of the Augustinians in the Place des Victoires, the Jesuits in the Faubourg Saint-Antoine, and the Feuillants.

These bare facts do not always present a realistic picture of performance practices. For special occasions, many instruments were used, and court as well as town musicians augmented the meager resources of the churches. Claude Binet wrote that Jacques Mauduit's (1557–1627) *Requiem*, which was performed at the funeral of Ronsard in 1586, was "animated by all sorts of instruments,"[3] and we remember that this is the same Mauduit who directed sixty-four voices, twenty-eight viols, and fourteen lutes for the performance of the *Ballet de la*

Délivrance de Renaud in 1617. A description of a ceremony at the Cathedral of Notre-Dame celebrating the Peace of Vervins in 1598, mentions the musicians "borrowed" from the king's Chamber to augment the musicians of the Chapel:

> *Those from the Chamber, with gentle and bigger voices joined by lutes, viols, and other gentle instruments were placed on the right side (of the altar) in order to be better heard . . . . Those from the Chapel, blending their stronger, fuller voices with the cornetts and trumpets, were on the other side (cited by Brenet 1909, 283).*

The *Mercure galant* of October 1682 (1:243) described another ceremony at Notre-Dame almost one hundred years later in celebration of the birth of the Duc de Bourgogne: "A concert of trumpets, oboes, and violins began the Vespers, which was sung by an excellent group composed of all the best voices of the two chapters (of St. Étienne and St. Saturnin) and of the town." Note that this took place some twelve years before Campra's modest request for violins at Notre-Dame was granted.

The musical conservatism of France in the first half of the seventeenth century is nowhere more dramatically displayed than in the reluctance of her composers to make use of the basso continuo. The first printed work in France in which the continuo is used throughout is not even by a Frenchman; it is the *Pathodia sacra et profana* by Constantin Huygens. Ballard printed it in 1647. Although isolated continuo-like passages for lute are found in some *airs de cour* by Guédron and Boesset that date from earlier in the century, they are just that: isolated passages. Étienne Moulinié's *Meslanges de sujets chrétiens, cantiques, litanies et motets, mis en musique à 2, 3, 4 & 5 parties avec une basse continue* was printed by Jacques de Senlecque in 1658 but was in circulation before 1650 and therefore preceded the publication of Du Mont's *Cantica sacra* by Ballard in 1652. In the preface to *Cantica sacra*, Du Mont wrote: "This kind of music, with basso continuo, has not been printed before in France . . . . My plan was to join the Motets and a Mass for five voices with the *Basse continue*; however, I was advised to print them separately." Thus, Du Mont was the first to use figures and, through Ballard, to print separate continuo parts.

The concomitant practice of adding continuo parts to earlier polyphonic vocal music was also slow to develop in France. Writing about the Ballard edition of Claude Le Jeune's *Octonaires de la Vanité* printed in 1641, Brossard chose to ignore the musical conservatism of the 1640s and blamed Ballard instead. He commented:

It is surprising that when [Ballard] had this second or third Edition [of Octonaires] printed in 1641, he did not add a Basse continue, *which certainly would not have spoiled this work . . . . But that is the way of Printers; laziness and often fear of expense prevents them from perfecting their Works as much as they ought, even for their honor (1724; 1725–1730, 271).*

Settings of the Ordinary of the Mass remained the stronghold of the *stile antico* throughout the seventeenth century. Stylistically static, these Mass settings had their origins in Flemish a cappella and Roman polychoral Masses. This conservative bias was reflected by Ballard, who, when he deigned to print Masses, generally chose the most archaic examples by Charles d'Helfer, Henri Frémart, François Cosset, and others as opposed to those written in *concertato* style. The Renaissance tradition in liturgical music was also supported by the official documents regulating church ceremonies—especially in the Paris area. The stern voice of the Council of Trent is heard again in the *Ceremoniale parisiense* (1662), which was written by a Parisian priest, Martin Sonnet, in an important attempt to establish uniformity in the celebration of the Divine Office and other ceremonies in Parisian churches. Sonnet admonished church musicians who used instruments other than the organ: "tubae, tibiae aut cornea" (trumpets, flutes, or cornetts) (cited by Launay 1963, 189). In 1674 an ordinance of the Archbishop of Paris strictly forbade singing "secular or profane music" in any church or chapel, and proscribed the following:

Playing on the organ any chansons *or other airs unworthy of the modesty and gravity of sacred song, singing in chorus or playing on instruments during Tenebrae; or inviting others, by means of tickets or publicity announcements, to come hear the music as though it were a spectacle or a theater performance (cited by Launay 1963, 189).*

The list of conservative Mass composers in France in the first sixty years of the seventeenth century is a long one. Beginning with Du Caurroy, it includes the Cambrai and Arras composers J. Solon, Antoine Penne, and Valérien Gonet, whose extant double choir music is rooted in the Franco-Netherlands tradition. The peripatetic Jean de Bournonville (1580?–1632), *Maître de Chapelle* at Rouen, Evreux, Saint-Quentin, Abbeville, and Amiens, left us eight Magnificats and about twenty Masses. Two four-voice Masses by Valentin de Bournonville, son of Jean, have been found in the Petit Séminaire in Quebec (see Schwandt 1980). Eight of Pierre Lauverjat's Masses were printed by Ballard between 1613 and 1623, and the Jesuit Charles d'Ambleville included two of his own Masses in his *Harmonia sacra* (1636). Artus Auxcousteaux (1590–1656), *Maître de Musique* at the Sainte-Chapelle from 1643 to 1651 and former student of Jean de Bournonville, used each of the eight ecclesiastical modes in turn to compose eight Masses—one Mass for each mode. Only four of these Masses survive. According to Brossard, Auxcousteaux was so conservative that he "never wanted to hear talk of adding *Basses continues* to his works" (1724; 1725–1730, 275). Annibal Gantez (1600–1668), whose charming *L'Entretien des musiciens* (1643) gives us such a lively picture of his musical peers, remained conservative in his four- and six-part Masses. However, he wrote that he found the progressive music of Jean Veillot "most pleasing" in contrast to the conservative music of André Péchon, which he found "most serious." Péchon, who was at Saint-German-l'Auxerrois in 1640, favored the archaic use of a cantus firmus in augmented note values in his motets. Henri Frémart (died after 1646) and François Cosset (died 1673) both left several Masses, some of which were printed by Ballard. Brossard himself added a *symphonie* to Cosset's *a*5 *Missa Gaudeamus* for a performance at the Royal Chapel in 1688. There are four extant Masses by Charles d'Helfer (died ca.1664), who was *Maître de Chapelle* at Soissons in the 1650s. His *Missa pro defunctis a*4 of 1656 was performed on 27 July 1774 for the repose of the soul of Louis XV (see Launay 1963, 178). Between 1676 and 1693, Ballard published a Vespers, for double chorus and instruments, and five polyphonic *a*5 and *a*6 Masses by Pierre Menault (1642–1694), who directed the choir school of Saint-Étienne in Dijon. Only lightly scored sections of these Masses include unfigured continuo parts (Christe eleyson, Benedictus, Elevation).[4] From the early years of the eighteenth century, instrumental parts were grafted onto these museum pieces to make them palatable to the contemporary listener.

An opinion attributed by Brossard to Pierre Tabart, his immediate predecessor at Meaux, shows awareness of the reaction late in the seventeenth century against this conservative style:

> *In spite of his cleverness in writing counterpoint, [Tabart] set things right with everyone and confessed many times to me that in the end, these kinds of counterpoint were only good for pleasing the eyes and not the ears, and that he was astonished to find that they had made such magnificent foundations for having pieces composed that could please very few people and only very rarely (1724; 1725–1730, 491).*

Much earlier, Étienne Moulinié, in his preface to the *Meslanges de sujets chrétiens* (1658), was already an outspoken partisan of the *agrémens* of the "new manner" as opposed to the "austerity" of the old. In 1659 Thomas Gobert wrote new music for the *Paraphrase des Psaumes de David en vers françois*, although these verses by Antoine Godeau, dilettante bishop of Vence, had been set to music by Auxcousteaux in 1654. Why a new setting only five years later? Gobert's printer, Pierre le Petit, took the trouble in his preface to justify the new effort on grounds that "the original intention of the Monseigneur of Vence [Godeau] was to render the psalms in 'simple counterpoint' appropriate for those who know only a little music." He added that the earlier settings by Auxcousteau "did not have all the grace desirable for such admirable verses."

Clearly then, we must turn to the motets, to the psalm paraphrases, the sacred hymns and spiritual odes, to noels and parodies of *airs de cour* instead of to the Masses to trace the development of the *stile moderno* in France. The *airs de cour* and *récits* from the court ballets as well as elements from the Italian *concertato* style served as models for the new style in France. Also discreetly admired and imitated were early seventeenth-century Italian motets for solo voice and continuo by Pietro Pace, Girolamo Marinoni, Antonio Burlini, Severo Bonini, and others. The Bibliothèque Nationale is rich in such collections, and estate inventories in documents of the *Minutier central* from 1600 to 1650 show the amazing extent to which Italian music permeated private libraries.

Nicolas Formé (1567–1638) was first to move the double chorus motet and Mass in the direction of the Baroque *concertante* motet. He was Du Caurroy's successor as *sous-maître* at the Royal Chapel (1609). In a curious contract dated 30 January 1638, he gave Pierre and Robert Ballard three double chorus Masses in the new style to publish in return for a promise that they would print "no other music [than his] similar to that of the aforementioned three Masses . . . during the lifetime of Sieur Formé" (cited by Lesure 1964). Unfortunately, these three Masses are not extant, but another double chorus Mass, composed the same year and dedicated to Louis XIII, is definitely in the Venetian *stile concertato*. It has a *petit choeur a*4 of soloists and a *grand choeur a*5. This distribution of vocal parts conforms to the description of double choruses found in the letter to Huygens by Formé's successor, Thomas Gobert, in 1646. Thus, one generation removed from Du Caurroy and only three years after the Ballard publication of Charles d'Ambleville's conservative double chorus motets (*Harmonia sacra*), Nicolas Formé tried to corner the market on the "new" manner of composing religious music. Undoubtedly by virtue of Louis XIII's approval and the subsequent performances of these works, Formé was looked upon by later generations as the originator of the double chorus motet in France. Contributing to this myth was Henri Sauval's account:[5]

> *[Formé] invented the double chorus Motets that everyone esteems and that the* Maîtres de Musique *of the King so often copy and imitate. He surpassed all those who had preceded him in Counterpoint and fine invention . . . . The King esteemed his works so much that after his [Formé's] death in 1638 . . . [the King] had them performed often. More than that, he had them locked in a cabinet which he had had built for this purpose and for which he always had the key . . . . At the death of the King, they passed with all other furnishings of his apartment to Jean de Souvre in his capacity as* Gentilhomme de la Chambre *. . . and a few days later they fell into the hands of Jean Villet [Veillot],* Sous-maître de la Chapelle, *who used them for his profit (1724, 1:326–327).*

Rarely has the direct influence of an important stylistic change been so clearly documented; the more's the pity that only two Formé motets for double chorus have survived (one of these, *Ecce tu pulchra es*, is reproduced in Denise Launay's *Anthologie du motet latin polyphonique en France [1609–1661]*, Paris: Société Française de Musicoligie, 1963, 106).

Although Jean Veillot (Villot, Villet, died 1662) was not the first to add instruments to motets and Masses (we recall the Mass *"avec symphonie"* by Jehan Titelouze performed in 1632 in Rouen), he was surely one of the first to add *symphonies* to Formé's plan of *grand choeur* and *petit choeur*. The "most agreeable" (Gantez) music of Veillot prefigures the *grand motet* of the next generation and thereby is an important link between Formé and Henry Du Mont, Veillot's successor at the Royal Chapel. Three double chorus motets by Veillot survive, two of which were copied by Philidor, perhaps because of their popularity. They are *O filii et filiae* and *Sacris solemnis*, which were conceived in a grand manner suitable for royalty. The orchestra has independent *ritournelles* and doubles the voices of the *grand choeur*; the soloists of the *a6 petit choeur* are sustained by a continuo. Unfortunately, the third of these double chorus motets *Angeli archangeli* (1644), is lost except for the parts for its first chorus. (For a fourth and possibly a fifth motet by Veillot, see Burke 1981, 28–29.)

Also lost is a *Te Deum* composed by Veillot and performed in April 1660 for the double celebration of the Peace of the Pyrenees and the marriage of Louis XIV. It drew upon the *Vingt-quatre Violons* as well as "all the best instrumentalists of Paris" (see Launay, preface to *Anthologie du motet latin polyphonique en France*, xxxiv). It is tempting, though fruitless, to conjecture a direct bearing of this motet upon the earliest *grands motets* by Henry Du Mont, dating before 1666, or upon the *Miserere* of 1664 by Lully.

Thomas Gobert (died 1672) was a composer of the *avant-garde* in France along with Formé and Veillot. He admitted to admiring many "beautiful and good things" in Monteverdi's madrigals (Jonckbloet and Land 1882, ccxiv), and he did much to stabilize the double chorus motet. Unfortunately, none of Gobert's motets survive. His lost *Antiennes recitatives* may have used the basso continuo before Huygens's *Pathodia sacra* of 1647. His peers and superiors alike thought well of him. Gantez noted his "good jump into the employ cf Monsieur le Cardinal [Richelieu] and a better jump yet to the service of the King, since he is now his chapelmaster" (1643; ed. of 1878, 142).

Gobert's *Paraphrase des Psaumes de David*, first printed in 1659, was reprinted in 1661, 1672, 1676, and 1686. Antoine Godeau's paraphrases of the psalms of David were immensely popular and were even recited and sung at the Hôtel de Rambouillet, the headquarters of *préciosité* itself. As we have seen above, the old-fashioned settings by Auxcousteaux would not do for this elegant and worldly Catholic milieu; it remained for Gobert to render them in a simple counterpoint that was far removed from the archaic Renaissance polyphony of Auxcousteaux. Gobert found the paraphrases ideally suited for two voices and continuo, which could be reduced to solo voice and continuo for the convenience of the performer.

Étienne Moulinié (1599–1676) was *Maître de Musique* for Gaston d'Orléans, Louis XIII's brother, from 1627 until 1660. Better known today as a composer of *airs de cour* (from 1625 to 1668), he also has significance as a composer for the church. His *Missa pro defunctis*, printed by Ballard in 1636, is in the austere style of Du Caurroy, but the influence of the *airs de cour* and Italian solo motets may be seen in his *Meslanges de sujets chrétiens* of 1658.

In the preface to the *Meslanges*, Moulinié felt it necessary to defend his use of daring intervals and cross relations:

> *I am obliged to remark here concerning my particular manner of composing. There are some places where I have employed certain passages . . . which are rather bold and which may pass for license in the opinion of those who prefer the austerity of the old style to the* agrémens *of the new.*

Certainly to ears accustomed to Monteverdi, or even Cavalli and Rossi, the few harmonic audacities of Moulinié simply emphasize the conservative nature of French religious music in the mid-seventeenth century. More significant is the importance he accorded the solo voice in his *Meslanges*. The motet was well on the way to becoming a concert piece with solo passages that at times approached true airs.

The late motets Moulinié mentioned in his preface to the *Airs à 4 parties* (1668) are unfortunately lost; also gone are the motets (?) he presumably wrote to texts by Abbé Perrin. We owe many religious texts to Perrin, who was quite specific in indicating voice parts and even the names of composers and performers. Moulinié's name appears at the head of a number of poems which appear to have been written by Perrin with a sacred cantata or even an oratorio in mind.

Included among the many pieces copied by Brossard and found today in the Bibliothèque Nationale (*Rés. Vma Ms. 571*) are works by Boesset: three Masses (*a3, a4,* and *a5*); four motets with continuo; and a *Magnificat* for two sopranos, *haute-contre*, and continuo. Brossard stated that he believed the Masses were probably works of Jean-Baptiste Boesset (1614–1685), not his father, Antoine (ca. 1587–1643). We have not progressed beyond Brossard in assigning these works definitely to one Boesset or the other. Launay supports Brossard primarily on the basis of internal stylistic evidence and attributes the music to Jean-Baptiste. Certainly the unequivocal tonal direction of the harmony, the symmetrical phrase groupings, the frequency of cadences, and, above all, the continuo (albeit unfigured) of viols and organ would be more appropriate for works composed in the 1660s than in the 1630s. However, most French scholars treat the above as an example of a "new esthetic" (Verchaly 1953–1954, 83) and follow the lead of Henri Quittard (1906, 97) in assigning the works to Antoine Boesset.[6]

More remarkable and even more mysterious is the music presumably written by a Languedoc composer, Guillaume Bouzignac (before 1587–ca. 1643). Most of it is conserved in two principal manuscripts.[7] There are many lacunae in the biography of Bouzignac. We know that in 1609 he was *Maître de Musique des Enfants* at the Cathedral of Saint-André in Grenoble. Although we do not know the dates of his birth or death, textual references in some of his motets place him in Carcassonne, Rodez, and Tours at different times in his life, and he may have ended his career in Clermont-Ferrand, where he was appointed *Maître de Musique* in 1643. Most of the music found in the two principal manuscripts dates from 1628 to 1643. There are forty-five works common to both manuscripts with minor variants, but only nine compositions carry his name. On stylistic grounds, however, most of the remaining anonymous works may be attributed to him.

His music has a degree of individuality altogether remarkable in a period of general conformity within a prescribed genre. No other music of the time looks the same on the page or sounds the same as the motets of Bouzignac. This in itself argues against the music's having been composed by a Provençal school with Bouzignac as musical mentor. Even though the Ballard presses ignored Bouzignac's manuscripts, some of them may have reached Paris. In any case, he may be legitimately considered one of the precursors of Marc-Antoine Charpentier in the introduction of the oratorio in France, but it seems doubtful that Charpentier was familiar with his music.

Bouzignac is the first composer of religious music in France with a real dramatic flair, nurtured by his exposure to Italian and possibly to Catalan influences which penetrated the Midi to a much greater degree than the north. Speech rhythms (see Example 12-1a) and repeated short fragments of text in some of the music give it a mosaic-like quality that recalls Giovanni Gabrieli. Certain two-syllable words must have suggested certain rhythmic dialogues to the composer, for these passages recur throughout the motets (Example 12-1b,c).

Madrigalisms and word painting are used to a greater degree than is normally found in French music of the period. In the *a*5 motet *Alleluya, Deus dixit*, the *grand choeur* acts as a unifying agent through its music and text ("et factum est ita, ita Alleluya")—a procedure similar to that used by Giovanni Gabrieli in his famous *In Ecclesiis*. The *petit choeur* is sometimes reduced to one soloist who dialogues with the *grand choeur*. In such a motet as *Ex ore infantium* (1628), Bouzignac exploited the sound of a solo baritone in dialogue with the chorus. Similarly, a solo soprano, representing the angel Gabriel in the Christmas motet *Noë, noë pastores*, dialogues with the chorus of shepherds. These embryonic oratorios antedate the *histoires sacrées* by Charpentier by some seventy years.

Bouzignac is representative of many composers who thrived on the rich musical soil of Provence and whose names today are no more than footnotes in a history of French music (see *Encyclopédie des musiques sacrées* 1969, 2:541–552). Music was performed on a regular basis at the church of Saint-Sauveur in Aix-en-Provence as early as the thirteenth century. There, Guillaume Poitevin (1646–1708), himself a composer of Masses and motets, held the position of *Maître de Musique* for thirty-five years (1667 to 1702) and served as a teacher and inspiration to generations of composers: André Campra, Jean Gilles, Jacques Cabassol, Laurent Belissen, Claude-Mathieu Pellegrin, and Esprit Blanchard (see Raugel 1954). With Michel Mazarin (brother of the Cardinal) Archbishop in 1644 and with Jérôme de Grimaldi succeeding him in 1655, the music of Rossi, Cavalli, and Carissimi must have formed an important part of the repertoire of the church choir.

Example 12-1. Extracts from motets by Bouzignac. (a) *Alleluya, Deus dixit.* (b,c) *Cantate Domino.*

The progressive trends described on the last several pages were consolidated and systematized in the religious music of a northerner, Henry de Thier (1610–1684), born near Liège, who in the 1630s replaced his Walloon family name *Thier* with the French equivalent, *Mont*. Du Mont gave us the earliest printed example in France of the *petit motet* for two or three voices and continuo in his *Cantica sacra*. He also was chiefly responsible for creating the classic model for the *grand motet* that was rapidly elevated by the royal imprimatur of Louis XIV to the most favored position among all religious genres—a position it kept throughout the remainder of the *grand siècle*.

Music in Flanders was infused with Italianisms during Du Mont's youth. The *stile recitativo* was welcomed by Belgian composers, and the assimilation of the basso continuo in Belgium antedated its adoption in France by some thirty years. Du Mont was surely acquainted with the motets for two, three, and four voices and continuo and occasional independent violin parts by Alessandro Grandi, Antonio Cifra, Felice and Giovanni Francesco Anerio, and other Venetian and Roman composers which formed part of the repertory of the Flemish churches. He may also have known the Italian prototype for the *petit motet*, the *Concerti ecclesiastici* (1602) by Viadana, or the dramatic dialogues found in Vecchi's *Dialoghi* of 1608. This exposure acted as effective armor with which to combat the conservative bias the young composer found when he arrived in France about 1638.

Du Mont composed at least two hundred works set to Latin texts, of which sixty-two are lost (see Sawkins 1989, 61). He exploited the use of trio texture (two solo voices and continuo) in his *Cantica sacra*, which was first printed by Ballard in 1652. Only eleven of the thirty-five motets are scored for four voices. In his preface he not only explains the use of a second printed part for the basso continuo, he also states that he added an optional treble viol or violin part (found in nine of the motets). *Cantate Domino* (No. 28) is a *concertato* motet in which four solo voices alternate with a four-part chorus labeled "omnes." Many of the motets exhibit the short, highly contrasting, and mosaic-like structural divisions so typical of the early Italian Baroque. *Tristitia vestra* (No. 5) and *Alleluia haec dies* (No. 8) are examples of multi-sectional motets unified through the use of recurring sections and Alleluia refrains, while *O Gloriosa Domine* (No. 26) is a long motet in two large sections, each introduced by its own twelve-measure *symphonie*.

In their inventive apposition of contrasting rhythms, their treatment of dissonance, and their restrained use of affective melodic intervals and text painting, the *petits motets* of the *Cantica sacra* show how well Du Mont had assimilated many features of contemporary Italian religious music.

The *petits motets* composed by Du Mont after his *Cantica sacra* include hymns, antiphons, settings of Godeau's psalms of David, and some works in dialogue form. The latter are perhaps Du Mont's most original and far-reaching musical contributions. In the Brossard collection at the Bibliothèque Nationale is a *Dialogus de anima* (1668) for five voices, viol, and organ, which is a dialogue among God, a sinner, and an angel. Its organization into three scenes, each preceded by a *symphonie,* and its use of a *petit* and *grand choeur* as well as solo *récits* justify Brossard's description of this work as a "type of oratorio" (1724; 1725–1730, 483).[8]

Du Mont organized five of the thirty motets included in *Motets à deux voix avec la basse continue* (1668) as dialogues for specific characters such as sinners and angels or brides and bridegrooms. *O fideles miseremini* (No. 30) shows Du Mont's exploitation of the technique of dramatic monody. The affective intervals and repeated text fragments owe a debt to Carissimi and mark this work along with the dialogues as an important precursor of Charpentier's *histoires sacrées* (see Example 12-2).

Example 12-2. Du Mont: Extract from *O fideles miseremini* (after ed. of 1668).

With *Motets à II, III et IV parties pour voix et instruments avec la basse continue* (1681), Du Mont moved the *petit motet* closer to French models. This collection contains thirty-seven motets and three independent *symphonies.* Co-existing with Italianate dialogues and pieces with echo effects are motets in the style of popular airs based on French dance rhythms. *Regina divina* (No. 25), for example, borrows the phrase structure and rhythmic organization of a minuet. The collection includes a doubled continuo bass air "accompanied" by two violins (*Sub ombra noctis*).

In his *Airs à quatre parties avec la basse continue* (1663), Du Mont joined the company of Antoine Lardenois, de Gouy, Auxcousteaux, and Gobert in providing music for the psalm paraphrases by Antoine Godeau. With their binary structure, asymmetrical phrases, occasional meter shifts, and syllabic settings, the *Airs* are French to the core. Only six years earlier, Du Mont had drawn upon the rich polyphonic tradition of his Flemish heritage in his setting of Godeau's *Quand l'esprit accablé* (paraphrase of Psalm IV, *Cum invocarem*), found as Number 20 in the *Meslanges à II, III, IV et V parties avec la basse continue* (1657) (see Example 12-3).

Example 12-3. Du Mont: Extract from *Quand l'esprit accablé* (after ed. of 1657).

To conclude the survey of the development of religious music in France prior to the majority of Louis XIV (1661), some attention should be given to the music written and arranged for use in convents and monasteries. If the seventeenth century was the century of Antoine Godeau, Bishop of Vence and "maître de la galanterie," it was also the century of François de Sales and Vincent de Paul. If it was the

century of the dissolute Abbess of Metz who incurred the wrath of
Bossuet, it was also the century of Mme Accarie who introduced the
cult of Saint Theresa and the order of the Carmelites. The founding
of new orders and the reform of old ones in a spirit of penitence and
austerity was characteristic of the century. The Jesuits were recalled to
France in 1603. In 1618 they founded their Collège de Clermont,
which was called Collège Louis-le-Grand after 1683.

To meet the needs of so many new religious institutions, the
Ballards printed many collections of music designed primarily for performers of limited ability and modest means. The necessity of supplying simple music for the Mass gave rise to the so-called *plain-chant
musical* composed for choirs singing in unison. The task of creating a
new style of plain chant fell mainly to the Congregation of the
Oratoriens, founded in 1611. In 1634 Pierre Ballard began publishing
liturgical chants (*Brevis Psalmodiae Ratio ad usum Presbyterorum
Congregationis Oratorii*) in versions composed by François Bourgoing,
a priest of the Oratoire. These simple melodies have nothing in common with the infinite variety and long melismas of Gregorian chant.

Henry Du Mont's five *Messes en plain-chant* (inexplicably called
"Messes royales" in the fourth edition of 1701) first appeared in 1669
and were the most popular of what Brenet called "grotesque carica-
tures of true liturgical chant" (1899, 32). They were reprinted four
times and used in country churches into the twentieth century. The
second printing is lost. The third, fourth, and fifth editions were
printed in 1685, 1701, and 1711. There exists an Alexandre Guilmant
edition, "harmonisées à 4 voix." The Bibliothèque Nationale holds
one of them "arranged for military band" (1852).

The six liturgical books by Guillaume Gabriel Nivers, published
between 1658 and 1706, help round out any study of the seventeenth-
century view of the *plain-chant musical*. His *Graduale romanum juxta
missale* (1658) and *Antiphonarium romanum juxta breviarium* (1658)
predate Sonnet's *Ceremoniale parisiense* (1662). In his chant books,
Nivers uses two note values, the *longa* and the *breve*. Nivers's most
important ideas concerning the performance of chant are found in two
tutors, *Dissertation sur le chant grégorien* (1683) and *Méthode certaine
pour apprendre le plain-chant de l'Église* (1698). He sanctions the use of
ornaments such as the *port de voix* if performed "naturally and without
being affected" (cited by Pruitt 1974, 38). Nivers claimed to have
based his plain chant on Roman models, and at the end of his
Dissertation, he described his method as having "purged [plain chant]
of all abuses" (cited by Launay 1993, 420).

Collections of psalm translations were available to composers
throughout the seventeenth century. The most popular were by
Philippe Desportes (1546–1604), whose translations appeared between

1591 and 1603 and were given musical settings until mid-century.[9] He made some in *vers mesurés*. Denis Caignet (died 1625) was the best known and most prolific of the composers who set Desportes's psalm translations to music. In 1607 Pierre Ballard printed fifty of them "set to music in 3, 4, 5, 6, 7, and 8 parts" by Caignet. In 1624 the same publisher brought out the 150 psalms of David "put into French verse" by Desportes and set by Caignet for solo voice.

Beginning in the 1630s, composers such as de Gouy, Lardenois, Auxcousteaux, Moulinié, Gobert, and Du Mont chose the psalm paraphrases by Godeau in preference to the literal or rhyming translations by the earlier generation. Of interest is the fact that Louis XIII was the first to compose music for the Godeau psalm paraphrases, and did so even before they were first printed in 1633. Unfortunately, the music for four voices by the king has not survived.

Many simple pieces were collected with an eye to their potential performance possibilities and their adaptability to the requirements of individual institutions. In the *Airs sur les hymnes sacrez, odes et noëls pour chanter au catechisme* (published by Ballard, 1623), the first soprano, "being the main part, may be sung alone, but one may also sing in four parts by utilizing several excellent *faux-bourdons* on the eight modes." Parodies of *airs de cour* were especially popular. Typical are the three books of *Airs de dévotion à deux parties* by the priest François Berthod, which were published by Ballard in 1656, 1658, and 1662. These two part settings are parodies of some of the best known airs by Lambert and Moulinié.

The collection of parodies of *airs de cour*, *La Despouille d'Aegipte* (1629), includes fifty tunes for one voice only. More than half of these are by Antoine Boesset; fifteen are by Guédron; and five, by Moulinié. The melodies of this collection conform closely to their models, and in spite of Pierre Ballard's comment that they were destined for the "hands of shepherds and nuns," musical difficulties abound (see Launay 1993, 231). Clearly, not all of this "simple" music performed at convents was necessarily sterile. Later in the century and in the century to follow, composers of the caliber of Charpentier, Couperin, Nivers, and Clérambault all composed works of the highest musical integrity "proper for all sorts of monks and nuns" ("*propres pour toutes sortes de Religieux et Religieuses*").

Chapter 13

The Motet: From Du Mont to Delalande

Generation of Du Mont, Lully, and Robert

"Printed by the express order of His Majesty" we read on the title pages of the collection of fifty *grands motets* composed by Henry Du Mont, Pierre Robert, and Jean-Baptiste Lully and printed by Ballard from 1684–1686. Designed as much to glorify the King of France as the King of Heaven, these motets became the officially sanctioned models for works in the same genre that formed the basic repertory of the Royal Chapel, the Concert Spirituel, and provincial music academies up to the eve of the Revolution. Composed and printed as they were on the "express order of His Majesty," they are a musical byproduct of the passion for order and uniformity that dominated the *grand siècle*.

As early as 1663, the king had appointed four *sous-maîtres* of the Royal Chapel: Henry Du Mont, Gabriel Expilly, Pierre Robert, and Thomas Gobert. In point of fact, Gobert and Expilly retired in 1669, leaving Du Mont and Robert as the only *sous-maîtres* until their retirement in 1683. Loret's carefully chosen words show that, in the minds of many, Du Mont and Robert carried the burden of composing for the Royal Chapel:

> Le Roy, dont l'oreille est scavante
> En cette science charmante,
> Par un vray jugement d'expert
> A choizi Du Mont et Robert (7 July 1663).

> *The King, whose ear is knowing*
> *In this charming science,*
> *with the true judgment of an expert*
> *Has chosen Du Mont and Robert.*

By 1671, the last of the royal academies, that of architecture, had been created; by 1682, the king had taken up permanent residence at Versailles; also in 1682, the "Église Gallican" declared its virtual independence from Rome, and the revocation of the Edict of Nantes was but three short years away. The Catholic church in France marched in willing lockstep with all other institutions, subservient to the will and manner of the *Roi Soleil*. The year 1682 saw the completion of a new Royal Chapel at Versailles, a chapel that could draw upon as many as eighty musicians to perform a *grand motet* for a special occasion or for the celebration of the king's Mass.

Louis XIV had been impressed by the opulence and heroic mien of such early Lully *grands motets* as the *Miserere* (1664) and the *Te Deum* (1677). He had also enjoyed the *Motets à 1, 2, 3, 4 et 5 parties avec symphonies et basse-continue* by Paolo Lorenzani, which had been heard at the court as early as 1678. It was only to be expected that he would want similar music for his Chapel.

The king preferred to attend low Mass (*Messe basse solennelle*) in his Chapel; for high Mass, he went to a royal parish in Paris, to Saint-Germain-en-Laye or, after 1690, to Notre-Dame of Versailles. The format of the low Mass gave him a chance to hear at least one *grand* and perhaps two *petits motets*. Abbé Perrin described the arrangement of motets in the service in his preface to *Cantica pro Capella Regis* (published by Ballard in 1665), a valuable collection of his motet texts for use at the Royal Chapel that includes the text for Lully's *petits motets*, *Ave coeli munus supernum* and *O lachrymae fideles*. Perrin wrote as follows:

> *For the King's Mass, there are ordinarily three [motets] sung: a* grand, *a* petit *for the Elevation, and a* Domine salvum fac Regem.[1] *I have made the* grands *long enough, so that they can last a quarter of an hour . . . and occupy the beginning of the Mass up to the Elevation. Those of the Elevation are smaller and can last up to the Post-Communion where the* Domine *begins.*

In the same preface, Perrin gave one of the earliest definitions of the motet in France. This definition, in common with all later ones, does not attempt to differentiate between a *grand* or *petit motet* but does emphasize the sectional nature of the genre:

> *The Motet is a piece varied by several vocal or musical sections, which are allied but are different [from each other] . . . . The variety of the piece will always be still greater and the composition always easier for the Musician, when there is variation in the Stanzas and Verses and when they are composed with a continual*

> *change in mind . . . . For this reason, I have followed this method in*
> *composing motet texts for the King's Chapel.*

The Brossard definition, found under *Motetto* in his *Dictionnaire de musique* (1703) is all-inclusive in its vagueness:

> *[The motet] is a composition of Music, complex (fort figurée) and*
> *enriched by all that is finest in the art of composition for 1, 2, 3, 4,*
> *5, 6, 7, 8 & even more Voices or Parts, often with Instruments, but*
> *ordinarily and almost always with at least a Basse continue . . . .*
> *At present, one extends the meaning of this term further to embrace*
> *all pieces composed for Latin words no matter on what subject, such*
> *as the praising of the Saints, the Elevations, etc. One even composes*
> *entire Psalms in the form of a Motet.*

Du Mont created the classical model of the *grand motet*, which, with only minor modifications, was to remain in place up to the Revolution. He achieved a position in French religious music "somewhat comparable to that of Haydn in the symphony and string quartet" (Garros 1960, 1:1598; see also Decobert 1994, 39). The twenty *grands motets*, chosen for inclusion in *Motets pour la chapelle du Roy* and published posthumously in 1686, were probably composed during the twenty years when Du Mont served in the Royal Chapel. Recent research by Lionel Sawkins shows that the repertory of the Royal Chapel included thirty-one of Du Mont's *grands motets* by 1666 (1989, 58). Sawkins based this work largely upon study of the *Livres du Roy*, the books that were printed quarterly and contained the texts of the *grands motets* and Elevations sung at the king's Mass. This research suggests that the bulk of Du Mont's *grands motets* were composed before Lully's *Miserere* of 1664 and may be viewed as an extension or a "natural evolution" (Sawkins) of the earlier examples of the genre by Gobert, Formé, and Veillot.

Du Mont quite possibly wrote his *grands motets* in reaction to the formal constraints put upon him by the *petits motets*. A dedication to the king, found in *Motets à II, III et IV parties* (1681), suggests that the composer of these *petits motets* was troubled:

> *Sire, several years ago I had the honor of presenting to your Majesty*
> *my motets for two voices . . . . I have since ascertained that two*
> *voices are assuredly too weak to allow me to be heard on a subject on*
> *which I wished to express myself better: and I imagined that Your*
> *Majesty would permit me to employ three or four voices . . . . But,*
> *Sire, I begin to see that I have scarcely succeeded any better.*

He had already "succeeded better" in his *grands motets* where he had created a type of extended cantata employing polyphonic and homophonic choruses and choral fragments, *récits*, duos and trios, *symphonies* and *ritournelles*.

The distribution of parts in Du Mont's *grands motets* remained more or less standard throughout the seventeenth century. Brossard gave this description:

> To perform them [Du Mont's motets] it is necessary to have five solo voices that constitute the petit choeur, that is: C [soprano], A [alto], T [tenor], T [tenor], B [bass]; five voices for the grand choeur, that is: CATTB;[2] and five instrumental parts to include two dessus de violon, one haute-contre, one taille, one basse de violon, and one basse continue. Thus, it is necessary to have as large a group as would normally be found in the King's music to perform all of this well; but if need be, five solo voices, two violins, a basse de violon, and a basse continue will suffice (1724; 1725–1730, 140).

Du Mont composed his motets as a series of unbroken episodes in which he interspersed solo voice (or voices) between music for the *grand* and *petit choeurs*. These episodes occasionally border on the autonomous (see, for example, *Cantemus Domino*), thereby anticipating the structure of the later motets by Charpentier and Delalande (see Decobert 1994, 60). More often, however, the parts merge or elide, one with the next. The whole is usually preceded by a *symphonie*, while *ritournelles* may define structural points of division in the body of a motet.

The introductory *symphonies* to Du Mont's motets present considerable variety and are themselves worthy of a separate study. The *symphonies* introducing *Quemadmodum desiderata* (No. 19) and *O Dulcissima* (No. 16) have closed binary forms somewhat like allemandes and have little to do with what follows. *Confitebimur tibi Deus* (No. 4) begins with a *symphonie* of thirty-five measures, whereas *Domine in virtute tuo* (No. 6) commences with a tutti chorus instead of a *symphonie*. Perhaps most impressive is the beginning of the Magnificat (No. 13) for which Du Mont employed a *symphonie* twenty-one measures long that begins with a theme closely based on the incipit of the Gregorian Magnificat. The voices of the orchestra weave a contrapuntal fabric, rich in dissonance that exposes genuinely independent part writing relating more to the composer's Flemish heritage than to the music of seventeenth-century France. The basses, who enter in measure eleven to sing the ancient Gregorian formula in unison, are absorbed into the polyphonic web of sound (see Example 13-1).

Example 13-1. Du Mont: Opening of Magnificat (after ed. of 1686).

Du Mont achieved more independence than Lully or Robert in the instrumental accompaniments to choruses. Normally the first violin doubles the soprano vocal line, leaving the second violin to embroider in free counterpoint. Notable are the accompaniments to the *petit choeur*, where the strings occasionally introduce an independent motif to be treated later by chorus and orchestra.

Whereas some of Du Mont's large syllabic choruses lack the compensatory drive of Lully's finest works in the genre, the five-part polyphony of the "Gloria Patri" from the *Magnificat* is worthy of Delalande. Du Mont's *grands motets* were impressive models for the next generation. Many of their devices were used by Charpentier and the young Delalande, whose first motets were certainly contemporary with the last of Du Mont's.

Between 1664 and 1685, Lully composed twenty-six motets, twelve of which are *grands motets*. In 1684 "by express order of His Majesty," Ballard printed six of the twelve *grands motets* by Lully in seventeen part books labeled *Motets à deux choeurs pour la chapelle du Roi*. These are *Miserere* (1664); *Plaude laetare* (1668); *Te Deum* (1677); *Dies irae* (1683); *De profundis* (1683); and *Benedictus Dominus* (1685). The six other *grands motets* are *Domine salvum fac regem* (date unknown); *Jubilate Deo* (date unknown);[3] *Notus in Judaea* (date unknown); *O lachrymae fideles* (1664); *Quare fremuerunt* (1685); and *Exaudiat te Dominus* (1687). These remain in manuscript copies, which may be found today in such diverse places as the Bibliothèque Nationale in Paris, the Bibliothèque Royale in Brussels, and the Westdeutsche Bibliothek in Marburg.

Lully used a six-part orchestra including first and second violins, three *parties de remplissage* (*haute-contre, quinte,* and *taille*), a *basse de violon* and continuo. In practice, however, this distribution of instruments results most often in the typical five-part texture of the opera orchestra with the first and second violins doubling. The distribution of parts for the *grand* and *petit choeur* builds in contrasting sonorities: the *petit choeur*, with its two sopranos, *haute-contre*, tenor, and bass, emphasizes the higher voices; whereas the *grand choeur* includes a baritone (*basse-taille*) and eliminates the second soprano.

The early *Miserere* of 1664 is the most impressive of all the *grands motets* by Lully. According to the *Mémoires* of Le Sieur Dubois, gentleman of the king's Chamber, it was a great favorite of Louis XIV.[4] It was performed in 1666 and again in 1672 at the Church of the Oratoire. The latter performance for the funeral of Chancellor Séguier was heard by Mme de Sévigné, who wrote that during the "Libera me," "all eyes were filled with tears. I do not believe any other music to exist in heaven."[5]

When Lully's motet orchestra is not supplying independent *symphonies* or *ritournelles*, it doubles the choral parts rigidly. It is unusual to find in these works any of the independent instrumental counterpoint that was timorously used by Du Mont and later exploited by Delalande. A notable exception occurs near the end of the final chorus of the *Miserere*, where the first violins, probably more inspired by practical considerations of range than by any artistic principle, initiate the final stretto-like entrance of the subject.

The year 1664 was also the year of *Le Mariage forcé, Les Amours déguisés*, and *La Princesse d'Élide*. The supple melodic lines found in the *récits* of the *Miserere* owe something to the vocal solos and ensembles of these court and comedy ballets. The *récit en duo*, "Amplius lava me," with its sham polyphony and parallel thirds, has the same sensuous quality as the duo of Climène and Philis from the fifth *Intermède* of *La*

Princesse d'Élide. The sequence of descending seventh chords, the melodic diminished seventh in "et in peccatis concepit me" (see Example 13-2), and the melodic diminished fourth on the word "iniquitate" in "Amplius lava me" clearly stem from an Italianate vocabulary of affections.

Example 13-2. Lully: Extract from the *récit* "Ecce enim," *Miserere* (after MS *Rés*. F. 663 in Bibliothèque Nationale).

Lully's Te Deum was first heard at Fontainebleau on 8 September 1677 to celebrate the baptism of his eldest son (then aged thirteen). It was subsequently performed in October 1679 at Versailles and again on that fateful 8 January 1687 at the Paris chapel of the Feuillants (a religious order of St. Bernard), when Lully, beating the measure with a long stick to keep hundreds of performers together, received the injury to his foot that resulted in his death from blood poisoning two months later.

This Te Deum is too long and has many musically arid moments, but the sound of trumpets and drums and the kinetic drive of the big double choruses, with their relentless speech rhythms wedded to massive blocks of homophony, give voice to the real spirit of Versailles. It is a secularized *concert spirituel* and is the source for bellicose operatic choruses such as those found later in *Bellérophon* and *Thésée*. Surprisingly, in only one other *grand motet* (*Exaudiat te Dominus*) do some of the manuscripts specify trumpets, bassoons, and drums. It is clear, however, from the description of the 1679 performance of the Te Deum found in the *Mercure galant* of October of the same year that the manuscripts and printed editions indicated only minimum performance possibilities:

> *The musicians were placed in the tribune before a large amphitheater raised up near the vault; those from the Chamber were at the right, and those from the Chapel at the left. There were oboes, flutes, trumpets, and drums along with the* Vingt-quatre Violons. *At least 120 persons sang or played instruments.*[6]

Like Du Mont, Lully composed his *grands motets* in loosely organized sections. Extended *symphonies* define the large structural divisions of the Te Deum. In the opening section, elements from the opening *symphonie* unify the section in rondo fashion. Shorter divisions, which are seldom autonomous units in themselves, are created within the larger units by dividing textual phrases, sentences, or lines into solo *récits* or short recitative-like passages, or by treating the *petit coeur* and *grand choeur* in a *concertato* manner. Thus, the text acts as a form-determinant. The contrast achieved by fragmentation had appeal if we are to believe the report of the *Mercure galant* of September 1677: "What was particularly admired was that each couplet was of different music. The king found it so beautiful that he wished to hear it again."[7]

The vertical sonorities in Lully's *grands motets* coupled with a predominantly syllabic rendering of the text invite a rather simple, even static, harmony for long stretches at a time. Chromatic inflections, when they occur, are usually the result of secondary dominant chords used to effect a transitory modulation to a closely related key. Yet Lully's motets are not totally devoid of harmonic interest, although they are far less imposing from a harmonic point of view than those by Delalande and Charpentier. Lully's borrowing of chords from the opposite mode results in a type of bi-modality common in French music of the Baroque period. An entire section may exploit a region of the opposite mode. When combined with a dramatic tempo change, this is an effective means of underscoring the text. The four-measure "Sanctus" from the Te Deum is a good example (see Example 13-3). Set within a larger harmonic frame of C and G major, this three-fold "Sanctus" in G minor forms the structural center of the first section of the motet and affords needed relief from the driving speech rhythms by which it is surrounded.

In outward appearances, the twenty-four *grands motets* chosen by Pierre Robert (ca. 1618–1690) for inclusion in the 1684 printing by Ballard of *Motets pour la chapelle du Roy* differ little from those by Du Mont and Lully. The *grand choeur* has the same distribution of voices; and the orchestra has the six-part division found in the Lully motets, although according to Brossard, "it is necessary to have seven instrumental parts, namely: First and Second violins, *Haute-contre, Taille, Quinte*, a *Basse continue* for the Viol and Bassoon, and finally, a figured *Basse continue* for the organ, harpsichord, and theorbo" (1724; 1725–1730, 160). This quotation emphasizes again the variance between printed editions or manuscripts and actual performance practices.

Robert differs most markedly from his contemporaries in his organization of the *petit choeur*, which he formed into ensemble combinations, labeled *récits*, from the following eight solo voices: first and second soprano, first and second *haute-contre*, first and second tenor, baritone, and bass. Through these "*ensembles de récits*" he exploited the contrast of sonorities more than either Lully or Du Mont. For example, within sixteen short measures in the verse, "Testimonium in Joseph," from *Exultate Deo adjutori nostro* (Number 9 of the motets), Robert juxtaposed solo, duo, trio, and quartet, with soloists including the baritone, first *haute-contre*, first tenor, and first and second soprano.[8]

Example 13-3. Lully: Extract from Te Deum (after MS *Rés.* F. 666 in Bibliothèque Nationale).

There is little evidence that Robert used this wide range of sonorities for text painting. The *récits*, alongside those of Du Mont, seem austere and impersonal. Indeed, with a change of sonority often occurring every few measures, the effect is that of textual fragmentation, and one can only conclude that purely musical features of the sonorities justified their use for Robert.

Freed from the compulsion of heroic posturing, the *petits motets* of Lully and Robert are intrinsically more musical than their *grands motets*. Several were copied in 1688 in the Philidor atelier and are included in the Bibliothèque Nationale manuscript (*Rés*. Vmb. Ms. 6) entitled *Petits motets et Élévations de MM. Carissimi, de Lully, de Robert, de Daniélis et Foggia à 2, 3 et 4 voix et quelques unes avec des violons*. This important manuscript adds to the testimony pointing to the use of Italian music at the Royal Chapel during Lully's lifetime. Out of seventy-two *petits motets*, thirty-two are by Carissimi, thirteen by Daniel Daniélis, seven by Francesco Foggia, and ten each by Robert and Lully.

Robert and Lully were more sensitive in their *petits motets* to the expressive power of dissonance, affective intervals, and modulation. It would be difficult to find, in any of the *récits* of Robert's *grands motets*, a melodic line so at one with the text and so Italianate in its use of textual repetition, melodic sequence, and chromaticism as the line in Example 13-4 extracted from his *petit motet O Flamma*. If the vocal scoring practices of the two composers are compared, clearly here, as in the *grands motets*, Robert was more concerned with contrasting sonorities. Lully scored seven of his motets for three high voices (*dessus*) and three for two high voices and bass. Robert scored four of his motets for various combinations of three voices; he scored five for combinations of two voices; and one, for a second tenor, two violins, and continuo.

Example 13-4. Robert: Extract from *O Flamma* (after Philidor copy).

Generation of Charpentier and Delalande

In 1683, well advanced in years after two decades of service at the king's Chapel, Du Mont and Robert retired. This left the prestigious post of *sous-maître* to be filled. The king, undoubtedly eager to dramatize his personal interest in the music of his Chapel, established a solemn competition for the position of four *sous-maîtres*. Thirty-five musicians from all over the realm competed. Among them were Jean Mignon of Notre-Dame; Guillaume Minoret of Saint-Germain l'Auxerrois; Jacques Lesueur from Rouen; Nicolas Coupillet (Goupillet) from the Cathedral of Meaux; Mallet from Avignon; Paolo Lorenzani, who was *Maître de Musique* for the queen; Guillaume-Gabriel Nivers, who was the king's organist; Daniel Daniélis; Jean Rebel; Pascal Collasse; Henry Desmarest; Marc-Antoine Charpentier; and Michel-Richard Delalande (who spelled his name this way on legal documents, but was also known as Lalande, de Lalande, De la Lande).

Each had a motet of his own composition performed, after which the king eliminated twenty from the competition. Those that remained were kept in isolation for several days while each composed a motet to the text of Psalm 31, *Beati quorum remissiae sunt*. From this final competition, four *sous-maîtres* were chosen: Coupillet, Collasse, Minoret, and Delalande. Charpentier, who was "extremely ill at the time of the isolation of the musicians" (*Mercure galant* 1683 [April], 313), did not take part in the final test and was awarded a consolation prize by the king in the form of a generous pension.

From the results of the competition, it is all too clear that outside influences determined the choice of most of the *sous-maîtres*. The first three were "safe" composers who offered no threat to Lully. Nicolas Coupillet was a mediocre composer from Senlis, whose subsequent *grands motets* for the Royal Chapel were actually ghost written for him by Henry Desmarest. Coupillet's ruse was discovered in a scandal which cost him his job in 1693. Collasse remained at the Royal Chapel until 1704, and Minoret, until 1714. In 1722 Delalande, in semi-retirement, shared his duties with Campra, Bernier, and Gervais.

Fortunately, the king insisted on his choice for the fourth *sous-maître*. "I have accepted, Messieurs, those whom you have chosen; it is only right that I choose one who conforms to my taste. It is Lalande whom I choose to be responsible for the quarter beginning in January" (Tannevot 1729, reprinted in *Notes et références pour servir à une histoire de Michel-Richard Delalande*, 1957, 150–151).

The *grand motet* reached full flower in France at the hands of two composers who led totally dissimilar lives. The one, Michel-Richard Delalande (1657–1726), received all but one of the possible official court appointments available to musicians; and the other, Marc-Antoine Charpentier (1643–1704), never received a direct court appointment. Between them, these two composers wrote more than three hundred motets; those of Delalande forming the basic repertoire of the Royal Chapel and later the Concert Spirituel, those of Charpentier serving the chapel of the Dauphin, the Jesuit church of Saint-Louis where he was employed after 1684, or the Sainte-Chapelle from 1698 to his death.

Charpentier certainly flourished without recourse to direct court patronage. More than five hundred of his compositions (sacred and secular vocal works, stage music, and instrumental works) exist in the twenty-eight volumes of autographs called the *Recueil des oeuvres manuscrites de musique du Sr Charpentier* (commonly referred to as the *Meslanges autographes*) which were sold in 1727 to the Royal Library by his nephew and are now preserved on microfilm at the Bibliothèque Nationale (see Ranum 1993). Undoubtedly, Lully considered Charpentier his most serious rival. Charpentier was an Italian-trained composer. He may well have aspired to composition for the lyric stage. Had he participated in the finals of the competition, Lully might have tried to block his appointment as *sous-maître*. Baptiste, however, seems to have made no overt effort to prevent Charpentier from receiving lucrative musical employment from a variety of Parisian sources. Nor did Charpentier lack royal favor. The king made it known in many ways that he was aware of Charpentier's worth as a composer and teacher. He saw to it that Charpentier was employed as the teacher of both his nephew, Philippe d'Orléans (the future Regent), and his oldest son, the *grand Dauphin*, for whose chapel Charpentier also served as *Maître de Musique*; in addition, the king offered no resistance to Charpentier's serving as a "composer-in-residence" for his cousin, Mlle de Guise (Marie de Lorraine) from about 1683 to her death in 1688.

How often did the paths of Charpentier and Delalande cross? What was their professional relationship at the Jesuit college, Louis-le-Grand, during the two years (1683–1685) of Delalande's employment there? Was it Charpentier who, fresh from his sojourn in Italy and from his lessons with Carissimi, introduced Delalande to the coterie surrounding Abbé Mathieu in Paris? Was it this introduction that led eventually to Delalande's inheritance of Italian cantatas and motets, the prize possessions of the *curé* of Saint-André-des-Arts? Did the Italian music introduced by Innocenzo Fede, the Master of Music at the court of the exiled Stuart monarchs James II and James III at Saint-Germain-en-Laye have an impact on Delaland? He had relatives living there who were closely connected with the English court (see Corp 1995, 227).

Delalande and Charpentier enjoyed popular success, although little of their music was published in their lifetime. Delalande's motets were considered "masterpieces of the genre" (Rousseau) and were known beyond the boundaries of France. "Delalande always enjoys a bright reputation, which nothing dims," wrote Nougaret. "They even perform most of his motets in Italy" (1769, 2:262).

Charpentier's reputation survived the vitriol of Lecerf: "I do not understand by what miracle Charpentier could have been expressive, that is, natural, vital, and correct, in his Latin music, he who was excessively harsh, dry, and affected in his French music" (1725; rpt. 1966, 4:121). He received the warm approbation of Brossard and the admiration of the brothers Parfaict: "a harmony and science [of composition] up to now unknown in France" (ca. 1741, 1:80). Serré de Rieux was impressed by Charpentier's dissonances: "In beautiful Harmony he pointed the way. Ninths and tritones shimmer under his hand" (1734, 112–113).

Happily, it is no longer possible to write as I did in the first edition of *French Baroque Music* that "for all practical purposes, both composers [Charpentier and Delalande] have barely survived the eighteenth century" (1974, 185). Since the publication of the first edition, Charpentier, in particular, has been well served by the publication of many performing editions of both sacred and secular works, two studies of his life and works (Cessac 1988 [Eng. trans. 1995] and Hitchcock 1990), a thematic catalogue (Hitchcock 1982), by doctoral theses (Parmley 1985, Burke 1985, and Powell 1982), the projected publication of all the volumes of the *Meslanges autographes* (Minkoff), by a semiannual Bulletin: *Société Marc-Antoine Charpentier* (edited by Cessac), and an impressive discography.

Unfortunately, the situation for Delalande is less encouraging. A thematic catalogue prepared by Sawkins is in progress. Two important doctoral theses (Coeyman 1987 and Sawkins 1993b), a handful of performing editions (most by Sawkins and Oboussier), a few articles and encyclopedia references, and a modest discography are available. A section on Delalande's *grands motets* was added to the third edition of Claude Palisca's *Baroque Music*.[9] Although out of date, *Notes et références pour servir à une histoire de Michel-Richard Delalande* (1957), edited by Norbert Dufourcq, remains a principal source for Delalande. Most of his seventy-one *grands motets* continue to slumber undisturbed in the archives of the Bibliothèque Nationale and the Bibliothèque Municipale de Versailles. It is a cruel fate that Delalande, who two years before his death was knighted a *Chevalier de Saint-Michel* by Louis XV, receives, as a motet composer, almost the same space (six lines) as Brossard in Prunières's *A New History of Music* (trans. Lockspeiser, 1943), and that he receives four lines in the standard English language text on the Baroque period (Bukofzer).

Gregorian chant and popular noels, Italian oratorio and cantata, French overture and dance measure, archaic polyphony and regal Versailles motet—all combine in the religious music of Charpentier. These elements document the composer's advice to his student, Philippe d'Orléans: "Diversity gives it [music] all its perfection, even as uniformity renders it insipid" (*Règles de Composition par Mr Charpentier*).[10]

Charpentier's motets range more widely in function than those by the Royal Chapel composers during the *grand siècle*. His motets group naturally into four divisions: hymns of praise to the Virgin or a Saint; psalms and Te Deums; Elevations, Lessons and Responses of Tenebrae; and miscelanea.

Charpentier composed *grands motets* for the Dauphin's chapel, the Sainte-Chapelle, and the most important Jesuit church, Église Saint-Louis. Some of his simpler *grands motets* and many *petits motets* were destined for convents, others for performances at Mlle de Guise's Hôtel du Marais; still others served as music for the many processions that were a regular feature of religious life in seventeenth-century Paris. The ceremony of the Benediction of the Blessed Sacrament (*Salut du Saint Sacrament*) during feasts such as Corpus Christi, Rogations, and Assumption, was the most common procession. Those in the procession would visit a series of street altars (*reposoirs*) where the Sacrament was exposed. At each altar of repose, a motet or a portion thereof was performed.

Unfortunately, we are in the dark concerning the dating of many of Charpentier's motets. Sometimes he wrote down the performers' names on the manuscript of a composition. These same names are also often found on the list of the six male and six female singers employed by Mlle de Guise during Charpentier's residency at her Hôtel du Marais. Occasionally the names correspond to musicians known to have worked at the Sainte-Chapelle. Certain *"pièces d'occasion,"* such as *In Obitum* (H. 409) composed for the death of Marie Thérèse in 1683, are, of course, datable. (For the chronology of Charpentier's works, see the interesting, albeit controversial, study of water marks and paper by Ranum 1994.)

Charpentier's motets lie in the middle ground between those by Du Mont and Lully, on the one hand, and those by Delalande, on the other. Some are almost without sectional divisions and constantly elide the different combinations of voices and instruments; others are virtual cantatas that include some autonomous sections in the style of certain Du Mont motets and the later motets by Delalande. Many make use of the type of structure already thoroughly explored by Du

Mont, in which an extended section is composed of episodes of motto-prelude, solo, ensemble, and chorus—all following one another without breaks. From time to time, Charpentier organized his motets in rondo form—rare in French religious music of the period and perhaps based on the rondo-cantatas popular in Rome or on his own Italian cantata, *Epithalamio* (H. 473), whose opening chorus recurs at the end (see, for example, *O filii et filiae* [H. 356], which is unified by an Alleluia refrain). Some motets are loosely organized in a chain of contrasting sections conforming more or less to Perrin's definition (see Chapter 12); others show remarkably tight organization similar to that found from time to time in Charpentier's own oratorios and Masses. The *Magnificat* (H. 74) for eight voices and eight instruments (one of ten settings of this text) is a symmetrical structure with a double chorus in the center flanked on both sides by solo or ensemble, the whole being framed by two double choruses (see Dufourcq 1963, 214).

In vocal and instrumental distribution of parts, Charpentier exhibits more imagination and sense of color than his predecessors. In many of his double chorus motets, the *grand* and *petit choeur* are both *a*4, with the composer favoring the soprano, *haute-contre*, tenor, and bass combination. We have already mentioned in Chapter 3 that Charpentier avoided the *a*5 vocal and instrumental texture so prevalent in French music of his day. Motets such as the *Miserere des Jésuites* (H. 193) in its second version and the antiphon *Salve Regina à trois choeurs* (H. 24) build up large choral sonorities unusual even for French music. In contrast, the *petit motet Sub tuum praesidium* (H. 28), obviously written for a convent and bearing the subtitle *Antiphona sine organo ad virginem*, is a rare example of an a cappella motet in the late seventeenth century. Its tender, personal intimacy is completely different from the official sound of the four extant Te Deums, which were written in the style of Lully during, perhaps, the last five years of Charpentier's life when he held the position of *Maître de Musique des Enfants* at the Sainte-Chapelle.

In some manuscripts, Charpentier was specific in his demands down to the last oboe; others are maddeningly incomplete. In the Te Deum (H. 145) edited by Denise Launay (1969, "Le Pupitre" series, Paris: Heugel), the title reads: *Te Deum à 8 voix, avec fl. et violons.* There is no indication whether or not one choir is a *petit choeur* of soloists, nor is there much specific information regarding instrumental scoring. Yet, in the couplet "Judex crederis esse venturus," for bass solo, Charpentier specified unequivocally, "Tous les Violons des 2 choeurs sans Flutes ny Hautbois" and carefully directed the violinists to play with mutes.

Charpentier was more of a colorist in his use of harmony than any other French composer of his generation. Like Purcell, he represents a transition from modality to tonality, and his cross-relations and other dissonant clashes are usually the result of the same tonal-modal conflict that so enriches the music of his English contemporary.

"Why different keys?" asked Charpentier in his little treatise, *Règles de Composition par Mr Charpentier*. He gave two reasons: the first, and less important, is to accommodate vocal ranges; the second, and principal, is "for the expression of different passions, for which the different key properties [*energies*] are appropriate." He included a list of keys, each followed by its corresponding affection.

Properties of the Modes

C major: Gay and warlike
C minor: Obscure and sad
D minor: Grave and pious
D major: Joyous and very warlike
E minor: Effeminate, amorous, and plaintive
E major: Quarrelsome and peevish
E-flat major: Cruel and severe
E-flat minor: Horrible, frightful
F major: Furious and quick tempered
F minor: Obscure and plaintive
G major: Quietly joyful
G minor: Serious and magnificent
A minor: Tender and plaintive
A major: Joyous and pastoral
B-flat major: Magnificent and joyous
B-flat minor: Obscure and terrifying
B minor: Lonely and melancholy
B major: Severe and plaintive

This chart, which precedes by thirty years Rameau's "De la propriété des Modes & des Tons" from the *Traité de l'harmonie*, has significance also in illustrating the wide range of keys that Charpentier felt were available to composers for expressing emotions.

Turning to two motets based on the Marian antiphon *Salve Regina*, we observe a striking example of Charpentier's use of harmony to dramatize the text. One, *Salve Regina* (H. 24), is scored for triple chorus and orchestra; the other, *Salve Regina* (H. 23), is a *petit motet* for "three like voices." In both settings, at the words, "Ad te clamamus, exsules, filii Hevae. Ad te suspira, gementes et flentes in hac lacrymarum valle" (To thee we cry out, exiled children of Eve; to thee we sigh, we mourn and weep in this vale of tears), Charpentier made use of the same material, obviously well pleased with the musical formula he had chosen for these words. In the *petit motet*, he extended by four measures the chromatically moving, parallel augmented triads found in the *grand motet* (Example 13-5a,b). As if to compensate for this audacity, he conventionalized the descending, chromatic harmonization of the concluding phrase of text, "In hac lacrymarum valle" (Example 13-5c). Perhaps nowhere in French Baroque music is there a more striking example of text painting than Charpentier's setting of this last phrase in the *grand motet* version (Example 13-5d). An almost Gesualdo-like series of descending augmented triads finally reaches a "very plaintive" augmented sixth chord just before the final A major triad. How this would have chilled the heart of Lecerf is easy to understand.

Example 13-5. Charpentier: *Salve Regina* motets. (a) *Grand motet* version (after the *Meslanges*, vol. 3). (b) *Petit motet* version (after the *Meslanges*, vol. 2). (c) *Petit motet* version (after the *Meslanges*, vol. 2). (d) *Grand motet* version (after the *Meslanges*, vol. 3).

The theoretical basis for Charpentier's treatment of dissonance is found in his *Règles de Composition par Mr Charpentier*. He ruled: "Several consecutive fourths or fifths are permissible between upper voices providing they move in conjunct motion and are of different types," but his example shows three consecutive perfect fifths followed by a diminished fifth (see Example 13-6a). He gives examples of augmented octaves and an augmented sixth chord (Example 13-6b), adding that "the augmented octave may only be used as in A and B and may be accompanied by the augmented sixth [*6^e plusque majeur*] as is shown in C." In the Brossard copy of the treatise, the augmented sixth chord is described thus: "This chord is very plaintive." The treatise also gives examples of cross-relations as seen in Example 13-6c.

Example 13-6. (a–c) Extract from Charpentier's *Règles de Composition*.

Dissonant intervals in Charpentier's music such as augmented fifths, parallel fifths, and augmented octaves are always by-products of complex part writing or are specifically chosen to express the text. Example 13-7 illustrates a build-up of eight independent vocal lines that results in some dissonance as well as in parallel fifths in the closing measures of the opening chorus of the Te Deum (H. 145).

Example 13-7. Charpentier: Extract from a Te Deum (after the *Meslanges*, vol. 15).

A favorite sonority of Charpentier was obtained by constructing a ninth chord on the third degree of a minor scale; its components included a major seventh and an augmented fifth. This mediant ninth chord, which often substituted for the dominant, was far from unique to Charpentier. Striking examples may be found in the motets of Delalande and the vocal and instrumental music of Couperin, among others. Its wide use was recognized by Nicolas Bernier, who mentioned it in his manuscript treatise *Principes de composition* as one type of augmented fifth that "can be used only on the mediant in the minor mode and then only when one is able to make thereby a ninth occurring on a strong beat" (see Bernier in translation by Nelson 1964, 14).

In his *Traité de l'harmonie*, Jean-Philippe Rameau treated this chord as an example of "chords by supposition, with which we may also avoid cadences while imitating them" (1722; English translation 1971, 88–91). Charpentier was always careful to let the text dictate the use of so dissonant a combination of tones. Example 13-8, from the six-part *Miserere des Jésuites* (H. 193), shows a typical use of this harmony with the $^9_7$ chord reserved for the words *a peccatis meis* (from my sins).
#5

Example 13-8. Charpentier: Extract from *Miserere des Jésuites* (after the *Meslanges*, vol. 7).

Rapid, expressive modulations, as well as chains of suspensions over a circle of fifths, are found in Charpentier's motets, yet surprisingly for someone with his interest in Italian music, he made little use of the diminished seventh or Neapolitan sixth chords.

Charpentier was never more Italian, however, than in his use of harmony to dramatize the texts of his motets. His three years in Rome had sensitized him to the dramatic possibilities of words in his motets as in his operas. His harmonic palette is certainly richer and more varied than that of his teacher, Carissimi. Nevertheless, he was no French Gesualdo nor even a Monteverdi. It would be a serious error to assume that the practices described above dominate his music stylistically. If anything, their judicious and sparing use increase their effectiveness. Charpentier's Italianism was tempered and restrained by the French tradition to which he adhered in most of his music. For him, this tradition embraced a melodic style derived from the court air and the dance. Although more contrapuntally oriented than Lully, his polyphony is often more suggested than real; points of imitation tend to line up in vertical sonorities after the initial entrances. The penetration of this tradition by influences from across the Alps gives Charpentier's motets their characteristic sound which justifies their being regarded as ideal examples of *goûts réunis*.

Of all the composers discussed thus far, Michel-Richard Delalande was most at home in the idiom of the *grand motet*. He was able to bring together totally dissimilar elements in a convincing manner and with an unprecedented depth of feeling. Co-existing in Delalande's motets are the official Versailles style and *galants* airs borrowed from opera; cantus-firmus treatment of Gregorian melodies in finely wrought polyphony are juxtaposed with homophonic "battle" choruses worthy of *Bellérophon*, as though, for him, there were no other way to praise his God and, incidentally, his king.

Like the music of Bach, the motets of Delalande are imbued with an overall spirituality that transcends Chapel and concert hall alike. Their eloquent message touched the favored few, who attended the king's Mass at Versailles, and the crowds who applauded them after 1725 at the Concert Spirituel in Paris. Far from just representing the "most conservative spirit of the period" (Bukofzer 1947, 259), they exhibit certain progressive tendencies in orchestral scoring, treatment of harmony and form, and attention to text. More restrained than Charpentier in their use of Italianisms, they nonetheless succeeded in humanizing what was in danger of becoming cold formulas of obeisance in the late Lully motets.

Colin de Blamont, a former student of Delalande, summarized his teacher's style succinctly in a letter to Alexandre Tannevot that is more perceptive than many present-day analyses. Tannevot included the letter in his *Avertissement* to the posthumous engraved edition of forty *grands motets* (1729) by Delalande. Colin de Blamont aptly labeled Delalande a "Latin Lully" and continued:

> *His great merit consisted in a wonderful choice of melody, a judicious choice of harmony, and a nobility of expression. He always sustained the value of the words he chose to treat and rendered musically their true meaning, their majesty and the holy enthusiasm of the Prophets . . . . Profound and learned on the one hand, simple and natural on the other, he applied all his study to touch the soul by richness of expression and vivid pictorialism; the mind is refreshed by the pleasing variety not only from one work to the next, but within the same piece . . . by the ingenious disparities with which he ornaments his works, by the graceful melodies that serve as contrasting episodes to the most complex choral sections (reprinted in* Notes et références, *1957, 155–156).*

That none of Delalande's seventy-one extant motets (seven are lost) was printed during his lifetime seems to suggest that a composer of his stature, completely secure in the paternalism of the regime, had no need to publish. Unfortunately, the 1729 edition is only complete with regard to the vocal and obbligato instrumental parts. The *a*5 orchestra is reduced to a trio texture for two first violins and bass—a less than satisfactory arrangement for a composer whose inner voice writing was generally more independent than that of his contemporaries.

In form, Delalande's later motets call to mind the German church cantata at the time of Bach. Most include autonomous movements, which are a succession of airs and ensembles (often with obbligato instruments) interspersed between choral sections. Most have opening *symphonies*; and in some motets, such as *Sacris solemnis* (1709), the use of a Gregorian hymn treated in cantus-firmus style in the opening chorus resembles a chorale "fantasia" typical of the opening movement of a Bach cantata. At the same time, many Delalande motets look back to Du Mont and Lully in that their opening section is based on a motto-prelude, followed by solo *récit*, ensemble, and chorus. Generally, however, each episode is considerably expanded and may be self-contained. In choosing psalms in preference to all other texts, Delalande was able to let the verses of the psalms dictate the musical form. Some are organized in recitative and air combinations; others, as solo and ensembles; still others, as choral movements.

Delalande placed solo instruments in dialogue with vocal solos and ensembles more than any other composer of *grands motets*. The air "Anima nostra," from Psalm 123, *Nisi quia Dominus* (1703), is accompanied by a solo recorder and solo violin that weave counterpoint around the vocal line. The *récit* "Ad vesperum," from Psalm 29, *Exaltabo te, Domine* (1704), juxtaposes transverse flutes and recorders; and the *récit* "Noctes recolitur," from *Sacris solemnis*, uses a bassoon line that is independent from the continuo. Borrowed from opera are airs such as "Ut eruat a morte" from Psalm 32, *Exsultate* (1710), in which a solo *haute-contre* supports melodic material delicately scored for two flutes and violins.

Delalande's use of counterpoint, both melodic and rhythmic, was not pedantic. A favorite device of his was to present the subject and counter-subject separately, in the *symphonie* and following solo *récit*, and then to combine them in a large fugal chorus. In the hymn *Veni Creator Spiritus* (before 1689), the text of the fifth verse is first set for solo *récit* (tenor) in which two clearly differentiated musical ideas are assigned to "Hostem repellas longius" (Repel afar our earthly foes) and to "Pacemque dones protinus" (Let us dwell henceforth in peace). These two ideas are then combined in a double chorus setting of ten different voice parts; the first choir is predominantly homophonic and the second, polyphonic (see Example 13-9, below).

Example 13-9. Delalande: Extract from *Veni Creator Spiritus* (after Philidor copy).

In spite of an occasional subordination of textual clarity to musical devices as in Example 13-9, Delalande understood Latin prosody better than most of his contemporaries, and he took pains to choose the musical motives best suited for individual words or phrases. Single key words, such as *non, portantes, mors, ploremus*, receive dramatic impetus by means of repetition and above all by the effective use of rests. Triadic motives appropriate for certain words recur with those words in several motets (see Example 13-10).

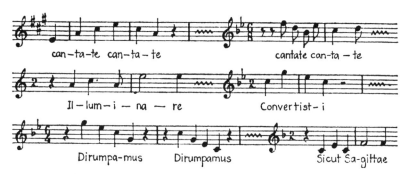

Example 13-10. Use of triadic motives in selected motets of Delalande.

Delalande sought maximum musical contrast between textual ideas in apposition. This is generally achieved either through the choice of melodic materials that, because of built-in rhythmic differences, combine effectively in counterpoint, or it is achieved through a clear contrast of mood resulting from the direction and choice of intervals and change in modality.

Delalande's use of harmony undoubtedly owes something to his exposure to the music of Charpentier. The $^{9}_{7}$ chord on the mediant, found so often in the music of Charpentier, is no stranger to the motets of his younger contemporary. Perhaps more than any other French composer before Rameau, Delalande viewed the diminished seventh chord as vested with a compelling dramatic quality. In Example 13-11, from *Pange lingua*, the careful choice of diminished seventh chords, coupled with a dramatic "silence" (the word is found in the score), is yet another example of the great care he took to find the most effective musical setting for the text.

Example 13-11. Delalande: Extract from *Pange lingua* (after the ed. of 1729).

Plate 1. Louis XIV as the Sun in the *Ballet de la Nuit*, 1653 (Bibliothèque Nationale, Cabinet des Estampes).

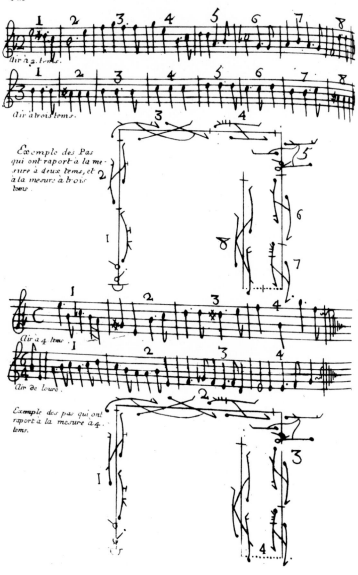

Plate 2. Example of choreography relating to measures of music from Feuillet's *Chorégraphie ou l'art de décrire*, 1713 edition (Special Collections, University of California at Los Angeles).

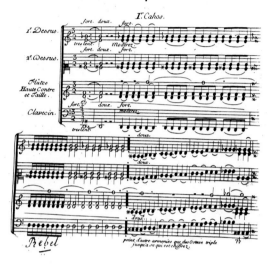

Plate 3. Opening page of Rebel's *Les Éléments* in the edition of 1737 (Bibliothèque Nationale Vm^7 1153).

Plate 4. Adagio of the sonata, Opus 9, No. 5 from Book 4 of the violin sonatas by Leclair (Bibliothèque Nationale Vm^7 748).

Plate 5. Adagio of the sonata, Opus 5, No. 12 from Book 3 of the violin sonatas by Leclair (Bibliothèque Nationale, Vm⁷ 747).

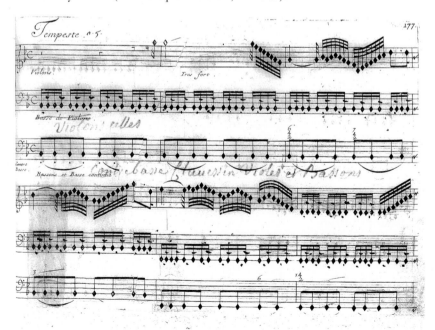

Plate 6. Handwritten *inégales* from Marais's Alcyone (Bibliothèque de l'Opéra, Baussen edition, MS A.69c).

Delalande's orchestra plays both a supportive and an independent role in his *grands motets*. Usually, it functions in both capacities at the same time. That is, some of the voices double the choral lines, while others weave an independent counterpoint around the voice parts, as we see in the chorus "Et ipse redimet Israël" from *De profundis* (Example 13-12a below). Example 13-12b shows the first violins and sopranos in "Desiderium peccatorum peribit" from Psalm 111 *Beatus vir qui timet Dominum*, in which a simple and adorned version of the same melody is used simultaneously, resulting in a kind of heterophony. In contrapuntal choruses, the orchestra often contributes a fugal entrance, independent of the voices. In *De profundis*, the subject of the "Requiem aeternam" is treated in imitative entrances spaced one measure apart and shared by voices and instruments (see Example 13-12c). In Psalm 45, *Deus noster* (1699), the orchestra supports the double chorus "Conturbatae sunt gentes" with ostinato rhythms to create an operatic battle scene of great power.

The "graceful melodies," noted by Colin de Blamont in his letter to Tannevot, form contrasting episodes. Borrowed from opera, they probably served as performance vehicles for Delalande's two daughters, both of whom had excellent voices, or for his wife, Anne Rebel, who was the sister of composer-performer Jean Féry Rebel, and who was one of the best singers of the king's Chamber. Like the da capo arias of Bach cantatas, they are "ingenious disparities" when placed in apposition to large double choruses. Some were written in a virtuoso and bravura style; others are more restrained in the manner of an operatic air by Lully. In the air "Illumina oculos meos," from Psalm 12, *Usquequo, Domine* (1692), the arpeggiated accompaniment pattern prefigures the *style galant* of the later eighteenth century (see Example 13-13). In certain *grands motets*, Delalande set the words of the verses to a series of airs (labeled *récits*) in much the same manner as Lully organized entire scenes in his operas around short dialogue airs interspersed with recitatives. *Exultate justi in Domino*, for example, contains five consecutive *récits* and one recitative. These give musical expression to six verses (see Anthony 1986b, 24–25).

The majority of Delalande's motets are found in three large collections: (1) the manuscript copy of twenty-seven motets made by Philidor in 1689 and 1690, now located at the Bibliothèque Municipale de Versailles (MSS 8–17); (2) the posthumously printed edition of forty motets mentioned above; and (3) the manuscript copy of forty-one motets and some shorter pieces made for, or by, a certain Gaspard-Alexis Cauvin and now housed, except for the last volume, at the Bibliothèque Municipale de Versailles (MSS 216–235).[11] The Cauvin manuscript seems to be a later eighteenth-century copy of the 1729 printed edition with a changed sequence of motets and the addition of one motet, *Exaudi Deus*. The Cauvin manuscript has the great advantage of including the instrumental inner voices ("parties de remplissage") in contrast to the printed edition which reduces Delalande's large orchestra to two violins and continuo. Eight motets in the early Philidor copy also appear in the Cauvin manuscript and, with one exception, in the printed edition.[12] Delalande continually revised his motets. Thirty-two exist in more than one version; some in three, and one, the Te Deum, in four (see Sawkins 1993b, 186). According to Tannevot's preface:

> *From the time of the former king [Louis XIV], he had begun to make changes in several of his earlier motets. Noting this, His Majesty prevented him from continuing, possibly to render more obvious the progress made under his aegis by the composer, possibly to preserve the grace and naïvety of the first works, or finally, because of fear that this occupation, which took so much time, would prevent him from composing new music (reprinted in* Notes et références, *1957, 152).*

A study of the revisions gives insight into Delalande's development. The Philidor copy of 1689 and 1690 represents an early style. These motets exploit the vertical sonorities and syllabic treatment of text that characterized the earlier Versailles motet. Many *récits*, often accompanied by *a*5 strings, are open-ended and elide with choral sections. Perhaps Tannevot judged them too harshly when he wrote that the "first compositions of M^r De La Lande are not as well worked as the last pieces; they are more simple than profound and are less the fruits of art than of Nature" (reprinted in *Notes et références*, 1957, 149). Soon after the turn of the century, Delalande suffered a crisis of conflicting styles engendered, at least in part, by his exposure to Italian music. He, like Charpentier, was a member of the coterie surrounding the Italophile Nicolas Mathieu, the *curé* of Saint-André-des Arts, and we recall that Delalande inherited Abbé Mathieu's Italian cantatas and motets.

Example 13-12. (a) Extract from *De profundis* (after ed. of 1729). (b) Extract from *Beatus vir* (after ed. of 1729). (c) Extract from *De profundis*.

The 1729 engraved edition and the Cauvin manuscript offer the most complete picture of the *grands motets* by the mature Delalande. In general, the changes that occur in the revisions and in the motets written after 1710 are the following: (1) change from a loosely organized structure with elided sectional divisions to autonomous movements of chorus, solo, and ensemble that resemble the so-called reform cantata by J. S. Bach or the Restoration anthem by Humfrey or Purcell; (2) creation of autonomous, elaborate concert "arias," which are accompanied by one or more obbligato instruments, out of simple *récits* with five-part homophonic accompaniment; (3) change from a predominantly homophonic choral texture to one that is more polyphonic; (4) change from an orchestra used primarily to double choral lines to one that is more independent of the voices; and (5) greater economy in the use of some material while other material is expanded.

Example 13-13. Delalande: Extract from *Usquequo Domine* (after the ed. of 1729).

A fine example of the fifth category is the "Requiem aeternam" from *De profundis*. The Philidor copy includes a *symphonie* of fourteen measures, a solo *récit* of eight measures, a second *symphonie* of six measures, and a chorus of thirty-one measures up to the "Et lux perpetua." The chorus is basically homophonic with clear separation of textual elements (Example 13-14a). The later and best-known version has only one *symphonie* of nine measures that merges with a fifty-three-measure chorus up to "Et lux perpetua." The chorus, this time, unifies textual elements and is written in dense, five-part polyphony of Bach-like intensity in which both voices and instruments participate (Example 13-14b).

Example 13-14. Delalande: *De profundis.* (a) First version (after Philidor copy). (b) Second version (after the ed. of 1729).

The bond between Michel-Richard Delalande, the fifteenth son of a Parisian tailor, and his king, the favored scion of the Bourbon dynasty, was a strong one, apparently nourished by adversity. In 1711 death took Delalande's two daughters, then came for the king's son. Tannevot relates that after the loss of the Dauphin, Louis XIV told Delalande, "You have lost two daughters, who were deserving of merit: I have lost Monseigneur. Lalande, it is necessary to submit [to the will of God]" (reprinted in *Notes et références*, 1957, 151).

Working in 1710 from the plans of his late brother-in-law, Jules-Hardouin Mansart, Robert de Cotte finished a project dear to the heart of the aging Sun King—the building of the new and final Versailles Chapel. In a figurative and literal sense, it was the *grands motets* of Delalande that gave to the new Chapel its most eloquent voice. The grand conception now could be realized with a choir and orchestra totaling close to ninety members and with the magnificent organ of Robert Clicquot, which possessed four manuals and thirty-six stops.

Out of her vast knowledge of French religious music of the *grand siècle*, Michel Brenet penned a moving tribute to the new Chapel, its composer, its musicians, and its king:

The old sovereign crosses by foot the galleries of Versailles to come to his recently finished chapel, brilliant with gold and light; one hundred Swiss guards line the way of his passage; the body guards await him at the Tribune, the chaplain at the holy water basin, the priests in the choir, the ladies in the balcony, the courtiers in the nave, the musicians behind their stands: he passes, noble, handsome, always the king; . . . the celebrant begins the Office, and Lalande lifts his baton; the music, indifferent to any liturgical chronology, is a motet for large chorus . . . . At first there is a symphonie *played by all the musicians of the chamber; then the two daughters of Lalande, the Italian Favalli or Sieur Borel de Miracle, sing some* récits *and duos accompanied by Philibert Rebillé on the transverse flute or Marais playing a bass viol solo; singers and virtuosi compete; there are the* gracieux, *the* tendrement, *the* légers *and the* loure . . . *all the* agréments *that suggest French melody; all this, set off by the overwhelming effect of the choruses . . . that follow the instruments and prepare for the end of the ceremony and the departure of the King (1899, 12–13).*

Chapter 14

The Motet in the Eighteenth Century

*B*ecause of its function as the chief musical element in the king's Mass, the *grand motet* in France took on the aspects of a sacred concert right from its inception. Its composers favored musical settings of non- or para-liturgical texts, as opposed to the words of the liturgy, and apparently Delalande himself made no effort to coordinate his *grands motets* with the liturgical year.

No one pretended that the motet was an integral part of the liturgy. This should not imply that somehow it was less religious than a polyphonic Mass, for example. What makes a composition religious other than text is impossible to define unless one arbitrarily chooses Gregorian chant or Palestrina Mass as the only true measure. The *grand motet* could not isolate itself from the aggressive state religion it served. The battle chorus of Delalande's *Deus noster* expresses the tone of the church of a Bossuet as much as Handel's "Hallelujah Chorus" speaks for the muscular protestantism of eighteenth-century England.

It should come as no surprise to find an acceleration in the secularization of religious music as the *grand siècle* gave way to the Regency. Thus, the motets by Brossard and Morin include Alleluia finales organized as instrumental gigues, and a *petit motet* by Mouret (*O sacrum convivium*) even allows the soprano soloist a cadenza. Only the musical integrity of a Couperin allows us to accept Gregorian melodies which, at first glance, seem over-laden with *tremblements* and *ports de voix*. The motets by Campra and Gilles are permeated by the popular tunes of their meridional homeland.

Secularization was inevitable, especially in a religion that used all its musical resources to parade its opulence and to orchestrate its power. The *Mercure* of June 1716 describes a religious procession *de luxe* that made use of an altar of repose (*reposoir*) near the Palais de Luxembourg in Paris:

All the court had been decorated with the most beautiful and richest tapestries of the Gobelins, the same as in the Marble Court where all the paving was covered with tapestries . . . . On the left, they had set up a theater for the musicians who were all the best voices of the Opera and several players of all kinds of instruments . . . . As soon as the banner of the Procession approached, the Duchesse de Berry went out of the doorway of the palace . . . to receive the Procession and adore the Holy Sacrament, which she then accompanied to the reposoir. *During all this time, the trumpets, drums, oboes, and bassoons that were on the balcony were heard. Then the musicians sang a motet composed by M. Destouches (218–221).*

Undoubtedly, the convents of the *Théatins* and the *Feuillants* and the Abbey of Longchamp had long deserved the admonition of Mme de Maintenon that they had made an opera house of their church. Lecerf has left us a vivid description of performances at convents by popular singers who were followed by groups of their fashionable admirers when the opera was closed:

One pays them to perform the most pious and solemn Motets! We have been doing better for several years: one hires singers, who sing a Lesson on Good Friday or a solo motet on Easter behind a curtain that they draw apart from time to time to smile at their friends among the listeners. One goes to hear them at an appointed Convent. In their honor, one pays the price for a seat at the Church that one would pay at the door of the Opera. One recognizes Urgande *and* Arcabonne *[characters in Lully's* Amadis*] and claps one's hands. (I have seen clapping at Tenebrae and Assumption Services; I do not recall whether it was for* la Moreau *or for* Madame Cheret*); and these Spectacles replace those that cease during this fifteen-day period) (1725; rpt. 1966, 4:162).*

Secularization is no stranger to religious music. At its best, it results in healthy cross-fertilization, beneficial to both the secular and the religious. *Trouvère* melodies soften the harsh contours of the Gothic motet; *motet-chanson*, as a term, indicates its dual origins; and the secular musical world of Baroque opera, dance suite, French overture, Italian concerto, and Italian sonata is synthesized in the church cantatas of J. S. Bach. In France, secularization was more a symptom than a cause of the decline of religious music in the eighteenth century. It was the reflection of an age grown tired of heroic posturing and a King-God.

Lacking any firm liturgical base, deprived of a ruling monarch, dependent upon a disinterested Regency, and on purely stylistic grounds, the *grand motet* should never have survived the *grand siècle*. It was out of joint with the frivolous and feminine world of the Regency; its grandiloquent gesture, hollow; its form, an empty shell. Yet, survive it did—a monolithic vestige of the age of the Sun King, permanently stabilized, it seemed, as part of the repertory of the Royal Chapel and the Concert Spirituel.

This of itself need not have precipitated a decline had there been composers of the caliber of Delalande who might have infused the *grand motet* with new life; but who now would revive the *grands motets* of Philippe Courbois, of Charles Gauzarques, or Abbé Gaveau?

French composers of the rank of Rameau or Leclair were almost totally committed to stage or instrumental music from the 1730s on. Perhaps they had the instinct, or good sense, to realize that the frivolity of the times, coupled with a strong anti-clericalism—the natural issue of the repressive religious atmosphere at the close of the *grand siècle*—was not the best intellectual or moral climate in which to promote significant religious music.

Grands motets, written for the most part in the early and middle years of the century by composers who had mastered the old style, dominated the repertory of the Royal Chapel up to the very eve of the Revolution. For example, the titles and texts of motets performed at the Royal Chapel from January to June in 1792 appear in the volume of the *Livre de motets pour la Chapelle du Roy* (Ballard, 1787–1792) that was published that year. Included are twenty-five by Madin, fourteen by Delalande, thirteen by Campra, five by Gervais, and four by Bernier.

Henry Desmarest (1663–1741) (Desmarets, Desmarais) might have enjoyed a more prosaic but secure career as composer for the court and Royal Chapel had he not become involved in an amorous imbroglio resulting in his expulsion from the realm.[1] From Titon du Tillet, we learn that the motet by Desmarest, performed for Louis XIV at the time of the 1683 competition, was "one of the most beautiful . . . but the King thought him to be too young to hold one of the appointments . . . and gave him a nine hundred *livres* pension instead" (1732; supplement 1743, 755).

As a student or follower of Du Mont, Robert, and Lully and as a successor to Charpentier at the Jesuit College, Desmarest, by training and apparently by inclination, would have been ideally suited to work with Delalande at the Royal Chapel. Of all Delalande's younger contemporaries, he was the best able to fill the large dimensions of the *grand motet* with convincing music.

Motets in manuscript, now at the Bibliothèque Nationale and the Bibliothèque Municipale de Lyon, show Desmarest's style at its best. Four of those at the Bibliothèque Nationale are psalm settings, each averaging over one hundred pages! From Delalande, he had learned how to treat his orchestra independently from the chorus. Desmarest "thought" more polyphonically than any other composer of his generation in France. The *grand motet* setting of Psalm 6, *Domine, ne in furore*,[2] which was composed about 1707 for the Duc de Lorraine, includes a vocal quartet (two sopranos, *haute-contre*, bass) accompanied by flutes and strings for the verse "Laboravi in gemitu meo." Here is dense polyphony involving voices and instruments, in which individual lines maintain their direction and tension. Without any linear clogging, all parts share in the overlapping descending motif on the words, "Lacrymis meis stratum meum rigabo" (I will water my couch with my tears) (see Example 14-1 below).

All that remain of the *grands motets* of Guillaume Minoret (ca. 1650–1720), one of the winners of the 1683 competition, are six motets copied by Philidor in 1697. Judging from these works, Minoret's style appears conservative; the instrumental accompaniment is reduced to a continuo in some double choir motets. Yet, remarks by Titon du Tillet provoke interest and remind us of the dangers of generalizing from such a small sample. In *Le Parnasse françois*, Titon wrote as follows:

> *Several pieces have singular beauty and may be called masterpieces of Music. I speak here only of the third Verse of the Psalm* Nisi Dominum . . . . *For this Verse, Minoret composed Music for four different Voices with an accompaniment for Violins and Basses, which also have independent parts—the whole results in a very beautiful piece that one can say is almost unique (1732, 561).*

Jean Gilles (1668–1705)[3] directed successively the choir schools at Aix-en-Provence, Agde, and at Saint-Étienne of Toulouse, where he remained from 1697 to his death. His known music consists of eleven *grands motets*, a Te Deum, three Lamentations, two Masses, and several *petits motets*, all of which are conserved today in manuscripts at the Bibliothèque Nationale and the Bibliothèque Méjanes at Aix-en-Provence.

Gilles, who had studied with Poitevin at Aix, was far away from direct influence of the Royal Chapel and consequently from pressure to compose "official" religious music. His motets are more personal and intimate. Although heavy with ornament, the melodic line of the *récits* is often popular in nature, reflecting the irregular phrase length of Provençal melody.

Example 14-1. Desmarest: Extract from *Domine, ne in furore* (after MS *Rés.* F 928 in Bibliothèque Nationale).

At the close of the seventeenth century, the *petit motet* had not as yet succumbed to virtuoso elements stemming from the Italian cantata and opera. The *Motets à voix seule avec la basse continue* by Guillaume-Gabriel Nivers (1632–1714) are representative. These sixty-one motets were written and published in 1689 for the young women of the Maison Royale de Saint-Louis at Saint-Cyr, where the composer served as organist and choir director. They are intimate works, obviously composed with the resources of the "Dames de Saint-Louis" in mind, and thirteen of them contain dialogues for solo voices and unison chorus. Nivers eschewed both vocal virtuosity and overt dramatic expression. Even so, Mme de Maintenon, who had founded Saint-Cyr in 1686 for the education of young noble women (see Bert 1963, 1964, and 1965), forbade the performance of one of the motets, *Adjuro Vos*, because it was "too tender."

The motets are short. Some are in binary and some in rondo form with an Alleluia acting as refrain. French vocal *agréments*, especially the *port de voix* and the *coulé*, inundate the melodic line. Short vocalises, sometimes placed rather arbitrarily on unimportant words, contribute to the creation of a busy melody (see Example 14-2).

[Pu-] tri   et   fi — li-o

Example 14-2. Nivers: Extract from Magnificat (after ed. of 1689).

Louis-Nicolas Clérambault (1676–1749), who served as *Maître de Chapelle* at Saint-Cyr along with Nivers, also contributed several *petits motets*. Clérambault composed his *petits motets* for one or two solo voices that alternate with a unison or two-part chorus. In addition, Jean-Baptiste Moreau (1656–1733), Delalande, Collasse, and Louis Marchand (1669–1732) all furnished settings of Racine's *Cantiques spirituels* for the young ladies of Saint-Cyr. Mme de Maintenon requested Racine to write a biblical tragedy, with recitatives and choruses to be provided by Moreau. On 26 January 1689, Racine and Moreau's tragedy *Esther* was performed in the presence of Louis XIV and Bossuet. It was so successful that a second tragedy with music by Moreau was requested by Mme de Maintenon. The result was *Athalie*, first performed on 5 January 1691.

Daniel Daniélis (1635–1696), like Du Mont, a Walloon born near Liège, was named *Maître de Chapelle* at Saint-Pierre in 1684 in Vannes, where his motets remained popular throughout the eighteenth century. He left us seventy-two motets ranging from one to four voices, which are scattered today in various manuscript copies at the Bibliothèque Nationale and the University library at Uppsala (see Bourligneux 1964). They are replete with textual repetitions, vocalises, chromaticism, text painting, and rapid and frequent modulations. No wonder Lecerf thought him to have been an Italian and coupled his name with that of Lorenzani as rare examples of Italian composers worthy of commendation.

Sébastien de Brossard (1655–1730) wrote three *grands motets* (probably for the Cathedral of Strasbourg), six shorter choral works, and about thirty *petits motets*.[4] He also orchestrated and composed additional music for the unaccompanied Masses by Bartolomo Baldrati, François Cosset, Pietro Antonio Fiocco, and Charles

D'Helfer. He was quite capable of writing in the *stile antico* as well. His *Cantique à l'honneur de Sainte-Cécile*, for example, is a highly imitative, unaccompanied motet for chorus *a*4.[5]

Among Brossard's most important religious compositions are the eight *petits motets* for solo voice of his *Élévations et motets* of 1695 (published again in 1698 and 1702). Musically, they stem more from Lully than from Charpentier and appear almost devoid of any real Italian influence—surprising in a composer so aware of and so partisan to the Italian musical penetration of France. Their main interest lies in their formal structure, which divides the music into several autonomous, contrasting sections that often end with an Alleluia or an Amen finale. The latter are well-developed compositions in their own right that, the composer informs us, can be performed as separate pieces. Typical in its sectionizing is number six of the set, *Angele sancte*, which has the following movement and meter scheme:

Adagio e affettuoso	Presto e Allegro	Adagio
(3/2)	(C)	(3/4)
Largo	Allegro e Presto	Presto e Allegro
(C)	(C)	(12/8)

The last "Presto e Allegro" amounts to an "Amen, Alleluia" and is, in truth, an instrumental gigue with words (see Example 14-3).

Example 14-3. Brossard: Extract from *Angele sancte* (after ed. of 1695).

Brossard's Avertissement suggests a practical reason for defining these sections so clearly:

Although these Motets may appear to be a little too long, they are only as long as one wishes, because they are arranged so that, in nearly every case, one may end at the place where one finds the mark A over a note.

As early as 1701 in his edition of the motets by Jacques-François Lochon (born ca. 1660), Ballard anticipated the fad of a fusion of Italian and French taste in the French cantata and other genres. The printer promoted his publication in an *Avertissement*:

Persuaded that what is new always pleases, I give these Motets to the Public with pleasure; the well-informed have found them in such good taste and the Nuns have found them so appropriate for the Choir, that I dare hope for an agreeable reception for them—all the more so because, in performing them, one will acknowledge that the Composer's genius has found the secret of uniting the structure, scheme, & expression of Italian music with the turn of phrase, delicateness, & gentleness of the French.

The motets include Italian terms taken from Brossard and a profusion of repeated text fragments, worked into long vocal melismas. This undoubtedly convinced Lecerf that he could expect nothing good from the new motets in "Franco-Italian taste" by Lochon. He objected: "I would never intentionally promote a profession of half-copying Italian composers. I cannot repeat too often that their use of dissonance, changes of key, broken melodic lines etc. does not conform at all to our Music" (1725; rpt. 1966, 4:143).

By 1703 André Campra let it be known in the title to his third book of motets that he had included a motet "*à la manière italienne.*" In fact, his first four books of motets provide the best material for studying the effect of the Italian cantata upon the French motet. Coming from Aix-en-Provence, Campra surely was no stranger to Italian religious music, and it is quite possible that soon after his arrival in Paris (1694) he became familiar with the popular motets by Paolo Lorenzani that had been in print for a year.

As the eighteenth century progressed, the *petit motet* and the *cantate françoise* tended to differ only in subject matter and language. They employed almost identical melodic formulas shaped by French ornamentation and Italian melisma. Both make use of recitatives and share da capo airs, and in both genres the driving rhythms of the Italian concerto and the gentle homophony of a French *sommeil* co-exist.

Campra's *petits motets* appear to have been preliminary studies in "*la manière italienne.*" Significantly, all four books[6] of his *petits motets* appeared before his first book of *Cantates Françoises* in which he elevated the combining of French *delicatesse* and Italian *vivacité* to a guiding principle.

The first book of Campra's *Motets à I, II et III voix avec la basse continue* was printed by Ballard in the same year as Brossard's *Élévations et motets* (1695). Three of the fourteen *petits motets* include parts for two violins—instruments, it will be remembered, that Campra introduced at Notre-Dame Cathedral where he had replaced Jean Mignon as director of the choir school in 1694. The melodies of this first set still have some of the simplicity and freshness that spring from the sun-drenched soil of Provence. They are similar to the melodies Campra composed two years later for his *opéra-ballet L'Europe galante.* Vocal melismas are restrained, but the harmony is richer, the modulations are more rapid and often move to more distant keys than is true in the motets of Brossard. *Tota pulchra es* (text from the *Song of Songs*) is an Italian chamber duet wed to a French passacaille (see Example 14-4). A sensuous melody moving predominantly in parallel thirds creates attractive double suspensions with the rigid bass line; the identical bass was used later by Campra to support the magnificent air "Sommeil qui chaque nuit" from the second *entrée* ("L'Espagne") of *L'Europe galante*.

Example 14-4. Campra: Extract from *Tota pulchra es* (after ed. of 1695).

Books 2 and 3 have more variety than the earlier set in terms of instrumental accompaniment (flutes and violins) and musical forms. *Immensus es Domine* from Book 2 uses two flutes and includes a thirty-two-measure *ritournelle*. *O Jesu amantissime*, from the same collection, includes a passage bristling with cross-relations and stark chromaticism over a dominant pedal (see Example 14-5).

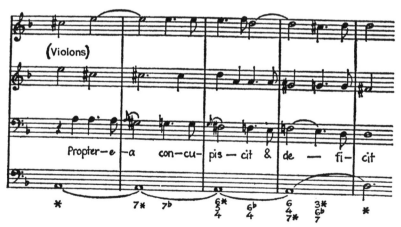

Example 14-5. Campra: Extract from *O Jesu amantissime* (after ed. of 1699).

Book 3 is closer yet to the Italian cantata. Two da capo arias frame *O Dulcis amor* (No. 3). There are more *airs de vitesse* and demanding vocalises. The third book was less successful than the earlier two, and Lecerf lost no time in placing the blame for this on Campra's "imitation of the Italians," adding smugly that the "price and power of true and false beauty are quite different" (1725; rpt. 1966, 4:118).

Book 4 of 1706 completed the process of Italianizing the *petit motet*. Da capo airs dominate, and frequent textual repetitions give rise to sequential patterns and long melismas that do little to illuminate the text and much to tire the listener.

Campra returned to the *petit motet* after fourteen years (Book 5, 1720). The final motet in this volume, *Ecce panis angelorum*, is a grand work that stretches the boundaries of the *petit motet*. It is scored for three voices, violins, flutes, and trumpets or oboes, and it is not surprising that years later Campra revised the final movement, "Cantate Domino," for chorus and full orchestra.

The most impressive of Campra's fifty-one *grands motets* were composed late in his life and formed part of the repertory of the Royal Chapel. They include two books of *Psaumes à grand choeur*, which were published in 1737 and 1738, respectively, as well as many manuscript copies found in the Bibliothèque Nationale and the Bibliothèque Méjanes in Aix-en-Provence. These motets borrow indiscriminately from the style of the composer's own *tragédies en musique*. Bravura passages for soloists abound and are often accompanied by virtuoso instrumental obbligatos; duos and trios are sometimes unified by recurring *ritournelles*; exciting, war-like choruses are set against a background of rapid violin figurations; and Psalm 75, *Notus in Judaea Deus*, includes an operatic *sommeil*. As in the earlier motet collections and his stage music, Campra displays great skill in constructing large-scaled movements over emphatic ostinato patterns such as the double fugue "Et lux perpetua" from *De profundis* and the opening of the *Magnificat* in the Aix collection.

More Italian than the motets of Campra are the two books of motets (1704, 1709) by Jean-Baptiste Morin (1677–1754), who, like Campra and Bernier, was in the employ of Philippe d'Orléans. Da capo arias include sequences of sevenths and circles of fifths. Like the *Élévations et motets* by Brossard, many contain detachable Alleluia finales, one of which is also a vocal gigue.

The twelve *Motets à I, II et III voix* of 1711 by Edme Foliot (died before 1752) are in the tradition of Nivers. Although they are more French than Italian, these motets include some sentimental duos where paired voices create chains of suspensions (for example, "Ora pro nobis" from *Regina coeli*). As though to dispel fears that his motets were other than a type of *Gebrauchsmusik* for the convent, Foliot wrote in his *Avertissement*: "I have had no other purpose in mind in composing these works than to render them useful to the Nuns . . . . I have restricted myself to the flowing and natural melody, so sought after by all people of good taste." Foliot designed his motets so that they may be abridged, like Brossard's, "in order not to prolong the Divine Office."

The motets by Nicolas Bernier (1665–1734)[7] are more important musically. His first book, which appeared in 1703, was criticized by Lecerf, who found his duos and trios "disagreeably marked with the stamp of Italy" (1725; rpt. 1966, 4:141). A total of forty-five *petits motets* were printed in three volumes widely spaced in time (1703, 1713, 1741). Thirty are for solo voice, and some include violin, two violins, or flute *ritournelles*. The restrained vocalises and the use of motto beginnings are discreetly Italian. Most conform to Perrin's definition of being "several pieces loosely strung together," although a few use rondo structure.

Bernier composed eleven *grands motets* for the Royal Chapel, where he was employed with Campra, Delalande, and Gervais from 1723 until his death. They are all in manuscript. Less operatic than those of Campra, they lie clearly in the tradition of the Versailles motet. The orchestra of five-part strings doubles the *grand choeur*. The *petit choeur* emphasizes the high voices of sopranos and *hautes-contres*. The harmonic language is conservative when compared with that of Charpentier or Delalande, although with considerably more harmonic interest than is found in the later motets of Lully.

The high musical quality of the two extant *grands motets* by François Pétouille (1681–1730), who followed Lalouette at Notre-Dame, gives us cause to regret the loss of so many others. Like Delalande, Pétouille "thought" polyphonically. Also like Delalande, he was gifted in choosing contrasting motives for different text phrases that combine in a natural manner (see, for example, "Et in saecula saeculorum," and "Amen" in the "Gloria Patri" of *Confitebor tibi*). Like those by Delalande, his airs, labeled *gracieusement* or *tendrement*, are "ingenious disparities" when placed next to the large choruses.

Virtually ignored by Lecerf, who considered him only as a "*serviteur passionné de l'Italie*" (1725; rpt. 1966, 4:210), François Couperin (1668–1733) succeeded better than all his contemporaries in the creation of a musical language compounded of French and Italian elements. In the *petits motets*, these *goûts réunis* appear to have been a natural musical expression for Couperin, whose personal style was rarely lost in self-conscious imitation of "*la manière italienne*." French are the short phrases, the many perfect cadences, and the melodic formulas derived from *airs sérieux* or dance measures. French, too, is the ornamentation, carefully calculated here, as in the keyboard works, for maximum expressiveness—used now as an accent, now as a built-in rubato; placed here to lend a sense of harmonic urgency, there to serve as decorative arabesque. Italian are the vivid musical images that underscore the text and the ability to paint a dramatic scene albeit in miniature. Italian also are the infusion of vocalises in the melodic line, the abrupt changes of tonality, and the frequent chromaticism.

Most commonly, elements of both styles co-exist harmoniously in the same composition. However, there are examples of pure Italian vocal and instrumental style in immediate apposition to what is unmistakably French. Such are the first two movements of the *Motet de Sainte-Suzanne*. The opening *haute-contre* solo, "Veni, veni sponsa Christi," with its light polyphony, its use of an introductory phrase that generates small rhythmic cells to be later employed in counterpoint, could be by Vivaldi or Handel. It is followed by a duet for soprano and *haute-contre*, "Date serta," which, with its note-against-note style, lack of melisma, and short phrases, could be by Lully.

The *petits motets* and Elevations by Couperin are not operatic, although they borrow freely from opera. An over-riding sense of balance and propriety subordinate virtuoso elements to purity of expression. Only in some of the large-scale works, the *Motet pour le jour de Pâques* or the Magnificat, is there a straining for effect and a surface brilliance that appears somewhat contrived.

As a miniaturist, Couperin wisely left to others the setting of complete psalm texts. Rather, he chose verses that seemed to him best suited for musical rendering. He often purposely selected the more lyric sentiments rather than those of the blood and thunder variety. The three collections of psalm verses published in 1703, 1704, and 1705, composed "by order of the King" and performed at Versailles, are among Couperin's most intimate and finely wrought motets. These and the *Leçons de Ténèbres* were the only sacred works by the composer to be printed in his lifetime.

The three collections of psalm extracts are very different in their vocal and instrumental sonorities. The sound of the *Quatre versets d'un motet* of 1703 is the sound of two high sopranos, one of whom was Mlle Marguerite-Louise Couperin, daughter of François the elder and cousin of François "the Great"; it is the sound of violins in the role of continuo that supports voice and recorders. The verses are the eleventh, twelfth, thirteenth, and fourteenth of Psalm 118 *Mirabilia testimonia tua*. It is a tender, gentle work in which the characteristic sound of the two sopranos is heard at the very beginning, before any *symphonie*, in a highly original duo, "*sans Basse Continue ny aucun Instrument.*" Verse 13 for soprano solo opens with a *ritournelle* scored for recorders and accompanied by "all the first violins." The motet closes, as it began, with a duo for two sopranos; this time, however, they are supported by violins, some of which double the voices on alternate strophes while others take over the function of the continuo.

Part of the refinement of Couperin's melodic style comes from the infinite variety, yet economy, of his vocalises. The four-fold repetition of *in aeternum* from the final duo is characteristic. The entire passage is only seventeen measures long, yet each of the four melismas has its own character—and the inner two are allowed to expand through totally different sequential patterns.

Sept versets du motet of 1704, on the other hand, is dominated by the male voice, although its last two verses were written for the voice of Mlle Couperin. It exploits the more brilliant sound of transverse flute and oboe as opposed to the gentler recorder. It gives us tenor and bass in recitatives, duos, and triple meter dance measures. It includes Verses 4, 5, 7, 8, 11, 12, and 13 of Psalm 84, *Benedixisti Domine terram tuam*. Verse 5 is a lively choral duet scored for "all tenors" and "all basses" in the style of Handel. The penultimate verse provides one of the most striking examples of a bimodality common in French music of the period: the use of chords borrowed from the parallel minor mode (see Example 14-6). The final verse is scored for oboe and transverse flute, each doubling a melodic line that resembles a thinly scored dance song. There is no continuo, and flute and oboe continue to double after the entrance of the solo soprano.

Example 14-6. Couperin: Extract from Verset 12 of *Benedixisti Domine* (after ed. of 1704).

The *Sept versets du motet* of 1705, based on Verses 1, 3, 9, 10, 11, 12, and 15 of Psalm 80, *Qui Regis Israel, intende*, is the most elaborate of the three sets. It is dominated by the sound of its instrumental *symphonies* and obbligato accompaniments. Elements from the concerto, overture, and dance merge to create short *symphonies* of great variety.

Again, all is expressed in the musical space of a few measures. The central point in the motet, the tenth verse, is defined by a "Symphonie à deux choeurs" in which oboes and flutes play in animated dialogue and the strings continue to support the bass solo, "Dux itineris fuisti," in *concertato* fashion. It is also the central point of the psalm, the description of the vine of Egypt which, when planted by God, took root and spread over the land. In dramatic contrast, the next verse uses the *tirades*, dotted rhythms, and wide melodic profile of the French overture, with leaps of diminished sevenths and minor tenths as well as melodic tritones, to introduce the soprano monologue, "O peruit montes umbra ejus." Verse 12, marked *"gratieusement,"* is a gentle nature scene. Extended melismas on *"flumen,"* echoed in the string accompaniment, suggest the murmuring of waters described in the text. The final verse, which includes the longest *symphonie* (twenty-four measures), features continuous light counterpoint between flute and oboe melodies and an independent bass line scored for bass viols that supports an *haute-contre* solo. The variety among verses is also reflected in the choice of tonalities, which move abruptly from C minor (Verses 1 and 3), to B-flat major (Verses 9 and 10), to F minor (Verses 11, 12), and back to C minor (Verse 15).

Couperin's twenty-six *Motets à voix seules, deux et trois parties et symphonies* were formerly part of the Toulouse-Philidor collection at Tenbury and now are in the Bibliothèque Nationale (see Oboussier 1971, 429–430).[8]

Before turning to Couperin's last and best religious work, the three *Leçons de Ténèbres* for Holy Thursday, it is important to trace the development of this genre that was so popular during the *grand siècle*. The Tenebrae Lessons are part of the extended service that takes place during the first Nocturn of the Office of Matins from midnight to four in the morning on each of the three days preceding Easter. Because of the lateness of the hour and possibly to encourage participation, the Tenebrae in the France of Louis XIV were celebrated in the afternoon instead on Wednesdays, Thursdays, and Fridays of Holy Week. The service includes psalms, antiphons, readings, responses, and canticles. The Office for each day contains three "Lessons" (for a total of nine) selected from the Lamentations attributed to Jeremiah, which deal with the destruction of the Temple of Jerusalem in 587 B.C. that was brought about by the sins of Israel. A vocalise on ritualistic Hebrew letters introduces each verse, and the whole is preceded by the Gregorian melody for the "Incipit Lamentatio Jeremiae Prophetae" (*Liber Usualis*, 631). Each Lesson concludes with the words *Jerusalem convertere ad Dominum Deum tuum* (Jerusalem turn back to your Lord

God). A second Gregorian source is the set of austere formulas for the Hebrew letters themselves (*Liber Usualis*, 631–637).

In France the musical style of the Tenebrae Lessons remained virtually unchanged for over seventy years. It was born of a synthesis between Italian monody of the early seventeenth century and the French *air de cour* with its melismatic *doubles*. The style consists of a nearly continual alternation between the highly ornamented melismas (used mainly for the Hebrew letters) and a more declamatory manner of composition that borders on recitative and arioso. This style is first found in the two sets of *Leçons de Ténèbres* by Michel Lambert, which were performed in 1662 and 1663. The fifty-four Lessons and Responsories by Charpentier appear to be closely modeled on those by Lambert, but Charpentier employed a much richer harmonic language to dramatize the text, as he did in his motets. This richness is especially evident in the poignant series of double suspensions for the words *ego vadem consolere pro vobis* (and I go to be sacrificed for you) from the response after the second Lesson of Holy Wednesday.

In about 1692 Jean Gilles composed three *Premiers Leçons* for each of the three days. As if to emphasize his isolation from the common style, the Provençal composer wrote for a string orchestra, four soloists, and a chorus. Brossard composed nine Lessons for solo voice and continuo, which were published in 1721. The three extant Lessons by Delalande were sung at the Sainte-Chapelle in 1680. The nine Lessons by Bernier were composed between 1704 and 1726.

François Couperin's three Lessons for Holy Thursday[9] were composed between 1713 and 1717 "at the request of the Nuns of L." (undoubtedly, the Abbey of Longchamp near Paris). The moving words of the prophet have a musical intensity rare for Couperin. At heightened moments amidst the recitatives, Couperin introduced closed musical forms such as the loosely organized rondeau airs that end the first two Lessons and the great lament, "Plorans ploravit in nocte," of the first Lesson, which is organized in an ABACC form. The pathetic opening line of this lament describing Jerusalem as a poor widow weeping in the night, makes its way inexorably from f" down a minor tenth to d', its passage impeded by repeated notes, expressive ornaments, and pauses.

Couperin reserves the wrenching chord of the mediant ninth for two places that portray desolation in the Lessons. The first (Example 14-7 below) occurs in the above-mentioned lament on the words *ex omnibus charis ejus* (of all her lovers, she hath none to comfort her); the second is found in the third Lesson on the words *posuit me desolatam* (he hath made me desolate).

Example 14-7. Couperin: Extract from first *Leçon de Ténèbres* (after F. du Plessy ed., n.d.).

Couperin united French and Italian practices —even in dissonance. The chains of suspensions and the chromaticism are Italian, but the selective use of the mediant ninth chord and the stacking up of dissonant tones over a pedal (see the verse "Omnis populus ejus gemens," from the third Lesson) were relatively common post-Lully harmonic procedures in France.

The first two Lessons are scored for high voice and continuo; the third adds a second high voice. These are minimum requirements, however, as Couperin stated in his informative *Avertissement*, which also illuminates some performance practices of his time: namely, the organist's ability to transpose could be assumed, and the harpsichord as well as the organ might be used in church performances. Couperin wrote:

> *The first and second Lessons of each day will always be performed by one voice and the third, by two: thus, two voices will suffice to execute all three; although the melody has been notated in the soprano clef, all other types of voices can sing it, in as much as most persons who accompany today know how to transpose . . . . It would be good if one could add a bass viol or a bass violin to the accompaniment by the organ or the harpsichord.*

The third Lesson is the most impressive from the point of view of consistency of mood and setting. It is a deeply felt and almost continuous recitative and *recitative en duo*, whose origins stretch back from the *tragédie lyrique* to Carissimi or even Monteverdi. Yet, it is a recitative in which French ornamentation is an organic part of the melodic line and a critical means of rendering the music expressive (see Example 14-8).

Example 14-8. Couperin: Extract from third *Leçon de Ténèbres* (after du Plessy ed.).

The long, undulating vocal melismas that make up the initial Hebrew letters afford the greatest possible contrast to the sections in recitative. Their point of departure is the Gregorian formula, now extended to an expressive *cantilena*. They are closer to Corelli than Bach, and their polyphony is that of a portion of a slow movement of a trio sonata whose chains of suspensions, evasions of cadence, and improvised ornaments now are written out in full (see Example 14-9).

Example 14-9. Couperin: Extract from third *Leçon de Ténèbres* (after du Plessy ed.).

Important in sustaining the tradition of the *grand motet* as a concert piece far into the eighteenth century are the motets by Jean-Philippe Rameau (1683–1764), Charles-Hubert Gervais (1672–1744), Joseph Bodin de Boismortier (1689–1755), Esprit Blanchard (1696–1770), Henry Madin (1698–1748), and Jean-Joseph Cassanéa de Mondonville (1711–1772).

Rameau composed less religious music than the others—even though he held posts as a church musician for about twenty-six years. All but one of these posts were as church organist, not *maître de musique*. Therefore, he was under no obligation to compose *grands motets*. Four *grands motets* may be attributed to Rameau: *Laboravi clamans*, *In convertendo*, *Quam dilecta*, and *Deus noster refugium*.

Laboravi clamans, which consists of a musical setting of the third verse of Psalm 69 and may have been extracted from a lost *grand motet*, was printed in Book 3 of the *Traité de l'harmonie* (1722) to illustrate *fugue*. "Fugue, like imitation," wrote Rameau, "consists of a certain passage of melody repeated at will and in any part we like" (1722; trans. 1971, 349).[10] This definition is followed by twelve general rules of fugue writing, after which Rameau concluded that the fugue is essentially "an adornment of Music governed by good taste alone" (1722; trans. 1971, 368).

This illustrative motet, scored for five-part chorus (two sopranos, *haute-contre*, tenor, and bass), is in one movement. The two sentences of the verse are divided into four clauses, and each clause is assigned a fugue subject. Rameau combined all this in a rather academic fashion with little attention to textual clarity. With the exception of the final stretto, not much use is made of the contrapuntal complexities described in some of his rules. There is little real tension or pull between the parts. Voices line up in homophony for measures at a time. Thus, by observing the music itself, rather than the rules it claims to illustrate, we can see how far Rameau was from the fugal procedures of J. S. Bach.

Composed between 1713 and 1715, *In convertendo* underwent complete revision for performance during Holy Week 1751 at the Concert Spirituel, where it was coolly received. The *Mercure* tried to justify the poor reception on the shaky grounds that *In convertendo* had been composed forty years before. Girdlestone suggests that "between thirty and forty would have been a truer statement" (1957, 96). The primitive version is lost. The autograph copy at the Bibliothèque Nationale documents the many stages of revision undertaken by Rameau for the concert performance. The motet is based on Psalm 126, whose eight verses are concerned with the Jews held captive by the Babylonians. The opening *haute-contre* solo, "In convertendo, Dominus," is an elegiac monologue worthy to stand beside its operatic counterparts: "Ah faut-il" from *Hippolyte* (Act IV, scene i), "Coulez mes pleurs" from *Zaïs* (Act III, scene iii), or "Séjour de l'éternelle paix" from *Castor et Pollux* (Act IV, scene i). It employs the shifting meter of French recitative, which is rarely found in Latin music. Its profuse ornamentation is organically shaped to the melodic line to assure the greatest expressiveness. Although it seems freely declamatory, it is, in fact, a rondeau air preceded and followed by a *ritournelle*. The baritone solo of Verse 4 makes use of elaborate melismas that are sung at great speed to illustrate the force of the torrents of water. Verse 5 for soprano and chorus, "Laudate nomen Dei cum cantico" (Praise the name of God with a song) is actually Verse 31 of Psalm 68, which Rameau inserted into Psalm 126. The extremely melismatic soprano solo contrasts markedly with the simple, even folk-like chorus. The elaborate writing for winds (at one place there is a wind quintet for three oboes and two bassoons) would have been unthinkable in the early version of 1713. Verse 6, "Qui seminant in lacrimis" (Who sows in tears will harvest in joy) is an animated trio for soprano, *haute-contre*, and bass. Accompanied by unison violins, this dance-like episode reinforces joy rather than sorrow.

Girdlestone is probably correct in rating the concluding chorus of this motet as the "greatest piece in all Rameau's church music" (1957, 98). It is a setting of the seventh verse, "Euntes ibant et flebant, mittentes semina sua. Venientes autem venient cum exultatione, portantes manipulos suos" (He that goeth forth and weepeth, bearing precious seed, shall doubtless come again with rejoicing, bringing his sheaves with him). Rameau used two contrasting motifs (Example 14-10a below) to express the initial textual idea ("Euntes ibant et flebant"). The affective descending chromaticism on the word *flebant* is often used independently of the first musical idea. The third motif (Example 14-10b), a predominantly sixteenth-note scalar melody, is ideally suited to the expression of "come again rejoicing." During the remainder of the chorus, these three motives are expanded and combined with great skill, as is shown in Example 14-10c.

Example 14-10. (a–c) Rameau: Motivic use in final chorus of *In Convertendo* (after autograph *Rés.* Vm¹ 218 in Bibliothèque Nationale).

Quam dilecta, composed between 1713 and 1722, is a setting of Psalm 83, which is based on David's desire to see the temple again. As is true of all three of Rameau's complete *grands motets*, the opening movement is a solo air. In this case, it is a rondeau air sung by a soprano and accompanied by strings and divided flutes. Verse 2, "Cor meum et caro mea exultaverunt in Deum vivum" (My heart and my flesh rejoice after the living God), is a masterpiece of contrapuntal writing. It is a five-part double fugue for chorus and orchestra. The first violins present the first subject, which is composed of quarter- and eighth-notes in conjunct motion and serves later for the text *exultaverunt*. The second subject, "Cor meum," is introduced by the sopranos. It consists of interlocking, ascending perfect fourths in slow-moving half- and whole-notes. All manner of fugal procedures are used, including inversion and multiple strettos, making this a much more convincing example of fugue than the *Laboravi clamans* found in the *Traité de l'harmonie*.

Deus noster refugium, the longest of Rameau's *grands motets*, may have been composed in 1713 for the Lyons Concert Society. The vivid imagery found in the eleven verses extracted from Psalm 45 must have appealed to the awakening dramatic and theatrical instincts of the composer. The eleven verses are divided into three major sections, each concluding with a chorus. Verse 3, "Sonuerunt et turbatae sunt" (The waters have been agitated), is a large four-part chorus with string orchestra. As Girdlestone has observed, it is organized as a *concerto grosso* in which the orchestra carries the burden of the recurring *ritournelles*. It is really a storm scene marked "*vivement*" and uses the forward motion and mechanical pulsations of the Italian concerto to describe the roar of waters and the mountains that "shake with the swelling thereof." The chorus appears distinctly subordinate to the orchestra, which continually penetrates the voices with the main thematic material.

Rameau's vocal writing in the solos and ensembles is more brilliant and more melismatic than that of Couperin or Delalande. Descriptive passages abound, and in the trio (two sopranos and bass) of Verse 2, string tremolos describe the mountains borne down to the sea in the upheaval of the earth. This is part of the raw material from which the storm *symphonies* emerge in the stage music of Rameau. Verse 4, "Fluminis impetus" (Impetuous river), for soprano solo with obbligato violin and bass viol, includes some complex rhythmic counterpoint, which at times is terraced in simultaneous triplets and in eighth-note and sixteenth-note patterns (see Example 14-11).

Example 14-11. Rameau: Extract from air "Fluminis impetus," *Deus noster refugium* (after MS *Rés*. Vm[1] 507 in Bibliothèque Nationale).

Verse 8, "Venite et videte" (Come and see), is a true aria da capo, which is scored for *haute-contre*, violin obbligato, and continuo. Italian text repetitions and short phrases are countered by French vocal restraint. Unfortunately, the music for Verse 10 contains only an instrumental introduction for flute and continuo—the vocal air has never surfaced.

Gervais left us more than forty *grands motets* in manuscript, which are found today in the Bibliothèque Nationale. Most of them were composed during his tenure at the Royal Chapel, where he was appointed in 1723 as one of four *sous-maîtres*. At first glance, the *grands motets* by Gervais are conservative and close to the Versailles model, with massive instrumental doublings of the vocal lines and largely homophonic choruses. A closer study, however, reveals a composer sensitive to the meaning of the text and adept at achieving contrast through shifts of texture. (See Jean-Paul Montagnier 1994.)

Boismortier and Blanchard accorded more importance to the orchestra of the *grand motet*. Boismortier's setting of Psalm 19, *Exaudiat te Dominus*, of 1730 includes parts for two oboes, trumpet, and timpani in addition to the usual strings. The use of more operatic orchestration and long da capo airs was an attempt to bring the *grand motet* up to date without basically altering its format. At the same time, the search for novelty resulted in the incorporation of popular elements into the motet which, if anything, emphasized the archaic nature of the genre. Thus, Boismortier's *Fugit nox* of 1741 included several well-known noels and was so well received that it was traditionally programmed every December twenty-fifth at the Concert Spirituel for more than twenty years. Late in the century, it was praised by La Borde: "Boismortier had the secret of interspersing noels [in his motet], whose melodies combined pleasantly with the *récits*, choruses, and *symphonies* with which they appeared to have nothing in common" (1780, 3:393).

Blanchard was yet another pupil of Poitevin. Following a series of appointments at Marseilles, Toulon, Besançon, and Amiens, Blanchard served at the Royal Chapel after the death of Bernier (1734). More than thirty of his motets are preserved in manuscript at the Bibliothèque Nationale. The voice of Delalande can be heard again in some of the large polyphonic choruses. Blanchard's technique of orchestration derives from the Italian concerto, and he was the first to introduce the clarinet into the orchestra of the Royal Chapel.

Henry Madin, appointed as one of four *sous-maîtres* at the Royal Chapel in January 1738,[11] was described by Titon du Tillet as an "Irish gentleman and one of the best motet composers of this century." Titon added that because of their musical value and popularity,

Madin's motets "merited being printed" (1732; supplement 1755, 21–22). Brenet informs us that the motet *Diligam Te* was indeed in the repertory at the Concert Spirituel as late as 1762.

The twenty-six *grands motets* by Madin, in manuscript at the Bibliothèque Nationale, show some of the same technical workmanship found in those by Delalande and Rameau in the creation of musical motives that may be used in apposition or in combination. A good example is the theme that opens Psalm 130, *De profundis*. Madin divides the text *De profundis clamavi* into two strikingly different motives that underscore the meaning of the words and at the same time present material that is effective in vertical combination (see Example 14-12).

Example 14-12. Madin: Motivic use in *De profundis* (after MS H53 in Bibliothèque Nationale).

The nine surviving *grands motets* by Mondonville were composed between 1734 and 1758. They received much extravagant praise when first heard in the Concert Spirituel in the 1740s. They appeared to be the *dernier cri* in the *grand motet* idiom, although their superficial pictorialism was attacked by Marmontel, who wrote: "Musicians, who compose pretty tunes and light choruses on the words of David, appear to me to profane his harp" ("Concert Spirituel," in the Supplement 2:537 to Diderot's *Encyclopédie* 1751–1780). The most important and arguably the best of these motets is the *De profundis*[12] composed in 1748 for the obsequies on 17 February of Henry Madin, Mondonville's colleague at the Royal Chapel. The opening chorus, "De profundis clamavi," was highly regarded. The *Mercure* of April spoke of its "sublime beauties." An octave jump downward depicts the depths; this forces the cry of "clamavi" to shift direction and leap upwards through a three-measure span—Mondonville was undoubtedly familiar with the *De profundis* by Delalande and that by Madin, in both of which a similar reversal of direction takes place. It must be confessed, however, that in spite of Mondonville's keen sense of orchestral sonorities and his fashionable Italianate airs, his *grands motets* point up the superiority of the one composer of religious music in France whose *grands motets* did not seem to date or suffer from style shifts: Delalande.

Chapter 15

Mass and Oratorio: The Domain of Marc-Antoine Charpentier

Mass

During the reign of Louis XIV, there were no musical settings of the Ordinary of the Mass whose title pages were graced by the caption, "printed by the express order of His Majesty." By showing his marked preference for the motet, the king virtually doomed the composition of Masses by composers connected with his Chapel. Regal taste became official policy, and many composers not directly involved with composing music for the Royal Chapel quite naturally took the Delalande motet as the accepted model for their religious music.

There is no known polyphonic setting of the Mass by Delalande, although a plainsong *Messe des deffuns* by him does exist in the Bibliothèque Nationale in a manuscript collection that also includes plainsong Masses and Mass fragments by Henry Du Mont, André Campra, Jean-François Lalouette, François David, and Charles Piroye.

Even so, polyphonic Masses continued to be written in France in substantial numbers. One hundred eighteen a capella Masses by forty-three composers, from Lassus to Campra, are listed in the *Catalogue des messes imprimées en musique*, which Ballard added at the end of his 1707 edition of Jean Mignon's *Missa Laetitia sempiterna*. Danièle Taitz-Destouches identified ninety-four Masses published between 1640 and 1707 (1974, 140–141).[1] Most of the above Masses are by conservative, provincial composers caught in a musical backwater.

Exceptional are the *Messe à deux choeurs* by Desmarest, which was copied by Philidor in 1704; the Brossard *Missa quinti toni per nocte ac dies Festis Natalis Domini* (1700), based on noel tunes; Minoret's *Missa pro tempore nativitate à deux choeurs*, also based on noels; the Lalouette Mass printed by Ballard in 1744; and five Masses by Madin that date after his appointment to the Royal Chapel in 1738 and were sung at Rouen, Rennes, Paris, and Cambrai.

André Campra left us two polyphonic settings of the Mass: an early a cappella *Missa ad majorem Dei gloriam*, *a*4, which Ballard printed in 1699 and again in 1700; and a *Messe des morts* (Requiem), *a*5 that was found in manuscript bound together with works by Gilles and Pellegrin in the Bibliothèque Méjanes in Aix-en-Provence. Barthélemy conjectures it to be a late work (1957a, 159), but Baker suggests that it was originally composed while Campra was at Notre-Dame (1694–1700) and that it was revised between 1716 and 1722 (1984, 113).[2] In any case, it is an impressive work, with finely wrought polyphony over Gregorian chant (see Introit), powerful homophonic choruses that have dramatic text repetitions (see the Gradual), and *récits* completely in the *style galant* (see "Lux aeterna" in the Post-Communion).

Jean Mignon (1636–1710), Campra's predecessor at Notre-Dame, composed a cappella Masses, six of which Ballard published between 1671 and 1707.

François Couperin, in company with Nicolas de Grigny and Nicolas Lebègue, preferred to write organ Masses, a Renaissance genre that continued to be popular in France (see Chapter 18).

One of the most popular Masses of the entire eighteenth century, and a work still performed in Paris churches, was actually composed in the closing years of the seventeenth century. It is a *Messe des Morts*[3] by Jean Gilles, a Provençal composer, who at the time was director of the choir school at Saint-Étienne of Toulouse. This Mass caught the fancy of audiences of the Concert Spirituel when it was performed there on 1 November 1750, almost fifty years after its first performance at the funeral for Gilles, who died prematurely in 1705. By 1750, the Mass was undoubtedly "pepped-up" by the addition of many instruments to make it more appealing to late eighteenth-century tastes. Michel Corrette even composed a Carillon "pour la fin de la Messe." The Mass was so popular that it was chosen for performances at a service in memory of J.-N. Pancrace Royer (director of the Concert Spirituel from 1748–1755) in 1756, at the obsequies for Rameau in 1764, and in 1774 for Louis XV. It must have been known outside of France, since Sir John Hawkins, in *A General History of the Science and Practice of Music* (1776, 778), described it as "the capital work" of Gilles.

The reasons for its success are not hard to find. It has melodic freshness, even sweetness, that cuts through its stiff Lullian exterior. This gives it immediate appeal—a characteristic of a much later Requiem by Gabriel Fauré. Its freshness springs, in part, from the folk music of Gilles's Provençal heritage. Dance-like melodies in triple meter, organized in asymmetrical phrases, are juxtaposed with *a*4 and *a*5 choral homophony and with string *symphonies* reminiscent of Du Mont. The "Et tibi," which alternates between four- and five-measure phrase groupings, is typical. The first Kyrie eleison, a tenor solo having irregular phrases and syncopated bass line (see Example 15-1 below), is contrasted with the short, second Kyrie scored for an *a*5 chorus. There is little real polyphony, and, as in his motets, Gilles often begins his choruses with a florid soprano line superimposed over the remaining voice parts in note-against-note style.

Example 15-1. Gilles: Extract from Requiem (after MS Vm[1] 1375 at Bibliothèque Nationale).

As we have noted, the composer who made the most significant contribution to the Mass in the French Baroque period is a man who had no official connection with the court or the Royal Chapel: Marc-Antoine Charpentier. The twelve Masses by Charpentier[4] serve as a glossary of the types of Masses cultivated during the Baroque period. They range from a simple, straightforward Mass for solo voices and unison chorus, to one for four *a*4 choruses, and from a Mass that parodies popular noels to one built over a Gregorian cantus firmus.

As is so often the case with the music of Charpentier, it is difficult to determine the chronology of his Masses. Hitchcock believes that H. 1 through H. 4 were composed in the early 1700s. The others date from the late 1680s and 1690s. Only the *Missa Assumpta est Maria* has a verifiable date from the Sainte-Chapelle period (1698–1704), because its manuscript includes the names of singers known to have been at the Sainte-Chapelle during Charpentier's tenure there. The titles indicate that many are *pièces d'occasion*. They must have been performed at the Dauphin's chapel or at the Jesuit church of Saint-Louis. One, we learn from the title, was written for the nuns of Port Royal, the headquarters of Jansenism. Clarence Barber suggests that the *Messe à quatre choeurs* may be an early work written when the sounds of Roman polychoral music were still fresh in Charpentier's ear (1955, 83). If so, it would be a natural implementation of his careful analysis ("Remarques sur les Messes à 16 parties d'Italie") found on his copy of Francesco Beretta's sixteen-part *Missa mirabilis elationes maris*, also in four choirs, which Charpentier had brought back from Italy. The *Messe à quatre choeurs* is a large *concertato* Mass—perhaps the only one of its kind in seventeenth-century France. Whether it was ever performed is conjectural.

Another Charpentier Mass with few French precedents is the *Messe pour plusieurs instruments au lieu des orgues* (Mass for Several Instruments Instead of Organ). The title tells us that this Mass alternates its verses between instruments and sung plainsong instead of between organ and sung plainsong as found in the traditional organ Mass. Charpentier used a variety of instruments that afford much color contrast. He scored the Mass for four recorders, three transverse flutes, four bass flutes, two oboes, one cromorne, and four-part strings. The lack of a continuo is exceptional in music of this late date. The organization of the Kyrie eleison demonstrates how Charpentier aimed for maximum color contrast in his ensembles. The numbering shown below duplicates that of the original, where the Kyrie-Christe-Kyrie complex was labeled Kyrie I to Kyrie IX. The even-numbered Kyries, not found below, are simply labeled, "for the priests."

Kyrie I: For all instruments

Kyrie III: For oboes

Kyrie V: For violins of the petit choeur

Kyrie VII: For recorders

Kyrie IX: For all instruments

Kyries I, VII, and IX, as well as sections of the Gloria, all make use of the Gregorian cantus firmus *Cunctipotens Genitor Deus* (*Liber Usualis*, 25). There is no Credo, and the Agnus Dei is incomplete. The cantus firmus is presented in whole notes and restricted to the bass, which undoubtedly rendered a basso continuo superfluous. The upper parts employ rhythmic, as opposed to melodic, counterpoint and often resemble an *air sérieux*. As in Couperin's organ Masses, elements from the dance are introduced. The Offertory for a wind and string choir resembles a French overture.

In spite of their popularity and their use as a basis for organ and instrumental ensemble pieces, French noels appear to have been only rarely cultivated as parody tunes for Masses or motets. The earliest extant example of one of these rare Masses may well be the *Messe de minuit pour Noël* by Charpentier. Perhaps this Mass and Minoret's *Missa pro tempore Nativitatis* served as models for Brossard's *Missa quinti toni per nocte ac dies Festis Natalis Domini* of 1700. In addition to these examples, only a Boismortier *grand motet, Fugit nox* of 1741, and the much later *Messe-Oratorio de Noël* of 1786 by Jean-François Le Sueur (1760–1837) use noel tunes.

Charpentier chose eleven noels for his *Messe de minuit pour Noël*, including one for which no music was provided, but which, we learn from the score, was to be performed independently during the Offertory.[5] The Mass is scored for solo voices, an *a*4 chorus, flutes, strings, and organ. Short orchestral interludes introduce the noels to be employed subsequently in the vocal settings. Example 15-2, below, illustrates Charpentier's use of parody technique. The opening phrase of the second part of the noel, "Où s'en vont ces gais bergers," is lightly exchanged between the voices before lining up in vertical sonorities. The whole is a tender, moving work in which popular elements lend exactly the right amount of naiveté and simple wonder appropriate to the subject.

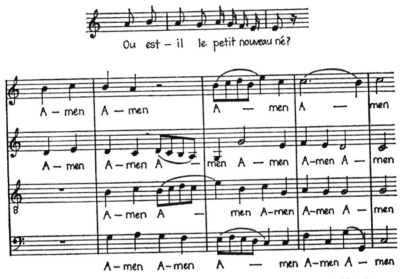

Example 15-2. Charpentier: Parody technique in the *Messe de Minuit* (after the *Meslanges autographes*, vol. 25).

Although generally less interesting than some of the other Masses by Charpentier, the [Mass for soloists, chorus, and two treble instruments . . .][6] is less conservative from the point of view of harmonic practices (see Example 15-3). The series of descending cross-relations, staggered between the voices in the "Passus et sepultus est" from the "Crucifixus," is a vivid example of text painting. Another is the astonishing augmented octave in close apposition to the often used mediant ninth chord in the "Miserere nobis" of the Agnus Dei.

Example 15-3. Charpentier: Use of harmony in the only untitled Mass in the *Meslanges autographes*, vol. 14.

In no other work do the compositional skills of Charpentier's late years show to better advantage than in the *Assumpta est Maria* Mass.[7] A balance is achieved here between chorus and orchestra, between polyphony and homophony, and between prayerful introspection and a dramatic sense of musical characterization. Its dimensions illustrate the healthy state of the performance groups at the Sainte-Chapelle at the turn of the century. A chorus *a*6 is used (first and second sopranos, *haute-contre*, tenor, baritone, bass); the orchestra is *a*4 and includes two flutes, strings, and organ. Co-existing with age-old practices, such as the use of "familiar style" (homophony) for the setting of the "Et Incarnatus est," are the melodic diminished fourths and augmented fifths and the searing harmonies of the "Miserere nobis" section of the "Qui tollis." Charpentier used vocal range and timbre in addition to harmony to delineate contrasting moods. Thus, only solo tenor, baritone, and bass sing for the "Crucifixus," the voices entering in that order, whereas the "Et Resurrexit" employs only the high voices of *haute-contre*, second soprano, and first soprano, in that order. Refined melodic style characterizes the *Assumpta est Maria* Mass. Many melodies are quiet and move with the predominantly conjunct motion of liturgical chant (Kyrie and Agnus Dei); others include joyful and quite vocal melismas on such words as *gratias*, *amen*, and *resurrexit*; others are "*fort et guay*" dances (Laudamus Te); and still others are well-suited for their extended fugal treatment (Cum Sancto Spiritu). Although the orchestra most commonly doubles the voices in the choral movements, the first and final Kyries, the first Sanctus, and the first and final Agnus Dei are long, autonomous *symphonies*. This is instrumental music of high seriousness which, with its contrapuntal lines, stems from the idiom of the ensemble fantasies and ricercare of the earlier seventeenth century.

Oratorio

The term *oratorio* was rarely used in France during the seventeenth century. Marc-Antoine Charpentier used the terms *historia*, *canticum*, *motet*, or *dialogue*. Others used the term *histoire sacrée*. H. Wiley Hitchcock prefers the functionally descriptive term *dramatic motet* rather than the term *oratorio* for the works by Charpentier that most resemble the oratorios by his mentor, Carissimi (1990, 52–61), because Charpentier's were performed in church to serve the same purpose as a motet. I suspect, however, that those of us who persist in using inexact terminology, such as *Landini sixth* or *Corelli clash*, will continue to use the word *oratorio*. For us, the stylistic features linking the oratorios of Charpentier and Carissimi will continue to take precedence over the musical function that separates them.

Charpentier's oratorios appear to have been antedated by certain *histoires en musique* composed by the theorist René Ouvrard (1624–1694) and described briefly in his letters to Claude Nicaise (1623–1701), canon at the Cathedral of Dijon.[8] Albert Cohen has found references to the following titles: *Histoire du Publicain et du Pharisien* (letter of 1 September 1664); *Histoire en musique de Jéricho* (letter of 29 October 1674); and *Histoire de Joseph* (letter of 24 February 1665). Unfortunately, none of Ouvrard's music for these works has survived. Pierre Perrin supplied Latin texts for certain dramatic dialogues in his *Cantica pro capella regis* (1665) and his *Recueil de paroles de musique* (ca. 1666). One of them, *In elevatione dialogus: Anima et Peccator*, was set to music by Thomas Gobert. The dramatic solos that dialogue with the chorus in several Bouzignac motets may be considered a precursor of the oratorio, and Brossard was correct to have viewed the *Dialogus de Anima* by Du Mont as a "type of oratorio" (1724; 1725–1730, 483).

In his *Catalogue raisonné* (1982), Hitchcock identifies thirty-five oratorios by Charpentier (H. 391–H. 425), which he calls "Dramatic Motets." Thirteen of these are genuine *histoires sacrées*. The remainder are various occasional pieces, *cantiques*, and *dialogues*.[9] For Hitchcock, the oratorios by Charpentier represent "exactly the midpoint between those of Carissimi and those of Handel" (1954, 384).

Charpentier's thirteen *histoires sacrées* are large-scale works in the manner of Carissimi's *Jephte* or *Judicium extremum*. They employ a narrator (*historicus*), solo *récits*, ensembles, chorus, and orchestra. The eight *cantica* are shorter, demand fewer performers, and include some works that are less dramatic and more introspective. The term *cantica* is included by Brossard in his dictionary as a synonym for *motet*. Similar to the *cantica* are five short *Méditations pour le Carême* scored for three male voices and continuo. The seven *dialogi*, like the *cantica*, are modest works written for two protagonists who are either two individuals or two groups. Charpentier may have been familiar with the *Dialogus de Anima* by Du Mont as well as the dialogues by Carissimi.

Only the *historia Judicium Salomonis*[10] may be dated. It was performed 11 November 1702 "*pour la messe rouge du Palais.*" The "Red Mass" was an annual event in the Grande Salle of the Palais de Justice to observe the convening of Parlement.

That Charpentier composed other oratorios for the Jesuit church of Saint-Louis is reasonable to assume, and we know that he composed some for the private chapel of the Duchesse de Guise at her home in the Marais.

In Hitchcock's words, the oratorios by Charpentier combine Italian and French traits "almost in equal measure" (1954, 384). The basic format of a sequence of *symphonies*, solo *récits* and airs, ensembles, and choruses, with the dramatic narrative controlled by a *historicus*, is familiar to us from the oratorios by Carissimi. The subject matter is also similar. Generally, although not exclusively, they are based on Old and New Testament stories. Three *historiae* by Charpentier treat subjects that had already been used by Carissimi: *Extremum Dei Judicium*, *Sacrificium Abrahae*, and *Judicium Salomonis*.

In his choral writing, Charpentier employed both the *concertato* principle of the *grands motets* by Lully and Delalande and the Roman polychoral style, which had been exploited with such telling results in Carissimi's *Judicium extremum*. Although basically homophonic, some choruses have a polyphonic integrity that is worthy of Delalande. A good example is "Flevit amare" which closes *Le Reniement de St Pierre*. On the other hand, there are choruses from some of the nativity *cantica* (see "Pastores undique" from *In Nativitate Domini Canticum*) that are labeled *chansons* and resemble popular noels.

Much of the solo vocal music is simple recitative, accompanied recitative, or arioso. Charpentier's more expansive recitative resembles its Italian model—perhaps because of the Latin text. The airs are few and relatively insignificant from a dramatic point of view. Some are modeled on French dance measures; a few, having extended vocalises and *ritournelles*, resemble the Italian aria da capo (see Solomon's air, "Benedictus es" from *Judicium Salomonis*).

Charpentier exhibited a dramatic gift comparable to the best pages of his *Médée* in the recitatives and the dialogues that he organized as ensembles. Few French operas of the seventeenth century achieve the high level of musical characterization found in the denial scene from *Le Reniement de St Pierre*, where Peter's repeated denials cut through the persistent questioning by the maidservants and the relatives of Molchus.[11]

Like Carissimi, Charpentier utilized harmony to underscore the meaning of the text. There are examples of augmented triads and cross-relations like those in his motets. Rests, harmony (Neapolitan sixth chord), and a vocal line that terminates before the final resolution are all agents of dramatic characterization in the death scene from the *historia*, *Caecilia virgo et martyr* (see Example 15-4).

Example 15-4. Charpentier: Extract from death scene in *Caecilia* (after the *Meslanges* autographes, vol. 3).

The oratorios by Charpentier may be most clearly differentiated from those by his teacher in the domain of instrumental music. Carissimi normally employed only two violins and continuo for his *symphonies*; Charpentier preferred a larger orchestra. *Caecilia virgo et martyr* is scored for two four-part string orchestras and includes a *concertante* part for solo organ in the final section. *Extremum Dei judicium* uses two trumpets to "play a fanfare" announcing the Last Judgment; and *Judicium Salomonis* employs a string orchestra with flutes, oboes, and bassoons.

The operas by Lully and *préramiste* composers influenced Charpentier's descriptive *symphonies*, which have no counterpart in the Italian oratorio. *Sommeils*, called "*Nuit*," are found in the nativity oratorios as well as in such large works as *Judith* and *Judicium Salomonis*. Typical is the prelude to the second part of *Judicium Salomonis*, which resembles the *sommeil* from Lully's *Atys* (Act III, scene iv). The Charpentier *sommeil* is richer in harmony and more thinly scored, but both use paired flutes and strings (muted in Charpentier) and similar melodic patterns.

Although these impressive compositions surpass those by Charpentier's teacher in some ways, they were, by a wry twist of fate, without significant musical issue in France; therefore, what has much musical merit is of little importance historically. The lack of historical follow-through on Charpentier's oratorios has blinded some to their intrinsic merits in spite of important studies (for the most part by French and American scholars). How else can one explain the two-sentence entry at the conclusion of "Das Oratorium in Italien im 17. Jahrhundert" in the *MGG* article "Oratorium" (vol. 10, columns 124–128).[12]

Over 130 years separate André Maugars's ecstatic description (1639; rpt. 1993, 11) of the *"admirable et ravissante"* music of the *"Comédie Spirituelle"* (his term for the Italian oratorios he heard on his Rome journey) from Marmontel's oblique suggestion that French composers might consider the Italian oratorio as an alternative to the *grand motet* ("Concert Spirituel" article in the Supplement 2:536–537 to Diderot's *Encyclopédie* 1751–1780). Except for Charpentier, the French were unwilling to attempt any naturalization of the Italian genre during this period, although copies of some Carissimi oratorios found their way into Parisian collections. To accept Rousseau's hypothesis that some in-born deficiency made the French "ill-suited to the dramatic genre" would be ridiculous (1768, 353). More likely, as Marmontel observed, most composers (and audiences) were habit-bound to the officially sanctioned vehicle for religious expression in music—the *grand motet* of the Royal Chapel or of the Concert Spirituel.

Marmontel defined Italian oratorios as "small sacred dramas, not staged but only executed in concert." He added parenthetically that some "weak essays in this genre have been performed at the Concert Spirituel in Paris." His "weak essays" must refer to the two sacred oratorios by Mondonville entitled "motets français." The first, *Les Israélites à la montagne d'Horeb*, was performed at the Concert Spirituel in 1758; its immediate success precipitated a second effort, *Les Fureurs de Saul*, which was performed the following year. From the *livret* of *Les Israélites*, we read that "Monsieur Mondonville has enriched our music with a *new genre*" (italics mine).

In his *Present State of Music in France and Italy* Charles Burney wrote: "The French have never yet had . . . a regular oratorio of any sort performed in their country" (1771; 1773 ed., 23). Clearly, neither Burney, Marmontel, nor Mondonville knew of the existence of the oratorios by Charpentier. It is possible that the only works that may stem from direct contact with them are a short *Oratorio à 4 voix . . . pour la Naissance de l'enfant Jésus* by Lochon and the *Histoire de la femme adultère* by Clérambault, which is found in an undated copy that Brossard once owned. Lochon's oratorio,[13] which includes chorus, dialogues, and a *symphonie* for two violins and continuo, bears little resemblance to the nativity *cantica* by Charpentier. Donald Foster, however, finds several similarities between the Clérambault oratorio and those by Charpentier (1975, 74).

❧ Part Three ❧

Music for the Lute, Guitar, and Keyboard Instruments

⇀ Chapter 16 ↽

The Lute and Guitar

One makes the lute speak as one wishes, and one controls one's audience as one wishes. When a good player picks up his lute and fingers its strings, when he places himself at the end of a table to seek out a fantaisie; *he has no sooner plucked three chords and begun the tune of a* fredon, *then all eyes and ears are drawn to him. If he chooses to let the strings die away under his fingers, he transports all these people and charms them with a gay melancholy; so that one lets his chin fall upon his chest; another, on his hand, which slowly extends full length as if pulled by his ear; another, with eyes wide open or with mouth half opened as though all his attention were riveted on the strings. You would have said that all were deprived of feeling, except for hearing, as if soul, having abandoned all senses, withdrew to the rim of the ears to delight more comfortably in such powerful harmony. But if he reawakens the strings by changing the way he plays, he brings all the audience back to life, and he who had stolen heart and soul returns them and does what he wants with men (François 1621, 474).*

This language rings with the clarity of true observation. Eschewing the euphemisms of preciosity, René François described the power of that most *précieux* of instruments, the lute, to move the listeners of his day. The seventeenth century inherited the previous century's mystique with regard to the lute as a superior social instrument. Nobleman and bourgeois alike sought the secrets of its elusive language. With demonstrable skill as lutenist, one might indeed enhance his social position. It was no accident that François I, in creating the division between the music of the *Chambre* and that of the *Écurie*, at first accepted only the lute among stringed instruments for his *Musique de Chambre.*

The notarial archives of the *Minutier Central* contain many references to *maistre joueurs de luth* up to 1640. Here, a Parisian merchant hires a teacher to instruct his thirteen-year-old son in the arts of "writing, arithmetic, music, and lute playing"; there, a nobleman and member of Parliament, engages a *maistre joueur de luth* to teach him "how to play the lute as perfectly as possible" within five years.

Marie de Médici appointed Robert Ballard as *Maistre Joueur de Luth* in 1612, and he lost no time in beginning to teach the child, Louis XIII. When Ennemond Gaultier was chosen by Anne d' Autriche as her private lute teacher, everyone at the court felt called upon to follow her example, and the "*vieux Gaultier*" became the most sought-after of teachers. Even Richelieu tried his hand at a few lessons, although Tallemant des Réaux confides that "it would be difficult to imagine anything more ridiculous than to see him (Richelieu) take his lessons from Gaultier" (1657; ed. of 1960, 1:238). In 1636 Mersenne could write in the "Livre second des instruments" in his *Harmonie universelle* that the lute "has taken such a lead over other stringed instruments, either because honest men gave it this advantage or because of its own excellence and perfection, that one hardly notices the other instruments" (1636; rpt. 1965, 3:56).

The lute was at the peak of its popularity during the reign of Louis XIII. Professional performers and lute makers were in great demand. Mersenne mentioned the Vosmeny (Vaumesnil) brothers, Charles and Jacques Hedington from Scotland, Julien Perichon, the "*Polonais*" (Jacob Reys), the Gaultiers, Enclos, Marande, René Mésangeau, and Vincent among those who excelled in playing the lute. In addition there were Charles Bocquet; Mercure; Merville; Bouvier; Jacques, Sieur de Belleville; François, Sieur de Chancy; Nicolas Chevalier; Estienne Houselot (called Dubuisson); Vignon; the Pinel and Gallot dynasties; Edinthon; Raël; the Dubuts (father and son); La Grotte; Montbuysson; and many others. Several of these composer-performers have left no trace of their music or, in some cases, their identity.[1]

This hue and cry for lutenists was not to endure. The vogue for the lute peaked by 1640, and the instrument was already into its long decline even at the time Denis Gaultier was composing *La Rhétorique des dieux* in the early 1650s. For only a few years did it enjoy harmonious co-existence with the harpsichord, whose music had already taken over many of the characteristic features of lute style. The increasing demand for more bass instruments in the later seventeenth century brought about the construction of double-necked lutes, or archlutes, that included a second pegbox for bass courses. The lute competed in vain with its stronger cousin, the theorbo (a "short" archlute), and at the end of the century suffered the indignity of being converted into a theorbo by the addition of supplementary strings and a widening of its neck.

The eventual adoption of the basso continuo in France hastened the downfall of the lute. The theorbo and harpsichord became the preferred realization instruments by virtue of their greater carrying power. In 1660, Ballard printed a *Méthode pour apprendre facilement à toucher le théorbe sur la basse continue* by Nicolas Fleury, *haute-contre* in the service of the Duc d'Orléans. In the preface to Denis Delair's *Traité d'accompagnement pour le théorbe et le clavessin* of 1690, we read that by following the rules one may gain a "perfect knowledge of this art as much on the theorbo as on the harpsichord, which are the two instruments most in use for accompanying."

By the third decade of the eighteenth century, lute, theorbo, and guitar had virtually disappeared in France, although a Sieur Marlière did hold an administrative post at court entitled *joueur de petit luth de la chambre* as late as 1759. Perhaps the last lutenist of the period to be heard in public performance in Paris was Wenzel Josef Kohault, who played some duos for lute and violoncello with Jean-Pierre Duport at the Concert Spirituel in 1763 and 1764.

Lecerf and Titon du Tillet blamed the disappearance of the lute on the difficulty of mastering the instrument. Titon du Tillet wrote: "I do not believe that one would find more than three or four old, venerable men who play the instrument today in Paris" (1732, 406). The limited volume of the instrument may have contributed to its decline in a period increasingly sympathetic to the brilliant sound of the violin.

If we believe Abbé Carbasus (pseudonym for François Campion), the lute was a victim of the mania that struck the Parisian public for musettes, vielles, and other *instruments champêtres* in the 1720s. In his satirical polemic in the form of a *Lettre . . . sur la mode des instruments de musique*, he wrote sarcastically: "You are not then informed as to the sole use made today of theorbos, lutes, and guitars? These gothic and contemptible instruments have been metamorphosed into *vielles*: that is their tomb" (1739, 18).

François Campion, theorbo player at the Opera, had previously blamed the "pernicious" tablature for the downfall of the lute in his 1716 *Traité d'accompagnement et de composition*. This theory had been expressed as early as 1680 in Perrine's *Livre de musique pour le lut* that included a "new and easy Method for playing the lute with notes of music." Perrine was the first lutenist to discard the tablature and write in keyboard score. In his preface he explained: "The disaffection of the public comes only from the great difficulty in learning the tabla-ture of A.b.c. that has been in use up to now . . . . This has caused most people to abandon this Royal instrument."

Unfortunately, the entire repertory of sixteenth- and early seventeenth-century lute music was abandoned, too, in the closing years of the seventeenth century. The composers, who had created the *style brisé* and bequeathed to the Chambonnières and Couperins an important element in their harpsichord style, sank into oblivion.

Jean Jacquot, editor of *Le Luth et sa musique*, has commented on the curious phenomenon whereby there were two distinct schools of lute composers in France in the seventeenth century (vol. 1, 1958: ed. of 1976, 164). One wrote primarily autonomous instrumental music, and the other composed *airs de cour* with lute accompaniments. This appears to have been a traditional division of labor. Composers did not cross these boundaries except in a very few cases. The *air de cour* composers were more conservative as a rule and stuck with the "old tuning" (*vieil ton*), whereas the instrumental composers were more adventurous with tunings and other modifications of their instruments.

The sixteenth-century lute was normally an eleven-string instrument. Five strings were doubled to make five pairs or *courses*, and there was one solo string, the *chanterelle*, which had the highest voice. The lute was expanded in the seventeenth century to include more courses. Antoine Francisque's *Le Trésor d'Orphée*, coming at the very turn of the century, for example, was written for a nine-course instrument. That lively source of information on French lutenists, Miss Mary Burwell, reported in her manuscript, *Instructions for the Lute*, that Mésangeau used a lute with nineteen strings (1670; rpt. 1958, 13). Up to six basscourses were added, each with a fixed pitch (generally G-F-E-D).

The "old tuning" (G-c-f-a-d'-g'), dating back at least to Attaingnant's two 1529 publications (*Dixhuit basses dances garnies de recoupes et tordions . . .* and *Très breve et familière introduction . . .*), was commonly used through the first twenty years of the seventeenth century. In time, the same spirit of experimentation that modified the instrument itself justified the use of new tunings. Ballard's 1623 *Tablature de luth de différents autheurs sur l'accord ordinaire et extraordinaire* was an early result of this experimentation in new tunings. Unfortunately, only the title page remains. In his *Harmonie universelle*, Mersenne includes both the "Accord ordinaire" and "Accord nouveau, ou extraordinaire" (G-c-f-a-c'-e') (1936; rpt. 1965). A subsequent publication by Pierre Ballard, *Tablature de luth de différents autheurs sur les accords nouveaux* (1638), is perhaps the first to introduce the tuning that eventually superseded all others in France and ended up as the favored tuning at the culmination of lute music in eighteenth-century Germany. This is the *nouveau-ton* (A-d-f-a-d'-f') which was *not* introduced by Denis Gaultier. It was exploited first by Denis's cousin, Ennemond Gaultier, and brought by him to England where Mary

Burwell quaintly referred to it as "Old Gaultier's new tuning, called the 'goat tuning,' because the first lesson he made upon that tuning is called 'The Goat' (and indeed represents the leaps and skippings of a goat)" (1670; rpt. 1958, 21). Varieties of this D minor tuning were common. One such variant tuned courses one and four up to F-sharp, resulting in two D major triads. This tuning also suited the key of F-sharp minor, another "goat's tuning" (*ton de la chèvre*) often found in French Baroque lute music (see Ledbetter 1987, 39).

The first seventeenth-century collection of lute music is *Le Trésor d'Orphée* (1600) by Antoine Francisque (ca. 1570–1605). The complete title gives us much information concerning the contents and also demonstrates the willingness of the composer-arranger to experiment with some new tunings ("*cordes avalées*"): *Le Trésor d'Orphée, livre de tablature de luth contenant: une Suzane un jour, plusieurs fantaisies, préludes, passemaises, gaillardes, pavanes d'Angleterre, pavane Espagnolle, fin de gaillarde, suittes de bransles, tant à cordes avalées qu'austres. Voltes et courantes.* There are about seventy pieces, the majority of which are dances. Only two are transcriptions of vocal works: "Suzanne un jour" by Lassus and "La Cassandre" from Arbeau's *Orchésographie*. Thus, at the very beginning of the century the transcriptions of vocal chansons, so important a part of the Renaissance lute repertory, were virtually abandoned.

More important musically and more international in scope is the *Thesaurus harmonicus* collection (printed in Cologne in 1603) made by Jean-Baptiste Besard (ca. 1567–1625), a Frenchman schooled in Italy and employed in Germany. The 403 compositions arranged by genres in ten books represent music by twenty-one composers and give a good cross-section of all types of lute music composed in Europe at the turn of the century. Here, as in Francisque, we find the newer dances, the allemandes, courantes, and even the gavottes appearing in substantial numbers. Besard published a second collection of lute music, *Novus partus, sive concertationes musicae* (1617), which includes several lute duos and other ensemble pieces for three lutes with voices and viols."[2]

In Amsterdam, Nicolas Vallet (ca. 1583–ca. 1642) published his *Secret des Muses* in two books (1615/1616 in Dutch, 1618/1619 in French). The *Secret des Muses* contains 109 pieces for one lute and seven pieces for four lutes. Although the preludes and fantasies are in Renaissance style, the collection also includes nineteen courantes, three bourrées, and one example each of a sarabande, allemande, and chaconne.

The "Balardus parisiensis," included in Besard, is Robert Ballard II (ca. 1575–after 1640), son of Robert Ballard I, founder of the Ballard printing dynasty. Robert Ballard II dedicated his first book of compositions for the lute (1611) to Marie de Médicis. This is the first lute tablature printed in France after Francisque. Some of the dances in Ballard's book are grouped together in miniature suites. The *Ballet de la Reine*, for example, includes four dances, the last a courante. The large number of courantes in this collection indicates a trend favoring this dance. In addition to the fourteen titled courantes, the "ten Angéliques" are all courantes called "Favorite d'Angélique" after Angélique Paulet, a lute virtuoso, who first appeared at court in 1609 when she was eighteen years old (*Angélique* is also the French name for the "angel lute," a double-necked instrument with twenty-three single strings). In many ways, the collection of nine *entrées de luth*, sixteen ballets, twelve courantes, ten "Angéliques," two "other" courantes, and six voltes is prophetic. Transcriptions of vocal pieces and polyphonically oriented fantasies are gone completely. The dances are graceful and homophonic, with short, ornamental figures supplanting the fuller chords of the previous century, and the texture is dominated by the *style brisé*.

The *style brisé* is a modern term used to describe this classic case of a musical style that exploits the very limitations of the instrument that created it. Chords are arpeggiated and inner voices shredded, so that any linear writing is more implied than actual, although Jacques Gallot insisted that should one wish to reconstruct the original polyphonic composition for performance by an ensemble, "he will find all the desired parts, upper and lower, in the work of this composer" (cited by Buch 1985b, 57). In the *style brisé*, consecutive notes from different octaves pass freely in and out of the texture only to disappear into thin air. Ornaments help sustain a melodic line. The texture continually thins and thickens. At the same time, as David Buch points out, there are several pieces in the immense lute repertory with well-defined melodic lines, consistent texture, clear harmonic direction, and clear rhythmic character (1985b, 52–67). The *style brisé* may already be observed in lute pieces by Francisque and in those of the Besard collection. It is not an innovation of the seventeenth century; actually, it is no more than an extension of a style in evidence from the earliest French lute tablatures (see Heartz 1955, 66).

With Ballard's collection, we have reached the point where the direction of development is away from purely choreographic considerations of the dance and toward an abstraction or idealization of certain characteristic features. The hemiola, which was characteristic of the French courante throughout the Baroque period, may be clearly seen in Example 16-1 below.

Example 16-1. Robert Ballard II: Hemiola formula in *Première Courante* (after Souris).

The "classical" ordering of the movements of the Baroque dance suite first appears in the lute repertory. François de Chancy's *Tablature de mandore* (1629) is the first collection to exploit an allemande-courante-sarabande order. A few years later two collections followed it: the *Tablature de luth des différents autheurs* of 1631 and 1638 by Pierre Ballard, the son of Robert Ballard II (see Buch 1985b, 95). The allemande-courante-sarabande ordering is not compromised by the fact that certain dances, especially the courante, are found in clusters. A Dufaut "suite" in Pierre Ballard's 1631 collection, for example, has four allemandes, six courantes, and two sarabandes. Presumably, one could make a selection for purposes of performance. David Buch has suggested that because many lute composers wrote dances for court ballets, the order in which dances were performed in several court ballets from 1600 to 1630 may have provided lute composers with a "general shape when grouping dances in their suites" (1985b, 107).

> *Many musical lights have risen in France, amongst whom a single one—as the sun among the stars—hath drawn the admiration and praises of all the world. It is the first Gaultier (who is named, in regard of his age and his merit, "old" Gaultier) (Burwell 1670; 1958, 13).*

Such is the simple homage rendered by Miss Burwell to Ennemond Gaultier, Sieur de Nèves (ca. 1575–1651), who was the first lutenist bearing this illustrious name. In spite of the prestige accorded him as court lutenist to both the queen mother, Marie de Médicis, and later to Anne d'Autriche, nothing by him was published in his lifetime. In the series "Corpus des luthistes français" (1966), André Souris has collected eighty-five pieces from a variety of sources—all composed for the lute (or harpsichord) by the "Vieux Gaultier." These miniatures have a charm and sophistication that should make them a source of pleasure to performer and listener alike. The melodic writing shows a great diversity in range and above all in asymmetrical phrase groupings. The use of written-out *ports de voix* and *coulés* with simultaneous ornament and resolution add pungency to the music (see measures one and three, respectively, of Example 16-2 below).

Example 16-2. Gaultier: Use of written-out ornamentation in a courante (after Perrine).

There is no better example of the transfer of style, or perhaps more accurately, the sharing of a common stylistic identity in the music for two different instruments, than in the two chaconne extracts found below. Example 16-3a is the *Chaconne, ou Cascade de Mr, de Launay* for lute by Gaultier; Example 16-3b is the *Chaconne* for harpsichord attributed to Jacques Champion de Chambonnières, considered the father of the French seventeenth-century harpsichord school. Each example exploits the lower range of its instrument, and each makes use of similar ornamental and nonharmonic tones that are absorbed into the chords themselves.

Example 16-3. (a) Gaultier: chaconne (after Souris). (b) Chambonnières: chaconne (after Bauyn MS in Bibliothèque Nationale).

The transcriptions of six Gaultier compositions from lute tablature to keyboard score made by Perrine in his *Pièces de luth en musique avec des règles pour les toucher parfaitement sur le luth, et sur le clavessin* (1680) appear to be quite literal except for some rhythmic changes. In contrast, the twelve Gaultier compositions that found their way into a manuscript of harpsichord pieces, copied by D'Anglebert after 1677 and now at the Bibliothèque Nationale (*Pièces de clavecin de différents auteurs Rés.* 89ter), show how the texture of the original lute pieces could be thickened, the syncopations ironed out, and the ornamentation increased (see Example 16-4a,b).

Example 16-4. Gaultier: A comparison of "La Superbe" in lute original with harpsichord transcription: (a) lute (after Souris), (b) harpsichord transcription.

Over half of Gaultier's compositions are courantes. Many bear descriptive titles such as "La Belle homicide," "Cléopatre amante," "La Petite bergère," "L'Adieu," "La Pleureuse," "Rossignol," etc. There are twelve allemandes, eleven gigues, eight sarabandes, and two chaconnes. Also, some of the earliest examples of *tombeaux* are among the allemandes—including one for Gaultier's teacher, Mésangeau, and one for the lutenist, L'Enclos, mentioned by Mersenne. While the tendency is to favor René François's "gay melancholy," reading into these idealized dances any pictorialism other than that of an overall mood would be a mistake.

Typical of the problems besetting André Souris and others who would rescue some of the lute repertoire for us from the period of Louis XIII, is the case of one Dufaut (Dufault, du Fault) about whom Miss Burwell wrote, "Mr Dufault would have made a good organist, because his way is heavy and affects too much the pedantic rules of music " (1670; rpt. 1958, 60). Who was François (?) Dufaut? According to Titon du Tillet, he was a student of Gaultier, but beyond that we have no information regarding his life or work or even his approximate dates of birth and death. Yet music by him kept turning up in various manuscripts such as the 1631 and 1638 collections by Pierre Ballard of lute tablatures. The extant music reveals Dufaut to have been an experimenter who never used the "old tuning" and who enjoyed some of the complexities of phrasing already noted in the music of his teacher. More importantly, he may have introduced the type of prelude later known as the free or non-measured prelude. There are six semi-measured preludes scattered throughout the lute pieces by Dufaut. The first of these, labeled "Recherche" and found in the *Airs de différents auteurs mis en tablature sur les accords nouveaux* (Ballard, 1631),[3] lacks bar lines and gives only an occasional suggestion of rhythmic values. Born of improvisation and the necessity of testing or "seeking out" the new tunings, the non-measured preludes reached an apogee in the harpsichord music of Louis Couperin and persisted through the third decade of the eighteenth century.

Denis Gaultier (ca. 1603–1672), or "le jeune Gaultier," or "Gaultier de Paris," was a younger cousin of "Le vieux Gaultier." "Young Gaultier" was one of the first composers to take some important steps toward the creation of the Baroque dance suite. He grouped together a number of different dances that he unified with a single tonality. *La Rhétorique des dieux*, which he composed between 1648 and 1652 for a wealthy patron, Anne de Chambré,[4] contains fifty-six lute pieces grouped by tonality into eleven suites. The suites generally open with an unmeasured prelude, a pavane, or an allemande; one or more courantes usually follow; and in more than half the cases, the suites conclude with a sarabande. By generally eschewing a random order of dances and following the lead of Chancy, Mésangeau, and Dufaut, Denis Gaultier moved the Baroque suite in mid-century closer yet to what became the normal order of its dances.

Like his cousin, Denis excelled in writing music marked by a tender melancholy. Unlike "old Gaultier," he tried from time to time to relate a descriptive title to descriptive music. In this, he pointed the way toward the late seventeenth-century composers of French lute music, Jacques Gallot and Charles Mouton, who may have been his students. As one example of this tendency, consider the courante "La Coquette virtuose" and its coquettish skips in the melody line, or the gentle lyricism of the *tombeau* for his wife in the key of F-sharp minor.

Along with Gallot and Mouton, Denis Gaultier was a master of the *tombeau*. *La Rhétorique des dieux* concludes with three compositions that form a sort of program suite. The "Tombeau du Sieur Lenclos," which opens this "suite," is an allemande filled with the dotted rhythms and syncopations that often characterize this dance; this is followed by "Consolation des amis de Sieur Lenclos," a courante in a much simpler style; and the suite concludes with a sarabande bearing the title "Résolution sur sa mort."

The seventeenth-century French lute school closes with the lute collections of the Gallot dynasty and Charles Mouton (1626–1699). Jacques Gallot (died ca. 1690), called "vieux Gallot de Paris," is the most important member of the Gallot dynasty. He composed 106 lute pieces, the most important of which are found in his *Pièces de luth composées sur differens modes* (ca. 1670). This collection is divided into two large sections, each preceded by a prelude; the whole concludes with variations on the "Folies d'Espagne." The dances include allemandes, courantes, sarabandes, gavottes, a minuet, gigues, chaconnes, canaries, and a volte. The collection contains only one of Gallot's ten *tombeaux*—a courante labeled "Tombeau de Madame."

Charles Mouton published four books of lute pieces; only two survive (see Rollin 1955). Both books bear the title *Pièces de luth composées sur differens modes* and were published in Paris "chez l'autheur" in 1698. Between them, they contain eight suites. Each suite has a variable number of dances ranging from four (Suite 2) to eleven (Suite 1). Each suite begins with a prelude that is generally followed by a pavane or allemande. Mouton avoided the allemande-courante-sarabande ordering frequently adopted by Denis Gaultier and certain of his predecessors. Most of the dances carry descriptive titles, and Mouton, unlike Denis Gaultier and his predecessors, tried to use the idealized dance movements to suggest miniature portraits of "La Belle Iris," "La Complaisance," "La Belle Angélique," and one self-portrait, a canarie entitled "Le Mouton." With the exception of a gaillarde and a passacaille, Mouton's choice of dances paralleled that of Gallot, listed above. More than any other lute composer, Mouton aimed for stylistic unity within the same composition. The "Tombeau de Gogo" that follows the prelude of Book 1, the allemande "Le Dialogue des grâces sur Iris," and the courante "Le Changeant" all have continuous flow—rare in lute music. Part of this search for unity is also reflected in the number of binary dances having both sections in exact balance.

In considering the music of a sister instrument, the guitar, it is important to realize that in the early years of the seventeenth century, the guitar was no longer considered "appropriate for musicians" the way it had been throughout the sixteenth century along with the lute. Pierre Trichet considered it little better than a "Spanish monkey" in his *Traité des instrumens de musique* and added that everyone knew the lute was "the most agreeable of all musical instruments" for the French (ca. 1640; 1956 [4]: 216).

The fortunes of the guitar improved later in the century. In 1629 Moulinié's third book of *airs de cour* included guitar as well as lute accompaniments. Perhaps the guitar was aided by Louis XIV's partiality for the instrument. Jacques Bonnet went so far as to declare that after eighteen months of practice, the king was the "equal of his guitar teacher" (1715, 331). The guitar was used to evoke the idea of Spain in *entrées* of certain court ballets by Lully and his predecessors.

The Italian guitarist-composer, Francesco Corbetta (ca. 1615–1681) began his sojourn in Paris in 1654. Two years later, he participated in Lully's ballet, *La Galanterie du temps*. At the restoration of the English monarchy in 1660, Corbetta left Paris for the court of Charles II. By the time he returned to Paris in 1670, François Martin had already printed his own *Pièces de guitarre* (1663), which contains two guitar suites, each introduced by a prelude followed by the now familiar ordering of allemande, courante, and sarabande, to which were appended optional dances such as gavottes, chaconnes, minuets, gigues, and bourrées.

Corbetta had returned to France to oversee the publication of his *Guitarre royalle* (1670) and to give guitar lessons to the Dauphin. The *Guitarre royalle*, which had been composed in England, was dedicated "au Roy de la Grande Bretagne." It contains fourteen suites for the five-string guitar and two allemandes, a sarabande, and a gavotte arranged for four voices and guitar continuo. Most of the suites have the format of prelude–allemande–courante–sarabande–optional dance. One (Number 12) achieves the classic ordering of the Baroque dance suite by adding a gigue to these dances. A second collection, also entitled *Guitarre royalle* but this time dedicated to Louis XIV, was published in Paris in 1673. The first twelve of its thirty-nine pieces are guitar duets, whose second parts (*contres parties*) are found "at the end of the Book in a detachable pocket."[5]

Robert de Visée (ca. 1660–after 1720), who undoubtedly had studied with Corbetta and who became Louis XIV's guitar teacher after 1695, is the most important composer of guitar music in France during the *grand siècle*. In addition to being a guitar virtuoso, he was also a fine singer and theorbist. We owe two books of guitar dances to him. The first book, *Livre de guittarre, dédié au Roy* (1682), includes eight dance "suites"; the second book, *Livre de pièces pour la guittarre* (1686), has four "suites."[6] These two books present a consistent ordering of dances within each suite more clearly than any lute pieces or, indeed, harpsichord pieces to this date. Most of the suites are structured in the order of prelude, allemande, courante, sarabande, and gigue, with such optional dances as gavottes, bourrées, minuets, chaconnes, and passacailles following the gigue in random order. With the exception of the beautiful allemande from the sixth suite, which serves as a *tombeau* for Corbetta, there are no descriptive titles. The courantes and allemandes are all of the French type, and certain minuets, labeled *rondeau*, are actually early examples of the rounded binary form A | B A' |.

The first third of the eighteenth century was dominated by François Campion (ca. 1686–1747), who pushed the virtuoso elements of the guitar to its limits. He added a sonatina and fugues to the basic repertory of dances and descriptive pieces. His most important collection of guitar music is the *Nouvelles découvertes sur la guitarre contenantes plusieurs suittes de pièces sur huit manières différentes d'accorder* (1705).[7]

As was true with the lute, the decline of the guitar in France was hastened by the difficulty of its tablature. Few composers attempted to write in keyboard score. All that remains of one such effort by Campion is the title, *Version de tablature en musique* [notes of music] *des pièces de guitarre*, and the privilege date, 14 June 1705 (see Brenet 1907, 419).

French lute music (and to a lesser degree, French guitar music) of the seventeenth century, although mannered and often precious, is never pretentious; it rarely demands more from the instrument than the instrument can give. In its own fragile way, it is true to itself, and many of its most salient features live on in French keyboard music.

Chapter 17

The Harpsichord

Seventeenth Century

*T*hat a transfer of elements of the lute *style brisé* to the harpsichord did occur in seventeenth-century France has ample documentation.[1] The final flowering of this style may be observed beyond the boundaries of France in the keyboard music of that greatest of all synthesizers of national styles, J. S. Bach. What is Example 17-1 below, from the allemande of the C minor *French Suite*, if not a total absorption of elements of the lute *style brisé*? What in the lute pieces was a *brisé* style pretending to be linear, has here become a linear style pretending to be *brisé*.

Example 17-1. Bach: Extract from Allemande of French Suite in C Minor.

One must, nevertheless, guard against the assumption that the lute *style brisé* was the only stylistic element to influence French composers of harpsichord music. Chambonnières, for instance, like Bach in Example 17-1, basically confined the *brisé* elements in his allemandes and courantes to inner-voice syncopations. His polyphonic texture of four real parts owes more to the seventeenth-century viol ricercare than to the lute repertory. Similarly, the free preludes by Louis Couperin draw as much from the toccatas of Johann Jakob Froberger as they do from lute preludes.

The earliest examples of French seventeenth- century harpsichord music antedate the collections of Chambonnières by many years. The so-called Copenhagen manuscript contains preludes, allemandes, courantes, and sarabandes dating from about 1626–1639. They are presumably of French authorship, although they are written, oddly enough, in German organ tablature (see P. Hamburger 1930–1931, 138–140). These dances, as well as those written for harpsichord by the lutenist René Mésangeau (died 1638),[2] show little evidence of the *style brisé* in their consistent *a2* and *a3* part writing. Thus, Daniel Heartz's observation concerning the lute and harpsichord repertory of the mid-sixteenth century could also apply to the mid-seventeenth century:

The style brisé *is already present in the* recueil *of Attaignant [1529], the first monument of French music for the lute. Keyboard music at this time maintained its own stylistic characteristics and only appropriated the* style brisé *of the lutenists at a much later date" (1955, 72).*

Only after the publication of Chambonnières's *Pièces de clavecin* in 1670, and only during the generation of D'Anglebert, did the *style brisé* became so pronounced in harpsichord music that we can legitimately speak of a "common language shared by both instruments" (Ledbetter 1987, 139). At that point, lutenist and harpsichordist shared a musical language that had its literary counterpart in the galant and frivolous verses by Vincent Voiture, who with his coterie at the Hôtel de Rambouillet had begun by 1620 to play a role in the Parisian world of letters. With a few changes of words, Pirro's description of the lute-harpsichord style might also describe the literary conceits stemming from the Hôtel de Rambouillet, which maintained its literary importance until 1650:

Instead of saying all, scrupulously and laboriously, the musician [lutenist or harpsichordist] tries to suggest what he has neglected to explain. Inconsistency, doubt, prodigious promises, the delights of a vaporous style, with its flashes of light that surprise or disturb, without ever imposing the continuous light whose brilliance dominates. Lutenists and harpsichordists made a virtue of their fragility (1925, 62).

Our knowledge of the instrument for which Chambonnières and Louis Couperin wrote their *Pièces de clavecin* is hampered because of the high mortality rate of seventeenth- and eighteenth-century French harpsichords. The earliest French harpsichord to survive is dated 1652 and was probably built by Claude Jacquet. Very few signed instruments from the seventeenth century are left. With the help of Mersenne and the few remaining instruments, we can, however, deduce the following: whereas the normal range of the sixteenth-century harpsichord was four octaves from C to c''', the seventeenth century extended the compass downward to GG and later to FF. This was accomplished at first by retuning to produce a short octave in the bass: that is, the lowest bass note, which appeared to be BB, was tuned down to GG; and the C-sharp, to AA; the D-sharp, to BB. Consequently, the instrument lacked certain notes in this short octave (GG-sharp, AA-sharp, for example) that were rarely called for in the music of the period. By the 1760s, a full five octave compass (from FF to f''' was normal). The short octave became obsolete, and by the turn of the century, the compass of the instrument had more or less stabilized.[3] The French harpsichord was a two-manual instrument about eight feet long that had three sets of strings, two registers of eight-foot pitch, and one of four-foot pitch. The best instruments from the workshop of the Blanchets or Taskin (preferably Flemish instruments _"refait par Pascal Taskin"_) had clarity of tone, lightness of touch, and contrast of timbres that were highly prized.

The most important dynasty of harpsichord makers was the Blanchet family, whose members spanned a 150-year period and included Pascal Taskin, who married the widow of François-Étienne Blanchet II in 1766. Very few instruments from the Blanchet-Taskin workshop survive. Incredible though it may seem, many French harpsichords belonging to the royalty and surviving the Terror were chopped up for firewood to warm the Conservatory classrooms during the bitter winter of 1816. Furthermore, much of the work of Blanchet and Taskin was in the enlargement and general restoration (known as _ravalement_) of older Flemish instruments, among which the Ruckers was most in demand. "It is in the art of enlarging the Flemish harpsichords of the Ruckers and of Couchet," one reads in the _Encyclopédie méthodique, ou par ordre de matières_ (1782–1832) "that Blanchet, a French maker, has perfectly succeeded" (cited by Frank Hubbard 1965, 119).

The vast repertory of seventeenth-century harpsichord music (over seven hundred compositions) consists almost entirely of binary dances; the only exceptions are preludes, chaconnes, passacailles, occasional descriptive pieces, and the keyboard transcriptions of lute music, instrumental music, and airs (mainly from Lully's operas).

Albeit with much freedom, French harpsichord composers continued the process of standardizing the principal dance types that make up the nucleus of the Baroque dance suite—a process already begun by lutenists. The allemande, usually placed near the beginning of the suite, is the most serious, the most "learned" dance. It employs points of imitation and a busy texture. The courante, the most popular of all French seventeenth-century dances, is the most complex rhythmically and, along with the allemande, the most irregular in phrase organization. The sarabande is the most predictable and most unified, due to its persistent use of standardized rhythmic patterns and symmetrical phrase groupings. The gigue, even though it carries a number of different meter signatures (3; 6/4; 12/8), is unified by some use of dotted rhythms and a relatively fast tempo. Generally, it is the longest of the seventeenth-century dances and the one most likely to use imitation.

From the Gaultiers's lute chaconnes, Chambonnières and Louis Couperin fashioned their own chaconnes or passacailles, which became prototypes for the monumental works in the same genre by François Couperin, Gaspard Le Roux, and Jacques Duphly. Other optional dances found in the repertory of seventeenth-century harpsichord music are minuets, galliards, gavottes, pavannes, bourées, canaries, voltes, and branles. Dances carrying descriptive titles are numerous and, unlike later examples, rarely deviate from a recognizable dance type.

In spite of an evident attempt to highlight certain characteristic features of each dance type, this music, like that for the lute, remains one step removed from improvisation. In spite of the unity that exists unavoidably between dances of the same type (all allemandes or all courantes, for example), there is almost an insistence on disunity within individual dances, which is achieved through constant change of texture, avoidance of melodic sequence, lack of harmonic stability, and a perverse reluctance to have Part A of the dance share its motivic material and melodic shape with Part B.

Six composers dominated the scene and created the bulk of the seventeenth-century harpsichord repertory. They are Jacques Champion de Chambonnières (1602–1672), Louis Couperin (1626–1661), Jean-Henri D'Anglebert (ca. 1628–1691), Jean-Nicolas Geoffroy (died 1694), Jean-Nicolas-Antoine Lebègue (1631–1702), and Elisabeth-Claude Jacquet de La Guerre (1665–1729). Although all shared in the creation of a common language, some individual differences are worth noting. Louis Couperin was certainly the most adventurous harmonically; Chambonnières, the greatest melodist; Lebègue, the most academic and predictable; D'Anglebert, the most difficult; Geoffroy, the most obscure; and Jacquet de La Guerre, the most eloquent.

By virtue of his finely structured allemandes, courantes, and his single pavanne, Henry Du Mont should be added to this list. The intrinsic musical value of the few manuscript pieces by Chambonnières's student, Jacques Hardel (1643–1678), is worth acknowledging. They are scattered here and there in collections of keyboard music.

For all practical purposes, we may consider Chambonnières to be the founder of the French school of harpsichordists. He numbered among his students and disciples Louis Couperin and Couperin's brothers—François ("the elder") and Charles—as well as Cambert, D'Anglebert, Lebègue, Hardel, and Nivers.

We have much evidence from Chambonnières's contemporaries concerning his manner of playing. Mersenne commented on the beauty of touch, the lightness and rapidity of his hand and added that the harpsichord had "met its finest master" in Chambonnières (1636; rpt. 1965, preface). More specific is the account by Jean Le Gallois in the *Lettre de Mr le Gallois à Mlle Regnault de Solier touchant la musique* (1680), which comments on Chambonnières's "lightness of touch" and describes how, each time he played a piece, he would add *ports de voix*, *passages* (probably filled-in skips), and *double cadences* (according to the composer's table, these are turns). Le Gallois's letter explains that one can always find new "graces" in such diversified performances. Already, the battle lines were drawn between those who favored a more virtuoso, brilliant style and the adherents of the *coulant* style exemplified by Chambonnières's performance. Le Gallois condemned the proliferation of ornaments in other musicians' performances, complaining that "only a perpetual trill (*cadence*) can be heard in their playing, which prevents the melody from being distinctly perceived, and they play *passages* continually, particularly between one pitch and its octave" (see Fuller 1976).

Chambonnières's harpsichord music appeared in two books,[4] both published in one volume at the end of his career in 1670, although presumably the music was composed over a thirty-year period. Perhaps needing a fillip after his "falling-out" with the king (or with Lully) in 1662, Chambonnières wrote in the preface that his music had been disseminated among the *"personnes les plus augustes de l'Europe"* and had reached "all cities of the world where there is some knowledge of the harpsichord." Chambonnières also related the story, familiar by then, of breaking into print because of the wide distribution of faulty copies of his music.

Each of the two books has thirty pieces grouped into suites, which are usually of four or five and never more than eight separate dances. Each suite begins with an allemande or pavanne, which is usually followed by a series of courantes, although in some instances gigues are inserted between the allemandes and courantes, thus showing how far he was from any standard dance order. Nearly half the dances (twenty-eight out of sixty) are courantes.

In addition to the printed sets above, some music by Chambonnières remains in manuscript. There are 126 of his compositions in the first volume of the Bauyn manuscript, named after Bauyn d'Angervilliers, whose coat of arms (along with that of the Mathefelon family) appears on the cover of its two volumes. This most important source of seventeenth-century harpsichord music is anonymous and cannot be dated with accuracy.[5] On the basis of paper analysis, Bruce Gustafson has suggested that it could not have been compiled before 1676 (Gustafson and Fuller 1990, 356). It also contains harpsichord music by Louis Couperin and other French *clavecinistes*, as well as compositions by Frescobaldi and Froberger. Brunold and Tessier point out in their edition of the *Oeuvres complètes* of Chambonnières that the Bauyn manuscript is to the French harpsichord school of the seventeenth century what the *Fitzwilliam Virginal Book* is to late Renaissance English keyboard music.

Example 17-2 illustrates Chambonnières's melodic gift. It is from Part B of a D minor sarabande and shows an appearance, rare in seventeenth-century French harpsichord music, of a melodic sequence being used to shift tonal centers (from D minor to F major), followed by a clear consolidation of the new harmony. This example is atypical of much seventeenth-century harpsichord music, whose harmony operates in part in a pre-tonal shadow zone. It is both an irritant to those of us who unfortunately began life with a built-in tonal bias, and at the same time a delight to have one's tonal compass totally disoriented. Perfect cadences, often built around secondary chords, follow rapidly one upon the other with little time in between for defining the key center. The wonder is that Chambonnières's melodies succeed so well in becoming airborne in spite of the gravitational pull of their many cadences.

His dances that carry descriptive titles rarely deliver more than a general musical mood corresponding with the title. (Note the allemande "dite l'affligée" in G minor with a lentement indicated by the composer.) Flashes of humor appear from time to time, however, especially in some gigues. At least one composition is purely descriptive, with no relationship to any recognizable dance-type: "La Drollerie," in which the nine measures of Part A are tightly organized around one descending conjunct motive treated in close imitation; whereas Part B introduces two meter changes, alludes briefly to the motive of Part A, and engages in sudden changes of texture—all within the brief span of thirteen measures!

Example 17-2. Chambonnières: Extract from Part B of the Sarabande in D Minor (after ed. of 1670).

Titon du Tillet tells the story of the three sons of Charles Couperin (Louis, François "the elder," and Charles), who played some of Louis's viol pieces for Chambonnières at his chateau near Chaumes-en-Brie. Chambonnières was reported to have told Louis that "a man, such as he, was not made to stay in the provinces and that he should absolutely come with him [Chambonnières] to Paris" (1732, 402). In any case, Louis Couperin was introduced at court by Chambonnières and, by 1657, was already an *Ordinaire de la Musique du Roy.*

Much of the keyboard music by Louis Couperin[6] is conserved in the second volume of the Bauyn manuscript and in the so-called Parville Manuscript, today at the University of California at Berkeley (see Curtis 1970). It is music that is filled with surprises when compared with Chambonnières's. Couperin was less conservative than his master in the choice of keys, for he used E minor, B minor, C minor, and A major in addition to the more usual keys. The key of F-sharp minor, found in a pavanne, is most unusual for an instrument utilizing mean-tone tuning. This may be the only keyboard piece of the French seventeenth century to attempt the cry of the *chèvre* (goat), as the lutenists called it.

Louis Couperin wrote sixteen non-measured preludes,[7] the greatest number by any harpsichord composer. He lavished much care on these compositions, whose genre he borrowed as much from the toccatas of Froberger as from the simple lute free preludes. Indeed, in the Parville Manuscript, there is a free prelude in A minor entitled "à l'imitation de Mr Froberger." This prelude (No. 6 in the Moroney edition) opens with a free quotation from the famous "Plainte faite à Londres pour passer la mélancholie" by Froberger.

In four of the preludes, Couperin introduced measured sections labeled *"changement de mouvement."* These preludes have three distinct parts: an imitative, ricercare-like middle section is sandwiched between non-measured sections. Most interesting is the prelude in F Major. Conceived as one large unit, its free sections merge without break with the measured, and its final section is a long, free melisma that decorates an F pedal. Is it possible that Jean-Philippe Rameau knew this prelude? His only non-measured prelude opens his *Pièces de clavecin* of 1706 and uses the same smooth transition device between free and measured sections. In both instances, the measured section is organized around a gigue-like rhythm.

In common with most seventeenth-century harpsichord composers, Louis Couperin made little effort to unify the two sections of his dances. Sometimes the disparity is considerable, as in Example 17-3 below, taken from a C major allemande; other times, however, he achieved a unity of sorts, especially in allemandes based primarily on continuous sixteenth-note movement.

Example 17-3. Louis Couperin: Extracts from two sections of the Allemande in C Major (after the Bauyn MS in Bibliothèque Nationale).

The expressive power of Louis Couperin comes, in part, through harmonic language richer than Chambonnières's. This is especially true in the cross-relations of the allemande in G minor, in the alternating couplets of the chaconnes (which reminded Pirro of bass viol solos and oboe duos) and in the seventh and ninth chords of the multi-sectioned "Tombeau de Mr de Blancrocher"—surely the most moving of all the many *tombeaux* to the dead lutenist.

The ordering of dances in the two books of *Pièces de clavecin* (1677, 1687)[8] by Nicolas-Antoine Lebègue is more consistent than in the "suites" by Chambonnières and Couperin. In fact, this very uniformity, carried down into the individual dances themselves, robs this music of the charm and whimsy of a Louis Couperin. Only the first book by Lebègue contains unmeasured preludes. Unlike Couperin, Lebègue employed a semi-measured notation to which he added diagonal bar lines to indicate chord changes (see Gustafson 1977).

In the title to his second book, Lebègue used the word *suitte* for the first time in French harpsichord music to identify each of the orderings of dances contained within. In this case, the title calls each of the six orderings of dances in the book a *suitte* and further identifies each by its tonality (for example, "Suitte en de la ré"). The majority of these suites are much closer to what we generally consider the norm of the Baroque dance suite, with its nucleus of allemande, courante, sarabande, and gigue. The optional dances, generally placed after the gigue, are a rondeau, gavottes, minuets, canaries, bourées, passacailles, and chaconnes. Gone are the archaic pavannes and galliards, the voltes and branles. The "Air de hautbois" from the Sixth Suite is an early example of the transfer to harpsichord of a dance from an operatic *divertissement*. The large number of minuets, which were the most popular of the optional dances, is also progressive. Only one suite in the second book lacks minuets. Several suites include minuet pairs, which are occasionally written in opposing modalities.

Key schemes are also of some interest. Lebègue planned some of his suites so that the last four or five dances would be in the parallel modality. The Second Suite, in G minor, ends oddly with a gavotte and minuet in the relative major key, which raises the question as to whether the order of performance is necessarily governed by the order found in the printed editions.

Jean-Henri D'Anglebert, who succeeded Chambonnières in 1662 as Louis XIV's harpsichordist, brought out his *Pièces de clavecin*[9] in 1689 and wisely dedicated them to the king's daughter, the Princesse de Conti. In the preface, D'Anglebert seems to be apologizing for using only four keys (G and D major and their parallel minors), insisting that he had already "composed in all the others." He added that he hoped to bring out the "others" in a second book (which apparently never did appear). The book contains a curious hodge-podge of four long suites, five rather academic organ fugues, a quartet on plainsong material appropriate for performance on the organ or on multiple harpsichords, and a short treatise on the "Principes de l'accompagnement."

Compared to the neat ordering of suites by Lebègue, D'Anglebert's work seems chaotic. Mixed in with normal dance components are fifteen keyboard reductions from Lully's stageworks. These include the overtures to *Cadmus*, *Le Carnaval mascarade*, and *Proserpine*; the chanconnes from *Acis et Galatée* and *Phaëton*; the passacaille from *Armide*; and other instrumental works.[10] D'Anglebert also included short *vaudevilles* in popular style "principally to fill up the ends of pages." This fact in itself, plus the inordinate length of the suites, makes one suspect that the order and choice of pieces was a matter of personal whim.

The "horror vacui" that compelled D'Anglebert to fill up all available space affected the music itself. The pages are black with notes; and the music is extremely *travaillée*. Ornaments, both indicated by symbols and written out, thicken the texture. An example of this style in Apel and Davison's *Historical Anthology of Music* (2:96–98) quotes the prelude, allemande, and sarabande from the Suite in G Minor. The semi-measured prelude is an impressive piece that derives its particular quality from the melodic interval of the tritone (see Example 17-4 below). This interval recurs many times and in many different guises. When the notes are held down as indicated, one imagines their wash of sound as stemming from a source like Fauré (or even Debussy) rather than from a seventeenth-century harpsichord composer.

Example 17-4. D'Anglebert: Use of melodic tritone in Prelude to the Suite in G Minor from ed. of 1689.

D'Anglebert included a set of twenty-two variations "Sur les Folies d'Espagne" in the suites. Pirro called them "*bien pauvres*" (very poor). They have historical interest as the only set of seventeenth-century French keyboard variations on the *Folia* tune that carries an attribution, although there are several anonymous examples of *Folia* variations in various keyboard manuscripts (see Gustafson 1979, 1:88–89). It is unlikely that D'Anglebert's variations served as a model for the very different eighteenth-century *Folies françoises* by François Couperin or *Folies amusantes* by Dandrieu.

The heavy, five-voiced texture of Lully was retained by D'Anglebert in his keyboard transcriptions. This "orchestral" style evidently affected D'Anglebert's dances as well. His allemandes and gigues often make use of full, five-voiced chords and busy inner parts that preclude a fast tempo for the gigues. The two 12/8 gigues are among the first of their type in France. Both are reasonably polyphonic and unified by a concentrated use of motivic material.

D'Anglebert's skill as a transcriber can be seen to good advantage in the keyboard manuscript in his hand, found today at the Bibliothèque Nationale (*Rés.* 89 ter). In addition to transcribing music from Lully's operas, D'Anglebert was one of the very few French composers who transcribed the pieces of lute composers such as Pinel (one), Mésangeau (one), E. Gaultier (twelve), and D. Gaultier (one) for harpsichord use. As Ledbetter pointed out, D'Anglebert's skill as an arranger of lute music on the harpsichord is evident not so much in the music that most closely reflects lute style, but in his "resourcefulness in finding natural keyboard equivalents for effects special to the lute" (1987, 69).

Although known to André Tessier and Paul Brunold, the 255 pieces by Jean-Nicolas Geoffroy in his *Livre des pièces de clavessin de tous les tons* have been the object of only one serious study—that by Martine Roche (1967). Roche suggested 1689 to 1702 as the possible chronological limits for this manuscript collection (Bibliothèque Nationale, *Rés.* 475) by the organist of Saint Nicolas du Chardonnet in Paris.

Geoffroy's book opens with fourteen suites in parallel modes on the diatonic scale degrees from C to A; Suites Nos. 13 and 14 are in the keys of B-flat major and B minor, respectively. Four of these suites also occur in transposed versions. With few exceptions, the dances within each suite follow the order of allemande, courante, sarabande, gavotte, minuet, and a concluding dance chosen from the following: rondeau, gigue, canarie, or chaconne. In addition to the wide range of keys, unprecedented in French keyboard music, Geoffroy's dances exhibit such harmonic daring that one wonders whether they are "experiments, spoofs, or very wrongly copied"[11] (see, for example, Roche 1967, 56–57). Since no piece by Geoffroy found its way into any other manuscript, it is doubtful that they were known by any of his contemporaries.

Elisabeth-Claude Jacquet de La Guerre, the wife of Marin de La Guerre (organist at Saint Severin and the Sainte Chapelle) and a protégée of Mme de Montespan, was highly regarded at court as a harpsichordist from her early teens. Her first book of *Pièces de clavecin*[12] was dedicated to Louis XIV and printed in 1687 when she was twenty-two years old. The book contains four suites in the keys of D minor, G minor, A minor, and F major. Each suite places allemande, two courantes, sarabande, and gigue in that order and ends with a minuet. The other optional dances, all placed after the gigue, are canaries, chaconnes, and a gavotte. The most eloquent and original music by Jacquet de La Guerre is found in the three preludes (Suites Nos. 1–3) and one *tocade* (*sic*) (Suite No. 4) that introduce the suites. The three preludes are semi-measured; their completely measured middle sections are written in freely imitative style. In contrast, except for an initial improvisatory flourish, the widely ranging *tocade* is measured throughout. It is the only example of a French harpsichord toccata in the seventeenth century.

Eighteenth Century

French harpsichord music of the eighteenth century[13] follows the tradition established by the composers of the previous century. The stabilization of the dance suite, begun by Lebègue and Jacquet de La Guerre and continued by Gaspard Le Roux and Louis Marchand, was never entirely completed in France—the only true "text book" examples being the six *Suittes* by Charles François Dieupart, which he composed not in France but in England.

Inevitably, French harpsichord music came to terms with the Italian influences that flooded Paris at the turn of the century in the form of cantatas and sonatas. Italian *vivacité* co-exists with French *douceur* in the keyboard works of François Couperin and Rameau as it does in the cantatas and *opéras-ballets* by André Campra. At first this was felt in matters of tempo and texture, and only to a lesser degree in melodic shape and harmony. Italian *vivacité* exists in the kinetic drive of the Italian giga in 12/8 with its continuous eighth-note movement; Italian *vivacité* is in Couperin's sprightly and unsophisticated character pieces, such as "L'Étincelante ou La Bontems" (Book 2, *Ordre* 11) or his "L'Atalante" (Book 2, *Ordre* 12), whose clean two-part writing and mechanical rhythmic pulsations derive from the Italian sonata and concerto.

Early eighteenth-century harpsichord composers gradually modified the *style brisé* with more continuous part writing. They also gradually unified the two sections of the binary dance, although striking examples of dissimilar sections endure throughout the period of François Couperin and Rameau. In addition to binary dances and character pieces, the rondeau became increasingly popular. Its possibilities for contrast and unity were exploited with telling effect by both Couperin and Rameau. Sixty out of over 240 compositions by Couperin are in this form.

Harmonically, French eighteenth-century harpsichord music remained essentially conservative. Such a well-known avant-garde example as Rameau's "L'Enharmonique" is really a demonstration piece and cannot be considered typical. Most of the pre-tonal edges of the previous century were smoothed out as tonal direction became more stable and tonal centers were used as important determinants in the musical architecture. This, however, was in the order of things: it was, after all, the century of Rameau's *Traité de l'harmonie*.

The harmonic outlook of the first part of the century with regard to keyboard music remained essentially French; the practices of an earlier age were given direction and more depth. Italian chromaticism, as an expressive device, is relatively rare although beautiful examples of its use may be found in François Couperin's last two books (see particularly, "La Mistérieuse" and "Les Ombres errantes" of the fourth book) and in Rameau's courante in A minor from the *Nouvelles suites de pièces de clavecin* of about 1729. Dissonance resulting from the use of non-harmonic chord tones in French ornamentation co-exists with dissonance that results from Italianate chains of suspensions or seventh chords in sequence.

The use of melodic sequence as a means of expanding motivic material became much more common in the eighteenth century, reaching such proportions in the Rameau A minor courante, mentioned above, that the entire piece is built on interlocking sequences. It is odd, however, that even the most adventurous and startling sequences, such as the sudden drop from A major to G major in the Rameau sarabande from the *Nouvelles suites de pièces de clavecin*, have a way of leading nowhere harmonically (see Example 17-5).

Example 17-5. Rameau: Use of sequence in Sarabande in A Major (after the Roussel engraved ed., n.d.).

The physical production of harpsichord music in the eighteenth century in France was enormous. In their catalogue of eighteenth-century harpsichord music, Gustafson and Fuller identified more than 180 titles of printed solo harpsichord music (with or without the "accompaniment of violin") by single composers from 1699 to 1780. To be sure, the musical high point was reached early in the century with the four books by François Couperin and the collections by Rameau. Hosts of imitators inevitably led to mannerism. Couperin's engaging program *ordres*, such as the "Folies françoises" or the "Fastes de la grande et ancienne Mxnxstrxndxsx," led to *Pièces de clavecin contenant plusieurs divertissemens* (Dandrieu). Powerfully descriptive pieces by Rameau, such as "Les Cyclopes" or "Les Tourbillons," degenerated in the hands of his imitators into "Les Vents en couroux," which describes the "Sea Agitated by Winds and Storm" (d'Aquin).

Yet, the well of inspiration that had sustained the French harpsichord school through Couperin and Rameau did not completely dry up in manneristic "Coo-coo" and other bird lore or in empty virtuoso display pieces like d'Aquin's "Les Trois cadences" with its double and triple trills. Nor was French imagination restricted to the making of folding harpsichords (*clavecin brisé*), "which can be torn down and put together so easily that one can carry [them] on a voyage" (Supplement 2:457 to Diderot's *Encyclopédie* 1751–1780), or limited to the invention of that ancestor of the color organ, Pierre Castel's color harpsichord (*clavecin oculaire*) of 1725, which, the *Encyclopédie* assures us, "was destined to give the soul the same agreeable sensations of melody and harmony of color via the eyes as the ordinary harpsichord communicates in sound via the ears" (1751–1780, 3:511).

French composers, always sensitive to quality of sound, continued to experiment with the harpsichord not only in combination with another harpsichord but also as an equal partner with other instruments. On the outer reaches of our survey are the innovative *Pièces de clavecin en sonates avec accompagnement de violon* of 1734 by Mondonville, which not only ushered the keyboard sonata into France, but also continued the development of the keyboard sonata with violin "accompaniment" that became extremely popular later in the century.

The very first decade itself opened the eighteenth century with a flourish. Ten collections of harpsichord pieces were published within those ten years. This remarkably productive period bridges the gap between the 1689 collection of D'Anglebert and the appearance of François Couperin's first book in 1713. These ten collections undoubtedly contain much music that was actually composed in the last two decades of the seventeenth century; this, of course, makes an attempt to postulate influences and priorities on the basis of publication dates virtually impossible. The collections of pieces are by Charles Dieupart (1701), Louis Marchand (two books in 1702), Nicolas Clérambault (1703), Jean-François Dandrieu (three books, about 1704), Gaspard Le Roux (1705), Jean-Philippe Rameau (1706), and Elisabeth-Claude Jacquet de La Guerre (second book, 1707).

Charles Dieupart (after 1667–1740) spent the last forty years of his life in England and is consequently somewhat outside the mainstream of development of the French eighteenth-century harpsichord school. His *Six suittes de clavessin*[14] are among the very few examples of French dance suites that adhere consistently to the order of overture, allemande, courante, sarabande, optional dances (for Dieupart, these were minuets, passepieds, and gavottes), and gigue. Published in 1701 in Amsterdam, it is also one of the earliest collections to be "*mise en concert*," that is, to include alternate performance possibilities with separately available parts for violin, flute, bass viol, and archlute (see Fuller 1974, 233–234). The music is more through-composed than much French music of the period and shows the careful attention paid to part writing that obviously impressed Bach, who copied the entire collection in about 1713. The similarity between the gigue of Dieupart's Suite No. 1 in A Major and the prelude to Bach's First English Suite in the same key has been observed by Dannreuther and others (see Example 17-6a,c below).

Just as interesting in this link up of influences is the role of Gaspard Le Roux (died ca. 1707), about whom we have practically no concrete information.[15] Surely much of the music of Le Roux's *Pièces de clavessin* was composed many years before the 1705 engraved edition. Some of it may even be contemporaneous with the 1689 collection by D'Anglebert. In this respect, Le Roux may be thought of as a connecting link between Louis Couperin and his nephew, François "le grand." Although Le Roux generally followed the classic order of allemande, courante, and sarabande (four of the seven suites begin with a prelude), only two suites contain a gigue, and the sarabande is missing from two suites. Each suite ends with one or more optional dances from the following: minuets, passepieds, gavottes, and a chaconne. Pirro (1907b, 430–431) was the first to notice that an alliance with Dieupart is suggested by the comparison of their two gigues in A major with the subsequent Bach copy (see Example 17-6a–c).

Example 17-6. (a) Dieupart: Gigue from A Major Suite. (b) Le Roux: Gigue from A Major Suite. (c) Bach: Prelude to English Suite in A Major.

Certain progressive tendencies in the keyboard music of Le Roux make him an important transitional composer in the development of eighteenth-century keyboard style. The "Courante luthée" from the First Suite, in D minor, is an early example of a binary dance whose two sections are unified—in this case by a tiny, four-note motivic cell ♪♪♪♪ that is almost always present in the texture at various pitch levels. Also progressive is the use of a rounded-binary form found in the sarabande of the Sixth Suite, in F-sharp minor. This apparently appeared so novel to Le Roux that he labeled it "Sarabande grave en rondeau," although its structure remains unequivocally binary, with each section repeated. Le Roux's music exhibits a discreet use of melodic sequence, sometimes combined with dissonant harmony, that clearly foreshadows Rameau (see Example 17-7a,b).

Example 17-7. (a) Le Roux: Extract from Courante in D Major (after ed. of 1705). (b) Rameau: Extract from Courante in A Minor (after Roussel ed. of 1706).

Each of the two books of *Pièces de clavecin* (1699, 1702) by the organist Louis Marchand (1669–1732)[16] contains but one suite (in D minor and G minor, respectively). Each suite maintains the order typical of Le Roux: prelude, allemande, courante, sarabande, and, in the case of Marchand, a gigue, which is then followed by optional dances (chaconne, gavotte, minuet). The consistent part writing of the organist forces greater unity between sections of the binary dances. In the gigue of the First Suite, this even extends to the use of a free inversion technique, whereby the direction of the opening melodic material is inverted at the beginning of Part B. This, of course, became standard practice in the gigues of the high Baroque dance suite in Germany.

Elisabeth-Claude Jacquet de La Guerre was the only French harpsichord composer to have her collections of harpsichord pieces published in both the seventeenth and eighteenth centuries. We have discussed her first book (1687). Her second book (1707), also dedicated to Louis XIV, was issued in a double volume that could be sold as a pair or separately. Part One is *Pièces de clavecin qui peuvent se jouer sur le viollon*, and Part Two is *Sonates pour le viollon et pour le clavecin*.

The fourteen harpsichord pieces fall naturally into two suites in D minor/major and G major, respectively. The following order is maintained throughout: allemande, courante, sarabande, and gigue, followed by optional dances (rigaudon, chaconne, minuet, rondeau). Only the opening allemande bears a descriptive title, "La Flammande." The fact that the treble line of the harpsichord may be doubled by a violin places this collection at the very beginning of the development of keyboard music with violin accompaniment. Nothing in the music itself suggests that, should this performance option occur, the harpsichordist would then, perforce, treat the bass line as a continuo and supply a realization. By the same token, the lack of a figured bass does not, in itself, preclude the possibility of this manner of performance. Most likely, however, the violin, played softly, would add another sound dimension to the melodic line. An early reference to this practice appeared in the *Mercure* of August 1729 (1874) describing a performance at the court by Marguerite-Antoinette Couperin, François's daughter, who was accompanied on the violin by Sieur Besson: "Besson . . . has made a particular study in order to play this sort of piece perfectly, softening his violin extremely."

The music in Jacquet de La Guerre's second book has some harmonic imagination and a nice blend of traditional features (note the extreme *style brisé* of the allemande, "La Flammande") with more progressive traits. One can only imagine the excitement that she brought to her *extempore* performances of these pieces. "She had, above all, a marvelous talent for playing preludes and fantasies on the spot. Sometimes, she would follow a prelude and fantasy for an entire half hour with melodies and harmonies that were extremely varied and in excellent taste" (Titon du Tillet, 1732, 636).

The paucity of our analytical vocabulary in music is nowhere more evident than in an attempt to deal adequately with the four books of *Pièces de clavecin* by François Couperin (1713, 1717, 1722, 1730). To label this music collectively as "Rococo worldliness" as was done in the 1969 edition of the *Harvard Dictionary of Music* (331) eliminates from consideration magnificent Baroque pieces such as the passacaille (Book 2, *Ordre* 8), "La Ténébreuse" (Book 1, *Ordre* 3) or "La Logivière" (Book 1, *Ordre* 5). It ignores the poetry and depth of feeling in "La Couperin" (Book 4, *Ordre* 21) or "La Convalescente" (Book 4, *Ordre* 26), and it is somewhat akin to Schumann's description of Mozart's Symphony in G Minor as "Grecian lightness and grace."

The *Pièces de clavecin* is an immense corpus of keyboard music embracing over 240 pieces that are distributed unequally among twenty-seven *ordres*. In point of fact, we would add more than eighty pieces to the four books of *Pièces de clavecin* were we to follow Couperin's own suggestions that his four *Concerts royaux* are appropriate for solo harpsichord as well as violin, flute, oboe, viol, and bassoon and that the trios of *Les Nations*, the *Apothéose de Corelli*, and the *Apothéose de Lulli* can be performed on two harpsichords, since "I perform them in my family and with my students with great success" (preface).

The music of these four books has been classified and codified by dance types and structural organization, by melodic and harmonic analysis, and by a systematic review of each *ordre* (the term is the composer's).[17] The meaning of the often ambiguous and enigmatic titles has been ferreted out when possible by Mellers (1950, 356–362; see also Beaussant 1980 [Eng. trans. 1990, 220–343] and Fuller 1990b). Couperin's musical language has been compared to the verse of Racine and the brushstrokes of Watteau.

All of this has value, but it gives us little of the essence of the music and tells us almost nothing of the mysterious alchemy that makes Couperin's harpsichord pieces so elusive yet so compelling. For in company with some of Chopin's mazurkas and Debussy's preludes, much of Couperin's keyboard music is more a communication between instrument and performer in the intimacy of the music-room than it is between performer on the stage and an unseen audience. It reveals itself only gradually and only after repeated playings; it is wed to its instrument as is no other music. Only through such intimate acquaintanceship with the music do the many dimensions of Couperin's art unfold.

Examples of "Rococo worldliness" and hedonism are abundant, indeed; witness the contrived fifes and *tambours* of "La Basque" (Book 2, *Ordre* 7) or the burlesque pieces that climax in the "Troisième Acte" of the satiric "Les Fastes de la grande et ancienne Mxnxstrxndxsx" (Book 2, *Ordre* 11) with its traveling circus of jugglers, tumblers, mountebanks, bears, and monkeys. Rococo is the unpretentious grace of "Soeur Monique" (Book 3, *Ordre* 18) and the well-named "Les Graces naturèles" (Book 2, *Ordre* 11), the playfulness of "Les Bagatelles" (Book 2, *Ordre* 10), the charming "nothingness" of "Le Petit-rien" (Book 3, *Ordre* 14). This is music far removed from either Baroque exuberance or the classical grandeur of the *grand siècle*. It breathes the spirit of the Regency, and, at the same time, its genre pieces have the effective immediacy and the accurate commentary of some Watteau sketches.

But there is also the Couperin of "La Ténébreuse" (Book 1, *Ordre* 3), whose explosive utterances almost break out of its narrow, formal boundaries. Part A is a French overture; Part B, a continuous variation that gains in power by a thickening of the texture until it achieves an almost Beethovenian urgency at its climax.

Similar use of contrasting sections within binary structures may be seen in "La Logivière" (Book 1, *Ordre* 5) and in "La Visionaire," which opens *Ordre* 25 of Book 4. Part B of "La Logivière" is made up of figurations unravelling over pedal points in a manner resembling the North German toccata. "La Visionaire" occupies the place normally accorded the allemande, but has severed its connection with the dance; its two sections are complete contrasts in tempo and texture.

Then there is the Couperin who can organize his material with the greatest economy, deriving all from a single motif. (See "La Laborieuse" and "Les Idées heureuses," both from *Ordre* 2 of Book 1.) Often this tight organization is combined with refined part writing that would do honor to J. S. Bach, himself. It should be emphasized that Couperin did not carry this contrapuntal play consistently through an entire composition except in a very few cases where it is the result of his attempt to transfer the particular texture of the Italian sonata to the harpsichord. Proof of this comes in the allemande, bearing the performance direction *légèrement*, which the composer included in his *L'Art de toucher le clavecin* to demonstrate an alternative to the *style brisé*—an alternative style, born of the sonata, in which "the melody and bass work together throughout the piece." This is a fine example of two-part writing and the expansion of motivic material unimpeded by too many regularly recurring cadences.

Couperin was not an innovator nor did he seek to experiment unduly with the binary and rondeau forms he had inherited. He did, however, enrich these simple forms in a wide variety of ways. Rameau may have learned from him the art of having each contrasting couplet of a rondeau move from the simple through the more complex, where complexity is achieved by a change in texture or increased harmonic activity. Such is the final couplet of "Les Baricades mistérieuses" (Book 2, *Ordre* 6), which, in its broken-chord spacing and in its delayed resolutions of suspensions, has the sound of Fauré or even of Schumann.[18]

Like other harpsichord composers around him, Couperin from time to time singled out certain pieces for multiple performance possibilities. For the popular "Le Rossignol-en-amour" (Book 3, *Ordre* 14), he suggested a performance on transverse flute; for the two musettes ("Muséte de choisi" and "Muséte de taverne") of Book 3, *Ordre* 15, he supplied both a *sujet* and a *contre partie* and added that they would be appropriate for "all sorts of instruments of equal pitch." In the preface to his third book, he described his "Pièces-croisées" as suitable for "two flutes or oboes, as well as for two violins, two viols, or other instruments of equal pitch."

This freedom to choose among several instruments is markedly different from Couperin's insistence that what he wrote must be scrupulously observed in performance. For him, keyboard ornamentation was not merely decoration but also a tool for deepening the expressive content of the piece. That he was aware of the limitations of the harpsichord as an expressive instrument is evident from his preface to the first book:

> *The harpsichord is perfect with regard to its compass and its brilliance; but as one can neither swell nor diminish the sound, I am always grateful to those who, by an art sustained by taste, are able to render the instrument susceptible to expression.*

He detailed (not always too clearly) his performance wishes with regard to ornamentation more than any other composer; yet apparently these instructions were not followed to the degree that he wished. In the preface to Book 3, he observed with some annoyance:

> *(After taking such care to mark the ornaments suitable for my Pieces, for which I have separately given an easily understood explanation in a particular Method known by the title* L'Art de toucher le clavecin*), I am always surprised to hear of people who have learned them without heeding my instructions. This is unpardonable negligence, the more so as it is no arbitrary matter to put in any ornament that one may wish. I declare, therefore, that my pieces must be executed as I have marked them, and that they will never make an impression on persons of real taste unless one observes to the letter all that I have marked, without any additions or deletions.*

Couperin's wish to assure performances of musical integrity may have accounted for his measuring the eight preludes placed at the end of *L'Art de toucher le clavecin*. Beginning with Dandrieu's 1705 collections, the free preludes were more commonly measured, although the non-measured or semi-measured types did persist here and there up to 1777, which is the date of a manuscript of an unmeasured prelude by Claude Bénigne Balbastre. Couperin justified measuring the preludes for a pedagogical reason: namely, they are easier to learn and to teach.

One suspects from his opening remarks, however, that he had little faith in the ability of most performers to sustain the non-measured prelude successfully.

Parodies were a measure of success for Couperin just as they were for an opera composer. André Tessier (1929) found parodies of Couperin's harpsichord pieces in the *Recueil d'Airs sérieux et à boire* that was published by Ballard in 1711, two years before Couperin's first book had been printed. In the preface to his third book, Couperin acknowledged the parodies and offered the broad suggestion that his "obliging associates" would find "a vast field for exercising their Minerva" in his most recent book.

The effect of François Couperin's first publication, *Pièces de clavecin* 1713, was electrifying. The genre piece rapidly rose in importance to the level of established types of dances and brought into general notice the concept of descriptive music as an end in itself rather than as an agent of the dance.

The impact of Couperin's four harpsichord books catapulted the genre piece to a position of prominence. The dance suite, as it existed in the first decade of the eighteenth century, appeared doomed. Significantly, there was an appreciable drop in the number of collections published between the year of Couperin's Book 1 (1713) and his Book 4 (1730). Only the collections of Nicolas Siret (1719), Rameau (1724, ca. 1728), and Jean-François Dandrieu (1724, 1728, 1734) were printed.

Jean-François Dandrieu (1682–1738), organist at Saint-Merri and, after 1721, at the Royal Chapel, had already written three collections of *Pièces de clavecin* dating from about 1705.[19] None of the three contains a dance bearing a descriptive title. His three books of 1724, 1728, and 1734, on the other hand, comprise descriptive pieces for the most part. Further, he labeled them *Premier livre*, *Second livre*, and *Troisième livre*, as if he wished to obliterate his earlier efforts. Paul Brunold discovered that many pieces from the *Troisième livre de pièces de clavecin* were actually taken from the earlier books and given descriptive titles (1932). It may be that Dandrieu wished to capitalize on Couperin's successes and, in particular, to exploit the program suite suggested by "Les Fastes de la grande et ancienne Mxnx-strxndxsx" among others.

The *Premier livre de pièces de clavecin* (actually his fourth book) carries the subtitle "*contenant plusieurs divertissemens dont les principaux sont Les Caractères de la guerre, ceux de La Chasse et les Fêtes de vilage.*" The "Caractères de la guerre," which follows the First Suite, is descriptive music with a vengeance. What was suggested in Couperin is here pounded home with little attention paid to the sensibilities of performer or listener. The fifty-three measures of tonic harmony in the "charge" incorporate cannon shots that, we are told in the preface, are marked only by four notes forming a "perfect chord. But instead of these four notes, one may strike the lowest notes of the Harpsichord with the entire flat of the hand as many times as one wishes the better to express the noise of the cannon." Thus, special effects on the keyboard two hundred years before Charles Ives and Henry Cowell!

In the *Second livre de pièces de clavecin* of 1728, which also includes two *divertissements*, "La Pastorale" and "L'Aubade," Dandrieu borrowed Couperin's concept of the *goûts réunis*. The First Suite opens with a French overture appropriately titled "La Lully,"[20] which is followed immediately by "La Corelli" and a *double* that is a clever parody of the great Italian's style.

François d'Agincourt (1684–1758) aimed only to give as good an imitation of Couperin as possible in his collection of 1733.[21] He went so far as to appropriate Couperin's designation *ordre* for the four suites of the collection. Louis-Claude d'Aquin (1694–1772) included one *divertissement* in his first book of 1735.[22] It is "Les Plaisirs de la chasse," which, we learn, may be performed with "hunting horns, oboes, violins, flutes, musettes, and vielles." D'Aquin's 1735 collection also includes some virtuoso descriptive pieces highlighted by a "storm at sea" with crossed-hand passages representing the "fury of the waves and the brilliance of the lightning."

In pieces like these with their veneer of special effects coming just two years after the death of Couperin, we are already far removed from his concept of genre pieces as *"espèces de portraits"* (kinds of portraits) (preface, Book 1) and even farther removed from his attitude toward performance: "I prefer much more that which moves me to that which surprises me" (preface, Book 1).

The vogue for descriptive keyboard *divertissements* continued throughout the century, reaching a nadir with Michel Corrette's *Divertissements pour le clavecin ou le forte piano* (1779) "containing echoes from Boston and a naval victory won by a frigate against several assembled privateers; the harmony expresses the noise of arms, of cannon, cries of the wounded, plaints of the prisoners in this combat."

Of the composers who published collections under the very nose of Couperin, only Nicolas Siret and Rameau were able to keep their identities and not succumb to the fashion of the moment. Siret (1663–1754), who was a student of Couperin's, adhered to the older practice of titled dances in his two books of harpsichord pieces (ca. 1710–1715, 1719). They keep the traditional order of allemande, courante, sarabande, and gigue followed by optional dances (gavotte, minuet, passacaille, chaconne, rigaudon, rondeau). There seems to have been a conscious effort on the part of Siret to sum up the various types of introductory pieces found in French collections of harpsichord dances. Thickly scored French overtures reminiscent of D'Anglebert introduce the two suites of the first book. Two of the three suites in the second book begin with preludes; the first, a semi-measured, free prelude, and the second, a multi-sectioned piece having toccata-like flourishes.

Every page of Rameau's first book of *Pièces de clavecin* of 1706 bears the personal stamp of its composer. The book consists of a single suite in A minor. The twenty-three-year-old Rameau was already equipped to deal effectively with the most progressive musical language. Most of the binary dances are titled and in the traditional order. The optional dances (two sarabandes, a gavotte, and a minuet) follow the gigue. The only descriptive piece is a rondeau, "La Vénitienne," inserted between the second sarabande and the gavotte. Most of the dances achieve a unity of texture and melodic material rare for this early date. Rameau's use of bold harmonies, both to lend color and for structural purposes, is evident from the first piece, a prelude, that combines an opening free section with a measured, gigue-like conclusion in the tradition of Louis Couperin. Some strikingly dissonant cross-relations in the measured section culminate in the diminished octave (see Example 17-8 below) that apparently so offended the timorous editors of the *Oeuvres complètes* that it was expurgated from their edition.[23] The first allemande could be viewed as a sketch in miniature for the great allemande in the same key (A minor) composed about twenty years later and included in the *Nouvelles suites des pièces de clavecin* (ca. 1729). In addition to the unity of texture and motive already alluded to, the piece is an interesting study of Rameau's harmonic practices at this date. The diminished seventh chord is given special prominence by its placement in the measure (see, for example, Part A, measures 7 and 12; Part B, measure 13). The use of sequence to extend musical space is already an adumbration of his later music. The courante, in addition to its striking sequence of sevenths and bass line chromaticism, also uses the diminished seventh chord—this time to delay the final cadence in Part A.

Example 17-8. Rameau: Use of dissonance in the Prelude from *Pièces de Clavecin* (after Roussel ed. of 1706).

Rameau's *Pièces de clavecin* of 1724 (revised 1731) includes a manual *De la méchanique des doigts sur le clavessin* (On the Technique of the Fingers on the Harpsichord). Contrary to the first collection, character pieces and dances of a popular nature (rigaudons, musettes, and tambourins) far outnumber the traditional dances. Here, also, Rameau used virtuoso elements for the first time for character pieces such as "Les Niais de Sologne," "Les Tourbillons," and "Les Cyclops." "Les Cyclops" is probably unique in the French harpsichord repertory. A brilliant piece, it makes its effect through the Scarlatti technique of rapid crossed-hand passages[24] and a driving, pulsating rhythm, broken dramatically here and there by sudden stops. Quite different from these are many gentle pieces in the Couperin tradition such as "Les Soupirs," "L'Entretien des Muses," and "Les Tendres plaintes."

The big, aggressive dances, represented by "Les Cyclops" and "Les Sauvages" with their bursts of kinetic energy, as well as the popular tambourines and musettes suggest all manner of choreographic treatment. That Rameau transcribed this music for orchestra many years later in the *divertissements* of his *tragédies lyriques* and *opéras-ballets* is no accident.[25]

In certain of his descriptive pieces, Rameau was able to capture the essence of the *"espèce de portrait"* with the greatest economy. In just sixteen measures, we are given a shocking picture of a cripple ("La Boiteuse") that is cruel in its incisiveness; undoubtedly, a later century would have viewed as social criticism what Rameau saw simply as a descriptive piece in the burlesque genre.

The later collections are those of the *Nouvelles suites de pièces de clavecin* of about 1729, mentioned above, and the *Cinq pièces* (1741) arranged for solo harpsichord by the composer from his *Pièces de clavecin en concerts* published the same year. In addition, Rameau transcribed for harpsichord thirty-seven *symphonies* grouped into four *concerts* from his *opéra ballet, Les Indes galantes* (see Sadler 1979; and Gustafson and Fuller 1990, 206–208).

The allemande that opens the *Nouvelles suites de pièces de clavecin* is one of the longest allemandes in the repertory; one section alone has the length appropriate for most other allemandes. Its length is achieved in part by a series of sequences that flow into one another with great ease. Characteristic of Rameau's later harpsichord writing is the total assimilation of earlier techniques, such as the *style brisé* and textual shifts, into an overall unity. There is an occasional thinning of texture (see, especially, the nearly linear quality of the triplet passages at the end of each section), but the whole appears to be consistent three-part writing with the *style brisé* hidden in the inner voice syncopations (see, for example, measures 8 and 9 of Part A).

His later rondeaux display a greater difference between the contrasting couplets, which move, as in Couperin, from the simpler to the more complex. This is climaxed by the final couplet of the second rondeau from "La Timide" (*Cinq pièces*). This couplet is in itself an excellent example of diversity amid unity. Here, in three-measure units, is a real patchwork of harmonies and textures that range from thickly voiced sequential chords, which would not be out of place in a French café tune of today (Example 17-9a), to Beethoven-like arpeggios that extend over three octaves and slow down the harmonic rhythm to one chord change per measure (Example 17-9b). Unification is achieved by means of the arpeggio figuration, which is never completely absent from the texture, and by the surprising transformation of the beginning of the first rondeau in the first three-measure unit (Example 17-9c).

Example 17-9. (a–c) Rameau: Extract from final couplet of "La Timide" (after Walsh ed., London, c. 1755).

The last harpsichord pieces by Rameau are *Les Petits marteaux* (see Fuller 1983) and *La Dauphine*. The latter piece was said to have been extemporized for the marriage of the Dauphin to Maria-Josepha of Saxony in 1747 and did not appear in print until 1895. It bristles with harmonic audacities and revels in the forbidden. Are there any more blatant, more exposed parallel fifths in the period of common practice than those implied by the trills that close the first measure?

Jean-Joseph Cassanéa de Mondonville (1711–1772)[26] composed the first keyboard sonatas ever to be published in France. These six sonatas appeared about 1738 as the *Pièces de clavecin en sonates avec accompagnement de violon, opus 3*. He wrote them for harpsichord solo or harpsichord with violin accompaniment. Unlike Elisabeth-Claude Jacquet de La Guerre (1707), Mondonville succeeded in writing an independent obbligato line for the violin in his sonatas. His violin only doubles the treble line of the harpsichord in two places: the slow part of the French overture that opens the set and again in the tutti sections of the first movement of Sonata No. 6.

Mondonville's preface tells us something about the vogue for the sonata in France at the time of his writing:

> *Perhaps it is rash to give instrumental Music to the Public today: there have been such a prodigious number of Sonatas of all types in the past few years, that everyone believes the genre to be exhausted. Nevertheless . . . I have attempted something new.*

The sonatas generally show a nice balance between the two instruments with, however, none of the tight polyphony that characterizes the violin-harpsichord sonatas of J. S. Bach. Mondonville cast all six of his sonatas in a three-movement format: Fast Slow Fast. The last movement is often a gigue; and the middle movement, a type of "aria" in moderate tempo. The Sixth Sonata, labeled Concerto by the composer, contrasts the tutti and solo groups clearly. These sonatas anticipate the variety of textures and techniques in much future chamber music having obbligato keyboard (see Fuller 1974, 239–240).

In 1748 Mondonville printed another set of innovative harpsichord pieces, *Pièces de clavecin avec voix ou violon*, Opus 5.[27] In his preface, he wrote:

> *It is composed of pieces for the Harpsichord, with a part that may be sung by a high voice, or played on a Violin. I believed that this format would particularly interest those who join vocal talent to a talent for the Harpsichord, since they could then perform this genre of music alone . . . . One must begin with one of the pieces bearing the words, "Paratum cor meum" or "Benefac, Domine, bonis," learning the vocal line first, and [one must] above all, distinguish the phrases in French taste from those in Italian taste. Afterwards, [one must] learn the Harpsichord piece that serves as an accompaniment, [one must] observe attentively the ornaments that I have taken care to notate . . . . People, who play the Harpsichord and who do not have a voice, can have the vocal line played on a Violin. If a Violin and voice are lacking, the accompaniment will stand alone.*

> *When the voice, Violin, and Harpsichord are united (this is possible to achieve with two persons), it is necessary to adjust the sound of the voice and Violin to the strength of the Harpsichord so that each part can be heard.*

There are eight *petits motets* in the collection—all based on psalm texts. All but one use the violin. The keyboard part is a true obbligato with no continuo.

The concept of a sonata for keyboard with violin accompaniment was not long in taking hold. By mid-century, Michel Corrette (*Sonates pour le clavecin avec un accompagnement de violon*, 1742) and Louis-Gabriel Guillemain (*Pièces de clavecin en sonates avec accompagnement de violon*, 1745) had collections in print. The preface to the collection of Guillemain (1705–1770) reflects the stylistic conflict engendered by the new genre and confirms the paramount role of the keyboard instrument:

> *Having noticed that the Violin would often cover [the harpsichord] a bit too much (making it difficult to distinguish the true subject), my first idea, when I composed these Pièces en sonates, was to let them be for the Harpsichord alone, without any accompaniment; but to conform to present day taste, I believed I could not dispense with this [accompaniment] part, which demands great gentleness in its execution, so that the Harpsichord may be heard with ease on its own.*

Clearly in the same tradition is Rameau's only example of chamber music, a set of five *concerts* for harpsichord with the accompaniment of violin (or flute) and viol (or second violin), called *Pièces de clavecin en concerts* (1741). In his *Avis*, Rameau insisted that these pieces "leave nothing to be desired if played as harpsichord solos." While this comment is generally true, in some pieces the harpsichord switches roles with the other instruments and serves as an accompaniment (see, for example, "La Livri" and "La Timide").

Italian influence increasingly modified the more traditional keyboard elements stemming from France. The *Sonates et pièces pour le clavecin* of 1740 by Jean-Baptiste Barrière (ca. 1705–1747) are characteristic of this trend. The collection includes six sonatas in which typical string figurations are coupled with elaborate broken octaves, scales, and arpeggios divided between the hands. These sonatas are the first that were composed by a Frenchman for keyboard alone.

Italian influence also compromised French *style brisé* in the *Pièces de clavecin* (1734) by Pierre Février (1696–1790)[28] and the *Premier livre de pièces de clavecin* (1735) by Charles (not Jean-Odéo) Demars (1702–1774), where traditional French dances and descriptive pieces are often rendered in clean, two-part writing. The former collection contains the only examples of French harpsichord fugues (used to introduce the Second and Third Suites) in the first half of the eighteenth century (see Montagnier 1990).

On the other hand, the mid-century keyboard collections of Joseph-Nicolas Pancrace Royer (ca. 1705–1755) and Pierre-Charles Fouquet (1694–1772) derive from the elaborate and virtuosic descriptive pieces found in earlier collections of Dandrieu, d'Aquin, and Corrette and exhibit little Italian influence. The early *Pièces de clavecin* (1759) of Claude Balbastre (1727–1799) follow in the wake of the François Couperin of the "*espèce de portraits*" in providing us, often with great elegance, keyboard portraits of minor personages, many of whom have been identified by Alan Curtis.[29]

French and Italian styles, as exemplified by dances and descriptive pieces on the one hand and sonatas on the other, co-exist harmoniously in the first two books by Jacques Duphly (1715–1789), written before mid-century,[30] and in the six books by Christophe Moyreau (ca. 1690—1772), all published after 1750. The first book by Duphly includes fifteen pieces with some musical "portraits" and some traditional dances. The courante in Example 17-10, below, clearly juxtaposes the *style brisé* and elements from the Italian corrente (the 2 meter sign may be thought of as two measures of 3/8). The last piece, labeled simply *légèrement*, resembles the *Sonates pour le clavessin sur le goût italien* by Giovanni Benedetto Platti, which was published in Nürnberg in 1742. It is an Italian sonata movement that has an embryonic second theme in the dominant key, a "Development" that begins with the main theme transposed to the dominant, and an incomplete "Recapitulation" of secondary thematic material transposed back to the tonic key.

Example 17-10. Duphly: Extracts from Courante, Book One (after Vandome ed., 1744).

This sonata, with its thin texture and lively tempo, its repeated notes and "patter" sequence, stems from the same source as those by Platti; that is, the Italian *opera buffa*. Thus, two years before the first performance of Pergolesi's *La Serva padrona* in France and many years before the *Querelle des Bouffons*, we see that the fashionable *goût Italien* has become a part of French keyboard music.

≈ Chapter 18 ≈

Organ Music of the Grand Siècle

he French organ school of the *grand siècle* was born in Normandy. There the prototype of the French classical organ was created despite the fearful ravages of religious wars that included wholesale destruction of church organs. In 1580 at Gisors, Nicholas Barbier finished the organ for the Church of Saint-Gervais et Saint-Protais. This superbly designed instrument, with its *Grand Orgue* of forty-eight keys, its *Positif* and Pedal, exhibited the general form of the later French classical organ.

To Normandy, to the Cathedral of Rouen, came young Jehan Titelouze (1563–1633) in 1588, and Titelouze, the organ specialist, had the foresight to bring the builder Crespin Carlier from Paris to restore the cathedral organ and make of it an instrument worthy of Titelouze, the composer.

In 1623 Ballard printed the first collection of organ compositions by Titelouze, *Hymnes de l'Église pour toucher sur l'orgue, avec les fugues et recherches sur leur plain-chant.*[1] Three years later his *Magnificat, ou cantiques de la Vierge, pour toucher sur l'orgue suivant les huits tons de l'Église* appeared. These two collections contain thirty-nine and fifty-six verses, respectively, designed to alternate with the *plain-chant musical.* The musical language is that of Renaissance polyphony. However, the occasional use of free dissonance and some chromaticism remind us that this is also the period of the Italian ricercare, labeled *"recherche"* by Titelouze, and that Frescobaldi's *Ricercari e canzoni francese* had appeared in print only eight years before.

Drawing upon the full resources of his organ, Titelouze required the first verse of each hymn to be performed on the *Plein-Jeu* (foundations and mixtures of full organ).[2] In verses like these the plainsong melody was often given to the Trumpet and Clarion of the Pedal to contrast with the *Plein-Jeu.* In the best "learned" fashion, material in the other voices was often derived from the cantus firmus as in Example 18-1 below, extracted from the first verse of *Iste Confessor.*

Example 18-1. Titelouze: Extract from first verse of *Iste Confessor* (after ed. of 1623).

The musically rewarding and technically refined compositions by Titelouze could scarcely have existed in a vacuum, yet very little survives of French organ music between Attaingnant's publications of 1530–1531 and Titelouze's hymns almost 100 years later. The nine *chanson* intabulations for organ date from the mid-sixteenth century and are found today in the Bayerische Staatsbibliothek of Munich (MS Mus. 2987).[3] A *Fantaisie* by Nicolas de La Grotte on Cipriano de Rore's *Ancor che col partire* survives and also a short *Fantaisie sus orgue ou espinette* by Guillaume Costeley, in the Bibliothèque Nationale (MS fr. 9152), which scarcely represents the best work of this "organiste et vallet de Chambre du Roy." The three *Fantaisies* for organ or viols by Claude Le Jeune were printed posthumously in 1612. The third of these is based on the Gregorian melody *Benedicta est coelorum Regina.* Also posthumously published are the *Fantaisies à III, IV, V et VI parties* by Du Caurroy, of which fourteen are based on plainsong and four paraphrase a Huguenot psalm (see Bonfils 1961–1962, 5–31). In 1610 Ballard printed the twenty-four *Fantaisies à quatre parties* by the Flemish composer Charles Guillet (ca. 1575–1654), who wrote them for "those who study Music as well as for those who are learning how to play the Organ" (preface).[4]

Even more surprising is the sparsity of collections of organ music in the thirty-four years between Titelouze's *Magnificat ou cantiques* and François Roberday's *Fugues et Caprices* of 1660. Surprising, because the number of excellent organs in Paris and the provinces presupposes a certain body of original literature; and because the archives hold recurring names of organists such as Florent Bienvenu at the Sainte-Chapelle, Jean Lesecq at Saint-Eustache, Marin Deslions at Saint-Étienne-du-Mont, Pierre Chabanceau de La Barre, royal organist, and Charles Racquet at Notre-Dame (see Dufourcq 1941; 2nd ed. 1949, 49).

Florent Bienvenu, called Helbic (1568–1623), was "the most excellent organist of his day," according to his student, Jean Denis (1650, 19), who also mentioned Bienvenu's monothematic fugues, yet no music by Bienvenu has survived. Of the organ music by Charles Racquet (1597–1664), from whom Mersenne acquired so much information for his study of the organ, a fantasy in manuscript, found in

Mersenne's personal copy of his *Harmonie universelle*,[5] and twelve *Versets de psaumes en duo sur les douze modes* (in "Livre cinquiesme de la composition" from *Harmonie universelle*, 1636; rpt. 1965, 2:283–289) are all that survive.

The *Fugues et Caprices* (1660) by François Roberday *fils* (1624–1680), organist at the Petits-Pères in Paris and *valet de chambre* of Anne d'Autriche and Marie Thérèse, are among the last examples of organ music in France to make a conscious effort to be "learned." At the same time they show Roberday to have been receptive to influences from outside of France. He based certain of his fugues on themes by Cambert, Pierre Chabanceau de La Barre, Louis (or Charles ?) Couperin, D'Anglebert, Froberger, Antonio Bertalli, and Francesco Cavalli. Unlike Titelouze, Roberday employed the scoring found in Samuel Scheidt's *Tabulatura nova* (1624): that is, a separate line for each of the four parts. He did this, he tells us, to facilitate performance on "viols or other similar instruments." Along with fugues that are conservative and academically competent, there are others in which Roberday appears to wish to convince that he is able to change with the changing times. The subject of such a fugue is extracted in Example 18-2 below. Three extracts from the Caprice "*sur le mesme sujet*" appear in Example 18-2a–c.

Example 18-2. Roberday: Extract from a fugue subject and three sections (a–c) of a caprice on the same subject (after Guilmant ed.).

Étienne Richard, Henry Du Mont, and Louis Couperin are more important than Roberday, for as transitional composers between Titelouze and Nivers, they helped forge a new style of organ music oriented more toward homophony and rhythms of the dance and less toward continuous polyphony. Du Mont was organist at Saint-Paul's

Church, in the fashionable Marais quarter, from 1643 until the year of his death (1684). That he was a fine performer was attested to by the inscription on his tomb at Saint-Paul's. Both church and tomb were destroyed in 1802, but the words can be clearly read in a drawing of the tomb found in the Gaignières collection at the Bibliothèque Nationale: "It was a delight to hear him play the organ as he did in this church for more than forty-five [sic] years. He was admired by all the most illustrious persons of his time." It is, therefore, surprising that among Du Mont's extant works, only scattered preludes and allemandes are specified for organ.[6]

From Étienne Richard (ca. 1620–1669), organist at Saint-Jacques-de-la-Boucherie, Saint-Nicolas-des-Champs, and Saint-Martin-des-Champs, we have four allemandes, three courantes, two sarabandes, two gigues, and two preludes for organ. The prelude in D minor, found in Pirro's "L'Art des organistes" (Lavignac and La Laurencie's *Encyclopédie de la musique*, Part II, 2:1272), is interesting. Its contrapuntal writing is more natural and supple than that of Roberday, and the middle section is composed of a graceful, dance like piece in triple meter that is as appropriate for the harpsichord as for the organ.

A final judgment of the role of Louis Couperin in this move away from polyphonic forms to dance-oriented homophony must await scrutiny (publication expected in 1997 by Éditions de L'Oiseau-Lyre) of the manuscript in Guy Oldham's possession that includes seventy organ pieces by Couperin, dating from 1650 to 1659 (see Oldham 1960, 51–59). They are preludes, fantasies, *basses de trompettes* (possibly the first examples of this genre), duos, and verses. Some of their titles indicate the registrations Couperin desired, which resemble those later required by Nivers in 1665 in his first book of organ pieces.

Among Couperin's pieces in the *Bauyn* manuscript are a *Fantaisie sur une basse de trompette* and a duo in G minor. The nervous and capricious counterpoint of the duo may reflect Couperin's admiration for the music of Frescobaldi (see Dufourcq 1971–1982, 4:61). Philidor copied a *Carillon* "composed by M. Couperin to imitate the carillons of Paris." Philidor added the information that on All Saints Day this *Carillon* "was always played on the organ of Saint-Gervais." The style of the *Carillon* (see Example 18-3 below) is completely different from that of Titelouze or Roberday. It is homophonic and closely modeled on dance rhythms.

Example 18-3. Louis Couperin: Extract from a *Carillon* (after Philidor copy at Versailles).

Some of the organ music composed by Richard, Du Mont, and Louis Couperin during this transition period from Titelouze to Nivers appears to be equally suitable for the harpsichord. All these composers were known harpsichordists (Du Mont and Richard both held court appointments). At the same time, their organ music remains close in spirit to an earlier generation; its general mood of sobriety even affected their dances and worked against a transfer of idiom from harpsichord to organ similar to the transfer of the *style brisé* from lute to harpsichord. Nevertheless, Jean Denis, organist at Saint-Barthélemy and Saint-Severin, felt it necessary as early as 1650 to warn the organist against "too much movement and wriggling of fingers . . . that prevents hearing consonances and [correct] tempos" (1650, 40). Performers who make suitable use of such ornaments as trills and mordents, he added, must be regarded as "very learned."

The *Premier livre d'orgue* (1665) by Guillaume-Gabriel Nivers is the first extant organ book after Titelouze's *Magnificat ou cantique de la Vierge . . .* (1626). What occurred stylistically between these two musical landmarks determined the direction of organ music in France for over 100 years. Up to this point it might have been possible to have postulated a development of organ music in France that would have run parallel to that of her northern neighbors. That this did not take place is due in large part to two factors: (1) the stabilization of the French classical organ, with its unique built-in timbre components and its light and responsive key action; and (2) the predominant influence on organ repertory of secular genres such as the *air de cour*, dance, vocal *récits* and dialogues, the harpsichord suite, and the sound-complex of Lully's opera orchestra.

No other organ music before the nineteenth century relates instrument and music more clearly than that of the French *grand siècle*. A prelude and fugue by Bach will not lose its musical integrity even when performed on an electric organ or transcribed for the piano; but a trio, "scored" by Lebègue for a *Dessus de Cromorne, Tierce en Taille,* and *Récit de Voix Humaine,* was composed with particular colors in mind and loses much of its *raison d'être* if it is performed with substitute registration—a fact which prompted Lebègue to state baldly in the preface to his *Premier livre d'orgue* that several pieces in his collection were of little use to organists whose instruments lacked the necessary stops to perform them.

The French classical organ largely evolved from the Norman instruments described earlier. Even by the time of Mersenne's *Harmonie universelle* (1636) it had reached a level of standardization that was to remain constant except for minor changes until Dom Bedos de Celles's *L'Art du facteur d'orgues* (1766–1770) (see Douglass 1973). Between 1660 and 1690, the building of organs in France was in the hands of relatively few masters. De Héman, Claude de Villiers,

Delaunay, Pierre and Alexandre Thierry, Étienne Énocq, Pierre Desenclos, and Robert Clicquot received the commissions and built in the degree of standardization mentioned above (see Dufourcq 1957c). By 1670 the French organ normally had four keyboards and pedal. The *Grand Orgue* and the *Positif* both had forty-eight keys; the *Écho* and the *Récit* keyboards had a restricted compass of two to three octaves; and the pedal had about twenty-four keys. The *Positif* or *Positif à dos* (so-called because its case was at the back of the player) was a copy in miniature of the *Grand Orgue* to which it could be coupled. It was the most important second manual and served the *Grand Orgue* in the capacity of an antiphonal instrument or as a solo group. The *Récit* and the *Écho*, whose chests were above and below the *Grand Orgue*, respectively, were utilized mainly for solo *récits*. Thus the French classical organ had manuals devoted to one or two solo stops, unlike the German instruments of the same period in which normally every manual controlled a complete division.

The standardization of stops (*jeux*)[7] and the concomitant standardization of registration called for in the prefaces of most organ books beginning with Nivers brought a consistency of sound to French organ music of the period that was and is unique in Europe. It is the sound of the reeds of the *Grand Jeu*, the *Cornets* of the *Récits*, the *Cromornes* of the *Positif*, and the shrill *Trompette* of the Pedal. It is the sound of duos of *Cromorne en Taille* and *Basse de Trompette*, of the solo *Récits* of the *Voix Humaine*, the *Nasard*, and, above all, the *Tierce en Taille*, which Williams called "the great French contribution to organ music" (1967, 189).[8] The special sound of the French classical organ comes from understanding that the *Plein Jeu* of the *Positif* "must be played in a lively, well-formed manner, marking the *cadences* or [other] trills. One must raise the fingers in the fast sections and [cultivate] a touch as light as that for the harpsichord" (G. Corrette, *Messe du 8ᵉ ton*, 1703), whereas the *Plein Jeu* of the *Grand Orgue* must be of a "serious and majestic" nature (Dom Bedos de Celles 1770, 3:523). (For French key action, see Douglass 1986, 19–34.) In short, the French organ music of the period is a common legacy of sound uniting the organists of Saint-Louis-des-Invalides with Notre-Dame, of Saint-Germain-des-Prés with Saint-Gervais, of Saint-Merri with Saint-Paul.[9]

The uniform content of the seventeenth-century organ books by Guillaume-Gabriel Nivers (1665, 1667, 1675), Nicolas Lebègue (1676, 1678, ca. 1685), Nicolas Gigault (1685), André Raison (1688), Jacques Boyvin (1689), François Couperin (1690), Gilles Jullien (1690), and Nicolas de Grigny (1699) can best be explained against the background of the important *Ceremoniale parisiense*, the so-called "Ceremonial of the Bishops," drafted by a Parisian priest, Martin Sonnet, and published in 1662 by order of the Archbishop of Paris, J. F. P. de Gondy. In the hierarchical spirit of the age, this document laid down the ground rules for all aspects of the celebration of the Divine Office in the Paris diocese. It brought up to date the earlier *Ceremoniale* by Clement VIII (Rome 1600), which had been printed in France in 1632. (For a detailed account of all the *Cérémoniaux*, see Launay 1993, 65–80 and 277–305).

The *Ceremoniale parisiense* carefully specified the use of the organ during the Mass and the Office. The organist was instructed to use the appropriate Gregorian melodies in alternation with the choir for portions of the Kyrie, Gloria, Sanctus, Agnus Dei, and the Domine Salvum. For the rest of the Ordinary, the organist was permitted to perform short *récits*, duos, trios, and other suitable compositions (see Dufourcq 1955). The *Ceremoniale parisiense*, therefore, provided Parisian church organists with considerable incentive to supply the formidable demands of the church year with a body of original music and music based on Gregorian chant.

Altogether typical are the three books by Nivers, who was organist at Saint-Sulpice from 1654 to 1714 and was appointed one of four organists at the Royal Chapel in 1678. Nivers's *Premier livre d'orgue* (1665) consists of "one hundred Pieces in all the church modes."[10] None has a Gregorian melody. Nivers organized them into twelve suites unified by key. Each suite opens with a prelude that should be played on the *Plein Jeu* (preface). Two suites have ten verses each, and each of the remaining suites has eight verses designed to alternate with the sung chant. In addition to the first extensive instructions for registration since Mersenne, the book contains some observations on hand positions and fingering that bear comparison with those supplied by François Couperin some fifty years later in his *L'Art de toucher le clavecin* (see Example 18-4a,b). Nivers emphasized the importance of a flowing style *("bien couler les notes")* and offered the suggestion that performers "consult the method of singing, because in this manner of playing, the Organ should imitate the Voice." The new style is particularly evident if we examine the fugues, which have become almost totally disassociated from polyphony! The part writing produces little tension or independence. Many sections line up the parts in a type of harpsichord homophony in which shifts of texture destroy linear integrity. The dialogues and *récits* exploit solo effects (there are ten *récits de cromorne*) and clearly show the transfer of vocal melody and harpsichord ornamentation to the organ.

Example 18-4a. Nivers's fingering.

Example 18-4b. Couperin's fingering.

The *Second livre d'orgue* (1667)[11] "containing a Mass and Hymns of the Church" is comparatively restricted. It provides alternating liturgical comments for the organist in one setting of the Ordinary of the Mass, which are followed by twenty-six hymns. The essence of the shift in style from Titelouze to Nivers is epitomized in Example 18-5a,b below, which gives two settings of the same Gregorian hymn, "Pange lingua." Example 18-5a comes from the beginning of the third verse of Titelouze's setting (*Les Hymnes de l' Église . . .*). Example 18-5b is a couplet "en Récit de Voix humaine" from Nivers's *Second livre d'orgue.*

Example 18-5a. Titelouze: "Pange lingua" (after ed. of 1624).

Example 18-5b. Nivers: "Pange lingua" (after ed. of 1667).

Nivers's third *Livre d'orgue* (1675)[12] "on the eight church modes" is similar to the first book. Its 105 compositions are grouped in eight suites, all of which have the same symmetrical architecture: a diptych composed of (1) prelude, fugue, *récit*, duo, *basse*, echo, dialogue for two choirs; and (2) fugue grave, *récit*, duo, *basse*, *dialogues de récits*, dialogue for two choirs.

Nivers is a significant figure in the history of French organ music as much for his extra-musical contributions as for the intrinsic merit of his music. It was he who showed the way, he who established the basic format of the organ book, and he who utilized to full capacity the color potential of the new organs.

Of some interest is an anonymous *Livre d'orgue* that was probably collected between 1670 and 1675. It is found today in the Bibliothèque Nationale (*Rés.* 476). The manuscript has been attributed falsely, it is believed, to Jean-Nicolas Geoffroy, organist at Saint-Nicolas du Chardonnet.[13] The collection illustrates a variety of ways of alternating the *plain chant musical* (here supplied with accompaniments) with short verses that often paraphrase the chant melody.

An important manuscript collection was brought from France to Montreal in 1724 by Jean Girard (1696–1765), organist at Montreal's Notre-Dame Church. It contains 398 *pièces d'orgue* from the seventeenth and early eighteenth centuries. To date, only sixteen pieces, all by Lebègue, have been identified.[14]

Nicolas-Antoine Lebègue (1631–1702) was organist at Saint-Merri for forty years and a colleague of Nivers at the Royal Chapel. Acknowledgment of the uniformity of registration in the Paris area comes in the subtitle of Lebègue's *Les Pièces d'orgue* (1676, new editions in 1678 and 1685) "composed . . . for the present manner of playing the Organ with all stops and particularly those that are in little use in the provinces, such as the *Tierces* and *Cromornes en Taille*."

Every suite in Lebègue's first book opens with a prelude and closes with a *Plein Jeu*. Occasionally, Lebègue inserts a trio with a nice feeling for independent line. He is a master of *récits* and dialogues that exploit the sounds of the *Tierce* or *Cromorne en Taille*, "the most beautiful and distinctive" sounds on the instrument (preface).

The *Second livre d'orgue* (1678) is an example of *Gebrauchsmusik* that contains "short and easy pieces based on the eight modes of the church and the Mass of solemn feasts." No pedal is necessary; the music may have been intended for Lebègue's own use on the rather primitive instrument at the Royal Chapel.

Both the first and second books contain a wealth of melodies in popular style that, it must be confessed, owe more to the *divertissements* of the opera than to the "eight modes of the church." They have charm and natural grace that influenced most of the French organ composers who followed (see Example 18-6).

Example 18-6. Lebègue: Popular types of melodies found in Book I of *Pièces d'orgues*, 1676.

The subtitle of the third book (1685) tacitly acknowledges the secularization of the organ repertory as well as the transference of the harpsichord medium to the organ keyboard: *Troisième livre d'orgue*, "containing large Offertories and Elevations; And all the best known Noels, *Symphonies* and carillons that one can play on the Organ and the Harpsichord." The four *symphonies* are large preludes in binary form that are clearly modeled on the French overture. One resembles the type of allemande with dotted rhythms and *tirades* already familiar in the harpsichord collections of D'Anglebert and others. Lebègue was probably inspired to set the popular noels by Gigault's settings that had already been printed in 1682. Here, Lebègue transferred elements from the *style brisé* to the organ for the first time.

Nicolas Gigault (ca. 1627–1707), organist at Saint-Nicolas-des-Champs, Saint-Honoré, and Saint-Martin-des-Champs, and at the Hôpital du Saint-Esprit, and quite possibly Lully's composition teacher, published a *Livre de musique pour l'orgue* dedicated to "la très Sainct Vierge" in 1683. The collection is made up entirely of popular noels, each treated in a variety of ways ranging from dialogues *à2* to full organ choir. Taking a leaf from some of the harpsichord books, Gigault suggested alternate performance possibilities on "lute, viols, violin, flute, and other instruments." Included in the 1683 collection is a demonstration piece, an Allemande, written for those who wished to achieve a certain "tendresse" in their manner of playing. "Tendresse" refers here to keyboard ornamentation labeled generically *ports de voix* by Gigault. The Allemande is presented first in its simple version. Then in order to give an idea of how ornaments "might be applied to all other types of pieces," an ornamented version is included. It is more important as a historical document than as living music. It is singularly awkward; incessant, dotted *ports de voix* tend to work at cross-purposes with the melodic frame.

In 1685, Gigault published his second *Livre de musique pour l'orgue*, a compendium of all genres of the French organ repertory in the late seventeenth century. The collection contains more than 183 compositions that "may be played on 1, 2, 3 and 4 keyboards," including several Masses and hymns along with some fugues "treated in the Italian manner." Like the motets of Brossard that have optional points of conclusion, these compositions were constructed so that "one might finish in several places." Many pieces are very short indeed; for instance, a "Glorificamus Te" has seven measures and a "Benedicamus Te" has ten measures. Others are overly long, including a fugue of sixty measures based almost exclusively on a dotted rhythmic formula that could be viewed as written-out *notes inégales* ♩. ♪ ♩. ♪ ♩. ♪. In fact, Gigault seemed curiously bound to patterns of dotted rhythms. Sequences, circles of fifths, and some dissonances "treated according to the Modern practice" (preface) dominate the fugues composed "in the Italian manner." In one two-voice fugue, Gigault anticipates the fashionable 12/8 Italian *Giga* used later in organ pieces by both Couperin and Grigny as well as in many harpsichord collections of the later seventeenth century.

The strong connection between dance rhythms and much of the organ music of the late seventeenth century is acknowledged by André Raison (died 1719) in his *Livre d'orgue* of 1688. As an aid in interpreting this collection of five Masses and an Offertory for the "happy convalescence of the King in 1687," Raison stated that "It is necessary to observe the Meter of the Piece that you are to play and to consider whether it has some rapport with a Sarabande, Gigue, Gavotte, Bourrée, Canarie, Passacaille, Chaconne, or the tempo of the Blacksmith dance [a characteristic dance of *divertissements*]. You must give it the same Air that you would were you performing it on the Harpsichord, except that you should play the trills a little slower because of the sanctity of the Place." A *"trio en passacaille"* from the "Christe" of the Mass in the twelfth mode gave Bach the first four measures of his great Passacaglia and Fugue in C minor. Unlike most of his contemporaries, Raison allowed for more latitude in the registration of his pieces, observing sensibly that he, himself, greatly varied the choice of stops and manuals in performance.

Jacques Boyvin (ca. 1650–1703) in his two organ books of 1690[15] and 1700 was less bound by the dance rhythms that so intrigued his contemporaries. Even the shorter preludes, such as the "Prélude facile" in the fourth mode, have achieved greater amplitude by their less static harmony and their evasion of cadence. In the "Avis" of his *Premier livre d'orgue*, Boyvin justified his explanations of stop combinations and registration, which he understandably assumed were well known and routine to all his readers, by supposing that his book might fall into the hands of foreign musicians not acquainted with the style.

Gilles Jullien's (ca. 1650–1703) *Premier livre d'orgue* of 1690[16] includes eighty pieces in the eight church modes. Because the subject of stop combinations had been dealt with so often, he stated that it would be "of little use to discuss it further here." Nonetheless, he proceeded to give much valuable information on registration. Jullien was primarily a colorist, who, in the "Avis" to his readers, admitted to some freedom from the "sense of ordinary chords." Example 18-7 with its three parallel seventh chords is perhaps an illustration of this freedom.

Example 18-7. Jullien: Extract from a "Prélude du Quatrième Ton" (after ed. of 1690).

In 1689 harpsichordist D'Anglebert included five fugues on the same subject, and a *Quatuor sur le Kyrie* for the organ in his *Pièces de clavecin*. The quartet, based on Gregorian melodies (*Cunctipotens* and *Salve Regina*), is written in open score with each part designed for a different keyboard.

The French organ school of the seventeenth century reached its highest musical level with the works of two composers—François Couperin, organist at Saint-Gervais from 1685 to 1723, and Nicolas de Grigny. The amount of organ music left by each is modest, but their music has a sincerity and depth of expression too often lacking in that of their contemporaries, whose collections favor the depressing weight of quantity over quality. Both composers were concerned with the liturgical considerations spelled out in the *Ceremoniale parisiense*; and the popular elements, the operatic influences, the profusion of ornamentation are all there with no loss of charm, but there is a greater sense of continuity and more evidence of control over the musical forms.

The Royal Privilege permitting François Couperin to have his *Pièces d'orgue* published was given 2 September 1690 upon Delalande's certifying that "I have found (them) very fine and worthy of being given to the Public." A routine matter, it would seem. Delalande had replaced Charles Couperin, the composer's father, as organist at Saint-Gervais after Charles's death in 1679; François had in turn replaced Delalande only five years before the privilege date at the age of eighteen years.

Yet for some reason Ballard never published the Couperin *Pièces d'orgue*, and the music remained in manuscript copies. Until the earlier years of this century when the research of Pirro, Bouvet, Tessier, Brunold, and Tiersot proved otherwise, the music was credited to François Couperin "the Elder," uncle of François "le Grand." It seemed to Danjou and Fétis and others that this music was simply too mature, too refined for such a young composer, and that the "F. Couperin, Sieur de Crouilly, Organiste de l'Église Saint-Gervais de Paris" must be the elder François Couperin of whom Titon de Tillet wrote: "He was a little man who loved good wine" (1732, 403).

The *Pièces* consist of two Masses; one for parishes for everyday use as well as for solemn feasts, and the other suitable for use in convents or monasteries. Although both contain twenty-one pieces in the identical ordering of Kyrie (5), Gloria (9), Offertory (1), Sanctus-Benedictus (3), Agnus Dei (2), and Deo Gratias (1), the convent Mass is considerably shorter and less demanding for the performer.

Whereas the Masses reveal Couperin's absorption of the tradition of Nivers, Lebègue, Raison, and Gigault, they also show the personal mark of the young composer in what may be one of his first compositions. It is a style nurtured at this point more by French than by Italian elements. The trios lack the crossing of parts, the chains of suspensions, and circles of fifths borrowed from the Italian trio sonata. They resemble more the homophonic trios of Lully's operas and his instrumental chamber music. Couperin created a noble cantilena in the Benedictus of the parish Mass and the fifth couplet of the Gloria of the convent Mass, both scored for *Cromorne en Taille*. The rhythmic pattern, the generally restricted range, the discreet ornamentation, and the use of affective intervals speak the language of Lully's monologues.

The Gregorian melodies of the parish Mass are taken from the *Cunctipotens Genitor Deus*. In accordance with the *Ceremoniale*, they are not ornamented and are treated in a sober manner, usually as a whole-note cantus firmus in the tenor or bass. The contrapuntal writing in the fugues and elsewhere strikes a nice balance between the continuous polyphony of Titelouze and the "homophonic" fugues of Lebègue. In general, Couperin's contrapuntal line is not compromised by the too regularly recurring internal cadences that give a short-breathed quality to so much French music of the period. The part writing engenders some cross-relations, and dissonant harmony colors the music without distracting from the general sobriety of mood. Such are the major seventh, the augmented fifth, and the melodic diminished fourth in Example 18-8, which was extracted from the "Fugue sur les jeux d'anches," the second couplet of the Kyrie of the parish Mass.

Example 18-8. Couperin: Extract from the *Messe pour les paroisses* (after Guilmant).

The Offertories of both Masses gave Couperin a chance to create a larger musical structure. The Offertory of the Mass of the convent resembles a set of free variations on a popular type of dance melody. Chaconne-like, the middle section is in the tonic minor key. The *Positif* and *Grand Orgue* are in constant juxtaposition as *ripieno* and *concertino*, and the texture of the *Positif* is usually restricted to three voices. In the parish Mass, the Offertory is a large tripartite structure beginning with a French overture in C major; following is a trio-quartet combination in C minor.

Popular dance forms invade several of the non-Gregorian pieces. The third couplet of the Gloria in the parish Mass is a gigue having the continuous eighth-note movement of the Italian form of the dance; the fourth couplet of the same Gloria is a large march—a virtual *entrée* for an operatic *divertissement*—dominated by its trumpet-like melody.

Nicolas de Grigny (1672–1703) dwelt outside the sphere of most Parisian organists. Although a student of Lebègue and organist from 1695 at Saint-Denis, he lived most of his life in Rheims and, like his father and grandfather before him, served at the Cathedral. Although Bach accorded him the greatest compliment by copying his *Premier livre d'orgue* at Lüneburg, he was little known in the eighteenth century and practically ignored by Fétis in the nineteenth century. He had to wait for recognition until 1904 when Guilmant and Pirro placed him in his own particular pantheon in volume 5 of their *Archives des Maîtres de l'Orgue*.

The *Premier livre d'orgue* (1699) includes a Mass (based on the *Cunctipotens Genitor Deus*) and, in the tradition of Titelouze, it is followed by paraphrases on Gregorian hymns. The scarcely fifty pieces of this collection show Grigny more able than any other French organ composer of his time to synthesize the archaic polyphony of a Titelouze with the grace of a Lebègue *récit*.

He often chose a five-part texture, with the Pedal acting as an harmonic support for the busy inner voices. Six of the eight fugues in the collection are for five voices. Grigny's part writing is generally consistent, and he avoided the shifts in texture that are so much a part of the French keyboard tradition. This consistency and his logical sense of development combined with depth of feeling may have attracted Bach to Grigny's organ music. These are especially evident in some of the hymn paraphrases such as the *Ave Maris Stella*. Indeed, certain paraphrases have a similarity to some of the chorale preludes of the German master's *Orgelbüchlein*.

Grigny, like Couperin, built from the French tradition. The dotted rhythms and *tirades* of the French overture are prominent. The trios often pair the upper voices in thirds or sixths. The dialogues and offertories *"sur les grands Jeux"* are more powerful statements than the offertories and *symphonies* of Lebègue from which they derive. Along with those of Couperin, they are superb musical illustrations for Dom Bedos de Celle's description of what is appropriate for the *Plein Jeu*: "great harmonic sweep, interlaced with syncopations, dissonant chords, suspensions, and harmonic audacities" (1766–1778, Part III, Chapter 4, 523).

Grigny's harmonic audacities are also more French than Italian although with an increased use of modulation and some effective chromatic writing. Again it is a question of using ornamentation to deepen the harmonic expressiveness of the music. Along with this, however, is a frequent use of cross-relations that stems from principles of voice leading. The final measures of the *Point d'Orgue*, a large, fantasy type of composition that closes the collection, are a striking example of passages in double counterpoint that combine the major and minor modes of E simultaneously.

Long before the French harpsichord school reached its climax in the music of Couperin and Rameau, the French organ school had slipped into mannerisms and decadence. To be sure there were composers such as Louis Marchand (1669–1732), Gaspard Corrette (dates unknown), Guillaume Freinsberg (called Guilain, dates unknown), Pierre Du Mage (1674–1751), Jean-François Dandrieu (1682–1738), and Louis-Nicolas Clérambault (1676–1749), who continued to compose books of liturgical suites in the tradition of the seventeenth-century masters. Even their music, however, shows the inroads of secular elements that do little to improve the musical content and much to detract from the legitimate purpose of a musical comment on the liturgy.

Few composers were tempted to write in the "learned" style so out of joint with the mode of the Regency. A study of the few labeled fugues by Clérambault or Marchand, for example, shows how far removed they are in spirit and technique from a fugue *a*5 by Grigny. The subject of the Clérambault fugue from his first suite (*Livre d'orgue*, 1710) is submerged in non-functional ornaments that cannot help but impede its forward motion. The Marchand fugue, although devoid of any indicated ornamentation, makes no pretense of guarding a linear texture; all voices line up in homophony after the second entrance of the subject.

At the same time, there are some fine pages in the organ music of the above composers. Louis Marchand[17] was much in demand as an organist and held posts at three Paris churches (Saint-Benoit, Saint-Honoré, Convent of the Cordeliers) as well as at the Royal Chapel. His music and performing ability were recognized outside of France, and Bach seemed to have held him in high regard in spite of the Frenchman's inglorious last minute defection in the Dresden "contest" of September 1717. Some of the music of his five short organ books has dramatic sweep and an adventurous sense of harmony that demands attention. As a study in dissonant counterpoint within a chordal frame, the E minor piece in the second book is perhaps unprecedented in French music of the period. The constant evasion of cadences and feints toward B minor, G minor, and D major help sustain tension throughout the thirty-four-measure piece.

The two suites, each with seven numbers, that constitute Clérambault's *Livre d'orgue* contain much music with unpretentious charm and naiveté implied in tempo designations such as *Gayement et gratieusement*. A Lullian chaconne, a real French overture with its two sections (*Fort grave*) and (*Gay*) in clear apposition, and an Italian "Sicilienne" are all found in these suites by the organist of Saint-Sulpice (1714), who also served at Mme de Maintenon's convent at Saint-Cyr.

Italian violin sonatas and concertos inevitably left their mark on French organ music of the eighteenth century. The trio in Example 18-9 was extracted from the *Pièces d'orgue pour le magnificat* (1706) by Guilain, a composer of German origins who reached Paris after 1702. Its chains of suspensions and voice crossings clearly show the influence of Corelli. The *Grand Jeu* from the same collection has the mechanical rhythmic pulsations and wide melodic profile of the Italian concerto. The piece is constructed around one motive and structured like a short concerto movement. The *Grand Jeu* serves as *ripieno* in rapid alternation with solo *Cornet* passages.

Example 18-9. Guilain: Extract from an organ trio (after Guilmant).

Dandrieu probably felt the stylistic conflict that could exist between what was appropriate in liturgical music and what was popular when he wrote in the *Avertissement* to his *Premier livre des pièces d'orgue* (1739): "The difficulty of composing *Pièces d'orgue* worthy of the majesty of the Place where the instrument is played . . . made me reluctant for a long time to undertake this work." The "noble and elegant simplicity" that Dandrieu decided was appropriate for organ music results in overall ennui for performer and listener. The collection includes six suites, each followed by a Magnificat. There are also two "Muzetes," bearing the performance directions "*Naivement et louré,*" and a Duo "*en cors de chasse sur la Trompette.*" The Offertory "*pour le jour de Pâques*" is similar to a set of harpsichord variations. Here, the eighth variation uses an Alberti bass formula.

No such compunctions concerning suitability bothered Nicolas Siret (c. 1664–1754), François d'Agincourt (1684–1758), Antoine Dornel (ca. 1685–1765), Louis-Claude d'Aquin (1694–1772), Guillaume-Antoine Calvière (1700–1755), Michel Corrette (1709–1795), or Claude-Benigne Balbastre (1727–1799), all of whom became increasingly concerned with virtuoso effects and the use of the French classical organ as a concert instrument. Elements from the theater and the dance, already present in organ suites, were exaggerated, and a new dimension was added: the color potential of the organ was thought of as a vehicle for descriptive music second only to that of the orchestra itself.

The *Premier livre d'orgue* (1737) by Michel Corrette contains, in addition to four Magnificats "for the use of nuns," a "Table of pieces from my *Livre de clavecin* that may be played on the organ." Corrette gives the titles of six harpsichord pieces and subverts the sacrosanct registration of the French classical organ to descriptive ends. Thus, "Les Giboulées de Mars," "Le Courier," "Les Bottes de sept lieues," "Les Fantastiques," and "La Prise de Jericho" all are to be played on the *Grand Jeu*; whereas "Les Amants enchantés" belongs on the Flutes and "Les Étoiles," on the *Tierce* of the *Positif.*

Louis-Claude d'Aquin, a virtuoso at the age of twelve at the church of the Petit Saint-Antoine, was the successor to Marchand at the Cordeliers and to Dandrieu at the Royal Chapel. D'Aquin had no rivals as an organ virtuoso after the death of Marchand. His major publications of organ music consist of collections of noels which were conceived of not only for organ but for harpsichord and in most instances for violin, flute, and oboe as well. The *Nouveau livre de noëls pour l'orgue et le clavecin* (1757) contains twelve noels with extensive and difficult variations (see Montagnier 1992, 134–137).

Foreign observers of the French musical scene as far removed in time as J. C. Nemeitz and Charles Burney commented on the introduction of popular elements into the organ music of the liturgy in France. Concerning a midnight Mass, Nemeitz wrote that "the music that is performed in the churches is not too devout since the organ plays minuets and all types of worldly tunes" (1727, 232). Years later in the *Present State of Music in France and Italy* (1771; 2nd ed. 1773, 38), Burney made essentially the same observations with regard to Balbastre's playing at Saint-Roch: "When they sang the Magnificat, he, in the same manner between each verse, played several minuets, fugues, imitations, and every species of music, even to hunting pieces and jigs, without surprising or offending the congregation."

The installation of a large organ at the hall of the Concert Spirituel in 1748 was a final step in this process of secularization. Little by little, from Nivers to d'Aquin, the French school of organists had compromised the liturgical functions of their instrument. Of an organ that could reveal the introspection of an Agnus Dei by Grigny, they made an organ that could "sound storm and thunder."

The critical time for forming a new and vital literature was at the turn of the century, yet the most important composers were already occupied elsewhere. The organ composer and the harpsichord composer did no more than reflect the tastes of the Regency and the period of Louis XV. Couperin, had he chosen to write a series of *Livres d'orgue* of the caliber of his *Pièces de clavecin*, might have been the catalyst for a new generation of organ composers in France with something musically significant to say. The harpsichord, not the organ, was the preferred instrument at court. Couperin must have known it. Why else would the Royal Chapel have only a mediocre positive organ? By the time the final Chapel at Versailles was finished and its magnificent Robert Clicquot organ installed, it was already too late.

Part Four

Instrumental Ensemble and Solo Music

Chapter 19

Instrumental Ensemble and Orchestral Music of the Seventeenth Century

$\mathcal{T}$here were many opportunities for ensemble performances in the France of Henry III, Henry IV, and Louis XIII. Performance in groups was a natural byproduct of the musical division of labor at court. It was a means of livelihood for the town musicians of the Confrérie of Saint-Julien-des-Ménétriers, and in the guise of private concerts it was the happy companion of the leisure hours of some of the most famous composers and musicians of the time (see Brenet 1900).

The literature of the period is rich in descriptions of concerts, some of which were organized on a more or less regular basis. The earliest concerts may have been those at Baïf's and Thibaut de Courville's Académie de Poésie et de Musique, founded in 1570. The statutes of the Académie show that the weekly concerts at Baïf's home might give a twentieth-century impresario reason for envy (Yates 1947, 320).

It is not certain whether the performances at the Académie included independent instrumental ensemble music during Baïf's lifetime or whether instruments were used exclusively to support the voices. In 1589, Baïf died, and Jacques Mauduit (1557–1627) took over direction of the concerts from this date until long after the Académie itself had ceased functioning as an organized group.

If Henri Sauval, writing perhaps fifty years later, was accurate, the concerts directed by Mauduit were no modest undertaking: "All sorts of things were sung in dialogues and in choirs; sometimes by vocal soloists, sometimes by performers on instruments and singers together. Ordinarily there were from sixty to eighty people [performing], often up to one hundred and twenty" (1724, 2:493). Instrumental music independent of the voices is suggested by Sauval's observation that "In Mauduit's Concerts there were not only these instruments [flutes, lutes, pandoras] but also spinets and viols that he [Mauduit] made fashionable" (1724, 2:494). In a letter, the Protestant poet Agrippa d'Aubigné described having heard "an excellent concert in Paris of guitars, twelve viols, four spinets, four lutes, two pandoras, and two theorbos" (cited by Reese 1959, 566). The large number of performers could mean that some works were performed with more than one player on a part.

The use of viols and harpsichords together in ensemble music is also confirmed by Mersenne in his description of concerts given by Maugars, Lazarin, La Barre (Pierre), and Du Buisson. In addition to concerts of voices and instruments and concerts of viols and harpsichord, Mersenne mentioned concerts "of Sieur Ballard (Pierre) in which five or six Lutes play together." Mersenne's concept of an ideal concert shows the catholicity of the great philosopher-mathematician at the very outset of the heated debate on national styles that was to preoccupy French aestheticians and musicians for 150 years:

> *If we wish to have all the pleasure which can issue successfully from Music, we should have all the [different] kinds of singing performed one after the other, in order to judge in what way one surpasses another: for example, it would be necessary to have one or two Madrigals or other Airs from Italy sung by a dozen good Italian voices, as many Sarabandes [sung] by Spaniards, as many Courantes & Airs [sung] by the French; and then have one or two of the best pieces of Music for Instruments performed so that six Lutes, or as many as one wishes, would begin, and then a concert of Viols would follow, and finally a concert of Violins similar to the 24 of the King (1636; rpt. 1965, 2:394).*

For Jacques de Gouy (died ca. 1650), the "first concerts" were some *concerts spirituels* given before 1650 at the home of Pierre de Chabanceau de La Barre (1592–1656), organist of the Royal Chapel. In the preface to his *Airs à quatre parties sur la Paraphrase des Psaumes de Godeau* (1650), he wrote: "The renown of these *concerts spirituels* . . . was so great that several Archbishops, Bishops, Dukes, Counts, Marquis, and other very important people honored them with their presence."

In 1655 Christian Huygens, who was traveling in France, wrote to his father describing the weekly concerts given by the *"Assemblée des honestes curieux,"* instituted by Chambonnières. Chambonnières's group had apparently been officially in existence for fourteen years when Huygens first heard them. A notarial entry in the *Minutier Central* of 17 October 1641 obliged seven musicians to present themselves before "Messire Jacques de Champion, chevallier, seigneur de Chambonnière, gentilhomme ordinaire de la Chambre du Roy" (in *Documents*, 435–436). For one year only, they were to arrive "punctually at the hour of noon twice weekly on Wednesdays and Saturdays at a hall that pleases the said sieur de Chambonnière, in order to give a concert there." Confirmation of the success of Chambonnières's amusingly titled Assembly of the Honest Curious comes in a notarial entry for the following 13 December, which authorized the group to perform in the "largest hall of the house of Mandosse." At this time the Assemblée must have already received royal patronage, since it is referred to in the minutes as the "accadémye instituée par le Roy."

Huygens also wrote to his father in glowing terms about the concerts given by "Monsieur Lambert and Mademoiselle Hilaire, his sister-in-law, who sings like an angel." Michel Lambert was Lully's father-in-law and a renowned teacher. According to Titon du Tillet, he had his best students perform in concerts held at his country house at Puteaux near Paris.

Descriptions in the memoirs and letters of Mlle de Scudéry, Mlle de Montpensier, and Mme de Sévigné and scattered references in the *Mercure* and Dangeau's *Journal* show a flowering of private concerts during the reign of Louis XIV. We learn through the pages of the *Mercure*, for example, that Sainte-Colombe, who was a bass viol player and the teacher of Marais, gave family concerts in which he and his two daughters all played viols; that Jacques Gallot, of the dynasty of lutenists, gave a concert at his home every Saturday; and that a certain Monsieur Médard had a concert at his home every fifteen days (Brenet 1900, 71). In fact, the wealthy bourgeoisie (who were prototypes for the eighteenth-century financier La Pouplinière) found it a distinct social advantage to present concerts in their salons—an attitude recorded in Molière's *Le Bourgeois gentilhomme*, where Monsieur Jourdain is advised to have a concert in his home "every Wednesday or Thursday" if he wishes to do things well (Act II, scene i).

There were so many private concerts in Paris in the early years of the eighteenth century that a young gentleman of means fortunate enough to be visiting that city, as was Joachim Christoph Nemeitz, could not only perfect his performance skills (which would assure an "*entrée* into the *grand monde*"), but could also hear a concert every day. Nemeitz lists some of the concerts he attended:

> *At the homes of the Duc d'* Aumont, *who was Ambassador to England, . . . Abbé* Grave, *Mademoiselle de* Maes, *who gave one a week* ordinarily; *and then at the home of Mons*[r] Clérambault,

> *who had one about every 15 days or three weeks. All these*
> Concerts *were performed by the best* masters *of Paris (1727, 69).*

By the last years of the Grand Monarch's reign, the normal routine of concerts to accompany his rising and his dining was augmented by Mme de Maintenon, who had some musical sensitivity in spite of her prudery. She arranged almost daily performances in her apartments by such well-known musicians as Robert de Visée (guitarist), René Descoteaux (flutist), Antoine Forqueray (bass viol player), and Jean-Baptiste Buterne (harpsichordist).

The instruments favored for private concerts through the first half of the seventeenth century were, as we have seen, lutes, viols, and harpsichords, with occasional use of guitar or flute. These were the "instruments of repose, destined for serious and tranquil pleasures, whose languid harmony is the enemy of all action and who demand only sedentary Auditors" (Michel de Pure 1668, 274). Much of the time, these instruments were used to support the voice, although the large number of extant fantasies suggests that there was a considerable body of independent literature available for ensemble performances. In fact, the existence of independent literature for viols in conjunction with other instruments is confirmed by Pierre Trichet, who wrote: "Viols . . . are very suitable for concerts of music, whether one wishes to use them with voices or whether one wishes to join them with other instruments" (ca. 1640; rpt. 1956 [4]:225).

It was only in the later seventeenth century that flutes, recorders, oboes, and violins began to supplant the viols as treble instruments, and we arrive at the combination of instruments suggested by the Music Master to Monsieur Jourdain for his weekly concerts: "bass viol, a theorbo, and a harpsichord for the *basse-continue*, with two violins to play the *ritournelles*" (*Le Bourgeois gentilhomme*, Act V, scene i).

The nature of ensemble performances at court was determined in large part by the categories of the King's Music discussed in Chapter 1. As has been noted, these divisions were often more semantic than actual.

The *Vingt-quatre Violons* and the *Petits Violons*, together with some of the best players from the *Écurie*, formed the orchestra for big court ballets—at least after 1661 when Lully had made his peace with the *Grande Bande*. All the king's musicians joined forces for special ceremonies such as coronations, entries of foreign dignitaries, royal births and marriages, and the like.

After Louis XIII had officially established the *Vingt-quatre Violons Ordinaires* in 1618, violins were apparently no longer found in the music of the king's Chamber. This was an elite group that was dominated by solo performers, who included singers, lutenists, violists, harpsichordists, and organists. That the violin should have been excluded was natural, for as early as Philibert Jambe-de-Fer's *L'Epitôme musical* (1556), the French considered the violin ideal for accompanying the dance. In about 1640 Trichet wrote: "Violins are principally destined for dances, balls, ballets, masquerades, serenades, morning songs (*aubades*), festivals, and all joyous pastimes—having been judged more suitable than any other instrument for this type of recreation" (ca. 1640; rpt. 1956 [4]:228). Writing in 1668, Michel de Pure recognized the violin as capable of sustaining a *grand ballet* "with equity and justice." "The glory of the Violin," he stressed, "is simply to play the measure and tempo accurately as soon as the *Entrée* commences" (276–277). His repeated warnings to performers to avoid "a thousand *coups d'archet*" and excessive ornamentation seem to vindicate Lully's distress at the performance practices of the *Vingt-quatre Violons*. In the "Livre quatriesme des instrumens" of his *Harmonie universelle*, Mersenne provided diminutions for the first thirty measures of a Jehan Henry fantasy, so that "one may observe the customary manner in which the violins [*Vingt-quatre Violons*] *diminuer* all sorts of melodies" (1636; rpt. 1965, 3:189). This indicates that such a practice was already well established by Lully's time.

Considered the instrument "most suitable of all to accompany dance" (Mersenne 1636; rpt. 1965, 3:177) and deemed appropriate for all manner of outdoor music,[1] the violin was not accorded the recognition and prestige that it received in Italy, where it was also viewed as a concert instrument. Rather, the violin was regarded as the instrument of street fiddlers, an attitude that the imperious demands of the Confrérie de Saint-Julien-des-Ménétriers did little to dispel. Even after the appearance of the first French sonatas, Lecerf could write, "That instrument [the violin] is not *noble* in France . . . . That is, Mademoiselle, one sees few gentlemen of means who play it and many lowly Musicians who make their living by it" (1725; rpt. 1966, 3:105). His sentiment echoes almost word-for-word that of Jambe-de-Fer about 170 years earlier: "There are few people who perform it [the violin] except those who make a living from it" (1556; rpt. 1958–1963, 6:63). To be sure, by 1738 the *Mercure de France* (June, 838) could write that it was no longer "shameful" for honest men to cultivate the violin. Nevertheless, striking documentation of the extent to which deprecation of the violin had slipped into common speech is offered by the *Dictionnaire de Trévoux* (1743). One of the meanings found under the heading *Violon* follows:

Violin is also a term of abuse and scorn that means fool, impertinent fellow. To consider a man a Violon *is as if one were to place him in the ranks of the* Ménestriers *who go from cabaret to cabaret*

playing a violin and increasing the pleasure of the drunkards
(6:814).

Violins, which were used in great numbers for court functions, were rarely used in private concerts before the late seventeenth century. The viol was preferred as the chamber instrument *par excellence*— both for independent ensemble performance and for the accompaniment of voices. All twentieth-century performers on instruments of the *viola da gamba* family understand, as did their forebears, that the sonorities of these instruments only superficially resemble those of the violin family. Substitution of violas or violoncellos for viols (or flutes for recorders) in Bach's Cantata 106, the *Actus tragicus*, for example, completely changes the desired sound complex: makes full what was thin and distinct, brightens what was delicate. Any modern performer could confirm the words of Trichet, who, in discussing the preference for viols, wrote that the "cleanness of their sound, the ease with which they are handled, and the gentle harmony that results makes them more willingly employed than other instruments" (ca. 1640; rpt. 1956 [4]:225).

The arbitrary functional division that saw viol as chamber instrument and violin as dance and outdoor instrument kept the technique of violin playing from developing as quickly in France as it did in Italy. French violin literature rarely leaves the first position until the time of Lully, and the wide leaps, rapid arpeggios, and string crossing associated with typical violin figurations are conspicuously absent from seventeenth-century French solo and ensemble music. André Maugars (ca. 1580–1654), who visited Italy in 1637–1638, was quick to notice that there were "ten or twelve" violinists in Rome who performed marvels on their instruments (1639; rpt. 1993, 14); whereas no one in Italy excelled on the viol, and it was "little used in Rome" (17).

French virtuoso viol players, beginning with Maugars and extending through Antoine Forqueray (1672–1745), formed a strong, closed group that had no wish to see the violin in a position of supremacy. Time was against the viol, however, although this unequal rivalry endured into the eighteenth century even as French composers borrowed more and more techniques from the Italian violin sonatas and concertos. The final, rather desperate attempt to bolster the fading fortunes of the viol was the treatise by Hubert Le Blanc, *Défense de la basse de viole contre les entreprises du violon et les prétensions du violoncelle* (1740). It calls the violoncello a "miserable canker" (36) and assures us that "the heightened Tone and explosive Sound of the Violin does not agree at all with persons of quality or of noble education" (89–90). Its polemical tone and tired shibboleths did little to sustain the viol against the onslaught of violin sonatas and concertos by Corelli,

Vivaldi, and Geminiani, which were played at the Concert Spirituel by popular French and Italian virtuosi.

The repertory performed at private concerts during the first half of the seventeenth century is difficult to trace. The bulk of independent ensemble music may have been fantasias for viols (and/or keyboard), since over 130 examples remain.[2] French and English fantasias reached the height of their popularity at about the same time. Although direct influence is conjectural, the French were acquainted with English examples of the genre. In Mersenne ("Livre quatriesme des instrumens"), for instance, there is a fantasia *a*6 for viols "composed by an excellent viol player, English by nationality"[3] (1636; rpt. 1965, 3:200–201).

In 1610, fifteen years after the first important set of English fantasias appeared, two collections were printed in France: the *Fantaisies à III, IV, V et VI parties* by Eustache Du Caurroy and the *Vingt-quatre fantaisies à quatre parties* by Charles Guillet. These were followed two years later by three *Fantaisies* by Claude Le Jeune that were included in the posthumous *Second livre des meslanges*. The fantasias by Du Caurroy, Guillet, and Le Jeune may certainly be thought of as both chamber and organ music (see Chapter 18). There must have been fantasias before the appearance of these collections, but only a few for lute and guitar are left. They date from the middle of the sixteenth century. Du Caurroy's and Guillet's collections form a sizeable body of well-crafted, refined examples. How could they have been composed in a vacuum? This question also continues to plague us with respect to the *Hymnes de l'Église* for organ by Titelouze and the *Pièces de clavecin* by Chambonnières.

An important link in the development of the viol fantasia in France was undoubtedly the very man responsible for the introduction of the large, six-stringed bass viol: Jacques Mauduit. He wrote fantasias that may have been part of the repertoire of his concerts for the Académie de Poésie et de Musique. Mersenne confirmed their existence but, regrettably, did not preserve them for posterity as he did so many other compositions.

The set by Du Caurroy consists of forty-two fantasias ranging in texture from *a*3 to *a*6. The four-part texture is favored. Almost half the total number fall into this category. Du Caurroy's contemporaries held him in high esteem and would not have agreed with Charles Burney, who found Du Caurroy's fantasias "extremely dry and destitute of idea"—a comment that tells us more about the late eighteenth-century approach to the "learned style" than it does about Du Caurroy's music. For "learned" they are, but in the best sense of the word. Most of the fantasias are based on pre-composed material used as a cantus firmus or employed in paraphrase technique. Some fantasias break up the cantus firmus in classic motet style and let each fragment serve as the subject of a small fugal exposition; in others, the cantus firmus, in long note values, acts as a source for imitative material in the surrounding voices; in still others, the melodic shape of the cantus firmus shows no relationship to the free counterpoint exhibited in the other voices.

The *Vingt-quatre fantaisies* by the Bruges composer, Charles Guillet (ca. 1575–1654), are pedagogical compositions designed to give those who would play them on the organ an opportunity to "exercise their fingers on the keyboard" and a means of understanding the church modes. Guillet's ordering and nomenclature of the modes is part Zarlino, part Glareanus. That is, the Zarlino disposition of the modes (their finals on C, D, E, F, G, A) are given the Glareanus titles of Dorian through Aeolian. There are two sets of twelve fantasias each. The music lacks the contrapuntal suppleness of Du Caurroy, and linear tension is often decreased through over-use of parallel motion between voices. Some ingenious structural devices are employed, however, such as the seven-note cantus firmus in No. 10 of the first set, that migrates in turn from the soprano, alto, tenor, and bass. Number 12 of the first set resembles a variation canzona. Its eight short, highly contrasting, sections all have different mensuration signs.

The three fantasias by Claude Le Jeune (ca. 1530–1611) are extended compositions that are generally less conservative than those by Du Caurroy or Guillet. Each fantasia is divided into two unequal parts. Each of the first two fantasias has a meter change and new material introduced into its second part. There are more modulations and some cross-relations. The rhythmic activity is rather complex. The many examples of crossing parts, especially between the *cinquiesme* or *haute-contre* and the *taille*, suggest viols rather than a keyboard instrument as an appropriate medium of performance.

During the reign of Louis XIII, fantasia composers such as Jehan Henry, called Henry Le Jeune (1560–1635), Antoine de [or du] Cousu (ca. 1600–1658), Étienne Moulinié (baptized 1599–1676), and Nicolas Métru (ca. 1610–1663) all wrote fantasias that derived as much from the *air de cour* and dance as from the older imitative style of writing—especially in the case of Henry and Moulinié. Jehan Henry, "violon ordinaire du Roy," composed fantasias ranging in texture from *a*2 to *a*6. Two of these compositions were apparently intended for court performances. They are found in "Livre quatriesme des instrumens" and "Livre cinqiesme des instrumens" of Mersenne's *Harmonie universelle* where they illustrate compositions well-suited for violins and cornetts, respectively (1636; rpt. 1965, 3:186–189 and 277). Both are stylistically removed from the viol fantasias discussed above. The heavy *a*6 texture allows little breathing space in the music, and there is none of the pervading imitation that characterizes the fantasias of the earlier generation, although points of imitation do occur occasionally between two voices.

Étienne Moulinié composed three *Fantaisies à quatre pour les violes* and included them in his *Cinquiesme livre d'airs de cour* (Paris, 1639). Each fantasia is divided into short and highly contrasting sections—some imitative, some homophonic, but most stemming from the dance rhythms and melodic formulae found in Moulinié's own court airs.

The golden age of the French ensemble fantasia closes with the collection of thirty-six *Fantaisies à deux parties pour les violles* (Paris 1642) by Nicolas Métru.[4] These short, unpretentious works conceal some masterful two-part writing, the more so because it appears so effortless. The fantasias are monothematic; the subject is answered at the fifth and constantly set off by independent counterpoint. Some of the tunes have a fresh, almost folk-like sound that provides clear tonal direction in the music. See Example 19-1 below.

Example 19-1. Métru: Selected "subjects" from the Fantasias (after ed. of 1642).

By the time of Louis Couperin, imitative fantasias were already a thing of the past. Couperin gave his fantasias a figured bass and a binary structure that resemble the French overture and dance.

At the end of the seventeenth century, any distinction that served earlier to delineate the genre was lost. For Brossard, *fantaisie* was synonymous with *capriccio* and *sonata*. Common to all three of his definitions is the idea of creation "according to the *fantaisie* of the composer, who, unfettered by general rules of counterpoint or fixed numbers and types of measure, lets the fire of his genius dictate change of measure and mood" (1703, "Capriccio").

Dances constitute the earliest printed examples of ensemble music in France. The twelve volumes of *Danceries*, brought out between 1530 and 1557 by Attaingnant, form the bulk of this repertory with their *basses danses*, branles, pavanes, galliards, and tordions (see Reese 1959, 563). After Thoinot Arbeau's *Orchésographie* of 1588, which included some dance tunes as illustrative material, French dance music for ensemble was not printed until the *Terpsichore* of Praetorius in 1612. Yet this was a period rich in the production of court ballets when some of the better composer-performers of the Confrérie de Saint-Julien were accepted into the *Violons de la Chambre du Roi*—musicians who would form the nucleus of the first generation of the *Vingt-quatre Violons* of the king.

Perhaps the dearth of printed collections of dance music in the early eighteenth century may be partly attributed to the composing techniques of the members of the Confrérie. Like modern jazz musicians with their lead sheets or fake books, many of the men simply worked from a dance melody to which they improvised the bass and inner voices (in rehearsal one hopes). Conceivably, much of the repertory served both the Confrérie and the court and was committed to memory much the same as are the standard "pop" tunes of today.

A small amount of the total repertory of the *"joueurs d'instruments tant haut que bas"* of the Confrérie and the first generation of the *Vingt-quatre Violons* survives in the 312 dances and *airs de ballet* that were collected and harmonized by Michael Praetorius (1571–1621) and Pierre-Francisque Caroubel (died 1611) and printed at Wolfenbüttel in 1612 under the title of *Terpsichore musarum.* According to the dedicatory page, Praetorius received the melodies for certain dances from Antoine Emaraud, dancing master of Duke Friedrich Ulrich of Brunswick. Praetorius and Caroubel, a *Violon de la Chambre* sojourning at Brunswick, were faced with the not inconsiderable task of harmonizing the majority of these tunes in four and five parts. Some other dances already were provided with both melody and bass, and a few, which are identified by composer in the collection, had all parts extant.

Among the composers represented in this important source are Pierre de La Grène, Jean Perrichon, Claude Nyon (called La Fons or De La Font), Pierre Beauchamps, Jean de La Motte, François Richomme, Jean Lebret, and Caroubel. Most of them were both members of the Confrérie and musicians of the king's Chamber.[5]

The dances give a good cross-section of the most popular types of dances at the turn of the century. They are arranged by category. The number of examples in each category, according to the title page, is as follows: twenty-one branles, thirteen other dances with special names (such as "Pavane de Spaigne," "La Bourée," "La Canarie"), one hundred sixty-two courantes, forty-eight voltes, thirty-seven ballets, three passamezzi, twenty-three galliards, and four doubles.

From time to time, the characteristic features of the dances that eventually made up the constituent members of the Baroque dance suite emerge clearly in the *Terpsichore musarum.* However, the courante category, by far the largest, illustrates how distant we are here from a consistent courante type. Along with courantes that exploit the shift of accent from two to three, thought of as a marked characteristic of French courantes, there are some that closely resemble the canarie, some that borrow the rhythmic pattern ♩. ♩ ♩ from the sarabande, and even a few that are programmatic tone paintings (see, for example, "Courante de Bataglia"). In spite of the inevitable monotony due to grouping so many dances together, the artistry of the harmonizers is evident on many pages. Inner voices often have melodic integrity of their own, and rhythmic counterpoint seldom allows the dances to become static.

About 1690, Philidor *l'aîné* copied music into four manuscripts that are of greater significance in transmitting the dance music of early court ballets and the repertory of the first and second generations of the *Vingt-quatre Violons*. This collection, entitled *Recueil de plusieurs anciens ballets dancez sous les Règnes de Henry IV et Louis XIII*, is now located in the Bibliothèque Nationale (*Rés.* F. 494, 496, 497, 498). Its principal contents are melody and bass settings of dances taken from about 130 ballets (see Buch 1994, 15). In one manuscript, *Rés.* F 494, Philidor supplied the names of the following composers whose music is represented in this source: François de Chancy, Jacques de Belleville, Michel Mazuel, Guillaume Dumanoir, Louis Constantin, and Lazarin.

For the second generation of the *Vingt-quatre Violons*, another rich source is the so-called Manuscript of Kassel, edited by Jules Écorcheville as the *Vingt suites d'orchestre du XVIIᵉ siècle français* (Paris, 1906). The manuscript contains 200 pieces that are grouped into twenty "suites." Among the composers represented in this collection are the Parisians Michel Mazuel (1603–1676), Louis Constantin (1585–1657), Michel Verdier (dates unknown), and De La Haye (dates unknown). The collection also includes music by Guillaume Dumanoir (1615–ca. 1697), the "King of Violinists," who was the conductor of the *Vingt-quatre Violons* as well. The music in the collection was taken from or modeled on French court ballet dance music and formed part of the *divertissements* at the court of Hesse.

The contents include twenty-five *"Pièces symphoniques,"* three *Ballets*, and 113 dances. As was true in the *Terpsichore*, more than half the dances are courantes, with the sarabande next in line, a situation that parallels that of the Chambonnières harpsichord collection. Surprisingly, the collection contains only one gigue and one minuet.

The allemandes are located among the symphonic pieces—a clear indication, as Écorcheville points out, that this dance had already lost much of its choreographic character and had, in effect, become a type of overture to the suite. As early as 1636 in "Livre second des chants" of *Harmonie universelle*, Mersenne had observed that "One is content today to play it [allemande] on instruments without dancing it . . . if it is not in a Ballet" (1636; rpt. 1965, 2:164–165). Example 19-2 below gives the incipit from a typical allemande from the Kassel Manuscript. It lacks an upbeat, and its wide melodic profile and dotted rhythms have affinity with the type of overture that had already been in use to introduce court ballets.

Example 19-2. Allemande from the Kassel Manuscript (after Écorcheville).

A manuscript that was copied by Philidor in 1705 and is now at Versailles (Bibliothèque Municipale, MS 168) provides a cross-section of the repertory of the Great Stable. It bears a long, descriptive title: *Partition de plusieurs marches et batteries de tambour tant françoises qu' étrangères avec les airs de fifre et de hautbois à 3 et 4 parties et plusieurs marches de timballes et de trompettes à cheval avec l'air du carrousel en 1686. Et les appels et fanfares de trompes pour la chasse.* Gathered here are pieces by some of the best performers and composers in the service of the king. Three members of the Philidor dynasty are included: namely the copyist himself, André Danican Philidor l'*aîné*, his brother, Jacques *le cadet*, and his nephew, Pierre. It also includes pieces by Martin Hotteterre, Delalande, and the oboist of the Musketeers, Jean-Baptiste Desjardins.

This is a collection of *pièces d'occasion*, and many of the compositions bear inscriptions that indicate the occasion. For example, the "Air de trompettes, timballes et hautbois" by Lully was composed "by order of the King for the carrousel of Monseigneur, in the year 1686." It is a dance suite consisting of prelude, minuet, gigue, and gavotte. The prelude is scored *a*9 (5 trumpets, 4 oboes), although the texture is actually much thinner because of massive doublings. In the year 1672, the king had ordered Lully to compose an "Air de hautbois" based on the *Folies d'Espagne*. Philidor's comments on the margin of the "Quatrième air de hautbois fait par M. de Luly" imply that this type of occasional work was not always to Lully's taste: "Philidor composed the *parties*, M. de Luly not having wished to do so."

Two additional sources that include dance music of the seventeenth century are the *Pièces pour le violon à quatre parties*, which was printed by Ballard (Paris, 1665),[6] and the Gustaf Düben collection, which is found today in the University Library at Uppsala (*Instrumental musik i handshrift* 409).[7]

Ballard's edition includes music from the *Ballet du Roy dansé à Fontainebleau* in 1664, several *Branles de Monsieur Brular*, which differ considerably from the pieces with this title in the Kassel Manuscript, some independent dances, and two short dance suites, both in B-flat major.

Gustaf Düben (1624–1690) copied 206 dances from the repertory of the *Vingt-quatre Violons* for performance at the court of Queen Cristina of Sweden (reigned 1644–1654). By far the most numerous dances in the collection are courantes (75), allemandes (37), and sarabandes (28). About sixteen composers are represented. Most of them were active in the courts of Louis XIII and Louis XIV.

An impressive amount of instrumental ensemble and orchestral music is included in the twenty-eight volumes of Marc-Antoine Charpentier's *Meslanges autographes*. Many of these pieces serve as preludes or overtures to motets, and many have a liturgical function: included are verses of hymns, *symphonies* for the instrumental music that alternated with sung chant during Mass, a *Messe pour plusieurs instruments* (see Chapter 15), and *symphonies* for consecrations and street processions. These volumes also contain a category of instrumental secular music that was composed for Molière's troupe at the Comédie Française, for Latin plays at the Jesuit College Louis-le-Grand, for the Académie Royale de Musique, and for more than twenty-five stage works that Charpentier wrote for the private *fêtes* of the Duchesse de Guise. Lastly, there are a few independent compositions, which include overtures, marches, minuets, a fanfare for two trumpets, *symphonies*, noels, and a *Concert pour quatre parties de violes* (see Hitchcock 1961).

The independent ensemble and orchestral music by Charpentier is a good meld of elements from Italian and French styles. The continued use of viols in ensemble writing, often in conjunction with violins, is French. So is the conservative writing for the first violins. But the predominantly four-part texture of the orchestral pieces and the exploitation of *concertato* effects are Italian.

The set of compositions that were used when the Corpus Christi processions paused at street altars (*reposoirs*) combines French overture, verses of hymns in archaic cantus firmus style, and, in two instances, an Allemande grave. Here again stripped of its choreographic past, the allemande presents itself as a symphonic piece. Significantly, as Hitchcock points out, there are no titled allemandes among the 110 dances by Charpentier, which include minuets, marches, gigues, sarabandes, gavottes, chaconnes, bourrées, loures, galliards, passacailles, passepieds, courantes, and canaries.

The unpretentious charm of the ten ensemble noels (H. 534) belies their artful counterpoint and fresh harmony. In the setting for violins of "Or nous dites Marie" (No. 5), Charpentier juxtaposes two strikingly different harmonizations of the same short melodic phrase. The use of mutes for the lower strings in the second harmonization adds to the contrast (see Example 19-3).

Example 19-3. Charpentier: Extract from an ensemble noel, "Or nous dites Marie" (after the *Meslanges*, vol. 5).

The *Concert pour quatre parties de violes* is a six-movement ensemble dance suite: Prelude No. 1, Prelude No. 2, Sarabande "en rondeau," English Gigue, French Gigue, and Passacaille. The opening prelude is a throwback to the earlier style of the ensemble fantasia, and the second prelude resembles an allemande. The two contrasting gigues foreshadow the *goûts réunis* of Couperin's *Concerts royaux*. No figured bass is provided, and due to the careful spacing of parts, none is needed.

Research by Julie Anne Sadie appears to confirm attribution to Charpentier of a *Sonate à huit instruments* found in a seventeenth-century manuscript at the Bibliothèque Nationale (Vm[7] 4813; see Sadie 1979b). It is an ensemble sonata in part books and is scored for two flutes, two violins, bass viol, bass violin, harpsichord, and theorbo. Its nine movements include two *Récits*: one for bass viol, the other for bass violin. The latter *récit* has an extremely wide range and a virtuoso Italianate style. It is unique among Charpentier's compositions and contrasts strongly with the rest of the sonata, which is dominated by dance movements (sarabande, bourée, gavotte, gigue, passacaille, chaconne), most of which are in trio texture.

Among the most imaginative and apparently popular of the many *symphonies* for the king's supper are those by Delalande that exist in three manuscripts (1703, 1727, and 1745). Philidor *l'aîné* and his son, Anne, made the manuscript of 1703 in part books for the Comte de Toulouse. It contains ten suites (154 movements), which were partly taken from the ballets and *divertissements* composed by Delalande between 1682 and 1700. The order of dances appears to be random, and there is no attempt to guard tonal unity in the suites. The title page helps corroborate the division of labor between the *Grande Bande* and the *Petits Violons*, for it asserts that these *symphonies* were performed "ordinarily at the King's supper by the *Troupe des petits violons.*"

The Philidor manuscript of 1727 contains thirteen suites (one hundred and thirty-nine movements), again with a random mixture of overture, prelude, titled dances, character dances, and free compositions such as caprices or fantasias. Included at the end of the volume are four *Symphonies des noëls* that, according to the manuscript, were "played in the King's Chapel on Christmas night."

The third manuscript is truly a manuscript *de luxe*. Copied out in 1745 in two small volumes, it bears the title *Simphonies de M. De La Lande* "which he had performed every fifteen days during the supper of Louis XIV and Louis XV." Although this collection was based on that of 1727, it carefully orders the suites and numbers the supper for which each suite was performed. It includes some examples of outdoor music "in which are mixed six Trumpet Airs from the *concert* given on the canal at Versailles" (Suite No. 4). Suites Nos. 6, 7, and 8 are entitled *Caprices* or *Caprices ou Fantaisies*. These imaginative works are a classic illustration of the Brossard definition of fantasia as a composition "created according to the *fantaisie* of the composer." They are free symphonic pieces, divorced from any specific dances. Each caprice has over-all key unity and reflects the sonorities that result from placing solo violin and oboe in apposition with the *tous*. The seventh suite, "which the King often asked for," is divided into five movements, which are designated only by tempo indications that move from slow to fast: (1) Un Peu lent; (2) Doucement; (3) Gratieusement; (4) Gayement; (5) Vivement. The final caprice (Suite No. 8) is made up of a series of *airs* and includes a set of free variations as the second *air*. The variations increase in complexity and, contrary to normal procedures, the *tous* sections appear more complex than the solos.

The genesis of the Baroque orchestral dance suite, known as an *Ouverture* or more literally as *Ouverture avec tous les airs*, can be found in the many collections of orchestral dances printed in Amsterdam by Heus, Pointel, and Roger between 1682 and 1715 (see Schneider 1989). Most of the music here is taken from the operas and ballets by Lully. All of the Amsterdam collections were printed in part books; unlike the original *a*5 scoring, all use the *a*4 scoring of violins I and II, viola, and bass favored in Italy. The fact that Roger's editions in particular were widely circulated in Rotterdam, London, Cologne, Berlin, Liège, Brussels, Halle, and Hamburg contributed to the wide dissemination of Lully's orchestral music, albeit in a bowdlerized version.

Chapter 20

Instrumental Ensemble and Orchestral Music of the Eighteenth Century

The first half of the eighteenth century saw such a variety of instrumental ensemble and orchestral music in France that exact classification of genres poses a very knotty problem. It was a period of experimentation and a period that witnessed the rapid absorption of elements from the Italian sonata and concerto, which by then co-existed with the traditional French forms of overture and dance suite. Added to this was the penchant, particularly French, for descriptive or programmatic music, which had been virtually elevated to aesthetic dogma by the end of the seventeenth century. The descriptive *symphonies* of the *tragédie lyrique*, oratorio, and cantata spread naturally to independent ensemble and orchestral music. Even Rousseau, certainly no partisan of French music, deprecated the "pure *symphonie* in which one only tries to show off the instruments" (1768; rpt. 1969, 452). He quoted with obvious approbation the slogan from the famous words of Fontenelle: "*Sonate, que me veux-tu?*" (Sonata, what do you want of me?).

Classification is further confounded by the numerous performance possibilities and indefinite terminology that fails to distinguish among different genres. Sonata, suite, concerto, and *symphonie*, as they were used, might mean the same thing. The head spins, the mind rebels at the mixture of genres found in such titles as *Livre de symphonies contenant six suittes en trio* (Dornel), *Sonades et suites de simphonies en trio* (Couperin), *Concert de simphonies* (M. Corrette), *Concert de violon avec voix* (Mondonville), and *Suites de concerts de simphonie en trio* (J. Aubert). These titles are confusing to the modern reader, accustomed as he is to the later eighteenth- and nineteenth-century definitions of symphony and concerto. However, the difficulties are more imagined than real if we remember that a source as late as Diderot's *Encyclopédie* defines *symphonie* as "all instrumental music, whether it be compositions destined only for instruments, like sonatas and concertos, or whether it be works where instruments are found mixed with voices, as in our operas" (1751–1780, 15:628).

Whether the composer desired performance of a work with one or more than one player on a part is often impossible to tell; but where his intention can be understood, the music may be divided into two classifications. This chapter considers only the ensemble music intended for performance by more than one person on a part; that is, the titles or the *avertissements* indicate that this was desired. (Nevertheless, the possibility of performance by one person on a part, despite the composer's intention, must not be ruled out for these pieces.) The next chapter considers the ensemble compositions that are restricted, at least in principle, to one performer on a part.

In view of the performance practices of the period, however, this division is in no way meant to be air-tight. The titles or subtitles of collected pieces may show that there should be more than one player on a part but we may read in the *avertissement* that the entire collection "can be performed with just one treble and one bass instrument," as is the case with Montéclair's *Sérénade ou concert* of 1697. At the same time, compositions that seem to be appropriate for solo instruments were occasionally performed with a multiple instrumental doubling of the solo lines. Why else would "M. de L. T." in his important "Dissertation sur la musique italienne & françoise," have felt it necessary to emphasize that Italian solo violin sonatas, "Should only be played by a single violin, which arches the line and shows off its brilliance as much as it pleases; they [the sonatas] would become very confused if the same part were to be performed by several instruments" (*Mercure galant* of November 1713, 23). This statement carries a hint of admonition for what was, in all likelihood, a common performance practice. Therefore, our classification is clearly artificial and designed only to deal with a bulk of music in some systematic manner.

In order to give greater focus to the music that concerns us in this chapter, we may establish two subclassifications based on texture and instrumentation:

1. Compositions in the first group are thinly scored (*a2* or *a3*) and are designed for small ensemble performance with more than one instrument on a part. They usually offer some latitude in the choice of instrumentation and some use of *concertato* effects between solo instruments and *tous*.

2. Compositions in the second group were conceived for orchestral performance and have predominantly *a*4 texture (at least for the *tous*). They have less latitude in the choice of instruments.

There is also a shadow zone in which we find compositions for small ensemble that derive from collections originally scored for one or two solo instruments. Through the *avertissements* of solo harpsichord collections (Dieupart, Le Roux, Couperin, and others) and the *avertissements* of compositions for one or two viols (Marais), we learn that some or, in some cases, all the pieces may be *mises en concert* with the help of a supplied list of suggested instruments. The only problem, it would seem, was "to know how to make a choice between each of the instruments" (Marais, *Avertissement*, Book 3 of *Pièces de viole*). Because these works derive from solo literature, and, indeed, much of the time the solo original is all that we have, they are discussed in the next chapter.

Properly belonging to the first category of ensemble pieces with more than one instrument on a part are the many collections that, according to their title pages, were composed for violins, flutes, and the like. Much of this music is in trio texture, which was favored for instrumental ensembles from the late years of the seventeenth century.

To subdivide this category further into collections that indicate specific instrumentation and those that merely suggest appropriate instruments would be helpful. Without a complete survey of each individual piece in any given collection, however, this is untenable. French composers of the period were not bound by what their title pages or subtitles suggest. In Dornel's *Livre de simphonies contenant six suittes en trio*, for example, we read that the six suites were composed for flutes, violins, and oboes, yet they are very rarely specified. Contrast this with Montéclair's *Sérénade ou concert*, where titles often give specific instrumentation, but a look at the music shows that Montéclair, himself, added instruments not found in the titles (trumpet, *tambour de Basque*, etc.).

The history of the chamber trio in France has only recently been studied. Herbert Schneider (1984a) has identified fifty-seven publications of French chamber trios, from Du Mont's *Meslanges à II, III, IV et V parties* (1657) to Couperin's *Les Nations* (1726). By the turn of the century, the demand for manuscript copies of trios and other chamber combinations was evidently great, because a considerable number were in circulation. For example, the *Suites des symphonies des vieux ballets de M. de Lully*, copied by Philidor for the Comte de Toulouse in

1703, contains over 500 extracts from Lully's court ballets. They are arranged for two violins (or oboes) and *basse de violon*.

Among the late seventeenth-century works meant for more than one player on a part are the twenty-six chamber trios by Lully, which can be found in the Bibliothèque Nationale (MS *Rés.* 1397),[1] and the *Pièces en trio pour les flûtes, violons, et dessus de viole* by Marin Marais, which was published in 1692.

Lully's twenty-six chamber trios owe little to Italian counterparts. Their harmonic language is conservative, and although there are many examples of part crossings, these do not generate the harmonic tension and suspension chains found in the Italian trios. Parallel thirds and sixths, crossed or uncrossed, are the norm. The collection consists almost entirely of binary dances. Irregular groups of phrases are often found. One minuet, for example, has a five-plus-five phrase grouping in Part A, which is followed by a normal four-measure grouping in Part B.

Marais gathered a total of six suites together for his 1692 collection of trios. These are scored in part books for *Dessus* I, *Dessus* II, and a *Basse-continue*, thereby allowing the performer to choose his instruments. Each suite is introduced similarly—by a prelude—but each ends in its own way with a different type of composition—either with a character piece or a dance. The dance components within the six suites are sarabandes, loures, gigues, gavottes, minuets, branles, and rigaudons. There are also some free forms, such as caprices and fantasias, as well as some descriptive pieces ("La Marienne," "La Bagatelle," etc.). The trios show little evidence of Italian influence. They stem more from the note-against-note style of the trios in Lully's operas. Even the fantasias found in five of the six suites are predominantly homophonic after an initial point of imitation. On the other hand, there is rich harmony, and the frequent crossing of voices helps to counteract the static rhythmic organization.

At the turn of the century, several collections of trios were scored for violins, flutes, and oboes. Typical of this kind of *Gebrauchsmusik* is Montéclair's *Sérénade ou concert, divisé en trois suites pour les violons, flûtes & hautbois* (Paris, 1697). We are informed that the set includes pieces "suitable for dancing" and, as mentioned above, that the entire collection could be reduced to just a treble and bass instrument. In spite of the subtitle's vagueness regarding instrumentation, each suite is cleverly built around a particular instrumental color and mood. Indeed, the rather thin musical substance of the suites is rendered quite tolerable because of Montéclair's marked and sometimes quite sudden contrasts. The first suite revels in the typically French *trio des hautbois's* contrasting with a *tous*. It includes some trumpet fanfares as well as an amusing two-part fantasia that imitates C major fife flourishes. The second suite, subtitled "Air tendre," is night music filled with the poetry of flutes and violins. An extensive *sommeil*, with solo sections for violin, bass viol, and *basse de violon*, frames the suite. Musettes and a *tambour de Basque* color the third suite, "Air champêtre."

Similar in style, although with less attention paid to contrasts of sonorities, are the seven suites included in the three collections of *Pièces en trio pour les violons, flûtes et hautbois* (1694, 1700, 1707) by Michel de La Barre (ca. 1675–1745). Brossard described the composer as "the most excellent player of the transverse flute in Paris, and the one responsible for creating the vogue for this instrument" (1724; 1725–1730, 352). The music gives little evidence, however, that La Barre sought to exploit the technical limits of his instrument or, indeed, considered the flute lines, when indicated, as any different from those accorded the violins or oboes.

Louis-Antoine Dornel (ca. 1681–ca. 1756) brought out four instrumental collections (1709, 1711, 1713, 1738), the first of which, a *Livre de simphonies*, is of interest. It contains six suites *en trio* for flutes, violins, oboes, "etc." as well as a *Sonate en quatuor*. Only the prelude to the sixth suite gives specific instrumentation ("*flûtes allemandes et violons*"). Perhaps due to his background as organist,[2] Dornel's suites and the sonata give the illusion of being more polyphonic than they actually are. Initial points of imitation are sustained over a longer time span than was normal, and there is some attractive rhythmic counterpoint; but in approaching a cadence, the upper voices inevitably fall into parallel motion. More important than this semblance of polyphony is the influence stemming from Corelli. Chains of suspensions, circles of fifths, and series of diatonically harmonized first inversion chords are evident. Unfortunately, Dornel's mediocre melodic gifts rob these procedures of any real character and reduce them to formulae.

The suites were printed in part books, but the *Sonate en quatuor*, found only in the part book labeled *Basse continue*, was printed in score, which may indicate that it is to be performed by solo instruments. It is divided into four sections approximating the Slow-Fast-Slow-Fast ordering of the Italian church sonata. The third movement is broadly paced and sarabande-like. Its many stops and starts show how Dornel, in common with many of his contemporaries, had not learned to use, or perhaps chose not to use, the Corelli vocabulary to allow expansion rather than contraction of a musical idea.

François Couperin composed fourteen *Concerts*, which were performed at Versailles in 1714 and 1715—possibly to brighten the deepening shadows of Louis XIV's last years. The first four were published in 1722 (the same year the third book of *Pièces de clavecin* appeared) and bear the title, *Concerts royaux*. The remaining ten were brought out two years later under the title *Les Goûts réunis ou nouveaux concerts*. The 1722 set is printed on two staves as though originally planned for harpsichord. Rarely is specific instrumentation supplied, but Couperin informed us in the preface that the pieces are "suitable not only for harpsichord, but also for Violin, Flute, Oboe, Viol, and Bassoon." Helpfully, he even supplied the names of his musicians in the *"petits Concerts de Chambre"* that took place on Sundays before the king: François Duval (violin), Philidor (oboe and bassoon), Hilaire Verloge Alarius (viol), and Pierre Dubois (oboe and bassoon). Couperin, himself, played the harpsichord (see Mellers 1950, 235). Meller's suggestion of "two stringed instruments, two wind instruments, and continuo, the strings and winds playing either together or alternately," provides a practical solution to the problem of the choice of instruments if we remember to seek out the affection of each piece. In seventeenth- and eighteenth-century France in particular, instrumental color could be as carefully compartmentalized as the choice of certain dances or the use of certain keys.

A study of textures of the *Concerts royaux*, coupled with an examination of the few places where instrumentation is specified, strongly suggests the use of some sort of *concertato* principle. The clearest example is in the "Courante à l'italienne" from *Concert* No. 4. Each of the two sections of the binary dance includes a thickening of texture from *a*2 to *a*3. Except for an occasional full-voiced chord at cadence points, the sections in *a*3 texture are consistently maintained, with their individual lines clearly differentiated. At the first occurrence of the *a*3 texture in Part A, Couperin indicated *"viole,"* perhaps referring to a treble viol for the upper melodic line or, conceivably, for a *concertino* group of solo viols. Were this the case, the *a*2 sections of the dance would then be performed by the full group. The fact that this suggestion of *concertato* performance occurs in a composition *à l'italienne* is perhaps not fortuitous.

A similar possibility exists in "Échos" from *Concert* No. 2, where specific solo sections are marked for one viol and one harpsichord playing together or for a single viol in apposition to the harpsichord. The prelude to *Concert* No. 3 includes a middle part (*contre partie*) for viol or for "violin, flute, oboe, etc." The prelude and the Sarabande grave from the same suite contain the thickest texture of any of the *Concerts*. Only in the *contre partie* is the linear writing consistently maintained. The upper and lower staves divide continually, suggesting the possibility of more than one instrument on a part.

Each of the four *Concerts* begins with a prelude, usually of a serious nature and resembling the opening movement of a Corelli church sonata. A series of freely disposed dances follows. These include allemandes, courantes, sarabandes, gigues, minuets, gavottes, chaconnes, rigaudons, and a forlane. French and Italian elements are frequently juxtaposed. In *Concert* No. 2, the prelude, labeled *"gracieusement,"* is a French dance; the Allemande *"Fuguée,"* which follows with its bass *"travaillée toujours,"* is Italian; the "Air tendre," with its expressive *port de voix, coulés,* and cross-relations (see Measure 13 of Part B), is the quintessence of a French air; the "Air contrefugué" and the concluding "Échos" pair national styles in a similar manner.

Overall, however, the four *Concerts royaux* are basically French. Much of their source material is rooted in the *Pièces de clavecin.* Their dissonance comes from French ornamentation and linear clashes rather than from suspensions or sequences of seventh chords. Noble melodic lines, elegant part writing, and strong dissonant clashes give the sarabandes from *Concerts* Nos. 3 and 4 a depth of feeling that goes "far beyond the normal confines of entertainment music" (Mellers 1950, 245).

The ten *Concerts* (Nos. 5 to 15) that comprise *Les Goûts réunis ou nouveaux concerts* are numbered as though they were a continuation of the *Concerts royaux* but exhibit many differences from the latter. Added to the typical French dances that make up most of the movements of the *Concerts royaux* are many descriptive pieces and independent *symphonies* drawn from a much broader milieu.

Except for certain portions of *Concert* No. 8, "Dans le goût théâtral," the texture of these *Concerts* is more consistently *a2,* and the writing more idiomatic for non-keyboard instruments and somewhat less harpsichordic. The scope and development of these *Concerts* are also greater than in the first group. No instrumentation is suggested except for *Concert* No. 12, *Concert* No. 13, and a *plainte* for viols in *Concert* No. 10. Two viols "or other instruments of the same pitch" are clearly specified for *Concert* No. 12 and *Concert* No. 13. In fact, after stating that the harpsichord or theorbo could be used as accompaniment in *Concert* No. 12, Couperin recommends two viols "with nothing more" for the best performance. Perhaps to emphasize this, he eliminates the figured bass after the prelude for the only time in the *Concerts.*

Couperin not only achieved a *goût réuni* by the juxtaposition of the two styles in a series of dances, but he also composed a few *Concerts* to illustrate a single *goût.* Thus, *Concert* No. 8 contains in microcosm the *symphonies* usually found in a Lully opera. A fine French overture and a *"Grande ritournelle"* open the *Concert* and are followed by a cross-section of the *airs de danse* that might be found in an operatic *divertissement.* The next *Concert,* entitled "Ritratto dell'Amore," includes some lively genre pieces ("Le je-ne-sçais quoy," "L'Et Coetera"), and a composition called simply "La Vivacité," whose fire, driving rhythms, and economy of thematic material deliberately imitate the closing movement of a Corelli or a Vivaldi violin sonata.

In some compositions, Couperin combined Italian and French styles. The "Sarabande mesurée" from *Concert* No. 6, for example, is the only sarabande of the entire collection of *Concerts* that bears the typically Italian meter signature of 3/4 (all the remainder are 3). Its use of triplet figures in the bass line comes dangerously close at times to converting the dance into an Italian sicilienne. The French element of profuse ornamentation results in considerable rhythmic freedom between the parts.

A similar, if somewhat more startling, example is the Allemande from *Concert* No. 11, which begins like the allemandes that have characteristics of the French overture. Choreographic origins are lost in a maze of dotted rhythms that give to the piece a true dramatic mien. Suddenly, the dotted rhythms give way to even sixteenth-notes, and we are catapulted into a circle of fifths having the string figurations typical of pure Corelli—all this within nine short measures.

Could Couperin have entertained second thoughts about the uninhibited nature of his Franco-Italian alliance in this Allemande? He followed it immediately with a *"Seconde allemande plus légère,"* which poses no problems. The situation reminds us of the introduction to the eighth *Ordre* from Book 2 of the *Pièces de clavecin*, in which the powerfully dramatic allemande, "La Raphaèl," is followed by a second allemande, "L'Ausonières," carrying the performance direction *légèrement.*

Concert No. 14, which closes the series, is one of Couperin's best realizations of *goûts réunis*. The musical language seems natural to the composer, without the conceit of mimicry or self-conscious imitation. French ornaments and melodic elegance coalesce with Italian formal direction and greater sense of development. The whole is cast in the four movement scheme (Slow-Fast-Slow-Fast) of the Italian sonata. The final movement is a busy "Fugueté" that sacrifices fugal integrity to overall vigor and kinetic drive in the manner of many closing movements of Corelli, Vivaldi, and Handel sonatas. The fugal process, itself, is fragmented and even abandoned in the wake of episodic concerto-like passages that assume considerable importance.

Couperin's *Concerts* stand at the very pinnacle of the chamber music for small ensemble that allows for the greatest latitude in performance possibilities. At the opposite end of the small ensemble's territory lie collections, written in the late 1720s and early 1730s, that inch the small ensemble closer to an orchestral concept by their more symphonic use of specific instruments, and thereby form a transition between our two categories.

Representative of these collections are the *Suites de simphonies*[3] by Jean-Joseph Mouret, the *Suites de concerts de symphonies en trio* by Jacques Aubert, and the *Concerts de symphonies* by Étienne Mangean. Dating from 1729, Mouret's suites are carefully scored with unusual attention paid to combinations of timbres. The first suite carries the title *Fanfares pour les trompettes, violons et hautbois* and is written for trumpet in D, violins I and II, oboes, bassoon, bass, and timpani. Trio texture is maintained throughout; violins and oboes generally double the upper lines. The suite has four movements, the first of which has achieved great popularity as the theme song of the popular television series *Masterpiece Theater*.

The second suite, *Symphonies pour les viollons, des hautbois, et des cors de chasse*, was performed before the king at the Hôtel de Ville (*Mercure*, October 1729) and, in Viollier's words, is *"joyeuse musique de table"* (1950, 208). It includes six binary dances—three with *doubles*. The instrumentation, which is clearly indicated, exploits the color contrast between horns and strings.

The *Suites de concerts de symphonies en trio pour les violons, flûtes et hautbois* (Opus 8–13) by Jacques Aubert (1689–1753) date from 1730 to 1733. There are six suites in this collection, which is the first item listed by Barry Brook as an antecedent of the French symphony (1962, 1:45). The preface informs us that these pieces "may be performed with a large group (*à grand choeur*) like Concertos."

The *Concert de symphonie pour les violons, flûtes et hautbois* (1735) by Étienne Mangean (ca. 1710–ca. 1756) includes some dances scored *a3* for specific soloists and other dances labeled *tous*. It also includes two suites with precise instructions concerning which instruments are to be used. Because of this precision, we can hypothesize some of the performance possibilities for the innumerable *concerts en trio* where little or no information is found regarding exact scoring.

We may consider Aubert's suggestion that his *Concerts de symphonie* be performed *"à grand choeur comme les Concertos"* an appropriate point of departure for our discussion of ensemble music that was composed for larger instrumental forces. In 1730 Aubert was obviously thinking of *concerto* in the sense of the original Italian meaning of the word; that is, "to work or join together," rather than in the sense of the original Latin term (*concertare*), which means "to compete, to contend" (see Boyden 1957).

In France, the type of concerto that places one instrument or a group of solo instruments "in competition" with a full group was rather late to appear as a distinct genre. After 1750 the Italian concept of symphony merged with the idea then current that a concerto in its broad sense was instrumental music played by a whole orchestra together. In his *Dictionnaire de musique*, Rousseau gave both the general and the narrow meaning of the word. In the first sense, a concerto is a *"Simphonie* made for execution by an entire orchestra"; for the more particular meaning, Rousseau gave a succinct summary of the *ritornello* principle as applied to a solo instrument and *tutti* (1768, 112). Rousseau added in his "Concerto" article for Diderot's *Encyclopédie* that "as for those [concertos] where all play together [*en choeur*] and where no instrument solos, Italians also call them *Symphonies*" (1751–1780, 3:804).

As early as 1727, the Italian expatriate Michele Mascitti (1664–1760) gave the first clear models for the Italian concerto in Paris with his *Sonate a Violino solo e Basso e quattro Concerti a sei*. The "*quattro Concerti*" were numbered nine to twelve and so were considered an extension of his first eight sonatas. The four concertos, however, are entirely distinct from the sonatas. They are genuine *concerti grossi*, scored for a *concertino* of two violins and a "*basso del concertino*," plus another violin, viola, and bass to make up the *ripieno*.

Although they belong in the category of music for small ensemble, the *VI Concertos pour 5 flûtes traversières ou autres instruments sans basse* (Opus 15) by the prolific Joseph Bodin de Boismortier also appeared in 1727. The subtitle adds the helpful information that the concertos "may also be played with a Bass," and a figured bass is included in the part book for the *Flauto quinto*. Of interest in the history of the concerto in France is the fact that all the concertos are cast in three movements; three are Slow-Fast-Slow, and the remainder are Fast-Slow-Fast. Furthermore, much of the music is organized in alternating solo and *tutti* groups. The thematic material, however, is more French than Italian. An occasional theme that begins in the style of a Corelli or Torelli often reaches a cadence point before the forward drive has been consolidated.

In 1728 The *VI concertos pour les flûtes, violons ou hautbois, avec la basse chiffrée pour le clavecin*, Opus 3, by Michel Corrette was printed. These may rightfully be considered the first concertos in France, written by a native Frenchman, that conform to the typical features of the Italian concerto. The conventionalized title (*"flûtes, violon ou hautbois"*) may well be partly responsible for the neglect of these works in their role of the first French *concerti grossi*. This emphasizes the need of looking beyond the title into each work itself—in French music especially. All six concertos follow an Allegro-Adagio-Allegro ordering of movements. Each has a clearly indicated *concertino*, which is composed of either two or three "*Flauti e Violoncello obbligato*." Three of the concertos (Nos. 1, 3, and 5) cast the allegro in binary form; each section is normally repeated. In one way or another, the even-numbered concertos adapt the *ritornello* principle that was systematized and published

nineteen years earlier in 1709 in the Opus 8 *Concerti Grossi* of Giuseppe Torelli (1658–1709). Typical is Concerto No. 2, "*con Tre Flauti e Violoncello obbligato,*" whose opening Allegro has four *tuttis*: after the dominant minor key of the second *tutti* and the relative major key of the third *tutti*, the tonic key returns in the fourth. The Adagio movement, in typically Corelli fashion, ends on a Phrygian cadence.

For the most productive part of his long life, Corrette was involved in some fashion with the concerto, and although the musical ideas are not always commensurate with the imaginative formats, it is curious that these works have been ignored in studies of Baroque instrumental music.[4] The *VI Concerti a sei strumenti* (Opus 26) of 1756 advertises itself in its title as being scored for harpsichord or organ obbligato, three violins, flute, viola, and violoncello. Most of the time the first violin doubles the right hand of the keyboard instrument or adds nonmelodic chord outlines, which reminds us that Corrette's Opus 25, presumably composed fourteen years before the six concertos, comprises *Sonates pour le clavecin avec accompagnement de violon ou viole*. However, in part of Concerto No. 3 and in much of Concerto No. 6, the keyboard acts as a legitimate obbligato instrument, sharing its solo material with the first and second violins. The thin keyboard writing, with its persistent use of the Alberti bass, is much in the character of the *style galant* (see Example 20-1). We learn from the *Avertissement* that, with the exception of Concerto No. 3, all may be performed on the organ "without *symphonie*." Corrette carefully specified the organ registration: "One must play the Allegros on the *Grand Jeu*; the Adagios on the *Flûtes*; and the Solos on the *Cornet de Récit*."

Example 20-1. Corrette: Extract from Allegro of Concerto No. 6 "a sei strumenti" (after ed. of 1756).

Corrette also composed a series of concertos in simulated *champêtre* style (*VI Concertos pour musette ou vielles composés sur les vaudevilles les plus connus*, Opus 7 of about 1731) and five *Concertos de noël* (from before 1733 to before 1753) for three treble instruments and bass, with material drawn from popular noels and even Gregorian themes (*Christe redemptor*, for example).

In addition, Corrette composed twenty-five *Concertos comiques* for various instrumental combinations, which range in time from 1732 to 1760 and are examples of descriptive concertos. Many of these works are of a popular nature; some even employ such rustic instruments as musettes and hurdy-gurdies.[5] Certain concertos were performed at the Fair theaters and the Comédie Italienne. At least three of them ("L'Allure," "La Servante au bon tabac," and "Biron") were probably choreographed at the Opéra Comique in 1732, 1733, and 1734, respectively (see Paillard 1954–1955, 146–148). In the *Avertissement* for the last of the *Concertos comiques* "La Prise de Port-Mahon," Corrette wrote: "In a *grand concert* it is necessary to add Trumpets and Drums (*Timbales et Tambour*) in order to render the concerto well. The composer will consider it a pleasure to supply the parts for Trumpet and *Timbale*."

Such a work would have surely resembled a *grande symphonie*, which, as defined by Rousseau, needed only two additional instrumental parts (normally the *taille* and *quinte*) between the treble and bass instruments. This gives the orchestral music of Corrette some significance as a transition between concerto and symphony in France.

From the above information, it is clear that the role of wind instruments (especially the transverse flute) in the history of the concerto in France must not be underestimated. In about 1735, Jacques-Christophe Naudot (ca. 1690–1762) introduced the flute concerto to France with his *Six concertos en 7 parties pour une flûte traversière*. The "*7 parties*" refer to the flute plus the accompanying parts of three violins, one viola, and two basses (violoncello or bassoon and continuo). All six concertos have a Fast-Slow-Fast movement scheme, and all use the *ritornello* principle. Boismortier, in ten publications following his Opus 15 of 1727, made use of one or more flutes in his concertos, and in the 1730s, Corrette and others composed many chamber concertos for flutes with other instruments.

Yet, French composers seemed curiously reluctant to engage in writing concertos in the Italian style. Jacques Aubert's first book of *Concertos à quatre violons et violoncelle*, Opus 17 was not published until 1734, six years after Corrette's Opus 3 (Aubert's Book 2, Opus 26, bears the same title and was printed in 1739). This is a marked change from the early absorption of the Italian sonata: Couperin's first two sonatas date from 1692, and François Duval's solo violin sonatas were published in 1705.

Advance publicity for Aubert's first book appeared in the *Mercure* of November 1734, in which the author, ignorant of Corrette's Opus 3, wrote that Aubert's concertos would be "the first works of this genre to have left the pen of a Frenchman."

The concertos were printed in six part books: violins I, II, III, and IV, violoncello, and *basso organo*. All are in the three-movement form of the Italian concerto; the middle movement is an Aria in three of the concertos and a *Gavotta* in those remaining. In two instances (Concertos Nos. 1 and 5) the final Allegro is a *Minuetto*.

The first violin is given the burden of the solo passages, while the remaining violins act as *ripieno* instruments. Although Aubert was conservative in his handling of the solo instrument when compared to his Italian contemporaries, the influence of Torelli and Corelli is fairly obvious (see especially Torelli's Opus 8). Mechanical rhythmic pulsations, circles of fifths, and typical Italian violin figurations spring from every page. The opening Allegros generally begin *tutti e forte* with unison passages. Indeed, the opening *tutti* of Concerto No. 2 is arranged in two- or four-measure phrases that repeat exactly, much in the manner of the early Italian symphonies. The music has gestic drive and a wide melodic profile. Its *tutti* themes are constructed in short, contrasting motifs, with clearly differentiated rhythms that allow for motivic expansion or contraction in subsequent *tutti* or solo groups.

The only French concerto composer that could seriously rival the Italian school is Jean-Marie Leclair (1697–1764), who was dubbed the "Corelli of France" by Blainville (1754, 88). Leclair, who had been a violin student of Giovanni Battista Somis in Turin, was the *Premier Symphonist du Roi* and a featured performer at the Concert Spirituel between 1728 and 1736.

Leclair composed two sets of violin concertos having six concertos in each set. The first book, *Six concertos à tre violini, alto e basso per organo e violoncello* (Opus 7), was printed in about 1737; the second book (Opus 10), in about 1743. All but two concertos are in the typical concerto format of three movements. Although all were written for a *violino principale*, No. 3 of Opus 7 may be performed "on the transverse flute or oboe."

The influence of Torelli and Vivaldi is very much in evidence, but here, as compared with Aubert or Corrette, the violin solo is a real challenge to the performer. The second book, especially, exploits the solo instrument. The finale of Concerto No. 5 has a seventy-two-measure solo, and the Allegro of the same concerto reaches the seventh position. Many concertos in both sets include dazzling passages in double stops and difficult arpeggio figures.

As in Vivaldi, some of the Allegro movements suffer from sequential patterns that are too long and too abundant, but in general, the thematic material is to the point and adaptable for the greatest motivic concentration. Moreover, this music achieves more than a skillful parroting of Italian models. In essence, the Italianisms contribute to the total architecture and to surface gesture, but the inner core of the music contains the strong, personal stamp of Leclair. The composer's harmonic language is bolder than that of most of his French contemporaries, and some of his key relationships between movements are more adventurous than, for example, those in the concertos of Torelli. The slow middle movements are usually cast in relative keys, but in Concerto No. 5 (Book 1) in A minor, the slow movement, a *sicilienne*, is in F major, which permitted the composer the luxury of an expressive five-measure modulatory Adagio designed to restore tonal equilibrium. The opening movement of this same concerto in A minor has an extended *tutti* section in B-flat major, the key of the Neapolitan.

Arthur Hutchings has mentioned Leclair's treatment of motivic material by an almost ever-present extension and variation technique (1961, 315). At times the solo is clearly a variation of the *tutti*; at times a motivic fragment extracted from the main *tutti* accompanies independent melodic material, thus modestly suggesting the beginnings of the obbligato technique that reached fruition in the symphonies of Joseph Haydn.

The variety with which Leclair approached *tutti* and solo rivalry attracts attention. Some concertos are clearly cast in a *ritornello* form, with constant alternation of *tutti* and solo; others rival Vivaldi in their use of solo penetration of the *tutti* section. In the Allegro of Concerto No. 2 (Book 2), it is the solo that rounds off the main theme (Example 20-2a); in the aria from Concerto No. 4 (Book 2), the solo interrupts the *tutti* over and over again to add its own commentary as in Example 20-2b, below.

Example 20-2. Leclair: Solo penetration of *tutti* in (a) Allegro of Concerto No. 2, Book 2, (b) Aria from Concerto No. 4, Book 2.

The music of Jean-Féry Rebel (1666–1747), more than that of any other composer, highlights the particularly French preoccupation with both descriptive music and ballet. Jean-Féry was the most famous member of the Rebel dynasty of musicians, who for over 100 years served in the corps of the king's musicians and in the opera. His knowledge of ballet and descriptive *symphonies* was a natural by-product of his close association with the Académie Royale de Musique, where in 1699 he entered the orchestra and became its conductor about sixteen years later.

Out of this experience, Rebel created the first choreographic and program *symphonies*, which, if they were not to find issue during the eighteenth century, would serve as isolated monuments to one man's imaginative power and sense of fantasy. The series begins with *Caprice* (1711), which was scored for five string instruments and was planned as background music for the choreographic skills of Mlle Prévost. Much more impressive is *Les Caractères de la danse* (subtitled *Fantaisie*) of 1715, which perhaps was also created for Mlle Prévost, but which later became a popular vehicle for young Mlle Camargo, who first danced it on 5 May 1726 "with all the vivacity and intelligence that one could expect from a young person of fifteen or sixteen years" (*Mercure* 1726, cited by Dacier 1905, 324).

The object of this *Fantaisie* appears to have been to give a summary of the most popular dances of the period. The entire work is a type of suite in which all the dance components are fragmented and telescoped together so as to create one large dance. This device may be observed in a much more modest way as early as the repertory of the *Vingt-quatre Violons* (see Écorcheville 1906c, 2:235), and Lully made use of it in the first *intermède* of *Le Bourgeois gentilhomme*. It was exploited in particular in the *opéras-ballets* by such *préramiste* composers as Campra, Bourgeois, and Mouret.

Table 20-1, below, shows the distribution and key schemes of the dances of this *Fantaisie*. The shortest dance fragment is an eight-measure courante; the longest, a chaconne of thirty-six measures. The *Fantaisie* also acknowledges the *goûts réunis* by including two sonata movements written in a much more genuine Italian style than, for example, the French concertos of the 1720s. If examined closely, the second sonata is actually seen to be a development and extension of the first one, with transitory modulations to the keys of B and E minor.

Only the Chaconne and the Musette are autonomous. The Musette is in binary form, with each part repeated. Unfortunately, the score is a *partition réduite*, and only a few of the dances give exact instrumentation.

Table 20-1. Dances of *Les Caractères de la Danse* by Rebel showing distribution and key schemes (I = D major).

Dance:	Prelude	Courante	Menuet	Bourrée	Chaconne
Key scheme:	I – V	I – V	I – V	I – I	I – I
Dance:	Sarabande	Gigue	Rigaudon	Passepied	
Key scheme:	i – v	i – i	i – v	i – III	
Dance:	Gavotte	Sonate	Loure	Musette	Sonate
Key scheme:	I – I	I – I	I – V	I – I	vi – I

The *Fantaisie* of 1729 and *Les Plaisirs champêtres* of 1734 are similar choreographic *symphonies*—their components are telescoped into one large dance. The *Fantaisie* includes two chaconnes, here again closely related thematically. The final chaconne repeats the first, but eliminates one section and reverses the order of the others. Thus, the A B C of the first chaconne becomes C A in the second. Apparently, this work, too, could be converted into a *grande symphonie*, for we read in the *Avertissement* that the "Contrebasse, trumpets, and timpani add much embellishment to this piece."

The most spectacular of all is a veritable symphonic poem called *Les Élémens*, "*simphonie nouvelle*,"[6] of 1737. According to the *Avertissement*, this *symphonie* was printed in a manner that permits performance *en concert* by two violins, two flutes, and a bass. As is so often the case, however, the whole may be performed on a solo harpsichord or undoubtedly be converted into a *grande symphonie* by the addition of other instruments (which, incidentally, are called for in any case).

Rebel's *Avertissement* gives us a capsule version of the program and the instruments as well as the harmonies to be used for specific descriptive ends:

> *The introduction to this* Simphonie *was natural. It was chaos itself—the confusion that reigned among the elements before the Instant when, subjected to unchanging laws, they took the place prescribed them by the order of Nature.*
>
> *To designate each particular Element in this confusion, I resorted to the most recognized conventions. The Bass expresses Earth in notes slurred together and played with tremolos ["secousses"]; the Flutes, in the rise and descent of their melody, imitate the course and murmur of Water; Air is painted by sustained tones followed by trills played on the piccolos; Finally, the violins represent Fire by their liveliness and brilliance.*
>
> *The distinct characters of the Elements can be recognized, separated or intermingled, in all or in part, in the diverse repetitions that I*

have named Chaos ["Cahos"], which mark the efforts of the Elements to shake themselves loose from one another.

I have dared to undertake joining to the idea of the confusion of the Elements that of the confusion of Harmony. I have risked having all the sounds heard mixed together at first, or rather, all the notes of the Octave united in a single sound. Then these notes develop, climbing to a Unison in the progression natural to them, and after a Dissonance, one hears a perfect chord.

The program symphony is constructed in two large sections. The first, the introduction labeled "Cahos," has seven *cahos* intrusions; all but the initial one are interspersed between airs and dances that represent the autonomous Elements. The final *cahos* is followed by an "Air pour l'Amour" for flute and two violins, which leads into the second large section entitled "Les Élemens." This section is composed of a random collection of nine airs, dances, and descriptive pieces exhibiting a wide range of instrumental scoring. "L'Eau," for example, is scored for oboes, violins, bassoons, and *tambours*, whereas the final air is written for flute alone.

Unfortunately, Rebel's fertile imagination is not sustained throughout by a commensurate musical inventiveness. Nonetheless, the Chaos sections are perhaps without precedent in the eighteenth century. Plate 3 reproduces the first page of the score and shows the opening chord described above by Rebel (note the figuring of the bass). The score directs the timpani to begin at the sixteenth-notes (measure 5) and to continue through the half-notes up to the sign ∤. One thinks immediately of the more restrained "Representation of Chaos" from *The Creation* by Haydn, but it is not until Beethoven combines all the notes of the same D minor scale in the "chaotic" opening chord of the Presto episode directly before the baritone recitative in the final movement of the Ninth Symphony that we have a sound complex of such descriptive power.

Chapter 21

The Sonata and Suite for Solo Instruments

Sonatas and Suites for Violin

*T*wo large categories, the sonata and the suite, cover the bulk of the instrumental music composed for a single instrument on each part during the Baroque period in France. That is, every indication by the composer in the title, the *avertissement*, or the score suggests this mode of solo instrumental performance.

Of all ultramontane importations, the sonata caused the French musical pulse to beat most rapidly, and it was the sonata, in company with the cantata, that gave the sharpest focus to the confrontation of national styles during the first decades of the eighteenth century.[1]

If we accept Couperin's statement in his preface to *Les Goûts réunis* (1724) that the first Italian sonatas appeared in Paris over thirty years before that publication, we arrive at a date sometime before 1694. In fact, Couperin himself may have written his first sonata *en trio* as early as 1692. He modeled it upon the trio sonatas of Corelli, whose first two *opere* had been in print since 1681 and 1685, respectively.

Corelli's sonatas were not printed in France until Foucault's publication of Opus 5 about 1701 (see Pincherle 1954; trans. of 1956, 169), but they surely had been circulated and heard within the small Parisian groups dedicated to the performance of Italian music. Michel Corrette unequivocally stated in his treatise, *Le Maître de clavecin pour l'accompagnement*:

> The trios of Corelli, which had been printed in Rome, appeared for the first time at a concert given by Abbé Mathieu, the curé of Saint-André-des-Arts. This new kind of music encouraged all composers to work in a more brilliant style . . . . All concerts took on a different form; scenes and symphonies from opera were replaced by sonatas (1753, preface).

Lecerf made reference to this kind of milieu in his resigned observation that there were "not only professional musicians, but men of quality and Prelates who sing nothing else and have nothing else played in their homes but Italian Pieces and Sonatas" (1725; rpt. 1966, 2:54). Brossard remarked that "At that time [1695], all the composers of Paris, the Organists above all, had the craze, so to speak, to compose *Sonates à la manière italienne*" (1724; 1725–1730, 544).

In rare agreement, both Lecerf and Couperin admitted that "novelty and the love of change" (Lecerf) and the "greed of the French for foreign novelties above all else" (Couperin) first stimulated French interest in Italian music. At the turn of the century, the solo sonatas that comprise Corelli's Opus 5 were considered the most modern and progressive music available in Paris—a position that was eventually usurped by the incredible popularity of Vivaldi's *L'Estro armonico*, which resulted in a true "Vivaldian snobbism" in the French capital between 1715 and about 1750 (see Pincherle 1948, 259).

Certainly there was snob appeal in the cultivation of a taste for the sonata. After all, had not Louis XIV himself, as early as 1682, so thoroughly enjoyed a performance by the Dutch violinist Johann Paul Westhoff (1656–1705) of his solo violin sonata that the king nicknamed the work "La Guerre" after its programmatic movement (William S. Newman 1966, 235 and 252). And now twenty years later, it was fashionable to declare oneself a partisan of Italian music, safe in the knowledge that arbiters of style, such as the Duc d'Orléans, made no effort to hide their admiration for this music. It is with heavy sarcasm that Lecerf wrote, "What joy, what a good opinion of himself has a man who knows something of the fifth opus of Corelli!" (1725; rpt. 1966, 4:201). Foolishly, Lecerf launched a diatribe against the eleventh sonata of Corelli's Opus 5 (1725; rpt. 1966, 4:203). He denounced such harmonic practices as the use of "24 consecutive sevenths in three measures," and what is even more surprising in the light of Corelli's great melodic gifts, Lecerf found the melodic line to be "poverty-stricken, to have only scraps of melody." Perhaps this unconsidered attack was precipitated not only by Abbé Raguenet's allusions to Lecerf's lack of critical acumen, but also out of a frustrated awareness of the extent to which the younger generation of French composers was falling under the influence of the great Italian's music.

This same feeling may help to explain the ambivalence of Titon du Tillet, who, after admitting to having listened with pleasure to Italian music for over seven years at the home of the harpsichord virtuosi, Mme and Mlle Duhallay, suddenly felt compelled to cry out that as a good Frenchman, his loyalty was to Lully, Campra, Destouches, Delalande, and Couperin, as opposed to Corelli, Gasparini, Scarlatti, or Tartini (1732; supplement 1743, 756).

An alliance between sonata and dance suite had already been accomplished in the *sonata da camera*, but the vogue for sonatas in France became so great as the eighteenth century progressed that they actually invaded the realm of choreographically oriented dance music. We have already seen in the previous chapter the important place accorded an Italianate sonata in Rebel's choreographic fantasy *Les Caractères de la danse* of 1715. In 1725, Montéclair brought out a set of *Menuets tant anciens que nouveaux*, which contains 100 minuets! In his *Avertissement*, Montéclair stated that his collection was divided into two parts; the first containing "graceful and easy Minuets suitable for dancing," whereas the second part includes "more difficult Minuets in the *goût des Sonates*." Unfortunately, the major difference seems to lie in Montéclair's neat categories themselves, for the minuets of both parts are practically indistinguishable and totally undistinguished.

It is appropriate that the person who was most concerned about the efficacy of a judicious union of French and Italian styles should have composed the first French sonatas "*à la manière italienne*." Conserved in manuscript at the Bibliothèque Nationale (Brossard Collection) are "La Pucelle," "La Visonnaire," "L'Astrée" and "La Steinquerque"—the first four of François Couperin's eight trio sonatas. The Bibliothèque de Lyon has two other sonatas entitled "La Sultane" and "La Superbe." "La Superbe" is a trio sonata, but "La Sultane" is Couperin's only "*sonade en quatuor*." Its fourth part is scored for bass viol. All these sonatas date from about 1692 to about 1695. In 1726, Couperin recast three of these sonatas for use in his *Les Nations, sonades et suites de simphonies en trio*. In an "Aveu de l'autheur au public," Couperin described a subterfuge through which he had the first French sonata, his "La Pucelle," performed under the name of a fictitious Italian composer. The ruse had worked. The sonata had been well received, and Couperin was encouraged to continue composing in the same genre. The three early sonatas chosen later for inclusion in *Les Nations* were "La Pucelle," "La Visonnaire," and "L'Astrée." The only important change made by Couperin was to retitle the sonatas in order to conform better with the generic title. Thus "La Pucelle," "La Visonnaire," and "L'Astrée" became "La Françoise," "L'Espagnole," and "La Piémontoise," respectively. For the bellicose and not too interesting "La Steinquerque," Couperin substituted a more mature sonata entitled "L'Impériale."

Two programmatic sonatas, apothéoses for Corelli and Lully, crown Couperin's achievements in this genre. The Corelli "Apothéose" appears after the ten *concerts* in *Les Goûts réunis* (1724). The Lully "Apothéose" was published separately in 1725.

There is very little to indicate specific instrumentation for any of the eight trio sonatas. Only in the Lully "Apothéose" did Couperin suggest "Flutes or Violins" for the "Plainte" and "two violins" for the two short airs. Moreover, in the *Avis* for the Lully "Apothéose," he emphasized that the two "Apothéose" as well as *Les Nations* "may be performed on two Harpsichords as well as on all other instruments." As was true in the *Concerts royaux* and *Les Goûts réunis*, the latitude for performance possibilities is very great indeed.

In the case of the trio sonatas, however, Couperin was careful to mark the three staves of "La Françoise," which introduces *Les Nations* as follows: *premier dessus, deuxième dessus,* and *basse d'archet.* This undoubtedly served as a model for the rest of the collection. The upper two parts are ideal for two violins, and the numerous textual and stylistic references to Corelli strongly suggest that violins were the favored instruments for performance of these sonatas. The writing, although completely idiomatic for the violin, rarely extends beyond the third position, and no double stops are employed.

On the other hand, the Lully "Apothéose" is called a "*concert instrumental,*" and the words "*de simphonie*" are added to the first and second *dessus* designations. The fact that many of the movements in the Lully "Apothéose" derive from the type of orchestral *symphonies* used in the opera suggests that this *concert* could have been performed with more than one instrument on a part and in that situation would conform to the compositions discussed in the previous chapter.

The four sonatas of *Les Nations*, "serve only," in Couperin's words, "as Preludes or kinds of introductions" to extended dance suites. Each sonata is grouped with its suite under the generic title *Ordre.* Couperin placed Italian sonata and French dance suite in apposition on a grander scale here than in *Les Goûts réunis*, and created a series of diptychs that are reminiscent of the Bach violin sonatas and partitas (see Mellers 1950, 103). In terms of scope and breadth of material, these four sonatas far transcend any introductory role. Most have seven or eight movements ("L'Impériale" has six), whose titles, with the exception of "airs," only indicate relative tempos.

Each sonata opens with a Gravement or a Grave movement corresponding to the first movement of an Italian *sonata da chiesa.* Here, as elsewhere, is an interpenetration of national styles. The long-breathed melodies remind us of Corelli or even Handel. The closely knit part writing, with much crossing of voices, and the chains of suspensions are Italian; but the ornamentation and certain harmonic practices, such as the use of the mediant ninth chord with an augmented fifth (see, for example, "La Françoise," measure 11), are French. Only the Gravement of "L'Impériale" has the steady eighth-note bass line, the *basse travaillée* so typical of Corelli, which here supports continually intertwining melodies of great lyric sweep. In contrast, the Gravement of "La Piémontoise," with its expressive use of rests and its basically homophonic texture, resembles an operatic lament more than a sonata movement.

Most of the quick movements, usually titled Gayement or Vivement, have some form of free fugal writing. Most notable is the concluding *Vivement et marqué* of "L'Espagnole," which is a skillful cross between a chaconne and a fugue. The chaconne bass, in the minor form of the descending tetrachord, is first presented by the continuo and is accompanied only by a lively *"Badinage pour le Clavecin si l'on veut"* (Badinage for the harpsichord, if one wishes). Unfortunately, Couperin wrote out only the first eight measures of the optional harpsichord part, but this does leave clues to a possible manner of realization. Chaconne merges with fugue as the music of the bass line transfers to the second violin and becomes subject. The counter-subject is so distinctive and so consistently carried out that it is possible to view this movement as a combination of chaconne and double fugue.

The most tightly organized of all Couperin's fugal movements is the Vivement that concludes "L'Impériale." This is music particularly well suited to the violin. It has wide leaps juxtaposed with rapid scale passages. In spite of its length, it never becomes diffused. The authoritative octaves that open its long subject (reproduced in Mellers 1950, 117) generate exciting episodes that build to *stretto* passages of Bach-like concentration.

In most of the quick movements, the bass shares in the melodic material, and in the concluding Gayement of "La Françoise," it is in perpetual motion, a vortex of swirling sixteenth-notes. The fourth movement (Gayement) of the same sonata is yet another example of Couperin's ability to expand and develop his material, often in combination with independent motifs that pass in and out of the texture—sometimes never to return. This results in free variation that rarely repeats the initial melodic material exactly.

Airs figure in three of the four sonatas of *Les Nations*. (Only "L'Impériale" has none.) The airs are an entirely French contribution to the sonatas and are always framed by fast movements. In this context, they offer the greatest possible contrast of tempo and style. Their simple, symmetrical tunes almost cry out for parody treatment and have much in common with the popular *brunettes* and *air tendre* repertory.

In my opinion, the suites introduced by the sonatas of *Les Nations* are less interesting musically than the suites of *Les Goûts réunis*. To be sure, the dances are exquisitely fashioned, but it is as though Couperin were summing up the heritage of French dance types. He carefully preserved and labeled the essence of each dance for all to see. Nothing ruffles the surface; all is neatly arranged, predictable, and quite conservative. Each suite begins with an allemande, which is followed by two courantes, a sarabande, gigue, and optional dances; sometimes an optional dance has been inserted between the sarabande and gigue. Most of the allemandes revert to the earlier type, which has little unity between its two sections. In these suites, one misses the occasional dramatic outbursts of an allemande like "La Raphaéle" or that of *Ordre 11* of *Les Goûts réunis*; one looks for some sign of the pathos of the "Sarabande très grave" behind the elegantly shaped melodies of these sarabandes.

Only the chaconnes, the passacailles, and the rondeaux capture some of the fantasy and imagination we have come to expect from mature Couperin. Three of the four *ordres* include one chaconne or passacaille. Couperin himself made little distinction between the two genres, for he labeled the example from the first *ordre* "Chaconne ou Passacaille." Most of these use techniques borrowed from the large orchestral chaconnes of Lully's operatic *divertissements*. The D major chaconne of "L'Impériale" is the most extensive. The middle section of its large three-part form is in the tonic minor key. All chaconnes show increased rhythmic activity as they progress, and several include episodes in which the bass line is in the treble clef—resembling the scoring found in Lully's orchestral chaconnes for two flutes (usually recorders) with a viola (or violin) continuo.

Along with the ten *concerts* of *Les Goûts réunis*, the two "Apothéoses" climax Couperin's efforts to achieve a synthesis between French and Italian musical styles. *Le Parnasse ou L'Apothéose de Corelli* is subtitled "Grande sonade en trio." It is divided into seven contrasting movements that bear programmatic titles as well as tempo indications. The program concerns Corelli's happy welcome by the Muses at Mount Parnassus. There are opportunities here for the apposition of Italian *vivacité* with French *douceur*: the former in the scenes of general rejoicing (Nos. 2, 6, 7) and Corelli's enthusiasm (No. 4) and the latter in the charming pastoral scenes describing Corelli's drinking at the Spring of Hypocrene (No. 3) and sleeping to the accompaniment of a *sommeil* (No. 5).

The opening movement is a Gravement representing Corelli "at the foot of Parnassus asking the Muses to allow him to be received among them." It is like the first movement of an Italian church sonata that exhibits great purity of style. The upper lines have direction and purpose; their melodies combine in wide arches supported by an eighth-note bass line that is nearly always present.

The fugal movements (Nos. 2 and 7) show Couperin's skill in devising subjects that work convincingly in short *stretti* and generate much forward motion. Exciting passage work interpenetrates the fugal texture; fugal procedures are never adhered to consistently throughout, and this may make the movements more effective as pieces of pure chamber music.

Number 3 ("Corelli drinking at the spring of Hypocrene") is a bucolic mood piece. The hypnotic spell of murmuring waters is achieved by the continuous, gentle motion of eighth-notes slurred in groups of four. It is a Lullian nature scene infused with Corelli's suspension chains, which help sustain the motion by cadence evasion.

Number 5 is a *Sommeil*, and Number 6 ("The Muses Awaken Corelli") is a piece of theater music in which trumpet calls blazon forth Corelli's arrival before Apollo. Unlike real trumpet fanfares with their static harmony, this simulated version is free to range far and wide in its harmonic organization. The short composition begins in D major and ends in F-sharp minor after rapid excursions through A major and C-sharp minor.

The *concert instrumental* entitled *Apothéose composé à la mémoire immortelle de l'incomparable Monsieur de Lully* is a trio sonata only by virtue of its final section, "La Paix de Parnasse." Couperin used a series of twelve descriptive pieces and airs to "introduce" the final movement, a "Sonade en trio."

The twelve programmatic pieces that form the bulk of the "Apothéose" draw heavily for their inspiration from the descriptive *symphonies* of Lully's *tragédie lyrique*. Again, it is a Lully seen through the enlightened eye of Couperin, with all the harmonic resources, color effects, and sense of fantasy used on a scale unknown by the Florentine. The harmonic range of the twelve pieces is in itself much greater than is normally found in a Couperin *ordre*. Flanked by movements in G minor and G major, the inner portions of the "Apothéose" are in the keys of B-flat, E-flat, and C minor.

The opening movement ("Lully in the Elysian Fields") is an elegiac operatic *ritournelle*, its expressiveness enhanced by the sharp dissonances that result naturally from the linear writing. Numbers 3, 4, 5, 6, and 7, entitled "Flight of Mercury," "Descent of Apollo," "Subterranean Clamor," "Laments," and "Rising up of Lully," respectively, are all examples of stage music for which any number of models could be found in the court ballets or *tragédies lyriques* of the *grand siècle*. Indeed, the source for "Subterranean Clamor" is undoubtedly the "Trembleurs" scene from *Isis* (Act IV, scene i), and the sighs of the two flutes in the "Plainte" resemble the flute passages in the "Plainte de Pan" in the same key, also from *Isis* (Act III, scene vi).

Putting together the two styles begins in earnest with Number 10, at which point "Apollo persuades Lully and Corelli that the joining of French and Italian taste can only result in the perfection of Music." The joining includes an "Essai en forme d'ouverture," two Airs, and the concluding "Sonade en trio." In each case, "Lully," "Corelli," and their Muses are assigned their respective roles on the staves of music. Lully's part is always scored in the French violin clef (G on the first line); Corelli's, on the other hand, is in the normal violin clef (G on the second line).

The "Essai en forme d'ouverture" exploits both the dotted rhythms of the French overture and the chains of triplets so characteristically Italian. The faster middle section unites arpeggio figuration and circles of fifths with a discreet use of French ornamentation. "Lully" and "Corelli," play the two short *a2* "airs," each taking a turn with his solo violin on the subject while the other plays the accompaniment—a delightful artifice of combining French ornamentation (see especially the chains of *coulés* played by "Lully") with Italian sequences and continuous eighth-note motion.

In the concluding "Sonade en trio," we are informed that because of complaints by the French Muses, "One should henceforth say *Sonade, Cantade*, in speaking their language, just as one says *Ballade, Sérénade*, etc." Couperin's attempts to appease the "complaining French Muses" are not as far afield as the obstinate use of French titles in Book 2 of the solo sonatas of Jean-Baptiste Anet (1676–1755), in which "Allaigre" is substituted for "Allegro."

The "Sonade en trio" is an excellent example of a church sonata. Its four movements are Gravement, Vivement, Rondement, and Vivement. The opening Gravement begins like a French allemande, but introduces consecutive and combined passages that best characterize the two *goûts*. Example 21-1 below illustrates the extent of the contrast between these passages in which a French nature scene gives way to a forceful Italian statement that is organized in sequences and is practically devoid of ornamentation.

Example 21-1. Couperin: Extract from Gravement of the *Apothéose . . . de Lulli* (after the ed. of 1725).

Couperin had chosen to cap another of his most important chamber works with a sonata. The final *concert* of *Les Goûts réunis* is an excellent example of a chamber sonata (if it is played by one instrument and continuo). It also is organized in the classic four-movement scheme; the movements here are Prelude, Allemande, Sarabande grave, and *Fuguété* (see Chapter 20).

During the period 1692–1695 when Couperin was composing his earliest sonatas, Sébastien de Brossard, Elisabeth-Claude Jacquet de La Guerre, and Jean-Féry Rebel were also experimenting with the new genre. Brossard was well acquainted with the Italian sonata. In his dictionary he gave us one of the first classifications of the sonata into *da chiesa* and *da camera*. In fact, he had copied the Opus 5 sonatas by Giovanni Battista Bassani (ca. 1647–1716) from the second edition of 1688. Brossard composed four sonatas, two of which are for violins and an obbligato bass viol; the other two, which were never completed, are for solo violin and continuo. The style is conservative and austere with little ornamentation, and reflects the influence of Lully more than Corelli. A clue as to why Brossard, a partisan of Italian music, should compose in such a conservative style is offered by his comments regarding the Bassani sonatas, which he described as

> *completely charming and excellent and not too difficult to perform, in contrast to the typical [ones] of the Italians, who believe they have not written a beautiful sonata unless they have stuffed it with fast movements that are often extravagant and without basis other than their fantasy, and with a perpetual wrangling more suitable for grating on one's ears than soothing them (1724; 1725–1730, 545).*

Of greater musical merit are the sonatas by Elisabeth-Claude Jacquet de La Guerre. A set of six sonatas is in manuscript, and six were printed in 1707 with the *Pièces de clavecin qui peuvent se jouer sur le viollon* (see Borroff 1966, 87–95 and Cessac 1994, 2:263–336). The manuscript sonatas, loaned or given to Brossard in 1695, comprise two sonatas "a violino solo e viol da gamba obbligata" with organ or harpsichord continuo, and a set of four trio sonatas. The two solo sonatas along with those by Brossard and Rebel are among the first examples of the genre in France. The solo and trio sonatas by Jacquet de La Guerre exhibit some progressive features, including what may be the first use of double stops in French solo violin music. Interesting shifts of texture also result where the obbligato bass viol occasionally separates from the continuo line and takes on a solo role.

Regarding the printed set of six sonatas, Edith Borroff takes issue with La Laurencie's comment that "One can hardly understand how

the King . . . could feel any surprise in hearing this innocent music."
La Laurencie, objects Miss Borroff:

does not do La Guerre justice, for she used strong materials from the
modern style of her own day, presenting them with taste and
assurance and wielding them into effective forms with a power and
style both personal and representative of the best of that remarkable
generation of which she was an honored member (1966, 158).

Based on Borroff's study, it is clear that the printed sonatas combine
Italian light polyphony and harmonic procedures in the quick movements with French formal ingenuity that ranges from a highly developed French overture (Sonata No. 4) to long free-form structures that
eschew exact repetitions. As in the manuscript sonatas, the solo role of
the bass viol at times thickens the *a*2 texture.

The *Recueil de douze sonates à II et III parties avec la basse chiffrée* by
Jean-Féry Rebel was published in 1712–1713 but dates from about
1695. Brossard owned copies of these sonatas and wrote: "They are all
magnificent; and I have heard them performed many times by the
Composer himself in a charming manner" (1724; 1725–1730, 335).
The collection includes seven trio sonatas and five solo sonatas. The
writing for the solo instrument is conservative; it displays far fewer
Italian traits than are found, for example, in the earlier sonatas of
Couperin or the sonatas of Jacquet de La Guerre. In fact, Lecerf was
so pleased with Rebel's restraint that he singled him out as one com-
poser who "has the taste and care to temper it [Italian fire] with
French wisdom and gentleness, and he has abstained from those
frightening and monstrous cadenza passages [*chutes*] that so delight the
Italians" (1725; rpt. 1966, 2:95–96).

Also published in 1713 was Rebel's *12 Sonates à violon seul mellées*
de plusieurs récits pour la viole. The collection is divided into two parts:
most of the first six sonatas have tempo or descriptive titles, the second six are composed of the typical dances of the French dance suite.
More advanced technically than the earlier set of twelve sonatas, this
collection makes some use of double stops and tremolo passages,
although the music remains mostly in the first three positions. The
récits for bass viol convert several movements into an *a*3 texture. At
times, the viol *récit* is no more than an elaboration of the continuo
line; at other times, it is independent of the continuo and vies for
dominance with the solo line itself.

The most prolific among the first generation of French sonata
composers was François Duval (ca. 1673–1728), whose seven collections span the years 1704–1720. Duval was also the first composer in
France to publish sonatas for the violin, and beginning with his Book

4 (1708), he was the first French composer of violin sonatas to favor the more common G clef over the French violin clef. In his *Premier livre de sonates et autres pièces pour le violon et la basse* of 1704, French dance measures and descriptive touches blend artfully with more advanced Italian instrumental techniques such as new bowing styles, double stops, and passages that go beyond the third position (La Laurencie 1922–1924, 1:117–120). This collection is "the first officially sanctioned acknowledgement of the French taste for such Italianisms" (W. S. Newman 1966, 365).

Undoubtedly, Louis-Nicolas Clérambault and Jean-François Dandrieu were among the organists described by Brossard as having the "craze" to compose Italianate sonatas. As might be anticipated, the six sonatas by Clérambault (all in manuscript) and the *Livre de sonates en trio* (1705) by Dandrieu reflect the polyphonic bias of the organist, as do the later collections by Louis-Antoine Dornel.

In the case of Dandrieu, this bias results from time to time in the use of the violoncello obbligato part as a linear partner in its own right, thereby thickening the texture to *a*4. Most of Dandrieu's sonatas are church sonatas, which often have a short transitional third movement (Adagio or Largo) that, in typical Corelli fashion, ends in a Phrygian cadence on the dominant of a minor key. Instead of progressing to the expected tonic, it moves to the tonic of the relative major key for the final movement.[2] Much of Corelli is heard in the trio sonatas of Dandrieu, as Example 21-2, below, from the Adagio of Sonata No. 5, illustrates.

Example 21-2. Dandrieu: Extract from Adagio of Sonata No. 5 (after ed. of 1705).

Couperin and Leclair are the two pillars of the Baroque sonata in France. In the generation of composers between these two monumental figures there were perhaps as many as thirty-five minor masters (see W. S. Newman, 1966, 367) who were busily engaged in supplying the increasing demand of the French public for sonata literature. In a study of some of the eighteenth-century editions of selected composers, one observes certain trends in the composition of sonatas that culminated in the four books of Jean-Marie Leclair.

Among the composers who published collections of violin sonatas before the appearance of Leclair's first book in 1723 are Joseph Marchand (1673–1747), Jean-Baptiste Senallié (ca. 1687–1730), Louis Francoeur "the elder" (ca. 1692–1745), François Francoeur "the younger" (1698–1787), and two Italian composers residing in Paris: Michele (called Michel) Mascitti (ca. 1664–1760) and Antonio Piani, called "Desplanes napolitano" (1678–after1757).

The violinist Mascitti published nine collections of sonatas between 1704 and 1738. In a reversal of the general trend of French composers seeking to absorb the style of the Italian sonata, Mascitti admitted in his *Avertissement* to his Opus 11 (1706) that "I have found such beautiful things in French music that I have applied myself to rendering this [French music] compatible with *le goût italien* in some of my Sonatas." Except for a more conspicuous use of double stops, Mascitti's sonatas do not progress technically beyond those of his teacher, Corelli.

In 1707 Joseph Marchand published his *Suites des pièces mêlées de sonates pour le violon et la basse*, dedicated to Louis XIV. An independent *fantaisie* opens the collection. Seven groups of pieces follow. Each contains six to ten movements. No functional difference between suite and sonata is discernable, and the prevailing homophonic texture discourages overt Italian influences.

The single collection of solo sonatas by Piani, published in 1712, is worth noting because of its increased technical difficulties (use of triple stops, for example) and explicit performance directions (such as ◄■■ and ■■► to indicate crescendo and diminuendo) (La Laurencie 1922–1924, 1:171).[3]

Louis Francoeur and his younger brother, François each composed two books of sonatas published in 1715 and 1726 (Louis) and in 1720 and 1730 (François). They advanced the technique of violin writing in France by offering varieties of bowings, use of the first five positions, use of triple and quadruple stops, wide leaps, and rapid arpeggio figurations that demand the left-hand thumb on the fingerboard in some instances (see La Laurencie, 1922–1924, 1:200 and 259).

In the development of a more technically demanding repertory for the solo violin in France, however, Jean-Baptiste Senallié (or Senaillé) is the most important composer between Couperin and Leclair. A violinist himself, who had studied in Modena with Tomasso Antonio Vitali, the son of the great Giovanni Battista Vitali, Senallié published fifty solo violin sonatas in five books from 1710 to 1727. The *Mercure* of June 1738 is explicit in assigning responsibility to

Senallié for the greater development of technical violin writing during the 1720s:

> *He had done some visiting in Italy and had brought back enough of this ultramontane taste to blend it artfully with beautiful French melody. The progress that the violin has made in France since then is due to him, because he mixed things that were difficult to execute into his Music; and as his* Airs de symphonie *were agreeable and had a certain brilliance, everybody was charmed by them and wished to learn how to play them, especially at that time when we had scarcely begun to familiarize ourselves with music that was a little difficult (cited by La Laurencie 1922–1924, 1:171).*

In addition to his elaborate passage work, long and frequent trills, his attainment of the seventh position, and his use of up to twenty-four notes on a bow stroke (see La Laurencie 1922–1924, 1:178–179), Senallié enriched the harmonic vocabulary of the violin sonata. Of considerable interest is his use of the bi-modality that had intrigued French composers since the middle years of the seventeenth century. Leclair carried this purposeful ambiguity of mode to its highest point, especially in his third and fourth books, but Senallié is the most important precursor of Leclair in this practice (see an extract from the Adagio of Sonata No. 9 in Senallié's Book 4 of 1721 in Example 21-3).

Senallié also experimented with deriving thematic material to unify different movements of the sonata. He used this device in a systematic manner in the ninth sonata from his Book 3 (1716) and the fifth sonata from Book 4. In the former case, as shown in Example 21-4, three movements of the sonata evolve from one basic "head-motive."

The forty-nine sonatas for solo violin and continuo, the twenty-five trio sonatas, and the twelve sonatas for two violins *en duo* by Jean-Marie Leclair crown the history of the violin sonata in France. The impressive list of secondary sources attests to the increased awareness of the importance of Leclair as a major Baroque composer of sonatas.[4] The solo violin sonatas are grouped into four books of twelve sonatas each (Book 1, Opus 1, 1723; Book 2, Opus 2, ca. 1728; Book 3, Opus 5, ca. 1734; and Book 4, Opus 9, ca. 1743). The forty-ninth sonata is a posthumous publication, Opus 15. It was printed in 1767. The majority of the sonatas are cast in the typical Slow-Fast-Slow-Fast movement scheme. There is no attempt to adhere to either chamber or church distinction. Rather, the sonatas mix elements of both within the same composition. Often the first two movements use only tempo designations, and the final movements (or movement) use dance titles.

Such, for example, are the first and third sonatas of Book 4, whose movements appear in the following orders, respectively: Adagio, Allegro assai, Andante, Minuetto; and Andante, Allegro, Sarabande, Tambourin. Reflecting the growing popularity of the transverse flute, many sonatas bear the direction "may be played on the *flûte allemande.*" This carries into the title of Book 2: "Pour le violon et pour la flûte traversière." In some of the sonatas that are marked this way, Leclair added a more difficult part "pour le violon seul" (see, for example, Sonatas No. 2 and No. 7 from Book 4).

There is evidence that Leclair, like Senallié before him, unified some of his sonatas through free use of a "head-motive" technique. The clearest example (Example 21-5) is that of Sonata No. 12 from Book 1, in which the two Allegro movements find their genesis in the opening Largo.

Example 21-3. Senallié: Extract from Adagio of Sonata No. 9, Book 4 (after ed. of 1721).

Example 21-4. Senallié: Thematic unity in Sonata No. 9, Book 3 (after ed. of 1716).

Example 21-5. Leclair: Thematic unity in Sonata No. 12, Book 1 (after ed. of 1723).

Leclair is French to the core in the *beau chant* of dance movements like minuets, sarabandes, gavottes, tambourins, musettes, and rondeaux. Here and there, he composed some dances with variations. The largo theme of the Sarabande of Sonata No. 9 of Book 1, for example, is followed by an allegro variation that resembles the old technique of diminution; this in turn is followed by a closing variation that employs the Alberti bass throughout.

Through Somis and others, Leclair had thoroughly absorbed the technical advances made in Italian violin music after Corelli. The *Mercure* of June 1738 erroneously claimed that Leclair was "the first Frenchman who, in imitation of the Italians, used double stops . . . he pushed this device so far that the Italians themselves confessed that he was a master of the genre" (1115). As we have seen, Mlle de La Guerre had used double stops as early as 1695. Leclair did, to be sure, "push" their use along with triple and quadruple stops to a degree never before realized in France. Furthermore, he developed the use of double trills in thirds and sixths, a left-hand tremolo, a great variety of bow strokes—all carefully notated (Lemoine recognizes five different combinations of legato, spiccato, and détaché in the sonatas)—and by the eighth sonata of Book 4, he had reached the eighth position.

One should remember, however, that in spite of the technical competence required to play these sonatas by Leclair, the virtuoso elements were not used as ends in themselves, and they never compromise the musical integrity of the sonatas. In spite of the number of allegro or allegro assai movements, Leclair took pains to emphasize in the *Avertissement* to his *Ouvertures et sonates en trio* of 1753 that he did not mean "too fast a movement" by the term *allegro*: "It is a gay movement. Those who push the tempo too much, above all in the pieces of character like the Fugues in 4/4 meter, render the melody trivial." Like Couperin, he insisted on scrupulous reading of his ornamentation, which was written out and symbolized. In the *Avertissement* to

Book 4, he commented forcefully: "One important point, on which one cannot insist too much, is to avoid the confusion of notes that are sometimes added to the melodic and expressive passages but which serve only to disfigure them."

Robert Preston has convincingly demonstrated that the sophisticated harmonic language of the Leclair sonatas is as important to any study of the composer's style as are his advanced violinistic techniques. After his first book, Leclair frequently used augmented sixth chords, Neapolitan sixths (often with a major seventh added), and diminished sevenths. He often used the latter chord, as did Rameau, to climax a long phrase or to evade a cadence (see, for example, the Adagio of Sonata 10, Book 2). The modulatory schemes are as expansive and original as may be found anywhere in the music of the French Baroque, and Leclair's sensitivity to key contrasts, both from one movement to the next and within the same movement, is highly developed.

The adagio movements of the fifth and ninth sonatas of Book 4 contain the quintessence of Leclair's refinement of harmony. His greatly expanded harmonic vocabulary parallels that of Rameau and even rivals that of J. S. Bach. In these movements, Leclair, like Bach, appears isolated from the music of his generation. Most of the composers contemporary to Leclair had already succumbed to the short, symmetrical melodies and the slow harmonic rhythm of the *style galant*.

The adagio of the fifth sonata is reproduced in facsimile from the ca. 1743 edition as Plate 4. It begins in F major and cadences in C minor in the eighth measure. A new section in A-flat major follows with transitory modulations to B-flat minor (measure 13), F minor (measure 19), and G minor (measure 25), and the movement closes with a Phrygian cadence on the dominant of A major. These are just the bare harmonic bones, however, and tell us nothing of the poetry of the forceful participation by the bass in close imitation (measures 5–6) or of a continually unfolding melodic line, widely arched and rich in invention, that only turns back on itself at the A-flat statement in measure 9.

The adagio of the ninth sonata can be found in facsimile at the end of Geoffrey Nutting's article in *The Musical Quarterly* (facing page 517). It begins in A major with a melodic and harmonic innocence that gradually gives way before the darkening colors of chords borrowed from the tonic minor key, a remarkable enharmonic modulation to C-sharp minor, and the use of triple and quadruple stops. Only the bass line remains undisturbed, and as so often is the case in Bach, its abstract pattern unifies the entire movement.

Worlds apart is the opening adagio of the twelfth sonata of Book 3, which is reproduced from the 1734 edition as Plate 5. This movement dramatically reveals the extent to which Leclair could make use of decorative arabesques, sweeping *tirades*, and double trills, set off by the sharply pointed rhythms of the overture and by a harmonic background that ranges from passages in slow harmonic rhythm to a series of rapid transitory modulations achieved through secondary dominants.

The twelve trio sonatas that comprise Leclair's Opus 4 (ca. 1730) and Opus 13 (1753) are impressive works that should be better known. In Nutting's words, here is Leclair, the "great craftsman-composer, undistracted by his pursuit of violin virtuosity" (1964, 507). The *Sonates à deux violons sans basse*, Opus 3, another work destined for the amateur performer, is superior musically to similar sets by La Barre, Boismortier, Aubert, and Guignon. Leclair's combinations of sonorities and his ability to "orchestrate" (Pincherle) the violins give pleasure to listener and performer alike.

Although they are outside the scope of this book, contemporaries and successors of Leclair such as de Tremais, Boismortier, Mondonville, Louis-Gabriel Guillemain (1705–1770), and Jean-Pierre Guignon (1702–1774) all contributed to the later development of the violin sonata in France. Of these composers, de Tremais, Mondonville, and Guillemain were the most experimental. A virtuoso performer, de Tremais (first name unknown)[5] is thought to have studied with Tartini. De Tremais was the first French composer to require pizzicati. Three of the six solo sonatas of his Opus 4 (1740) make use of scordatura tuning. His music is fraught with harmonic audacities and technical difficulties. There are multiple stops and as many as sixteen notes to a bow stroke. In Guillemain's *Amusements pour le violon seul* (Opus 18, 1762), we have the first use in France of sonatas *senza basso*. Mondonville's *Sonates pour le violon & B. C.*, Opus 1 of 1733, are already technically advanced over most of the sonatas of his contemporaries. His "Les Sons harmoniques," *Sonatas à violon seul avec B. C.* (Opus 4, 1738), constitutes the first extensive use of harmonics on the violin. "The same sounds are found on all sorts of instruments . . . . Why should we not use them with the same sensitivity?" (*Avertissement*). The harmonics are indicated with a trill sign and are often used in alternation with double stops.

Sonatas and Suites for Flute

"The instruments that are the most popular now in Paris are the harpsichord and the transverse or German flute. Today, the French play these instruments with unparalleled *delicatesse*." So wrote Nemeitz in his *Le Séjour de Paris* (1727, 70–71) about twenty years after the publication of Jacques Hotteterre's treatise, *Principes de la flûte traversière ou flûte d'Allemagne* (Paris, 1707, later editions in 1713, 1720, 1721, 1722, ca. 1728, 1741, and ca. 1765). We have seen that Leclair and others had specified the use of the transverse flute as a substitute instrument in certain of their violin sonatas and that Dornel, in 1711, had gathered eight violin sonatas and four flute suites together in one collection.

At this time, the transverse flute co-existed with the recorder in much the same way as the violoncello did with the bass viol, but gradually, solo performance on the recorder was restricted more and more to the amateur who could not achieve a high degree of performance skill on the flute. At first much flute repertory indicated in its titles that the music could be performed on the recorder or oboe—this again was a practical means of stimulating a wider dissemination of the music. Later in the century, however, it was evident that the recorder had become an instrument of last resort. Thus, in his Opus 34, which includes six sonatas for four parts "différentes et également travaillées" (1731), Boismortier specified "transverse flutes, violins, or other instruments" for the upper parts, but added that the treble part could be played on the recorder "in case of need."

Interest in the transverse flute was stimulated by the virtuoso performances of Philibert Rébillé (called Philibert, ca. 1639–1717), René-Pignon Descoteaux (ca. 1646–1728), and Michel de la Barre (ca. 1675–1745) that took place at court near the turn of the century. These men were all part of the king's musicians (*Chambre* and *Écurie*) and were flutists in the Paris Opera. The *Mercure de France* of June 1725 reveals that Louis XIV took great pleasure in hearing Philibert and Descoteaux and had them come often to play in his apartments and in the wooded glades of Versailles. Beginning with the appearance of Michel Blavet (1700–1768) as flute soloist at the Concert Spirituel on 1 October 1726, the flute surpassed the recorder and began to rival the violin as a virtuoso solo instrument.

An enormous amount of eighteenth century French literature was written for the flute beginning with La Barre's *Pièces pour la flûte traversière avec la basse continue* of 1702 and going through the thirty solo and eighteen trio sonatas by Jacques-Christophe Naudot (ca. 1690–1762). This repertory is less of a *terra incognita* today thanks to the pioneering work of Jane Bowers.[6]

Between 1702 and 1722, Michel de La Barre brought out eighteen books of pieces for the flute or the flute with other instruments. The personal rapport that could exist between composer and consumer is documented by La Barre's statement in his *Avertissement* for the *Deuxième livre de pièces pour la flûte traversière avec basse continue*

(1710). In discussing the total compass of the instrument, La Barre commented:

> *There are two or three notes that I believe no one knows [how to produce] and I would not know how to tell him in writing how to perform these notes; But if those who would like to learn would take the trouble to pass by my home, . . . it would give me great pleasure to show them how, with no obligation to them.*

La Barre's *Troisième livre des trios pour les violons, flûtes et hautbois* of 1707 contains five trio sonatas for *violon, flûtes et hautbois* as well as six trio sonatas for two flutes and continuo that, curiously, W. S. Newman did not mention. They are all four-movement sonatas that mix dances (gigues, gavottes, rondeaux) with Italianate preludes. Three of the six trio sonatas include two fugues (movements two and four), and all but one end with a fugue. La Barre's "fugues" are far from academic exercises in the "learned style"; except for initial points of imitation, they usually ignore consistent application of fugal procedures. The final movement of the last sonata is yet another example of a combination "fugue" and "gigue."

La Barre composed pieces scored for two treble instruments without bass and was the first to have this kind of work published in collections. Thirteen of his collections of suites for two flutes *sans basse* were published between 1709 and 1731. As is so often the case during this period of wide latitude in performance possibilities, one must beware of categorizing and tabulating on the basis of title alone. Composers and publishers were often so eager to propagate performances and sales or both that their *avertissements* at times belied their titles. The *Avertissement* to La Barre's first book for flute and continuo points out that the accompaniment may be dropped for most of the pieces.

Jacques Hotteterre, "le Romain," (1674–1763) was more influential as a flute virtuoso and writer of instruction manuals than as a composer for his instrument, although Jane Bowers vouches for the high musical quality of his works, which "are more consistently imaginative and well wrought than the works of La Barre" (1971, 159). Of some interest is the little instruction book, *L'Art de préluder sur la flûte traversière, sur la flûte à bec, sur le hautbois, et autres instrumens de dessus* of 1719, which includes exercises called preludes along with many musical examples to illustrate various problems of performance. Lully heads the list of composers from whom Hotteterre draws his examples. Lully is cited thirty-two times here thirty-two years after his death, while Corelli comes in a poor second with ten examples.

Joseph Bodin de Boismortier was the most prolific composer of flute music in the first half of the eighteenth century. Bowers lists forty-eight opus numbers by Boismortier that include parts for flute. He was most influential in establishing the sonata rather than the suite as the preferred form for flute music in France. From 1724 to 1733, he composed eight books of sonatas for two flutes without bass. The flute duets of 1725 (Opus 6) include six sonatas and, as Example 21-6 from the Allemande of the last sonata shows, it is attractive music idiomatically conceived for the instrument. The four sets of sonatas for flute and continuo (Opus 3, 1724; Opus 9, 1725; Opus 19, 1727; Opus 44, 1733) are among the first of their kind in France. The six sonatas of Opus 3 are typical of his style. Each is in four movements and each is a *sonata da camera* dominated by French dances (allemandes, courantes, sarabandes, gavottes). The music is superficially elegant and makes few demands on listener or performer. The six sonatas of Opus 91 (1741)[7] are the only examples in France of works composed for flute and obbligato keyboard. Boismortier also left us ten sets of trio sonatas, composed between 1724 and 1740, that include parts for at least one flute, and during the decade 1720–1730, he published about thirty concertos that include parts for solo flute, which can be reduced to trio sonatas "by omitting the *ripieno*" (Paillard 1954–1955, 146).

Example 21-6. Boismortier: Extract from Allemande of Sonata No. 6, Opus 6, for two flutes without bass (after ed. of 1725).

Although mainly committed to the concerto (see Chapter 20), Michel Corrette followed the lead of Boismortier in composing sonatas for two flutes without bass (Opus 2, 1727). More important for the solo flute literature in France are the sonatas of two performer-composers: Jacques-Christophe Naudot and Michel Blavet. Naudot was less interested in duet sonatas and concentrated instead on pieces for flute and bass; six books are extant. On the other hand, Blavet's Opus 1 (1728) contains six sonatas for two flutes without bass, while his Opus 2 (1732) and Opus 3, (1740) are collections of sonatas for flute and bass. Between 1731 and 1735, Blavet rivaled the popularity of the violinists Leclair and Guignon at the Concert Spirituel.

Many other composers contributed to the burgeoning flute literature in France before a decline set in between 1740 and 1750. Chief among these are Pierre-Gabriel Buffardin, Louis de Caix d'Hervelois, Nicolas Chédeville, André Chéron, Louis-Gabriel Guillemain,

Jacques Louillet, Thomas Lot, J.-J. Cassanéa de Mondonville, Quentin Le Jeune, Clair-Nicolas Roger, and Alexandre Villeneuve.

Sonatas for Violoncello

The violoncello was introduced into French chamber music even before it reached the French opera orchestra.[8] The *Sonates à deux violons et violoncello obligato con organo* by Jacquet de La Guerre, although undated, were given by La Guerre to Brossard in 1695 (see Brossard 1724; 1725–1730, 544). In 1705, Dandrieu's *Livre des sonates en trio pour deux violons, violoncelle et basse continue* allows the cello a modest amount of independence from the continuo line.

Chapter 15 of Michel Corrette's *Méthode théorique et pratique pour apprendre . . . le violoncelle* (1741) is addressed to those who already "know how to play the Viol and who wish to learn the Violoncello . . . as the majority of those who play the Viol presently have a taste for playing the Violoncello" (43). Corrette's treatise appeared two years after the spectacular success of Martin Berteau (Berthau, Berteaud, 1709–1771) as violoncello soloist at the Concert Spirituel in 1739. Berteau's performance had captivated his audience ten years after the publication of the first solo sonatas for violoncello in 1729, the Opus 26 of Boismortier. As is often the case, multiple performance possibilities are allowed by its title, *Cinq sonates pour le violoncelle, viole ou basson*. The sonatas are all in the Slow-Fast-Slow-Fast tempo scheme and include at least one dance movement. This collection includes a concerto (for cello, viol, or bassoon) that qualifies for the position of the first French solo concerto. Boismortier followed this collection with a second set of five sonatas for violoncello (or bassoon or viol) and one trio sonata for violoncello, bassoon or viol, and bass (Opus 50, 1734). Neither collection makes difficult demands on the performer, and in spite of a compass of two octaves and a fifth, the tessitura rarely requires leaving the first position. The six sonatas for cello and viol or bassoon by Michel Corrette subtitled "Les Délices de la solitude" (Opus 20, ca. 1733) are of comparable difficulty.

Of much greater significance are the four books of *Six sonates pour le violoncelle avec la basse continue* (1733, 1737, 1739, 1740) by Jean-Baptiste Barrière (1707–1747). Indeed, Berteau's performance at the Concert Spirituel in 1739, the eventual publication in 1740 of Books 1–4 of Barrière's cello sonatas (see W. S. Newman 1966, 388), and Corrette's method of 1741 did more than anything else to popularize the cello in France and doom the bass viol as a solo instrument, in spite of the great prestige of such virtuosi as Antoine Forqueray 1672–1745) and Louis de Caix d'Hervelois (1680–1760).

A mere glance at the incipits of the Barrière sonatas (see Shaw 1963, 253–266) reveals that we are no longer in the realm of works for cello *or* other instruments sharing the same range. Double stops abound. Sweeping *tirades* of thirty-second notes found in certain Adagio movements (see, for example, Sonata No. 5, of Book 1) would not be out of place in a Bach cello suite. The movement scheme in Books 1–3 is basically Slow-Fast-Slow-Fast. In Book 4, however, Barrière adopted the three-movement scheme of the Italian concerto.

Suites for Viol

La Barre concluded the *Avertissement* to his 1710 set of suites for the transverse flute with a tribute to Marin Marais: "I believed that for the glory of my Flute and my own, I should follow the example of M. Marais, who took so much care and trouble to perfect the Viol and who succeeded so happily in this end." In like manner, we take a backward glance and conclude this chapter with a discussion of the extensive literature for one, two, or three viols by Marais and his followers.[9]

According to Jean Rousseau (1644–1699), "the first men to excel as performers on the Viol in France were Messieurs Maugard [André Maugars] and Hotman [Nicolas Hotman, before 1613–1663]" (1687, 23). Mersenne deemed Hotman to be one of the best viol players. However, it was Hotman's student, Sainte-Colombe (fl. 1670–1700) who was really responsible for developing both the instrument itself and the technique of viol performance in the seventeenth century. Rousseau dedicated his treatise to his teacher, Sainte-Colombe, and informs us that it was Sainte-Colombe who added the seventh string to the instrument, thus extending its range down to low A. The use of the seventh string may be easily observed in Sainte-Colombe's *Concerts à deux violes esgales*, a manuscript collection now in the Bibliothèque Nationale (*Rés.* Vma MS 866),[5] which contains sixty-seven *concerts*, each containing from two to three pieces that are unified by tonality. They show Sainte-Colombe to have been a composer full of fantasy and rich imagination. Dances and character pieces co-exist. The most frequently found titled dances in the *Concerts* are sarabandes (twenty-two), gavottes (twenty-six), and gigues (twenty). Surprisingly, it contains only twelve minuets and five courantes. Until recently, the little known of Sainte-Colombe's life we owed to Titon du Tillet, who wrote that Sainte-Colombe gave concerts in his home with his daughters. One played treble viol, the other played bass. Together with him, they formed a trio of viols.[11]

Another of Sainte-Colombe's students, Danoville (first name unknown, fl. 1687), published his *Art de toucher le dessus et la basse de viole* in the same year as Jean Rousseau's *Traité de la viole* (1687).

Danoville, like Rousseau, was concerned with hand positions, finger charts, and ornamentation, and even more than Rousseau with lavishing praise on his teacher, whom he characterized as the "Orphée de nostre temps."

The earliest extant music for solo viol in France is by Dubuisson, who composed four suites for bass viol without continuo that date from 1666 (manuscript in Library of Congress). The *Pièces de violle en musique et en tablature* (1685) composed by de Machy appears to be the first music printed for solo viol in France. It preceded by two years the viol tutors by Jean Rousseau and Danoville and by one year the first book of *Pièces à une et à deux violes* by Marais. The collection by de Machy, about whom little is known, contains eight suites, four in staff notation and four in tablature. De Machy's preface, with its support for two hand positions (one for melody, one for chords), instigated a strong attack by Jean Rousseau (see Lesure 1960). In any case, this burst of activity in the late 1680s documents Rousseau's observation that "until recently [the viol] has not been esteemed in France."

The most important of all Sainte-Colombe's students was Marin Marais (1656–1728). Johann Gottfried Walther in his *Musikalisches Lexicon . . .* of 1732 declared him to be "an incomparable Parisian violist whose works are known all over Europe" (382). His 596 pieces for one, two, or three viols and continuo are distributed in five books (Book 1, 1686; Book 2, 1701; Book 3, 1711; Book 4, 1717; and Book 5, 1725). In 1689 he published a *Basse-continue des pièces à une ou à deux violes*, which is actually the continuo part for the first book but also includes ten new compositions in score rather than in the customary part books.

Each book contains over 100 compositions arranged, as in Couperin, in suites with a mixture of titled dances and descriptive pieces. There are, indeed, some superficial parallels between the Marais in many collections of *Pièces de viole* and the Couperin in four books of *Pièces de clavecin*. Both composers are miniaturists who, at their best, show a sense of fantasy, a freedom of invention disciplined by melodic purity, and an unerring sense of rhythmic organization. Both make allowances for different media of performance (Marais sanctioned performances on organ, harpsichord, lute, theorbo, violin, treble viol, transverse flute, recorder, guitar, and oboe!—see *avertissements* to Books 2 and 3). Both Couperin and Marais left extensive *avertissements* with rather precise information on how they wanted their pieces performed.[12]

From the first book, Marais tried to balance the many pieces of each suite by including compositions that are relatively easy alongside those of considerable difficulty. The suites were probably never meant to be performed as a unit, but to be perused and chosen on the basis of taste or one's technical proficiency. In this respect, the suites are more loosely organized than those by Couperin and generally contain many more individual numbers. The policy of mixing the difficult with the easy is discreetly expressed by Marais in his *Avertissement* to the first book:

> *And because simple melodies meet the taste of a lot of people, I have composed some pieces with this in mind, where chords scarcely enter; one will find others where I have used them more, and several which are entirely filled with them for those who love harmony and who are more advanced.*

Marais differs markedly from Couperin in that he made little conscious effort to achieve anything resembling the *goûts réunis* in his viol suites. This is not surprising, since the music itself is so wedded to the instrument and so bound to the tradition of virtuoso solo performance in France. Many years prior to Marais, Maugars discovered that the Italians had already given up solo performance on the viol. Thus, the sources of Marais's suites are the French dance and earlier genres such as the *tombeaux* cultivated by the lutenists and harpsichordists. Included in Book 2 are two *tombeaux*: one for "Mons. de Lully" and the other for "M. de Sainte-Colombe"; Book 1 has a particularly moving example, the "Tombeau de M. Méliton."

Some of the expressive and quasi-improvisatory preludes, especially from Book 2, seem endebted to the lute repertory in particular. The same ornaments, the same melodic turns and rhythms are found. As we move through the suites, descriptive and genre pieces come more into view. In the final book, for example, the last suite includes twenty-five pieces, and only four lack descriptive titles. The increase in the number of descriptive pieces from Book 1 to Book 5 is undoubtedly due to the pervading influence of Couperin's *Pièces de clavecin*, and Marais himself clearly stated in the *Avertissement* to the fifth book that "since character pieces are received favorably today, I have judged it appropriate to insert several. The different titles will indicate the meaning easily." The most notorious of these character pieces is the famous "Le Tableau de l'opération de la taille" (Presentation of the operation to remove stones from the bladder),[13] which includes titles in the score proper such as "The Sight of the Equipment," "Shivering on Observing It," "The Descent of the Equipment," "Serious Reflections," etc.

The most demanding of all the books of viol suites is the fourth, which Marais divided into three sections. The first is composed of pieces that are "easy, of a singing nature and with few chords"; the second is aimed for those who are "advanced on the viol"; and the third consists of pieces for three viols "which has not been done before in France" (but see Chapter 19 for contradictory information). Section two contains a descriptive suite entitled "Suite d'un goût étranger," which has thirty-six pieces in several keys. Included are pieces bearing such titles as "Le Labyrinth" and "Allemande la bizarre." The former composition includes many different key signatures within the same piece, a series of melodic tritones with sudden shifts of register, and a progression through a thorny "labyrinth" of keys far removed from the home tonic.

When the quality of Couperin's *Pièces de violes* (Paris, 1728)[14] is considered, it is regrettable that he did not write more music for this instrument. The two suites that comprise the set are musically superior to the *concerts* from *Les Goûts réunis* written for "two viols or other instruments of the same pitch" (Nos. 12 and 13). Both suites are scored for two viols; the second viol part is designed as a continuo with harpsichord realization, although there is nothing to prevent the performance of the suites on two unaccompanied viols.

The two suites, of modest dimensions, present many different aspects of the French dance suite. The first, in E minor, contains only titled dances that follow a prelude (Allemande, Courante, Sarabande grave, Gavotte, Gigue, and Passacaille); the second, in A major, includes no titled dances and, as is true in the final *concert* of *Les Goûts réunis*, it approaches a four-movement sonata (Gravement, Fuguette, Pompe funèbre, "La Chemise blanche").

The prelude to the first suite is a compendium of French harmonic and melodic practices of the period. It employs dotted rhythms and *tirades*; its short phrases receive amplitude from a melodic contour that includes many expressive intervals; the use of melodic sequence and chromaticism is restrained; and dissonance is achieved mainly through the typical *ports de voix* and *coulés* of French ornamentation, with one striking dissonant use of the mediant $\frac{9}{7}_{\#5}$ chord in measure 33. As we have observed elsewhere in the music of Couperin, features of a particularly strong initial movement occasionally carry over into subsequent movements. In this first viol suite, the sarabande grave repeats the descending melodic patterns that are found in the prelude in dotted notes.

The second suite has the greatest possible contrast of material. The first two movements bring to mind those of a church sonata, in which the melodic material of the fugal second movement is shared equally by both instruments. The third movement, a Lullian "Tombeau," makes its effect through breadth of melody, rich harmonies achieved by the use of double stops, and a formal clarity resulting from the relatively infrequent use by Couperin of a rounded binary form. The last movement, bearing the enigmatic title "La Chemise blanche," comes as a complete surprise. It is a light-hearted piece that closes the suite in a continuous whirl of rapid sixteenth-note patterns.

As we have seen, the voice of the solo viol was stilled in France after the mid-eighteenth century in spite of the talents of such students of Marin Marais as his son Roland-Pierre (ca. 1680–1750), Jacques Morel (born ca. 1700), and Louis de Caix d'Hervelois (ca. 1680–ca. 1760). The adoption by viol composers of fashionable Italian clichés, on the one hand, and their retreat into ever more difficult performance techniques, on the other, pulled post-Marais viol music in two directions at once and did nothing to stem its decline. This may be observed in Book 5 (1748) of Louis de Caix d'Hervelois's *Pièces à deux violles*, where, for example, *da capo* forms are used within French dance suites.

The two most important members of the Forqueray dynasty are Antoine (1672–1745) and his son, Jean-Baptiste-Antoine (1699–1782).[15] Both were virtuoso performers and composers, although the *Mercure de France* of 1738 chided them for having written pieces "so difficult that only he [Forqueray, *père*] and his son can execute them with grace" (cited by J. Bonfils in *MGG* 4, col. 564).

With the exception of a few dances in manuscript, all that remains of the elder Forqueray's production are five suites for viol and continuo, published in a heavily edited version in 1747 by his son. Jean-Baptiste-Antoine sadly conceded that "the viol, in spite of its advantages, has fallen into oblivion." A poignant epitaph for the instrument can be seen in the earnest efforts of the younger Forqueray to perpetuate the musical heritage represented by his father. At the same time as the above publication, he made harpsichord transcriptions of his father's suites, adding three pieces of his own to the third suite "as it did not contain enough pieces."[16]

After 1730, the treble (*dessus*) and the *pardessus de viole* (see R. Green 1982) were favored over the bass viol as solo instruments. The *pardessus de viole* is a descant instrument that sounds a fourth or a fifth above the *dessus de viole*. Louis Heudelinne (fl. 1700–1710) left us two books (1701, 1710) of pieces for the *dessus de viole "qui peuvent se jouer sur le clavecin et sur le violon."* The first book contains suites; the second, sonatas. Charles Dollé (fl. 1735–1755) published four selections of pieces between 1737 and 1754 for one or two *pardessus de viole* with or without a bass instrument. More and more, the influence of the virtuoso Italian violin school permeates the compositions for the six-stringed *pardessus*. This change is especially evident in the sonatas for *pardessus* and continuo by the cellist, Jean-Baptiste Barrière, published in 1739.

Sonatas and Suites for Rustic Instruments

The craze for solo music composed for pastoral instruments like the musette and the *vielle* (a fiddle or hurdy-gurdy) requires some comment. From the late 1720s to the 1740s, approximately 170 publications specifying both *vielle* and musette on their title pages flooded the market (R. Green 1987, 470). Such are the six suites for two musettes (Opus 11) by Boismortier of 1726 that can be played equally well by *vielles*, recorders, transverse flutes, and oboes. In 1733 Charles Bâton le jeune (ca. 1700–1754) composed suites for the *vielle* and continuo whose range eliminates the musette as an alternate instrument in most cases. More and more, the *vielle* appears to have been the preferred rustic instrument. Both Naudot and Boismortier composed sonatas for *vielle* and continuo. The most sophisticated music for solo *vielle* is found in the sonatas and chamber pieces by Jean-Baptiste Dupuits (fl. 1741–1753), many of which are entitled "Suite d'amusemens en duo." Dupuits stretches the technical possibilities of the *vielle* to the limit from time to time by imitating the melodic configurations found in keyboard and violin music. His Opus 3 (1741) consists of *Sonates pour un clavecin et une vielle*, and as Green points out, the collection is related to the contemporary accompanied keyboard music that was popular in France during the same period.

❦ *Part Five* ❦

Vocal Chamber Music

Chapter 22

The Air de Cour and Related Genres

For almost 200 years the *air de cour* served French composers as a primary model for their vocal music.[1] Lully consulted it rather than Italian aria and recitative for the airs and dialogues of his court and comedy ballets and his *tragédies lyriques*; the *récits* of many seventeenth-century motets were nourished by it; and, in combination with dance measures, its influence was felt in instrumental music, where, for example, it initiated important stylistic changes in the organ repertory. Its restricted range and generally conservative harmony acted as a deterrent to the adoption of Italian vocal techniques throughout much of the *grand siècle*. Its identity was maintained well into the eighteenth century in the many volumes of *Recueil d'airs sérieux et à boire de différents autheurs*, which were begun by Christophe Ballard in 1679 and continued, from 1716 to 1724, by his son Jean-Baptiste-Christophe Ballard.

For Lecerf, the *air de cour* was the touchstone against which all French vocal writing was to be judged. Predictably, Italianate vocalises caused the melodies of many French cantatas to fail his test. "What has become of *le bon goût*," railed Bourdelot.

> *Must it too expire under the confused jumble of all these Cantatas? What would the Lamberts, the Boessets, the Le Camus, and the Baptistes say were it possible for them to return to earth only to find French melody so changed, so degraded, and so disfigured (1725; rpt. 1966, 1:302)?*

The sixteenth century used many different terms, such as *vaudeville*, *air*, *air de cour*, and *chansonette* for vocal airs. The first publication actually to bear the words *air de cour* was Adrian Le Roy and

Robert Ballard's *Livre d'airs de cour miz sur le luth* of 1571. In his dedication to the Comtesse de Retz, Le Roy pointed out the rise of the court air from the popular *vaudeville* and clearly differentiated it from the polyphonic *chanson*. He described the *chansons* of Lassus as "difficult and arduous" in contrast to his "much lighter little collection of court *chansons*, which were formerly called *voix de ville* and today, *Airs de Cour.*" "So it was," wrote Levy, "that the homophonic and popular genre of the *vaudeville* acquired new dignity in the guise of the court air" (1954, 187). The word *air* was applied indiscriminately both to polyphonic vocal compositions in four or five parts and to their transcriptions for solo voice and lute. Although more than 500 ensemble airs appeared from 1576 to 1600, no sixteenth-century collections for solo voice and lute are found after that of Le Roy in 1571.

While not specifically labeled *airs de cour*, the first collection of polyphonic airs is Fabrice Caietain's *Airs mis en musique à quatre parties*, which was printed in 1576. The *Livre d'airs de cour mis en musique à quatre & cinq parties de plusieurs autheurs*, printed by Pierre Ballard in 1596, is the first collection to refer unequivocally to the new genre in its title.

In the early years of the seventeenth century, emphasis shifted from a random mixture of many different types of airs in a collection to a clear separation of genres. The *air de cour* gradually severed its ties with the *vaudeville* and became more serious and at the same time more *précieux*. Reflecting this change was the poetry chosen for *airs de cour*. The genre was dominated by themes and images drawn from Petrarch and fashioned by Philippe Desportes and his followers into a sentimental, precious language. Through the first half of the seventeenth century, the verses of Desportes were among those most sought after by composers of court airs. In addition, the names of François de Malherbe, Honorat de Racan, Saint-Amant, Théophile de Viau, Jacques Davy Du Perron, Boisrobert, Honoré d'Urfé, and Tristan l'Hermite are conspicuous in many *recueils*.

André Verchaly pointed out that the *air de cour* had become significantly more important as a separate genre in the second of the two sets of collections of airs published by Jacques Mangeant in 1608 and 1615 (1955). In 1608 in Caen, Mangeant printed three collections of solo airs—all bearing the title *Airs nouveaux, accompagnez des plus belles chansons à dancer*. In his preface to the first of these three, he described how young people would often dance to songs in lieu of instrumental music if no instruments were available. He explained that this led him to solicit appropriate texts for dance songs from the poets among his friends. These collections then are a mixture of *chansons à danser*, with and without texts, and polyphonic *airs de cour* for which only the soprano part is provided. Branles, courantes, voltes, villanelles, pastorales, *airs de ballet, chansons à boire*, and *airs de cour* are found in a seemingly random mixture.

In 1615 Mangeant again published three collections of solo airs. The first volume is almost entirely filled with *airs de cour* extracted from various ensemble and solo collections of the time. These are serious and often elegant melodies that show little trace of their humble origins. They jar strangely with the title: *Recueil des plus beaux airs accompagnés de folâtres, bachanales autrement dites vaudevilles* (Collection of the most beautiful airs accompanied by frolicsome pieces, bacchanales otherwise called *vaudevilles*). This may be yet another example of a publisher misrepresenting the contents of his publication for commercial ends. In contrast, the second and third volumes of the 1615 collections contain the "most beautiful *Chansons de dancer* of this time" (vol. 2) and the "most beautiful *Chansons des Comédiens François*" (vol. 3).

In 1608 Pierre Ballard printed the first book of *Airs de différents autheurs mis en tablature de luth*. There are sixteen books in this important collection. Gabriel Bataille (1575–1630) was responsible for the intabulation of Books 1–6 (1608–1615), and Antoine Boesset (1587–1643) for Books 9–16 (1620–1643); Books 7 (1617) and 8 (1618) were intabulated by the composers of the airs themselves. In addition to Bataille, the following composers are the "*différents autheurs*" of this set: Pierre Guédron, Guillaume Tessier, Jacques Mauduit, Vincent, Antoine Boesset, J. Thibaut de Courville, Sauvage, and Jacques Le Fevre.

Other significant collections of court airs "put into lute tablature" are the five books (1624–1635) by Étienne Moulinié, Pierre Ballard's eight books of melodies only (1615–1628), and the collections of Jean Boyer (1621), Louis de Rigaud (1623), François Richard (1637), and Denis Caignet (1625). The above collections embrace over 1000 airs for solo voice and lute and include some examples for voice and guitar as well.

Co-existing with solo court airs intabulated for lute were the collections of ensemble airs in four or five parts that were the original source for most solo airs. The most important of the collections of *Airs de cour à quatre et cinq parties* that date from the first half of the seventeenth century are the six books of Guédron (from 1602–1620), nine books of Boesset (1617–1642), Books 3–5 of Moulinié (1635–1639; Books 1 and 2 are lost), and one book each by Boyer (1619) and Richard (1637).

In general, the ensemble version was printed first and given the signature of the composer. Afterwards, an intabulation for lute and solo voice was made—often by someone other than the composer. Some editions were published with solo voice only, and as we move along in the seventeenth century, some airs were printed as accompanied monodies or dialogues independent of any known polyphonic source. The melodic shape of the solo air remains fairly close to that of its ensemble original except for rhythmic changes to allow for the numerous *ports de voix* and diminutions which were added, sometimes to deepen the expressive content but more often to afford the singer a vehicle for display.

The formal structure of most *airs de cour* is simple. Short stanzas made up of four or six lines are arranged musically in a variety of binary forms; AB, AAB, or AA BB are the most common. In earlier collections, the stanzas usually are organized verbally by octosyllables or Alexandrines. Bar lines, which in the Le Roy 1571 collection actually mark the isometric divisions, have no metric function in the early seventeenth century. Instead, they mark the end of each line of poetry. Where meter signs appear, they have no metric significance and may be viewed merely as a convenient way of grouping time units; they must never be interpreted as depicting strong or weak accents.

Walker divides early seventeenth-century *airs de cour* into two distinct rhythmic groups: the first obeys a principle that emphasizes text meter by placing notes of longer duration at caesura points and at the ends of lines; the second group is completely free rhythmically, has no discernible metrical plan, and often disregards verbal prosody entirely (1948, 141). This distortion of verbal rhythm was noted in an English publication of *French Court Aires with their Ditties Englished*, printed in 1629 by a Mr. Ed. Filmer Gent, who wrote in the preface:

> *The French when they compose to a ditty in their own Language, being led rather by their free Fant'sie of Aire . . . than by any strict and artificiall scanning of the Line, doe often, by disproportion'd Musicall Quantities, invert the naturell Stroke of a Verse (cited by Walker 1948, 158).*

Although cautioning against blaming the influence of the *vers mesuré* for all the ills of text distortion in the early seventeenth-century *air de cour*, Walker concedes that application of some of the *vers mesuré* principles was a contributing factor. Its influence may be clearly seen in Example 22-1 below, which also illustrates Walker's first group by having longer note values at the point of caesura and the end of the octosyllabic line.

Example 22-1. Influence of *vers mesuré* on *air de cour* (after the *2ᵉ livre d'airs*, Bataille, 1609).

Disregard for the natural verbal rhythm of the text is nowhere more evident than in the craze for diminutions that converted all strophes coming after the first into true *doubles.* Musician ran roughshod over poet. The results of this practice may be observed in the airs by Boesset and Moulinié that Mersenne included in his *Harmonie universelle* (1636; rpt. 1965, 2:411–414) along with their following couplets "en diminution," so that "everyone might imitate the method of those who teach singing in Paris, & whose exercise and Art consists in knowing how to compose good Melodies & how to create diminutions and embellishments."[2] In many instances, a different composer provided the embellished strophe. According to Bénigne de Bacilly, Henry Le Bailly (died 1637) was a specialist "who dedicated himself entirely to the ornamentation of other men's works, without spending any time whatsoever at original composition" (translated by Caswell 1968, 29). Five airs composed by Le Bailly for court ballets have been identified by Durosoir in the *Dictionnaire de la musique en France* (387).

Pierre Guédron (ca. 1575–ca. 1620), who in 1601 succeeded Claude Le Jeune as composer of the *Chambre du Roi,* dominated the early years of seventeenth-century *air de cour* production. Although direct influence of Italian recitative upon his airs is minimal, he nonetheless exhibits genuine feeling for dramatic representation of the text—thus suggesting the possibility that he may have been impressed with the performances by Giulio Caccini at the French court in 1604 and 1605. Unlike most of his peers, Guédron took care to avoid the distortion of verbal rhythms described above. Some of his rhythms are in the tradition of the popular chanson (see Example 22-2a below), but his most important contribution was the creation of a supple and convincing melodic style in the *récits* of the court ballets. His *récits* may be numbered among the first models for French recitative. Example 22-2b, "Quel excès de douleur," is a *récit* with no polyphonic original. Its discreet use of affective intervals and its narrow melodic range are typical of Guédron, who held to the strophic tradition of the *air de cour* even in his *récits.*

Example 22-2. Melodic style in Guédron. (a) "Sus, sus bergers" (after the *5ᵉ livre d'airs,* Guédron, 1620). (b) "Quel excès de douleur" (after the *9ᵉ livre d'airs,* Boesset, 1620).

Guédron and, later, Boesset were the first in France to use the basso continuo, albeit timidly. They did this long before the Ballard publication of Du Mont's *Cantica sacra* in 1650 (see Chapter 12). Admittedly, Guédron's polyphonic setting of "Berger, que pensés-vous faire" (Book 3, 1617) contains no more than bass fragments scored *"Pour le luth,"* but as Verchaly points out, they represent the first appearance in France of a continuo—here used in support of a dramatic dialogue (1961, Introduction to *Air de cour pour voix et luth,* Paris: Société Française de Musicologie, xii; see also Durosoir 1991, 309). Bataille's intabulation of this air in his fourth book represents, then, the first genuine realization of a continuo line in France.

This innovation was not seized upon by the conservative French, although from 1620 on Boesset scored occasional passages in his polyphonic airs *"Pour le luth."* It was not until his seventh book (1630) that Boesset included a *"basse continue pour les instruments"* for the five-part air "Mourons, Tirsis" (see Verchaly in *Airs de cour pour voix et luth,* lxiv) and not until years later in his ninth book (1642) that the same composer included other ensemble airs with continuo.

François Richard (ca. 1585–1650) alluded to the pleasure the king took in the music of his Chamber: "I know that after the sounds of the Trumpets and Drums [of war], those of Lute and voices do not displease you" (dedication to Louis XIII *Airs de cour à quatre parties,* 1637). Richard is an important forerunner of Lambert and Lully in the development of dialogue airs. The dialogue "Cloris attends un peu" from the *Airs de cour avec le tablature de luth* (1637) concludes with an "operatic" duo sung by Tircis and Cloris.

Dialogues could also exist in polyphonic settings of *airs de cour.* Soprano and tenor share the dialogue of "Faut-il mourir sans espérance" by François de Chancy (ca. 1600–1656) from Book 1 (1635), and a four-part chorus sings the refrain.

Étienne Moulinié and Antoine Boesset are among the most important composers of court airs following Guédron. Unlike Guédron's, however, their airs display little feeling for the dramatic. Rather, there is a natural facility that created melodies of refined grace and suppleness. As early as 1628, Moulinié was the director of music for Louis XIII's brother, Gaston d'Orléans, whose household was one of the most musical in the realm. Gaston had recourse to the king's *Vingt-quatre Violons,* kept a vocal ensemble of seven or eight singers, and by 1643 had already modeled his musical estate on that of the king and had divided it into *Chambre* and *Chapelle.* Marolles commented that Gaston had "the best dancers in France" (1645, 1:114), which may account for the large number of vocal extracts from court ballets found among the works of Moulinié.

Moulinié[3] composed five books of *Airs de cour avec la tablature de luth* (1624–1635), and five books of *Airs de cour à 4 et 5 parties* (1625–1639). A sixth book of *Airs de cour à 4 et 5 parties avec la basse continue*, his last known work, was printed by Ballard in 1668, at which time the composer described himself as *"maistre de la musique des États de Languedoc."* Moulinié varied the contents of his collections more than any other composer of court airs. Book 3 of *Airs de cour avec la tablature de luth et de guitarre* (1629), for example, contains several dialogues, six Italian airs, five Spanish airs, and eight *airs à boire*.

The sixteen books of *airs de cour* by Antoine Boesset[4] give us the most complete picture of the development of the genre from Guédron to Michel Lambert. They contain more than 200 *airs de cour*. In nine of the books these are in four and five parts, 1617–1642; in seven books they are *airs de cour mis en tablature de luth*, 1620–1643. Boesset composed seventy-three of these *airs de cour* for twenty-five court ballets. This change of venue may have caused him to place more emphasis upon declamation and irregular verse schemes. Of all composers of court airs, Boesset was arguably the greatest melodist. The thought persists that Guédron was inhibited by the narrow frame of the air and that he would have wished a larger canvas to display his dramatic gifts. Not so with Boesset—the miniature design with all of its limitations, far from having a deleterious effect on this composer, actually seems to have stimulated him to shape and mould exquisite melodies of modest proportions. In his long career, Boesset became more and more sensitive to the setting of the text. As time passed, for example, he made less use of the purely abstract melodic patterns that had indiscriminately appeared in his earlier collections to the detriment of textual meaning. Even some of the best *récits* by Guédron are marred by the type of pattern illustrated in Example 22-3.

Example 22-3. Use of abstract melodic patterns in Guédron.

Boesset brought out his ninth book of *Airs de cour à quatre et cinq parties* in 1642 after ten years of silence. In the dedication to the king, he wrote:

My advancing age causes me to lose the ardor of youth little by little and diminishes the gaiety necessary for the embellishment of the Airs; thus I am unable to produce them in as great a number as when I had the force and vigor of my early years.

It is true that these products of Boesset's old age are tinted with a gay melancholy not unlike some of the lute pieces by his contemporaries; at the same time, however, the book contains some of the composer's best efforts. They display greater melodic amplitude due to longer phrases and a more extensive vocal range. They also have an intensity of expression rarely encountered in the *air de cour*, which is achieved by more conspicuous use of affective intervals, careful placement of rests for dramatic effect, and judicious use of repeated text fragments. The remarkable change of style reflected in Example 22-4 below surely owes something to Italian vocal writing; and it is no accident that, according to Lecerf, the melodies of Boesset were admired by Luigi Rossi.

Example 22-4. Melodic intensity in late Boesset (after ed. of 1642).

Undoubtedly the person most responsible for orienting the *air de cour* more toward expressive realization of the text was the singer Pierre de Nyert (ca. 1597–1682), friend of La Fontaine, who from 1633 to 1635 studied in Rome. According to Saint-Evremond, Nyert believed that "to render music pleasurable, one should hear Italian airs in the mouth of a Frenchman" (cited by Prunières 1913, 96). After 1640, Nyert's influence was felt everywhere among composers and performers of French vocal music. He was a favorite singer of Louis XIII and one of the strongest influences on Lambert and above all on Bénigne de Bacilly (ca. 1625–1690), who in his *Remarques curieuses sur l'art de bien chanter* (1668) attempted a reform of French singing by systematizing rules of pronunciation, ornamentation, prosody, and correct breathing.

Not all were convinced that the salvation of the *air de cour* lay in the method of Nyert or the more intensely personal language of Boesset's ninth book. In fact, opposition to the new style was in part responsible for confrontation between Boesset and the Dutch musician-priest Johannes Alertus Bannius (see Pirro 1907a, 114–120, and Walker 1976). Although only a minor skirmish, it involved some of the most important names in French music and aesthetics of the time, and it stemmed from the same age-old impulses that brought about a major battle between Giovanni Maria Artusi and Claudio Monteverdi at the beginning of the seventeenth century.

Both Bannius and Boesset composed an air on the text "Me veux-tu voir mourir." In a letter located today in the Bibliothèque Mazarine, Bannius complained in detail of Boesset's setting to Anne Maria van Schuurman. He found particular fault with Boesset's use of the tritone (actually a diminished fifth) in the opening phrase. Boesset received the support of Mersenne, who had been the prime mover behind the "little harmonic combat" (see Walker 1976, 234). In a letter to Huygens, Mersenne commented that Boesset had "divided the tritone into two minor thirds, thereby softening the harshness" (see "mourir" in Example 22-5 below). Descartes wrote to Mersenne in 1640 as follows: "With regard to the music of M. Ban [Bannius], I believe that it differs from the air of Boesset as the exercises in rhetoric of a student eager to practice all the rules differs from an oration of Cicero" (cited by Pirro 1907a, 119).

Me veux – tu voir mourir

Me veux-tu voir mourir

Example 22-5. Opening phrase of "Me veux-tu voir mourir" by Bannius (left) and Boesset (right).

Bannius had indeed composed his music by employing a "*science très certaine*" (Pirro) and had even contrived the key of F without a B-flat, because that to him expressed "indignation." Yet, we can tell instantly that his music is stillborn. His opening phrase is awkward and unconvincing, lacking rapport with the text, whereas the melody of Boesset is a little masterpiece of musico-dramatic expression.

The use of lute tablature became much less frequent after the last book of Boesset's *Airs de cour avec la tablature de luth* (1643). The theorbo was preferred as the principal accompanying instrument. Bacilly was of the opinion that the viol and harpsichord have not the "grace and accommodation found in the theorbo" (1668; trans. 1968). The change from lute tablature to continuo went hand in hand with the abandonment of the term *air de cour*. The collections of the second half of the seventeenth century were called *air* or *air sérieux* instead.

Perrin has given us a working definition of the air as seen by composers and authors of the period of Louis XIV:

The Air proceeds in a free though serious measure and movement and thus is more proper for the expression of honest love and the tender emotions of pain or of joy that it wakens in the heart . . . . [The air] does not exceed the length of six long lines, nor limit itself to less than the heroic couplet; the best in my opinion are the quatrains, cinquains, or sestets of irregular lines. It can be composed in three parts, but it succeeds best in two [parts], which correspond to the two statements of the melody. It may be structured as a Rondeau at the beginning, the middle, at the end, or at any place one wishes . . . .

The Chanson *differs from the* Air *in that the* Air, *as we have said, follows a free measure; and the* Chanson *follows a fixed meter, dance or other [sort], either entirely or in part (ca. 1667, 7).*

Bacilly created a separate category for "short airs . . . such as Gavottes, Sarabandes, and Minuets" and warned that one must always "maintain the metric proportions so as not to alter a minuet or a sarabande to such an extent that it becomes a song in free meter, such as is usually implied by the term *air*" (1668; trans. 1968, 49).

The various collections of airs published by Robert and Christophe Ballard and later by Jean-Baptiste-Christophe Ballard are among the richest sources of airs for the second half of the seventeenth century and the early years of the eighteenth century. Such a collection is the thirty-eight-volume *Airs de différents autheurs à 2 parties* printed and edited by Robert Ballard between 1658 and 1673, then by Christophe Ballard from 1674 to 1694. Unfortunately, neither Ballard identified composers or poets in this collection.

We must rely on Bacilly's three-part *Recueil des plus beaux vers qui ont esté mis en chant*, in which Bacilly helpfully provided the names of the "Authors of the Airs as well as of the Words." The first part of this important source was published in 1661. Bacilly attested to the popularity of the art of singing in France at mid-century: "The number of those who sing being infinite, there is no one who does not have his favorite *chanson*: And the collection would have little merit if he could not find it here in its proper category" (preface). The composer most often cited by Bacilly is Michel Lambert, followed in order of frequency by Sébastien Le Camus, Louis de Mollier, Antoine Boesset, Bénigne de Bacilly, Étienne Moulinié, Jean-Baptiste Boesset, Jean de Cambefort, François Richard, Jean Granouilhet de Sablières, Joseph Chabanceau de La Barre, and Jacques Champion de Chambonnières.

Of these composers, Michel Lambert (ca. 1610–1696)[5] is the most representative composer of airs in the second half of the seventeenth century. He owed his fame as much to his singing and teaching of voice as to his compositions themselves. In the words of Lecerf, the airs by Lambert represented the quintessence of French vocal music and the most important models for Lully. Seen in this light, the miniaturist Lambert received larger-than-life treatment:

After [Le Bailly] came Lambert, who, in the opinion of all Europe, was the best Master to have appeared for many centuries. His song was so natural, so clear, so graceful that one sensed its charm immediately . . . . There was no one in Paris, French or foreigner, who did not wish to study with him, and he led the way for such a long time that he had a thousand excellent Students. His method spread in a few years to the Provinces . . . . The Opera of Paris prescribed it (Lecerf 1725; rpt. 1966, 3:72–73).

Lambert's first collection was dedicated to Nyert and engraved by Richer in 1660. The *doubles* that were provided for each air in this collection by Lambert perpetuate the domination of poet by musician, so it is easy to understand why Lully, as a text-oriented composer, was opposed to the tradition of this vocal technique.

Gathered together from the work of many years, the airs in *Airs à une, deux, trois et quatre parties avec la basse continue* (1689) sum up the art of Michel Lambert. The chronology of these airs is difficult to determine. It may be that in such airs as "Ma bergère est tendre & fidelle" or "Vos mespris," both constructed over chaconne basses, Lambert was influenced by La Barre or even by his son-in-law, Lully. Most airs in the collection begin with a *ritournelle* for two violins and continuo followed by solo and ensemble settings that share the same melodic and harmonic materials. Most of Lambert's airs use the short binary structure so typical of the *air de cour*. There are some examples of rounded binary airs (see "Mes yeux, que vos plaisirs") and airs *en rondeau* (see "Ah! qui voudra desormais s'engager"). Some borrow the rhythmic organization of sarabandes and minuets, and some are organized as dialogues. Certain of his more dramatic airs (see "Ombre de mon amant") border on recitative and may have had an influence on the creators of French opera.

The *Airs à deux parties avec les seconds couplets en diminution* (1669) by the king's organist, Joseph Chabanceau de La Barre (1633–1678), are more innovative with regard to form than Lambert's airs. La Barre even experimented with the binary format: Part A of "Quand une âme est bien atteinte," for example, is a passacaille; Part B is a short dramatic scene whose changing tempo markings, "Lentement" and "Gayement," mirror the text. The technique of converting the second part of an air into a little "operatic" scene is also found in "Ah! je sens que mon coeur," whose text repetition, affective intervals, and changes of tempo combine to heighten the dramatic effect of this bucolic quarrel.

La Barre's dramatic techniques stem more from the French tradition than from any Italian influence, yet it is worth noting that his collection includes an "Air italien" some thirty years before Ballard's first *Recueil des meilleurs airs italiens*. The air, "Sospiri ohimè," contains many indications of expression and occasional archaic madrigalisms such as the "Presto" over "ridete" in the phrase "il mio morir ridete."

In later collections of *airs sérieux,* dramatic elements based on the dialogues by Richard, La Barre, Lambert, and others were expanded. Composers commonly grouped airs, recitatives, and ensembles together to form autonomous dramatic entities. Many of these are scattered throughout the Ballard collections of the late seventeenth century. Witness the "Adieu de Tircis à Climène" by Montéclair in the Ballard *Recueil d'airs sérieux et à boire* for the month of October 1695. The musical components of the little scene are as follows: (1) Recitative of Tircis; (2) Air of Climène; (3) Recitative of Tircis; (4) Duo. A systematic study of these air-recitative ensemble complexes might shed more light on the early history of the secular cantata in France.

Many of the collections in the later seventeenth century and early eighteenth century carry the generic label *"Airs sérieux et à boire,"* in which the healthy strains of lighter genres co-exist with the *airs sérieux*. With their broad base of popular appeal, the chansons, *vaudevilles, airs à boire, brunettes,* and *airs champêtres* had never really been seriously threatened by the precious, more esoteric *air de cour* and its progeny, the *air sérieux*. Typical of such collections are the *Brunettes ou petits airs tendres avec les doubles et la basse continue mélées de chansons à danser* printed by Ballard in 1703, 1704, and 1711. In one of the few studies of popular vocal genres of the French Baroque, Masson has recognized three main categories of *brunettes*: (1) pieces in which both music and words are of a popular nature; (2) pieces in which a more worldly type of poetry is combined with melodies of popular origin; and (3) pieces in which both poetry and music are more sophisticated.[6] The first category corresponds most closely to the *"chansons à danser."* The second and most important category is closely related to the *vaudeville*, and the third category generally resembles the *air sérieux*.

As we have seen, annual publication of *Airs sérieux et à boire* had been initiated by Christoph Ballard in 1679. Responding to the unprecedented demand for more airs, Ballard began a publication in 1694 bearing the same title and intended to appear at the beginning of every month—a practice that continued for over thirty consecutive years. Ballard also adopted the progressive use of a full score instead of the part books of his earlier collections. Scattered throughout these and similar collections are the illustrious names of such composers as Lully, Charpentier, Sicard, Couperin, Campra, Dandrieu, Dornel, Mouret, Montéclair, Boismortier, and Rameau.

The *airs à boire* had a great vogue throughout the seventeenth century. From 1627 to 1669, Pierre Ballard published collections of *Chansons pour dancer et pour boire* for which Bacilly contributed most of the chansons from 1661 to 1669 (see Poole 1987, 187). Example 22-6 is taken from the fifth book of 1637. Its note-against-note texture, its narrow range, symmetrical phrases, and contrasting concluding refrain are altogether typical of the genre for the first half of the century.

Example 22-6. A *chanson à boire* "Qu'il est bon" from Ballard collection of 1637.

Beginning with Bacilly and Sicard, the *airs à boire* became more musically significant. Jean Sicard (dates unknown) brought out 336 airs in seventeen books between 1666 and 1683, at the rate of one book per year (except for 1672). These collections vindicate the opinion of his peers, many of whom found Sicard the composer *par excellence* of the Bacchic genre. His range of invention and the variety of his musical settings are much greater than one would anticipate. Many of his *airs à boire* are scored for bass voice and two violins and are examples of the doubled continuo airs found in French opera up until Rameau. Some are virtuoso pieces for bass, far removed from the naive simplicity of Example 22-6 (see the fall of nearly two octaves in "Ne vous estonnez pas" from Book 5). There are even a few *airs à boire* organized as dialogues like some of the *airs sérieux*.

In his third book (1668), Sicard tells us that he had been advised that year "to mix some *Airs sérieux* in among my *Chansons Bachiques*." One of these *airs sérieux*, "Languir," which he wrote for soprano, violin ("If one wishes"), and continuo, is as moving a lament as exists in seventeenth-century French music (see Example 22-7).

Example 22-7. Sicard: Extract from "Languir" (after ed. of 1668).

In the *Advis* of the fourth book (1669), Sicard actually blurred the distinctions between his *airs sérieux* and *airs à boire* in stating that "Among the *Sérieux* there are those that are joyful and demand a fast tempo; there are also among the *Boire* those that demand a *Sérieux* tempo."

Sicard's first *Advis au lecteur* gives us a taste of his wit: "But I confess I have an extreme passion to divert those indifferent to good taste." Satire and a raucous humor are apparent in every collection. The duo "Amis, je suis triste" found in Book 5 (1670) uses the musical language of an *air tendre* to mourn a broken wine bottle.

Ballard printed many other collections that were made up of genres related to the *airs sérieux* and *airs à boire*. Among them are the *Recueil de chansonettes de différents autheurs*, which was printed from 1675 to 1694, the *Recueil d'airs des comédies modernes* (Book 1, 1706), and, above all, the *Recueil des meilleurs airs italiens,* which was printed from 1699 to 1708. The latter collection, more than any other, reflects the inroads made by Italian vocal music in France at the turn of the century. Its last volume (1708) contains all the Italian airs in its preceding volumes as well, for a total of over 115 airs. Most of the airs are really *arie da capo* taken from the *divertissements* of *tragédies lyriques* and *opéra-ballets.* There is a liberal sprinkling of airs and arias by Italian composers Carissimi and Scarlatti; some, although written expressly for the particular revival of an opera, exist only in this collection or in the later collection by J.- B.-C. Ballard: *Recueil d'airs ajoutez à différents opéra, depuis l'année 1698* (1734).[7]

Chapter 23

The Cantate Françoise

*One talks only of cantatas, only cantatas are advertised at the street
corners* (Dictionnaire de Trévoux *1743–1752, 1:1670*).

The early years of the eighteenth century in France witnessed a brief
but rich flowering of the secular cantata.[1] Most of the important collections were published between 1706 and 1730,[2] by which time the
genre had already gone out of fashion. It is no accident that cantata
and sonata are often coupled together in French sources of the time
that describe, sometimes with annoyance, the popularity of these two
totally different genres, because the cantata, like the sonata, was an
importation from across the Alps. In the *Mercure* of November 1714,
the cantatas and sonatas "which have inundated all Paris" (201) are
blamed squarely for the change in taste that caused Parisian audiences
to cool toward Lully's operas. A year previously, the same journal had
already observed that "a musician no longer arrives [in Paris] without
a sonata or cantata in his pocket" (1713, November, 34).

French eighteenth-century sources are almost unanimous in
attributing the birth of the cantata there to the poet, Jean-Baptiste
Rousseau (1671–1741). Similarly, most eighteenth-century writers
agree that Jean-Baptiste Morin (1677–1745), in setting Rousseau's
cantata texts to music (1706), was the "first composer of French cantatas" (Nemeitz 1727, 353) in spite of the earlier Privilege date (1703)
of Bernier's first book.

Nevertheless, there is some evidence that French composers had
experimented with cantatas or at least with cantata-like compositions
in the previous century. I have mentioned the striking similarities
to the cantata of some of the *airs sérieux* found in late seventeenth-
century collections. Pierre Perrin has left us the texts for two "*grands
récits*" (*Polyphème jaloux* and *La Mort de Tysbé*) in his manuscript *Recueil
de paroles de musique* (ca. 1666). They were set to music by Moulinié
and Sablières, respectively (music lost). The texts are laid out in the

format of the cantata, and Perrin took great care to indicate textual divisions into solo, ensemble, and chorus—even going so far as to specify the required voices (*dessus, taille*, etc.) for the solo portions.

Two works by Charpentier, dating from the early 1680s, must also figure in any pre-history of the French cantata, although since both exist only in manuscript and one is but a fragment, it is difficult to see how they could have had much influence on later composers—a regrettably recurring theme in the evaluation of Charpentier's position in French Baroque music. The first work, *Coulez, coulez charmans ruisseaux*, is of doubtful authenticity. It is identified as a "Cantate françoise" in an eighteenth-century manuscript at the Muséum Calvet in Avignon. It is a short fragment of little musical interest for solo voice (tenor), two violins, and continuo. The second work, dating from 1683, *Orphée descendant aux enfers* (H. 47) is a genuine cantata in the French style (see Quittard 1904b). It may have been composed for Mlle de Guise and was probably performed at a concert at her home, the Hôtel de Guise. It is scored for three voices, two violins, a recorder, a transverse flute, and continuo. The role of Orphée (tenor) may have been sung by Charpentier himself. A high point musically is the "Récit d'Orphée," which comes after the opening *Sinfonia* (see Example 23-1). It is an accompanied monologue in the tradition of those found in the later operas of Lully but has an Italianate richness of harmony, and text painting intensifies such lines as "laissez moy descendre aux ombres du trépas!"

23-1. Charpentier: Extract from *Orphée descendant aux enfers* (after the *Meslanges autographes*, vol. 6).

None of these seventeenth-century "cantatas" is mentioned in the many dictionary definitions of the genre in the eighteenth century. In 1703 Brossard still viewed the cantata as "an extended composition whose words are in Italian." Only in later editions of his dictionary did he offer the information that "recently French cantatas have been composed that have been very successful" (cited by Launay in *MGG 7*, col. 576). In his manuscript, *Dissertation sur cette espèce de concert qu'on nomme Cantate*, Brossard added that "there is nothing that has been more applauded in France, nothing whose performances have been more generally and widely disseminated than that which we now title *cantate* after the Italian *cantata*." The *Dictionnaire de Trévoux* gives a succinct, clear definition of the eighteenth-century French cantata: "A *cantate* is a piece varied by recitatives, *ariettes* or short airs in contrasting tempos. Ordinarily it is composed for solo voice and continuo, [but it is] often [accompanied by] two violins or by several instruments" (1743–1752, 1:1670).

The most important source to illuminate the early history of the French cantata is Bachelier's *Recueil de cantates, contenant toutes celles qui se chantent dans les concerts: pour l'usage des amateurs de la musique et de la poésie* (1728). This *Recueil* contains the texts of ninety-nine cantatas, including some set by Bernier (twenty-four), Clérambault (fourteen), Stuck (eleven), Morin (seven), Bourgeois (two), and Montéclair (twelve). Texts are by Rousseau, Mennesson, Serré de Rieux, Fuzelier, Thibault, La Grange, and three cantata texts by the Regent, Philippe d'Orléans.

In the preface, Bachelier acknowledges Jean-Baptiste Rousseau as the first to work in the genre in a manner to satisfy "the most discerning" tastes. He quotes in full Rousseau's own description of how he evolved the format of the cantata text:

> *The Italians called these short Poems* CANTATES, *because they are particularly well suited to song. They are ordinarily composed of three Recitatives interspersed with as many* Airs de mouvements; *which fact obliges them to diversify their Strophes, whose lines are sometimes long, sometimes short as in the Choruses of the ancient Tragedies and in the majority of the Pindaric Odes . . . . Since I had no other model than that of the Italians, who often sacrifice reason, as do we in France, to the convenience of the Musician, I noticed that after composing several [poems], I lost from the verse what was gained by the Music; I wrote nothing of value and was content to amass vain Poetic Phrases, one upon the other, lacking design or liaison with a subject. This is what gave me the idea of creating a form that would confine these small poems to exact,*

allegorical treatment in which Recitative would furnish the body of the cantata, and tuneful Airs, the soul. From among the ancient Fables, I chose those that I deemed most suitable to this design . . . & this way succeeded well enough for me to stimulate many other [poets] to adopt it. Whether or not it is the best plan that one might choose is not for me to determine, because in the case of something new, nothing is as deceiving as a first vogue, & only time can prove its merits & give it its true worth.

Heading up the *Recueil de cantates* is Rousseau's *Euterpe* set to music by Morin. Its prominent position is defended by Bachelier: "I believe that [Morin] is the first to have set Cantatas to Music; for this reason I have chosen *Euterpe,* the first of those composed [by Morin], to put at the head of the *Recueil.*"

Jean-Baptiste Morin (1677–1754), *Maître de Chapelle* for the Regent's daughter, the Abbesse de Chellesse, wrote three books of cantatas, most of which are in the form that Rousseau suggested in the preface quoted above: three recitatives alternating with three airs. Morin's *Avis* to his first book of *Cantates françoises à une et deux voix* suggests that at least some of its six cantatas had been widely circulated before the 1706 publication date. In the best tradition of *goûts réunis,* he claimed to have attempted a synthesis between the *douceur* of French melody and the more diversified accompaniments, tempo contrasts, and modulations found in Italian cantatas. To increase the range of performance possibilities, Morin added a modest *symphonie* of flute and violin to one cantata (*Enone*), and the final cantata (*Les Amants mécontents*) is for two solo voices. We are assured, however, that the collection may "easily be performed as *musique de chambre*" by a single voice, a harpsichord, and a bass viol.

Concerning the first book of *Cantates françoises ou musique de chambre à voix seule* (Privilege date, 1703) by Nicolas Bernier, Bachelier wrote: "I have heard some capable gentlemen from across the Mountains, who were scornful of French Music before this time, [now] admit to admiring *Diane, L'Absence, Les Muses,* and *Les Forges de Lemnos*[3] from the first book of M. Bernier" (1728, preface). As is the case with Morin, the cantatas of Bernier's first book are all in the format of Recitative / Air / Recitative / Air / Recitative / Air. It is impossible to tell from the privilege date whether or not Bernier's cantatas circulated before those of Morin.

In Bernier's third book (no date), two new elements were introduced to the French cantata: humor and descriptive *simphonies* borrowed from the lyric stage. An unequal contest between coffee and wine is the subject underlying *Le Caffé* (No. 4). The storm scene and the music describing the approach of the sea monster (see Example 23-2 below) in *Hipolite et Aricie* (No. 5) stem more from *préramiste* opera than from the earlier *tragédies lyriques* of Lully. The extract reproduced below from this scene is an accompanied recitative. The dramatic interpolation of rapid violin passages is an adumbration of the similar scene in the more famous *Hippolyte et Aricie* written almost thirty years later by Rameau.

23-2. Bernier: Extract from *Hipolite et Aricie* (after Book 3, n. d.).

Jean-Baptiste Stuck, called Batistin or Baptistin (ca. 1680–1755), was born in Florence to parents of German origin. He arrived in Paris about 1705 and entered the service of the Duc d' Orléans, to whom he dedicated his first book of *Cantates françoises* (1706). He was partisan to joining "the taste of Italian Music with French Words." Bachelier commented: "His Cantatas brought him infinite honor; those of his first Book, although the Recitative be not completely in the French manner, were favored . . . especially his *Philomèle*." *Philomèle*, the first

of the set of six cantatas, was organized in the by then familiar alternation of recitatives and airs. It includes parts for two violins. The only
French element in the final air of *Philomèle* ("Pourquoi plaintive,
Philomèle") is the French language itself; the music, a slow *siciliana*,
would do credit to Alessandro Scarlatti, as Example 23-3, taken from
the introduction, reveals.

23-3. Stuck: Italian influence in cantata movement (after ed. of 1706).

Stuck made considerably more use of obbligato instruments than
either Morin or Bernier, and he was careful to add the words *"avec
symphonie"* to each of his collections of cantatas. He wrote for violin,
flute, and oboe (*Le Calme de la nuit*, Book 1), for violin and obbligato
bass viol (*Mars jaloux*, Book 2, 1708), and even for trumpet and violins
(*Les Festes bolonnoises*, Book 4, 1714).

The *Cantades et ariettes françoises* (1708) by Brunet de Moland is a
curious mixture of four long cantatas and six *ariettes*. The *ariettes* are
all extensive *da capo* airs of the type often included in the *divertissements* of the contemporary *opéras-ballets*. *Apollon et Daphné*, which
opens the collection, is typical of his cantatas and has six recitatives in
alternation with as many airs.

Elisabeth-Claude Jacquet de La Guerre has given us some of the
very few examples of sacred cantatas in French Baroque music in the
twelve that make up her two books of *Cantates françoises sur des sujets
tirez de l'écriture* (1708–1711). Houdar de La Motte supplied all the
texts, which he took from the Old Testament. They are *Esther, Jacob et
Rachel, Jonas, Susanne, Judith, Adam, Jephté, Joseph, Samson*, and three
descriptive cantatas: *Le Passage de la mer rouge, Le Temple rebasti*, and
Le Déluge.

The subject matter itself obviously suggested numerous descriptive *symphonies*: the sounds of battle (*Le Passage de la mer rouge*), the
tempests (*Jonas*), and the *sommeils* (*Judith*). Although she adhered in
general to Rousseau's format, Mlle de La Guerre was more successful

in sustaining mood and intensity in these miniature dramas than in her one *tragédie lyrique, Céphale et Procris* (1694). This is particularly evident in her recitatives, which do indeed "furnish the body" of the cantatas as Rousseau had originally planned. The sudden shift of mode, the highlighting of certain key words, and the use of rests for maximum dramatic effect may be observed in the extract from *Jephté* found as Example 23-4 below.

23-4. La Guerre: Extract from *Jephté* (after ed. of 1711).

Mlle de La Guerre also composed three secular cantatas (*Sémélé, L'Ile de Délos,* and *Le Sommeil d'Ulisse*) for which she borrowed freely all manner of descriptive *symphonies* from opera. This further fragmented the traditional cantata format. In *L'Ile de Délos,* she added a prelude, a "*Muzette,*" a chaconne, and a "*Simphonie de rossignol & voix*" to the normal air-recitative components. In the collection of these three secular cantatas, she added a short recitative and duo, in *buffo* style, entitled *Le Racommodement comique de Pierrot et de Nicole.* The *haute-contre* voice was so popular in early eighteenth-century France that Mlle de La Guerre found it necessary to warn performers of this charming little "scene" against making any substitutions in the voice parts: "My wish is to have the piece known as I composed it. It is for a Bass and a Soprano; and it would be very difficult to execute it with a *haute-contre* without corrupting the harmony" (*Avertissement*).

In the *Avertissement* to his first book of cantatas (1708), André Campra presents us with a "veritable manifesto" (Barthélemy 1957a, 93) for those now committed to the fashionable *goûts réunis:*

> *Because Cantatas have become* à la mode, *I felt duty bound to heed the solicitations of many persons to give some of my own to the Public. I have tried as much as I could to mix in with the gentleness of French Music, the vivacity of Italian Music; perhaps those who*

have completely abandoned the former will not approve of the manner in which I have treated this small Work. I am persuaded as much as anyone concerning the merit of the Italians, but our language will not accommodate certain things in which they excel. Our Music has beauties that they cannot avoid admiring and trying to imitate, although these same beauties are neglected by some of our very own French composers. I have attempted above all to conserve the beauty of melody, expression, and our manner of recitative which, in my opinion, is the best: it is for those with good taste to decide whether I am wrong or right.

This "safe" paragraph was designed to offend no one and at the same time to create a rationale for the several elaborate vocalises found especially in the lively airs in compound meter. These airs, or more accurately *ariettes*, also make use of rapid modulations, another Italianism that had characterized the music of Campra from the days of *L'Europe galante* (1697). Essentially French, however, are the recitatives, instrumental music, and simple vocal lines of most of the airs, which are constructed in short phrases with many *coulés* and *ports de voix*.

Each of the six cantatas in Campra's first book contains at least one *ariette* in addition to airs and recitatives. For Campra, at least in 1708, *ariette* and air were not always clearly differentiated. Both may be *da capo* structures; both may have introductions and concluding *ritournelles*; and airs, on occasion, may even be longer than *ariettes*, the French equivalent of da capo arias. The only general difference seems to be the prevalence of compound meter and a more rapid tempo in the *ariettes*.

The final cantata of Book 1, *Les Femmes*, includes a gentle yet strikingly harmonized *sommeil* in F-sharp Minor used to introduce a *da capo* air, "Fils de la nuit," based on the same material. Campra's dramatic sense is shown to good advantage in the opening phrase of this doubled continuo air, in which the vocal line suddenly drops a major seventh, and again by the full measure rest following the word *silence* (see Example 23-5 below).

In his second and third books (1714, 1728), Campra treated his cantata texts as miniature dramas. This should come as no surprise when we realize that his librettists, Danchet and Fuzelier, contributed many of the texts. Campra even borrowed the common, effective technique, so often employed in operatic *divertissements*, of fragmenting the dance with interspersed sections of recitative. In *La Dispute de l'Amour* (Book 2), a bourée is interrupted in the best operatic fashion by such comments as "*Mais, qu'entends-je?*" *Énée et Didon* (Book 2), a virtual "cantata opera" with action for two protagonists, opens with a tempest that continues into the following duo "Quel bruit soudain"; and *La Colère d'Achille* (Book 3) includes a vengeance air of some dramatic power.

23-5. Campra: Beginning of air "Fils de la nuit," *Les Femmes* (after ed. of 1708).

During this same period, Campra expanded the role of obbligato instruments and displayed greater sensitivity to the contrast afforded by shifts in tonality within the components of a cantata. *La Colère d'Achille* is scored for strings, solo violin, flutes, oboes, and trumpets; *Les Plaisirs de la campagne* (Book 3) is scored for strings and flutes and uses an independent violoncello line in the "Air des musettes."

More operatic than Campra's cantatas are the twenty by Louis-Nicolas Clérambault printed in five books (1710, 1713, 1716, 1720, 1726) and his five separately published cantatas.[4] Bachelier attests to the unprecedented renown of Clérambault as a cantata composer in the first twenty-five years of the eighteenth century:

> *A Frenchman attending one of our concerts, at which some Cantatas of Ms. Batistin & Bernier were performed, exclaimed with surprise, Well, now! Messieurs, are you not familiar with Clérambault? What? You do not sing his* Orphée, *his* Médée, *his* Pigmalion, Léandre & Héro, *or his* Musette? *These are works of the greatest beauty, and there are few that can compare with their grace of melody, their forceful accompaniments, and the difficulty of their execution. They answered that they indeed knew these cantatas which he had just praised and which merited [it], and this was the reason that they did not profane them through daily use; rather, they reserved them for the most important Holidays & Sundays; and in order to prepare their performance better, they use those of M. Bernier and Batistin as lessons (1728, preface).*

The all too rare congruency of composer and genre may be observed in the cantatas of Clérambault. Competent but superficial in his keyboard music, often tentative or merely decorative in the *petits motets* he composed for the young ladies of Saint-Cyr, Clérambault wrote his cantatas with the assurance and self-discipline of one to the manner born. The best of these works, composed with equal part of felicitous grace and dramatic conviction, do indeed constitute a "repository of neglected masterpieces" (Tunley 1966a, 331).

From his first book on, Clérambault discreetly allowed content to determine form, and in so doing, he modified and bent the seemingly inflexible cantata format. This is especially evident in the musical structures chosen for the points of greatest dramatic intensity, which often occur near the center of a cantata. In *Orphée* (Book 1), the most admired French cantata of the entire century (see Tunley 1966a, 319), the key dramatic action in which Orpheus pleads with Pluto for the release of Euridice is rendered musically by two "ariosi" that are separated by a contrasting "*air tendre*" placed at the center of the cantata. The first "arioso," in B major ("Monarque redoute"), is scored for soprano, flute, and violin, with no bass line; the second, in B minor, adds the continuo and harmonically intensifies the pleading of Orpheus. By employing a mediant $\frac{9}{7}_{\#5}$ chord that never resolves (Example 23-6a) and a simultaneous cross-relation that results from a *port de voix* heard against the bass (Example 23-6b), Clérambault owes nothing in *Orphée* to any Italian model; rather, he draws upon the traditional French treatment of dissonance found in the works of Charpentier, Delalande, Couperin, and others.

23-6. (a, b) Clérambault: Extracts from *Orphée* (after ed. of 1710).

Médée (Book 1) includes both a virtuoso vengeance aria ("Courons à la vengeance") that is strongly influenced by the driving rhythms of the Vivaldi concerto, and a long accompanied monologue ("Cruelles filles des Enfers") that could have been lifted from Lully's *Armide*. Thus, a single mood of dark despair is sustained by means of entirely different musical styles.

In *Pirâme et Tisbé* (Book 2), the heart of the cantata lies where Pyramus discovers Thisbe's blood-soaked veil. It is a true operatic scene consisting of the following: Recitative / "Plainte" / "Prélude" and Monologue /. A final air, marked *"gracieusement et gai"* wrenches us free of the scene of Pyramus's tragic discovery and subsequent death and, in the best tradition of the Rousseau cantata, leaves us with a maxim in the guise of a gentle reproach to Love: *"Tu refuses tes récompenses aux plus fidelles coeurs"* (You refuse your rewards to the most faithful hearts).

In *Abraham* (1715), a sacred cantata published separately and dedicated to Mme de Maintenon, a recitative forms the center of the action with the appearance of the angel of the Lord, who stays the hand of Abraham.

La Muse de l'opéra ou les caractères lyriques, published separately in 1716, is one of Clérambault's most ambitious cantatas. It offers the listener a neat catalogue of operatic elements. It includes descriptive *symphonie*s: an opening prelude, a tempest, a *sommeil* and a *prélude infernal*. Its opening *da capo* air, scored for trumpet, first and second violins, bass violins, bass viols, and continuo, describes in turn the approach of Mars ("Au son des Trompettes"), Diana and her court ("Bruit de chasse"), and the inevitable shepherd and shepherdess ("Trio des hautbois")—all this within the formal confines of one long *da capo* air!

In my opinion, the twenty French and four Italian cantatas by Michel Pignolet de Montéclair, published in three books (ca. 1709, ca. 1717, 1728), also constitute a "repository of neglected masterpieces." Montéclair's originality is acknowledged by Bachelier, who wrote: "Montéclair, through his own particular taste, gives pleasure to those who hear him" (1728, preface). This is guarded praise, however, and Bachelier could not have been too happy with Montéclair's choice of texts, for he added that they were not "among the most regular," and he expressed the hope that some poems "in the taste of M. Rousseau" would fall into Montéclair's hands, so that he would have greater success and gain the "approbation of connoisseurs."

Like Clérambault, Montéclair borrowed liberally from operatic sources. His cantatas include a tempest (*La Mort de Didon*), the sounds of battle (*Le Retour de la Paix*), and a *sommeil* (*La Bergère*). Montéclair appropriated the use of a narrator (*historien*) from the oratorio for one cantata (*Pyrame et Thisbé*).

Montéclair gave a more prominent role to his obbligato instruments than any other composer of cantatas before Rameau. No doubled continuo airs are found in his cantatas, and if a bass voice is used, there is often an independent bass line. The extensive solo passages for the bass viol in *Le Triomphe de la constance* (Book 1) and *Ariane et Bacchus* (Book 3) never become the mere display pieces that on occasion mar the bass viol writing in the cantatas by Rameau (see, for example, the latter's cantata *L'Impatience*).

When we examine the solo airs of cantatas such as *L'Enlèvement d'Orithée* (Book 2) or *Tircis et Climène* (Book 3), we are reminded that Montéclair was also the author of a treatise on violin playing. In the *air léger* "Amants tout cède" (*L'Enlèvement*), for example, a solo violin maintains an independent line, sharing its motivic material with both vocal melody and bass in a degree of concentration that resembles an air from a Bach cantata more than an air from a *cantate françoise*.

In the *da capo* air, "Fille du ciel!" (*Le Retour de la Paix*, Book 1), persistent, detached, and often quite dissonant chords describe the destructive power of Mars as he overturns the altars of Peace. Momentary relief is afforded only through the brief recitative that makes up Part B of the air. The entire cantata *Le Retour de la Paix* is an impressive study in contrasts—contrasts of texture, mood, tempo, and key. Two violins and a bass viol comment throughout on the struggle between Mars and Peace. They suggest a background of warring strife, with fanfare and battle prelude, or they describe "gentle Peace," at which time the incisive notes of the harpsichord are stilled.

The longest and most dramatic of Montéclair's cantatas is *Pyrame et Thisbé* (Book 2), which was written for three voices (soprano, *haute-contre*, and baritone), violin, and continuo. It has four airs, two *ariettes*, ten recitatives, and three duos. For Montéclair, the *ariette* was not Campra's lively da capo air in compound meter; instead, it was a short, French binary air that repeated each of its balanced sections. Montéclair gave this description of *Pyrame et Thisbé*:

> *Although the Following Cantata has many more lines of text than any of the others I have written, I dare to flatter myself that it will not appear too long. I have cut out the repetitions ordinarily found in this type of work, and I have substituted a variety that perhaps will not displease. It is half Epic, half Dramatic. What is Epic is sung by a baritone, who represents the narrator, and what is Dramatic must be performed by a soprano and a* haute-contre, *who represent the protagonists (Book 2, 71).*

One of the musical highlights of the cantata is the first duo between the unfortunate lovers, "Que d'allarmes!" The opening measures are worth quoting in full in Example 23-7. The three-fold statement of the fanfare motif, with its interval expanded in repetition from a fourth to a sixth, is deprived of its forward motion each time by a searing dissonance followed by a delayed resolution every fifth measure.

23-7. Montéclair: Opening of duo "Que d'allarmes," *Pyrame et Thisbé* (after Book 2, ca. 1716).

As David Tunley has observed (1974, 154), Montéclair "seems to have drawn far closer to the French style than ever before" in his third volume of cantatas. Although nineteen out of thirty airs are *da capo*, Montéclair treated the Italian form with great originality (see Anthony 1977–1978). In most instances, a type of French binary air (usually an extended binary) is incorporated within the large A section. Montéclair divided the A section of his *da capo* airs into three parts. A "motto" *ritournelle* introduces Part 1 and is followed by a vocal statement of the initial motif, which is rounded off by a second *ritournelle*. Part 2 repeats and expands the motif. This section introduces additional text and new motivic material, modulates to a closely related key, and closes with a third *ritournelle* that re-establishes the original key. In Part 3, the most important musically, Montéclair created from the material of Part 2 a self-contained unit in the form of the extended binary air mentioned above, thus creating a synthesis between French and Italian formal procedures.[5]

André Cardinal Destouches composed two cantatas: *Oenone* (1716) and *Sémélé* (1719). In both cantatas, operatic techniques served Destouches well. The brilliant air "Volez grands Dieux" from *Oenone* is interrupted by a poignant recitative over a descending chromatic bass line. In *Sémélé* the abrupt change of key from A minor to F major gives dramatic import to the sound of thunder that follows.

Colin de Blamont left us three books of cantatas. This is music that borrows equally from French and Italian sources. His dramatic *symphonies* resemble those in French opera (see the tempest from *Didon*, Book 1); and his French monologue airs are pierced by exciting *tirades* for solo instruments (see "C'est ainsi" from *Circé*, Book 3). At the same time, the *da capo* aria structure dominates, and many *ritournelles* make use of the driving rhythms, melodic shapes, and harmonic practices of the Italian concerto.

The seven extant cantatas by Rameau[6] are all works of his first period except for the *Cantate pour le jour de la [fête de] Saint-Louis* (ca. 1745). They may be viewed as advanced studies for his later stage music.

The composer himself cited *Aquilon et Orithie* and *Thétis* in his letter to the librettist Houdar de La Motte (25 October 1727) as a measure of his skill in the composition of recitatives and airs and in the realization of a dramatic musical characterization. These two cantatas then are probably his first essays in the genre and date, as he stated in the letter, from 1715 a dozen years earlier. All the airs of *Aquilon et Orithie* contain Italianate elements. Brilliant, concerto-like violin obbligati climax in the rage aria, "Servez mes feux." *Thétis*, however, takes over from *préramiste* opera such descriptive *symphonies* as a thunder *symphonie* and a twenty-seven-measure storm. The prelude to *Thétis*, which is modeled on the *grave* section of the French overture, is also French.

Les Amants trahis (not later than 1721) is a rare example in the French Baroque of a comic cantata. It contains the earliest suggestions of a style perfected by Rameau in his lyric comedy, *Platée*, of 1745. The various musical means used to characterize laughing or weeping, although obvious and overworked, are at least justifiable from the standpoint of the subject matter; and the rapid Alberti bass patterns and awkward leaps of the obbligato bass viol add much to the *buffo* character of Damon's airs. How different this is from similar passages in his cantata *L'Impatience* (not later than 1722) that appear to have no function other than to test the skills of the viol player and to generate endless melismas in the vocal line on stereotyped words such as *chaîne* and *flamme*.

Orphée (not later than 1721) follows the format of a Rousseau cantata, with the addition of a long series of accompanied recitatives inserted abruptly before the last of too many virtuosi *airs gais*. The most effective contrast that results from this dramatic centerpiece of recitatives is that of a conflict of tonalities. We are catapulted without warning from an *air gracieux* in D major to a recitative in B-flat major. All of the following action recitatives now occur in flat keys (B-flat major, G minor, A-flat major, E-flat major, C minor, and D minor) until we are just as abruptly returned to G major in an *air gai* that closes the work.

The only cantata from which Rameau borrowed in his later work is the dramatic pastoral, *Le Berger fidèle* (ca. 1728). Its charming air, "L'Amour qui règne dans votre âme," recurs in the third *entrée* of *Les Fêtes d'Hébé* of 1739. As Girdlestone has observed, this cantata is one of the few by Rameau to include pages in which the composer's personal style breaks through the patina of Italianisms and *préramiste* imitations. In the opening recitative, the dramatic leap of an augmented sixth in the bass initiates, by means of a diminished seventh chord, a sudden shift of key from the relative major (F) to C minor. This is vintage Rameau, as is the correct declamation and the intensity of feeling in the elegiac air, "Faut-il qu'Amaryllis périsse?" that follows.

Although they contain some individual numbers of great charm, most of the cantatas by Charles-Hubert Gervais and Laurent Gervais, Philippe Courbois, Thomas-Louis Bourgeois, Boismortier,[7] François Bouvard, Bernard Burette, Nicolas Racot de Grandval, and Louis Néron cannot be classed with the best by Bernier, Campra, Clérambault, Montéclair, or Rameau.

Cantatas, especially those by Bernier and Clérambault, were widely disseminated throughout France and appear to have stimulated the composition of similar pieces by provincial composers. Such are the four cantatas found in a manuscript collection of *"Airs françois et italiens avec simphonie"* in the Bibliothèque du Muséum Calvet in Avignon (MS 1182). A high point of this collection is *Le Mauvais ménage* by a Sr Reboul. It is one of the scarce examples in France of a comic cantata. This scene of domestic strife is scored for soprano and tenor, with the unusual accompaniment of two *basses de viole*, a *basse de violon*, a bassoon, and harpsichord. A certain M. Malet, *"Maître de Musique de Saint-Pierre"* (Avignon), contributed a charming *cantate patoise* in Provençal dialect to this collection.

In an attempt to extend the life of the cantata into the later eighteenth century, composers wrote diminutive works bearing the generic title of *cantatille*. They were usually composed of two or three short airs and as many recitatives. Rousseau was probably too harsh in branding these works as "worse than the Cantata." At their best, they reflect the superficial yet elegant world of the Rococo. Jean-Joseph Mouret brought out a collection of nine *cantatilles* (no date), most of which were designed for performances at the *Concerts Français* at the Tuileries. At least two from this set (*Écho* and *Eglé*) date from as early as 1718. Mouret's *cantatilles* have a great deal of charm and subtlety, especially in their long melismas and asymmetrical phrases.

Louis Lemaire (ca. 1694–ca. 1750) left us sixty-six *cantatilles*. In view of the interest in rustic instruments during this period, it is understandable that several of Lemaire's *cantatilles* call for the accompaniment of *vielles* and musettes. *Cantatilles* were often tailor made for specific performers and performances. Thus, *Borée* by Louis Lemaire (privilege date, 1733) was "sung at the Concert of the Château des Tuileries by Mlle Petit-Pas" (score), and we read at the end of Lemaire's score for *Hébé* that he wrote this *cantatille* for "M. Jeyliot [Pierre Jelyotte], whose voice is of a great range. The composer has transposed it up a Fourth in order to accommodate Sopranos and Tenors."

So it was that the cantata lived on in the eighteenth century through the *cantatille* as an anachronistic vehicle of display for vain performers and an exercise in composition suited to the limited talents of minor composers. Its demise parallels the fate of the *grand motet* after Delalande and that of the descriptive harpsichord piece after Couperin. The fault lay not so much with the genre or the medium itself, or even with the eddies and tides of fickle fashion that had isolated it—rather, the critical fact was the dearth of composers of genius as the century progressed: there were no Rameaus at the height of their creative powers, none to become sufficiently interested in the cantata to compose examples of enduring musical value.

⋙ Chapter 24 ⋘

Epilogue: Thoughts on the Performance of French Baroque Music

Although it is quite possible to insist energetically that the most critical problems of ornamentation and rhythmic alteration arise in the music of the *grand siècle*, it is equally true that this music offers the greatest latitude of any for stylistically valid alternatives in performance. I do not propose to become embroiled in the endless polemics that heat the pages of our scholarly journals regarding "correct performance" of, for example, a Couperin trill. Rather, it is more appropriate to conclude a general survey of seventeenth- and eighteenth-century music in France with some general observations on performance problems connected with this music.

Only the twentieth century has shown an almost obsessive interest in the problems of performance of music of earlier centuries. Only in the twentieth century do we find book after book dealing with the "interpretation of early music" and entire journals devoted to performance problems (see, for example, the *Performance Practice Review* and *Historical Performance*, both founded within the last decade). This interest dates from the pioneering work of scholars such as Arnold Dolmetsch in the first decades of this century. Since the appearance of his *The Interpretation of the Music of the XVII and XVIII Centuries Revealed by Contemporary Evidence* in 1915, the bibliography on performance practices has reached monumental proportions.

With near methodical regularity, composers of keyboard music from Chambonnières to Balbastre provided a table of ornaments (*agréments*) in the prefaces to their *pièces de clavecin* or *pièces d'orgue*. For over 150 years, the tables maintained a fairly high degree of consistency in the interpretation of named ornaments, if not in the symbols given to the defined names. Now that many of the tables are available in secondary sources,[1] it is important that present day performers of this music consult them and note the discrepancies that do exist. In Couperin, for example, the *tremblement lié* results in a type of built-in rubato that is most effective in pieces of a moderate or slow tempo; this differs, however, from Marchand's interpretation of the same ornament and from the *cadence appuyée* of Rameau, by which the preceding note is considered an *appuy* and the actual oscillation begins on the main note (see Example 24-1).

24-1. Ornaments from three tables compared: (a) Couperin, (b) Marchand, (c) Rameau.

Yet we have become over-zealous, perhaps even puritanical, in our attempts to apply rules of ornamentation derived from these tables. Undoubtedly, the tables were designed to serve as guidelines for the performer and not necessarily as Holy Writ. Their authors might be startled were they to find the quasi-improvisational tone of their keyboard pieces sacrificed to an overly doctrinaire attitude toward ornamentation in our studios and classrooms. The number of twentieth-century specialists in the art of Baroque keyboard ornamentation is impressive, to be sure, but often one cannot help feeling a rigidity in their approach that converts *a* correct manner of application to *the* correct manner. It is amusing to contemplate the trauma of a piano teacher armed with Ralph Kirkpatrick's dictum, "It cannot be too emphatically stated that the Bach trill *always begins with the upper note* . . . [italics his],"[2] who is suddenly faced with the trill in the second *Two-Part Invention*: when begun on the upper note, this trill results in exposed parallel octaves.

Current reseachers of problems in Baroque interpretation would do well to heed Robert Donington's words:

> *No one interpretation of a Baroque ornament can be singled out as alone correct. There is no one right interpretation. There can be varied interpretations which are within the style, and therefore right, as well as others which are outside the style, and therefore wrong.*[3]

Also, that the "integrity of the French trill (beginning on the upper note) remains intact"[4] is less important than that the performer is immersed in the over-all style and sound-complex of French Baroque music.

In the performance of non-keyboard music, the problem of ornamentation is confounded by most composers' perverse insistence on indicating their ornamentation by a single sign (+). Such a sign was generally thought to indicate some sort of trill. Montéclair, for example, in his *Principes de musique* tells us that "teachers [of vocal music] designate the trill [*tremblement*] by a small cross placed before the note" (1736, 77).[5]

Couperin's oft-quoted observation in his *Art de toucher le clavecin* is one of the many comments of the period that attest to the importance of rhythmic alteration in performance traditions of French Baroque music: "We [French composers] write music differently from the way we play it . . . . The Italians, on the other hand, observe the exact value of the notes in composing their music" (1716, 39).

One common way of achieving a marked rhythmic deviation from the printed page was through the use of unequal notes (*notes inégales*) in place of the notated even-note values.[6] This widespread practice was undoubtedly sanctioned by the writings of most theorists and composers. From their treatises emerges a

> *picture remarkable for a high degree of uniformity with respect to (1) the manner of presentation; (2) the rules that determine which notes are to be even, and which are eligible for unevenness; (3) the nature of the inequality; and (4) the exceptions to the rules (Neumann 1965a, 319).*

The French mania for using *inégales* may be observed in Plate 6. In spite of warnings against their application to pieces having a brisk tempo or a series of repeated notes, an anonymous hand converted the fast, even sixteenth-notes of the famous tempest from Marais's *tragédie lyrique*, *Alcyone*, into an orgy of *inégales* in a reduced score that was used for performance in an eighteenth-century revival and is found today in the Bibliothèque de l'Opéra (A. 69c).

Naturally, the degree of inequality desired, its prohibition, and the application of this French practice to music beyond the borders of France is somewhat ambiguous. Composers could prohibit inequality by adding dots over the notes, by slurring together more than a pair of notes, or by writing clear instructions such as *notes égales, croches égales, marqué, également, martelées*, or *détachées*. Somewhat more equivocal are the general prohibitions against using *inégales* in pieces written in a fast tempo, in pieces in which the motion is prevailingly conjunct, and in dances such as allemandes. The allemandes posed no problem for Michel de Saint-Lambert, who wrote in his *Principes du clavecin* that inequality of eighth-notes need not occur here, "because of the slowness of their tempo." He was quick to add, however, that one could apply inequality to the sixteenth-notes "if there are any" (1702, 26). We recall that certain types of allemandes are closely related to the French overture and would benefit from the use of dotted rhythms. A suggestion that two possible interpretations of an allemande were acceptable is found in Perrine's *Pièces de luth en musique* (ca. 1680), in which two allemandes notated with even notes are followed by versions in dotted rhythms exemplifying the same piece played "*en gigue.*"

If the proliferation of rules for and against using *inégales* is confusing to us, we may take comfort from an eighteenth-century composer of excellent repute; Montéclair himself admitted that "it is very difficult to give general principles on the equality or inequality of notes, because it is the character of the Pieces one sings that governs them" (1709, 15).

In my opinion, we should use extreme discretion in applying rules of inequality to music composed outside France unless this music is unmistakably in the French style. In spite of their thinness of texture and idealizations of the *style brisé*, the so-called *French Suites* by Bach, for example, derive as much from Italian sources (note especially the courantes and gigues) as they do from Couperin and Dieupart. Dolmetsch's proposal that *inégales* be used in the sarabande from the first suite in D minor is difficult to justify (1915, 86), for they essentially convert Bach's sarabande into a siciliana!

Rhythmic alterations other than the *notes inégales* often result from the carelessness, or, at best, the indifference of many seventeenth- and eighteenth-century composers toward precise rhythmic notation. This is especially true of dotted rhythms following a rest. Measure four of Example 9-1b (Part Two, Chapter 9), an excerpt from a revised version of Lully's *Bellérophon*, illustrates this inexactitude. What is obviously meant is the precise vertical alignment of dotted rhythms between all voices, which would mean changing the oboe and bassoon parts to conform to that of the strings. A similar problem exists with the group of rapid upbeat notes (*tirades*) typically found in French overtures. No matter how notated, according to Newman Powell, they were played "as rapidly as possible" (1958, 184).

More controversial are the performance practices of double dotting (or overdotting) notes (and rests) within the context of passages dominated by dotted rhythms, and the rhythmic synchronization of all parts. For many, these remain the two most important characteristics of music written *à la française*. Two diametrically opposed points of view may be found in Thurston Dart and Frederick Neumann. Dart stated that in performance:

> *Conventional lengthening of the dotted note and shortening of the complementary note was in very widespread use over a very great length of time, and ignorance of this fact is one of the great defects of present-day performances of old music (1954, 81).*

Dart added that "All dotted rhythms should be adjusted so that they fit the shortest one in the piece." In 1965 in the *Revue de musicologie*, Neumann first challenged the view of Dart (and the majority of the musicological establishment) by claiming that the written double dot was known in France in the second half of the seventeenth century and therefore would have been employed if lengthening were desired; noting that no French treatises of the period mention it, he concluded that the concept of overdotting in performance is "essentially a legend" (1965b, 86). The battle of the double dot continues unabated, but charge and counter-charge often shed more heat than light on a complex performance problem.[7]

Whether or not a French overture is performed with double dotted rhythms and whether or not rhythmic synchronization is applied are less vital than that the style of the music itself spring from the kinetic energy of the French dance. Be the rhythms overdotted or played as notated, we have all known performances of the overture to *Messiah* sadly lacking the crisp, rhythmic incisiveness appropriate to heraldic gesture and taken so slowly in the initial *Grave* that musical impetus falters. Permeated by the all-enveloping sound of the modern symphony orchestra, such a performance too often succeeds in obliterating the music's dance origins—even though it is a French overture. One is immediately reminded of Igor Stravinsky's cogent observation that "Whether instrumental or vocal, whether sacred or secular, eighteenth-century music is, in one sense, *all* dance music" (1962, 128).

Some brief comments on an over-used term of the period are in order. If we only understood *le bon goût* in full, its meaning might help resolve some of the controversies described above. It was a musical court of last appeal to which both composer and performer might turn to vindicate their work. French aestheticians and philosophers of the eighteenth century, however, were no better equipped to define *le bon goût* than their twentieth-century counterparts.[8] "They speak without cease of *taste*, of good *taste*, of bad *taste*," despaired the author of the article "Goût" in the *Dictionnaire de Trévoux*, adding, "It is much easier to say what taste is not than what it is" (1743–1752, 3:865). For Lecerf, *le bon goût* was "merely natural sentiment aided by principles"

(1725; rpt. 1966, 2:273). For Père André in his *Essai sur le beau* (1741) and for the author of the *Dictionnaire de Trévoux* article, it was a sentiment perceived at first glance that revealed the nature of things in an instant. For Charles Batteux, good taste "must be satisfied when Nature is well chosen and well imitated by the Arts" (1746, 9), yet in the same year, Louis de Bollioud de Mermet wrote that the "imitation of nature is a road too well traveled, a too common and trivial device" (1746,16). He added the sensible comment that "true Taste demands . . . that he who performs follows to the letter the intention of the composer" (1746, 23). Germain Boffrand, recognizing that "every man claims to have it [good taste]" but aware that it was only vaguely defined as a certain *"je ne sais quoi* that pleases," suggested that one could find demonstrations of good taste only in the clearly defined principles of each art taken individually (1743, 3–4). Jean-Jacques Rousseau, in the long articles on "Goût" in his dictionary and in Diderot's *Encyclopédie*, made a valiant effort to bring a more systematic point of view to definitions of taste. He wisely refrained from arguing with what he called each man's *goût particulier* and concentrated on a *goût général*, concerning which "all well-organized men were in agreement." In Rousseau's opinion, it was reasonable that such men with sufficiently sensitive ears and well-trained minds would, upon attending a concert, reach a unanimous opinion on the relative value of the music heard.

We may be amused, annoyed, and often stimulated by the dialectical convolutions expressed in the felicitous language of most eighteenth-century French writings on good taste. To expect these sources to illuminate the music of a Couperin or a Rameau, however, is a *reductio ad absurdum*. French taste of the period, good or bad, can only be determined from the music itself. Through total immersion in the score and through detailed analysis of the music *qua* music, guided by one's own musical sensibilities and aided by some knowledge of the performance practices of the period, one may grasp the transcendent worth of a *grand motet* by Delalande or a simple noel setting by Charpentier.

Appendix: Preparation and Performance of a Seventeenth-Century Ballet de Cour

Ballet of the King at the Hôtel de Ville*

In the year 1626 on the fourth day of February, monsieur de Bailleul, knight & lord of Vattetot-sur-la-mer & of Soisi-sur-Seine, state counselor, civil lieutenant, & chief magistrate of the merchants of the town [prevost des marchands], reported to the aldermen [échevins] at the office that the previous day at the Louvre the king had told him that he wished to come dance his ballet at the said hôtel de ville & that he wished to honor the said town by this act; to which end he [the chief magistrate] was to order the necessary preparations & request all the most beautiful & highly placed ladies to attend. To which he replied to his majesty that this would be the greatest honor the town could ever receive. And forthwith the said chief magistrate of the merchants with the said aldermen, king's prosecutor [procureur du roy], town clerk [greffier], & tax collector [receveur] of the town resolved to issue orders for all the said preparations to receive his majesty there in the most sumptuous & superb manner possible.

And on Sunday the eighth day of the said month of February, the said chief magistrate of the merchants together with sieur Clement, the town clerk, went to see the king at the Louvre, to whom his majesty confirmed that he would come without fail to dance his said ballet at the said hôtel de ville about Shrovetide & that one should send for the beautiful ladies & the townswomen. To which the said chief magistrate of the merchants said that this news was already spread throughout the entire town which rejoiced in the hearing of it.

And on Monday the ninth day of the said month of February, the said chief magistrate of the merchants & aldermen initiated the said preparations to receive his majesty & to this end sent for the master-masons & master-carpenters of the town to make platforms, balconies, stages, & amphitheaters in the great hall of the hôtel de ville, in order to accommodate the ladies & guests there; they even sought out the advice of sieur Franchine.**

They also sent for the town grocer, whom they ordered to have ready a great quantity of white candles, both large & small, to put in the chandeliers & the candlestands that will be on the floors of the great halls, rooms, galleries, & offices of the said hôtel de ville & on the tables; also to prepare a great quantity of sweetmeats for the refreshment of the king, princes, maskers, & others.

They also sent for the town woodworker to have him ply his trade wherever necessary, to make all the said chandeliers & candlestands of wood, to have sconces to fix in place in all the rooms, along the stair-ways & galleries, ready to receive the small white candles.

They likewise sent for the town's captain of artillery whom they ordered to hold the town artillery, cannons, & mortar ready for firing when his majesty arrives to dance the ballet.

And on Tuesday the seventeenth of the said month of February, one of the gentlemen of the duc de Nemours came to the hôtel de ville to request the gentlemen to send him the said town clerk so he might speak with him on behalf of the king about his ballet. And forthwith, the said town clerk was conveyed there, to whom the said sieur de Nemours said that in his majesty's ballet there were a great number of machines which could not be transported from the Louvre to the hôtel de ville; that the said town would have to have similar ones made promptly & that to do this it was necessary to apply to a certain sculptor named Bourdin living in the hôtel de Nevers, who made the ones for the Louvre. That having been reported by the said town clerk to the said gentlemen of the town, they sent for the said Bourdin, who delivered the memorandum of all that he had to make; & among other things there was a great elephant, a camel, two mules, four parrots, & other pieces over which Bourdin & the said gentlemen of the town struck a bargain for the sum of 900 pounds without the paintings.

There also came to the said hôtel de ville the said sieur Franchine & monsieur Morel, who told the said gentlemen that it was necessary to prepare the hall of the hôtel de ville to accommodate the said machines that were the same as those in the Louvre; & to this end carpenters & joiners were ordered to work promptly there.

Similarly, they sent for the town painter whom they ordered to make the necessary paintings for the said stages, amphitheaters, & all else, just as at the Louvre.

The said gentlemen also sent for the tapestry-maker of the said town whom they ordered to have ready a great quantity of tapestries for adorning the hall where his majesty would take his refreshment, together with adorning all the rooms, offices, & private studies where his majesty, monsieur his brother, monsieur the comte de Soissons, & other princes & masked lords would retire to warm themselves & change clothes; likewise for the said tapestry-maker to have ready two beautiful canopies—one to be put in the great ballroom, the other, in the hall where refreshments will be served.

They also sent for twenty violinists & wind players who were contracted to play & have the town guests dance while awaiting the maskers.

They also sent for the town cooks to prepare the necessary refreshments.

And on Saturday the twenty-first of the said month of February, the said chief magistrate of the merchants, & aldermen, & town clerk went in the presence of his majesty, to assure themselves of which day he wished to dance his ballet, so that they could prepare the said refreshments & invite the ladies. To which gentlemen his majesty announced that it would be the night of the day of Shrove Tuesday.

Thus the said gentlemen of the town sent word to the cook, widow Coiffier, to prepare banquets of fish instead of meat, which she promised.

And on Sunday the twenty-second of the said month, the said gentlemen of the town were at the home of Monsieur the duc de Montbazon, governor of the town, to entreat him to honor the town with his presence in all solemnity, which he very willingly promised to do.

And on the same day, he, as well as sieur du Hallier, captain of the king's guards, & other lords, members of the ballet, came to dine at the said hôtel de ville to see & investigate the said preparations; the said sieur du Hallier with the said gentlemen of the town were even taken everywhere to check the doors, entryways, rooms, & places of the said hôtel de ville to have barriers made at the great door as well as at certain locations in the galleries & at the stairs to keep out the crowd of people; sieur du Hallier told the said gentlemen of the town that he had orders from the king to come with his company to the said hôtel de ville the day of the ballet; & that furthermore he would dispatch two other companies to the Grève[†]—one composed of his regiment of guards & the other, of Swiss guards—to prevent disorders.

On Monday the twenty-third of the said month of February, the said machines were brought to the hôtel de ville of the said town.

The same day the said gentlemen of the town invited all the most beautiful, high ranking ladies of Paris to come to the said hôtel de ville to see the ballet the next day.

The said gentlemen of the town ordered their wine steward & maître d'hôtel to have ready an abundance of wine, bread, & meat for the said day of Shrove Tuesday for the dinner & supper of the said governor, du Hallier, & other captains, & gentlemen of their retinue, as well as for several of the said guests, the same for the said guards of the king's corps as well as for other companies, & to put wood in the Grève to warm them; similarly to have wood brought into all the rooms & offices to warm the said guests & maskers when they arrive & when they change their clothing.

The said gentlemen of the town also invited messieurs the town counsellors & messieurs the district officers to be present.

It is noteworthy that the said sieur Clement, town clerk & consièrge of the hôtel de ville, had the particular charge of securing with good strong timber props the rooms & all places under the halls, the rooms & private studies where the king would be; together with having all the chimneys cleaned to avoid fire or other accidents.

Thus by the great care, order, & diligence that the said chief magistrate of the merchants, aldermen, & town clerk exercised, all was perfect & in a state of readiness by Monday evening.

And as much as the said gentlemen of the town had not had the coverings of embroidered satin made, nor the sky, nor the other scenery that was needed to accompany the machines, nor had they the live horse that was supposed to be there, the said gentlemen of the town beseeched his majesty to order those at the Louvre brought to the said hôtel de ville when they were no longer needed at the Louvre; this his majesty accorded & commanded the sieur de la Garde, his treasurer, to take care of it.

And on Tuesday the twenty-fourth of the said month, Shrove Tuesday, at six o'clock in the morning, there came to the said hôtel de ville sieur de la Coste, ensign of the guards of the king's corps, followed by two adjutants & a number of archers of the corps, who asked the said sieur Clement for all of the keys to the gates, rooms, & offices of the said hôtel   de ville, which he directly gave them with a tag attached to each key in order to identify it; & the said guards stationed themselves at all the gates & approaches to the said hôtel   de ville.

And at about eleven o'clock there came the said du Hallier, captain of the guards, followed by a number of archers; & a short time later the said sieur de Montbazon; & they all dined at the said hôtel de ville with the said chief magistrate of the merchants, aldermen, town clerk, & tax collector; the king's prosecutor not being there because of his indisposition.

At three o'clock in the afternoon two companies of relief guards came into the Grève, one was French & the other, Swiss, with drums sounding.

At four o'clock the guests began to arrive, who were seated one after the other in the said great hall by the said sieurs du Hallier & de la Coste, followed by the archers. And it can be said, & is true, that never has one seen such fine order & lack of confusion due to the care & foresight of the said monsieur du Hallier.

At seven o'clock the said governor, du Hallier, & several other gentlemen supped at the said hôtel de ville with the said chief magistrate of the merchants, aldermen, town clerk, & tax collector, & a few of the best-known gentry of the town.

The lords & ladies being placed on the stages & on the platforms, all the candles were lit, & then all the beautiful ladies were recognized, who were laden with pearls & diamonds & adorned to advantage.

At eleven o'clock in the evening there came *madame la première présidente* [wife of the president of Parliament, always called Premier Président], who was received by the said gentlemen of the town & given the first seat.

At midnight the refreshment of sweetmeats was laid out for the king in the little hall, on the side toward the church of Saint-Jean, where they also set out the town's silver service, guarded by four archers; for this refreshment there were brought more than six hundred little boxes of fine sweetmeats.

Moreover, three large tables were set up for the banquet of fish, which, however, was not cooked until the maskers were seen to arrive.

All night long the twenty violinists performed in the said great hall to entertain the guests without anyone's dancing, since the ladies did not wish to leave their seats.

The gentlemen of the town had the responsibility of seeing that the white candles were changed & replaced as they burned down, there being in the said hall thirty-two candelabra in which there were 128 candles which were replaced & changed twice during the night, & likewise in the other halls, rooms, & offices.

At four o'clock in the morning, the maskers began to arrive. The said chief magistrate of merchants, aldermen, & town clerk were dressed in their felt robes, each of two colors, except for the said chief magistrate who wore a robe of satin in two colors & went to meet the king, preceded by ten police officers of the town also dressed in their robes of two colors & each holding two lighted white tapers in his hands. And the said gentlemen of the town met the king on the stairs; to whom the said chief magistrate of the merchants offered a short welcome on his safe arrival & spoke of the honor that the town received this day by his presence. His majesty apologized for arriving so late, which was not his fault, but rather that of the workmen who had not completed preparations soon enough. His majesty was escorted by the said governor, chief magistrate of the merchants, aldermen, & town clerk into the private study of the said town clerk which had been prepared for his majesty where he took his shirt & masquerade costume. Monsieur, the king's only brother, was escorted into the room of the said town clerk near the said study where the king was. Monsieur the comte de Soissons, prince of the blood, was escorted into the small office that had been prepared for him. The other princes & lords who were members of the *grand ballet*, in the other rooms. The maskers in the large office. The masked musicians & the violinists, in the room of the first gallery; in each of which there was a fire, bread, wine & meats.

The said sieurs chief magistrate of the merchants, aldermen, & town clerk, thus dressed in their two-colored robes, always attended his majesty until he was ready to dance his ballet.

The said sieur du Hallier, just as had been planned, had removed the town violinists who were on the platforms & in their place had brought the king's violinists who would play for the ballet.

And at about five o'clock in the morning, his majesty & all the other maskers went into the great hall to dance the ballet. And then the violinists began to play. And while the first maskers made their entrances, his majesty, monsieur, & the other princes sat down in the loge of woodwork made expressly at the entrance to the hall so that they might see the dancing. The loge actually represented a tavern, which in the ballet stood for the town of Clamart. After the completion of some *entrées*, the king came masked & danced with the others. The machines also made their effect. And afterward, the *grand ballet* was danced by the king & twelve other princes & lords, among whom were monsieur the brother of the king, monsieur the comte de Soissons, monsieur the grand prior, monsieur the duc de Longueville, monsieur the duc d'Elbeuf, monsieur the comte d'Harcour, monsieur the comte de la Roche-guyon, monsieur de Liancour, monsieur de Baradas, monsieur the comte de Cramail, & monsieur the chevalier de Souvray, all dressed very richly.

After the conclusion of the said ballet which had lasted at least three hours, the violinists began to play a branle, & his majesty & the other maskers unmasked, & all the aforementioned each took a lady to dance the said branle, namely his majesty took *madame la première présidente*; monsieur the brother of the king, madame de Bailleul, wife of the said chief magistrate of the merchants; monsieur the comte [de Soissons?] afterward, & then the said princes & lords.

The said branle concluded, his majesty was escorted by the said gentlemen of the town into the hall where the banquet & refreshments had been prepared; this banquet, which consisted of very fine fish, was admired by the king who, standing the whole while, ate of the said banquet for a very long time, being accompanied by the said princes & lords named above, who likewise ate very much of the said victuals; the said gentlemen of the town with the said town clerk being still near his majesty at the time of the said banquet. And his majesty, having asked for drink, holding his glass in his hand, said loudly, addressing his words to the said chief magistrate of the merchants that he was going to drink to him & to the entire town, & turning towards the said aldermen, drank likewise to them; & particularly addressing himself to the said town clerk, afforded him the favor of drinking to him. And after his majesty had drunk, he ordered that wine be handed to the said chief magistrate of the merchants, aldermen, & to the said sieur Clement, & he said that he wished them to drink also to him, which they also did with unparalleled joy. And immediately, his majesty approached the table of sweetmeats, which was covered with two large, white cloths; these cloths being lifted, his majesty drawing back, admiring the great number of exquisite sweetmeats which were there, said loudly: *How beautiful it is!* And at the same time, his majesty himself chose three little boxes of the said sweetmeats. And forthwith all the said princes & lords & other persons threw themselves upon the said refreshments, which were taken, ravished, & dispersed, & half were turned upside down on the floor, from which scene the king took singular pleasure. This done, his majesty said to the said gentlemen of the town & to the said town clerk that he was very pleased with them & that he thanked them & that he had never seen better organization & had never eaten with greater appetite than he had just done; & wholly dressed in costume as he was when he danced the *grand ballet*, he departed & was escorted by the said gentlemen of the town & the said town clerk, who still wore their robes of two colors, to the staircase at the main entrance to the said hôtel de ville where, it being about nine o'clock in the morning, the artillery, cannon, & mortar of the town began to fire; from which his majesty took very great pleasure & remained a long time at the top of the said flight of stairs, being seen by all the people in the Grève, which Grève was entirely filled with people who shouted: *Long live the king* with a great acclamation of joy. And the king thanking anew the said gentlemen of the town, entered his carriage to go to his Louvre, Swiss guards walking before him, drums sounding.

And it is worthy of note that along the streets where the king passed in order to come from the Louvre to the said hôtel de ville, there were paper lanterns of sundry colors at each window of all the houses & shops, following the instructions sent by the said town to the district officers for this purpose; just as the said hôtel de ville was also filled with them, outside as well as inside, which was very fine to see.

And it cannot be said that the town was ever more honored by its king than it was by this act, for which there was general rejoicing.

And the next day, the twenty-sixth of the said month of February 1626, the chief magistrate of the merchants, aldermen, & clerk of the said town were at the Louvre to thank the king for the honor which he bestowed upon the town, to whom his majesty answered that he was very pleased with them & thanked them for it.

The king danced another ballet at the hôtel de ville again the sixteenth of February the following year.[‡] There were fireworks at the Grève set up and executed by Denis Caresme, firework-maker of the town. The king arrived at three o'clock in the morning.

---

*   The ballet described was the *Grand bal de la Douairière de Billebahaut*, which was first danced at the Louvre on 11 February 1626 (found in Lacroix, *Ballets et mascarades de cour*, 3:151–202). This description is an "extract from the registers of the hôtel de ville of Paris" found in *Histoire de la ville de Paris*, 1725, 5:568–572. Volumes 1 and 2 of this source were prepared by Michel de Félibien (1666–1719), and vols. 3–5, by Guy-Alexis Lobineau (1666–1727).

**   Tomasso Francini, Engineer of the king.

†   Large square in front of the hôtel de ville.

‡   Possibly the *Ballet du Sérieux et le grotesque*. See Lacroix 1868–1870, 3:298–321.

Abbreviations

AfMW	*Archiv für Musikwissenschaft*
AM	*Acta musicologica*
BSIM	*Bulletin de la Société Internationale de Musique*
CM	*Current Musicology*
CMBV	Centre de Musique Baroque de Versailles
EM	*Early Music*
FAM	*Fontes artis musicae*
GSJ	*Galpin Society Journal*
JAMS	*Journal of the American Musicological Society*
JMT	*Journal of Music Theory*
JVGSA	*Journal of the Viola da Gamba Society of America*
LWV	*Chronologisch-thematisches Verzeichnis sämtlicher Werke von Jean-Baptiste Lully* (*Lully Werke Verzeichnis*)
M&L	*Music and Letters*
MD	*Musica disciplina*
MF	*Die Musikforschung*
MGG	*Die Musik in Geschichte und Gegenwart*
MM	*Le Mercure musical*
MQ	*The Musical Quarterly*
MR	*The Music Review*
MT	*The Musical Times*
NOHM	*The New Oxford History of Music*
PRMA	*Proceedings of the Royal Musical Association*
RBdM	*Revue belge de musicologie*
RdM	*Revue de musicologie*

Recherches	*Recherches sur la musique française classique*
RM	*La Revue musicale* (Ed. H. Prunières)
RMC	*La Revue musicale* (Ed. Combarieu)
RMI	*Rivista musicale italiana*
RMS	*Revue musicale suisse*
SiM(AUS)	*Studies in Music* (University of Western Australia)
SiM(CND)	*Studies in Music* (University of Western Ontario)
SIMG	*Sammelbände der Internationalen Musik-Gesellschaft*
XVIIe siècle	*Revue publiée par la Société d'Étude du XVIIe Siècle*
ZfMW	*Zeitschrift für Musikwissenschaft*

Bibliography

Sources Before 1800

Amelot. No date. *Mémoires pour servir à l'histoire de l'Académie Royale de Musique, depuis son établissement jusqu' à présent*, Manuscript. Bibliothèque de l'Opéra. (*Rés.* 516).

André, Père Yves-Marie. 1741. *Essai sur le beau*. Paris: Hippolyte-Louis Guérin.

Aquin de Château-Lyon, Pierre-Louis d'. 1753. *Siècle littéraire de Louis XV ou Lettres sur les hommes célèbres*, 2 vols. Paris: Duchesne.

Argenson, René Louis de Voyer de Paulmy, Marquis d'. No date. *Notices sur les oeuvres de théâtre.* Manuscripts. Bibliothèque de l'Arsenal (Manuscripts 3448–3455). Abridged version. Ed. Henri Lagrave. In *Studies on Voltaire and the Eighteenth Century*, vols. 42 and 43. Ed. Theodore Besterman. Geneva: Institute et Musée Voltaire, 1960.

Bachelier, I. 1728. *Recueil de cantates.* The Hague: Albert and Vander Kloot. Rpt. Geneva: Minkoff, 1992.

Bacilly, Bénigne de. 1661. *Recueil des plus beaux vers qui ont esté mis en chant.* Paris: C. de Sercy.

———. 1668. *Remarques curieuses sur l'art de bien chanter.* [2nd ed.] Paris: Chez l'autheur, 1679. Rpt. Geneva: Minkoff, 1971. Trans. and ed. by Austin Caswell as *A Commentary Upon the Art of Proper Singing.* New York: The Institute of Medieval Music, 1968.

Batteux, Charles. 1746. *Les Beaux-Arts réduits à un même principe.* Paris: Durand. Rpt. of 1773 ed. Geneva: Minkoff, 1971.

Bauderon de Sénecé. 1688. *Lettre de Clément Marot à M. de *** touchant ce qui s'est passé à l'arrivée de J.-B. Lulli aux Champs-Elysées.* Cologne: P. Marteau. Printed in *Écho musical*, 1913 (5 February, 5 March, 5 April).

Beauchamps, Pierre-François Godard de. 1735. *Recherches sur les théâtres de France.* Paris: Prault père. Rpt. Geneva: Minkoff, 1968.

Beaujoyeulx, Baltasar de. 1582. *Balet comique de la Royne*. Paris: Adrian le Roy, Robert Ballard, & Mamert Patisson. Rpt. Binghamton, New York: Center for Medieval & Early Renaissance Studies, 1982. Trans. Carol and Lander MacClintock. [Dallas?]: American Institute of Musicology, 1971.

Bedos de Celles, Dom François. 1766–1778. *L'Art du facteur d'orgues*, 4 vols. Paris: L.-F. Delatour. Rpt. Kassel: Bärenreiter, 1963.

Beffara, Louis-François. 1783–1784. *Dictionnaire de l'Académie Royale de Musique*. Manuscript. Bibliothèque de l'Opéra (*Rés*. 602).

Bérard, Jean-Baptiste Antoine. 1755. *L'Art du chant*. Paris: Dessaint et Saillant. Rpt. Geneva: Minkoff, 1972.

Bernier, Nicolas. No date. *Principes de composition*. Manuscript. Bibliothèque Nationale (*Rés*. Vmb MS 2). Eng. trans. Philip Nelson. Brooklyn: Institute of Medieval Music, 1964.

Besche l'âiné. 1774. *Abrégé historique de la ménestrandie*. Versailles: No publisher.

Blainville, Charles-Henri de. 1754. *L'Esprit de l'art musical, ou Réflexions sur la musique*. Geneva: No publisher. Rpt. Geneva: Minkoff, 1975.

Boffrand, Germain. 1715. *Le Théatre de M. Quinault*, 5 vols. Paris: P. Ribou.

———. 1743. *Livre d'Architecture*. Paris: Guillaume Cavelier patrem. Rpt. Farnborough, Hants, England: Gregg Press Limited, 1969.

Boindin, Nicolas. 1719. *Lettres historiques sur tous les spectacles de Paris*. Paris: P. Prault.

Bollioud de Mermet, Louis de. 1746. *De la corruption du goust dans la musique françoise*. Lyons: A. Delaroche. Rpt. New York: AMS Press, 1978.

Bonnet, Jacques. 1715. *Histoire de la musique et de ses effets*. Paris: J. Cochart. Rpt. Geneva: Minkoff, 1969.

———. See Bourdelot, Pierre, and Jacques Bonnet.

Borjon de Scellery, Charles-Emmanuel. 1672. *Traité de la musette*. Lyons: J. Girin et B. Rivière. Rpt. Geneva: Minkoff, 1972.

Bourdelot, Pierre, and Jacques Bonnet. 1725. *Histoire de la musique et de ses effets*. 4 vols. Amsterdam: C. le Cene. Rpt. 4 vols. bound in 2. Graz, Austria: Akademische Druck und Verlagsanstalt, 1966.

Boyer, Abbé Claude. 1666. *Dessein de la tragédie des amours de Jupiter et Sémélé*. Paris: P. Promé.

Bricaire de la Dixmerie, Nicolas. 1769. *Les Deux âges du goût et du génie français*. Paris: Lacombe. Rpt. Geneva: Minkoff, 1971.

Brossard, Sébastien de. 1703. *Dictionnaire de musique*. Paris: C. Ballard. Rpt. Amsterdam: Antiqua Amsterdam, 1964.

———. 1724. *Catalogue des livres de musique théorique et pratique . . . qui sont dans le cabinet du sieur Séb. de Brossard*. Manuscript. Bibliothèque Nationale (*Rés*. Vm^8 20). Manuscript copy. Bibliothèque Nationale (*Rés*. Vm^8 21), made between 1725–1730. Ed. Yolande de Brossard, Paris: Bibliothèque Nationale, 1994.

―――. No date. *Dissertation sur cette espèce de concert qu'on nomme Cantate*. Manuscript. Paris, Bibliothèque Nationale, Nouv. acq. fr. 5269, fol. 75.

Burney, Charles. 1771. *Present State of Music in France and Italy*. London: T. Becket et al. 2nd ed. London: T. Becket et al., 1773. Rpt. of 2nd. ed. New York: Broude Bros., 1969.

Burwell, Mary, Miss. 1670. *Instructions for the Lute*. Manuscript. Printed 1958 in *GSJ* 11 (May): 3–62.

⌐ 🔲 ⌐

Cahusac, Louis de. 1754. *La Danse ancienne et moderne*, 3 vols. The Hague: J. Neaulme. Rpt. Geneva: Minkoff, 1971.

Callières, François de. 1688. *Histoire poétique de la guerre nouvellement déclarée entre les anciens et les modernes*. Paris: G. Aubonin.

Campion, François. 1716. *Traité d'accompagnement et de composition*. Paris: Veuve G. Adam. Rpt. Geneva: Minkoff, 1977.

―――. 1730. *Addition au traité d'accompagnement et de composition*. Paris: Veuve Ribou. Rpt. Geneva: Minkoff, 1977.

―――. See also Carbasus, Abbé.

Carbasus, Abbé (pseud. de François Campion). 1739. *Lettre de Monsieur l'abbé Carbasus à Monsieur D. . . . [Voltaire] . . . sur la mode des instruments de musique*. Paris: Veuve Allouel.

―――. See also Campion, François.

Chabanon, Michel-Paul Guy de. 1764. *Éloge de M. Rameau*. Paris: M. Lambert.

―――. 1785. *De la musique considérée en elle-même*. Paris: Pissot. Rpt. Geneva: Minkoff, 1969.

Chappuzeau, Samuel. 1674. *Le Théâtre françois*. 3 vols. Lyons: M. Mayer.

Chastellux, François-Jean. 1765. *Essai sur l'union de la poésie et de la musique*. Paris: Merlin. Rpt. Geneva: Minkoff, 1970.

Compan, Charles. 1787. *Dictionnaire de danse*. Paris: Cailleau. Rpt. Paris: J. Touzot, 1979.

Corrette, Michel. [1735]. *Méthode pour apprendre aisément à joüer de la flûte traversière*. Paris: Boivin et Le Clerc. Rpt. Hildesheim: Georg Olms Verlag, 1971. Trans. Carol R. Farrar. Brooklyn: Institute of Mediaeval Music, ca. 1970.

―――. 1738. *L'École d'Orphée: méthode pour apprendre facilement à jouer du violon*. Paris: Boivin et Le Clerc. Rpt. Geneva: Minkoff, 1973.

―――. 1741. *Méthode théorique et pratique pour apprendre en peu de temps le violoncelle dans sa perfection*. Paris: L'auteur. Rpt. Geneva: Minkoff, 1972.

―――. [1748.] *Méthode pour apprendre facilement à jouer du pardessus de viole à 5 et à 6 cordes*. Paris: Boivin et Le Clerc. Rpt. Geneva: Minkoff, 1983.

―――. 1753. *Le Maître de clavecin pour l'accompagnement*. Paris: L'Auteur. Rpt. Hildesheim: Georg Olms Verlag, 1971.

―――. 1758. *Le Parfait maître à chanter*. Paris: L'Auteur.

————. [1781.] *Méthode pour apprendre à jouer de la contre-basse à 3, à 4 et à 5 cordes* . . . . Paris: adresses ordinaires. Rpt. Geneva: Minkoff, 1978.

————. [1782.] *L'Art de se perfectionner dans le violon.* Paris: Mlle. Castagnery. Rpt. Geneva: Minkoff, 1973.

————. ca. 1783. *La Belle vielleuse, méthode pour apprendre facilement à jouer de la vielle.* Paris: Mlle. Castagnery. Rpt. Geneva: Minkoff, 1984.

Couperin, François. *Oeuvres complètes de François Couperin.* 12 vols. Ed. M. Cauchie et al. Paris: Éditions de l'Oiseau Lyre, 1932–1933. New ed. Ed. K. Gilbert and D. Moroney. Monaco: Éditions de l'Oiseau Lyre, 1979–.

————. ca. 1698. *Règles pour l'accompagnement.* Manuscript. Ed. Paul Brunold In *Oeuvres completes de François Couperin,* vol. 1. Paris: Éditions de l'Oiseau Lyre, 1933.

————. 1716. *L'Art de toucher le clavecin.* Paris: L'auteur. 2nd ed. revised. Paris: Boivin, 1717. Rpt. in *Oeuvres complètes de François Couperin,* vol. 1. Paris: Éditions de l'Oiseau Lyre, 1933. Rpt. New York: Broude Brothers, Ltd. 1969. Rpt. Geneva: Minkoff, 1986. Trans. and ed. by Anne Linde in French, German, and English. Wiesbaden: Breitkopf und Härtel, 1933. Trans. Margery Halford. Port Washington, New York: Alfred Publishing, 1974.

☙ 🔲 ❧

D'Alembert, Jean Le Rond. 1758. *De la liberté de la musique.* In *Oeuvres de d'Alembert.* Paris: A. Belin, 1821–1822, 1:515–546. Rpt. Geneva: Slatkine, 1967.

Dandrieu, Jean-François. ca. 1719. *Principes de l'accompagnement du clavecin.* Paris: L'auteur. Rpt. Geneva: Minkoff, 1972.

Danoville. 1687. *L'Art de toucher le dessus et basse de violle.* Paris: Ballard. Rpt. Geneva: Minkoff, 1972.

David, François. [1737.] *Méthode nouvelle ou Principes généraux pour apprendre facilement la musique et l'art de chanter.* Paris: Veuve Boivin.

Delair, Denis. 1690. *Traité d'accompagnement pour le théorbe et le clavessin.* Paris: L'auteur. Rpt. Geneva: Minkoff, 1972.

Denis, Jean. 1650. *Traité de l'accord de l'espinette.* Paris: Ballard. Rpt. New York: Da Capo Press, 1969.

Descartes, René. 1650. *Musicae compendium.* Utrecht: Girberti a Zyll & Theodori ab Ackersdyck. Rpt. New York: Broude Bros., 1968.

Dictionnaire de Trévoux. See Dictionnaire universel françois et latin.

Dictionnaire universel françois et latin (known as the *Dictionnaire de Trévoux*). 1743–1752. 7 vols. Paris: Delaune.

Diderot, Denis. See *Encyclopédie, ou Dictionnaire raisonné des sciences, des arts et des métiers.*

Documents du Minutier Central concernant l'histoire de la musique 1600–1650. 2 vols. Ed. Madeleine Jurgens. Vol. 1, Paris: SEVPEN, 1969; vol. 2, Paris: La Documentation française, 1974.

Dubos, Jean-Baptiste. 1719. *Réflexions critiques sur la poésie et sur la peinture.* 2 vols. Paris: J. Mariette. 7th ed., 3 vols. Paris: Pissot, 1770. Rpt. 7th ed. Geneva: Minkoff, 1967.

Dumanoir, Guillaume. 1664. *Le Mariage de la musique avec la danse.* Paris: G. de Luyne. New ed. Ed. J. Gallay. Paris: Librairie des bibliophiles, 1870.

Durey de Noinville, Jacques-Bernard. 1757. *Histoire du théâtre de l'Académie Royale de Musique en France.* 2 vols. 2nd ed. Paris: Duchesne. Rpt. (2 vols. in 1) Geneva: Minkoff, 1969.

Du Tralage, Jean-Nicolas. No date. *Notes et documents sur l'histoire des théâtres de Paris au XVIIe siècle, par Jean-Nicolas Du Tralage.* Ed. Paul Lacroix. Paris: Librairie des bibliophiles, 1880.

Encyclopédie, ou Dictionnaire raisonné des sciences, des arts et des métiers. 1751–1780. 35 vols. Ed. Denis Diderot. Paris: Briasson.

Estève, Pierre. 1753. *L'Esprit des beaux-arts.* Paris: C.-J.-B. Bauche. Rpt. Geneva: Minkoff, 1970.

Favart, Charles-Simon. 1763–1772. *Théâtre de M. (et Mme) Favart.* 10 vols. Paris: Duchesne. Rpt. Geneva: Minkoff, 1971.

Félibien, André. 1668. *Relation de la feste de Versailles du 18e juillet 1668.* Paris: P. Le Petit. Ed. of 1679. Paris: Impr. royale. Rpt. Paris: Dédalle Maisonneuve et Larose, 1994.

———. 1674. *Les Divertissemens de Versailles donnez par le Roy au retour de la conquete de la Franche-comté, en l'année 1674.* Paris: J.-B. Coignard.

———. 1689. *Recueil de descriptions de peintures et d'autres ouvrages faits pour le roi.* Paris: Veuve de S. Mabre-Cramoisy.

Félibien, Dom Michel, and Guy-Alexis Lobineau. 1725. *Histoire de la ville de Paris.* 5 vols. Paris: G. Desprez.

Feuillet, Raoul-Auger. 1700. *Chorégraphie ou l'art de décrire la dance par caractères, figures et signes démonstratifs.* Paris: L'auteur. Rpt. New York: Broude Bros., 1968.

Fleury, Nicolas. 1660. *Méthode pour apprendre facilement à toucher le théorbe sur la basse continue.* Paris: Robert Ballard. Rpt. Geneva: Minkoff, 1972.

Fontenay, Louis-Abel Bonafous (Abbé de). 1776. *Dictionnaire des artistes.* 2 vols. Paris: Vincent. Rpt. Geneva: Minkoff, 1972.

François, René (pseud. d' Étienne Binet). 1621. *Essai des merveilles de nature.* Rouen: R. de Beauvais.

Freillon-Poncein, Jean-Pierre. 1700. *La Véritable manière d'apprendre à jouer en perfection du hautbois, de la flûte et du flageolet.* Paris: J. Collombat. Rpt. Geneva: Minkoff, 1971.

Furetière, Antoine. 1690. *Dictionnaire universel.* 3 vols. The Hague: A. et R. Leers. Rpt. Paris: Le Robert, 1978.

⌐ ▦ ⌐

Gantez, Annibal. 1643. *L'Entretien des musiciens.* Auxerre: Jacques Bouquet. Ed. Thoinan et Claudin. Paris: A. Claudin, 1878. Rpt. Geneva: Minkoff, 1971.

Genest, Charles-Claude. 1712. *Les Divertissemens de Sceaux.* Trevaux and Paris: Étienne Ganeau.

Gherardi, Evaristo. 1700. *Le Théâtre italien . . . ou le Recueil général de toutes les comédies et scènes françoises jouées par les comédiens italiens du roy.* 6 vols. Paris: No publisher. London: J. Tonson, 1714.

Goldoni, Carlo. 1787. *Mémoires de M. Goldoni.* 3 vols. Paris: Veuve Duchesne.

Grandval, Nicolas Ragot de. 1732. *Essai sur le bon goût en musique.* Paris: Pierre Prault.

Grimarest, Jean-Léonard le Gallois de. 1707. *Traité du récitatif.* Paris: Jacques Le Fèvre et Pierre Ribou. Rpt. New York: AMS Press, 1978.

Grimm, Friedrich Melchior, Freiherr von. 1752. *Lettre de M. Grimm sur Omphale.* [Paris]: No publisher.

———. 1753. *Le Petit prophète de Boehmisch-Broda.* No city: No publisher. Trans. in O. Strunk. *Source Readings in Music History.* New York: W. W. Norton, 1950.

⌐ ▦ ⌐

Hawkins, Sir John. 1776. *A General History of the Science and Practice of Music.* 5 vols. London: T. Payne & Son. Rpt. in 2 vols. New York: Dover Publications, Inc., 1963.

Hotteterre, Jacques-Martin. 1707. *Principes de la flûte traversière ou flûte d'Allemagne. De la flûte à bec, ou flûte douce et du hautbois, divisés par traités.* Paris: Christophe Ballard. Rpt. Geneva: Minkoff, 1973.

———. 1737. *Méthode pour la musette.* Paris: J.-B.-C. Ballard. Rpt. Geneva: Minkoff, 1977.

⌐ ▦ ⌐

Jambe-de-Fer, Philibert. 1556. *L'Epitôme musical.* Lyons: Michel du Bois. Rpt. 1958–1963 in facsimile with its own pagination (1–71). In article "L'Epitôme musical de Philibert Jambe de Fer (1556)" by François Lesure. *Annales musicologiques* 6: inserted after page 346.

Jullien, Jean-Auguste. 1770. 2 vols. *Histoire du théâtre de l'opéra comique.* Paris: Lacombe.

Jumilhac, Pierre Benoît. 1673. *La Science et la pratique du plain-chant.* Paris: Louis Bilaine. Ed. J. Nisard and A. de Clercq. Paris: A. Le Clercq, 1847.

⌐ ▦ ⌐

La Borde, Jean-Benjamin de. 1780. *Essai sur la musique ancienne et moderne.* 4 vols. Paris: E. Onfroy. Rpt. Geneva: Minkoff, 1972.

La Bruyère, Jean de. 1688. *Des ouvrages de l'esprit.* New ed. Ed. G. Servois. New ed. Paris: Librairie de L. Hachette, 1865.

La Chapelle, Jacques-Alexandre de. 1736–1752. *Les Vrais principes de la musique.* 4 vols. Paris: Veuve Boivin.

Lacombe, Jacques. 1752. *Dictionnaire portatif des Beaux-arts.* Paris: Veuve Estienne & fils.

Ladvocat, Louis. [1694–1696.] *Lettres sur l'opéra à l'Abbé Dubos.* Ed. Jérôme de La Gorce. Paris: Cicero Éditeurs, 1993.

L'Affilard, Michel. 1694. *Principes très-faciles pour bien apprendre la musique.* Paris: Christophe Ballard. Rpt. Geneva: Minkoff, 1970.

La Fontaine, Jean de. 1677. "Épître à M. de Niert sur l'opéra." *Oeuvres diverses de Jean de La Fontaine,* vol. 2. Paris: Didot.

La Grange, Charles Varlet de. 1659–1685. *Le Registre de La Grange 1659–1685.* Manuscript. Paris: Archives of the Comédie Française. Rpt. with an index by B. E. Young and G. P. Young. 2 vols. Paris: Librairie E. Droz, 1947.

La Vallière, Louis César de La Baume Le Blanc, duc de. 1760. *Ballets, opéra et autres ouvrages lyriques.* Paris: J.-B. Bauche. Rpt. London: H. Baron, 1967.

La Voye, Mignot de. 1656. *Traité de musique.* Paris: R. Ballard. Rpt. Geneva: Éditions Minkoff, 1972.

Le Blanc, Hubert. 1740. *Défense de la basse de viole contre les entreprises du violon et les prétentions du violoncel.* Amsterdam: Pierre Mortier. Printed in *RM* 1927–1928, 9 (November–December); 9 (January–March and June). Rpt. Geneva: Minkoff, 1975.

Le Brun, Antoine-Louis. 1712. *Théâtre lyrique.* Paris: Pierre Ribou.

Lecerf de la Viéville, Jean-Laurent. 1725. *Comparaison de la musique italienne et de la musique françoise.* Reproduced without acknowledgement from 2nd ed. (1705–1706) in vols. 2–4 of Bourdelot, Pierre and Jacques Bonnet, *L'Histoire de la musique et de ses effets,* 4 vols. bound as 2. Amsterdam: C. Le Cène, 1725. Rpt. Graz, Austria: Akademische Druck und Verlagsanstalt, 1966. All vol. and page references come from the 1966 rpt. of Bourdelot and Bonnet, so do not match those of 2nd ed. which has 3 parts in 1 vol. Brussels: François Foppens, 1705–1706. Rpt. Geneva: Minkoff, 1972. 2nd ed. is a revised and enlarged ed. of the original (1st ed. Brussels: François Foppens, 1704).

———. For index to *Comparaison de la musique italienne et de la musique françoise,* see Carl B. Schmidt, 1993.

Le Gallois, Jean. 1680. *Lettre de Mr. le Gallois à Mlle Regnault de Solier touchant la musique.* Paris: Estienne Michallet et G. Guinet.

Leris, Antoine de. 1754. *Dictionnaire portatif des théâtres . . . de Paris.* Paris: C. A. Jombert. 2nd ed. 1763. Rpt. Geneva: Slatkine Reprints, 1970.

Le Sage, Alain-René, and D'Orneval [and Fuselier]. 1721–1737. *Le Théâtre de la foire ou l'opéra comique.* 10 vols. Paris: E. Graneau. Rpt. Geneva: Slatkine Reprints, 1968.

Lister, Dr. Martin. 1699. *A Journey to Paris in the Year 1698.* London: J. Tonson. Rpt. Urbana: University of Illinois Press, 1967.

Loret, Jean. 1650–1665. *La Muze historique.* Paris: C. Chenault. New ed. 4 vols. Paris: P. Jannet, 1857–1878.

Louis XIV. Ed. of 1978. *Louis XIV Mémoires.* Paris: Librairie Tallandier.

Loulié, Étienne. 1696. *Éléments ou principes de musique.* Paris: Christophe Ballard. Rpt. Geneva: Minkoff, 1972. *Elements or Principles of Music.* Trans. Albert Cohen. New York: Institute of Medieval Music, Ltd., 1965.

Lully, Jean-Baptiste. *Oeuvres complètes de J.-B. Lully.* 4 series, 10 vols. Ed. Henry Prunières. Paris: Éditions de la Revue musicale, 1930–1939.

Mably, Gabriel Bonnot de. 1741. *Lettres à Madame la Marquise de P[ompadour] sur l'opéra.* Paris: Didot. Rpt. Geneva: Minkoff, 1978.

Marmontel, Jean-François. 1787. *Eléments de littérature.* Vols. 12–15 of 1818–1820 ed. of *Oeuvres complètes de Marmontel.* Paris: Verdière.

Marolles, Michel de. 1645. *Mémoires.* Amsterdam: no publisher. New ed., 3 vols. Paris: A. de Sommaville, 1656–1657.

Masson, Charles. 1699. *Nouveau traité des règles de la composition de la musique.* 2nd ed. Paris: Christophe Ballard. 3rd ed. Paris: C. Ballard, 1705. Rpt. Geneva: Minkoff, 1971.

Mattheson, Johann. 1713. *Das neu-eröffnete Orchestre.* Hamburg: Der Autor.

Maugars, André. 1639. *Response faite à un curieux sur le sentiment de la musique d'Italie.* Rome: Maroscotti. Rpt. and English trans. H. Wiley Hitchcock. Geneva: Editions Minkoff, 1993.

Maupoint. 1733. *Bibliothèque des théatres.* Paris: Laurent-François Prault.

Mazarin, Jules, Cardinal. No date. *Lettres de Cardinal Mazarin.* 9 vols. Paris: M. A. Chervel, 1872–1906.

Ménestrier, Claude-François. 1658. *Remarques pour la conduite des ballets.* Ed. as appendix to *Le Ballet de cour de Louis XIV 1643–1672* by Marie-Françoise Christout. Paris: Picard, 1967.

———. 1669. *Traité des tournois, joustes, carrousels, et autres spectacles publics.* Lyons: J. Muguet. Rpt. New York: AMS Press, 1978.

———. 1681. *Des représentations en musique anciennes et modernes.* Paris: R. Goignard. Rpt. Geneva: Minkoff, 1972.

———. 1682. *Des ballets anciens et modernes selon des règles du théâtre.* Paris: R. Goignard. Rpt. Geneva: Minkoff, 1972.

Mersenne, Marin. 1636. *Harmonie universelle.* Paris: Sebastien Cramoisy. Rpt. in 3 vols. with annotations of the author. Paris: CNRS, 1965.

Mervesin, Dom Joseph. 1706. *Histoire de la poésie françoise.* Paris: P. Giffart.

Millet, Jean. 1666. *L'Art de bien chant*er. Lyons: J. Gregoire. Rpt. New York: Da Capo Press, 1973.

Montéclair, Michel Pignolet de. 1709. *Nouvelle méthode pour apprendre la musique.* Paris: L'auteur.
———. 1712. *Méthode facile pour apprendre à jouer du violon.* Paris: L'auteur.
———. [1735.] *Petite méthode pour apprendre la musique aux enfants . . . .* Paris: Boivin. Summary by M. Pincherle. 1948. *MQ* 24 (1) (January): 61–67.
———. 1736. *Principes de musique divisez en quatre parties.* Paris: Veuve Boivin. Rpt. Geneva: Minkoff, 1972.
Motteville, Françoise de. 1723. 5 vols. *Mémoires pour servir à l'histoire d'Anne d'Autriche.* Amsterdam: F. Changuion.
Muffat, Georg. 1695. "Preface" to *Florilegium primum.* Augsbourg: Wilhelmum Panneker. Trans. by O. Strunk. 1950. In *Source Readings in Music History.* New York: W. W. Norton. 442–444.
———. 1698. "Preface" to *Florilegium secundum.* Passau: Apud Authorem. Trans. by O. Strunk. 1950. In *Source Readings in Music History.* New York: W. W. Norton. 445–447. Trans. by Kenneth Cooper and Julieus Zsako. 1967. In "Georg Muffat's Observations on the Lully Style of Performance." *MQ* 53 (April): 220–245.

Nemeitz, Joachim Christoph. 1727. *Le Séjour de Paris.* Leyden: J. van Abcoude.
Nivers, Guillaume-Gabriel. 1667. *Traité de la composition de musique.* Paris: L'auteur et Robert Ballard.
———. 1683. *Dissertation sur le chant grégorien.* Paris: L'auteur et Christophe Ballard.
———. 1698. *Méthode certaine pour apprendre le plainchant de l'église.* Paris: Christophe Ballard.
Nodot. 1687. *Le Triomphe de Lully aux Champs-Elysées.* Manuscript. Published 1925. In *RM* 6 (3) (special number) (January): 89–106.
North, Roger. 1728. *Memoires of Musick.* Manuscript printed in *Roger North on Music.* Ed. John Wilson. London: Novello, 1959, 315–359.
Nougaret, Pierre-Jean-Baptiste. 1769. *De l'art du théâtre.* 2 vols. Paris: Cailleau. Rpt. Geneva: Minkoff, 1971.
Noverre, Jean-Georges. 1760. *Lettres sur la danse et sur les ballets.* Stuttgart and Lyons: A. Delaroche. Rpt. New York: Broude Bros., 1967. Modern ed. Ed. André Levenson. Paris: Éditions de la Tourelle, 1927. Trans. Cyril W. Beaumont. Brooklyn: *Dance Horizons,* 1966.

Oeuvres complètes de François Couperin. See Couperin, François.
Oeuvres complètes de J.-B. Lully. See Lully, Jean-Baptiste.
Oeuvres complètes de J.-P. Rameau. See Rameau, Jean-Philippe.
Les Oeuvres de P. de Ronsard. See Ronsard, P. de.
Ouvrard, René. No date. *La Musique rétablie depuis son origine.* Manuscript. Bibliothèque Municipale de Tours (MS 821–822).

⊂ ◈ ⊃

Parfaict, Claude, and François Parfaict. 1734. *Histoire du théâtre français depuis son origine jusqu'à présent.* Paris: A. Morin et Flahaut. (2nd ed.) 15 vols. Amsterdam: Aux dépens de la Compagnie, 1735–1749. (3rd ed.) 13 vols. Paris: P.–G. La Mercier, 1745–1749. Rpt. New York: B. Franklin, 1968.

————. ca. 1741. *Histoire de l'Académie Royale de Musique.* Manuscript. 2 vols. in 1. Bibliothèque Nationale (MS nouv. acq. fr. 6532).

————. 1743. *Mémoires pour servir à l'histoire des spectacles de la foire,* 2 vols. Paris: Briasson. Rpt. New York: AMS Press, 1978.

————. 1756. *Dictionnaire des théâtres de Paris,* 7 vols. Paris: Lambert. Rpt. Geneva: Minkoff, 1971.

Parran, Antoine. 1639. *Traité de la musique théorique et pratique.* Paris: Pierre Ballard. Rpt. Geneva: Minkoff, 1972.

Perrault, Charles. 1674. *Critique de l'opéra ou examen de la tragédie intitulée "Alceste ou le Triomphe d'Alcide."* Paris: C. Barbin.

————. 1687. *Le Siècle de Louis le Grand.* Paris: J.-B. Coignard.

————. 1696–1700. *Les Hommes illustres qui ont paru en France pendant ce siècle.* 2 vols. in 1. Paris: A. Dezollier.

Perrin, Pierre. 1661. *Les Oeuvres de poésie de M. Perrin.* Paris: E. Loyson.

————. 1665. *Cantica pro capella regis.* Paris: Robert Ballard.

————. ca. 1667. *Recueil de paroles de musique.* Manuscript. Bibliothèque Nationale (fr. 2208).

Peyrat, Guillaume du. 1645. *Histoire ecclésiastique de la cour, ou les antiquitez et recherches de la chapelle et oratoire du roy de France depuis Clovis 1ᵉʳ jusques à nostre temps, divisée en trois livres.* Paris: H. Sara.

Pluche, Abbé Antoine. 1732. *Le Spectacle de la nature.* 9 vols. Paris: Veuve Estienne.

Pradel, Abraham du [Nicolas de Blégny]. 1692. *Le Livre commode des adresses de Paris pour 1692.* Paris: Veuve de D. Nion. Annoted ed. Ed. E. Fournier. Paris: P. Daffis, 1878.

Pure, Michel de. 1668. *Idée des spectacles anciens et nouveaux.* Paris: M. Brunet. Rpt. Geneva: Minkoff, 1972.

⊂ ◈ ⊃

Quantz, Johann Joachim. 1752. *Versuch einer Anweisung die Flöte traversiere zu spielen.* Berlin: Johann Friedrich Voss. Rpt. Kassel: Bärenreiter, 1953. Trans. Edward Reilly. New York: Free Press, 1966.

La Querelle des bouffons; texte des pamphlets. 1752–1754. Rpt. (with introduction, commentary, and index by Denise Launay) Geneva: Minkoff, 1973.

⊂ ◈ ⊃

Raguenet, François. 1702. *Parallèle des Italiens et des Français en ce qui regarde la musique et les opéra.* Paris: Jean Moreau. Rpt. Geneva: Minkoff, 1976.

————. 1705. *Défense du parallèle des Italiens et des Français.* Paris: Veuve de Claude Barbin. Rpt. (with the *Parallèle des Italiens . . .*), Geneva: Minkoff, 1976.

Rameau, Jean-Philippe. *Oeuvres complètes de J.-P, Rameau.* 18 vols. Ed. C. Saint-Saëns, C. Malherbe et al. Paris: A. Durand et fils. 1895–1924.

————. *Complete Theoretical Writings.* Rpt. of French editions, articles, and letters. 6 vols. Ed. E. R. Jacobi. Rome: American Institute of Musicology, 1967–1972.

————. 1722. *Treatise on Harmony [Traité de l'harmonie].* Trans. Philip Gossett. New York: Dover Publications, Inc., 1971.

Rameau, Pierre. 1725. *Le Maître à danser.* Paris: J. Villette. Rpt. New York: Broude Bros., 1967. Trans. Cyril W. Beaumont. Brooklyn: A Dance Horizons Republication, 1970.

Recueil général des opéra. 1703–1746. 16 vols. Ed. J. N. de Francini. Paris: Christophe Ballard. Rpt. in 3 vols. Geneva: Minkoff, 1971.

Rémond de Saint-Mard, Toussaint. 1741. *Réflexions sur l'opéra.* The Hague: J. Neaulme. Rpt. Geneva: Minkoff, 1972.

Riccoboni, Luigi. 1738. *Réflexions historiques et critiques sur les différens théâtres de l'Europe.* Paris: J. Guérin. Trans. as *Reflexions upon Declamation: or the Art of Speaking in Publick; with an Historical and Critical Account of the Theatres in Europe.* London: Anon., 1741.

Robinet, Charles. 1665–1670. *Lettres en vers à Madame.* Paris: M. de Beaujeu. Also found in *Les Continuateurs de Loret.* 3 vols. Ed. James de Rothschild. Paris: D. Morgand et C. Fatout, 1881–1899.

————. Various dates. "Lettres en vers à Monsieur." In chronological order in *Les Continuateurs de Loret.* 3 vols. Ed. James de Rothschild. Paris: D. Morgand et C. Fatout, 1881–1899.

Rochemont, de. 1754. *Réflexions d'un patriote sur l'opéra françois et sur l'opéra italien.* Lausanne: No publisher.

Ronsard, P. de. *Les Oeuvres de P. de Ronsard.* Vol. 10 of 1587 edition. Ed. J. Galland et C. Binet. Paris: G. Buon.

Rousseau, Jean. 1683. *Méthode claire, certaine et facile pour apprendre à chanter la musique.* Paris: L'auteur. 5th ed. Amsterdam: P. Mortier, 1710. Rpt. Geneva: Minkoff, 1976.

————. 1687. *Traité de la viole.* Paris: Christophe Ballard. Rpt. Amsterdam, 1965. Rpt. with a preface by François Lesure. Geneva: Minkoff, 1975.

Rousseau, Jean-Jacques. 1743. *Dissertation sur la musique moderne.* Paris: G. F. Quillan, père.

————. 1753. *Lettre sur la musique françoise.* Paris: No publisher. English trans. in *Source Readings in Music History.* Ed. and trans. Oliver Strunk. New York: W. W. Norton, 1950.

————. 1768. *Dictionnaire de musique.* Amsterdam: M. M. Rey. Rpt. New York: Johnson Reprint Corporation, 1969.

Roy, Pierre-Charles. 1749. "Lettres sur l'opéra." In *Lettres sur quelques écrits de ce tems*, vol. 2. Ed. E. C. Fréron. Geneva: No publisher. 7–22. Rpt. Geneva: Slatkine, 1966.

⸙ ▣ ⸙

Saint-Évremond, Charles de Marguetel de Saint-Denis, Seigneur de. 1684a. *Les Opéra, comédie*. Paris: C. Barbin. In *Oeuvres de M. de Saint-Évremond*, 4th ed., vol. 3. Amsterdam: Covens et Mortier, 1726.

———. 1684b. "Sur les opéra." In *Oeuvres meslées*, vol. 11. Paris: C. Barbin, 1714.

Saint-Hubert. 1641. *La Manière de composer et faire réussir les ballets*. Paris: François Targa. Rpt. Geneva: Minkoff, 1993.

Saint-Lambert, Michel de. 1702. *Les Principes du clavecin*. Paris: Christophe Ballard. Rpt. Geneva: Minkoff, 1972. English trans. B. Harris-Warrick. London: Cambridge University Press, 1984.

———. 1707. *Nouveau traité de l'accompagnement*. Paris: Christophe Ballard. Rpt. Geneva: Minkoff, 1972.

Sauval, Henri. 1724. *Histoire et recherches des antiquités de la ville de Paris*. 3 vols. Paris: C. Moette. Rpt. Geneva: Minkoff, 1973.

Scarron, Paul. 1643. *La Foire Saint-Germain*. Paris: J. Bréquigny.

Sénecé. See Bauderon de Sénecé.

Serré de Rieux, Jean de. 1734. *Les Dons des enfants de Latone*. Paris: Pierre Prault.

Sonnet, Martin. 1662. *Caeremoniale parisiense ad usum omnium ecclesiarum collegiatarum, parochialium . . . et diocesis parisiensis*. Paris: Lutetiae Parisiorum.

⸙ ▣ ⸙

Tallemant Des Réaux, Gédéon. 1657–1659. *Historiettes*. Manuscript. Ed. A. Adam. 2 vols. Paris: Gallimard, 1960.

Terrasson, Antoine. 1741. *Dissertation historique sur la vielle*. Paris: J.-B. Lamesle. Rpt. Amsterdam: Antiqua, 1966.

Terrasson, Jean. 1715. *Dissertation critique sur l'Iliade d'Homère*. 2 vols. Paris: F. Fournier and A.-V. Coustelier.

Titon du Tillet, Évrard. 1732. *Le Parnasse françois*. Paris: J.-B. Coignard fils. Supplements in 1743, 1755, 1760. Rpt. of eds. of 1732–1743. Geneva: Minkoff, 1971. Rpt. of eds. of 1755–1760. Geneva: Minkoff, 1977.

Tralage. See Du Tralage, Jean-Nicolas.

Trichet, Pierre. ca. 1640. *Traité des instruments de musique*. Manuscript. Paris. Bibliothèque Sainte-Geneviève (1070). Printed with preface by François Lesure in *Annales musicologiques* 1955(3):283–387; 1956(4):175–248.

⸙ ▣ ⸙

Walther, Johann Gottfried. 1732. *Musikalisches Lexikon, oder, musikalische Bibliothek*. Leipzig: Wolfgang Deer. Rpt. Kassel: Bärenreiter-Verlag, 1953.

Sources After 1800

Adam, Antoine. 1948–1956. *Histoire de la littérature française au XVIIe siècle*. 4 vols. Paris: Domat.

Alderman, Pauline. 1946. *Anthoine Boësset and the air de cour*. Ph.D. Thesis, University of Southern California.

Aldrich, Putnam. 1942. *The Principal "agréments" of the Seventeenth and Eighteenth Centuries*. Ph.D. Thesis, Harvard University.

Amtmann, Willi. 1976. *La Musique au Québec: 1600–1875*. Montréal: Edition de l'Homme.

Anthony, James R. 1964. *The Opera-Ballets of André Campra: a Study of the First Period French Opera-Ballet*. Ph.D. Thesis, University of Southern California,

———. 1965. "The French Opera-Ballet in the Early 18th Century: Problems of Definition and Classification." *JAMS* 18 (2) (Summer): 197–206.

———. 1966. "Thematic Repetition in the Opera-Ballets of André Campra." *MQ* 52 (2) (April): 209–220.

———. 1969. "Some Uses of the Dance in the French Opéra-Ballet." *Recherches* 9:75–90.

———. 1970. "Printed Editions of André Campra's *L'Europe galante*." *MQ* 56 (1) (January): 54–73.

———. 1977–1978. "French Binary Air within Italian Aria da Capo in Montéclair's Third Book of Cantatas." *PRMA* 104: 47–56.

———. 1982. "A Source for Secular Vocal Music in 18th-Century Avignon: Manuscript 1182 of the Bibliothèque du Muséum Calvet." *AM* 54 (1–2) (January–December): 261–279.

———. 1986a. "Jean-Baptiste Lully." In *The New Grove French Baroque Masters*. Ed. Stanley Sadie. London: Macmillan London Limited. 1–72.

———. 1986b. "La Structure musicale des récits de Michel-Richard Delalande." In *Actes du colloque international sur le grand motet français (1663–1792)*. Ed. Jean Mongrédien and Yves Ferraton. Paris: Presses de l'Université de Paris-Sorbonne. 119–127.

———. 1986c. "Michel-Richard de Lalande." In *The New Grove French Baroque Masters*. Ed. Stanley Sadie. London: Macmillan London Limited. 119–150.

———. 1987a. "Lully's airs—French or Italian?" *MT* 128 (March): 126–129.

———. 1987b. "More faces than Proteus: Lully's *Ballet des muses*." *EM* 15 (3) (August): 336–344.

———. 1987c. "Towards a Principal Source for Lully's Court Ballets: Foucault vs. Philidor." *Recherches* 15:77–104.

———. 1990. "The Musical Structure of Jean-Baptiste Lully's Operatic Airs." In *Jean-Baptiste Lully. Actes du colloque*. Ed. Herbert Schneider and Jérôme de La Gorce. Laaber: Laaber-Verlag. 65–76.

————. 1991. "Air and Aria added to French Opera from the Death of Lully to 1720." *RdM* 77(2):201–219.

Antoine, Michel. 1952. "Autour de François Couperin." *RdM* 34 (December): 109–127.

————. 1965. *Henry Desmarest*. Paris: Picard.

Apel, Willi. 1937. "Du nouveau sur la musique française pour l'orgue au XVIIe siècle." *RM* 18 (February): 96–108.

————. 1967. *Geschichte der Orgel und Klaviermusik bis 1700*. Kassel: Bärenreiter Verlag. English trans. H. Tischler. Bloomington: Indiana University Press, 1972.

Appia, Edmond. 1950. "The Violin Sonatas of Leclair." *The Score* 3 (June): 3–19.

Arger, Jane. 1919. "Le Rôle expressif des 'agréments' dans l'école française de 1680 à 1760." *RdM* 1 (1) (December): 215–226.

————. 1921. *Les Agréments et le rythme*. Paris: Rouart.

Arnold, Franck Thomas. 1931. *The Art of Accompaniment from a Thorough-Bass*. London: Oxford University Press. Rpt. in 2 vols. New York: Dover Publications, 1965.

Astier, Régine. 1983. "Pierre Beauchamps and the Ballets de Collège." *Dance Chronicle* 6(2):138–163.

————. 1974–1975. "Pierre Beauchamps: The Illustrious Unknown Choreographer." *Dance Scope* 8(2):32–42, and 9(1):31–45.

Auld, Louis. 1968. *The Unity of Molière's Comedy-Ballets*. Ph.D. Thesis, Bryn Mawr College.

————. 1986. *The Lyric Art of Pierre Perrin, Founder of French Opera*. 3 vols. Henryville, NY: Institute of Medieval Music.

————. 1989. "'Dealing in Shepherds': The Pastoral Ploy in Nascent French Opera." In *French Musical Thought, 1600–1800*. Ed. G. Cowart. Ann Arbor: UMI Press. 53–79.

————. 1990. "Lully's Comic Art." In *Jean-Baptiste Lully. Actes du colloque*. Ed. Herbert Schneider and Jérôme de La Gorce. Laaber: Laaber-Verlag. 17–30.

L'Avant scène opéra. 1984 and 1987. "Médée." 68 (October 1984); and "Atys." 94 (January 1987).

Bailes, Anthony. 1984. "An Introduction to French Lute Music of the XVIIth Century." In *Le Luth et sa musique*, vol. 2. Ed. J. M. Vaccaro. Paris: Corpus des Luthistes Français. 213–228.

Baker, Anne. 1984. "The Church Music of André Campra. A Reconsideration of the Sources." *Recherches* 22:89–130.

————. 1986. "The *Exaudiat Te Dominus* of André Campra: A Celebrated Motet Rediscovered." In *Actes du colloque international sur le grand motet français (1663–1792)*. Ed. Jean Mongrédien and Yves Ferreton. Paris: Presses de l'Université de Paris-Sorbonne. 91–104.

Banducci, Antonia. 1990. *"Tancrède" by Antoine Danchet and André Campra: Performance History and Reception (1702–1764).* Ph.D. Thesis, Washington University.

———. 1993. "Staging a *tragédie en musique*: a 1748 promptbook of Campra's *Tancrède.*" *EM: French Baroque I* 21 (2) (May): 181–190.

Barber, Clarence. 1955. *The Liturgical Music of Marc-Antoine Charpentier.* Ph.D. Thesis, Harvard University.

———. 1963. "Les Oratorios de Marc-Antoine Charpentier." *Recherches* 3:90–130.

Bardet, Bernard. 1956. *Les Violons de la musique de la Chambre sous Louis XIV, 1634–1715.* Doctoral Thesis, École Nationale des Chartes, Paris.

Barksdale, Glen E. 1973. *The Chorus in French Baroque Opera.* Ph.D. Thesis, University of Utah.

Barnes, Clifford R. 1965. "Instruments and Instrumental Music at the 'Théâtres de la foire.'" *Recherches* 5:142–168.

———. 1968. "Vocal Music at the 'Théâtres de la Foire.'" *Recherches* 8:141–160.

Barnett, Dene. 1987. *The Art of Gesture: The Practice and Principles of Eighteenth-Century Acting.* Heidelberg: C. Winter.

Le Baroque au théâtre et la théâtralité du Baroque, Actes des journées internationales d'étude du baroque, 2e session. 1967. Montauban: Centre Nationale de Recherches du Baroque.

Le "Baroque" musical. 1963. Vol. 4, *Colloques de Wégimont.* Liège: Université de Liège.

Barthélemy, Maurice. 1953a. "Les Divertissements de Jean-Joseph Mouret pour les comédies de Dancourt." *RBdM* 7(1):47–51.

———. 1953b. "Les Opéras de Marin Marais." *RBdM* 7:136–146.

———. 1955. "L'Orchestre et l'orchestration des oeuvres de Campra." *RM* (special issue) 226:97–104.

———. 1956. "L'Opéra français et la querelle des Anciens et Modernes." *Lettres modernes* 10:379–391.

———. 1957a. *André Campra.* Paris: Picard. New ed. Arles: Actes Sud, 1995.

———. 1957b. "La Musique dramatique à Versailles de 1660 à 1715." *XVIIᵉ siècle* 34 (March): 7–18.

———. 1969. "Theobaldo di Gatti et la tragédie en musique, *Scylla.*" *Recherches* 9:55–66.

———. 1990. *Métamorphoses de l'opéra français au siècle des Lumières.* Arles: Actes Sud.

Barthélemy, Maurice, and Philippe Vendrix. 1991. "Le Rococo et la musique française? Deux points de vue." In *Rocaille Rococo.* Vol. 18, *Études sur le XVIIIᵉ siècle.* Ed. R. Mortier and H. Hasquin. Brussels: Université de Bruxelles. 25–33.

Bartlett, M. Elizabeth C. 1989. "A Musician's View of the French Baroque after the Advent of Gluck: Grétry's *Les trois âges de l'opéra* and Its Context." In *Jean-Baptiste Lully and the Music of the French*

Baroque. Ed. John Hajdu Heyer. Cambridge: Cambridge University Press. 291–318.

Bashford, Christina. 1991. "Perrin and Cambert's 'Ariane, ou Le Mariage de Bacchus' Re-examined." *M&L* 72 (1) (February): 1–26.

Bates, Carol Henry. 1975. *The Instrumental Music of Elisabeth-Claude Jacquet de La Guerre*. Ph.D. Thesis, Indiana University.

———. 1984. "Elizabeth Jacquet de La Guerre: a New Source of Seventeenth-Century French Harpsichord Music." *Recherches* 22:7–49.

———. 1989. "French Harpsichord Music in the First Decade of the Eighteenth Century." *EM* 18 (2) (May): 184–196.

———. 1991–1992. "The Early French Sonata for Solo Instruments." *Recherches* 27:71–95.

Bazzana, Kevin. 1991. "The Uses and Limits of Performance Practice in François Couperin's Huitième Ordre." *MQ* 75(1):12–30.

Beaussant, Philippe. 1980. *François Couperin*. Paris: Fayard. English trans. Alexandra Land. Portland, OR: Amadeus Press, 1990.

———. 1991. *Vous avez dit baroque? musique du passé, pratiques d'aujourd'hui*. Arles: Actes Sud.

———. 1992. *Lully ou le musicien du Soleil*. Paris: Gallinard.

Beechy, Guilym. 1989. "The Harpsichord Music of Jean-François Dandrieu." *The Consort* 45:19–42.

Beecker, David. 1987. "Aesthetics of the French Solo Viol Repertory." *JVGSA* 24:10–50.

Benoit, Marcelle. 1971a. *Musiques de cour: Chapelle, Chambre, Écurie, 1661–1733*. Paris: Picard.

———. 1971b. *Versailles et les musiciens du roi, 1661–1733: étude institutionelle et sociale*. Paris: Picard.

———. 1982. *Les Musiciens du Roi de France: étude sociale, 1661–1733*. Paris: Presses Universitaires de France.

———. 1986. "L'Apprentissage chez les facteurs d'instruments de musique à Paris, 1600–1661;1715–1774." *Recherches* 14:5–106.

———. 1989. "The Residences of Monsieur de Lully: a West Side Story." *Jean-Baptiste Lully and the Music of the French Baroque*. Ed. John Hajdu Heyer. Cambridge: Cambridge University Press. 159–182.

———. 1993. "Paris, 1661–87: The Age of Lully." In *The Early Baroque Era from the Late 16th Century to the 1660's*. Ed. Curtis Price. Vol. 3, *Music and Society*. London: The Macmillan Press Limited. 238–269.

———. See *Dictionnaire de la musique en France aux XVIIe et XVIIIe siècles*.

Benoit, Marcelle, and Norbert Dufourcq. 1957. "Une Vieille querelle: organistes et violonistes, luthiers et facteurs d'orgue à Paris à la fin du XVIIe siècle." *L'Orgue* 83:41–47.

―――. 1963. "Les Musiciens de Versailles à travers les minutes notariales de Maître Lamy versées aux Archives départementales de Seine-et-Oise, 1682–1733." *Recherches* 3:189–206.

―――. 1966. "Les Musiciens de Versailles à travers les minutes du Baillage du Versailles conservées aux Archives départmentales de Seine-et-Oise." *Recherches* 6:197–226.

―――. 1967, 1968a, 1969–1970. "Documents du Minutier Central: Musiciens français du XVIIIᵉ siècle: Actes transcrits." *Recherches* 7(1967):217–233; 8(1968):243–256; 9(1969):216–238; 10(1970): 197–220.

―――. 1968b. "À propos des Forqueray." *Recherches* 8:229–241.

―――. 1975. "Les Musiciens de Versailles à travers les minutes notariales de Maître Gayot versées aux Archives départementales des Yvelines. 1661–1733." *Recherches* 15:155–190.

―――. See also Dufourcq, Norbert, and Marcelle Benoit.

Bert, Henri. 1957. "Un Ballet de Michel-Richard Delalande." *XVIIᵉ siècle* 34 (March): 58–72.

Bert, Marie. 1963–1965. "La Musique à la maison royale Saint-Louis de Saint-Cyr." *Recherches* 3(1963):55–71; 4(1964):127–131; 5(1965):91–127.

Berton, Nathalie. 1994. "Le Petit opéra chez Marc-Antoine Charpentier." *Bulletin: Société Marc Antoine Charpentier* 11 (July): 12–23.

Betzwieser, Thomas. 1989. *Exotismus und "Türkenoper" in der französischen Musik von Lully bis Grétry*. Doctoral Thesis, University of Heidelberg.

―――. 1990. "Die Türkenszenen in 'Le Sicilien' und 'Le Bourgeois Gentilhomme' im Kontext der Türkenoper und des musikalischen Exotismus." *Jean-Baptiste Lully. Actes du colloque*. Ed. Herbert Schneider and Jérôme de La Gorce. Laaber: Laaber-Verlag. 51–63.

Bjurström, Per. 1962. *Giacomo Torelli and Baroque Stage Design*. 2nd ed. Stockholm: Almquist Hiksell.

Blaze, François-Henri-Joseph (known as Castil-Blaze). 1855. *L'Académie impériale de musique*. 2 vols. Paris: Castil-Blaze.

Bloch-Michel, Antoine. 1963. "Les Messes d'Aux-Cousteaux." *Recherches* 3:31–40.

Boalch, Donald H. 1956. *Makers of the Harpsichord and Clavichord 1440–1840*. New York: The MacMillan Company. 2nd ed. London: Oxford University Press, 1976.

Bobillier, Marie. See Brenet, Michel (pseud.).

Bol, Johan Hendrik Daniël. 1973. *La Basse de Viole du temps de Marin Marais et d'Antoine Forqueray*. Bilthoven, Holland: A. B. Creyghton.

Bond, Ann. 1994. "Between Two Worlds: the Music of Duphly." *MT* 135 (May): 274–278.

Bonfils, Jean. 1961–1962. "Les Fantaisies instrumentales d'Eustache Du Caurroy." *Recherches* 2:5–31.

———. 1965. "L'Oeuvre d'orgue de Jehan Titelouze." *Recherches* 5: 5–16.

Bonnet, Georges-Edgar. 1921. "La Naissance de l'opéra-comique en France." *RM* 2 (8) (June): 231–243.

Bonnet, Jean-Louis. 1988. *Bouzignac, Moulinié et les musiciens du pays l'Aude*. Béziers: Société de Musicologie de Languedoc.

———. 1989. "Musiciens audois du XVIIe siècle à la cour: Antoine et Étienne Molinier." *Bulletin de la Société d'études scientifiques de l'Aube*. 84:39–52.

Borowitz, Albert. 1974. "Lully and the Death of Cambert." *MR* 35 (November): 231–239.

———. 1986. "Finale Marked Presto: The Killing of Leclair." *MQ* 72(2):228–238.

Borrel, Eugène. 1929. "L'Interprétation de Lully après Rameau." *RdM* 10:17–25.

———. 1931a. "L'Interprétation de l'ancien récitatif français." *RdM* 12:13–21.

———. 1931b. "Les Notes inégales dans l'ancienne musique française." *RdM* 12:278–281.

———. 1934. *L'Interprétation de la musique française de Lully à la Révolution*. Paris: Librairie Félix Alcan. Rpt. New York: AMS Press, 1978.

———. 1949. *Jean-Baptiste Lully*. Paris: La Colombe.

———. 1954. "La Vie musicale de Marc-Antoine Charpentier d'après le *Mercure galant*." *XVIIe siècle* 21–22:433–441.

———. 1955. "Notes sur l'orchestration de l'opéra *Jephté* de Montéclair (1733) et de la symphonie des *Élémens* de J.-F. Rebel (1737)." *RM* 226 (special number): 105–116.

———. 1957. "Notes sur la musique de la Grande Écurie de 1650 à 1789." *XVIIe siècle* 34:33–41.

Borroff, Edith. 1958. *The Instrumental Works of Jean-Joseph Cassanéa de Mondonville*. Ph.D. Thesis, University of Michigan.

———. 1966. *An Introduction to Elisabeth-Claude Jacquet de La Guerre*. Brooklyn: Institute of Medieval Music.

———. 1967. "The Instrumental Style of Jean-Joseph Cassanéa de Mondonville." *Recherches* 7:165–204.

———. 1970. *The Music of the Baroque*. Dubuque: C. Brown.

Böttger, Friedrich. 1930. *Die "Comédie-Ballet" von Molière-Lully*, Berlin: P. Funk. Rpt. Hildesheim: Georg Olms Verlag, 1979.

Boucher, Thierry. 1990. "Un Haut lieu de l'Opéra de Lully: la salle de spectacles du château de Saint-Germain-en-Laye." In *Jean-Baptiste Lully. Actes du colloque*. Ed. Herbert Schneider and Jérôme de La Gorce. Laaber: Laaber-Verlag. 457–467.

Bouissou, Sylvie. 1993. "Les Fonctions dramatico-musicales de la tempête et de l'orage dans l'opéra français (1674–1774)." In *Penser l'opéra français de l'âge classique.* Ed. Catherine Kintzler. Paris: Collège International de Philosophie. 89–103.

Boulay, Laurence. 1955. "La Musique instrumentale de Marin Marais." *RM* 226 (special number): 61–75.

———. 1957. "Les Cantiques spirituels de Racine mis en musique au XVIIe siècle." *XVIIe siècle* 34 (March): 79–92.

———. 1960. "Notes sur quatre motets inédits de Michel-Richard Delalande." *Recherches* 1:77–86.

Bourligueux, Guy. 1964. "Le Mystérieux Daniel Daniélis." *Recherches* 4:146–178.

Bowers, Jane M. 1971. *The French Flute from 1700–1760.* Ph.D. Thesis, University of California, Berkeley.

———. 1977. "New Light on the Development of the Transverse Flute between about 1650 and about 1770." *Journal of the American Musical Instrument Society* 3:5–56.

———. 1978. "A Catalogue of French Works for the Transverse Flute." *Recherches* 18:89–125.

———. 1979. "'Flaüste traverseinne' and 'Flûte d'Allemagne'. The Flute in France from the Late Middle Ages up through 1702." *Recherches* 19:7–50.

Boyden, David. 1957. "When is a Concerto not a Concerto?" *MQ* 43 (2) (April): 220–232.

Boyer, Ferdinand. 1926. "Giulio Caccini à la cour d'Henri IV." *RM* 7 (October): 241–250.

Boyer, Jean. 1984. "Nouveau documents sur la jeunesse d'André Campra et la vie musicale à Aix-en-Provence au XVIIe siècle." *Recherches* 22:79–88.

Braun, Werner. 1990. "Lully und die französische Musik im Spiegel der Reisebeschreibungen." *Jean-Baptiste Lully. Actes du colloque.* Ed. Herbert Schneider and Jérôme de La Gorce. Laaber: Laaber-Verlag. 271–285.

Brenet, Michel (pseud. for Marie Bobillier). 1896. "Sébastien de Brossard, prêtre, compositeur, écrivain et bibliophile, d'après ses papiers inédits." *Mémoires de la Société de l'histoire de Paris et de l'Ile-de-France.* 23:72–124. Rpt. Tours: Librairie Ars Musicae, 1982.

———. 1899. *La Musique sacrée sous Louis XIV.* Paris: Bureau d'Édition de la Schola Cantorum.

———. 1900. *Les Concerts en France sous l'ancien régime.* Paris: Fischbacher. Rpt. New York: Da Capo Press, 1970.

———. 1902–1903. "La Jeunesse de Rameau." *RMI* 9(1902):868–893; 10(1903):185–286.

———. 1907. "La Librairie musicale en France de 1653 à 1790, d'après les registres de privilèges." *SIMG* 8 (April–June): 401–466.

———. 1909. "Notes sur l'introduction des instruments dans les églises de France." *Riemann Festschrift.* Leipzig: Max Hesses Verlag. 277–286.

———. 1910. *Les Musiciens de la Sainte-Chapelle du Palais.* Paris: Picard. Rpt. Geneva: Minkoff, 1973.

Bricqueville, Eugène de. 1887. *Le Livret d'Opéra de Lully à Gluck.* Paris: Maison Schott.

Bridgeman, Nanie. 1957. "L'Aristocratie française et le ballet de cour." In *Cahiers de l'Association Internationale des Études Françaises,* vol. 9. Paris: Société d'Éditions "Les Belles Lettres." 9–21.

Brobeck, John T. 1995. "Musical Patronage in the Royal Chapel of France under Francis I (R. 1515–1547)." *JAMS* 48 (2) (Summer): 187–239.

Brofsky, Howard. 1966. "Notes on the Early French Concerto." *JAMS* 19 (1) (Spring): 87–91.

———. 1985. "Rameau and the Indian: The Popularity of *Les Sauvages.*" In *Music in the Classic Period: Essays in Honor of Barry S. Brook.* Ed. A. Atlas. New York: Pendragon. 43–60.

Brook, Barry. 1962. *La Symphonie française dans la seconde moitié du XVIIIᵉ siècle.* 2 vols. Paris: Publication de l'institut de musicologie de l'Université de Paris.

Brossard, Yolande de. 1970. "La Vie musicale en France d'après Loret et ses continuateurs." *Recherches* 10:117–193.

———. 1987. *Sébastien de Brossard, théoricien et compositeur, encyclopédiste et maître de chapelle. 1677–1730.* Paris: Picard.

———. 1988. "Quelques commentaires de Brossard concernant Lully et Charpentier." *XVIIᵉ siècle* 16 (1) (October–December): 387–392.

———. See *Musiciens de Paris 1535–1792.*

———. See Sébastien de Brossard in Sources before 1800.

Brown, Leslie Ellen. 1978. *The "tragédie lyrique" of André Campra and his Contemporaries.* Ph.D. Thesis, University of North Carolina.

———. 1984a. "Departure from Lullian Convention in the *tragédie lyrique* of the *préramiste* Era." *Recherches* 22:59–78.

———. 1984b. "The *Récit* in the Eighteenth-Century *tragédie en musique.*" *MR* 45 (May): 96–111.

———. 1990. "Oratorical Thought and the *tragédie lyrique*: a Consideration of Musical-Rhetorical Figures." *College Music Symposium* 22:99–116.

Brunold, Paul. 1925. *Traité des signes et agréments employés par les clavecinistes français des XVIIᵉ et XVIIIᵉ siècles.* Lyons: Janin. Rpt. Nice: Delrieu, 1964.

———. 1932. "Trois Livres de pièces de clavecin de J.-F. Dandrieu." *RdM* 13:147–151.

Buch, David Joseph. 1983. *La Rhétorique des dieux: a Critical Study of Text, Illustration, and Musical Style.* Ph.D. Thesis, Northwestern University.

———. 1985a. "The Influence of the *Ballet de Cour* in the Genesis of the French Baroque Dance Suite." *AM* 57 (1) (January–June): 94–109.

————. 1985b. *"Style brisé,* style *luthé,* and the *Choses luthée." MQ* 71(1): 52–67; "Additional Remarks on '*Style brisé, Style luthée,* and the *Choses luthée.'" MQ* 71(2):220–221.

————. 1989. "The Coordination of Text, Illustration, and Music in a Seventeenth Century Lute Manuscript: *La Rhétorique des Dieux." Imago Musicae* 6:39–81.

————. 1994. *Dance Music from the Ballet de Cour 1575–1651.* Stuyvesant, NY: Pendragon Press.

Bukofzer, Manfred F. 1947. *Music in the Baroque Era.* New York: W. W. Norton.

Burke, John R. 1981. "Sacred Music at Notre-Dame-des-Victoires under Mazarin and Louis XIV." *Recherches* 20:19–44.

————. 1985. *Marc-Antoine Charpentier (c. 1634–1704): Sources of Style in the Liturgical Works.* Doctoral Thesis, Oxford University.

Burton, Humphrey. 1955. "Les Académies de musique en France au XVIIe siècle." *RdM* 37 (December): 122–147.

Busch, Hermann J. 1986. *Zur Interpretation der französischen Orgelmusik.* Merseburger: Gesellschaft der Orgelfreunde.

Buttrey, John. 1995. "New Light on Robert Cambert in London, and his *Ballet et Musique." EM* 23 (2) (May): 199–220.

Byrt, John. 1967. *"Notes inégales,* some misconceptions." *JAMS* 20 (3) (Fall): 476–480.

————. 1995. "Just a Habit with us." *MT* 136 (October): 536–539.

Cadell, Patrick. 1984. "La Musique française classique dans la collection des comtes de Panmure." *Recherches* 22:50–58.

Campardon, Émile. 1880. *Les Spectacles des Foires.* 2 vols. Paris: Berger-Levrault.

————. 1884. *L'Académie Royale de Musique au XVIIIe siècle: documents inédits découverts aux Archives Nationales.* 2 vols. Paris: Berger-Levrault. Rpt. New York: Da Capo Press, 1971.

Carlez, Jules. 1876. *La Musique à Caen de 1066 à 1848.* Caen: F. Le Blanc-Hardel. Rpt. Geneva: Minkoff, 1974.

Carmody, Francis J. 1933. *Le Répertoire de l'opéra-comique en vaudevilles de 1708 à 1764.* Berkeley: University of California Press.

Carstensen, Brigitte. 1992. *Die französische Triosonate von 1680–1750.* Doctoral Thesis, Frankfurt University.

Castanet, Pierre-Albert. 1987. "La Viole de gambe. Instrument soliste dans l'oeuvre de François Couperin." *Recherches* 25:139–186.

Castil-Blaze. See Blaze, François-Henri-Joseph.

Castle, Conan J. 1962. *The Grands Motets of André Campra.* Ph.D. Thesis, University of Michigan.

Caswell, Austin. 1964. *The Development of Seventeenth-Century French Vocal Ornamentation and Its Influence upon Later Baroque Ornamentation Practice.* Ph.D. Thesis, University of Minnesota.

————, trans. See Bacilly 1668.

Caswell, Judith Carls. 1973. *Rhythmic Inequality and Tempo in French Music between 1650 and 1740.* Ph.D. Thesis, University of Minnesota.

Cauchie, Maurice. 1920. "La Dynastie Boësset." *RdM* 2(6):13–26.

Cessac, Catherine. 1988. *Marc-Antoine Charpentier.* Paris: Fayard. English trans. E. Thomas Glasow. Portland, OR: Amadeus Press, 1995.

———. 1994. *Elizabeth Jacquet de la Guerre (1665–1729), claveciniste et compositeur.* Doctoral Thesis, University of Paris-Sorbonne.

———. 1995a. *Elisabeth Jacquet de La Guerre.* Arles: Actes Sud.

———. 1995b. *"Les Jeux à l'honneur de la Victoire* d'Elisabeth Jacquet de La Guerre: premier opéra-ballet?" *RdM* 81(2):235–47.

Chailley, Jacques. 1952. "Notes sur la famille de Lully." *RdM* 34 (December): 101–108.

Charnassé, Hélène. 1960. "Contribution à l'étude du récitatif chez l'abbé Pierre Robert." *Recherches* 1:61–67.

———. 1961–1962. "Quelques aspects des 'ensembles de récits' chez l'abbé Pierre Robert." *Recherches* 2:61–70.

———. 1963–1964. "Contribution à l'étude des grands motets de Pierre Robert." *Recherches* 3(1963):49–54; 4(1964):105–120.

———. 1986. "Un Aspect du grand motet à la fin du XVIIe siècle: Pierre Robert." In *Actes du colloque international sur le grand motet français (1663–1792).* Ed. Jean Mongrédien and Yves Ferraton. Paris: Presses de l'Université de Paris-Sorbonne. 39–65.

Chartier, François-Léon. 1897. *L'Ancien chapitre de Notre-Dame de Paris et sa maîtrise d'après les documents capitulaires (1326–1790).* Paris: Perrin et Cie. Rpt. Geneva: Minkoff, 1971.

Chastel, Anne. 1981. "Le Parlement de Provence et la musique." *Recherches* 20:205–248.

Cheilan-Cambolin, Jeanne. 1972. *Un Aspect de la vie musicale à Marseille au XVIIIe siècle: cinquante ans d'opéra.* Doctoral Thesis, Université d'Aix-en-Provence.

———. 1990. "La Première décentralisation des opéras de Lully en province: la création de l'Opéra de Marseille au XVIIe siècle." In *Jean-Baptiste Lully. Actes du colloque.* Ed. Herbert Schneider and Jérôme de La Gorce. Laaber: Laaber-Verlag. 529–538.

Cheney, Stuart C. 1990. "A Summary of Dubuisson's Life and Sources." *JVGSA* 27:7–21.

Chouquet, Gustave. 1873. *Histoire de la musique dramatique en France.* Paris: Firmin-Didot.

Christie, William. 1993. "The Elusive world of the French Baroque." *EM: French Baroque I* 21 (2) (May): 263–266.

Christout, Marie-Françoise. 1967. *Le ballet de cour de Louis XIV 1643–1672.* Paris: Picard.

———. 1987. *Le ballet de cour au XVIIe siècle.* Geneva: Minkoff.

———. 1990. "Baptiste, interprète des ballets de cour." In *Jean-Baptiste Lully. Actes du colloque*. Ed. Herbert Schneider and Jérôme de La Gorce. Laaber: Laaber-Verlag. 209–222.

Citron, Pierre. 1955. "Autour des folies françaises." *RM* 226 (special number): 89–96.

———. 1968. *Mélanges François Couperin. Publiées à l'occasion du tricentenaire de sa naissance*. Paris: Picard.

Clark, Jane. 1980. "Les Folies Françoises." *EM* 8 (2) (April): 163–169.

Clerval, J.-A. 1899. *L'Ancienne Maîtrise de Notre-Dame de Chartres*. Paris: C. Poussielgue. Rpt. Geneva: Minkoff, 1972.

Clerx, Suzanne. 1948. *Le Baroque et la musique*. Brussels: Librairie Enclopédique.

Coeurdevey, Annie. 1991. *La Formation du langage tonal en France dans la première moitié du dix-septième siècle: Étienne Moulinié*. Doctoral Thesis, University of Tours.

Coeyman, Barbara. 1987. *The Stage Works of Michel-Richard Delalande in the Musical-Cultural Context of the French Court, 1680–1726*. Ph.D. Thesis, City University of New York.

———. 1990a. "Lully's Influence on the Organization and Performance of the Ballet de Cour after 1672." In *Jean-Baptiste Lully. Actes du colloque*. Ed. Herbert Schneider and Jérôme de La Gorce. Laaber: Laaber-Verlag. 517–528.

———. 1990b. "Theaters for Opera and Ballet during the Reigns of Louis XIV and Louis XV." *EM* 18 (1) (February): 22–37.

Cohen, Albert. 1958. *The Evolution of the Fantasia and Works in Related Styles in the Seventeenth-Century Instrumental Ensemble Music of France and the Low Countries*. Ph.D. Thesis, New York University.

———. 1962a. "A Study of Instrumental Ensemble Practice in Seventeenth-Century France." *GSJ* 15 (March): 1–5.

———. 1962b. "The Fantaisie for Instrumental Ensemble in Seventeenth-Century France." *MQ* 48 (2) (April): 234–243.

———. 1965. "Étienne Loulié as a Music Theorist." *JAMS* 18 (1) (Spring): 70–72.

———. 1966. "Survivals of Renaissance Thought in French Theory, 1610–1670: a Bibliographical Study." In *Aspects of Medieval and Renaissance Music*. Ed. J. LaRue. New York: W. W. Norton. 62–95.

———. 1969. "L'Art de bien chanter (1666) of Jean Millet." *MQ* 55 (2) (April): 170–179.

———. 1972a. "René Ouvrard (1624–1694) and the Beginnings of French Baroque Theory." In *Report of the 11th Congress of the IMS*, vol. 1. Copenhagen: Edition Wilhelm Hansen. 336–342.

———. 1972b. "Symposium on Seventeenth-Century Music Theory: France." *JMT* 16(1–2):16–35.

———. 1975. "The Ouvrard-Nicaise Correspondance (1663–1693)." *M&L* 56 (3–4) (July–October): 356–363.

————. 1977a. "Early French Dictionaries as Musical Sources." *A Musical Offering: Essays in Honor of Martin Bernstein*. Ed. E. H. Clinkscale and C. Brook. New York: Pendragon. 97–112.

————. 1977b. "Music in the French Scientific Academy before the Revolution." *Stanford French Review* 1:29–37.

————. 1981. *Music in the French Royal Academy of Sciences*. Princeton: Princeton University Press.

————. 1989. "The Performance of French Baroque Music: A Report on the State of Current Research." *Performance Practice Review* 2(2):10–24.

————. 1992. "*L'État de la France*: One Hundred Years of Music at the French Court." *Notes* 48 (3) (March): 767–805.

————. 1993. "The King's Musicians: a Postscriptum." *Notes* 49 (4) (June): 1390–1394.

Cole, William P. 1967. *The Motets of J.-B. Lully*. Ph.D. Thesis, University of Michigan.

Collard, Louis-Henri. 1975. "Quelques documents sur Henry Du Mont." *Recherches* 15:244–261.

Collins, Michael B. 1966. "The Performance of Triplets in the 17th and 18th Centuries." *JAMS* 19 (3) (Autumn): 281–328.

————. 1969. "A Reconsideration of French Over-Dotting." *M&L* 50 (1) (January): 111–123.

————. 1973. "In Defence of the French Trill." *JAMS* 26 (3) (Autumn): 405–439.

Cooper, Kenneth, and Julius Zsako. 1967. "Georg Muffat's Observations on the Lully Style of Performance." *MQ* 53 (2) (April): 220–245.

Cooper, Martin. 1949. *Opéra-comique*. New York: M. Parrish.

Cordey, Jean. 1955. "Lulli d'après l'inventaire de ses biens." *RdM* 37 (July): 78–83.

Corp, Edward T. 1995. "The Exiled Court of James II and James III: a Centre of Italian Music in France, 1689–1712." *Journal of the Royal Musical Association* 120(2):216–231.

Courville, Xavier de. 1925. "Quinaut, poète d'opéra." *RM* 6 (3) (special number) (January): 74–89.

Couvreur, Manuel. 1989. *Le livret d'opéra en France de "Cadmus et Hermione" de Quinault et Lully (1673) aux "Boréades" de Cahusac et Rameau (1763)*. Doctoral Thesis, Free University of Brussels.

————. 1990. "Marie de Louvencourt, librettiste des *Cantates Françoises* de Bourgeois et de Clérambault." *RBdM* 44:25–40.

————. 1992. *Jean-Baptiste Lully: musicien et dramaturge au service du Prince*. Brussels: Vokar.

Cowart, Georgia. 1981. *The Origin of Modern Musical Criticism: French and Italian Music, 1600–1750*. Ann Arbor: UMI Press.

————. 1984. "Sense and Sensibility in Eighteenth-Century Musical Thought." *AM* 56 (2) (July–December): 251–266.

———. 1986a. "Lully *enjoué*: Galanterie in Seventeenth-Century France." In *Actes de Baton Rouge*. Ed. S. A. Zebouni. *Biblio* 17(25):35–51.

———. 1986b. "La Querelle musicale des Anciens et des Modernes au XVIIe siècle." In *D'un siècle à l'autre: anciens et modernes, XVIe colloque*. Paris: Centre Méridional de Rencontres sur le XVIIe siècle.259–268.

———. 1989a. "Inventing the Arts: Changing Critical Language in the Ancien Regime." In *French Musical Thought, 1600–1800*. Ed. G. Cowart. Ann Arbor: UMI Press. 212–238.

———, ed. 1989b. *French Musical Thought, 1600–1800*. Ann Arbor: UMI Press.

———. 1994. "Of Women, Sex and Folly: Opera under the Old Regime." *Cambridge Opera Journal* 6 (3) (November): 205–220.

Crussard, Claude. 1945. *Un Musicien français oublié, Marc-Antoine Charpentier*. Paris: Librairie Floury.

———. 1945. "Marc-Antoine Charpentier théoricien." *RdM* 27: 49–68.

Cucuel, Georges. 1913. "Sources et documents pour servir à l'histoire de l'opéra-comique en France." *L'Année musicale* 3:247–282.

———. 1914. *Les Créateurs de l'opéra-comique français*. Paris: F. Alcan.

Cudworth, Charles L. 1956–1957. "Baptist's Vein: French Orchestral Music and Its Influence." *PRMA* 83:29–47.

———. 1975. "Fitzwilliam and French Music of the Baroque." In *French Music and the Fitzwilliam, Cambridge*. Cambridge: Fitzwilliam Museum. 7–11.

Current Studies in Baroque Music. 1986 and 1990. 2 vols.: vol. 1. Ed. G. Dixon and J. Roles. Leicester: University of Leicester; vol. 2. Ed. C. Blazey. Durham: Words & Music.

Curtis, Alan. 1956. *Unmeasured Preludes in French Baroque Instrumental Music*. Master's Thesis, University of Illinois.

———. 1970. "Musique classique française à Berkeley: pièces inédites de Louis Couperin, Lebègue, La Barre, etc." *RdM* 56(2):123–164.

Cyr, Mary. 1975. *Rameau's "Les Fêtes d'Hébé."* Ph.D. Thesis, University of California, Berkeley.

———. 1977. "On Performing 18th-Century Haute-Contre Roles." *MT* 118 (April): 291–295.

———. 1979. "A New Rameau Cantata." *MT* 120 (November): 907–909.

———. 1982. "*Basses* and *basse continue* in the Orchestra of the Paris Opera 1700–1764." *EM* 10 (2) (April): 155–170.

———. 1983a. "Performing Rameau's Cantatas." *EM* 11 (4) (October): 480–489.

———. 1983b. "Towards a Chronology of Rameau's Cantatas." *MT* 124 (September): 539–541.

———. 1992. *Performing Baroque Music*. Portland, OR: Amadeus Press.

———. 1995. "The Dramatic Role of the Chorus in French Opera: Evidence for the Use of Gesture, 1670–1770." In *Opera and the Enlightenment.* Ed. Thomas Bauman and Marita P. McClymonds. Cambridge: Cambridge University Press. 105–118.

Dacier, Emile. 1905. "Les Caractères de la danse: histoire d'un divertissement pendant la première moitié du XVIIIe siècle." *RM* 5:324–335, 365–367.

Dart, Thurston. 1954. *The Interpretation of Music.* 4th ed. London: Hutchinson's University Library. Rpt. New York: Harper & Row, 1963.

———. 1969. "On Couperin's Harpsichord Music." *MT* 110 (June): 590–594.

Dartois-Lapeyre, Françoise. 1983. *La Danse au temps de l'opera-ballet.* Doctoral Thesis, University of Paris-Sorbonne.

———. 1992. "Du ballet de cour à l'opera-ballet." *Les premiers opéras en Europe et les formes dramatiques apparentées.* Ed. Irène Mamczarz. Paris: Klincksiek.

Daval, Pierre. 1961. *La Musique en France au XVIIIe siècle.* Paris: Payot.

Dean, Robert H. 1970. *The Music of Michele Mascitti (c. 1664–1760): A Neapolitan Violinist in Paris.* Ph.D. Thesis, University of Iowa.

DeBoer, Barbara Ann. 1983. *The Harpsichord Music of Jean Nicolas Geoffroy.* Ph.D. Thesis, Northwestern University.

Decobert, Laurence. 1989. *Henry Du Mont (1610–1684), sous-maître de la Chapelle de Louis XIV: contribution à l'histoire de la musique religieuse au Grand Siècle.* 4 vols. Doctoral Thesis, University of Paris-IV.

———. 1994. "Les Choeurs dans les *grands motets* de Henry Du Mont (1610–1684)." *RdM* 80(1):39–80.

Deierkauf-Holsboer, Wilma. 1958. *Le Théâtre du Marais II: le berceau de l'Opéra et de la Comédie-Française, 1648–1673.* Paris: Nizet.

Demuth, Norman. 1963. *French Opera, Its Development to the Revolution.* Sussex: Artemis Press.

Desautels, André. 1983. "Un Manuscrit autographe de Marc-Antoine Charpentier à Québec." *Recherches* 21:118–127.

Despois, Eugène. 1874. *Le Théâtre français sous Louis XIV.* Paris: Hachette.

Devriès, Anik. 1976. *Editions et Commerce de la musique gravée à Paris dans la première moitié du XVIIIe siècle. Les Boivin, les Leclerc.* Geneva: Minkoff.

Devriès, Anik, and François Lesure. 1979. *Dictionnaire des éditeurs de musique française: des origines à environ 1820,* vol 1. Geneva: Minkoff.

Deyris, Edith. 1991. *La Vie et l'oeuvre de Charles Levens, contribution à l'étude du milieu musical bordelais au XVIIIe siècle.* Doctoral Thesis, University of Bordeaux.

Dictionnaire de la musique. 1970–1976. 4 vols. Ed. Marc Honegger. Paris: Bordas.

Dictionnaire de la musique française aux XVIIe et XVIIIe siècles. 1992. Ed. Marcelle Benoit. Paris: Fayard.

Dictionnaire des oeuvres de l'art vocal. 1991. 3 vols. Ed. M. Honegger and P. Prévost. Strasbourg: Bordas.

Dill, Charles. 1994. "Rameau Reading Lully: Meaning and System in Rameau's Recitative Tradition." *Cambridge Opera Journal* 6 (1) (March): 1–17.

———. 1995. "Eighteenth-Century Models of French Recitative." *Journal of the Royal Musical Association* 120(2):232–250.

Documents du Minutier Central concernant l'histoire de la musique 1600–1650. 1969, 1974. 2 vols. Ed. Madeleine Jurgens. Vol. 1, Paris: STEVPEN; vol. 2, Paris: La Documentation Française.

Dolmetsch, Arnold. 1915. *The Interpretation of the Music of the XVIIth and XVIIIth Centuries Revealed by Contemporary Evidence.* 2 vols. London: Novello. New ed. London: Novello, 1946.

Donington, Robert. 1967. "A Problem of Inequality." *MQ* 53 (4) (October): 503–517.

———. 1973. *A Performer's Guide to Baroque Music.* London: Faber.

———. 1974. *The Interpretation of Early Music.* 3rd ed. New York: St. Martin's Press.

———. 1982. *Baroque Music-Style and Performance: a Handbook.* London: Faber.

Douglass, Fenner. 1969. *The Language of the Classical French Organ.* New Haven: Yale University Press. New and expanded ed., New Haven: Yale University Press, 1995.

———. 1973. "Should Dom Bedos play Lebègue." *The Organ Yearbook* 4:101–111.

———. 1986. "Towards the Restoration of Grace in Early French Organ Ornamentation." *Charles Brandon Fisk, Organ Builder: Essays in His Honor.* Ed. Fenner Douglass et al. Easthampton: Westfield Center for Early Keyboard Studies.

Ducrot, Ariane. 1961. *Recherches sur Jean-Baptiste Lully (1632–1687) et sur les débuts de l'Académie royale de Musique.* Doctoral Thesis, École Nationale des Chartes, Paris.

———. 1970. "Les Représentations de l'Académie royale de Musique au temps de Louis XIV." *Recherches* 10:19–55.

———. 1973. "Lully créateur de troupe." *XVIIe siècle* 98–99:91–107.

Dufourcq, Norbert. 1941. *La Musique d'orgue française de Jehan Titelouze à Jehan Alain.* Paris: Foury. 2nd ed. Paris: Foury, 1949.

———. 1953–1954. "La Musique religieuse française de 1660 à 1789." *RM* 222 (special number): 89–110.

———. 1954a. "Concerts parisiens et associations de symphonistes." *RBdM* 8:46–57.

———. 1954b. *La Vie musicale en France au siècle de Louis XIV: Nicolas Lebègue.* Paris: Picard.

————. 1955. "De l'emploi du temps des organistes parisiens sous les règnes de Louis XIII et Louis XIV et de leur participation à l'office." *RM* 226 (special number): 35–47.

————. 1957a. "Les Chapelles de musique de Saint-Sernin et de Saint-Étienne de Toulouse dans le dernier quart du XVIIe siècle." *RdM* 39 (July): 36–55.

————. 1957b. "Quelques réflexions sur les ballets et divertissements de Michel-Richard Delalande." In *Cahiers de l'Association Internationale des Études Françaises*, vol. 9. Paris: Société d'Éditions "Les Belles Lettres." 44–52.

————. 1957c. "Recent Researches into French Organ Building from the Fifteenth to the Seventeenth Century." *GSJ* 10:66–81.

————. 1960. "Retour à Michel-Richard Delalande." *Recherches* 1: 69–75.

————. 1962. *Jean-Baptiste de Boësset: un musicien, officier du roi et gentilhomme campagnard 1614–1685.* Paris: Picard.

————. 1963. "Le Disque et l'histoire de la musique." *Recherches* 3: 207–220.

————. 1965a. "Die klassische französische Musik, Deutschland und die deutsche Musikwissenschaft." *AfMW* 22 (3) September): 194–207.

————. 1965b. "La Musique française de 1661 à 1764." In *La Musique, les hommes, les instruments, les sources*, vol. 1. Ed. Norbert Dufourcq. Paris: Larousse. 285–384.

————. 1971–1982. *Le Livre de l'orgue français 1589–1789.* 5 vols. Paris: Picard.

————. 1973. "Les Baricades mistérieuses de François Couperin." *Recherches* 13:23–34.

————. 1979. "Contribution à l'histoire du Concert Spirituel dans la seconde moitié du XVIIIe siècle." *Recherches* 19:195–210.

————. 1981. "Une Association de symphonistes en France au XVIIe siècle." *Recherches* 20:255–260.

————. 1983. "François-Eustache Du Caurroy (1549–1609) et son entourage familial et professionnel." *Recherches* 21:9–40.

————. 1985. "En parcourant la 'Gazette,'" 1645–1654." *Recherches* 23:176–202.

————. 1987. "Autour de Nicolas Lebègue. Un recueil de motets inédits." *Recherches* 25:7–26.

————. See *Notes et références pour servir à une histoire de Michel-Richard Delalande.*

Dufourcq, Norbert, and Marcelle Benoit. 1957a. "À propos de Nicolas Bernier." *RdM* 39 (July): 78–91.

————. 1957b. *Dix années de la chapelle royale de musique d'après une correspondance inédite (1718–1728).* Paris: Picard.

————. See also Benoit, Marcelle, and Norbert Dufourcq.

Dufourcq, Norbert, and Jean-Yves Ribault. 1985. "Le Livre d'orgue de Montréal." *Orgue: cahiers et mémoires* 33:1–39.

Durand, Georges. 1922. *La Musique de la cathédrale d'Amiens avant la Révolution*. Amiens: Yvert et Tellier. Rpt. Geneva: Minkoff, 1972.

Durand, Henri-André. 1957. "Notes sur la diffusion de M. R. Delalande dans les chapitres provençaux au XVIIIe siècle." *RdM* 39:72–73.

Duron, Jean. 1977. *L'Oeuvre religieux de Henry Desmarest (1661–1741)*. Thesis, Conservatoire National Supérieur de Musique, Paris.

———. 1983. "L'Année musicale 1688." *XVIIe siècle* 139 (April–June): 229–241.

———. 1984. "L'Orchestre à cordes français avant 1715, nouveaux problèmes: les quintes de violon." *RdM* 70(2):260–269.

———. 1986a. "Le Grand motet: Rameau face à ses contemporains." In *Jean-Philippe Rameau. Colloque international*. Ed. Jérôme de La Gorce. Geneva: Champion-Slatkine. 331–370.

———. 1986b. "L'Orchestre de Marc-Antoine Charpentier." *RdM* 72(1):23–65.

———. 1986c. "La Structure-fugue dans le grand motet français avant Rameau." In *Actes du colloque international sur le grand motet français (1663–1792)*. Ed. Jean Mongrédien and Yves Ferraton. Paris: Presses de l'Université de Paris-Sorbonne. 129–166.

———. 1990. "Le Rapport choeur-orchestre dans les grands motets de Lully." In *Jean-Baptiste Lully. Actes du colloque*. Ed. Herbert Schneider and Jérôme de La Gorce. Laaber: Laaber-Verlag. 99–144.

———. 1991a. "'L'Instinct' de M. de Lully." In *La Tragédie lyrique*. Ed. P. Van Dieren. Paris: Cicero. 65–119.

———. 1991b. "Marc-Antoine Charpentier: *Mors Saülis et Jonathae—David et Jonathas*, de l'histoire sacrée à l'opéra biblique." *RdM* 77(2):221–268.

———. 1996. *L'Oeuvre de Sébastien de Brossard (1655–1730): catalogue thématique*. Versailles: Éditions du CNBV.

Durosoir, Georgie. 1991. *L'Air de cour en France, 1571–1655*. Liège: Pierre Mardaga.

———. 1994. "Pastorales avec musique et pastorales en musique en France au milieu du XVIIe siecle." In *Théâtre et musique au XVIIe siècle*, vol. 21. Ed. C. Mazouer. Paris: Klincksieck. 234–248.

Durosoir, Georgie, and André Verchaly. 1991. "Visages contrastés de l'Italie dans les ballets de cour de France dans la première moitié du XVIIe siècle." *RdM* 77(2):169–178.

———. In Press. *Catalogue de l'air de cour (1571–1664)*.

⁓ ▨ ⁓

Eastwood, Tony. 1984. "The French Air in the Eighteenth Century: A Neglected Area." *SiM(AUS)* 18:84–107.

Écorcheville, Jules-Armand-Joseph. 1900–1901. "Quelques documents sur la musique de la Grande Écurie du roi." *SIMG* 2:608–642.

———. 1906a. *Corneille et la musique*. Paris: L. Marcel Fortin.

———. 1906b. *De Lulli à Rameau 1690–1730: l'esthétique musicale.* Paris: L. Marcel Fortin. Rpt. Geneva: Minkoff, 1970.

———. 1906c. *Vingt suites d'orchestre du XVIIe siècle.* 2 vols. Paris: L.-Marcel Fortin. Rpt. New York: Broude Brothers, Ltd., 1970.

———. 1907. *Actes d'état-civil de musiciens insinués au Chatelet de Paris 1539–1650.* Paris: L. Marcel Fortin.

———. 1911. "Lully gentilhomme et sa descendance." *BSIM* 5 (15 May): 1–19; 6 (15 June): 1–27; 7 (15 July): 36–52.

Eighteenth-Century Keyboard Music. 1994. Ed. Robert L. Marshall. New York: Schirmer Books.

Ellis, Helen Meredith. 1967. *The Dances of J.-B. Lully.* Ph.D. Thesis, Stanford University.

———. 1968. "The Sources of Jean-Baptiste Lully's Secular Music." *Recherches* 8:89–130.

———. 1969. "Inventory of the Dances of Jean-Baptiste Lully." *Recherches* 9:21–55.

———. See also Little, Meredith Ellis.

Encyclopédie de la musique. 1958–1961. 3 vols. Ed. François Michel. Paris: Fasquelle.

Encyclopédie de la musique et Dictionnaire du Conservatoire. 1913–1931. 11 vols. Ed. Albert Lavignac and Lionel de La Laurencie. Paris: Delagrave.

Encyclopédie des musiques sacrées. 1968–1970. 4 vols. Ed. Jacques Porte. Paris: Labergerie.

Eppelsheim, Jurgen. 1961. *Das Orchester in den Werken Jean–Baptiste Lullys,* Tutzing: Hans Schneider.

Escudier, Monique. 1975. *Aperçus sur la société, la création et l'esthétique en France de la Renaissance au Grand Siècle, d'après les pièces liminaires accompagnant l'édition musicale, de 1589 à 1661.* Thesis, Conservatoire National Supérieur de Musique, Paris.

⌒ ▦ ⌒

Fajon, Robert. 1978. "Propositions pour une analyse rationalisée du récitatif de l'opéra lullyste." *RdM* 64:55–75.

———. 1982. *A. C. Destouches et l'évolution du répertoire de l'Académie Royale de Musique.* Doctoral Thesis, University of Paris-Sorbonne.

———. 1983. "Jean-Joseph Mouret, musicien de Marivaux." In *Jean-Joseph Mouret et le théâtre de son temps.* Aix-en-Provence: C. A. E. R. 89–129.

———. 1984. *L'Opéra à Paris du Roi-Soleil à Louis le Bien-aimé.* Geneva: Slatkine.

———. 1986. "Le Préramisme dans le répertoire de l'Opéra." In *Jean-Philippe Rameau. Colloque international.* Ed. Jérôme de La Gorce. Geneva: Champion-Slatkine. 307–329.

Falk, Margaret. 1973. *Les Parodies du Nouveau Théâtre Italien (1731). Histoire systematique des timbres.* Bilthoven, Holland: A. B. Creyghton.

Farrar, Carol R. 1970. *Michel Corrette and Flute Playing in the Eighteenth Century.* Brooklyn: Institute of Mediaeval Music.

Fau, Elisabeth. 1978. *La Gravure de musique à Paris des origines à la Révolution (1650–1789).* Thesis, École Nationale des Chartes, Paris.

Favre, George. 1971. "Un Prince mélomane au XVIIIe siècle: la vie musicale à la cour d'Antoine 1er prince de Monaco (1661–1731)." *RdM* 57:135–149.

Ferguson, Howard. 1975. *Keyboard Interpretation.* New York and London: Oxford University Press.

Fleck, Stephen H. 1995. *Music, Dance, and Laughter: Comic Creation in Molière's Comedy-Ballets.* Paris: Jean Touzot.

Fleurot, François. 1984. *Le Hautbois dans la musique française (1650–1800).* Paris: Picard.

Fleury, Louis. 1923. "The Flute and Flutists in the French Art of the Seventeenth and Eighteenth Centuries." *MQ* 9:515–537.

Flood, W. H. Grattan. 1928. "Quelques précisions nouvelles sur Cambert et Grabu à Londres." *RM* 9 (August): 351–361.

Font, Auguste. 1894. *Favart: l'opéra-comique et la comédie vaudeville aux XVIIe et XVIIIe siècles.* Paris, Fischbacher. Rpt. Geneva: Minkoff, 1970.

Fontijn, Claire. 1994. *Antonia Bembo: "Les goûts réunis," Royal Patronage and the Role of the Woman Composer during the Reign of Louis XIV.* Ph.D. Thesis, Duke University.

———. 1995. "Quantz's *unegal*: implications for the performance of 18th-century music." *EM* 23 (1) (February): 54–62.

Ford, Robert. 1978. "The Filmer Manuscript: A Handlist." *Notes* 34 (4) (June): 814–825.

———. 1981. "Nicolas Dieupart's Book of Trios." *Recherches* 20: 45–75.

Fortassier, Pierre. 1970. "Musique et paroles dans les opéras de Campra." In *La Régence.* Aix-en-Provence: C. A. E. R. 31–43.

Foster, Donald H. 1967. *Louis-Nicolas Clérambault and his "Cantates françaises."* Ph.D. Thesis, University of Michigan.

———. 1975. "The Oratorio in Paris in the 18th Century." *AM* 47 (1) (January–June): 67–133.

Fournel, Victor. 1863–1875. *Les Contemporains de Molière.* 3 vols. Paris: Firmin-Didot.

François-Sappey, Brigitte. 1974. "L'Oeuvre de clavecin de Jean-François Dandrieu 1682–1738." *Recherches* 14:155–235.

———. 1982. *Jean-François Dandrieu (1682–1738), Organiste du Roy.* Paris: Picard.

Fuller, David R. 1965. *Eighteenth-Century French Harpsichord Music.* Ph.D. Thesis, Harvard University.

———. 1974. "Accompanied Keyboard Music." *MQ* 60 (2) (April): 222–245.

————. 1976. "French Harpsichord Playing in the Seventeenth Century after Le Gallois." *EM* 4 (1) (January): 22–26.

————. 1977. "Dotting, the 'French style' and Frederick Neumann's Counter-Reformation." *EM* 5 (4) (October): 517–535.

————. 1978. "Harpsichord Registration." *The Diapason* (July): 1, 6–7.

————. 1981. "An Unknown French Ornament Table from 1699." *EM* 9 (1) (January): 55–61.

————. 1983. "Les Petits Marteaux de M. Rameau." *EM* 11 (4) (October): 516–517.

————. 1985. "The 'Dotted Style' in Bach, Handel and Scarlatti." In *Bach, Handel, Scarlatti: Tercentenary Essays*. Ed. Peter Williams. Cambridge: Cambridge University Press. 99–117.

————. 1987. "More on Triplets and Inequality." *EM* 15 (3) (August): 384–385.

————. 1989. "Notes and *inégales* Unjoined: Defining a Definition." *Journal of Musicology*. 7 (1) (Winter): 21–28.

————. 1990a. "Les Arrangements pour clavier des oeuvres de Lully." In *Jean-Baptiste Lully. Actes du colloque*. Ed. Herbert Schneider and Jérôme de La Gorce. Laaber: Laaber-Verlag. 471–482.

————. 1990b. "Portraits and Characters in Instrumental Music of Seventeenth and Eighteenth Century France." *Early Keyboard Journal* 8:33–59.

————. 1993. "Sous les doigts de Chambonnières." *EM: French Baroque I* 21 (2) (May): 191–202.

————. In Preparation. *French Harpsichord Music.*

————. See also Gustafson, Bruce, and David Fuller.

Garden, Greer. 1991. "'Les Amours de Venus' (1712) et le 'Second Livre de Cantates' (1714) de Campra." *RdM* 77(1):96–107.

————. 1993. "A Link between Opera and Cantata in France: Tonal Design in the Music of André Campra." *EM: French Baroque II* 21 (3) (August): 397–412.

Garros, Madeleine. 1943. "Mme de Maintenon et la musique." *RdM* 1 (Special series) (January): 8–17.

————. 1960. "La Musique religieuse en France de 1600 à 1750." In *Histoire de la musique*, vol. 1. Ed. Roland-Manuel. Paris: Gallimard. 1591–1613.

Gastoué, Amédée. 1905. "La Musique à Avignon et dans le Comtat du XIVe au XVIIIe siècle." *RMI* 12:555–578, 768–777.

Gaudefroy-Demombynes, Jean. 1941. *Les Jugements allemands sur la musique française au XVIIIe siècle*. Paris: G. P. Maisonneuve. Rpt. New York: AMS Press. 1978.

Gausson, François. 1960. "Actes d'état-civil de musiciens français 1651–1681." *Recherches* 1:53–203.

Genest, Emile. 1925. *L'Opéra-comique connu et inconnu*. Paris: Fischbacher.

Geoffroy-Dechaume, Antoine. 1964. *Les "secrets" de la musique ancienne*. Paris: Fasquelle.

Gérold, Théodore. 1921. *L'Art du chant en France au XVIIe siècle*. Strasbourg: Publications de la Faculté des Lettres, Palais de l'Université. Rpt. Geneva: Minkoff, 1971.

Gervais, Françoise. 1965. "La Musique pure au service du drame lyrique chez Rameau." *RM* 260 (special number): 37–45.

Gillespie, John Edward. 1951. *The Harpsichord Work of Nicolas Le Bègue*. Ph.D. Thesis, University of Southern California.

Giraud, Yves. 1973. "Quinault et Lully ou l'accord de deux styles." *Marseille* 95:195–212.

Girdlestone, Cuthbert. 1957. *Jean-Philippe Rameau: His Life and Work*. London: Cassell. 2nd ed. French trans. Paris: Desclée de Brouwer, 1962.

———. 1972. *La Tragédie en musique considérée comme genre littéraire, 1673–1750*. Geneva: Droz.

Goldschmidt, Hugo. 1901–1904. *Studien zur Geschichte der italienischen Oper im 17. Jahrhundert*. 2 vols. Leipzig: Breitkopf.

Green, Robert. 1979. *Annotated Translation and Commentary on the Works of Jean Rousseau*. Ph.D. Thesis, Indiana University.

———. 1982. "The *pardessus de viole* and its literature." *EM* 10 (3) (July): 301–307.

———. 1987. "Eighteenth-Century French Chamber Music for Vielle." *EM* 15 (4) (November): 468–479.

———. 1988. "The Treble Viol in 17th-Century France and the Origins of the Pardessus de viole." *JVGSA* 25:64–71.

Green, Thomas. 1992. *Early Rameau Sources: Studies in the Origins and Dating of the Operas and Other Musical Works*. Ph.D. Thesis, Brandeis University.

Gros, Étienne. 1926. *Philippe Quinault*. Paris: E. Champion. Rpt. Geneva: Slatkine, 1990.

———. 1928. "Les Origines de la tragédie-lyrique et la place des tragédies à machines dans l'évolution du théâtre vers l'opéra." *Revue d'histoire littéraire* (April–June): 161–193.

Grout, Donald. 1939. *The Origins of the Opéra-comique*. Ph.D. Thesis, Harvard University.

———. 1941a. "The Music of the Italian Theatre in Paris, 1682–1697." *Papers of the AMS* 20:158–170.

———. 1941b. "Seventeenth-Century Parodies of French Opera." *MQ* 27 (2) (April): 211–219, 514–526.

———. 1941c. "Some Forerunners of the Lully Opera." *M&L* 22 (1) (January): 1–25.

———. 1965. *A Short History of Opera*. 2nd ed. New York: W. W. Norton.

———. 1980. *A History of Western Music*. New York: W. W. Norton.

Guide de la musique sacrée et chorale profane: l'âge baroque, 1600–1750. 1992. Ed. E. Lemaître. Paris: Fayard.

Guilcher, Jean-Michel. 1969a. "André Lorin et l'invention de l'écriture chorégraphique." *Revue d'histoire du théâtre* 21:256–264.

―――. 1969b. *La Contredanse et les renouvellements de la danse française.* Paris: Mouton et Cie.

Guillo, Laurent. 1989. "Notes sur la Librairie musicale à Lyon et à Genève au XVIIᵉ siècle." *FAM* 36 (2) (April–June): 116–135.

Guillot, Pierre. 1971. "Les Livres de clavecin de Christophe Moyreau." *Recherches* 11:179–220.

1991. *Les Jésuites et la musique: le Collège de la Trinité à Lyon.* Liège: Mardaga.

Gürtelschmied, Walter. 1975. *Paolo Lorenzani (1640–1713): Leben, Werk, thematischer Katalog.* Doctoral Thesis, University of Vienna.

―――. 1995. "France." Im *Keyboard Music before 1700.* Ed. Alexander Silbiger. New York: Schirmer Books. 90–146.

Gustafson, Bruce. 1977. "A Letter from Mʳ Lebègue Concerning His Preludes." *Recherches* 17:7–14.

―――. 1979. *French Harpsichord Music of the 17th Century: A thematic Catalogue of the Sources with Commentary.* 3 vols. Ann Arbor: UMI Press.

―――. 1984. "Shapes and Meanings of Slurs in Unmeasured Harpsichord Preludes." *French Baroque Music: A Newsletter* 2 (October): 20–22.

―――. 1987. "The Lully Labyrinth. Cross References and Misattributions in the Lully-Werke-Verzeichnis." *Notes* 44 (1) (September): 33–39.

―――. 1989. *A Thematic Locator for the Works of Jean-Baptiste Lully.* New York: Performers' Editions.

―――. 1990. "The Legacy in Instrumental Music of Charles Babel, Prolific Transcriber of Lully's Music." In *Jean-Baptiste Lully. Actes du colloque.* Ed. Herbert Schneider and Jérôme de La Gorce. Laaber: Laaber-Verlag. 495–516.

Gustafson, Bruce, and David Fuller. 1990. *A Catalogue of French Harpsichord Music, 1699–1780.* New York: Clarendon Press.

Gutmann, Veronika. 1986. "Die französischen Quellen zu den Instrumentenartikeln in Johann Gottfried Walthers 'Musikalisches Lexicon.'" *Aufklärungen: Studien zur deutsch-französischen Musikgeschichte im 18. Jahrhundert.* Ed. W. Birtel and C. H. Mahling. Heidelberg: Winter. 14–21.

☙ ▨ ☙

Haas, Robert. 1929. *Die Musik des Barocks.* Wildpark-Potsdam: Akademische Verlags Gesellschaft Athenaion.

Hajdu Heyer, John. 1973. *The Life and Works of Jean Gilles.* Ph.D. Thesis, University of Colorado.

―――. 1986. "Recent Findings in the Sources of Lully's Motets: The Traditions of Philidor and Foucault." In *Actes du colloque international sur le grand motet français (1663–1792).* Ed. Jean

Mongrédien and Yves Ferraton. Paris: Presses de l'Université de Paris-Sorbonne. 77–87.

———. 1989. "The Sources of Lully's *grands motets*." *Jean-Baptiste Lully and the Music of the French Baroque.* Ed. John Hajdu Heyer. Cambridge: Cambridge University Press. 81–98.

———. 1990. "Lully's 'Jubilate Deo,' LWV 77/16: A Stylistic Anomaly." In *Jean-Baptiste Lully. Actes du colloque.* Ed. Herbert Schneider and Jérôme de La Gorce. Laaber: Laaber-Verlag. 145–154.

Hamburger, Paul. 1930–1931. "Ein handschriftliches Klavierbuch aus der ersten Hälfte des 17. Jahrhunderts." *ZfMW* 13:133–140, 556–558.

Hardouin, Pierre. 1957. "Harpsichord Making in Paris." *GSJ* 10:10–29; *GSJ* 12(1959): 72–85; *GSJ* 13(1960a):52–58.

———. 1960b. "François Roberday (1624–1680)." *RdM* 45 (July): 44–62.

Harris, Frances Claire. 1975. *Jean-Claude Gillier: Theater Musician of the Early Eighteenth Century.* Ph.D. Thesis, University of Minnesota.

Harris-Warrick, Rebecca. 1982. "The Tempo of French Baroque Dances: Indications from 18th-Century Metronome Devices." In *Proceedings of the Annual Meeting of the Society of Dance History Scholars.* Cambridge, MA: Society of Dance History Scholars. 14–23.

———. 1986. "Ballroom Dancing at the Court of Louis XIV." *EM* 14 (1) (February): 241–249.

———. 1989. "*La Mariée*: the History of a French Court Dance." In *Jean-Baptiste Lully and the Music of the French Baroque.* Ed. John Hajdu Heyer. Cambridge: Cambridge University Press. 239–257.

———. 1990a. "Contexts for Choreographies: Notated Dances set to the Music of Jean-Baptiste Lully." In *Jean-Baptiste Lully. Actes du colloque.* Ed. Herbert Schneider and Jérôme de La Gorce. Laaber: Laaber-Verlag. 433–455.

———. 1990b. "A Few Thoughts on Lully's *hautbois*." *EM* 18 (1) (February): 97–106.

———. 1992. "Interpretation of Pendulum Markings for 18th Century French Dance." In *The Marriage of Music and Dance.* Cambridge: Cambridge University Press. No pagination.

———. 1993a. "From Score into Sound: Questions of Scoring in Lully's Ballets." *EM: French Baroque II* 21 (3) (August): 355–362.

———. 1993b. "Interpreting Pendulum Markings for French Baroque Dances." *Historical Performance* 6 (1) (Spring): 9–22.

———. 1994. "Magnificence in Motion: State Musicians in Lully's Ballets and Operas." *Cambridge Opera Journal* 6(3):189–203.

Harris-Warrick, Rebecca, and Carol G. Marsh. 1994. *Musical Theater at the Court of Louis XIV: the Example of 'Le Mariage de la Grosse Cathos.'* Cambridge: Cambridge University Press.

Haymann, Emmanuel. 1991. *Lulli*. Paris: Flammarion.

Haynes, Bruce. 1988. "Lully and the Rise of the Oboe as Seen in Works of Art." *EM* 16 (3) (August): 324–338.

———. 1992. *Musical Pitch Standards in the Baroque and Classical Periods*. Ph.D. Thesis, University of Montreal.

Heartz, Daniel. 1955. "Les Styles instrumentaux de la Renaissance." In *La Musique instrumentale de la Renaissance*. Ed. Jean Jacquot. Paris: CNRS. 61–76.

———. 1969. "The Genesis of Mozart's *Idomeneo*." *MQ* 55 (1) (January): 1–19.

———. 1985. "Terpsichore at the Fair: Old and New Dance Airs in Two Vaudeville Comedies by Lesage." In *Music and Context: Essays for John M. Ward*. Cambridge, MA: Harvard University Press. 278–304.

———. 1993. "The Concert Spirituel in the Tuileries Palace." *EM: French Baroque I* 21 (2) (May): 241–248.

Hefling, Stephen E. 1993. *Rhythmic Alteration in Seventeenth- and Eighteenth-Century Music*. New York: Schirmer Books.

Hehr, Elizabeth. 1985. "How the French Viewed the Difference Between French and Italian Singing Styles of the 18th-Century." *International Review of the Aesthetics and Sociology of Music* 16 (1) (June): 73–85.

Hendrie, Gerald. 1988. "Some Reflections on the Keyboard Music of Rameau." *SiM(AUS)* 22:13-38.

Herlin, Denis. 1995. *Catalogue du fonds musical de la Bibliothèque de Versailles*. Paris: Éditions Klincksieck.

Hibberd, Lloyd. 1968. "Mme de Sévigné and the Operas of Lully." *Essays in Musicology: A Birthday Offering for Willi Apel*. Bloomington, in: University Press. 153–163.

Higginbottom, Edward. 1975. "'*Sonate, que me veux-tu?*' Classical French Music and the Theory of Imitation." In *French Music and the Fitzwilliam*. Cambridge: Fitzwilliam Museum. 12–22.

———. 1986. "François Couperin." In *The New Grove French Baroque Masters*. Ed. Stanley Sadie. London: MacMillan London Limited. 151–206.

Hilton, Wendy. 1977. "A Dance for Kings: The 17th-Century French Courante." *EM* 5 (2) (April): 160–172.

———. 1980. *Dance and Music of Court and Theater: The French Noble Style, 1690–1725*. Princeton: Princeton Book Company.

———. 1986. "Dances to Music by Jean-Baptiste Lully." *EM* 14 (1) (February): 51–63.

Himelfarb, Hélène. 1986. "Lieux éminents du grand motet: décor symbolique et occupation de l'espace dans les deux dernières chapelles royales de Versailles (1682 and 1710)." In *Actes du colloque international de musicologie sur le grand motet français (1663–1792)*. Ed. Jean Mongrédien and Yves Ferraton. Paris: University of Paris, Sorbonne. 17–27.

————. 1990. "Un Domaine méconnu de l'empire lullyste: le Trianon de Louis XIV, ses tableaux et les livrets d'opéras." In *Jean-Baptiste Lully. Actes du colloque.* Ed. Herbert Schneider and Jérôme de La Gorce. Laaber: Laaber-Verlag. 287–306.

Histoire de la musique. 1960–1963. Ed. Roland-Manuel, 2 vols. Paris: Gallimard.

Hitchcock, H. Wiley. 1954. *The Latin Oratorios of Marc-Antoine Charpentier.* Ph.D. Thesis, University of Michigan.

————. 1955. "The Latin Oratorios of Marc-Antoine Charpentier." *MQ* 41 (1) (January): 41–65.

————. 1961. "The Instrumental Music of Marc-Antoine Charpentier." *MQ* 47 (January): 58–72.

————. 1971. "Marc-Antoine Charpentier and the Comédie-Française." *JAMS* 24 (2) (Summer): 255–281.

————. 1972. "Problèmes d'édition de la musique de Marc-Antoine Charpentier pour *Le Malade imaginaire.*" *RdM* 58 (1): 3–15.

————. 1974. "Some Aspects of Notation in an *Alma Redemptoris Mater* (c. 1670) by Marc-Antoine Charpentier." *Notations and Editions.* Ed. Edith Borroff. Dubuque: C. Brown. 127–134.

————. 1982. *Les Oeuvres de/The Works of Marc-Antoine Charpentier: catalogue raisonné.* Paris: Picard.

————. 1984a. "Charpentier's 'Médée.'" *MT* 125 (October): 563–567.

————. 1984b. "Les Oeuvres de Marc-Antoine Charpentier: post-scriptum d'un catalogue." *RdM* 70(1):37–50.

————. 1985. "Marc-Antoine Charpentier: Memoires and Index." *Recherches* 23:5–44.

————. 1986. "Marc-Antoine Charpentier." In *The New Grove French Baroque Masters.* Ed. Stanley Sadie. London: MacMillan London Limited. 73–118.

————. 1990. *Marc-Antoine Charpentier.* Oxford: Oxford University Press.

Hofman, Shlomo. 1961. *L'Oeuvre de clavecin de François Couperin le Grand.* Paris: Picard.

Hogwood, Christopher. 1975. "Sources for the Performance of French Keyboard Music." In *French Music and the Fitzwilliam.* Cambridge: Fitzwilliam Museum. 23–30.

Horrix, Christoph. 1981. *Studien zur französischen Lautenmusik im 17. Jahrhundert.* Doctoral Thesis, University of Tübingen.

Houle, George. 1987. *Meter and Music 1600–1800: Performance, Perception and Notation.* Bloomington: Indiana University Press.

Howard, Patricia. 1974. *The Operas of Jean-Baptiste Lully.* Doctoral Thesis, University of Surrey.

————. 1975. "The Académie Royale and the Performances of Lully's Operas." *Consort* 31:109–115.

————. 1989. "Lully and the Ironic Convention." *Cambridge Opera Journal.* 1 (2) (July): 139–153.

————. 1990. "The Positioning of Woman in Quinault's World Picture." In *Jean-Baptiste Lully. Actes du colloque.* Ed. Herbert Schneider and Jérôme de La Gorce. Laaber: Laaber-Verlag. 193–199.

————. 1991. "The Influence of the Précieuses on Content and Structure in Quinault's and Lully's *Tragédies Lyriques.*" *AM* 63(1):57–72.

————. 1994. "Quinault, Lully and the Précieuses: images of women in seventeenth-century France." In *Cecilia Regained: Feminist Perspectives on Women and Music.* Urbana: University of Illinois Press. 70–89.

Hsu, John. 1978. "The Use of the Bow in French Solo Viol Playing of the 17th and 18th Centuries." *EM* 6 (4) (October): 526–529.

————. 1981. *A Handbook of French Baroque Viol Technique.* New York: Broude Brothers, Ltd.

Hubbard, Frank. 1965. *Three Centuries of Harpsichord Making.* Cambridge, MA: Harvard University Press.

Hutchings, Arthur. 1961. *The Baroque Concerto.* London: Faber and Faber. 3rd revised ed. London: Faber, 1973.

⤳ ▩ ⤶

L'Interprétation de la musique française aux XVIIe et XVIIIe siècles. 1974. Ed. Édith Weber. Paris: CNRS.

Isherwood, Robert M. 1969–1970. "The Centralization of Music in the Reign of Louis XIV." *French Historical Studies.* 6:156–171.

————. 1973. *Music in the Service of the King: France in the Seventeenth Century.* Ithaca, New York: Cornell University Press.

————. 1978. "Popular Music Entertainment in Eighteenth-Century Paris." *International Review of the Aesthetics and Sociology of Music.* 9:295–309.

————. 1986. *Farce and Fantasy: Popular Entertainment in Eighteenth-Century Paris.* New York: Oxford University Press.

Ishikawa Marvyama, Yumiko. 1996. *L'Opera-ballet des Indes galantes (1735) aux Fêtes d'Hébé (1739).* Doctoral Thesis. University of Paris-Sorbonne.

⤳ ▩ ⤶

Jacquot, Albert. 1882. *La Musique en Lorraine.* Paris: A. Quantin. Rpt. Geneva: Minkoff, 1972.

Jansen, Albert. 1884. *Jean-Jacques Rousseau als Musiker.* Berlin: G. Reimer. Rpt. Geneva: Minkoff, 1971.

Jean-Baptiste Lully. Actes du colloque. 1990. Ed. Schneider, Herbert, and Jérôme de La Gorce. Laaber: Laaber-Verlag.

Jean-Baptiste Lully and the Music of the French Baroque: Essays in Honor of James R. Anthony. 1989. Ed. John Hajdu Heyer. Cambridge: Cambridge University Press.

Jean-Philippe Rameau. Colloque international, 1986. Ed. Jérôme de La Gorce. Geneva: Champion-Slatkine.

Jeanselme, Christiane. 1991. *250 ans de vie musicale et théâtrale à Aix-en-Provence: du début du XVIIe siècle à la veille de la seconde République*. Doctoral Thesis, University of Aix-Marseille.

Johnson, James H. 1995. *Listening in Paris: A Cultural History*. Berkeley: University of California Press.

Jonckbloet, W. J. A., and J. P. N. Land. 1882. *Musique et musiciens au XVIIe siècle*. Leyden: Société pour l'Histoire Musicale des Pays-Bas.

Jullien, Adolphe. 1876. *Les Grandes Nuits de Sceaux: le théâtre de la duchesse du Maine*. Paris: J. Baur. Rpt. Geneva: Minkoff, 1978.

Jurgens, Madeleine. 1969, 1974. See *Documents du Minutier Central concernant l'histoire de la musique (1600–1650)*.

Kapp, Volker. 1990. "Benserade, librettiste de Lully et panégyriste du roi." In *Jean-Baptiste Lully. Actes du colloque*. Ed. Herbert Schneider and Jérôme de La Gorce. Laaber: Laaber-Verlag. 167–180.

Karro, Françoise. 1990. "L'Empire ottoman et l'Europe dans l'opéra français et viennois au temps de Lully." In *Jean-Baptiste Lully. Actes du colloque*. Ed. Herbert Schneider and Jérôme de La Gorce. Laaber: Laaber-Verlag. 251–269.

Käser, Theodore. 1966. *Die Leçon des Ténèbres im 17. und 18. Jahrhundert*. Bern: P. Haupt.

Kenyon, Nicolas, ed. 1988. *Authenticity and Early Music: A Symposium*. Oxford: Oxford University Press.

Kimbell, David R. B. 1968. "The 'Amadis' Operas of Destouches and Handel." *M&L* 49 (4) (October): 329–346.

Kinney, Gordon J. 1966. "Marin Marais as Editor of his Own Compositions." *JVGSA* 3:5–16.

———. 1968. "Problems of Melodic Ornamentation in French Viol Music." *JVGSA* 5:34–50.

Kintzler, Catherine. 1986a. "De la pastorale à la tragédie lyrique: quelques éléments d'un système poétique." *RdM* 72(1):67–96.

———. 1986b. "Essai de definition du récitatif." *Recherches* 24: 128–141.

———. 1991a. *Poétique de l'opéra français de Corneille à Rousseau*. Paris: Minerve.

———. 1991b. "La Tragédie lyrique et le double défi d'un théâtre classique." In *La Tragédie lyrique*. Ed. P. Van Dieren. Paris: Cicero. 51–63.

Kirkpatrick, Ralph. 1938. "Eighteenth-Century Metronomic Indications." In *Papers of the AMS*. No place: Privately printed by the Society (AMS). 30–50.

Kish, Anne L. 1964. *Jean-Baptiste Senallié: His Life, His Time, and His Music*. Ph.D. Thesis, Bryn Mawr College.

Kitchen, John P. 1979. *Harpsichord Music of Seventeenth-Century France: the Forms, Their Origin and Development, with Particular*

Emphasis on the Work of Louis Couperin. Doctoral Thesis, Cambridge University.

Kooiman, Ewald. 1986a. "Verzierungen in der klassischen französischen Orgelmusik." In *Zur Interpretation der französischen Orgelmusik.* Ed. H. J. Busch. Merseburger: Gesellschaft der Orgelfreunde. 65–77.

———. 1986b. "Die *Inégalité* in der französischen Barockmusik." In *Zur Interpretation der französischen Orgelmusik.* Ed. H. J. Busch. Merseburger: Gesellschaft der Orgelfreunde. 51–64.

Kroll, Mark. 1994. "French Masters." In *Eighteenth-century Keyboard Music.* Ed. Robert L. Marshall. New York: Schirmer Books. 124–133.

Krucker, Jérôme. 1989. *Sébastien de Brossard (1655–1730) et sa musique religieuse.* Doctoral Thesis, University of Paris-Sorbonne.

Kuntzmann, Vladia. 1993. *Jean-Féry Rebel (1666–1747) and His Instrumental Works.* Ph.D. Thesis, Columbia University.

Lacroix, Paul, ed. 1868–1870. *Ballets et Mascarades de cour de Henri III à Louis XIV.* 6 vols. Geneva: Gay. Rpt. Geneva: Minkoff, 1968.

———. 1875. *XVIIIe siècle: institutions, usages et costumes.* Paris: Firmin-Didot.

La France, Albert. 1986. *The Sacred Music of Paolo Lorenzani.* Doctoral Thesis, University of Victoria.

La Gorce, Jérôme de. 1978. *L'Opéra sous le règne de Louis XIV: le merveilleux ou les puissances surnaturelles (1671–1715).* Doctoral Thesis, University of Paris-Sorbonne.

———. 1979. "L'Académie Royale de Musique en 1704, d'après des documents inédits conservé dans les archives notariales." *RdM* 65(2):160–191.

———. 1981. "L'Opéra et son public au temps de Louis XIV." *Bulletin de la Société de l'Histoire de Paris et de L'ile-de-France.* 108:27–46.

———. 1983a. "Documents inédits relatifs à la vie de Jean-Joseph Mouret." In *Jean-Joseph Mouret et le théâtre de son temps.* Aix-en-Provence: C. A. E. R. 12–37.

———. 1983b–1984. "L'Opéra français à la cour de Louis XIV." *Revue d'histoire du théâtre.* 387–401.

———. 1984. "Un Opéra français représenté à la Cour de Louis XIV en 1671 et 1672: *Les Amours de Diane et d'Endymion*, pastorale mise en musique par Sablière" *XVIIe siècle* 142 (January–March): 37–46.

———. 1986a. "Une Académie de musique en province au temps du Roi-Soleil." In *La Musique et le rite sacré et profane.* Ed. M. Honegger and P. Prévost. Strasbourg: Bordas. 465–496.

———. 1986b. *Berain, dessinateur du Roi Soleil.* Paris: Herscher.

———. 1988. "Un Proche collaborateur de Lully: Philippe Quinault." *XVIIe siècle* 16 (1–4) (October–December): 365–370.

————. 1989. "Some notes on Lully's orchestra." In *Jean-Baptiste Lully and the Music of the French Baroque*. Ed. John Hajdu Heyer. Cambridge: Cambridge University Press. 99–112.

————. 1990a "Guillaume-Louis Pécour: a biographical essay." *Dance Research* 8(2):3–26.

————. 1990b. "L'Orchestre de l'Opéra et son evolution de Campra à Rameau." *RdM* 76(1):23–43.

————. 1991. *Lully, un age d'or de l'opéra français*. (Catalogue of the Drouot-Montaigne exhibition.) Paris: Drouot Montaigne.

————. 1992. *L'Opéra à Paris au temps de Louis XIV: histoire d'un théâtre*. Paris: Desjonquères.

Lagrave, Henri. 1972. *Le Théâtre et le public à Paris de 1715 à 1750*, Paris: Klincksieck.

Lajarte, Théodore. 1874. "Les Transformations d'un opéra au XVIIIe siècle." *Chronique musicale*. 4 (20) (April 15): 61–65.

————. 1878. *Bibliothèque musicale du théâtre de l'Opéra: catalogue historique, chronologique, anecdotique*. 2 vols. Paris: Librairie des Bibliophiles. Rpt. Geneva: Minkoff, 1971.

Lalague-Guilhemsans, Marie-Thérèse. 1979. *Une Famille de musiciens français aux XVIIe et XVIIIe siècles: les Forqueray*. Thesis, École Nationale des Chartes, Paris.

La Laurencie, Lionel de. 1905. *Le Goût musical en France*. Paris: A. Joanin. Rpt. Geneva: Slatkine, 1970.

————. 1907. "Quelques documents sur Jean-Philippe Rameau et sa famille." *BSIM* 3:541–614.

————. 1908a. *Rameau*. Paris: H. Laurens.

————. 1908b–1909. "Deux violistes célèbres: les Forqueray." *BSIM* (1908):1251–1274 and (1909):48–60.

————. 1908c–1909. "Notes sur la jeunesse d'André Campra." *SIMG* 10:159–258.

————. 1911. *Lully*, Paris: F. Alcan. Rpt. Paris: Éditions d'Aujourd'hui, 1977.

————. 1912. "Les Pastorales en musique au XVIIe siècle en France avant Lully et leur influence sur l'opéra." In *International Music Society, 4th Congress Report*. London: Novello. 139–146.

————. 1913. "André Campra, musicien profane." *L'Année musicale* 3:153–205.

————. 1920. *Les Créateurs de l'opéra français*. Paris: F. Alcan. Rpt. Paris: Éditions d'Aujourd'hui, 1975.

————. 1922a–1924. *L'École française de violon de Lully à Viotti*. 3 vols. Paris: Delagrave. Rpt. Geneva: Minkoff, 1971.

————. 1922b. "Un Musicien dramatique du XVIIe siècle, Pierre Guédron." *RMI* 29:445–472.

————. 1925. "L'Opéra français au XVIIe siècle." *RM* 6 (3) (special number) (January): 26–43.

————. 1928. "*L'Orfeo nell'inferni* d'André Campra." *RdM* 9:129–133.

———. 1934. "Les Débuts de la musique de chambre en France." *RdM* 15:25–34.

Lancaster, H. Carrington. 1940. "Comedy versus Opera in France 1683–1700." In *Essays and Studies in Honor of Carleton Brown.* New York: New York University Press. 257–263.

Lance, Evelyn B. 1974. "Molière the Musician: a Tercentenary View." *MR* 35 (2) (August): 120–130.

Lancelot, Francine. 1971. "Ecriture de la danse: le système Feuillet." *Revue de la Société d'ethnographie française* 1 (new series): 29–58.

Landowska, Wanda. 1910. "Bach und die französische Klaviermusik." *Bach-Jahrbuch* 7:33–44.

Lang, Paul Henry. 1935. *The Literary Aspects of the History of Opera in France.* Ph.D. Thesis, Cornell University.

———. 1941. *Music in Western Civilization.* New York: W. W. Norton.

Larousse de la musique. 1957. Ed. Norbert Dufourcq. 2 vols. Paris: Larousse.

La Rue, Jan. 1957. "Bi-focal Tonality." In *Essays on Music in Honor of Archibald Thompson Davison.* Cambridge: Harvard University Press. 173–184.

Launay, Denise. 1955a. "La Fantaisie en France jusqu'au milieu du XVIIe siècle." In *La Musique instrumentale de la Renaissance.* Ed. Jean Jacquot. Paris: CNRS. 327–338.

———. 1955b. "Notes sur Étienne Moulinié, maître de musique de Gaston d'Orléans." In *Mélanges d'histoire et d'esthetique musicales offerts à Paul-Marie Masson,* vol. 2. Paris: Richard-Masse. 67–78.

———. 1957. "Les Motets à double choeur." *RdM* 40 (December): 173–195.

———. 1963. "A propos d'une messe de Charles d'Helfer." In *Le "Baroque" musical.* Vol. 4, *Colloques de Wégimont.* Liège: Université de Liège. 177–199.

———. 1964. "La 'Paraphrase des psaumes' de Godeau et ses musiciens." *RdM* 50(1):30–75.

———. 1965. "Les Rapports de tempo entre mesures binaires et mesures ternaires dans la musique française (1600–1650)." *FAM* 12 (2–3) (May–December): 166–194.

———. 1975. "Church Music in France (a) 1630–1660." In *NOHM,* vol. 5. London: Oxford University Press. 414–437.

———. 1977. "La Querelle des Bouffons et ses incidences sur la musique." In *IMS Report* (at Berkeley). Kassel: Bärenreiter, 1981. 225–233.

———. 1982. "L'Enseignement de la composition dans les maîtrises en France aux XVIe et XVIIe siècles." In *Les Fantaisies du voyageur. XXXIII variation Schaeffner.* Ed. J. Gribenski and J. M. Nectoux. Paris: Société Française de Musicologie. 80–90.

———. 1984. "Le Thème du retour à l'antique et la musique religieuse en France au temps de la Contre-Reforme." In *Biblio* (supplement to *La Pensée religieuse dans la littérature et la civilisation du XVIIe siècle en France.* Ed. M. Tietz and V. Kapp.) 17:814–825.

———. 1986a. "Les Deux versions musicales d'*Andromède*: Une Étape dans l'histoire du théâtre dans ses rapports avec la musique." In *Colloque Pierre Corneille.* Paris: PUF. 413–441.

———. 1986b. "Les 'Enfances' du grand motet." In *Actes du colloque international sur le grand motet français (1663–1792).* Ed. Jean Mongrédien and Yves Ferraton. Paris: Presses de l'Université de Paris-Sorbonne. 29–37.

———. 1990. "Les Airs italiens et français dans les ballets et les comédies-ballets." In *Jean-Baptiste Lully. Actes du colloque.* Ed. Herbert Schneider and Jérôme de La Gorce. Laaber: Laaber-Verlag. 31–49.

———. 1993. *La Musique religieuse en France du Concile de Trent à 1804.* Paris: Société Française de Musicologie.

———. 1994. "Les Ballets franco-italiens de Lully: leur importance pour la formation de son style." *Ars lyrica* 8:105–122.

Lawrence, William J. 1936. "The French Opera in London: a Riddle of 1686." *Times Literary Supplement* (March 28): 268.

Leavis, Ralph. 1978. "Double-Dotting and Ultre-Dotting." *EM* 6:309.

Lebeau, Elisabeth. 1963. "La Musique des cérémonies à la mort de Marie-Thérèse, reine de France, 1683." In *Le "Baroque" musical.* Vol. 4, *Colloques de Wégimont.* Liège: Université de Liège. 200–219.

Leclerc, Hélène. 1953. "Les Indes galantes (1735–1952)." *Revue d'histoire du théâtre.* 5:259–285.

Ledbetter, David. 1982. "Aspects of 17c French Lute Style Reflected in the Works of the Clavecinistes." *Lute Society Journal.* 22(2):55–66.

———. 1987. *Harpsichord and Lute Music in 17th-Century France.* Bloomington: Indiana University Press

Lefebvre, Léon. 1893. *La Musique et les Beaux-Arts à Lille au XVIIIe siècle.* Lille: Lefebvre-Ducrocq. Rpt. Geneva: Minkoff, 1973.

Le Huray, Peter. 1990. "Couperin's Huitième ordre." In *Authenticity in Performance: Eighteenth-Century Case Studies.* Cambridge: Cambridge University Press. 45–69.

Lemaître, Edmond. 1983. "Le Premier opéra-ballet et la première tempête, deux originalités de l'oeuvre de Pascal Colasse." *XVIIe siècle.* 139 (2) (April–June): 243–255.

———. 1986a. "Hippolyte et Aricie: les 'haute-contre de violon' dans les parties séparées du fonds La Salle." In *Jean-Philippe Rameau. Colloque international.* Ed. Jérôme de La Gorce. Geneva: Champion-Slatkine. 235–243.

———. 1986b and 1988–1990. "L'Orchestre dans le théâtre lyrique français chez les continuateurs de Lully (1687–1715)." *Recherches* 24:107–127 and 26:83–131.

————. 1991. "Les Sources des Plaisirs de l'Isle enchantée." *RdM* 77(2):187–200.

Le Moël, Michel. 1960. "Les Dernières années de J. Champion de Chambonnières, 1655–1672." *Recherches* 1:31–46.

————. 1963. "Un Foyer d'italianisme à la fin du XVIIᵉ siècle." *Recherches* 3:43–48.

————. 1966. "La Chapelle de musique sous Henri IV et Louis XIII." *Recherches* 6:5–26.

Lemoine, Micheline. 1953–1954. "La Technique violonistique de Jean-Marie Leclair." *RM* 225:117–143.

Leppert, Richard D. 1978. *Arcadia at Versailles. Noble Amateur Musicians and Their Musettes and Hurdy-gurdies at the French Court (c. 1660–1789)*. Amsterdam: Swets & Zeitlinger.

Leroux, Martial. 1987. *Guillaume Bouzignac et son siècle*, Doctoral Thesis, University of Paris-Sorbonne.

————. 1988–1990. "La Musique religieuse de Pierre Bouteiller." *Recherches* 26:51–82.

————. 1993. *Guillaume Bouzignac (ca. 1587–ca. 1643)*. Béziers: Société de Musicologie de Languedoc.

Lespinard, Bernadette. 1974, 1975, 1976, and 1977. "Henry Madin (1698–1748), sous-maître de la Chapelle royale." *Recherches* 14:236–296; 15:107–145; 16:9–23; and 17:150–204.

Lester, Joel. 1994. "An Analysis of Lully from circa 1700." *Music Theory Spectrum*. 16 (1) (Spring): 41–61.

Lesure, François. 1949. "Réflexions sur les origines du concert parisien." *Polyphonie* 5:47–51.

————. 1952. "Die 'Terpsichore' von Michael Praetorius und die französische Instrumentalmusik unter Heinrich IV." *MF* 5:7–17.

————. 1953. "Marin Marais: sa carrière, sa famille." *RBdM* 7:129–136.

————. 1954. "Les Orchestres populaires à Paris vers la fin du XVIᵉ siècle." *RdM* 36 (July): 39–54.

————. 1956. "Le Recueil de ballets de Michel Henry." In *Les Fêtes de la Renaissance*, vol. 1. Ed. Jean Jacquot. Paris: CNRS. 205–219.

————. 1960. "Une Querelle sur le jeu de la viole en 1688: J. Rousseau contre Demarchy." *RdM* 46 (December): 181–199.

————. 1964. "Un Contrat d'exclusivité entre Nicolas Formé et Ballard, 1638." *RdM* 50 (2) (December): 228–229.

————. 1969. *Bibliographie des éditions musicales publiées par Estienne Roger et Michel Charles le Cène*. Paris: Société Française de Musicologie.

————. 1972. *L'Opéra classique français, XVIIᵉ et XVIIIᵉ siècles*. Vol. 1, *Iconographie musicale*. Geneva: Minkoff.

————. 1985. "Musical Academicism in France in the Eighteenth-Century: Evidence and Problems." *Music in the Classic Period: Essays in Honor of Barry S. Brook*. Ed. A. Atlas. New York: Pendragon. 159–180.

Levinson, André. 1925. "Notes sur le ballet du XVIIe siècle: les danseurs de Lully." *RM* 6 (3) (special number) (January): 44–55.

Levy, Kenneth. 1954. "Vaudeville, vers mesurés et airs de cour." In *Musique et poésie au XVIe siècle*. Paris: CNRS, 185–199.

Liberman, Mark L. 1984. *The Organ Works of Nicolas Lebègue in the Context of Contemporary Theory and Practice*. Ph.D. Thesis, Northwestern University.

Lindemann, Frayde E. 1978. *Pastoral Instruments in French Baroque Music: Musette and Vielle*. Ph.D. Thesis, Columbia University.

Lionnet, Jean. 1994. "Charpentier à Rome." *Bulletin de la Société Marc-Antoine Charpentier*. 10 (January): 2–10.

Little, Meredith E. 1975a. "The Contribution of Dance Step to Musical Analysis and Performance: *La Bourgogne*." *JAMS* 28 (1) (Spring): 112–124.

———. 1975b. "Dance under Louis XIV and XV." *EM* 3 (4) (October): 331–340.

———. 1981. "French Court Dance in Germany at the Time of Johann Sebastian Bach: *La Bourgogne* in Paris and Leipzig." In *Report of the Twelfth Congress, International Musicological Society*. Ed. D. Heartz and B. Wade. Kassel: Bärenreiter. 730–734.

———. 1990. "Problems of Repetition and Continuity in the Dance Music of Lully's 'Ballet des Arts.'" In *Jean-Baptiste Lully. Actes de colloque*. Ed. Herbert Schneider and Jérôme de La Gorce. Laaber: Laaber-Verlag. 423–432.

———. See also Ellis, Helen Meredith.

Little, Meredith E., and Natalie Jenne. 1991. *Dance and the Music of J. S. Bach*. Bloomington: Indiana University Press.

Little, Meredith E., and Carol Marsh. 1992. *La Danse Noble: An Inventory of Notated Dances and Sources*. New York: Broude Trust.

Loewenberg, Alfred. 1955. *Annals of Opera*. 3rd ed. Totowa, NJ: Rowman and Littlefield, 1978.

Lohmann, Ludger. 1990. "Zur Ornamentik in der Orgelmusik der Spätrenaissance und des Frühbarock." *Musik und Kirche* 60 (4) (July–August): 173–185.

Lote, Georges. 1912. "La Déclamation du vers français à la fin du XVIIe siècle." *Revue de phonétique* 2:313–363.

Loubet de Sceaury, Paul. 1949. *Musiciens et facteurs d'instruments de musique sous l'ancien régime: statuts corporatifs*. Paris: A. Pedone.

Lowe, Robert. 1950. "Les Représentations en musique dans les collèges de Paris et de province, 1632–1757." *Revue d'histoire du théâtre* 3:120–136.

———. 1966. *Marc-Antoine Charpentier et l'opéra de collège*. Paris: G.-P. Maisonneuve et Larose.

Le Luth et sa musique. 1958 and 1984. 2 vols. Vol. 1, ed. Jean Jacquot. Neuilly-sur-Seine: CNRS. 2nd ed. of vol. 1, Paris: CNRS, 1976. Vol. 2, ed. J. M. Vaccaro. Paris: Corpus des luthistes français, 1984.

Luc, Charles-Dominique. 1994. *Les Ménétriers français sous l'ancien régime*. Paris: Klincksieck.

Mace, Dean T. 1970. "Mersenne on Music and Language." *JMT* 14(1):2–35.

Malignon, Jean. 1966. "Zoroastre et Sarastro." *Recherches* 6:144–158.

Malloch, William. 1991. "Bach and the French Ouverture." *MQ* 75(2):174–197.

Mamczarz, Irène. 1972. *Les Intermèdes comiques italiens au XVIIIᵉ siècle en France et en Italie*. Paris: CNRS.

Mancardi, Sylvie. 1978. *Le Milieu socio-professionnel des maîtres de musique à Paris au XVIIIᵉ siècle*. Thesis, École Nationale des Chartes, Paris.

Maniates, Maria Rika. 1969. "'Sonate, que me veux-tu?' The Enigma of French Musical Aesthetics in the Eighteenth-Century." *CM* 9:117–140.

Marchard, Roberte. 1980. *Jean-Joseph Cassanéa de Mondonville, virtuose, compositeur, et chef d'orchestre*. Béziers: Société de Musicologie du Languedoc.

Marsan, Jules. 1905. *La Pastorale dramatique en France à la fin du XVIᵉ et au commencement du XVIIᵉ siècle*, Paris: Hachette. Rpt. New York: B. Franklin, 1971.

Marsh, Carol G. 1985. *French Court Dance in England, 1706–1740: a Study of the Sources*. Ph.D. Thesis, New York University.

Martin, Colette, 1986. "L'Ornementation dans les tablatures français de guitare au XVIIᵉ siècle." In *Instruments et musique instrumentale*. Ed. Hélène Charnassé. Paris: CNRS. 1:85–100.

Martin, Margot. 1995. "Préciosité, Dissimulation and le bon goût: Societal Conventions and Musical Aesthetics in 17th-Century French Harpsichord Music." *Consort* 51 (1) (Spring): 4–12.

Marx, Joseph. 1951. "The Tone of the Baroque Oboe." *GSJ* 4:3–19.

Massenkeil, Günther. 1967. "Marc-Antoine Charpentier als Messenkomponist." In *Colloquium Amicorum Joseph Schmidt-Görg zum 70. Geburtstag*. Ed. S. Kross and H. Schmidt. Bonn: Beethovenhaus. 228–238.

————. 1970. *Das Oratorium*. Cologne: Arno Volk Verlag.

Massip, Catherine. 1971. *François Collin de Blamont, musicien du roi*. Thesis, Conservatoire Nationale Supérieur de Musique, Paris.

————. 1976a. "Musique et musiciens à Saint-Germain-en-Laye. 1651–1683." *Recherches* 16:117–152.

————. 1976b. *La Vie des musiciens de Paris au temps de Mazarin (1643–1661)*. Paris: Picard.

————. 1978. *Cantates, motets, opéras, ballets . . . manuscrits de Philidor. Catalogue*. Paris: Bibliothèque Nationale.

————. 1983. "La Collection musicale Toulouse-Philidor à la Bibliothèque Nationale." *FAM* 30(4):184–207.

―――. 1985a. "Le Mécénat musical de Gaston d'Orléans." In *L'Âge d'or du mécénat (1598–1661). Actes du colloque international CNRS*. Paris: CNRS. 383–391.

―――. 1985b. *Michel Lambert (1610–1696): contribution à l'histoire de la monodie en France*. Doctorat d'État, University of Paris-Sorbonne.

―――. 1986a. "Maître et surintendants du roi au XVIIIᵉ siècle: Une nouvelle querelle." *Recherches* 24:222–226.

―――. 1986b. "Rameau et l'édition de ses oeuvres: bref aperçu historique et méthodologique." In *Jean-Philippe Rameau. Colloque international*. Ed. Jérôme de La Gorce. Geneva: Champion-Slatkine. 145–157.

―――. 1988. "Facteurs d'instruments et maîtres à danser parsiens du XVIIᵉ siècle." In *Instrumentistes et Luthiers parisiens, XVIIᵉ–XIXᵉ siècles*. Ed. F. Gétreau. Paris: Délégation à l'Action Artistique de la Ville de Paris.

―――. 1989. "Michel Lambert and Jean-Baptiste Lully: the Stakes of a Collaboration." In *Jean-Baptiste Lully and the Music of the French Baroque*. Ed. John Hajdu Heyer. Cambridge: Cambridge University Press. 25–39.

―――. 1990. "Les Petits motets de Jean-Baptiste Lully: de quelques problèmes d'authenticité et de style." In *Jean-Baptiste Lully. Actes du colloque*. Ed. Herbert Schneider and Jérôme de La Gorce. Laaber: Laaber-Verlag. 155–164.

―――. 1991. "Airs français et italiens dans l'édition française 1643–1710." *RdM* 77(2):179–185.

―――. 1993. "Paris, 1600–61." In *The Early Baroque Era from the Late 16th Century to the 1660s*. Ed. Curtis Price. Vol. 3, *Music and Society*. London: The Macmillan Press Limited. 218–237.

―――. 1994. "Les Sources musicales et littéraires des comédies-ballets de Molière et Lully présentes dans la collection Philidor." In *Théâtre et musique au XVIIᵉ siècle*, vol. 21. Ed. Charles Mazouer. Paris: Klincksieck. 59–64.

Masson, Chantal. 1961–1962. "Le Journal du Marquis de Dangeau, 1684–1720: extraits concernant la vie musicale à la cour." *Recherches* 2:193–223.

Masson, Paul-Marie. 1910–1911. "Les Brunettes." *SIMG* 12:347–368.

―――. 1911. "Lullistes et Ramistes." *L'Année musicale* 1:187–213.

―――. 1912. "Musique italienne et musique française." *RMI* 19: 519–545.

―――. 1928. "Le Ballet héroïque." *RM* 9:132–154.

―――. 1930. *L'Opéra de Rameau*. Paris: Henri Laurens. Rpt. New York: Da Capo Press, 1972.

―――. 1932. "*Les Fêtes vénitiennes* d'André Campra." *RdM* 13: 127–146, 214–226.

―――. 1939. "Rameau and Wagner." *MQ* 25:466–478.

―――. 1945. "La 'Lettre sur Omphale' (1752)." *RdM* 27:1–19.

———. 1954. "Les Deux versions du *Dardanus* de Rameau." *AM* 26:36–48.

———. 1975. "French Opera from Lully to Rameau." In *The New Oxford History of Music*, vol. 5. Ed. Anthony Lewis and Nigel Fortune. London: Oxford University Press. 206–266.

Masson, Renée Girardon. 1955. "André Destouches à Siam." In *Mélanges d'histoire et d'esthétique musicale offerts à Paul-Marie Masson*, vol. 2. Paris: Richard-Masse. 95–102.

———. 1959. "André Cardinal Destouches: surintendant de la Musique du Roy, directeur de l'Opéra, 1672–1749." *RdM* 43 (July): 81–98.

Mather, Betty Bang. 1973. *Interpretation of French Music from 1675 to 1775: for Woodwind and Other Performers*. New York: McGinnis & Marx.

———. 1989. "Tempos and Affects of French Baroque Dances, with Special Attention to Sarabandes." *The Flutist Quarterly* 14 (4) (Autumn): 7–11.

Mather, Betty Bang, and Dean H. Karns. 1988. *Dance Rhythms in the French Baroque: a Handbook for Performance*. Bloomington: Indiana University Press.

Mather, Betty Bang, and David Lasocki. 1984. *The Art of Preluding, 1700–1830, for Woodwind and Other Performers*. New York: McGinnis & Marx.

Maul, William. 1966. *The Organ Works of Nicolas de Grigny*. Ph.D. Thesis, Washington University.

Maurice-Amour, Lila. 1955. "Les Musiciens de Corneille, 1650–1699." *RdM* 37 (July): 43–75.

Mazouer, Charles. 1993. *Molière et ses comédies-ballets*. Paris: Klincksieck.

McDowell, Bonney. 1974. *Marais and Forqueray: a Historical and Analytical Study of their Music for Solo Basse de Viole*. Ph.D. Thesis, Columbia University.

McGowan, Margaret M. 1963. *L'Art du ballet de cour en France, 1581–1643*. Paris: CNRS.

McQuaide, Rosalie. 1978. *The Crozat Concerts, 1720–1727: a Study of Concert Life in Paris*. Ph.D. Thesis, New York University.

Mélèse, Pierre. 1934a. *Répertoire analytique des documents contemporains . . . concernant les théâtres à Paris sous Louis XIV 1659–1715*. Paris: E. Droz.

———. 1934b. *Le Théâtre et le public à Paris sous Louis XIV 1659–1715*. Paris: E. Droz.

Mellers, Wilfrid. 1950. *François Couperin and the French Classical Tradition*. London: D. Dobson. New revised ed. London: Faber, 1987.

Miehling, Klaus. 1990. "Einführung in die Tanztempi des Barock." *Tibia* 15:14–22.

Milliot, Sylvette. 1964. "Réflexion et recherches sur la viole de gambe et le violoncelle en France." *Recherches* 4:179–238.

———. 1968. "Le Testament de Michel Pignolet de Montéclair." *Recherches* 8:131–140.

———. 1970. *Documents inédits sur le luthier parisien au XVIIIᵉ siècle*. Paris: Société Française de Musicologie.

———. 1981. *Le Violoncelle en France au XVIIIᵉ siècle*. Paris: H. Champion.

Milliot, Sylvette, and Jérôme de La Gorce. 1991. *Marin Marais*. Paris: Fayard.

Mirimonde, A. P. de. 1975. *L'Iconographie musicale sous les rois Bourbons: la musique dans les arts plastiques (XVIIᵉ–XVIIIᵉ siècles)*. Paris: Picard.

Mongrédien, Georges. 1973. "Molière et Lully." *Marseilles* 95(4): 213–219.

Mongrédien, Jean, ed. 1984. *Cat* 1. 1990. "La Fugue pour clavier en France vers 1700–1730: à propos des deux fugues de Pierre Fevier." *RdM* 76(2):173–186.

———. 1992. *La Vie et l'oeuvre de Louis-Claude Daquin (1694–1772)*. Lyons: Aléas Éditeur.

———. 1993. "De l'air *da capo* à un embryon français de 'Forme Sonate.'" *RdM* 79(2):308–318.

———. 1994. *The Church Music of Charles-Hubert Gervais (1671–1744), Sous-maître de Musique at the Chapelle Royale*. Ph.D. Thesis, Duke University.

Moomaw, Charles J. 1985. *Augmented Mediant Chords in French Baroque Music*. Ph.D. Thesis, University of Cincinnati.

Morby, John E. 1971. *Musicians at the Royal Chapel of Versailles, 1683–1792*. Ph.D. Thesis, University of California, Berkeley.

Morche, Günther. 1979. *Muster und Nachahmung: Eine Untersuchung der klassischen französischen Orgelmusik*. Bern: Francke.

Morel, Jacques. 1973. "Poésie, musique, spectacle: la structure de *La Princesse d'Élide*." *Marseille* 95:213–219.

Moroney, Davitt. 1976. "The Performance of Unmeasured Harpsichord Preludes." *EM* 4 (2) (April): 143–151.

———. 1990. "Chambonnières and his 'Belle manière. '" In *Jean-Baptiste Lully. Actes du colloque*. Ed. Herbert Schneider and Jérôme de La Gorce. Laaber: Laaber-Verlag. 201–208.

Moureau, François. 1990. "Lully en visite chez Arlequin: parodies italiennes avant 1697." In *Jean-Baptiste Lully. Actes du colloque*. Ed. Herbert Schneider and Jérôme de La Gorce. Laaber: Laaber-Verlag. 235–250.

Mráček, Jaroslav. 1965. *Seventeenth-Century Instrumental Dances in Uppsala University Library IM hs 409: a Transcription and Study*. Ph.D. Thesis, Indiana University.

———. 1972. "An Unjustly Neglected Source for the Study and Performance of Seventeenth-Century Instrumental Dance Music."

Report of the 11th Congress of the IMS, vol. 2. Ed. H. Glahn et al. Copenhagen: W. Hansen. 563–571.

———. 1987. "Inaugurators of Bach's French Style: The Vingt-quatre Violons du Roi and their Contemporaries." In *Alte Musik als ästhetische Gegenwart: Bach, Händel, Schütz*. Ed. D. Berke and C. Hanemann. Kassel: Bärenreiter. 335–377.

Mullins, Margaret. 1978. "Music and Dance in the French Baroque." *SiM(AUS)* 12:45–67.

Murata, Margaret. 1995. "Why the first opera given in Paris wasn't Roman." *Cambridge Opera Journal* 7 (2) (July): 87–105.

Musiciens de Paris 1535–1792 d'après le fichier Laborde. 1965. Ed. Yolande de Brossard. Paris: Picard.

Die Musik in Geschichte und Gegenwart. 1949–1986. 17 vols. Ed. Friedrich Blume. Kassel: Bärenreiter.

La Musique, les hommes, les instruments, les sources. 1965. 2 vols. Ed. Norbert Dufourcq. Paris: Larousse.

Mussat, Marie-Claire. 1994. "La Bretagne dans l'art lyrique." *La Bretagne à l'Opéra*. Quimper: Musée Départemental Breton.

Nelson, Philip. 1958. *Nicolas Bernier: a Study of the Man and His Music*. Ph.D. Thesis, University of North Carolina.

———. 1960. "Nicolas Bernier: a Resumé of His Works." *Recherches* 1:93–98.

———. 1969. "Nicolas Bernier: a Bibliographic Study." *Studies in Musicology: Essays . . . in Memory of Glen Haydon*. Chapel Hill: University of North Carolina Press. 109–117.

———. 1978. "Nicolas Bernier." *Recherches* 18:51–87.

———. 1979. "Nicolas Bernier. 2ᵉ Partie." *Recherches* 19:51–101.

Neumann, Frederick. 1964. "Misconception about the French Trill in the 17th and 18th Centuries." *MQ* 50 (2) (April): 188–206.

———. 1965a. "The French Inégales, Quantz and Bach." *JAMS* 18 (3) (Autumn): 313–358.

———. 1965b. "La Note pointée et la soi-disant 'manière française.'" *RdM* 51(1):66–92. English trans. Raymond Harris and Edmund Shay, 1977 as "The Dotted Note and the So-called French Style." *EM* 5 (3) (July): 310–324.

———. 1966. "External Evidence and Uneven Notes." *MQ* 52 (4) (October): 448–464.

———. 1967. "The Use of Baroque Treatises on Musical Performance." *M&L* 48 (4) (October): 315–324.

———. 1969. "Couperin and the Downbeat Doctrine for Appoggiaturas." *AM* 41 (1–2) (January–June): 71–85.

———. 1974. "The Question of Rhythm in the Two Versions of Bach's French Overture, BWV 831." In *Studies in Renaissance and Baroque Music in Honor of Arthur Mendel*. Ed. R. Marshall. Kassel: Bärenreiter. 183–194.

————. 1977. "Facts and Fiction about Overdotting." *MQ* 63 (2) (April): 155–185.

————. 1978. *Ornamentation in Baroque and Post-Baroque Music.* Princeton: Princeton University Press.

————. 1979. "Once more: the 'French Overture Style.'" *EM* 7 (1) (January): 39–45.

————. 1981. "The Overdotting Syndrome: Anatomy of a Delusion." *MQ* 67 (3) (July): 305–347.

————. 1982. *Essays in Performance Practice.* Ann Arbor: UMI Press.

————. 1986. "Graham Pont's 'Paradigm of Inconsistency.'" *EM* 14 (3) (August): 403–406.

————. 1988. "The Notes *inégales* Revisited." *Journal of Musicology* 6 (2) (Spring): 137–149.

————. 1989. *New Essays on Performance Practice.* Ann Arbor: UMI Press.

————. 1993a. "Changing Times: Meter, Denomination, and Tempo in Music of the Seventeenth and Eighteenth Centuries." *Historical Performance* 6:23–29.

————. 1993b. *Performance Practices of the Seventeenth and Eighteenth Centuries.* The Early Music Series. New York: Macmillan.

The New Grove Dictionary of Music and Musicians. 1980. 20 vols. Ed. Stanley Sadie. London: Macmillan Publishers Ltd.

The New Grove Dictionary of Musical Instruments. 1984. 3 vols. Ed. Stanley Sadie. New York: Macmillan Press Ltd.

The New Grove Dictionary of Opera. 1992. 4 vols. Ed. Stanley Sadie. London: Macmillan Press Ltd.

The New Grove French Baroque Masters. 1986. Ed. Stanley Sadie. London: Macmillan Publishers Ltd.

The New Oxford History of Music (abbreviation: *NOHM*). 1975. Vol. 5. *Opera and Church Music, 1630–1750.* Ed. Anthony Lewis and Nigel Fortune; and 1986. Vol. 6. *Concert Music (1630–1750).* Ed. Gerald Abraham. New York: Oxford University Press.

Newman, Anthony. 1992. "Inequality (Inégales): a New Point of View." *MQ* 76 (2) (Summer): 169–183.

Newman, Joyce. 1979. *Jean-Baptiste de Lully and his tragédies lyriques.* Ann Arbor: UMI Press.

Newman, William S. 1966. *The Sonata in the Baroque Era.* Revised ed. Chapel Hill: University of North Carolina Press.

Newton, Richard. 1952. "Hommage à Marin Marais." *The Consort* 9 (June): 12–21.

Niderest, Alain. 1976. "L'Actualité politique dans l'opéra français à la fin du règne de Louis XIV, 1686–1715." In *Regards sur l'opéra du ballet comique de la reine à l'opéra de Pékin.* Paris: PUF. 187–212.

Noack, Friedrick. 1929. "Die Musik zu der Molièreschen Komödie 'Monsieur de Pourceaugnac' von Jean Baptists de Lully." In *Festschrift für Johanne Wolf zu seinem sechzigsten Geburtstage.* Ed.

W. Lott et al. Berlin: Martin Breslaver. 139–147. Rpt. Hildesheim: Georg Olms Verlag, 1978.

Noel, Jeanne. 1990. "Grandeur et décadence de la guitare en France au temps de Louis XIV." *Guitare* 35:20–24.

Norman, Buford. 1988. "The Vocabulary of Quinault's Opera Libretti: Drama without Drama." In *The Age of Theater in France.* Ed. D. Trott and N. Boursier. Edmonton: Academic Print. & Pub. 287–309.

————. 1989. "Ancients and Moderns, Tragedy and Opera: The Quarrel over *Alceste.*" In *French Musical Thought, 1600–1800.* Ed. G. Cowart. Ann Arbor: UMI Press. 176–196.

————. 1993. "The Tragedie-Lyrique of Lully and Quinault: Representation and Recognition of Emotion." *Continuum* 5:111–142.

————. 1994. "Les Folles conventions de langage musical dans les dernières comédies-ballets de Molière." In *Théâtre et musique au XVIIe siècle,* vol. 21. Ed. C. Mazouer. Paris: Klincksieck. 91–102.

Noske, Frits. "L'Influence de Lully en Hollande (1670–1700)." In *Jean-Baptiste Lully. Actes du colloque.* Ed. Herbert Schneider and Jérôme de La Gorce. Laaber: Laaber-Verlag. 591–598.

Notes et références pour servir à une histoire de Michel-Richard Delalande. 1957. Ed. Norbert Dufourcq. Paris: Picard.

Nuitter. See Truinet, Charles-Louis-Étienne.

Nutting, Geoffrey. 1964. "Jean-Marie Leclair, 1698–1764." *MQ* 50 (4) (October): 504–514.

Oboussier, Philippe. 1971. "A Couperin Discovery." *MT* 112 (May): 429–430.

————. 1971–1972. "Couperin Motets at Tenbury." *PRMA* 98:17–29.

————. 1976. "Lalande's Grands Motets." *MT* 117 (June): 483–486.

O'Donnell, John. 1979. "The French Style and the Overtures of Bach." *EM* 7 (2) (April): 190–196; and (3) (July): 336–345.

Oldham, Guy. 1960. "Louis Couperin. A New Source of French Keyboard Music of the Mid-Seventeenth Century." *Recherches* 1:51–59.

Oliver, Alfred. 1947. *The Encyclopedists as Critics of Music.* New York: Columbia University Press.

Oliver, Richard. 1947. "Molière's Contribution to the Lyric Stage." *MQ* 33 (3) (July): 350–364.

L'Opéra-comique en France au XVIIe siècle. 1992. Ed. Philippe Vendrix. Liège: Mardaga.

Packer, Dorothy S. 1970. "'La Calotte' and the Eighteenth-Century French Vaudeville." *JAMS* 23 (1) (Spring): 61–83.

Paillard, Jean-François. 1954–1955. "Les Premiers concertos français pour instruments à vents." *RM* 226 (Special number): 144–162.

————. 1960. *La Musique française classique.* Paris: PUF.

Palisca, Claude V. 1968. *Baroque Music*. Englewood Cliffs, NJ: Prentice Hall. 3rd ed. Englewood Cliffs, NJ: Prentice Hall, 1991.

————. 1986. "The Recitative of Lully's *Alceste*: French Declamation or Italian Melody." In *Actes de Baton Rouge*. Ed. S. A. Zebouni. *Biblio* 17(25):19–34.

————. 1989. "'Baroque' as a Music-Critical Term." In *French Musical Thought, 1600–1800*. Ed. G. Cowart. Ann Arbor: UMI Press. 7–21.

Pacquot, Maurice. C. 1933. *Les Étrangers dans les divertissements de cour de Beaujoyeulx à Molière, 1581–1673*. Brussels: La Renaissance du Livre.

Paquette, Daniel, ed. 1989. *Aspects de la musique baroque et classique à Lyon et en France*. Lyons: Presses Universitaires de Lyon.

Parmley, Andrew. 1985. *The Secular Stage Music of Marc-Antoine Charpentier*. Doctoral Thesis, University of London.

Performance Practice. Music after 1600. 1989. Ed. Howard Mayer Brown and Stanley Sadie. London: Macmillan Publishers Ltd.

Peterman, Lewis E. 1985. *The Instrumental Chamber Music of Joseph Bodin de Boismortier with Special Emphasis on the Trio Sonatas for Two Treble Instruments and Basso Continuo*. Ph.D. Thesis, University of Cincinnati.

————. 1991. "Michel Blavet's Breathing Marks: a Rare Source for Musical Phrasing in Eighteenth-Century France." *Performance Practice Review* 4(2):186–198.

Pfeiffer, Christel. 1979. "Das französische Prélude non mesuré für Cembalo: Notenbild, Interpretation, Einfluss auf Froberger, Bach, Händel." *Neue Zeitschrift für Musik* 62(2):132–136.

Picard, Evelyne. 1981. "Liturgie et musique à Sainte-Anne-la-Royale au XVIIᵉ siècle." *Recherche* 20:249–254.

Piejus, Anne. 1994. "La tragédie chrétienne: théâtre à Saint-Cyr." In *Théâtre et musique au XVIIᵉ siècle*, vol. 21. Ed. Charles Mazouer. Paris: Klincksieck. 139–148.

Pierre, Constant. 1975. *Histoire du Concert Spirituel, 1725–1790*. Paris: Heugel.

Pincherle, Marc. 1911. "La Technique du violon chez les premiers sonatistes français (1695–1723)." *BSIM* 7 (August–September): 1–32 and 8 (October): 19–35. Rpt. Geneva: Minkoff, 1973.

————. 1948. *Antonio Vivaldi et la musique instrumentale*. 2 vols. in one. Paris: Librairie Floury. Rpt. New York: Johnson Reprint Corp., 1968.

————. 1952. *Jean-Marie Leclair*. Paris: La Colombe. Rpt. Paris: Plan-de-la-Tour, 1985.

————. 1954. *Corelli et son temps*. Paris: Plon. English trans. Hubert Russell. *Corelli, His Life, His Work*. New York: W. W. Norton, 1956.

————. 1968. "François Couperin et la conciliation des 'goûts' français et italien." *Chigiana* 25(5):69–80.

Pinson, Jean-Pierre. 1984. "L'Action dans le récitatif pathétique de Lully: la déclamation." *Canadian University Music Review* 5:152–178.

Pirro, André. 1907a. *Descartes et la musique*. Paris: Librairie Fisch-bacher. Rpt. Geneva: Minkoff, 1973.

———. 1907b. *L'Esthétique de Jean Sébastien Bach*. Paris: Librairie Fisch-bacher. Rpt. Geneva: Minkoff, 1973.

———. 1920. "Louis Couperin." *RM* 1(1–2):1–21.

———. 1925. *Les Clavecinistes*. Paris: Laurens.

Pitou, Spire. 1983. *The Paris Opera: An Encyclopedia of Operas, Ballets, Composers, and Performers*. 2 vols. Westport, CT: Greenwood Press.

Pond, Celia. 1978. "Ornamental Style and the Virtuoso: Solo Bass Viol Music in France, c. 1680–1740." *EM* 6 (4) (October): 512–518.

Pont, Graham. 1978. "Rhythmic Alteration and the Majestic." *SiM (AUS)* 12:68–100.

———. 1980. "French Overtures at the Keyboard: 'How Handel Ren-dered the Playing of Them.'" *Musicology* 6:29–50.

———. 1983. "Handel's Overtures for Harpsichord or Organ: an Unrecognized Genre." *EM* 11 (3) (July): 309–322.

———. 1985. "Handel and Regularization: a Third Alternative." *EM* 13 (4) (November): 500–505.

———. 1986. "A Third Alternative." *EM* 14 (3) (August): 409–411.

———. 1987. "Handel's Keyboard Overtures: Problems of Authen-ticity and Interpretation." *SiM(AUS)* 21:39–68.

Poole, Elissa. 1987. "The *Brunetes* and Their Sources: A Study of the Transition from Modality to Tonality in France." *Recherches* 25:187–206.

Populus, Bernard. 1939. *L'Ancienne Maîtrise de Langres*. Langres: Lepitre-Jobard. Rpt. Geneva: Minkoff, 1973.

Pougin, Artur. 1881. *Les Vrais créateurs de l'opéra français, Perrin et Cambert*. Paris: Charavay.

Powell, John S. 1982. *Music in the Theater of Molière*. Ph.D. Thesis, University of Washington.

———. 1986a. "Charpentier's Music for Molière's 'Le malade imagi-naire' and Its Revisions." *JAMS* 39 (1) (Spring): 87–142.

———. 1986b. "The Musical Sources of the Bibliothèque-Musée de la Comédie-Française." *CM* 41:7–45.

———. 1991a. "L'Aspect protéiforme du Premier Intermède du 'Malade imaginaire.'" *Société Marc-Antoine Charpentier* 5 (July): 2–14.

———. 1991b. "La 'Sérénade pour Le Sicilien' de Marc-Antoine Charpentier et le crépuscule de la comédie-ballet." *RdM* 77(1):88–96.

———. 1992. "Music, Fantasy and Illusion in Molières 'Le malade imaginaire.'" *M&L* 73 (2) (May): 222–243.

———. 1993. "Music and the Self-fullfilling Prophecy in Molière's *Le Mariage forcé*." *EM: French Baroque I* 21 (2) (May): 213–230.

———. 1995. "Pierre Beauchamps, Choreographer to Molière's Troupe du Roy." *M&L* 76 (2) (May): 168–186.

———. 1996. "Musical Practices in the Theater of Molière." *RdM* 82(1):5–37.

Powell, Newman. 1958. *Rhythmic Freedom in the Performance of French Music from 1650–1735*. Ph.D. Thesis, Stanford University.

Powers, David M. 1988. *The "Pastorale héroïque": Origin and Development of a Genre of French Opera in the Seventeenth and Eighteenth Centuries*. Ph.D. Thesis, University of Chicago.

Prada, Michel. 1986. *Un Maître de musique en Province et en Languedoc: Jean Gilles*. Béziers: Société de Musicologie de Languedoc.

Preston, Robert E. 1959. *The Forty-Eight Sonatas for Violin and Figured Bass of Jean-Marie Leclair, l'Aîné*. Ph.D. Thesis, University of Michigan.

———. 1963. "The Treatment of Harmony in the Violin Sonatas of Jean-Marie Leclair." *Recherches* 3:131–144.

Prévost, Arthur-Emile. 1906. *Histoire de la maîtrise de la cathédrale de Troyes*. Troyes: P. Nouel. Rpt. Geneva: Minkoff, 1972.

Prévost, Paul. 1986. "Deux exemples de notation des préludes non mesurés pour clavecin vers 1660–1670: Louis Couperin et Nicolas Lebègue." *Instruments et musique instrumentale*. Ed. Hélène Charnassé. Paris: CNRS. 71–84.

———. 1987. *Le Prélude non mesuré pour clavecin (France, 1650–1700)*. Baden-Baden: Éditions Valentin Koerner.

Price, Charles Gower. 1973. *The Codification and Perseverance of a French National Style of Instrumental Composition between 1687 and 1733: Montéclair's "Sérénade ou Concert" (1697)* Ph.D. Thesis, Stanford University.

Prim, Jean. 1961. "'Chant sur le livre' in French Churches in the 18th Century." *JAMS* 14 (1) (Spring): 37–49.

Prod'homme, J.-G. 1903. "Les Forqueray." *RMI* 10:670–706.

———. 1925. *L'Opéra (1669–1725)*. Paris: Delagrave. Rpt. Geneva: Minkoff, 1972.

Pruitt, William. 1973. "Bibliographie des oeuvres de Guillaume-Gabriel Nivers." *Recherches* 13:133–156.

———. 1974. "The Organ Works of Guillaume-Gabriel Nivers (1632–1714)." *Recherches* 14(1974):7–81 and 15(1975):47–90.

———. 1986. "A 17th-Century French Manuscript on Organ Performance." *EM* 14 (2) (May): 237–251.

Prunières, Henry. 1908. "Lecerf de La Viéville et l'esthétique musicale classique au XVIIe siècle." *BSIM* 4:619–654.

———. 1909a. "La Jeunesse de Lully (1632–1662)." In *BSIM* 3 (15 March 1909): 234–242; 4 (15 April 1909): 329–353.

———. 1909b. *Lully*. Paris: Laurens. 2nd ed. Paris: Laurens, 1927.

————. 1910a–1911. "Notes sur l'origine de l'ouverture française." *SIMG* 12:565–585.

————. 1910b. "Recherches sur les années de jeunesse de J.-B. Lully." *RMI* 17:645–654.

————. 1911. "La Musique de la Chambre et de l'Écurie sous le règne de François Ier." *L'Année musicale* 1:215–251.

————. 1912a. "Jean de Cambefort, Surintendant de la musique du roi." *L'Année musicale* 2:205–226.

————. 1912b. "Lully, fils de meunier." *MM* 8:57–61.

————. 1913. *L'Opéra italien en France avant Lulli*. Paris: E. Champion. Rpt. New York: Johnson Reprint, 1971.

————. 1914. *Le Ballet de cour en France avant Benserade et Lully*. Paris: H. Laurens.

————. 1920. "Les Petits Violons de Lully." *Écho musical* 5 (April): 118–130.

————. 1922. "Paolo Lorenzani à la cour de France." *RM* 3:97–120.

————. 1923. "Un Maître de chant au XVIIe siècle: J. Bénigne de Bacilly." *RMI* 17:156–160.

————. 1925. "L'Académie Royale de Musique et de Danse." *RM* 6 (3) (special number) (January): 3–25.

————. 1929. *La Vie illustre et libertine de Jean-Baptiste Lully*. Paris: Les Petits Fils de Plon et Nourret.

————. 1931. "Les Premiers ballets de Lully." *RM* 12:1–17.

⌐ ▣ ⌐

Quittard, Henri. 1902. "Les Années de jeunesse de J.-P. Rameau." *Revue d'histoire et de critique musicales* 2:61–63, 100–114, 152–170, 208–218.

————. 1903. "Un Chanteur compositeur de musique sous Louis XIII: Nicolas Formé." *RMC* 3:362–367.

————. 1904a–1905. "Un Musicien oublié du XVIIe siècle français: G. Bouzignac." *SIMG* 6:356–417.

————. 1904b. "Orphée descendant aux Enfers." *RMC* 4:495–498.

————. 1906. *Un Musicien en France au XVIIe siècle: Henry Du Mont*. Paris: Société du Mercure de France. Rpt. Geneva: Minkoff, 1973.

————. 1908. "La Première comédie française en musique." *BSIM* 4:378–396, 497–537.

⌐ ▣ ⌐

Radet, Edmond. 1891. *Lully, homme d'affaires, propriétaire et musicien*. Paris: L. Allison.

Ranum, Patricia. 1985. "Les Caractères des danses françaises." *Recherches* 23:45–70.

————. 1986a. "Audible Rhetoric and Mute Rhetoric: the 17th Century French Sarabande." *EM* 14 (1) (February): 22–38.

————. 1986b. "Le Musicien tailleur: Étienne Loulié et la musique des anciens." In *D'un siècle à l'autre: anciens et modernes, XVIe col-*

loque. Marseilles; Aix-en-Provence: Centre Méridional de Rencontres sur le XVIIᵉ Siècle. 239–257.

———. 1987a and 1988–1990. "Étienne Loulié (1654–1702). Musicien de Madmoiselle de Guise, pédagogue et théoricien." *Recherches* 25:27–76, 26:5–49.

———. 1987b. "A Sweet Servitude: A Musician's Life at the Court of Mlle de Guise." *EM* 15 (3) (August): 346–360.

———. 1990. "'Mr de Lully en trio' Étienne Loulié, the Foucaults, and the Transcription of the Works of Jean-Baptiste Lully (1673–1702)." In *Jean-Baptiste Lully. Actes du colloque*. Ed. Herbert Schneider and Jérôme de La Gorce. Laaber: Laaber-Verlag. 309–330.

———. 1991. *Méthode de la prononciation latine dite vulgaire ou à la française: Petite méthode à l'usage des chanteurs et des récitants d'après le manuscrit de Dom Jacques Le Clerc*. Arles: Actes Sud.

———. 1993. "Meslanges, mélanges, cabinet, recueil, ouvrages: L'Entrée des manuscrits de Marc-Antoine Charpentier à la bibliothèque du Roi." *Bulletin: Société Marc-Antoine Charpentier* 9 (July): 2–9.

———. 1994. *Vers une chronologie des oeuvres de Marc-Antoine Charpentier*. Baltimore: Chez l'Auteur.

Raugel, Felix. 1925. "The Ancient French Organ School." *MQ* 11 (4) (October): 560–571.

———. 1954. "Une Maîtrise célèbre au Grand Siècle: la maîtrise de la cathédrale d'Aix-en-Provence." *XVIIᵉ siècle* 21–22:422–432.

———. 1957. "La Musique à la chapelle de Versailles sous Louis XIV." *XVIIᵉ siècle* 34:19–25.

Rave, Wallace. 1972. *Some Manuscripts of French Lute Music, 1630–1700: An Introductory Study*. Ph.D. Thesis, University of Illinois.

Réau, Louis. 1925–1926. *Histoire de la peinture française au XVIIIᵉ siècle*. 2 vols. Paris: G. van Oest.

———. 1946. *Le Rayonnement de Paris au XVIIIᵉ siècle*. Paris: R. Laffont.

Rebourd, René-Marie. 1954. "Messire Arthus Aux-Cousteaux, maître de musique de la Sainte-Chapelle au Palais." *XVIIᵉ siècle* 21–22:403–417.

Reese, Gustave. 1959. *Music in the Renaissance*. New York: W. W. Norton.

Reilly, Edward R. 1963. "Quantz on National Styles in Music." *MQ* 49 (2) (April): 163–187.

Reimann, Margarete. 1940. *Untersuchungen zur Formgeschichte der französischen Klavier-Suite mit besonderer Berücksichtigung von Couperins "Ordres."* Regensburg: Gustav Bosse Verlag.

Renken, Alice B. 1981. *Marin Marais's "Alcyone": An Edition with Commentary*. Ph.D. Thesis, Washington University.

Rice, Paul F. 1988. *The Performing Arts at Fontainbleau from Louis XIV to Louis XVI*. Ann Arbor: UMI Press.

Richards, James E. 1950. *The "Grand Motet" of the Late Baroque in France as exemplified by Michel-Richard de Lalande*. Ph.D. Thesis, University of Southern California.

———. 1958. "Structural Principles in the Grands Motets of de Lalande." *JAMS* 11 (2–3) (Summer–Autumn): 119–127.

Robert, Jean. 1965a. "Comédiens, musiciens et opéras à Avignon (1610–1715)." *Revue de la Société d'histoire du théâtre* 17:275–323.

———. 1965b. "Maîtres de chapelle à Avignon, 1610–1715." *RdM* 51(2):149–169.

———. 1967. "La Clientèle aristocratique des comédiens et des musiciens dans le Midi méditerranéen (1610–1720)." In *Dramaturgie et Société, XVIe et XVIIe siècles. Colloques internationaux du CNRS*, vol. 1. Paris: CNRS. 267–275.

Robinson, Lucy. 1975. "La Basse de viole." In *French Music and the Fitzwilliam*. Cambridge: Fitzwilliam Museum. 31–35.

Roche, Martine. 1967. "Un Livre de clavecin français de la fin du XVIIe siècle." *Recherches* 7:39–73.

Rolland, Romain. 1901. "Notes sur l'*Orfeo* de Luigi Rossi et sur les musiciens italiens à Paris sous Mazarin." *Revue d'histoire et de critique musicales* 1:225–236, 363–371.

———. 1914. *Musiciens d'autrefois*. 4th ed. Paris: Hachette. English trans. Mary Blaiklock. New York: Henry Holt and Co., 1915. Rpt. Freeport, New York: Essay Index Reprint Series, 1968.

Rollin, Monique. 1954. "Le 'Tombeau' chez les luthistes Denys Gautier, Jacques Gallot, Charles Mouton." *XVIIe siècle* 21–22:463–479.

———. 1955. "La Suite pour luth dans l'oeuvre de Charles Mouton." *RM* 226 (special number): 76–88.

———. 1984. Quelques échos des opéras de Lully dans la musique de luth." *Arts du spectacle et histoire des idées. Recueil offert en hommage à Jean Jacquot*. Ed. J. M. Vaccaro. Tours: CNRS. 229–234.

———. 1990. "Les Oeuvres de Lully transcrites pour le Luth." In *Jean-Baptiste Lully. Actes du colloque*. Ed. Herbert Schneider and Jérôme de La Gorce. Laaber: Laaber-Verlag. 483–494.

Ronez-Kubitschek, Marianne. 1987. "Die französischen Manieren des 18. Jahrhunderts in den Quellen der Violinmusik." In *Studien zur Aufführungspraxis und Interpretation der Musik des 18. Jahrhunderts*, vol. 32. Ed. E. Thom and W. Siegmund-Schultze. Blankenburg/Harz: Kultur und Forschungsstätte Michael Stein. 23–34.

Rose, Adrian. 1980. "The Solo Repertoire for Dessus and Pardessus de violes." *Chelys* 9:14–22.

———. 1985. "Elizabeth Claude Jacquet de La Guerre and the secular cantate française." *EM* 13 (4) (November): 529–541.

Rosow, Lois. 1980. "Lallemand and Durand: Two Eighteenth Century Music Copyists at the Paris Opéra." *JAMS* 33 (1) (Spring): 142–163.

———. 1981. *Lully's "Armide" at the Paris Opéra: A Performance History*. Ph.D. Thesis, Brandeis University.

———. 1983. "French Baroque Recitative as an Expression of Tragic Declamation." *EM* 11 (4) (October): 468–479.

———. 1987a. "From Destouches to Berton: Editorial Responsibility at the Paris Opéra." *JAMS* 40 (2) (Summer): 285–309.

———. 1987b. "Performing a Choral Dialogue by Lully." *EM* 15 (3) (August): 325–335.

———. 1989. "How Eighteenth-Century Parisians Heard Lully's Operas: the Case of *Armide*'s Fourth Act." *Jean-Baptiste Lully and the Music of the French Baroque*. Ed. John Hajdu Heyer. Cambridge: Cambridge University Press. 213–237.

———. 1990. "The Metrical Notation of Lully's Recitative." In *Jean-Baptiste Lully. Actes du colloque*. Ed. Herbert Schneider and Jérôme de La Gorce. Laaber: Laaber-Verlag. 405–422.

———. 1993. "Making Connections: Thoughts on Lully's Entr'actes." *EM: French Baroque I* 21 (2) (May): 231–238.

Royer, Louis. 1938. *Les Musiciens et la musique à l'ancienne collégiale Saint-André de Grenoble du XVᵉ au XVIIIᵉ siècle*. Paris: E. Droz. Rpt. Geneva: Minkoff, 1973.

Royster, Don Lee. 1972. *Pierre Guédron and the "air de cour," 1600–1620*. Ph.D. Thesis, Yale University.

Ruff, L. M. 1967. "M.-A. Charpentier's 'Règles de composition.'" *The Consort* 24:233–270.

Ryhming, Gudrun. 1982. "Quelques remarques sur l'art vocal français de la seconde moitié du 17ᵉ siècle." *RMS* 122(1):1–7.

⌐ ▦ ¬

Sadie, Julie Anne. 1978a–1979. "Bowed Continuo Instruments in French Baroque Chamber Music." *PRMA* 105:37–49.

———. 1978b. "Marin Marais and His Contemporaries." *MT* 119 (August): 672–674.

———. 1978c. "Montéclair, The Viol Player's Composer." *JVGSA* 15 (December): 41–50.

———. 1979. "Charpentier and the Early French Ensemble Sonatas." *EM* 7 (2) (July): 330–335.

———. 1980. *The Bass Viol in French Baroque Chamber Music*. Ann Arbor: UMI Press.

———. 1986. "*Musiciennes* of the Ancien Regime." In *Women Making Music*. Ed. Jane Bowers and Judith Tick. Urbana: University of Illinois. 191–223.

———. 1989. "Parnassus Revisited: The Musical Vantage Point of Titon du Tillet." In *Jean-Baptiste Lully and the Music of the French Baroque*. Ed. John Hajdu Heyer. Cambridge: Cambridge University Press. 131–157.

————, ed. 1991. *Companion to Baroque Music.* New York: Schirmer Books.

————. 1993. "Paris and Versailles." In *The Late Baroque Era.* Ed. George Buelow. Vol. 4, *Music and Society.* London: The Macmillan Press Limited. 129–189.

————. See Vertrees, Julie Anne.

Sadler, Graham. 1974. "Rameau, Piron and the Parisian Fair Theatres." *Soundings* 4:13–29.

————. 1979. "Rameau's Harpsichord Transcriptions from *Les Indes galantes.*" *EM* 6 (1) (January): 18–24.

————. 1980. "The Role of the Keyboard Continuo in French Opera, 1673–1776." *EM* 8 (2) (April): 148–157.

————. 1981–1982. "Rameau and the Orchestra." *PRMA* 108:47–88.

————. 1983. "Rameau, Pellegrin and the Opera: The Revision of 'Hippolyte et Aricie' during the First Season." *MT* 124 (September): 533–537.

————. 1986a. "Jean-Philippe Rameau." In *The New Grove French Baroque Masters.* Ed. Stanley Sadie. London: MacMillan London Limited. 207–277.

————. 1986b. "The Paris Opera Dancers in Rameau's Day: a Little-Known Inventory of 1738." In *Jean-Philippe Rameau. Colloque international.* Ed. Jérôme de La Gorce. Geneva: Champion-Slatkine. 519–532.

————. 1989. "A Re-examination of Rameau's Self-borrowings." In *Jean-Baptiste Lully and the Music of the French Baroque.* Ed. John Hajdu Heyer. Cambridge: Cambridge University Press. 259–289.

Sadler, Graham, and Neal Zaslaw. 1980. "Notes on Leclair's Theatre Music." *M&L* 61 (2) (April): 147–157.

Saint-Arroman, Jean. 1983 and 1988. *L'Interprétation de la musique française 1661–1789.* 2 vols. Paris: H. Champion.

Sajak, Rainer. 1973. *Sébastien de Brossard als Lexicograph, Bibliograph und Bearbeiter.* Doctoral Thesis, University of Bonn.

Samoyault-Verlet, Colombe. 1966. *Les Facteurs des clavecins parisiens, notices biographiques et documents (1550–1793).* Paris: Société Française de Musicologie.

Sandman, Susan Goertzel. 1977. "The Wind Band at Louis XIV's Court." *EM* 5 (1) (January): 27–37.

Sanford, Sally Allis. 1979. *Seventeenth and Eighteenth-Century Vocal Style and Technique.* D. M. A. Thesis, Stanford University.

Sawkins, Lionel. 1975. "Lalande and the Concert Spirituel." *MT* 116 (April): 333–335.

————. 1981. "An Encore to the Lexicographer's dilemma, or de Lalande et du Bon Sens." *FAM* 28(4):319–323. [Response by James R. Anthony. 1982. *FAM* 29(3):141.]

————. 1986a. "The brothers Bêche: an anecdotal history of court music." *Recherches* 24:192–221.

————. 1986b. "Nouvelles sources inédites de trois oeuvres de Rameau: leur signification pour l'instrumentation et l'interprétation du chant." In *Jean-Philippe Rameau. Colloque international.* Ed. Jérôme de La Gorce. Geneva: Champion-Slatkine. 171–200.

————. 1986c. "Performance practice in the *grands motets* of Michel-Richard de Lalande as determined by eighteenth-century timings." In *Actes du colloque international sur le grand motet français (1663–1792).* Ed. Jean Mongrédien and Yves Ferraton. Presses de l'Université de Paris-Sorbonne. 105–117.

————. 1987. "For and Against the Order of Nature. Who Sang the Soprano?" *EM* 15 (3) (August): 315–324.

————. 1989. "Chronology and evolution of the *grand motet* at the court of Louis XIV: evidence from the *Livres du Roi* and the works of Perrin, the *sous-maîtres,* and Lully." In *Jean-Baptiste Lully and the Music of the French Baroque.* Ed. John Hajdu Heyer. Cambridge, Cambridge University Press. 41–79.

————. 1990a. "Classic and Baroque: Paris and the Esterházy court." *Haydn Society of Great Britain Newsletter* 10:5–17.

————. 1990b. "Lully's Motets: Source, Edition and Performance." In *Jean-Baptiste Lully. Actes du colloque.* Ed. Herbert Schneider and Jérôme de La Gorce. Laaber: Laaber-Verlag. 383–403.

————. 1993a. "*Doucement* and *Légèrement*: Tempo in French Baroque Music." *EM: French Baroque II* 21 (3) (August): 365–374.

————. 1993b. *The Sacred Music of Michel-Richard de Lalande.* Doctoral Thesis, University of London.

————. 1995. "' . . . à l'admiration de tout Paris'*: Lalande's Sacred Music for Women's Voices." In *Essays in Honour of David Evatt Tunley.* Ed. Frank Calloway. Perth: University of Western Australia. 73–90.

————. In Press. *Catalogue raisonné et thématique des oeuvres de Michel-Richard de Lalande.*

Scheibert, Beverly. 1986. *Jean-Henry d'Anglebert and the Seventeenth-Century Clavecin School.* Bloomington: Indiana University Press.

————. 1987. "French Overdotting." *EM* 15 (3) (August) 443–444.

Scherpereel, Joseph. 1986. "Emplois et modes d'emploi du grand motet en Avignon et dans le comtat vernaissin." In *Actes du colloque international sur le grand motet français (1663–1792).* Ed. Jean Mongrédien and Yves Ferraton. Presses de l'Université de Paris-Sorbonne. 187–196.

Schmidt, Carl B. 1987. "Newly Identified Manuscript Sources for the Music of Jean-Baptiste Lully." *Notes* 44 (1) (September): 7–32.

————. 1988. "Une Parodie hollandaise peu connue sur la musique de Lully: les Opwekklyke Zedezangen." *XVIIᵉ siècle* 16 (4) (October–December): 371–386.

————. 1989. "The Geographical Spread of Lully's Operas during the late Seventeenth and Early Eighteenth Centuries: New Evidence from the Livrets." In *Jean-Baptiste Lully and the Music of the French*

Baroque. Ed. John Hajdu Heyer. Cambridge: Cambridge University Press. 183–211.

————. 1990. "Livrets for Lully's Ballets and Mascarades. Notes Toward a Publishing History and Chronology." In *Jean-Baptiste Lully. Actes du colloque.* Ed. Herbert Schneider and Jérôme de La Gorce. Laaber: Laaber-Verlag. 331–356.

————. 1992. "Berkeley MS454: Philador L'Aîné's 'Enigma Variations.'" *Journal of Musicology* (10) (3) (Summer): 362–404.

————. 1993. *Jean-Laurent Lecerf de la Viéville. Comparaison de la musique italienne et de la musique françoise: Index Compiled and Edited by Carl B. Schmidt.* Geneva: Éditions Minkoff.

————. 1995. *The Livrets of Jean-Baptiste Lully's Tragédies Lyriques: a Catalogue Raisonné.* New York: Performers' Editions.

Schmitz, Eugen. 1914. *Kontata und des geistlichen Konzerts: Geschichte der Weltlichen Solokantate.* Leipzig: Breitkopf & Härtel. Rpt. Weisbaden, 1966.

Schneider, Herbert. 1972. *Die französische Kompositionslehre in der ersten Hälfte des 17. Jahrhunderts.* Tutzing: Hans Schneider.

————. 1981a. *Chronologisch-thematisches Verzeichnis sämtlicher Werke von Jean-Baptiste Lully.* (LWV). Tutzing: Hans Schneider.

————. 1981b. "Dokumente zur französischen Oper von 1659 bis 1699." In *Quellentexte zur Konzeption der europäischen Oper im 17. Jahrhundert.* Kassel: Bärenreiter. 342–366.

————. 1982a. *Die Rezeption der Opern Lullys im Frankreich des Ancien Regime.* Tutzing: Hans Schneider.

————. 1982b. "Tragédie et tragédie en musique: querelle autour de l'autonomie d'un nouveau genre." *Komparistische Hefte* 5(6):43–58.

————. 1984a. "Die französische Kammersuite zwischen 1670 und 1720." In *Jacob Stainer und seine Zeit.* Ed. W. Salmen. Innsbruck: Helbling. 163–173.

————. 1984b. "La Parodie spirituelle de chansons et d'airs profanes chez Lully et chez ses contemporains." In *La Pensée religieuse dans la littérature et la civilisation du XVIIe siècle en France.* Ed. Manfred Tietz and Volker Kapp. Paris and Seattle: Papers on French Seventeenth Century Literature. 69–91.

————. 1985. "*Canevas* als Terminus der lyrischen Dichtung." *AfMW* 42(2):87–101.

————. 1986a. "Die Funktion des Divertissement und des Ballet de Cour in der höfischen Ideologie." In *La Musique et le rite sacré et profane.* Ed. M. Honegger and P. Prévost. Strasbourg: University of Strasbourg. 433–463.

————. 1986b. "Lullys Beitrag zur Entstehung des Grand Motet." In *Actes du colloque international sur le grand motet français (1663–1792).* Ed. Jean Mongrédien and Yves Ferraton. Presses de l'Université de Paris-Sorbonne. 67–76.

———. 1986c. "Rameau et la tradition lulliste." In *Jean-Philippe Rameau. Colloque international.* Ed. Jérôme de La Gorce. Geneva: Champion-Slatkine. 287–306.

———. 1986d. "Unbekannte Handschriften der Hofkapelle in Hannover: Zum Repertoire französischer Hofkapellen in Deutschland." In *Aufklärungen: Studien zur deutsch-französischen Musikgeschichte im 18. Jahrhundert.* Ed. W. Birtel and C. H. Mahling, Heidelberg: Winter. 180–193.

———. 1988. "Les Monologues dans l'opéra de Lully." *XVIIᵉ siècle* Special no. 161 (October–December): 353–363.

———. 1989. "The Amsterdam Editions of Lully's Orchestral Suites." In *Jean-Baptiste Lully and the Music of the French Baroque.* Ed. John Hajdu Heyer. Cambridge: Cambridge University Press. 113–130.

———. 1990a. "Chaconne und Passacaille bei Lully." In *Studi Corelliani*, vol. 4. Florence: L. S. Olschki. 319–334.

———. 1990b. "Händel und die französische Theatermusik in ihren dramatisch-szenischen Belangen." *Händel-Jahrbuch* 36:103–120.

———. 1990c. "Strukturen der Szenen und Akte in Lullys Opern." In *Jean-Baptiste Lully. Actes du colloque.* Ed. Herbert Schneider and Jérôme de La Gorce. Laaber: Laaber-Verlag. 77–98.

———. 1991. "Die Serenade in 'Bourgeois Gentilhomme.'" *Le Bourgeois Gentilhomme. Problèmes de la comédie-ballet.* Ed. Volker Kapp. In *Biblio* 17:139–162. Paris, Seattle, Tübingen.

———. 1992. "Structures métriques du menuet au XVIIᵉ et au début du XVIIIᵉ siècle." *RdM* 78(1):27–65.

———. 1994. "Airs de comédie de J.-Cl. Gillier pour différentes pièces de la Comédie-Française." In *Théâtre et musique au XVIIᵉ siècle*, vol. 21. Ed. C. Mazouer. Paris: Klincksieck. 175–192.

Schulze, Hans-Joachim. 1985. "The French Influence in Bach's Instrumental Music." *EM* 13 (2) (May): 180–184.

Schwandt, Erich. 1974. "L'Affilard on the French Court Dances." *MQ* 40 (3) (July): 389–400.

———. 1977. "L'Affilard's Published 'Sketchbooks.'" *MQ* 43 (1) (January): 99–113.

———. 1980. "Some 17th Century French Music in Canada: Notes for RISM." *FAM* 27(3–4):172–174.

———. 1981. "The Motet in New France. Some 17th and 18th Century Manuscripts in Quebec." *FAM* 28(3):194–219.

———. 1986. "Le Motet classique français en nouvelle France: cent années d'adaptation (1652–1755)." In *Actes du colloque international sur le grand motet français (1663–1792).* Ed. Jean Mongrédien and Yves Ferraton. Presses de l'Université de Paris-Sorbonne. 199–213.

Schwartz, Judith L., and Christena L. Schlundt. 1987. *French Court Dance and Dance Music: a Guide to Primary Source Writings.* Stuyvesant, New York: Pendragon.

Schwendowius, Barbara. 1970. *Die solistische Gambenmusik in Frankreich von 1650 bis 1740*. Regensburg: Gustav Vosse.

Scott, R. H. F. 1973. *Jean-Baptiste Lully*. London: Owen.

Seagrave, Barbara. 1958. *The French Style of Violin Bowing and Phrasing from Lully to Jacques Aubert*. Ph.D. Thesis, Stanford University.

Seares, Margaret. 1974. "Aspects of Performance Practice in the Recitatives of Jean-Baptiste Lully." *SiM(AUS)* 8:8–16.

―――. 1981. "The French Part-Songs of the Late Sixteenth and Early Seventeenth Centuries." *SiM(AUS)* 15:36–50.

―――. 1985. "Étienne Moulinié and the *Air de Cour*." *SiM(AUS)* 19: 61–79.

Seidel, Wilhelm. 1986. "Französische Musiktheorie im 16. und 17. Jahrhundert." *Entstehung nationaler Traditionen*. Darmstadt: Wissenschaftliche Buchgesellschaft. 4–140.

Semmens, Richard T. 1975. *Woodwind Treatment in the Early Ballets of Jean-Baptiste Lully*. Master's Thesis, University of British Columbia.

―――. 1980a. "The Debut of the Remodelled Transverse Flute." *SiM(CND)* 5:64–80.

―――. 1980b. *Étienne Loulié as Music Theorist: An Analysis of Items in Ms, Paris, Bibliothèque Nationale, fonds fr., n. a. 6355*. Ph.D. Thesis, Stanford University.

Shaw, Gertrude. 1963. *The Violoncello Sonata Literature in France during the Eighteenth Century*. Ph.D. Thesis, Catholic University.

Sicard, Michel. 1985. "The French Viol School: the Repertory from 1650 to Sainte-Colombe (about 1680)." *JVGSA* 22:42–55.

Silin, Charles. 1940. *Benserade and His Ballets de Cour*. Baltimore: John Hopkins Press.

Smith, Christine. 1988. *André Campra's "Idoménée": a Study of Its Structural Components and a Critical Edition of the Work*. Ph.D. Thesis, University of Kentucky.

Smither, Howard E. 1977. *The Oratorio in the Baroque Era: Italy, Vienna, Paris*. In *A History of the Oratorio*, vol. 1. Chapel Hill: University of North Carolina Press.

Snyders, Georges. 1968. *Le Goût musical en France aux XVIIe et XVIIIe siècles*. Paris: J. Vrin.

Stern, David Bruce. 1974. *The French Te Deum from 1677–1744: Its Esthetic Style and Development*. D.M.A. Thesis, University of Illinois.

Stevens, Jane R. 1989. "The Meanings and Uses of *Caractère* in Eighteenth-Century France." In *French Musical Thought, 1600–1800*. Ed. G. Cowart, Ann Arbor: UMI Press. 23–52.

Stravinsky, Igor (with Robert Craft). 1962. *Expositions and Developments*. Berkeley: University of California Press.

Stricker, Rémy. 1968. *Musique du baroque*. Paris: Gallimard.

Strunk, Oliver, ed. and trans. 1950. *Source Readings in Music History*. New York: W. W. Norton.

Sutton, Julia. 1985. "The Minuet: an Elegant Phoenix." *Dance Chronicle* 8(3–4):119–152.

꠸ ▣ ꠹

Taitz-Desouches, Danièle. 1974. "Jean Mignon: maître de chapelle de Notre-Dame." *Recherches* 14:82–153.

Tapié, Victor. 1957. *Baroque et classicisme*. Paris: Plon. New ed. Paris: Livres de poche, 1980. English trans. by A. Ross Williamson as *The Age of Grandeur: Baroque Art and Architecture*. New York: Praeger, 1966.

Teplow, Deborah A. 1986. *Performance Practice and Technique in Marin Marais' "Pièces de viole."* Ann Arbor: UMI Press.

———. 1987. "Rhetoric and Eloquence: Dramatic Expression in Marin Marais' *Pièces de viole*." *JVGSA* 24:22–50.

Térey-Smith, Mary. 1979. "French Baroque Partbooks in the Uppsala University Library." *Journal of The Canadian Association of University Schools of Music* 9(1):29–47.

———. 1989. "Orchestral Practice in the Paris Opera (1690–1764) and the Spread of French Influence in Europe." *Studia musicologica academiae scientiarum hungaricae* 31:81–159.

Tessier, André. 1924. "L'Oeuvre de Marin Marais." *Bulletin de la Société d'Histoire de l'Art Français.* 76–80.

———. 1926a–1927. "Correspondance d'André Cardinal des Touches et du Prince Antoine Ier de Monaco (1709–1731)." *RM* 7(2): 97–114; 8(4):104–117; 8(5) 209–224; and 8(6):149–162.

———. 1926b. *Couperin*. Paris: H. Laurens.

———. 1927. "Robert Cambert à Londres." *RM* 9 (2):101–122.

———. 1928a. "La Carrière versaillaise de La Lande." *RdM* 9: 134–148.

———. 1928b. "Giacomo Torelli a Parigi e la messa in scena delle *Nozze di Peleo e Teti* di Carlo Caproli." *Rassegna musicale* 1:573–590.

———. 1929. "Quelques parodies de Couperin." *RdM* 10:40–44.

Thoinan, Ernest (pseud. for A.-E. Roquet). 1894. *Les Hotteterre et les Chédeville*. Paris: E. Sagot.

Thompson, Clyde F. 1959. *The Music of Marin Marais*. Ph.D. Thesis, University of Michigan.

———. 1960. "Marin Marais's *Pièces de Viole*." *MQ* 46 (4) (October): 482–499.

———. 1963. "Instrumental Style in Marin Marais's *Pièces de Viole*." *Recherches* 3:79–89.

Tiersot, Julien. 1922a. "François II Couperin compositeur de musique religieuse." *RdM* 3:101–109.

———. 1922b. "La Musique des comédies de Molière à la Comédie-Française." *RdM* 3:20–28.

———. 1926. *Les Couperins*. Paris: F. Alcan.

Tilney, Colin. 1991. *The Art of the Unmeasured Prelude for Harpsichord: France, 1660–1720*. London: Schott.

Torrefranca, Fausto. 1929. "La prima opera francese in Italia? (L'Armida di Lulli, Roma, 1690)." *Festschrift für Johannes Wolf zu seinem sechzigsten Geburtstage.* Ed. W. Lott et al, Berlin: Martin Breslauer, 1929. 191–197. Rpt. Hildesheim: Georg Olms Verlag, 1978.

Tribout de Morembert, H. 1967. "Bodin de Boismortier: notes sur un musicien lorrain." *RdM* 53(1):41–52.

Troeger, Richard. 1983. "Metre in Unmeasured Preludes." *EM* 11 (3) (July): 340–345.

———. 1987. *Technique and Interpretation on the Harpsichord and Clavichord.* Bloomington: Indiana University Press.

Truinet, Charles-Louis-Étienne (pseud. Charles-Louis-Étienne Nuitter), and A. E. Roquet (pseud. A.-E. Thoinan). 1886. *Les Origines de l'opéra français.* Paris: Plon. Rpt. Geneva: Minkoff, 1972.

Tunley, David. 1966a. "The Cantatas of Louis-Nicolas Clérambault." *MQ* 52 (3) (July): 313–331.

———. 1966b. "Philidor's *Concerts français.*" *M&L* 43 (April): 130–134.

———. 1967a. "An Embarkment for Cythera—Social and Literary Aspects of the Eighteenth-Century Cantata." *Recherches* 7:103–114.

———. 1967b. "The Emergence of the Eighteenth-Century French Cantata." *SiM(AUS)* 1:67–88.

———. 1974. *The Eighteenth-Century French Cantata.* London: Dobson. Revised ed. Oxford: Clarendon Press, 1997.

———. 1982. *François Couperin.* London: Oxford University Press.

———. 1983a. "Couperin and French Lyricism." *MT* 124 (September): 543–545.

———. 1983b. "Couperin Over 250 Years." *SiM(AUS)* 17:87–90.

———. 1984. "The Union of Words and Music in Seventeenth-Century French Song—The Long and the Short of It." *Australian Journal of French Studies* 21(3):281–307.

———. 1986. "Solo Song and Vocal Duet: France." In *NOHM*, vol. 6. Ed. G. Abraham. Oxford: Oxford University Press. 172–185.

———. 1987. "Grimarest's *Traité de récitatif*: Glimpses of Performance Practice in Lully's Operas." *EM* 15 (3) (August): 361–364.

———. 1993. "Tunings and Transpositions in the Early 17th-Century French Lute Air. Some Implications." *EM: French Baroque I* 21 (2) (May): 203–209.

Turnbull, Michael. 1981. *A critical Edition of "Psyché," an Opera with Words by Thomas Corneille and Philippe Quinault and Music by Jean-Baptiste Lully.* Doctoral Thesis, Oxford University.

———. 1983. "The Metamorphosis of *Psyché.*" *M&L* 64 (1–2) (January–April): 12–24.

———. 1990. "The Sources for the Two Versions of 'Psyché' (1671 & 1678)." In *Jean-Baptiste Lully. Actes du colloque.* Ed. Herbert

Schneider and Jérôme de La Gorce. Laaber: Laaber-Verlag. 349–356.

☞ ◈ ☜

Underwood, T. Jervis. 1970. *The Works of Jacques-Christophe Naudot.* Ph.D. Thesis, North Texas State University.

Urquhart, M. I. J. 1970. *Style and Technique in the "Pièces de Viole" of Marin Marais.* Doctoral Thesis, University of Edinburgh.

☞ ◈ ☜

Vaissier, Louis. 1984. "Michel Blavet, 1700–1768. Essai de biographie." *Recherches* 22:131–159.

Vallas, Léon. 1932. *Un Siècle de musique et de théâtre à Lyon (1668–1789).* Lyons: P. Masson. Rpt. Geneva: Minkoff, 1971.

Van Wze, Benjamin. 1980. "Ritual Use of the Organ in France." *JAMS* 33 (2) (Summer): 287–325.

Vanuxem, Jacques. 1967. "Les Fêtes théâtrales de Louis XIV et le baroque de *La Finta Pazza* à *Psyché*." In *Le Baroque au théâtre et la théâtralité du Baroque, Actes des journées internationales d'étude du baroque, 2e session.* Montauban: Centre National de Recherches du Baroque. 31–41.

Vendrix, Philippe. 1987. "Le Tombeau en musique en France à l'époque baroque." *Recherches* 25:105–138.

———. 1988. "René Ouvrard et l'évolution de l'art musical." *RBdM* 42:193–197.

———. 1989. "Proportions harmoniques et proportions architecturales dans la théorie française des XVIIe et XVIIIe siècles." *International Review of the Aesthetics and Sociology of Music,* 20(1):3–10.

———. 1992. *Aux origines d'une discipline historique. La Musique et son histoire en France aux XVIIe et XVIIIe siècles.* Geneva: Droz.

Verchaly, André. 1947. "Gabriel Bataille et son oeuvre personnelle pour chant et luth." *RdM* 29:1–24.

———. 1953–1954. "La Musique religieuse française de Titelouze à 1660." *RM* 222 (special number): 77–88.

———. 1954a. "Desportes et la musique." *Annales musicologiques* 2: 271–328.

———. 1954b. "Poésie et airs de cour en France jusqu'à 1620." In *Musique et poésie au XVIe siècle.* Paris: CNRS. 211–223.

———. 1954c. "Un Précurseur de Lully: Pierre Guédron." *XVIIe siècle* 21–22:383–393.

———. 1955. "À propos des chansonniers de Jacques Mangeant." In *Mélanges d'histoire et d'esthétique musicales offerts à Paul-Marie Masson,* vol. 2. Paris: Richard-Masse. 169–177.

———. 1957. "Les Ballets de cour d'après les recueils de musique vocale." In *Cahiers de l'Association Internationale des Études Françaises,* vol. 9. Paris: Société d'Éditions "Les Belles Lettres." 198–218.

———. 1960. "Air de cour et ballet de cour." In *Histoire de la musique,* vol. 1. Ed. Roland-Manuel. Paris: Gallimard. 1529–1560.

————. 1961. "La Métrique et le rythme musical." In *Report of the Eighth Congress of the IMS*. Kassel and New York: Bärenreiter. 66–74.

————. 1968. "La Poésie française baroque et sa musique (1580–1645)." In *Actes des journées internationales d'étude du baroque*. Montauban: Centre international de synthèse du baroque. 127–136.

————. 1975. "À propos du récit français au début du XVIIe siècle." *Recherches* 15:39–46.

————. See also Durosoir, Georgie, and André Verchaly.

Vertrees, Julie Anne. 1977. *French Secular Chamber Music with Basse de Viole Obbligato*. Ph.D. Thesis. Cornell University.

————. See Sadie, Julie Anne.

Vidal, Henri. 1988–1990. "Le Grand motet aux États de Languedoc. Note sur la vie musicale à Montpellier au XVIIIe siècle." *Recherches* 26:222–229.

Viollier, Renée. 1939. "La Musique à la cour de la Duchesse du Maine." *RM* 20:96–105, 133–138.

————. 1950. *Jean-Joseph Mouret, le musicien des grâces*. Paris: Floury. Rpt. Geneva: Minkoff, 1976.

————. 1951. "Les Sonates pour violon et les sonates en trio d'Elisabeth de La Guerre et de Jean-François d'Andrieu." *RMS* 91(9):349–351.

Vollen, Gene E. 1982. *The French Cantata: A Survey and Thematic Catalogue*. Ann Arbor: UMI Press.

Voloshin, Metro J. 1984. *The Secular Cantatas of Nicolas Benier*. Ph.D. Thesis, University of Kentucky.

Walker, D. P. 1948. "The Influence of *Musique mesurée à l'antique*, particularly on the *Airs de Cour* of the Early Seventeenth Century." *MD* 2(1):141–163.

————. 1976. "Joan Albert Ban and Mersenne's Musical Competition of 1640." *M&L* 57 (3) (July): 233–255.

Wallon, Simone. 1956. "Un Recueil de pièces de clavecin de la seconde moitié du XVIIe siècle." *RdM* 38 (December): 105–114.

————. 1957. "Les Testaments d'Elisabeth Jacquet de La Guerre." *RdM* 40:206–214.

Weber, Édith, ed. 1974. *L'Interprétation de la musique française aux XVIIe et XVIIIe siècles*. Paris: CNRS.

————. 1988. "L'Influence du théâtre humaniste à participation musicale sur le théâtre jesuite." In *Les Jesuites parmi les hommes aux XVIe et XVIIe siècles, Actes du colloque international*. Clermont-Ferrand: University of Clermont-Ferrand. 445–460.

Weber, William. 1984. "*La Musique ancienne* in the Waning of the *Ancien régime*." *Journal of Modern History* 56:58–88.

————. 1990. "Lully and the Rise of Musical Classics in the 18th Century." In *Jean-Baptiste Lully. Actes du colloque*. Ed. Herbert

Schneider and Jérôme de La Gorce. Laaber: Laaber-Verlag. 581–590.

Wesolowski, Frantiszck. 1987. "Französische Vokalornamentik in der ersten Hälfte des 18. Jahrhunderts." In *Studien zur Aufführungspraxis und Interpretation der Musik des 18. Jahrhunderts,* vol. 32. Ed. E. Thom and W. Siegmund-Schultze. Blankenburg/Harz: Kultur und Forschungsstätte Michael Stein. 13–23.

Wild, Nicole. 1961. *La Vie musicale en France sous la Régence d'après le "Mercure."* Thesis, Conservatoire National Supérieur de Musique, Paris.

———. 1965. "Aspects de la musique sous la Régence. Les Foires: naissance de l'opéra-comique." *Recherches* 5:129–141.

Williams, Peter. 1967. *The European Organ 1450–1850.* Nashua, NH: Organ Literature Foundation.

———. 1980. *A New History of the Organ. From the Greeks to the Present Day.* London: Faber and Faber.

———. 1989. "French Overture Conventions in the Hands of the Young Bach and Handel." In *Bach Studies.* Ed. D. O. Franklin. Cambridge,: Cambridge University Press. 183–193.

Witherell, Anne L. 1983. *Louis Pécour's "Recueil de danses."* Ann Arbor: UMI Press.

Wolf, Robert Peter. 1978. "Metrical Relationships in French Recitative of the Seventeenth and Eighteenth Centuries." *Recherches* 18:29–49.

Wolff, Helmuth Christian. 1973. "Händel und Frankreich." In *Göttinger Händel-Festspiele.* Ed. W. Mayerhoff. Kassel: Bärenreiter. 19–27.

Wood, Caroline. 1981a. *Jean-Baptiste Lully and His Successors: Music and Drama in the "Tragédies en musique," 1673–1715.* Doctoral Thesis, University of Hull.

———. 1981b–1982. "Orchestra and Spectacle in the *Tragédie en musique,* 1673–1715: oracle, *sommeil* and *tempête.*" *PRMA* 108:25–46.

Wulstan, David. 1986. "Glorious Uncertainty." *EM* 14 (3) (August): 406–409.

Wurtz, Martha H. 1966. *The Sacred Vocal Works of François Couperin.* Ph.D. Thesis, Washington University.

Yannou, Demetre. 1980. *Die "Geschichte der Musik" (1715) von Bonnet et Bourdelot.* Regensburg: G. Bosse.

Yates, Francis A. 1947. *The French Academies of the Sixteenth Century.* London: The Warburg Institute.

Yvon-Briand, Anne-Marie. 1949. *La Vie musicale à Notre-Dame de Paris aux XVIIe et XVIIIe siècles.* Thesis, École Nationale des Chartes, Paris.

———. 1967. "La Maîtrise de Notre-Dame aux XVIIe et XVIIIe siècles." In *8e centenaire de Notre-Dame de Paris.* Paris: J. Vrin. 359–399.

⌐ ▣ ⌐

Zaslaw, Neal. 1970. *Materials for the Life and Works of Jean-Marie Leclair, l'Aîné*. Ph.D. Thesis, Columbia University.

———. 1972. "Mozart's Tempo Conventions." In *Report of the 11th Congress of the IMS*. Copenhagen: W. Hansen. 728–732.

———. 1974. "The Enigma of the Haute-Contre Roles." *MT* 115 (November): 939–941. [Response by James R. Anthony. 1975. *MT* 116 (March): 237.]

———. 1979. "Leclair's "Scylla et Glaucus." *MT* 120 (November): 900–907.

———. 1983. "At the Paris Opera in 1747." *EM* 11 (4) (October): 514–516.

———. 1986. "Rameau's Operatic Apprenticeship: The First Fifty Years." In *Jean-Philippe Rameau. Colloque international*. Ed. Jérôme de La Gorce. Geneva: Champion-Slatkine. 13–50.

———. 1988. "When is an Orchestra not an Orchestra?" *EM* 16 (4) (November): 483–495.

———. 1989. "The First Opera in Paris: a Study in the Politics of Art." In *Jean-Baptiste Lully and the Music of the French Baroque*. Ed. John Hajdu Heyer. Cambridge: Cambridge University Press. 7–23.

———. 1990. "Lully's Orchestra." In *Jean-Baptiste Lully. Actes du colloque*. Ed. Herbert Schneider and Jérôme de La Gorce. Laaber: Laaber-Verlag. 539–579.

———. 1993. "*Scylla et Glaucus*: A case study." *Cambridge Opera Journal* 4(3):199–228.

Zaslaw, Neal, and John Spitzer. 1986. "Improvised Ornamentation in Eighteenth-Century Orchestras." *JAMS* 39:524–577.

Notes

Chapter 1. *Institutions and Organizations of the* Grand Siècle

1. Titon du Tillet 1755, 57. *Le Parnasse françois* is a rich source of information on the musical life of France for almost a hundred-year period. There are three supplements to the original edition of 1732. Their dates are 1743, 1755, and 1760 (entitled *Description du parnasse françois*). The three supplements add names and biographies of the musicians "taken in death" between 1743 and 1760. For an index of musicians mentioned in the above, see Sadie 1989, 149–157.

2. Benoit's 1971b *Versailles et les musiciens du roi* and her *Musiques de cour* of the same year are the most complete studies. See also Massip 1976b, 25–36. For the Royal Chapel, see Morby 1971 and Raugel 1957. For the Great Stable *(La Grande Écurie)*, see Écorcheville 1900–1901; Borrel 1957; and Prunières 1911.

3. See "Jean de La Motte" in the index to *Documents du Minutier Central* (Jurgens 1969, 1974). From a selection of 1751 notarial documents covering a fifty-year period, Mlle Jurgens has fashioned a research tool of inestimable value for the first half of the seventeenth century.

4. *Dictionnaire de la musique en France au XVIIᵉ et XVIIIᵉ siècles* (1992, 724). Bardet's 1956 thesis, which, sadly, remains unpublished, is the most complete study of the string ensembles of the Chamber.

5. From 1649 to 1749 a handbook, *État de la France*, was printed on a more or less regular basis to give information concerning the organization and administration of the royal court. It is an important source of information on the musicians and function of music at the court. See Cohen 1992.

6. That some were still attached to the Stable as late as the period of Louis XIV is suggested by the *État de la France* for the year 1686,

mentioned above, in which a "band of violins from the Great Stable" joined the winds for certain court ceremonies (Prunières 1920, 130).

7. In the earlier English-language editions of this book, I used the word *counter-tenor*. The proper name for this voice in English has been the subject of some controversy. To be sure, the French *haute-contre* had nothing in common with the English counter-tenor (i.e., male falsettist). The *haute-contre*'s penetrating voice (*voix aiguë*) pushed into the highest tenor range with only an occasional switch to falsetto. Some have argued that the term *high tenor* should be used in English to avoid any confusion with the English counter-tenor. Yet the brothers Parfaict made a distinction between a high tenor (*haute-taille*) and an *haute-contre* when they described the voice of Du Mesny as being that of a very high tenor ("*du haute-taille des plus hautes*"), which permitted the singer to "pass for an *haute-contre*" (ca. 1741, 1:46). To avoid any confusion, I will use the French term *haute-contre* in this book. For additional information, see Zaslaw 1974; my response in the same journal in 1975; and Cyr 1977.

8. The most complete discussion of the Versailles chapels is found in Himelfarb 1986. See also Dufourcq 1965b, 1:286.

9. *Notes et références pour servir à une histoire de Michel-Richard Delalande*, 19. For a discussion of what constituted the soprano (*dessus*) section in French music from Lully onwards, see Sawkins 1987.

10. Cited by Morby (1971, 225). The "*grosse basse de violon*" probably referred to the larger of the two types of bass violins in use at court and at the Paris Opera, rather than the contrabass. It is doubtful that the latter instrument was used in France at this time.

11. For additional information on the situation at Notre-Dame and the Sainte-Chapelle, see Chartier 1897 and Brenet 1910.

12. This journal, an important mirror of official opinion, underwent many changes of title: in addition to the name *Mercure*, it was known at various times as *Mercure de France*, *Mercure galant*, *Nouveau Mercure*, and *Mercure français*.

13. Benoit 1971a, 155. For Philidor's *atelier*, see Massip 1983 and Anthony 1987c.

14. Lesure 1954, 47. For a study of the Confrérie that reproduces many of the pertinent royal patents and statuts, see Loubet de Sceaury 1949.

15. Besche 1774, 8. See also Benoit and Dufourcq 1957.

16. For a description of other associations of "*symphonistes*," see Dufourcq 1954a, 46–57, and 1981.

17. All the documents pertinent to the establishment of the Académie Royale de Musique are found in Truinet [Nuitter] and Roquet [Thoinan], 1886; rpt. 1972. See also Riccoboni 1738, 1741; Prunières 1925; Mélèse 1934a and 1934b; Demuth 1963, 97–118

(which includes a helpful series of appendices with many of the *Lettres Patentes)*; Ducrot 1970; Lagrave 1972; La Gorce 1981; Pitou 1983, 1:13–26; Coeyman 1990b; and La Gorce 1992.

18. Brenet's 1900 *Les Concerts en France sous l'ancien régime* remains the classic secondary source for information on French concerts during the seventeenth and eighteenth centuries. For the Concert Spirituel, see Pierre 1975. See also Dufourcq 1979; both Chapter 7 ("Les Concerts privés") and Chapter 8 ("Le Concert Spirituel") in Daval 1961; and Heartz 1993.

19. See Tunley 1966b. For a list of works performed at the Concerts Français from 1727 to 1733, see Tunley 1974, 241–249.

Chapter 2. Ballet de Cour *I: From Beaujoyeulx to Lully*

1. Important sources for information on the court ballet are Loret 1650–1655; Pierre-François Godard de Beauchamps 1735; La Vallière 1760; Lacroix 1868; Prunières 1914; Silin 1940; Yates 1947; McGowan 1963; Christout 1967; Buch 1985; Christout 1987 and 1990; Durosoir 1991; and Buch 1994. In the *Dictionnaire de la musique en France aux XVIIe et XVIIIe siècles* (Benoit 1992, 45–49), Christout identified 392 court ballets performed from 1572 to 1671 by title, year, specific date (if known), and place (if known).

2. A facsimile of the 1582 score, with an informative introduction by Margaret M. McGowan, was published by the Center for Medieval & Early Renaissance Studies (Binghampton, New York: 1982). An English translation, prepared by Carol and Lander MacClintok with a modern transcription of the music, was published by the American Institute of Musicology in 1971.

3. Parfaict and Parfaict ca. 1741, 1:2. The same statement by Jean-Laurent Lecerf de la Viéville may be found in the version of the 1705–1706 ed. of his *Comparaison de la musique italienne et de la musique françoise* that constitutes (without acknowledgement) vols. 2–4 of Bourdelot and Bonnet's *Histoire de la musique et de ses effets* (1725, 4 vols. bound as 2, 3:157), whose vol. numbers do not match the 1705–1706 (2nd) ed. All my references to Lecerf come from the 1966 reprint of Bourdelot and Bonnet's *Histoire de la musique*.

4. The extant music from *Renaud* is found in Prunières's Appendix (1914). For some reason, Prunières did not include Guédron's *récit*, "Pour Armide contente de posséder Renault," found in Book 7 of *Airs de differents autheurs mis en tablature de luth par eux-mesmes* (Paris: Ballard, 1617). For a modern transcription of the *récit*, see Verchaly 1975, 44.

5. Louis XIV as Apollo in the *Ballet du roy des fêtes de Bacchus* (1651) had already worn the attributes of the sun. For a reproduction of his costume, see Isherwood 1973, 137.

Chapter 3. Ballet de Cour *II: The Period of Lully*

1. Important sources that deal with the life of Lully are Radet 1891; Rolland 1914; Prunières 1909a and 1909b; Écorcheville 1911; La Laurencie 1911; Prunières 1912b, 1929, and prefaces to *Oeuvres complètes de J.-B. Lully* 1930–1939; Borrel 1949; Ducrot 1961; Scott 1973; Anthony 1986a, 1–17; Beaussant 1992; and Couvreur 1992. See also Schneider1981a, 1989, and 1990c.

2. Letter of 19 February 1656 from *La Muze historique* (1656; ed. of 1857–1878). Loret's *La Muze Historique* is a collection of letters in verse that comment on the newsworthy events of the day. Although poor as poetry, it is rich as a source of information on individuals and musical events.

3. Manfred Bukofzer's assertion that the use of triple meter in the second part of the French overture "was to become standard practice" and that the overture to *Serse* (1660) is "perhaps the first example of the fully developed French overture" (1947,154) is not borne out by the facts. Six of the overtures to Lully's *tragédies en musique* have their second sections constructed in duple meter.

4. *Catalogue des livres de musique théorique et pratique . . . qui sont dans le cabinet du Sieur Seb. de Brossard*, 1724, (see page 532 in manuscript copy). This autograph catalogue of the great bibliophile's personal library is an important source of information on all aspects of seventeenth- and early eighteenth-century music in France. All references to this 1724 catalogue, Bibliothèque Nationale (*Rés.* Vm^8 20), are taken from a copy made between 1725 and 1730 that contains valuable annotations by Brossard and is also found in the Bibliothèque Nationale (*Rés.* Vm^8 21). The autograph has been edited by Yolande de Brossard (1994).

5. Lully's protege, Pascal Collasse, "borrowed" the same chorus for the prologue to his *Ballet des saisons* (2nd ed., 1700).

6. An extract from the prelude may be found in Lavignac's *Encyclopédie de la musique et dictionnaire du Conservatoire* (1913–1931, Part II, 3:1508); a facsimile of the opening of the prelude is in *NG* 11:319.

7. The *Ballet de la jeunesse* was published in facsimile with an introduction by Barbara Coeyman, Stuyvesant, NY: Pendragon Press, 1996.

8. The appendix in Lowe 1966 lists all performances with or without music from 1579 to 1761 at the College Louis-le-Grand.

Chapter 4. *Italian Opera in France*

1. Margaret Murata (1995) questions Zaslaw's suggestion on the grounds that *Il guidizio* "lacks lyricism, demands no virtuoso singing, and requires good Italian . . . to understand its jokes and satire" (103).

2. For further information on Torelli's stage machinery, see Per Bjurström (1962).

3. *Oeuvres complètes de J.-B. Lully*, "Les Ballets," 2:xi. For *Orfeo* see also Rolland (1914, 63–103 with a "Supplement musical" 297–303) and Goldschmidt (1901–1904, 1:295–311).

4. On the completion of the theater, Gaspard and his two sons returned to Modena, but less than two months later Louis XIV recalled them to engineer *divertissements* and *ballets de cour*.

5. The *sommeil* from *L'Orfeo* is in Arnold Schering, *Geschichte der Musik in Beispielen*, Leipzig: Breitkopf & Härtel, 1931, 248–249; the *sommeil* from *Les Amants magnifiques* is in the *Oeuvres complètes de J.-B. Lully*, "Les Comédies-ballets," 3:184–187. Cavalli's *Ercole amante* also contains a *sommeil*, "Dormi, dormi, dormi, O sonno" (Act II, scene vi) found in the appendix to Prunières (1913, 27–32).

Chapter 5. *The* Comédie-Ballet *and Related Genres*

1. This ostentatious party proved disastrous to Fouquet, who was arrested soon afterwards by order of the king for mismanagement of funds. In the words of Victor Tapié, it meant that the king alone could mount such a lavish display (1957, 105.).

2. The *comédies-ballets* of Molière and Lully are *L'Impromptu de Versailles* (1663); *Le Mariage forcé* (1664); *Les Plaisirs de l'isle enchantée* (1664); *La Princesse d'Élide* (1664); *L'Amour médecin* (1665); *La Pastorale comique* (1667); *Le Sicilien ou L'Amour peintre* (1667); *George Dandin ou Le Grand Divertissement royal de Versailles* (1668); *Monsieur de Pourceaugnac* (1669); *Les Amants magnifiques* (1670); and *Le Bourgeois gentilhomme* (1670). In addition, Molière collaborated with Charpentier on comic *intermèdes* for the 1672 revivals of *La Comtesse d'Ascarbagnas* and its *divertissement*, *Le Mariage forcé*, and for the first performance run of *Le Malade imaginaire* in 1673. Charpentier was responsible for the music of the revivals of *Le Malade imaginaire* in 1674 and ca. 1686. He also composed music for the 1672 revival of *Les Fâcheux* (music lost) and for the 1695 (?) revival of *Le Sicilien*.

3. A detailed account of Charpentier's music for the French theater is found in H. Wiley Hitchcock (1971). On Charpentier's music for *Le Malade imaginaire*, see Hitchcock (1972); see also John S. Powell (1986a and 1992). By conflating the following two sources, all of the extant music composed by Charpentier for *Le Malade imaginaire*

may be recreated: *Prologue et intermèdes du Malade imaginaire de Molière* edited by Hitchcock (Geneva: Minkoff, 1973) and *Music for Molière's Comédies* edited by Powell (Madison: A-R Editions, 1992).

4. Charles Varlet de La Grange left a financial record coupled with anecdotal material for all spectacles given at the *salles* of the Palais Bourbon, Palais Royal, and the Théâtre Guenegard from 1659 through 1685.

5. See, for example, the chorus "Le Monstre est mort" from *Cadmus et Hermione* (prologue, scene iv).

Chapter 6. *The Pastorale*

1. See Pougin 1881; Auld 1986, especially vol. 1, 25–50. See also titles found in Endnote 1, Chapter 1 and see La Gorce 1992, 17–34.

2. See Tessier 1927 and Flood 1928. The circumstances of Cambert's death are obscure. In his polemical allegory against Lully, *Lettre de Clément Marot à M de *** touchant sur qui s'est passé à l'arrivée de J.-B. de Lulli aux Champs-Elysées* (1688), Bauderon de Sénecé referred to Cambert as a "furious spirit" who appeared "still totally disfigured by the wounds from his assassination in England." The fact that no seventeenth- or eighteenth-century source documents this murder makes one suspect that Bauderon de Sénecé's account is a fanciful literary conceit. For recent research on Cambert's musical activites in London, see Buttrey 1995.

3. See Powers 1988 on the *pastorale héroïque*. Pierre-Jean-Baptiste Nougaret defined the *pastorale héroïque* as a "Drama whose subject is more serious than simple and whose dénouement is sometimes tragic" (1769, 2:230). The following *pastorales héroïques* were performed at the Opera between Lully's *Acis et Galathé* and Rameau's *Zaïs*: *Coronis* (Gatti 1691), *Issé* (Destouches 1697), *Le Jugement de Paris* (Bertin de la Doué 1718), *Princesse d'Élide* (Villeneuve 1728), *La Pastorale héroïque* (Rebel 1730), and *Endimion* (Collin de Blamont 1731). Rameau composed four *pastorales héroïques*: *Zaïs* (1748), *Naïs* (1749), *Acante et Céphise* (1751), and *Daphnis et Églé* (1753).

Chapter 7. Tragédie en Musique *I: Dramatic Organization and Vocal Music*

1. Cited by Prunières in his preface to *Opéras*, vol. 1 of the *Oeuvres complètes de J.-B. Lully*.

2. Following are Lully's stage works performed at the Académie Royale de Musique. All are *tragédies en musique*, and all *livrets* are by Quinault, unless otherwise indicated. Dates of first performances are given. If a première occurred at court, the date of the stage work's first performance at the Académie Royale de Musique is also provided:

Les Fêtes de l'Amour et de Bacchus, pastorale, Quinault, Molière, and Périgny; 10 (?) Nov. 1672.

Cadmus et Hermione; 27 (?) Apr. 1673.

Alceste; 19 Jan. 1674.

Thésée; Saint-Germain-en-Laye, 11 Jan. 1675; Paris, Apr. 1675.

Atys; Saint-Germain-en-Laye, 10 Jan. 1676; Paris, Apr. 1676.

Isis; Saint-Germain-en-Laye, 5 Jan. 1677; Paris, Aug. 1677.

Psyché, Quinault, T. Corneille, and Fontenelle; 19 Apr. 1678.

Bellérophon, T. Corneille, Fontenelle, and Boileau; 31 Jan. 1679.

Proserpine; Saint-Germain-en-Laye, 3 Feb. 1680; Paris, Nov. 1680.

Le Triomphe de l'Amour (ballet), Quinault and Benserade; Saint-Germain-en-Laye, 21 Jan. 1681; Paris, May. 1681.

Persée; 18 Apr. 1682.

Phaëton; Versailles, 6 Jan. 1683; Paris, Apr. 1683.

Amadis; 18 Jan. 1684.

Le Temple de la Paix (ballet); Fontainebleau, 20 Oct. 1685; Paris, Nov. 1685.

Roland; Versailles, 8 Jan. 1686; Paris, 8 or 9 Mar. 1686.

Armide; 15 Feb. 1686.

Acis et Galathée (*pastorale-héroïque*), Campistron; Anet, 6 Sep. 1686; Paris, 13 or 17 Sep. 1686.

3. In France, *Opéra* was used from the beginning to describe a large-scale dramatic work that was sung throughout. Lecerf used the terms *Opéra* and *Tragédies en Musique* interchangeably (see, for example, 1725; rpt. 1966, 2:101). The plural *Opéras*, however, was not in general use until the late eighteenth century. "It seems to me," wrote Nougaret, "that the word *Opéra* is common enough among us to merit a plural form" (1769, 1:20).

4. Grimm 1753; trans. 1950, 631.

5. Racine's son Louis insisted, however, that those who believed that his father had made use of a high-flown (*enflée*) and singing manner of declamation onstage were in error (cited by Lote 1912, 321).

6. Lois Rosow cautions that by the late 1670s Lully began to mix all five signatures together in his recitatives (C, 3, ₵, 2, 3/2). Following Loulié's reasoning, there would simply be beat equivalence. "Still," she writes," when an individual passage . . . includes both 3 and 3/2, or both 2 and ₵, one has to wonder if there is not some significance to the choice of signatures" (1990, 408).

7. "Bois épais" has often been singled out as typical of the best among Lully's monologue airs. Donald Grout described it as "serious, restrained, elegantly proportioned, full of aristocratic yet sensuous charm" (1965, 348). Yet anyone who wants to hear a stylistically valid performance of "Bois épais" must be content with two recorded ver-

sions: one by Caruso and the other by Rosa Ponselle; both use an abridged and woefully inaccurate piano reduction. These recordings do little but document the popularity of "Bois épais" in the early twentieth century as a token "early music" piece with which to open a song recital.

8. For evidence of some choral gestures and movements onstage in the eighteenth century, see Banducci 1993, Harris-Warrick and Marsh 1994, and Cyr 1995.

9. A suggestion made by Denise Launay, for example, in her edition of a Charpentier Te Deum, "Le Pupitre" series, Paris: Heugel, 1969.

Chapter 8. Tragédie en Musique *II: Instrumental Music and the Dance*

1. From 1677 to 1687 (the year of Lully's death), Christophe Ballard printed 13 stage works by Lully, mainly in full score. According to a contractual arrangement dated 1680, Ballard would be the only printer of Lully's music, and he would agree to print 750 copies of each work (see Rosow 1981, 10).

2. The most complete treatment of the dance in the stage music of Lully is found in Helen Meredith Ellis's Ph.D. Thesis, Stanford University, 1967.

3. A helpful summary that compares eighteenth-century metronome markings is found in Appendix D of Mellers 1950. See also Kirkpatrick 1938; Zaslaw 1972, 730–731; and Neumann 1993a, 23–29. For a brief summary of the many pendulum devices and chronometers, see Mather 1989. See also Harris-Warrick 1992. For a discussion of tempi in Delalande's *grands motets*, in which he occasionally indicated exact timings, see Sawkins 1986c, and 1993a.

4. Performance of the minuets from Rameau's *Hippolyte et Aricie* (Act IV, scene iii) on two recordings dramatically demonstrates the importance of looking into eighteenth-century discussions of tempos. For an otherwise excellent interpretation, Anthony Lewis inexplicably chose the more moderate tempo of the minuet from *Don Giovanni* (L'Oiseau-Lyre record No. 286-7-8). Contrast this with the more appropriate tempo chosen by Roger Desormière in his performance of extracts from the same opera (L'Oiseau-Lyre record No. 50034). Zaslaw's table (see Endnote 3 above) gives the metronome marking of the minuet as = 70 from 1717 to 1747 and as = 53 in 1752.

5. See also the *Menuet de Poitou* to which Louis Couperin added a *double* (found in *Harvard Anthology of Music* 2:93).

6. Preface to his *Florilegium secundum*. For a summary, see Mellers 1950, 352–355.

7. Inexplicably, little work has been done until recently on the relationship between the musical components of dance (phrase structure, tempo) and choreography. Important sources dealing with this problem are the following: Little 1975a; Hilton 1977; Hilton 1980; Witherell 1983; Harris-Warrick 1989; Harris-Warrick 1990a; Little and Jenne 1991.

Chapter 9. Tragédie en Musique *III: From Lully to Rameau*

1. For the performances of *Atys* in Rennes beginning 21 October 1689, Lully's disciple Pascal Collasse composed a new, politically inspired prologue (music lost) set in Brittany. Under the guise of allegory, this prologue celebrates the rapport among France (La Nymphe de la Seine), Brittany (La Nymphe de la Loire), and the king (Apollon). (See Mussat 1994, 8–9.)

2. The *Journal* found at the Bibliothèque de l'Opéra is a handwritten, year by year account of the performances that took place at the Paris Opera. In spite of several lacunae, it is an important source for determining the number of performances of any opera. It includes some anecdotal material as well.

3. The reference is, of course, to the famous passage in a letter by Mme de Sévigné of 1 December 1673 describing a performance or rehearsal of *Alceste*, which she attended in the company of Mme de La Fayette.

4. After the deaths of Lully and Quinault, the question of authors' payment (*honoraires d'auteurs*) was first resolved in principle at the time of the first performance of *L'Europe galante* (1697), when Campra and La Motte refused to accept the paltry fee offered by an economy-minded administration. It remained for the 1713 Ordinance, however, to spell out the details.

5. Desmarest left France in 1699 and abandoned this opera. Campra composed the prologue; Act II, scene i; Act IV, scene ii; the last three scenes of Act V; and several recitatives and airs.

6. Some pages are not orchestrated, and there are many copyist errors. Jean Duron has corrected them in his edition of the opera, Paris: CNRS, 1981.

7. Such short, self-contained theater pieces are also known as "*petits opéras*" (see N. Berton 1994, 12–23).

8. Unfortunately, *Sémélé* exists only in a short score dating from the time of the first performance. I am grateful to Geoffrey Burgess, who brought to my attention a set of orchestral parts for the chaconne at the Bibliothèque de l'Opéra that was used for the revivals of

Collasse's popular *Thétis et Pélée* in 1750 and 1754. The chaconne was inserted after the final chorus in the last scene of Act V.

9. Rameau's stage works are as follows:

Tragédies en musique:
Hippolyte et Aricie, Pellegrin, 1 October 1733.
Samson, Voltaire (music lost).
Castor et Pollux, Bernard, 24 October 1737.
Dardanus, Le Clerc de la Bruère, 19 November 1739.
Zoroastre, Cahusac, 5 December 1749.
Linus, Le Clerc de la Bruère, not performed.

Opéra-ballets:
Les Boréades, Cahusac? not performed.
Les Indes galantes, Fuzelier, 23 August 1735.
Les Fêtes d'Hébé, Montdorge, 21 May 1739.
Les Fêtes de Polymnie, Cahusac, 12 October 1745.
Le Temple de la Gloire, Voltaire, 27 November 1745.
Les Fêtes de l'Hymen et de l'Amour, Cahusac 15 March 1747.
Les Surprises de l'Amour, Bernard, 27 November 1748.

Comédies lyriques:
Platée, Autreau, 31 March 1745.
Les Paladins, anon., 12 February 1760.

Pastorales héroïques:
Naïs, Cahusac, 22 April 1749.
Acante et Céphise, Marmontel, 19 November 1751.
Daphnis et Eglé, Collé, 30 October 1753.
Zaïs, Cahusac, 29 February 1748.

There are, in addition, one pastorale (?) (*Lysis et Délie*, Marmontel, not performed), one *comédie-ballet* (*La Princesse de Navarre*, Voltaire, 23 February 1745), ten *actes de ballet*, and incidental music composed for the Fair Theater and Comédie Française. Most of the latter is lost.

Rameau's operas have been the subject of several important studies, chief of which are: Émile Dacier (1903); Françoise Gervais (1965); Cuthbert Girdlestone (1957; 2nd ed. 1962); Hélène Leclerc (1953); Jean Malignon (1966); and Paul-Marie Masson (1930, 1939, 1954). For more recent studies, see the bibliographies contained in the articles found in *Jean-Philippe Rameau. Colloque international*, 1986, ed. J. de La Gorce.

Chapter 10. *The* Opéra-Ballet

1. The Dauphin, Louis XIV's only legitimate son, died in 1711; the king's eldest grandson, the Duc de Bourgogne, his wife, and elder son died in 1712.

2. Selected from the extracts found in Chantal Masson (1961).

3. For the *opéra-ballet*, see also the following: La Laurencie (1913); Paul-Marie Masson (1932); Anthony (1965, 1966, 1969, 1970); Fajon (1984); Barthélemy (1957b); Viollier (1950); Dartois-Lepeyre (1983, 1992); Lemaître (1983); Cessac (1995).

4. Recent research by Catherine Cessac suggests that the structural model for *L'Europe galante* may be the ballet *Les Jeux à l'honneur de la Victoire* (ca. 1691–1692), which predates the *Ballet des Saisons* by three or four years. Jacquet de La Guerre's music for this ballet is lost, but the livret reveals a stage work divided into a prologue and three "divertissments," each with its own plot and mythological characters (See Cessac 1995b; see also La Gorce 1992, 101–102).

5. The musical quotations are taken from the following: "Entrée des songes agréables" and "Entrée des songes funestes" from Lully's *Atys* (Act III, scene iv); the *sommeil* from Destouches's *Issé* (Act IV, scene ii); the woodland scene from *Issé* (Act V, scene i); and the tempest from Marais's *Alcyone* (Act IV, scene iv).

6. For the role of Folly in French Baroque opera, see Cowart 1994, 215–220.

7. Paul-Marie Masson suggested the term *opéra-ballet héroïque* to distinguish *ballets héroïques* that exhibit the structure of the *opéra-ballets* from the few examples that, although labeled *ballet héroïque*, have a continuous dramatic action (1928, 133).

8. Max Lütolf has edited *Les Fêtes vénitiennes*, "Le Pupitre" series, Paris: Heugel, 1971.

9. The La Laurencie quotation comes from Lavignac and La Laurencie's *Encyclopédie de la musique* (1913–1931, Part I, 3:1383). Unfamiliarity with the $\frac{9}{7}_{\#5}$ chord in French music of the period undoubtedly caused Mellers to dismiss it as an "abstruse dissonance" (1950, 242), and prompted F. T. Arnold to view the #5 as a "retarded 6 which is taken unprepared in a very unusual manner" (1931, 187). Charles J. Moomaw has written an entire dissertation on this chord (1985).

10. *Les Fêtes vénitiennes* contains two additional cantatas found in "L'Amour saltimbanque," scene iii, and in "Les Sérénades et les joueurs," scene iv.

Chapter 11. *From* Divertissement *to* Opéra Comique

1. The anonymity of the composer of *L'Europe galante* was a poorly guarded secret, as the following extract from a 1697 chanson shows:

Quand notre Archevêque sçaura
L'Auteur du nouvel Opéra [L'Europe galante]
De sa Cathédrale Campra
Décampera.

When our Archbishop knows who is
The composer of the new Opera,
From his Cathedral, Campra
Will decamp.

Le Carnaval de Venise with an introduction by this author was published in facsimile edition. Stuyvesant, NY: Pendragon Press, 1989.

2. *Don Quichotte chez la duchesse* has been edited by Roger Blanchard, "Le Pupitre" series, Paris: Heugel, 1971.

3. Important sources on the history of the *opéra comique* are Campardon 1880; Font 1894; Cucuel 1913; La Laurencie in Lavignac and La Laurencie's *Encyclopédie*, 1913–1931, Part I, 3:1457–1489; Cucuel 1914; Genest 1925; Carmody 1933; Grout 1939; Cooper 1949; Barnes 1965; Grout 1965; Wild 1965; Barnes 1968; Packer 1970; Cooper in NOHM, 1973, 7:200–256; Heartz 1985; Isherwood 1986; Moreau 1990; and *L'Opéra-comique en France au XVIIIe siècle*, 1992.

4. The harpsichord piece "Les Sauvages," from the *Nouvelles Suites de Pièces de clavecin* dating from about 1729, was adapted from a dance composed by Rameau for one of the Fair Theatre productions of 1725 (see Sadler 1974).

Chapter 12. *From Du Caurroy to Du Mont*

1. These are the chronological boundaries of *Anthologie du motet latin polyphonique en France*. Ed. Denise Launay. Paris: Société Française de Musicologie, 1963. The valuable introduction to this source and Launay 1957, 1975, and 1993 are among the few sources that deal with the French motet in the first half of the seventeenth century.

2. Modern edition by E. Martin and J. Burold, Paris: Rouart, Lerolle et Cie., 1951.

3. *Les Oeuvres de Pierre de Ronsard*, ed. of 1587, vol. 10.

4. Two Masses by Pierre Menault have been edited by Michel Cuvelier as *Messes pour Saint-Étienne de Dijon*, Versailles: Éditions du Centre de Musique Baroque de Versailles (Éditions du CMBV), 1993.

Other projected volumes include *Vespers* by Menault, Masses by Henri Hardouin, *Messe à deux choeurs* by Nicolas Formé, and the works of Pierre Tabart.

5. Henri Sauval (1623–1676) was a historian whose researches resulted in the invaluable *Histoire et recherches des antiquités de la ville de Paris*, which was not published until 1724 by C. Moette.

6. For a summary of arguments on both sides, see Launay writing in Dufourcq 1962, 57–63.

7. These are Bibliothèque de Tours MS 168 and Bibliothèque Nationale *Rés*. Vma. MS 571. For Bouzignac, see Quittard 1904a–1905, 356–417; Jean-Louis Bonnet 1988; Launay 1993, 158–167; and Leroux 1993. Many motets by Bouzignac have been edited by Denise Launay, Bernard Loth, and Félix Raugel for the Éditions Musicales de la Schola Cantorum in their series "Oeuvres françaises du temps de Richelieu et du XVIIe siècle." This music deserves a far greater audience than has been accorded it to date.

8. Modern edition by Jean Lionnet, Versailles: Éditions du CMBV, 1992.

9. For Desportes, see Verchaly 1954a, 271–328. The most complete discussion of psalm translations and paraphrases is found in Launay 1993 in those sections of her book labeled "chant français." Launay edited settings of Desportes's translations composed by Du Caurroy, Chastillon, La Tour, Jean Boyer, de Courbes, and Signac in her *Anthologie du Psaume français polyphonique, 1610-1663*, Paris: Éditions ouvrières, 1974.

Chapter 13. *The Motet: From Du Mont to Delalande*

1. Psalm 19:10, "Domine salvum fac regem: Et exaudi nos in die qua invocaverimus te." (Grant victory to the king, O Lord, and answer this day our appeal.) The *Domine salvum* was a salutation to the king that from the days of Louis XIII was traditionally used as a closing motet for both high and low Mass.

2. In fact, the Ballard edition labels them *dessus, haute-contre, haute-taille, basse-taille*, and *basse*.

3. John Hajdu Heyer questions the attribution of this motet to Lully on stylistic grounds (1990).

4. Cited by Prunières in preface to vol. 1 of *Les Motets*. In *Oeuvres complètes de J.-B. Lully*, 1931.

5. Cited by Prunières in preface to vol. 1 of *Les Motets*. In *Oeuvres complètes de J.-B. Lully*, 1931.

6. Cited by Prunières in preface to vol. 2 of *Les Motets*. In *Oeuvres complètes de J.-B. Lully*, 1935.

7. Cited by Prunières in preface to vol. 2 of *Les Motets*. In *Oeuvres complètes de J.-B. Lully*, 1935.

8. See Charnassé 1961–1962, 65. Hélène Charnassé has edited two *grands motets* by Robert: *Deus noster refugium* and *Quare fremuerunt gentes*, "Le Pupitre" series, Paris: Heugel, 1969.

9. First published in 1968. 3rd. ed. 1991.

10. This interesting document (written for Philippe d'Orléans between 1692 and 1698) is a short treatise on composition appended by an *"Abrégé des règles d'accompagnement"* (Summary of rules for accompaniment). The original, given to the future Regent, has not survived, but there are two copies in the Bibliothèque Nationale (MS nouv. acq. fr. 6355, fol. 1–15, and MS nouv. acq. fr. 6356, 26–33). For a facsimile and English trans., see Ruff 1967. See also Cessac 1988, English trans. 1995, 389–411.

11. The final volume of the Cauvin manuscript is at the Bibliothèque Nationale (*Rés.* Vmb. MS 16). Eleven *grands motets* by Delalande, formerly in the Toulouse-Philidor collection at Saint Michael's College, Tenbury Wells, are today at the Bibliothèque Nationale. For more information on this collection, see Massip 1983. Certain of these copies differ in detail from those in the Bibliothèque de Versailles (see, for example, *Super flumina*). Five motets and some shorter works are in the private collection of M. R. Lutz in Strasbourg. For more details, see Dufourcq 1960; see also Boulay 1960.

12. These are *De profundis*, *Dixit Dominus*, *Domine in virtute tua*, *Exaudi Deus*, *In convertendo*, *Lauda Jerusalem*, *Miserere mei*, and Te Deum. As is mentioned above, *Exaudi Deus* is not in the engraved edition.

Chapter 14. *The Motet in the Eighteenth Century*

1. Desmarest abducted the daughter of the director of taxation for the Senlis district, Mlle de Saint-Gobert, and was exiled from France before the turn of the century. In 1707 he was appointed *Surintendant* of music at the court of Leopold, Duc de Lorraine in Nancy—a position he held until his death. (For more on Desmarest, see Antoine 1965, 46–61.)

2. *Domine, ne in fuore* and *Confitebor tibi* have been edited by Jean Duron, Paris: Éditions musicales de Radio France, 1983.

3. For Gilles, see Hajdu Heyer 1973 and Prada 1986.

4. The CMBV is publishing the complete works of Brossard as part of their Patrimoine Musical Français series.

5. Modern edition by Jean Duron, Versailles: Éditions du CMBV, 1993.

6. For Campra's religious music, see La Laurencie 1908c–1909; Barthélemy 1957a, 28–41; Castle 1962; and Baker 1984.

7. For the motets of Bernier, see Nelson 1979, 51–94.

8. Of these 26 motets, 12 are unica. Nine of the 12 have been edited byPhilippe Oboussier, "Le Pupitre" series, Paris: Heugel, 1972. All of the 12 have been edited by Kenneth Gibert, Davitt Maroney, and Orhan Memed, Monaco: Éditions de L'Oiseau-Lyre, 1995.

9. Daniel Vidal has edited Couperin's three *Leçons de Ténèbres*, "Le Pupitre" series, Paris: Heugel, 1968.

10. For the fugue in French Baroque motet prior to Rameau, see Duron 1986c.

11. For Madin, see Lespinard 1974; and 1975.

12. Modern edition by Silvie Bouissou, Paris: Édition Salabert, 1993.

Chapter 15. *Mass and Oratorio: The Domain of Marc-Antoine Charpentier*

1. For omissions to the list by Taitz-Destouches, see Edward Higginbottom's 1976 review in *M&L* 57 (3) (July): 327–328.

2. Modern edition for "voice and piano" by Elisabeth Van Straeten, Paris: Costellat, 1983.

3. John Hajdu Heyer has prepared a modern edition of the Gilles *Requiem*, Madison: A-R Editions, 1984.

4. These are as follows: [Mass for soloists, chorus, two treble instruments, and continuo] (H. 1); *Messe pour les trépassés à 8* (H. 2); *Messe à 8 voix et 8 violons et flûtes* (H. 3); *Messe à quatre choeurs* (H. 4); *Messe pour le Port Royal* (H. 5); *Messe à 4 voix, 4 violons, 2 flûtes et 2 hautbois pour M. Mauroy* (H. 6); *Messe des morts à 4 voix* (H. 7); *Messe pour le samedi de Pâques* (H. 8); *Messe de minuit à 4 voix, flûtes et violons pour Noël* (H. 9); *Messe des morts à 4 voix et symphonie* (H. 10); *Assumpta est Maria: Missa sex vocibus cum simphonia* (H. 11); and *Messe pour plusieurs instruments au lieu des orgues* (H. 513).

5. For the noel tunes and texts, see Hitchcock's edition of this Mass for Concordia, St. Louis, 1962.

6. Modern edition by Martin Herman, Colorado Springs: Colorado College Music Series, 1958.

7. Modern edition by Jean Duron, Versailles: Éditions du CMBV, 1994.

8. For more on Ouvrard, see Cohen 1972a; 1975.

9. The thirteen *histoires sacrées* listed below will be published by the CMBV. There are four versions of *Caecilio virgo et martyr*, each having a slightly different name (H. 394, 397, 413, and 415). The other twelve *histoires sacrées* are *Judith sive Bethulia liberata* (H. 391), *Historia Esther* (H. 396), *Pestis Mediolanensis* (H. 398), *Filius prodigus* (H. 399), *Extremum Dei judicium* (H. 401), *Sacrificium abrahae* (H.

402), *Mors Saülis et Jonathae* (H. 403), *Josue* (H. 404), *Praelium Michaelis archangeli* [incomplete] (H. 410), *Caedes sanctorum innocentium* (H. 411), *Judicium Salomonis* (H. 422), *Le Reniement de St. Pierre* (H. 424).

10. Modern edition by Hitchcock, New Haven: A-R Editions, 1964.

11. The entire scene (inexplicably transposed down) is included in Carl Parrish, *A Treasury of Early Music*, New York: W. W. Norton, 1958, 244–252.

12. The bibliography of this article neglects to include either Hitchcock's important Ph.D. dissertation or his 1955 article, both of which were available before the 1962 date of the *MGG* article. See also Clarence H. Barber 1963.

13. Extract in Massenkeil 1970, 87–91.

Chapter 16. *The Lute and Guitar*

1. The Centre National de la Recherche Scientifique (CNRS) is publishing much of the extant repertory of seventeenth-century French lute music that is not already in modern editions in their series "Corpus des luthistes français." Most of the composers listed above are already included in this ambitious project edited by Monique Rollin, André Souris, Jean-Michel Vaccaro, Jean Jacquot, and Sylvie Spychet. Minkoff of Geneva has published facsimile editions of the following: *Thesaurus harmonicus* by Besard; *Le Trésor d'Orphée* by Francisque; *Les Pièces de luth* by Gallot; the *Livres de tablatures des pièces de luth* by Ennemond and Denis Gaultier; and the *Pièces de luth* by Mouton. Included also in the facsimile collection are the following manuscript anthologies that contain pieces by a variety of composers: *Manuscrit Bethune, Manuscrit Milleran*, and *Manuscrit Vaudry de Saizenay*.

2. Besard's solo works for lute have been transcribed by André Souris in the CNRS series, Paris: CNRS, 1969.

3. Transcribed and analyzed by Souris in *Le Luth et sa musique* (290–292). All six preludes are in *Oeuvres de Dufaut*, which has been transcribed by Souris in the CNRS series, Paris: CNRS, 1965.

4. André Tessier's facsimile and transcription of *La Rhétorique des dieux* (Paris: Société Française de Musicologie, 1932–1933) is incomplete and includes some concordant versions. A complete facsimile and transcription edited by David J. Buch may be found as volume 62 of *Recent Researches in the Music of the Baroque Era*, Madison: A-R Editions, 1990. See also Buch 1989, which is a discussion of the literary texts and elaborate ink-wash illustrations of the modes by Abraham Bosse that adorn *La Rhétorique des dieux*.

5. The 1670 edition of *Guitarre royalle* appears in facsimile, Geneva: Minkoff, 1975; the pieces for two guitars in the 1673 edition of the *Guitarre royalle* appear in facsimile, Florence: Studio per edizioni scelte, 1983.

6. These books, plus additional manuscript pieces by de Visée, have been transcribed by Robert W. Strizich, "Le Pupitre" series, Paris: Heugel, 1969.

7. Facsimile edition, Geneva: Minkoff, 1977.

Chapter 17. *The Harpsichord*

1. For a traditional treatment of the transfer, see Bukofzer (1947, 169–170); Quittard in Lavignac and Laurencie's *Encyclopédie de la musique et dictionnaire du Conservatoire*, Part 1, 3:1230–1240; and Apel (1967, 542).

2. Found in *Oeuvres de René Mésangeau*, ed. A. Souris, Paris: CNRS, 1971.

3. For the French harpsichord and harpsichord makers, see the following: Hardouin 1957; 1959; 1960a; Hubbard 1965; Samoyault-Verlet 1966; and Boalch 1956: 2nd. ed., 1976. For a brief summary, see Fuller's 1975 review of *French Baroque Music*, *JAMS* 28 (2) (Summer): 377–378. The fundamental study of the sources for seventeenth-century French harpsichord music is Gustafson 1979.

4. Chambonnières's extant harpsichord music is found in *Oeuvres complètes de Chambonnières*, ed. P. Brunold and A. Tessier, Paris: Senart, 1925. Thurston Dart has edited the *Pièces de clavecin*, Monaco: Éditions de L'Oiseau-Lyre, 1970. For a facsimile of the 1670 Paris edition, see New York: Broude Brothers, 1967. At the time of this writing, a new edition of the complete works of Chambonnières is "in preparation" by Davitt Moroney for Éditions de L'Oiseau-Lyre, Monaco.

5. The Bauyn Manuscript is found in the Bibliothèque Nationale (*Rés.* Vm^7 674–675). It is available in a facsimile editon, Geneva: Minkoff, 1977.

6. See the *Oeuvres complètes de Louis Couperin*, ed. Paul Brunold, Paris: L'Oiseau-Lyre, 1936; see also *Pièces de clavecin*, ed. Thurston Dart, Monaco: Éditions de L'Oiseau-Lyre, 1959. Alan Curtis has edited the harpsichord music of Louis Couperin, "Le Pupitre" series, Paris: Heugel, 1970. His edition includes four previously unknown pieces found in the Parville Manuscript. A new edition containing all the available pieces by Couperin has been provided by Davitt Moroney, Monaco: Éditions de L'Oiseau-Lyre, 1985. Moroney preserves the Bauyn Manuscript's grouping of pieces by order of ascending tonality.

7. For the unmeasured prelude, see Newman Powell 1958, 237–283; Ferguson 1975, 23–28; Gustafson 1977; Moroney 1976; Pfeiffer 1979; Prévost 1987; Troeger 1983; Tilney 1991. See also Moroney's Introduction (11–16) to his edition of *Pièces de clavecin de Louis Couperin*, Monaco: Éditions de L'Oiseau-Lyre, 1985.

8. Modern edition by Dufourcq, Monaco: Éditions de L'Oiseau-Lyre, 1956.

9. Modern edition by Marguerite Roesgen-Champion, Paris: Société Française de Musicologie, 1934; modern edition by Kenneth Gilbert, "Le Pupitre" series, Paris: Heugel, 1975. Facsimile edition, New York: Broude Brothers, 1965.

10. D'Anglebert was not the first to transcribe extracts from Lully's operas for keyboard. An anonymous transcription for organ of extracts from *Alceste*, *Thésée*, *Atys*, *Isis*, and *Bellérophon* exists in manuscript in the Bibliothèque Nationale (MS 2094). See Almonte C. Howell, *Nine Seventeenth Century Organ Transcriptions from the Operas of Lully*, Lexington, Kentucky: University of Kentucky Press, 1963.

11. See David Fuller's 1975 review of *French Baroque Music*, *JAMS* 28 (2) (Summer): 378.

12. Elisabeth-Claude Jacquet de La Guerre's first book of *Pièces de clavecin* was only recently discovered by Carol H. Bates in the library of the Benedetto Marcello Conservatory in Venice. Bates has edited the collection for the "Le Pupitre" series, Paris: Heugel, 1986. See also Bates 1984.

13. The only detailed survey of this music from its seventeenth-century origins through the many sonatas for "*clavecin ou piano-forte*" of the 1780s is David R. Fuller's 1965 unpublished Ph.D. dissertation, *Eighteenth-Century French Harpsichord Music*, which, it is hoped, will soon be available in book form. See also Gustafson and Fuller 1990. For a brief summary of eighteenth-century harpsichord music, see Mark Kroll 1994, 124–133.

14. Modern edition by Brunold, Paris: L'Oiseau-Lyre, 1934.

15. See introduction to Albert Fuller's edition of *Pieces for Harpsichord* (New York: Alpeg Press, 1956). This introduction contains much valuable information on many aspects of the performance of seventeenth- and eighteenth-century harpsichord music, including ornamentation, fingering, articulation, and phrasing, as well as comments on the instrument and its registration.

16. Modern edition by Thurston Dart, Monaco: Éditions de L'Oiseau-Lyre, 1960.

17. The most complete discussion of Couperin's harpsichord music may be found in Mellers 1950 (ed. of 1987, 171–212); Reimann 1940, 82–122; Hofman 1961; and Beaussant 1980, English trans. 1990, 220–343. The music of the four books is in *Oeuvres complètes de*

François Couperin, vols. 1–4. A welcome new edition was prepared by Kenneth Gilbert for "Le Pupitre" series, Paris: Heugel, 1969–1972. Sylvia Marlowe has edited selected pieces from each of the four books, New York: G. Schirmer, 1970. For a discussion of ornamentation and registration in Couperin's harpsichord pieces, see Gilbert's prefaces to his editions for "Le Pupitre" series and his "Le Clavecin français et la registration" in *L'Interprétation de la musique française*, 1974 203–211; and Dart in the same source, 213–220.

18. There is no reason, in my opinion, to think this piece a "technical joke [with] the continuous suspensions being a mysterious barricade to the basic harmony" (Mellers 1950, 358). It was a common conceit of the time to use military vocabulary in amorous war between the sexes. In this context, the "Baricades mistérieuses" are no more than the mysterious defenses employed by the fair sex against male assault. For further information on "Les Baricades mistérieuses" see Dufourcq 1973.

19. The three early books of *Pièces de clavecin* have been edited by François-Sappey under the title *Trois livres de clavecin de jeunesse*, Paris: Heugel, 1975; the three later books have been edited by Pauline Aubert and François-Sappey under the title of *Trois livres de clavecin*, Paris: Éditions de la Schola Cantorum, 1973. See also François-Sappey 1974; and Brunold 1932.

20. Note that the "La" in proper names need have nothing to do with the sex of the individual portrayed. Often, and certainly in the above case, it should be understood as "la pièce intitulée."

21. Modern edition by Howard Ferguson, "Le Pupitre" series, Paris: Heugel, 1969.

22. Modern edition by Brunold. Paris: Senart, ca. 1920. New edition by Christopher Hogwood. London: Faber, 1982.

23. The harpsichord music by Rameau is found in *Oeuvres complètes de J.-P, Rameau*, vol. 1. Erwin R. Jacobi edited Rameau's harpsichord works, Kassel: Bärenreiter, 1958. There is a recent edition by Kenneth Gilbert for the "Le Pupitre" series, Paris: Heugel, 1979.

24. There is no evidence that Rameau was familiar with the sonatas of Scarlatti. His comments in his manual regarding "Les Cyclopes" indicate that he believed these kinds of *batteries* had "never appeared before."

25. For a list of these transcriptions, see Girdlestone 1957, 53–54.

26. Modern edition by Pincherle. Paris: Droz, 1935. For the keyboard music by Mondonville, see Borroff 1967.

27. Pincherle prepared a facsimile edition, London: H. Baron, 1966. A modern edition may be found as vol. 2 of Borroff 1958.

28. Modern edition by Edward Smith, Monaco: Éditions de L'Oiseau-Lyre, 1995.

29. See Curtis's preface to his edition of Balbastre's *Pièces de clavecin, d'orgue et de forte-piano*, "Le Pupitre" series, Paris: Heugel, 1973.

30. All four books (First Book, 1744; Second Book, 1748; Third Book, 1756; and Fourth Book, 1768) are available in the "Le Pupitre" series, Paris: Heugel, 1967. For Duphly, see also Bond 1994.

Chapter 18. *Organ Music of the* Grand Siècle

1. Titelouze's complete works for organ as well as the works of Boyvin, Clérambault, Couperin, Dandrieu, d'Aquin, Du Mage, Gigault, Grigny, Guilain, Lebègue, and Raison are found in the ten volumes of the *Archives des maîtres de l'orgue* edited by Alexandre Guilmant and André Pirro, Paris: A. Durand et fils, 1898–1910; Rpt. New York: Johnson Reprint, 1972. Pirro's introductions, which include the composers' prefaces, are invaluable research aids. Selected works by d'Aquin, Dornel, Lebègue, Raison, and others are also included in the collection *Orgue et liturgie*, edited by Dufourcq, Raugel, and J. de Valois, Paris: Éditions Musicales de la Schola Cantorum. On the organ music of Titelouze, see Jean Bonfils 1965, 5:5–16.

2. The most helpful glossary of terms dealing with the French classical organ may be found in Williams 1967, 169–203; Douglass 1969, 217–221, 2nd ed. 1995, 235–237; Pruitt 1974, 68–81; Williams 1980, 104–110; and Williams in *The New Grove Dictionary of Musical Instruments*, 1984, 2:918–929. The most complete study of the French organ from 1589 to 1789 is by Dufourcq 1971–1982, *Le Livre de l'orgue français* in five volumes. For a discussion of French organ building in selected locations outside of Paris see *Recherches*, XII (1972), a special number devoted to "L'Histoire de l'orgue français aux XVIe, XVIIe et XVIIIe siècles."

3. See Apel 1937. These have been transcribed by Jean Bonfils as *Chansons françaises pour orgue, vers 1550*, "Le Pupitre" series, Paris: Heugel, 1968.

4. Modern editon by Jos. Watelet, *Monumenta Musica Belgicae*, vol. 4, Antwerp: "De Ring," 1938.

5. A modern edition of Racquet's organ music edited by Bonfils is found in *L'Organiste liturgique*, 1957, vols. 29–30.

6. The keyboard music of Du Mont edited by Bonfils is found in *L'Organiste liturgique*, 1953, vol. 13.

7. The word *jeu* may refer both to single stops (Mersenne's "*jeux simples*") and to combinations of stops (Mersenne's "*jeux composés*").

8. According to Williams, the *"Tierce en taille* is essentially a melodic registration for the left hand on the *Positif* under a soft accompaniment on the *Grand Orgue"* (1967, 189).

9. For more detailed information on the specifications and registration of French classical organs, see Douglass 1969, 78–114.

10. Modern edition by Dufourcq, Paris: Bornemann, 1963. For Nivers's organ music, see Pruitt 1974 and 1975.

11. Modern edition by Dufourcq, Paris: Éditions Musicales de la Schola Cantorum, 1956.

12. Modern edition by Dufourcq, Paris: Société Française de Musicologie, 1958.

13. See the preface to Jean Bonfils's edition of the *Livre d'orgue attribué à J. N. Geoffroy* for "Le Pupitre" series, Paris: Heugel, 1974. See also Dufourcq 1971–1982, 4:80–83.

14. The manuscript was discovered by Elisabeth Gallat-Morin at the Fondation Lionel Groulx in Montreal in 1978. It is published as *Un Monument de musique française classique: Le Livre d'orgue de Montréal*, edited by Gallat-Morin, Montreal: Les Presses de l'Université, 1988.

15. Modern edition by Dufourcq, Paris: Société Française de Musicologie, 1952.

16. Modern edition by Dufourcq, Paris: Société Française de Musicologie, 1952.

17. Two manuscript collections of Marchand's organ music located at the Bibliothèque Municipale de Versailles (MSS 61/1–2) have been edited by Jean Bonfils as *Pièces d'orgue du grand Marchand*, 3 vols., Paris: Les Éditions ouvrières, 1972–1974.

Chapter 19. *Instrumental Ensemble and Orchestral Music of the Seventeenth Century*

1. Trichet even commented that "formerly one accompanied the bride and groom to the church with the sound of oboes and returned them to their home with the sound of the violins" (ca. 1640; rpt. 1955 (3): 351).

2. See Cohen 1958 and 1962b, 234. See also Launay 1955a.

3. This fantasia, anonymous in Mersenne, has since been identified as part of a fancy by Alfonso Ferrabosco II. See Cohen 1962b, 236.

4. Modern edition by by Paul Hooreman, "Le Pupitre" series, Paris; Heugel, 1973.

5. For biographical details, see the index of the *Documents du Minutier Central* and Lesure 1952.

6. Modern edition by Martine Roche, Paris: Société Française de Musicologie, 1971.

7. See Mrácek 1972, 563–571. Mrácek has published 213 of these dances in *Monumenta musicae Svecicae*, vol. 8, Stockholm: Edition Reimars, 1976.

Chapter 20. *Instrumental Ensemble and Orchestral Music of the Eighteenth Century*

1. Modern edition by H. Schneider, "Le Pupitre" series, Paris: Heugel, 1987.

2. Dornel was one of six who competed for the position of organist at Sainte-Madeleine de la Cité. Young Rameau won the competition but chose not to accept the appointment, which went to Dornel.

3. Modern edition by Michel Sanvoisin, Paris: Heugel, 1970.

4. The composer's name is missing from the index of Claude Palisca's *Baroque Music* (even from the 3rd ed. of 1991) and Arthur Hutching's *The Baroque Concerto*, 1961.

5. Composers such as Corrette, Boismortier, Naudot, Bousset, and Chedeville composed many works featuring musettes and vielles in a solo capacity. Typical are the *Six concertos en quatre parties pour la vièle, musette, flûte traversière, flûte à bec ou hautbois* (Opus 17) of Naudot. (See Green 1987; see also Leppert 1978 and Lindemann 1978).

6. Modern edition by C. Cessac, "Musica Gallica" series, Paris: Salabert, 1993.

Chapter 21. *The Sonata and Suite for Solo Instruments*

1. Lionel de La Laurencie's (1922–1924) *L'École française de violon de Lully à Viotti* remains the most valuable source for a comprehensive style analysis of the violin literature in France of the period. For a discussion of problems of technique and interpretation, see Pincherle 1911; William S. Newman (1966, 352–392) includes a two-chapter summary of the sonata in France up to 1750. Many important extracts from the prefaces to Couperin's sonata collections are translated into English in this source. See also Bates 1991–1992.

2. This popular Baroque and Classic cadential procedure, in which a V of VI is substituted for the anticipated V of I, was labeled a "bi-focal cadence" by Jan La Rue (1957).

3. Montéclair claimed credit in his *Principes de musique* (1736, 88) for suggesting these symbols to Piani. The interesting passage follows:

> *There is no symbol to designate the swelling of a sound [son enflé] or the diminishing of a sound [son diminué]. Because of this,*

Mr. de Planes [Piani], an Italian, asked me what he could use to indicate this agrément in certain passages of his Sonatas. I advised him to use a line that would thicken according to the swelling of the sound and, on the contrary, would become thinner as the sound diminished. He used this innovation with success, and as it was my idea, I will make use of it below.

4. In addition to La Laurencie (1922–1924) and W. S. Newman (1966), the sources are Appia 1950; Pincherle 1952; Lemoine 1953–1954; Preston 1959; 1963; Nutting 1964; and Zaslaw 1970. Preston's preface to his edition of the Opus 5 violin sonatas (A-R Editions, Madison, 1968) is an important source for information on performance practices and ornamentation. Preston has also edited Opus 2 (1988) and Opus 9 (1969) for A-R Editions.

5. I am grateful to Reinhard Pauly, who shared with me his microfilm collection and selected photocopies of sonatas by this remarkable composer.

6. The most complete study to date dealing with French Baroque flute music is by Jane Bowers 1971; see also Bowers 1978; 1979. See also Mather 1973, and Mather and Lasocki 1984. Bowers has edited the *Pièces pour la flûte traversière avec la basse continue* by La Barre, "Le Pupitre" series, Paris: Heugel, 1976.

7. Modern edition by Pincherle, "Le Pupitre" series, Paris: Heugel, 1970.

8. On the history of the violoncello in France, see Shaw 1963, Milliot 1964; and Milliot 1981.

9. The most complete study of the viol and its music in the French Baroque is by Bol 1973. See also Schwendowius 1970. Minkoff in Geneva has published in facsimile collections of *pièces de viole* by the following composers: Barrière, Boismortier, Caix d'Hervelois, Couperin, Dautrecourt (Sainte-Colombe), Demachy, Dollé, Forqueray, Heudelinne, Hugard, Le Blanc, Lendormy, Marin and Roland Marais, Marc, Morel, André Danican Philidor, and Roget.

10. Modern edition by Paul Hooreman, Paris: Société Française de Musicologie, 1973.

11. Titon du Tillet 1732, 624–625. The extraordinary success of the film *Tous les matins du monde* (1992), which deals in a generally fanciful manner with the relationship between Sainte-Colombe and Marin Marais, has stimulated research into Sainte-Colombe's background. Pierre Guillot, writing in *Le Monde* of 18 January 1992, has identified Sainte-Colombe as Augustin Dautrecourt from the Sainte-Colombe region near Lyons.

12. All the *avertissements* from the five books have been translated into English and are included in Kinney 1966. For a discussion of the

viol suites by Marais, see Boulay 1955 and Thompson 1959; 1960; 1963. See also Tessier 1924; Newton 1952; Lesure 1953; McDowell 1974; Urquhart 1970; Vertrees 1977; Sadie 1978b; Milliot and La Gorce 1991. The instrumental works of Marais are being edited by John Hsu for Broude Trust (formerly known as Broude Brothers Limited). To date, Books 1–3 of the *Pièces à une et à deux violes* have appeared (1980, 1986, 1996).

13. Reproduced in Lavignac's *Encyclopédie*, Part II, 3:1776.

14. Modern edition by Lucy Robinson, "Le Pupitre" series, Paris: Heugel, 1973.

15. On the Forqueray family, see Prod'homme 1903; La Laurencie 1908b–1909; Benoit and Dufourcq 1968b; and Lalague-Guilhemsans 1979.

16. Modern edition of the *Pièces de violes mises en pièces du clavecin*, edited by C. Tilney, "Le Pupitre" series, Paris: Heugel, 1970.

Chapter 22. *The* Air de Cour *and Related Genres*

1. Among the most important references are Gérold 1921; Walker 1948; Levy 1954; Verchaly 1954b; 1960; 1961; Tunley 1986; and Durosoir 1991. See also the introductions to two anthologies: *Chansons au luth et airs de cour français du XVIe siècle*, ed. Lionel de La Laurencie and Adrienne Mairy, Paris: Société Française de Musicologie, 1934; and *Airs de cour pour voix et luth (1603–1643)*, ed. Verchaly, Paris: Société Française de Musicologie, 1961.

2. Examples of Boesset's "N'espérez plus mes yeux," with a diminution by Le Bailly and a second diminution by the composer, were taken from Mersenne by Walker (1948, 162–163).

3. For Mouliné, see Launay 1955b and Durosoir 1991.

4. For Boesset, see Alderman 1946 and Durosoir 1991.

5. For Lambert, see Massip 1985b and 1989.

6. P.-M. Masson 1910–1911, 354. See also Schwandt 1977 and Poole 1987.

7. Such is the case with Louis Marchand's "Io provo nel core," which was added to Campra's *L'Europe galante* and is found in Book 1 of the *Recueil des meilleurs airs italiens* for 1699.

Chapter 23. *The* Cantate Françoise

1. Important sources concerning the history of the French cantata are La Laurencie in Lavignac and La Laurencie's *Encyclopédie*, 1913–1931, Part I, vol. 3:1546–1562; Malherbe's preface to *Oeuvres complètes de Rameau*, 3; Tunley 1967a; 1967b; 1974; and 1986; and Vollen 1982. From 1990–1991 Garland Press published 17 volumes of facsimile editions of the basic repertory of the eighteenth-century

French cantata with introductions by Tunley. A list of modern performing editions may be found in Tunley 1974 (Appendix A, ii). This list will be updated in the new edition of Tunley's *The Eighteenth Century French Cantata*, to be published by Oxford University Press.

2. In chronological order, these are Bernier (7 books, 1703–1723); Morin (3 books, 1706–1712); Stuck (4 books, 1706–1714); Brunet de Moland (1 book, 1708); Jacquet de La Guerre (2 books, 1708 and 1711); Bourgeois (2 books, 1708 and 1718); Campra (3 books, 1708–1728); Montéclair (3 books, ca. 1709–1728); Bousset (1 book before 1710); Brossard (6 cantatas, no date); Courbois (1 book, 1710); Clérambault (5 books, 1710–1726); Charles-Hubert Gervais (1 book, 1712 and a separate cantata 1720); Rameau (7 cantatas, ca. 1715–ca. 1740); Destouches (2 cantatas, 1716 and 1719); Mouret (1 book, 1718); Grandval (1 book, 1720); Colin de Blamont 3 books, 1723–1729); Boismortier (2 books, 1724 and 1729); and Laurent Gervais (2 books, 1727 and 1732).

3. *Les Forges de Lemnos* may be found in a modern edition prepared by Tunley in "Music Series 2," which is a supplement to *Studies in Music* 1967, vol. 1. *Le Caffé* from Book 3 has been edited by Hinnenthal, Kassel: Bärenreiter, 1959.

4. For background information and style studies of Clérambault cantatas, see Tunley 1966a; Tunley 1974, 120–149; and Foster 1967.

5. Diran Akmajian and I edited Book 3 of Montéclair's cantatas, Madison: A-R Editions, 1978.

6. See Girdlestone 1957, 65–73; and Malherbe's preface to the *Oeuvres complètes de J.-P. Rameau*, vol. 3. Mary Cyr has discovered a previously unknown late cantata by Rameau (*Cantate pour le jour de la [fête de] Saint-Louis*) (see Cyr 1979). For the chronology of Rameau's cantatas, see Cyr 1983b.

7. Boismortier's *Actéon* of 1732 may be seen under the title *Diane et Actéon*, incorrectly attributed to Rameau, in the *Oeuvres complètes de J.-P. Rameau*, vol. 3.

Chapter 24. *Epilogue: Thoughts on the Performance of French Baroque Music*

1. See, e.g., the table of "Keyboard Ornaments Used in France" in Ferguson 1975, 138–141; the 26 tables reproduced in Brunold 1925; the Appendix ("Selective Glossary of Terms and Symbols") in Neumann 1978, 577–604; and Donington "Ornaments" in *NG* 13:827–867. See also Donington 1982, 107–145; Cyr 1992, 132–138; and Neumann 1993b.

2. Preface to Ralph Kirkpatrick's edition of the Bach *Goldberg Variations*, New York: G. Schirmer, 1938.

3. From a letter sent to the editor and published in 1965, *M&L* 46 (4) (October): 381.

4. Collins, Michael. 1970. "Jean Rousseau and the Integrity of the French Trill." In *Abstracts of Papers Read at the 36th Annual Meeting of the American Musicological Society*, 40.

5. On page 5 of the same treatise, Montéclair explained that the trill is "indicated in foreign countries and in music printed in France by a small t. Apparently, negligence in curving the base of the t resulted in the small + or x, which only the French use in manuscripts and in engraved editions to designate this ornament." For other possible interpretations of the cross in instrumental music, see Brunold 1925, 25–31; Dart 1954, 85; and Robert Preston's edition of Leclair's *Sonatas for Violin and Continuo*, Op. 5, New Haven: A-R Editions, 1968, xv–xxii. The choice of a suitable ornament, often a trill or a mordent, presupposed sufficient general knowledge of the style on the part of the performer. The appoggiatura (*port de voix*) was usually indicated by notes in small print.

6. For *notes inégales*, see Neumann 1965a; Fuller, "Notes inégales" in *NG* 13:420–427; Neumann 1993b, 120–134; and Hefling 1993, Chapters 1–3. The latter source contains a list of primary sources dating from 1535 to 1787. For information on the performance of *notes inégales* outside of France, see Byrt 1967, 1995; Hefling 1993; and Fontijin 1995.

7. Michael Collins was first to respond to Neumann's challenge (1969). Neumann answered in 1977, David Fuller joined the fray in 1977, and Neumann was quick to respond in 1979. Neumann's original *Rdm* article received a wider audience by virtue of its translation into English by Harris and Shay in 1977 (all articles dealing with overdotting subsequent to Neumann 1965b have been in English). See also Leavis 1978; Pont 1978; O'Donnell 1979; Neumann 1981; and 1982; Fuller 1985; Neumann 1986; Wulstan 1986; Scheibert 1987; Neumann 1989; and 1993b; and Hefling 1993.

8. Following are some modern sources that discuss musical taste in the France of the *grand siècle*: La Laurencie 1905; Écorcheville 1906b; Prunières 1908; Oliver 1947; Snyders 1968; Maniates 1969; and William Weber 1984.

Index

Note: Page numbers in italics indicate the more important references. Musical compositions and theoretical writings by composers are indexed by name of composer. Indexed by title are all literary works and collections containing compositions by more than one composer. Nineteenth- and twentieth-century authors are excluded.